XML: The Complete Reference

Heather Williamson

Osborne/**McGraw-Hill**
New York Chicago San Francisco
Lisbon London Madrid Mexico City
Milan New Delhi San Juan
Seoul Singapore Sydney Toronto

Osborne/**McGraw-Hill**
2600 Tenth Street
Berkeley, California 94710
U.S.A.

To arrange bulk purchase discounts for sales promotions, premiums, or fund-raisers, please contact Osborne/**McGraw-Hill** at the above address. For information on translations or book distributors outside the U.S.A., please see the International Contact Information page immediately following the index of this book.

XML: The Complete Reference

1234567890 DOC DOC 01987654321

ISBN 0-07-212734-1

Publisher
Brandon A. Nordin

Vice President & Associate Publisher
Scott Rogers

Acquisitions Editor
Rebekah Young

Project Editor
Jenn Tust

Acquisitions Coordinator
Paulina Pobocha

Technical Editor
Simon St. Laurent

Copy Editor
Karyn DiCastri

Proofreader
Paul Medoff

Indexer
Jack Lewis

Computer Designers
Tara Davis, Carie Malnekoff,
Melinda Moore Lytle, Roberta Steele

Illustrators
Michael Mueller, Lyssa Sieben-Wald

Series Design
Peter F. Hancik

This book was composed with Corel VENTURA™ Publisher.

To the creative minds at the W3C
that see where the Internet should go ... and who make it happen.

About the Author

Heather Williamson has spent the last five years designing and developing HTML documents for both corporate intranets and public Internet sites. When corporate mergers forced her to look for alternative forms of employment, she started a small Web development and consulting company, which provides a variety of programming and development services to companies in the Pacific Northwest, New York, and Arizona. These services include Web page development, e-commerce solutions, graphic and multimedia design, developing computer-based training, and applications development.

In her free time, between writing and raising her family, Heather raises American quarter horses, moves cattle, and generally metamorphoses from your typical techno-nerd into a downright "tomboy-ish" country-raised farm kid.

Contents

Part I
XML Basics

1 Getting a Global Perspective 3
The Early Beginnings 4
A Foundation in SGML 4
XML Requirements 6
The Current Standards 10
XML 1.0 10
XML Namespaces 11
Document Type Definitions 11
Cascading Style Sheets 12
Extensible Stylesheet Language 12
XML Schemas 13
XML Query Language 13
XLinks 14
XPointers 14
XPath 14
XML Digital Signatures 15
The Resource Description Framework Schema 15
Canonical XML 15
XHTML 16

XML Software 16
Nonvalidating Parsers 16
Validating Parsers 18
Don't Forget the DOM 19

2 Reviewing XML Validating and Nonvalidating Parsers 21
Getting XML Documents Written 22
XML Nonvalidating Parsers 27
Starting with a Basic Parser 28
Online Parsers 28
XML Validating Parsers 29
Validation Requirements 30
Online Validators 31
Schema Checkers 33

3 Saying "Hello World" in XML 35
XML Structure 36
XML Elements 39
Writing Your First Document 40
Parsing Your Document 41
Using Layers of Elements 42
Commenting Your XML Code 43
Data Structures and Organization 45

4 Organizing XML Data 47
Creating Layers of Information from Your Data 48
Identifying Information Importance 48
Adding Detail to Your List 49
Structuring Your Data 51
Identifying Your Elements 51
Identifying Your Attributes 56
Ensuring That Your Data Works with the Document Object Model (DOM) 56

5 Creating Well-Formed XML 59
Document Basics 60
<?xml> Declaration 60
The Root Element 65
Creating and Describing Elements 66
Opening and Closing Element Tags 66
Element Content 66
Empty Element Tags 68
Naming Elements 68
Child Elements 71

6 Adding Attributes 73
When to Use Attributes 75
Metadata 75
Attributes Are Not Extensible 76
Using Attributes to Enhance Elements 79

Attribute Rules ... 81
Naming Attributes ... 81
Attribute Values ... 82
Using Attributes to Enhance Empty Elements ... 83
Sharing Attributes ... 83
Using Style Sheets with Attributes ... 84
Adding a Style Sheet ... 84
A Quick Cascading Style Sheet ... 86
A Quick XSL Style Sheet ... 86

7 XML Namespaces ... 91
What Are Namespaces? ... 92
Using Namespaces Within Documents ... 94
Identifying Namespaces ... 94
The Syntax ... 96
Default Namespaces ... 96
Adding Namespaces to DTDs ... 97

Part II
Working with DTD

8 Validating Your XML Documents ... 103
DTDs and Validation ... 104
Adding DTDs to Your Documents ... 105
Linking to Document Type Definitions ... 106
Embedding Document Type Definitions ... 107
`PUBLIC` Versus `SYSTEM` DTDs ... 108
Referencing `SYSTEM` DTDs ... 108
Referencing `PUBLIC` DTDs ... 109
Declaring `Element` Types ... 109
Controlling Element Content ... 114
Empty Elements ... 117
Adding Comments ... 118

9 Defining DTD Entities ... 121
Understanding Entities ... 122
Internal Entities ... 123
External Entities ... 123
General Entities ... 124
Parameter Entities ... 124
Defining General Entities ... 125
Internal General Entities ... 125
Using Entities Within Entities ... 127
General Entity Restrictions ... 127
Putting It All Together ... 128
External General Entities ... 130
Defining Parameter Entities ... 134
Internal Parameter Entities ... 135
External Parameter Entities ... 138

10 Working with Attributes 141
Delving into Attributes 142
Attribute or Element? 143
Defining Attributes 144
Controlling Attribute Types 145
Setting Default Values 150
Defining Multiple Attributes 152
Using Predefined Attributes 156
`xml:space` 156
`xml:lang` 157

11 Adding Other Data 159
Exploring Notations 160
Unparsed External Entities 162
Conditional Statements 165
Adding Processing Instructions 167

Part III

Adding Style

12 When to Use Style Sheets 173
What Are Style Sheets? 174
Where Does CSS Shine? 174
Forward and Backward Compatibility 175
Complementary Structure 175
Independence from All Companies 175
Easy Maintenance 175
Simplicity 175
Rich Variety of Scripts 176
Accessibility 176
Where Does XSL Shine? 179
Paging and Scrolling 179
Selectors and Tree Construction 179
Extended Page Layout Model 179
An Area Model 179
Internationalization and Writing Modes 180
Linking Controls 180
Using One or the Other 181

13 CSS Basics 185
The Basic CSS Statement 186
Adding CSS to Your Document 187
CSS Selections 187
Selecting Elements 191
Selecting Classes 192
Selecting IDs 193
Selecting in Context 193
Using Pseudo-Elements 193
Using Pseudo-Classes 194
Controlling Your Fonts 197
Setting `font-family` 197
Setting `font-size` 197

Setting font-stretch 198
Setting font-style 199
Setting font-variant 199
Setting font-weight 200
Setting font shorthand 200
Setting font color 201
Controlling Your Text 202
Setting letter-spacing 202
Setting line-height 203
Setting text-align 203
Setting word-spacing 204
Setting Your Alignment 204
Indenting Text 205
Using Text Decorations 205
Using `text-shadow` 206
Using Text Transformations 206
Controlling Your Object Boxes 207
Setting Borders 207
Setting `border-collapse` 210
Setting Outlines 211
Setting Margins 213
Adding Padding 215
Setting Backgrounds 217
Putting Together a Style Sheet 221

14 CSS: The Next Step 229
Adding Content 230
Adding `:before` 230
Adding `:after` 231
Creating Counters and Automatic Numbering 233
Using CSS Pseudo-Classes and Pseudo-Elements 234
Working with `:first-child` 235
Working with `:first-line` 235
Working with `:first-letter` 237
Visually Formatting Your Objects 240
`display` Property 240
Setting Object Position 245
Setting Object Size 250
Controlling Object Visibility 252
Controlling Object `overflow` and `clip` Properties 252
Controlling Your Cursors 253
Setting Object Importance 254
Using Media Types 255
Using `@media` 255
Using the `@import` Alternative 257
A Look at Aural Style Sheets 257

15 XSL Basics 263
Background 264
The Need for XSL 264
XSL History and Status 265
XSL Basics 267
Styling Through Transformation: XSLT 267
CSS via XML: XSL-FO 269

XSL Software and XSLT Software 272
Editors/Authoring Tools 272
Processors (Engines) 274
XSL-FO Software 277
Native XSL-FO Renderers 278
Formatting Objects-to-PDF Converters 279

16 XSL Transformations 283
XSLT Concepts 284
Source and Result Trees 284
Nodes and Node Types 286
The XPath Standard 287
Context 291
Location Step Syntax 291
XPath Location Path Examples 297
Node Values 299
XPath Functions 300
Transforming XML with XSLT 309
Style Sheet Structure 309
Template Rules 317
Conditional Processing 331
Sorting 334
Generating Content in the Result Tree 338
Variables and Parameters 345
Importing and Including Style Sheets 353
Special Result Tree Output 358
Copying Nodes from Source to Result Tree 360
Template Rule Modes 364
Issuing Messages from Style Sheets 367
XSLT Functions 369

17 XSL: Completing Your Application 397
XSL-FO Document Structure 398
Creating an XSL-FO Document 399
Layout Master Sets: Page Layouts and Sequences 399
Page Layouts 400
Page Sequences 404
Adding Content: Page Sequences 405
Block Versus Inline Formatting 408
Fixed Content within a Page Sequence 408
Content That Varies from Page to Page 410
Viewing the Resulting Document 410
Modifying a Region's Display Properties 413
Inserting Images 414
XSL-FO Tables 415

Part IV
Using Schemas

18 Introducing Schemas 427
What Are Schemas? 428
Comparing DTDs and Schemas 430

Writing a Basic Schema 434
A Hierarchical Schema 435
Flat Catalog of Schema Elements 437
What Software Is Available? 439
Schema Editors 439
Schema Validators and Parsers 441

19 Schema Elements, Types, and Groups 445
Schema Element Descriptions 446
Element Types 454
Complex Types 454
Simple Types 456
Defining Your Own Simple Types 461
Using Groups of Elements 463
Element Content 464
Attributes and Simple Values 464
Mixed Content 465
Empty Content 466

20 Defining Schema Attributes 469
Schema Attributes Descriptions 470
Attribute Groups 473
Using Schema Annotations 475
Using Constraints 476
Making a <choice> 476
Creating a <sequence> 477
Using <all> 478
Creating Unique Elements and Attributes 479
Schemas and Namespaces 480
Using Entities 482

21 Advanced Concepts with Schemas 485
Target Namespaces and Schemas 486
Undeclared Target Namespaces 489
Schema Constraints Versus ID Attributes 489
Global Versus Local Declarations 489
Using Schemas as Multiple Documents 492
Substitution Groups 493
Abstract Elements and Types 494

Part V
Using XML Query

22 Introducing XML Query 499
XML Query Requirements 500
XML Query Data Model 501
XML Query Algebra 502
Data and Types 504
Projection 506
Atomic Data 506
Iteration 507

Selection 507
Quantification 508
Join 509
Sorting 510
Utilizing XML Query 510

23 XLinks 515
Understanding XLink 516
XLink Syntax 517
The XLink Namespace 518
The XLink Attributes 519
Types of Links 524
A Glance at XBase 531

24 Using XPointer 535
Understanding XPointer 536
XPointer Schemes 536
XPointer Syntax 538
The Full Form 538
Bare Names 539
Child Sequence 540
XPointer Escaping 540
Escaping XPointer Specific Characters 541
Escaping Characters in URIs 541
Escaping Characters for Use in XML Text 541
XPointer Functions 543
Identifying a `location-set` 543
Point Location Type 544
Range Location Type 544
`string-range` Function 544
`range-to` Function 546
`here` Function 546
`origin` Function 547
`start-point` Function 547
`end-point` Function 548

25 Resource Description Framework 551
What Is the RDF and the RDF Schema? 552
RDF 552
RDF Schema 553
Implementing the RDF Basic Model 553
Resources 554
Properties 554
Statements 554
RDF Basic Syntax 555
Using RDF Containers 557
RDF Container Syntax 558
Container Objects 558
Statements 560
URI Patterns 561

Part VI
XML in Action

26 XHTML 567
What Is XHTML 568
HTML to XHTML Conversions 569
Element Conversions 570
A Quick Conversion from HTML to XHTML 571
Future XHTML Modules 572
Structure Module 573
Text Module 574
Hypertext Module 581
List Module 582
Presentation Module 583
Edit Module 586
Bidirectional Text Module 587
Forms Module 588
Table Module 592
Image Module 595
Client-Side Image Map Module 596

27 Manipulating XML with JavaScript 599
The Process 600
The XML Document 600
Our Schema 601
Our Style Sheet 603
Writing the Script 605
Putting It All Together 605

28 Collecting and Writing Data with CGI 613
Setting Up the Variables and Opening the Script 614
Format of the Flat-File Database 615
Creating the XML File 616
Opening the Database and Starting the Loop 616
Reading the Data 617
Writing Your Data 618
Saving Your XML File and Ending the Program 618
The Complete Script 618

Part VII
XML Child Languages

29 SYMM and SMIL 625
SYMM Basics 626
Understanding SMIL 626
SMIL Editors and Players 627
SMIL and HTML 629
SMIL Media Elements 630
Unknown Media Types 632
SMIL Media Attributes 632

SMIL Layout and Formatting Elements 635
Setting Up the Presentation: <smil>, <head>, and <body> 636
Using Meta Information 639
Using <layout> 641
Using <root-layout> 642
Using <region> 643
Using <viewport> 646
Providing Display Options 647
Setting Up SMIL Timing 650
Synchronizing Your Site 650
The Timing and Synchronization Attributes 652
Linking Between Objects and Presentations 652
Using <a> 652
Using <area> 655
Link Attributes 656
Creating SMIL Animations and Transformations 658
Animation Effects 658
Transformation Effects 660

30 Using Scalable Vector Graphics (SVG) 663
A Quick Look at SVG 664
SVG Syntax 665
SVG DataTypes 667
SVG Elements 668
SVG Attributes 683
An SVG Example 692

31 Scientific Languages: MathML and CML 695
The Language of Mathematicians: MathML 696
MathML Elements 696
MathML Examples 714
The Language of Chemists: CML 716
CML Elements 716
CML Examples 717

Part VIII
The Appendixes

A DTD Key Codes and a Sample DTD 729
DTD Elements 730
Attribute Declarations 731
DTD General Entities 732
Internal General Entities 733
External General Entities 734
Parameter Entities 734
Notations 734
External Unparsed Entities 734
DTD Comments 735
Conditional Statements 735
Processing Instructions 736
Sample DTD: The Strict XHTML DTD 736

B CSS Language Reference 757
Basic Concepts and @-Rules 758
Comments 758
<?xml-stylesheet…?> 758
Selectors 758
Contextual Selector 759
class Selector 760
ID selector 761
@charset 761
@fontface 761
@import 762
@media 762
@page 763
!important 764
Pseudo-Elements and Pseudo-Classes 764
:active 765
:after 765
:before 765
:first 766
:first-child 766
:first-letter 767
:first-line 768
:focus 768
:hover 769
:lang 769
:left 769
:link 770
:right 770
:visited 771
Units of Measurement 771
<length> 771
<percentage> 772
<color> 772
Font and Text Properties 774
font 774
font-family 774
font-size 775
font-size-adjust 775
font-stretch 776
font-style 777
font-weight 777
letter-spacing 778
line-height 778
text-align 779
text-decoration 779
text-indent 780
text-shadow 780
text-transform 781
vertical-align 781
word-spacing 782
Color and Background Properties 782
background 783
background-attachment 783

background-color 783
background-image 784
background-position 784
background-repeat 785
color 785
Generated Content and Cursors 786
content 786
counter-increment 787
counter-reset 787
cursor 787
Containment Box Properties 788
border 788
border-bottom 789
border-bottom-color 789
border-bottom-style 790
border-bottom-width 790
border-collapse 791
border-color 791
border-left 792
border-left-color 792
border-left-style 793
border-left-width 793
border-right 794
border-right-color 794
border-right-style 795
border-right-width 795
border-style 796
border-top 796
border-top-color 797
border-top-style 797
border-top-width 798
border-width 798
bottom 798
clear 799
clip 799
float 800
height 800
left 801
margin 801
margin-bottom 802
margin-left 802
margin-right 803
margin-top 803
marker-offset 804
marks 804
max-height 804
max-width 805
min-height 805
min-width 806
orphans 806
outline 807
outline-color 807

- outline-style 808
- outline-width 808
- overflow 809
- padding 809
- padding-bottom 810
- padding-left 810
- padding-right 810
- padding-top 811
- page 811
- page-break-after 812
- page-break-before 812
- page-break-inside 813
- position 813
- quotes 814
- right 814
- size 815
- top 815
- visibility 816
- widows 816
- width 817
- z-index 817

Classification Properties 818
- direction 818
- display 818
- list-style 819
- list-style-image 820
- list-style-position 820
- list-style-type 820
- unicode-bidi 821
- white-space 822

Table Properties 822
- caption-side 822
- cell-spacing 823
- column-span 823
- empty-cells 824
- table-layout 824

Aural Properties 824
- azimuth 825
- cue 825
- cue-after 826
- cue-before 826
- elevation 827
- pause 827
- pause-after 828
- pause-before 828
- pitch 829
- pitch-range 829
- play-during 830
- richness 830
- speak 830
- speak-header 831

speak-numeral ... 831
speak-punctuation ... 832
speech-rate ... 832
stress ... 833
voice-family ... 833
volume ... 834

C XSL Formatting Objects Reference ... 835
XSL Formatting Objects ... 836
Declarations, Pagination, and Layout ... 836
Block-Level Objects ... 844
Inline-Level Objects ... 845
Table Formatting Objects ... 853
List Formatting Objects ... 858
Link and Multi-Formatting Objects ... 860
Out-of-Line Formatting Objects ... 862
Other Formatting Objects ... 863
Formatting Properties ... 864
Accessibility Properties ... 865
Absolute Position Properties ... 865
Border, Padding, and Background Properties ... 865
Font Properties ... 870
Table Properties ... 871
Hyphenation Properties ... 872
Margin Properties-Block ... 873
Margin Properties-Inline ... 874
Area Alignment Properties ... 875
Area Dimension Properties ... 876
Block and Line-Related Properties ... 877
Character Properties ... 879
Color-Related Properties ... 880
Float-Related Properties ... 880
Keeps and Breaks Properties ... 880
Layout-Related Properties ... 881
Leader and Rule Properties ... 882
Properties for Links ... 882
Document Properties ... 883
Properties for Markers ... 883
Properties for Number to String Conversion ... 885
Pagination and Layout Properties ... 885
Writing-Mode-Related Properties ... 887
Miscellaneous Properties ... 887
Aural Properties ... 887

D UNICODE Character Sets ... 891
Math-Related Character Codes ... 898

Index ... 949

Acknowledgments

My hat goes off to the great team at Osborne/McGraw-Hill and Studio B for their constant faith in me throughout the long, arduous task of publishing this book. I definitely couldn't have done it without all of their help. Thanks to Rebekah Young, Jenn Tust, Paulina Pobacha, Jody McKenzie, Karyn DiCastri, Paul Medoff, Simon St. Laurent, Neil Salkind (at Studio B), and all of the great production crew that I never saw, or heard from, but saw the wondrous results of their work in my writing. And I can't forget the illustrators, binders, papermakers, and everyone else working on this book. I might not know your names, but my thanks go out to all of you. The team at Osborne/McGraw-Hill was wonderful to work with and should be commended on their perseverance with this extremely long project.

I also would like to thank Ann for being such a wonderful, understanding daughter while I was working on this book. There is no one better than you. Mom, Dad, thank you for encouraging me to keep up the hard work and giving me a "never quit" attitude. And Luis, just whatever you do, never change. Your support makes light work out of the heaviest load.

Introduction

Have you ever seen another industry that moves as fast as the computer industry? What would you do if your car had to be replaced every year because this year's gas wasn't compatible with last year's car? This is the problem that Internet developers—no matter what language they are working in—face on a daily basis: this year's hottest Internet development language doesn't work fully in last year's Web browser.

With XML you no longer have to worry about your document not being compatible with the next, latest and greatest development. As long as you have basic XML-compliant software you can see your basic XML document. This book will help you with your XML, and it leaves the software development to companies like Microsoft and Netscape.

Who Should Read This Book

The audience for *XML: The Complete Reference* is any Web aficionado, who wants to create their own Web site using advanced features and capabilities of XML and its brethren. You could be either an experienced Web developer, who simply wants a quick reference to both languages and how they are used, or a beginning XML developer, who needs to know how to make something happen that you just can't quite figure out.

Whoever you are, you should already have these basic skills:

- Know the basic syntax of an SGML-based language, such as HTML
- Know the basic process used in creating an HTML page
- Have a basic familiarity with the concepts associated with using a browser, links, URL, etc.
- Understand the SGML document element-attribute hierarchy

You do not need to understand or even know any XML child languages, but you should have the interest in following the text intensive style of this book.

What's in This Book

At this time, XML is one of the hottest topics on the Internet. It is becoming the programmer's fix-all for information. The goal of *XML: The Complete Reference* is to provide you with "everything" you need to know about XML. You can find everything from the simple basics of writing your first XML document to the advanced topics in the field of XML, including parsers, validators, schemas, Document Type Definitions (DTDs), style sheets (CSS and XSL), namespaces, XLink, XPointer, XBase, and XML Query. In addition, this text covers a lot of supporting XML standards—the Resource Description Framework (RDF), XHTML, Synchronized Markup Languages (SYMM), such as SMIL, and Scalable Vector Graphic (SVG) formats.

I begin this reference by covering XML basics, such as creating simple documents that can be properly parsed by the current XML parsers. This information expands as you read about the creation of the DTD for the XML document and validating the document and its DTD. From there, the addition of style sheets adds both color and functionality to the document as you grow from simple Cascading Style Sheet (CSS) additions to the more complex Extensible Style Sheet Language (XSL) and XSL Transformations (XSLT) additions. Once you have completed an XML document with functioning style sheets, you will learn about XML Schemas, XHTML, XLink, XPointer, and the RDF. You will also explore the Document Object Model (DOM) through the use of scripts (JavaScript and Perl) by manipulating information contained within an XML document and flat-file database related to the document. Finally, you are introduced to the popular, and heavily used, XML child languages, such as MathML and SMIL. The chapters and parts are broken down in the next few pages.

Part I: XML Basics

Part I introduces the basic structure of XML documents. You'll learn how to identify XML elements and attributes, explore the purpose of validating XML documents, and examine some of the software that will perform that validation. You will also find a chapter covering XML namespaces and how they are used in your documents for validation purposes.

Chapter 1, "Getting a Global Perspective," provides a general overview of all the related technologies and requirements for XML. You'll find a bit of its history and a quick overview of the software that works with the current standard—and the software that is expected to work with the upcoming standards. In addition, this chapter covers the requirements of XML applications, what they do, and where they can take your development projects.

Chapter 2, "Reviewing XML Validating and Nonvalidating Parsers," discusses the various software that works with XML, including parsers, editors, and validators.

Chapter 3, "Saying 'Hello World' in XML," explains the requirements for correct information parsing and how to use validating software with your document. You will begin to build a simple

XML document, learn how to save, view, and add comments to it as well as how to check that it is parsing correctly.

Chapter 4, "Organizing XML Data," explores how to organize your data so that it will make sense when it is turned into an XML application. This chapter extensively covers the DOM, so you'll know what users are creating when they plan for the formatting of their data. Also, you'll look at how style sheets will affect your data presentation and examine how and when data should be used as an attribute not an element and vice versa.

Chapter 5, "Creating Well-Formed XML," discusses the rules associated with XML elements, opening and closing tags, identifying elements, and their child elements. It also contains all of the information you need to utilize empty tags and non-empty tags, the `<!xml>` statement, and it also explores the importance of the root element.

Chapter 6, "Adding Attributes" looks at the specifics of implementing XML attributes and reveals how attributes relate to elements and where attributes should be used within your document.

Chapter 7, "XML Namespaces" explores basic XML namespace concepts as well as the purpose of namespaces and the syntax used to reference namespaces.

Part II: Working with DTD

Document Type Definitions (DTDs) provide the instructions that control how your XML documents must be configured. In the four chapters in this part, you'll see how XML elements and attributes are defined using DTDs, and you'll discover how entities and notations are used within XML documents.

Chapter 8, "Validating Your XML Documents," covers both embedded and external DTDs, including specific validating software, what validation is, and why it is needed. You will also learn the general rules for defining DTD statements and using public DTDs.

Chapter 9, "Defining DTD Entities," addresses the identification of XML entities as well as using both general and parameter entities. You'll explore how to create an entity reference in the XML document using an entity reference linked from an external document.

Chapter 10, "Working with Attributes," identifies attributes in DTDs and explains how to identify them and their default values. Other topics discussed include attribute data types, predefined attributes, and declaring multiple attributes for one element.

Chapter 11, "Adding Other Data" covers the addition of comments, notations, and unparsed entities to the DTD. It also addresses the use of processing instructions for your data and identifying conditional statements in DTDs.

Part III: Adding Style

This entire Part is devoted to the use and implementation of style sheets, both Cascading Style Sheets (CSS) and the Extensible Stylesheet Language (XSL), in your XML documents.

Chapter 12, "When to Use Style Sheets," explores when and where to use style sheets, including how to decide whether to use CSS or XSL.

Chapter 13, "CSS Basics," examines the use of external style sheets in your XML documents, which includes both creating and saving them in XML documents. You'll learn how to use CSS to control the basic appearance of a document utilizing fonts, backgrounds, borders, margins, padding, and other general appearance settings.

Chapter 14, "CSS: The Next Step" covers the CSS properties that control visibility, overflow, indexing, object dimensions, and object display style. You will find a discussion of aural style sheet properties—both the `first-line` and `first-letter` pseudo-classes—the use of `!important`, and the properties controlling the appearance of your list elements.

Chapter 15, "XSL Basics" provides a simpler XSL introduction, explaining what XSL and XSLT do and the software that can be used to create, view, and validate your XSL and XSLT documents.

Chapter 16, "XSL Transformations," explores the XSLT language giving explicit detail on what it is, how it works, what it does, and why it does it. You will also find an extensive discussion of XPath.

Chapter 17, "XSL: Completing Your Application," explores formatting concepts for the XML content using the XSL-FO elements discussed in Appendix C.

Part IV: Using Schemas

In this Part you will find a relatively complete discussion of XML Schemas as far as the scope of this book, and the current state of the schema specification, allows. Because XML Schemas are a topic for a book in and of itself, you won't find every detail on XML Schemas here, but you will find all of the information that is required to begin writing and developing your own schemas.

Chapter 18, "Introducing Schemas," covers XML Schemas and the differences between XML Schemas and XML namespaces, and it includes the information you'll need to understand XML Schemas. It also provides examples of basic schema documents and the software that supports them.

Chapter 19, "Schema Elements, Types, and Groups" expands upon the use of XML Schema elements by showing you how to define both `complexType` and `simpleType` elements. It also covers the grouping of elements within your document.

Chapter 20, "Defining Schema Attributes," expands on the use of XML Schema attributes, including identifying attributes, creating groups of attributes, and introducing simple data types.

Chapter 21, "Advanced Concepts with Schemas" covers the rest of the information that you may have been looking for in the other schema chapters. You'll find a discussion on using target namespaces, setting up schema constraints, and using local versus global variables, as well as other Schema-related topics.

Part V: Using XML Query

With the constant developments in the growing field of XML you can always expand the information that you include within your document, or how you retrieve that information. Part V examines many of the XML related "hot topics" that are currently making inroads into the world of XML documents.

Chapter 22, "Introducing XML Query," covers the XML Query language, including what the language is designed to do and where and how it can be used, as well as the current state of the XML Query working draft. You will find a discussion of each of the XML Query working drafts that were available since February 2001.

Chapter 23, "XLinks," offers a general introduction to the XML Linking Language, its structure, and how to use and create XLink statements. This chapter also explores the creation of a DTD for your linking elements, such as attributes, and the definition of local and remote resources used in the links.

Chapter 24, "Using XPointer," provides a general introduction to the XML Pointer language by explaining why XPointers are used and what their structure is. Chapter 24 also includes examples of how to use XPointers.

Chapter 25, "Resource Description Framework," discusses the use of metadata in your XML documents and covers the framework used, why to use it, and offers examples of how RDF is used.

Part VI: XML in Action

XML doesn't do you a lot of good if you can't apply it to your everyday situations. The chapters in Part VI provide you with this grounding in reality.

Chapter 26, "XHTML," covers the conversion of HTML to XHTML and offers examples of the conversion process and an in-depth discussion of the modularization of XHTML.

Chapter 27, "Manipulating XML with JavaScript," examines how to use the DOM and JavaScript/JScript to modify the appearance and visibility of information in an XML document.

Chapter 28, "Collecting and Writing Data with CGI," provides a well-commented example of using CGI/Perl to collect information from a flat-file database and how to convert it to an XML document.

Part VII: XML Child Languages

Because of the popularity of XML, and its ease of application to so many areas of industry, XML is having children. There are three varieties of XML child languages discussed in Chapters 29 through 31.

Chapter 29, "SYMM and SMIL," covers the basic use and syntax of SMIL and the purpose of using XML-based languages for creating universally accessible synchronized multimedia documents. It also discusses the software that is available to read and view these documents.

Chapter 30, "Using Scalable Vector Graphics (SVG)" examines the basic use and syntax of SVG and the purpose of using XML-based language for creating vector graphics for use on networked systems.

Chapter 31, "Scientific Languages: MathML and CML," explores the basic use and syntax of both MathML and CML, including the application of XML-based languages for sharing scientific data over a variety of systems. XML provides both MathML and CML with the ability to identify various special notations used in the scientific industry.

Part VIII: The Appendixes

XML: The Complete Reference has a lot of Appendix-styled reference material that includes references for CSS and XSL as well as the key for writing a standard XML DTD. These Appendixes are formatted in easy-to-read tables or lists that should make the retrieval of information quick and painless. Appendix A offers "DTD Key Codes and a Sample DTD," Appendix B is a "CSS Language Reference," Appendix C is an "XSL Formatting Objects Reference" for formatting elements, and Appendix D, "UNICODE Character Sets," is a reference for MathML and CML as well as other UNICODE languages.

Conventions Used in This Book

There are very few conventions used in this book, but if you familiarize yourself with them now, reading the multitude of code examples will be much easier.

- All code is shown in a monospaced font.
- Bolded code in long examples helps you pinpoint the exact portion of code that is being discussed in the paragraphs around the code example.
- Note fields provide additional information about the topic being discussed in the chapter.
- All variables will appear in italics. If those variables are both code and variable, then they will appear in an italicized monospaced font.

Getting the Latest Information

Information on XML changes frequently so you will need to check out the World Wide Web Consortium site at http://www.w3.org to find out the current state of many of the XML-related specifications. You will also find a lot of information on XML sites, such as:

- http://www.xmlhack.com
- http://www.xml.com
- http://www.xslt.com
- http://www.internet.com
- http://www.xmlinfo.com
- http://www.xslinfo.com
- http://msdn.microsoft.com/xml
- http://www.schema.net
- http://www.xmlsoftware.com

The Complete Reference

Part I

XML Basics

Chapter 1

Getting a Global Perspective

The Extensible Markup Language (XML) is simply a set of rules. This set of rules identifies how you can define tags (text markup) that separate a document into individual parts and subparts. XML is a markup language like HTML, but it has been defined in such a way that it is not restricted to one particular vocabulary, industry, or use. XML is the epitome of extensibility for the Internet. It can be personalized for each corporate or private endeavor for which you may wish to apply it.

XML's markup rules are based upon an earlier markup language called the Standard Generalized Markup Language (SGML). Using SGML as its foundation and learning a few lessons from HTML (another SGML based language), XML creates text files to store your structured information. Don't worry, XML is much more straightforward to use than SGML, and it allows you, the document creator, as much freedom as you need for your own creation. XML is a very easy to use, easy to read by a computer (and not too difficult for a human being), easy to debug, and easy to use to create extensible markup language suitable for any industry that uses structured data such as spreadsheets, databases, financial information, and technical drawings.

The Early Beginnings

The human race has been creating solutions to problems since our first step on this world. When Alexander Graham Bell invented the first telephone, he was attempting to solve one of the common communication problems of the era. Today we have highly skilled technogeeks developing languages such as XML to share and display information with anyone, anywhere, no matter what software they are using, whether they are connected to the Internet or swapping disks across an office hall. That is what XML does. Perfectly. XML uses its strong SGML foundation to fulfill a series of requirements for identifying the pieces of a document so that it can be shared in its entirety or in part with any software, any user, anywhere, whether the user is connected to the Internet or simply working with a variety of database file formats throughout a company project.

A Foundation in SGML

XML has its foundation in the Standard Generalized Markup Language (SGML). SGML was developed to provide a method to identify the portions and content of a document, not by the actual content or line numbers, but by the type of information that it contains. For example, you could use SGML marked-up documents and search for a string such as "h1" to identify a level 1 heading, no matter what the content of that heading would be. You could then use scripts to find all of the level 1 headings by looking for that `<h1>` text marker, to show only the level 1 headings or copy them into another document to create a table of contents, and to sort out all of the text other than the level 1 headings.

SGML was developed out of the General Markup Language (GML), which was developed by IBM in the late 1960s. Only a few large organizations, educational institutes, and government offices used this language prior to its becoming a recognized document standard in 1986. A large boost to SGML's acceptance as an official standard was its official incorporation by the U.S. Internal Revenue Service and the U.S. Department of Defense. Upon these two organizations' acceptance, and their requirement for all of their contractors to also incorporate it, SGML received the extra boost it needed to become a standard. When the concept of documents that could be shared over a network, Web documents, was first brewing, the developers looked toward SGML as a model for the creation of HTML. Then with the explosion of the Internet, SGML received a new "lease on life" in the form of its newest child: XML.

HTML, unlike SGML and XML, controls the presentation of information. HTML is strictly a formatting language. SGML and XML are both sets of rules that are used to control the creation of markup languages that identify document content so that information can be formatted consistently throughout the document. Both SGML and XML are best suited for use in documents that have large amounts of similarly organized information such as catalogs, address books, mathematical functions, and even accounting records. Both SGML and XML are great for displaying information that would otherwise be found in a database structure.

The beauty of SGML, and XML, is that it allows one team of designers to identify the structures that are available for use in all documents. Think about this book. The original document was written using Microsoft Word, and all of the section headings, page headers and footers, and paragraph text were formatted, or styled, using Word styles. If this book would have been written in either SGML or XML, the markup from these languages would have been used to create the headings, footers, paragraphs, code segments, figure captions, callouts, and other document configurations used. You may ask yourself, if word processors can already do this, why the interest in XML? The answer is simple: Word processors can't share their style information. For instance, neither Corel's WordPerfect nor Sun's StarOffice word processing software can immediately read styles that you create in Microsoft Word. The document has to undergo a conversion process for any other type of software to read the information, and even then the conversion of the document styles is not always exact. SGML and XML allow the document to be read by any type of software, with the document author being able to specify how each portion of the document's content will be interpreted by all software. However, since XML only describes the content of your document, you have to provide a style sheet if you wish to format your information beyond normal text. The two main style sheet languages used with XML are Cascading Style Sheets (CCS) and Extensible Style Sheet Transformations (XSLT), both of which are discussed later in this chapter.

XML Requirements

When you create XML vocabularies and document structures, you have two tasks that must be completed to create a valid document. (See Chapter 5 for more information on validating XML documents.) First you need to identify all of the types of information, the content, you will be placing in your document. This task must be completed whether you want your document validated or simply parsed so your browser can view it. Second, you should provide a definition for the structure surrounding each piece of information you are identifying within your document. Without a document definition (Document Type Definition, DTD) describing the structure of the content used in your XML document, it can't be validated. Because you can create your own content identifiers (labels) and content descriptions, you can use XML to describe any type of information that can be sorted into specific content types. For example, you could as easily use XML to track the results of the National Finals Rodeo as you could to identify all of the parts of complex mathematical equations. You simply provide the identifying markup structure by identifying the content types and describing the content.

HTML was the first language that was popularly accepted to format documents using markup languages so they could be read by anyone, but HTML has one major flaw: it is a formatting language that does not regard document structure or content. This means that document designers can use a variety of HTML tags to control their document's appearance, but they have nothing to control the physical structure of the document. This system can create documents that appear professional, but it doesn't help you to create well-structured documents, based on the rules of XML or documents with universally identifiable parts.

The first step toward separating formatting from content control occurred with the development of Cascading Style Sheets (CSS). Style sheets allow all occurrences of a specific type of tag to be formatted in a specific way. Style sheets also allow a tag with a specific identifier to be formatted in a specific way. This is the first step toward removing the clustered HTML `<P><FONT><B>` tags from around the headings and paragraphs in your HTML documents. Using style sheets for formatting information works just as well, if not better, with XML as it does with HTML. This is in large part due to the strict content-centric focus of XML. Check out Chapter 13 and 14 for more information on Cascading Style Sheets.

For XML to perform its job of identifying document content correctly, you have to know how it is working. You need to understand how you can mark up your information so that other software, or style sheets, can interpret the structure of the document and apply formatting to the information.

Describing Structure

XML's tags describe the structure of a document, as well as identify the content of a document. XML tags, just like HTML, are opened and closed with angle brackets, "<" and ">". Within those brackets is the identifying name, or label, of the content. After this opening tag you will place the actual content being marked up by the XML. Finally, XML requires that you have a closing tag sharing the same name exactly as the starting tag (XML is case specific), other than the addition of a forward slash to the opening angle bracket: "</."

```
<TAGNAME> content </TAGNAME>
```

These tags include *attributes* that provide additional information about the content of the tag or the tag itself. Attributes are matched sets of name/value pairs in the form of `name="value"`. These attributes reside within the tags themselves as shown in the following code snippet:

```
<TAGNAME attributename="attributevalue"> content </TAGNAME>
```

Just because XML is formatted in the familiar HTML style, don't be fooled into thinking that it is as lax in its rules as HTML. If you have written HTML, you know that you can forget quotation marks around most of your attributes and the document will still load into your Web browser. You can even forget to add closing tags to some of your elements such as `<P>` and `<BR>`. XML is much more strict. Every attribute value must be enclosed in quotation marks, and every opening tag has to have a closing tag, unless it is an empty tag, but you will read more about those in Chapter 5. Applications that read XML documents are not allowed to ignore errors or to attempt to second-guess the document author; they must stop right at the error in the document and issue an error message to the viewer of the document. This makes XML documents relatively easy to debug because you know exactly which line is causing the error when you view the document. The rules relating to how the document has to be marked up control the *well-formedness* of the document. According to your XML software, a document is *well-formed* if the document meets all of the criteria identified within the XML specification. You can find more information on well-formed documents in Chapter 5.

If you view an XML document in a Web browser like Internet Explorer 5, you will see that there is no formatting being performed. All of your information is displayed in an outline structure (see Figure 1-1). The controls built into the software allow you to open and close segments of data, but they do not format the information.

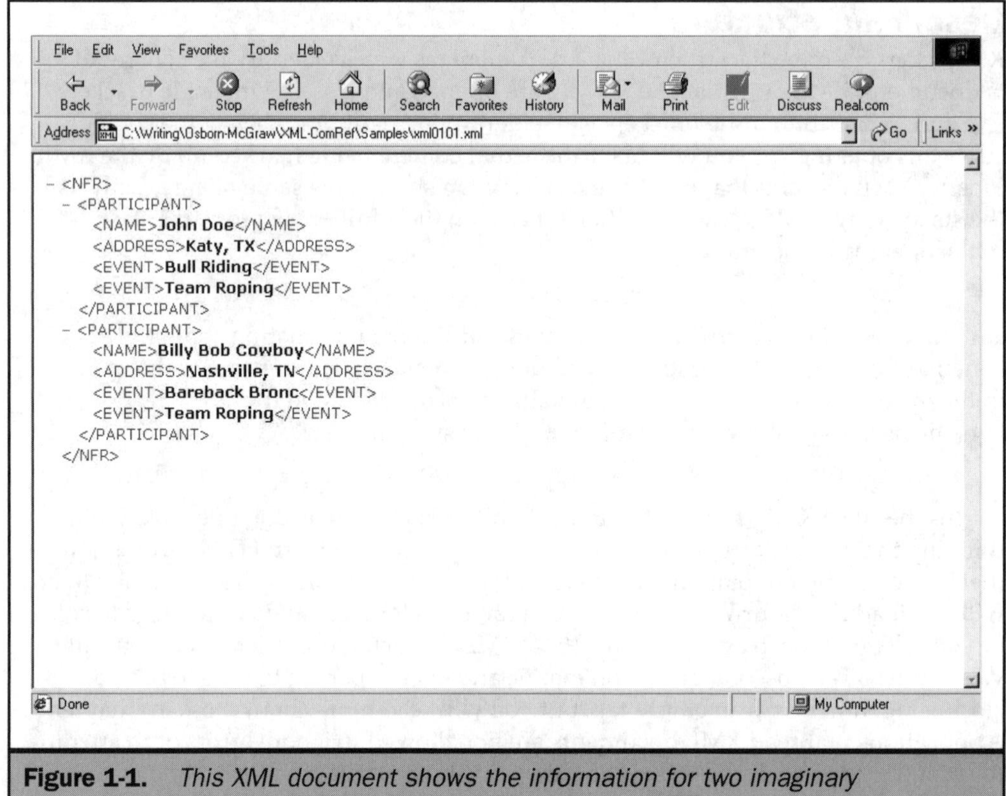

Figure 1-1. *This XML document shows the information for two imaginary participants in the National Finals Rodeo (NFR).*

There is nothing inherent in XML, or its child languages, that controls the formatting of the information when the Web browser, or other document reader, views your XML document. With XML, unlike HTML, style sheets control all of the formatting, unless the formatting controls are already built into the software viewing the document, as is the practice with Synchronized Multimedia Integration Language (SMIL) players such as Real Networks RealPlayer 8.

The structure that XML gives to its document content becomes an inverted tree if you were to break each set of markup tags into its own branch on a document. This tree structure, the same as is created in SGML documents, allows you to see the architecture and tag hierarchy of the XML document easily. You can see this structure in Figure 1-1 with the `<NFR>` and the two `<PARTICIPANT>` headings. This tree structure, shown in general in Figure 1-2, places the document root as a foundation for all of the headings, subheadings, and text that appears on the document. If you were to superimpose this structure over the NFR example, the `<NFR>` element would replace the Document Root, and each of the `<PARTICIPANT>` tags would replace a level 1 heading.

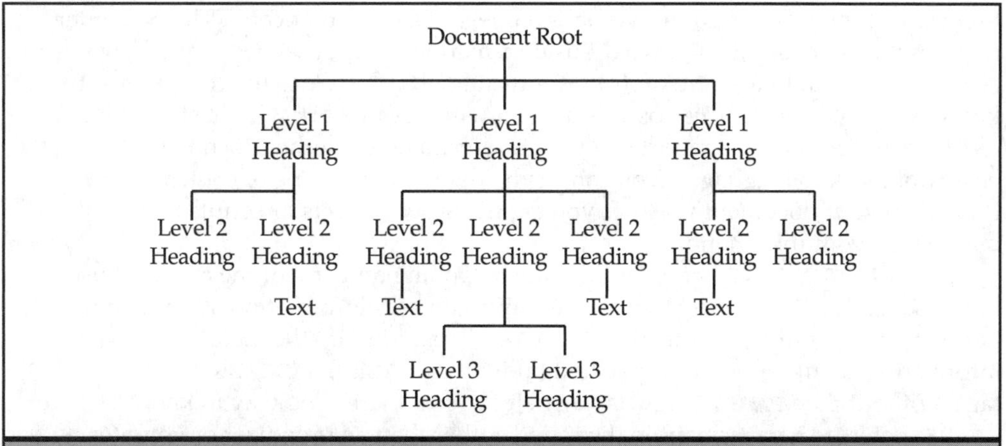

Figure 1-2. *The general structure of an XML document resembles this inverted tree and the structure of most books.*

In addition to marking up the individual segments of a document, XML provides additional information about each of those segments.

A Meta Language

XML markup is a meta language. This means that the markup can be used to describe other languages. This allows you to create your own XML tags that provide information about the information for which you are creating the XML based document structure. In the case of a National Finals Rodeo participant you would use the XML markup to identify the rodeo participant's name, separate from their mailing address, and still separate from the rodeo event or events in which they are participating, and separate from every other participant in the rodeo:

```
<NFR>
  <PARTICIPANT>
    <NAME> John Doe </NAME>
    <ADDRESS> Katy, TX </ADDRESS>
    <EVENT> Bull Riding </EVENT>
    <EVENT> Team Roping </EVENT>
  </PARTICIPANT>
</NFR>
```

The XML tags `<NAME>`, `<ADDRESS>`, and `<EVENT>` provide the descriptive information, or markup text label, for the content found within the tags. `<NAME>` identifies the name of the person, in this case John Doe, that the remaining information is discussing. This is meta information. A person would recognize the string "John Doe" as an individual's name, but a computer can't. The computer requires that something tell it what this information is supposed to be and how it is to be used or stored. In the case of XML it is the tag `<NAME>`. Once the computer software knows what type of information it is dealing with, it can work with it, storing it in a database, or formatting a report on either a Web page or another document. That is the beauty of markup languages. You can easily identify every type of content that is located on your document whether you are using style sheets or scripts to format and manipulate your information.

The `<PARTICIPANT>` tag identifies the beginning and end of the *record*, to use a database term, within the XML document that contains information about a single participant. Not only does the `<PARTICIPANT>` tag identify the record, it also provides information about the content specified under the `<NAME>`, `<ADDRESS>`, and `<EVENT>` tags. Without the `<PARTICIPANT>` tag helping out, there is no way to know that the `<NAME>` refers to a participant in the rodeo, rather than an organizer or volunteer.

```
<NFR>
  <ORGANIZER>
    <NAME> Jimmy Parker </NAME>
    <ADDRESS> Houma, LA </ADDRESS>
    <EVENT> Bull Riding </EVENT>
  </ORGANIZER>
  <PARTICIPANT>
    <NAME> John Doe </NAME>
    <ADDRESS> Katy, TX </ADDRESS>
    <EVENT> Bull Riding </EVENT>
    <EVENT> Team Roping </EVENT>
  </PARTICIPANT>
</NFR>
```

The Current Standards

XML is a standards-based set of rules. This means that every document has to be compatible with the set of rules that has been defined for all XML documents by the World Wide Web Consortium (W3C). The goal of these standards is to create a series of technologies that all work together, creating an extensible universe of document formatting controls allowing for the reuse of document definitions throughout any combination of documents and their needs.

XML 1.0

This primary specification that set up the rules for XML was released in February 1998. This standard identifies the requirements of a well-formed XML document, as well as the origin and goals of XML. The goals of XML are quite simple actually. They include the following ideals:

- XML shall easily be implemented over the Internet.
- XML shall be usable in a vast variety of applications.
- XML shall be compatible with SGML.
- XML documents shall be legible to humans.
- XML document design shall be done swiftly.
- XML document design shall be formal and to the point.
- XML documents shall be easy to create.
- XML markup is not required to be terse.

You can read the specification itself on the W3C Web site located at http://www.w3.org/XML.

XML Namespaces

The XML Namespaces recommendation was released in January 1999. This standard provides the rules for associating XML element and attribute names with a collection of element and attribute names that have been identified by a specific Uniform Resource Identifier (URI). The goal of XML Namespaces was to create a mechanism in which a single document could use elements and attributes in previously identified sets of vocabularies, without worrying about duplication of element and attribute names. This system works by adding a prefix to the names of elements and attributes so that each attribute is properly associated with its originating document. You can find more information on using XML Namespaces in XML documents in Chapter 7.

You can read the specification itself on the W3C Web site located at http://www.w3.org/TR/1999/REC-xml-names-19990114/.

Document Type Definitions

Document Type Definitions (DTDs) provide the rules by which information within your XML document can be validated. These documents provide the controls, defined using Backus-Naur Form (BNF) grammar, to identify which elements are valid for a particular document and which attributes are then valid to use with each of those elements. With a DTD, you will find a list of all the elements, attributes, notations, and entities that can be used within a single XML document. In the process of identifying the valid parts of the XML document, it also defines the relationship of each part to every other part. For example, a DTD would identify that the root element of a document has to be `<NFR>` and it can contain as many `<PARTICIPANT>` and `<ORGANIZER>` elements as you, the document author, wish to include. It will also specify that the `<NFR>` element can't contain any `<NAME>` elements, and that each `<PARTICIPANT>` and `<ORGANIZER>` element is allowed one `<NAME>` within it. Read Part II for more information on Document Type Definitions.

Cascading Style Sheets

Cascading Style Sheets (CSS) became a standard in 1996. In its first draft, it defined a very simple visual formatting model for working with HTML documents. In May of 1998, Cascading Style Sheet 2 (CSS2) became a recommendation. This updated version of CSS included more advanced formatting options, including controls for paged and printed media, which are followed when you print from a Web site, as well as aural style, which control the verbose reading of Web pages through speech synthesizers. CSS2 included support for document element positioning, downloadable fonts, and advanced functions for tables.

Cascading Style Sheet development hasn't stopped there. Cascading Style Sheet 3 (CSS3) is currently in the works, and it is going to be dramatically different in format than CSS2. CSS3 is being written as a series of modules covering such things as paged media, color profiles, multicolumn layouts, behaviors, accessibility features, international layouts and characters, CSS namespaces, and user interface designs. This will allow for the acceptance of portions of CSS3 as they are completed and therefore should increase the acceptance and implementation of CSS3 in our favorite browsers and XML editors, validators, and parsers. Chapters 13 and 14 will help you use CSS with your XML documents.

Note *You can collect more information on the various Cascading Style Sheet specifications from the W3C Web site located at http://www.w3.org/Style/CSS/.*

Extensible Stylesheet Language

The Extensible Stylesheet Language (XSL) is a language designed for creating style sheets specifically with XML pages. It is based on XML and has two primary parts. The first goal of XSL is to provide a language for transforming XML documents. The second is to provide an XML-based vocabulary for formatting XML structured documents. XSL style sheets control the presentation of your XML information by converting the original XML document into an XSL document using the formatting controls specified in the XSL language. For more information on creating and using XSL with XML documents read Chapters 15, 16, and 17.

The XSL specification is broken down into two parts. The first is XSL Transformations (XSLT), which became a W3C recommendation in November of 1999. This recommendation defines the syntax and semantics that are used in converting standard XML documents into new XML documents using XSL formatting controls.

The second portion of the specification is very much like CSS. It provides a series of formatting objects and properties that are applied to the XML classes found within your document, and they control its appearance when a Web browser or other supporting software renders the document.

Note *You can collect more information on the various XSL stylesheet specifications from the W3C Web site located at http://www.w3.org/Style/XSL/.*

XML Schemas

XML Schemas are still in a working draft form as of this writing, but they are intended to provide more functionality built into your XML documents than is currently provided for with DTDs. The XML Schema draft is broken down into three separate documents: two of the documents identify and define a specific aspect of schemas, and the third document, the Primer, identifies how to use them. Schemas work with XML and XML Namespaces to create a specific class of XML documents using namespaces. The goal is that XML documents will conform to a specific schema, which is much like a DTD in conceptual approach, but much more advanced. This schema is then used on a variety of XML documents, each of which is often referred to as an *instance document*, to constrain it, much the same way a DTD would, but with the following considerations taken into account:

- Schemas must be more expressive than XML DTDs.
- Schemas must be expressed in XML.
- Schemas must be usable by a wide variety of applications that employ XML.
- Schemas must be easily usable on the Internet.
- Schemas must be optimized for interoperability.
- Schemas must be simple to implement using modest design and runtime resources.
- Schemas must be coordinated with relevant W3C specifications, including XML Information Set, XLinks, XML Namespaces, XPointers, and style sheets recommendations, as well as the Document Object Model (DOM), HTML, and the Resource Description Framework (RDF) Schema.

XML Schemas can be quite difficult to learn the first time around, so check out Part IV for more information on what they do and how they do it.

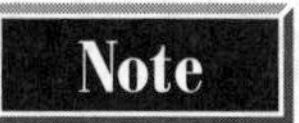

You can collect more information on the various XML Schema working drafts from the W3C Web site located at http://www.w3.org/TR/xmlschema-0/, http://www.w3.org/TR/xmlschema-1/, and http://www.w3.org/TR/xmlschema-2/.

XML Query Language

The XML Query Language is currently not much more than a list of goals to be completed. When this new recommendation is available, it will provide a data model to use with XML documents, as well as a complete query language and set of operators for use with the data model. For more information on the XML Query Language read Chapter 21.

You can collect more information on the XML Query Language working drafts from the W3C Web site located at http://www.w3.org/TR/xmlquery-req/.

XLinks

The XML Linking Language (XLink), discussed in detail in Chapter 23, is used in XML documents to create and define links between resources in a much more informative and flexible manner than is provided in the linking abilities of HTML documents. XLink provides a framework for creating a wide variety of links from a basic unidirectional link to more complex linking structures allowing XML documents to do the following.

- Create links among more than two resources
- Associate metadata with the link
- Create databases of links capable of being located away from the linked documents and resources

You can collect more information on the XML Linking Language working drafts from the W3C Web site located at http://www.w3.org/TR/xlink/.

XPointers

The XML Pointer Language (XPointer), the topic of Chapter 24, is designed as a tool for identifying fragments of the Uniform Resource Identifier (URI) references that locate XML Internet media types such as `<text/xml>` or `<application/xml>`. XPointers are used to identify the internal structure of an XML document by selecting specific internal parts of the document based upon information in the document tree. Using XPointers, you can select any part of a document, including the element type, attribute value, character content, and the part's relative position within the document tree.

You can collect more information on the XML Pointer language working drafts from the W3C Web site located at http://www.w3.org/TR/xptr/.

XPath

The XML Path (XPath) W3C recommendation, completed in November 1999 and discussed in Chapter 16, was designed as a means of referring to specific portions of an XML document using XSLT and XPointer. This recommendation provides a standard means of referencing addresses and locations within XML documents as well as manipulating and comparing strings, numbers, and Boolean values.

You can collect more information on the XPath specification from the W3C Web site located at http://www.w3.org/TR/xpath.

XML Digital Signatures

The XML Digital Signatures working draft, covered in Chapter 25, identifies the processing rules and syntax for representing digital signatures within XML documents. These signatures can be applied to any XML document as either an enveloped (included within the XML document) or detached signature (included in an external data file).

You can collect more information on the XML Digital Signatures working draft from the W3C Web site located at http://www.w3.org/TR/xmldsig-core/.

The Resource Description Framework Schema

The Resource Description Framework (RDF) Schema, discussed in detail in Chapter 26 along with the original Resource Description Framework specification, was designed as a means of exchanging computer-readable descriptions of the resources on the Internet. This means that the RDF Schema provides a means of processing metadata about Web resources. This schema uses XML to exchange information about resources, although the resource itself could be any type of file from an XML document to a Java application. RDF could be used for a variety of purposes, including sharing information about resources with search engines, creating a catalog about the information contained within a Web site, or even as a means of rating document content.

You can collect more information on the Resource Description Framework (RDF) Schema working draft from the W3C Web site located at http://www.w3.org/RDF/.

Canonical XML

The goal of the Canonical XML working draft, discussed in Chapter 27, is to identify a way of comparing XML documents on a syntactical level. Since most XML documents, even describing similar types of data, will not have the same structure, or the same content, they appear to have no association to each other using byte-for-byte comparisons. Canonical XML creates a subset of the original XML document that can be compared to other documents using the same, or similar, syntax.

You can collect more information on the Canonical XML working drafts from the W3C Web site located at http://www.w3.org/TR/xml-c14n/.

XHTML

The Extensible Hypertext Markup Language (XHTML), described in Chapter 28, is not a new language at all, it is simply a reformulation of the exiting HTML 4.0 specification into modules that follow the rules imposed by the XML specification. The current browsers don't automatically support this reformulation of HTML, since they still lack full support for XML. As XML becomes more fully supported in Web browsers and other software, XHTML will be more fully supported. XHTML does not remove any of the syntax of the existing HTML 4.0 specification, and it continues to support the HTML DOM (Document Object Model). XHTML allows document authors to create documents that will be functional in the future XML-centric world and still work in today's HTML-centric Web.

You can collect more information on the XHTML1.0 specification and the XHTML 1.1 working draft by checking out the W3C Web site located at http://www.w3.org/TR/XHTML1/ and http://www.w3.org/TR/XHTML-basic/, respectively.

XML Software

XML documents, or applications as they are often called, are designed to be very easy for computer software to manipulate and legible for human readers and developers. This software reads the XML document or application. The most current versions of Microsoft Internet Explorer and Netscape Navigator can both display XML documents, but they require the assistance of other software to read the XML document. There are two different types of software that can read XML documents: nonvalidating parsers and validating parsers.

Nonvalidating Parsers

Nonvalidating parsing software, detailed in Table 1-1, is the easiest software to use with your XML documents. It simply verifies that your document is well-formed: all of the opening tags have closing tags, and all of the attribute name/value pairs are properly expressed. The parsing software then takes apart the document, breaking it into its identifiable parts, and displays it for the reader. Both Netscape Navigator and Microsoft Internet Explorer provide these parsers within their newest browsing software. Internet Explorer has included an XML parser since version 4, while Netscape Navigator did not start supporting XML until the 6.0 release.

Note *Netscape Navigator 6.0 requires a style sheet to show the contents of your XML document.*

Parser Name	Description and Location
expat	This XML 1.0 parser has been developed in C. This parser should be fully conforming to the standard. http://www.jclark.com/xml/expat.html ftp://ftp.jclark.com/pub/xml/expat.zip
Lark	This XML 1.0 parser has been implemented using Java. It is covered under a general public license. Lark has a validating version in beta called Larval that is available from the same Web page. http://www.textuality.com/Lark/
XP	XP is an XML 1.0 parser that has been developed using Java. It conforms to all XML 1.0 specifications and identifies well-formed documents. http://www.jclark.com/xml/xp/index.html
TclXML	This TCL-based parser includes a completely TCL-based XML parser, as well as a TCL interface to the expat XML parser. http://www.zveno.com/zm.cgi/in-tclxml/
XML Testbed	The XML Testbed software is a collection of XML applications written in Java that includes an XML parser, editor, and viewer. http://www.w3.org/XML/1998/08withall/
Jumbo	This XML parser was originally designed to parse the Chemical Markup Language (CML) but can also be used with other XML applications. xml-cml.org/jumbo
RUWF at xml.com	This is an online XML parser that will check the URL of your XML page and report back with any errors that it has found. http://www.xml.com/xml/pub/tools/ruwf/check.html

Table 1-1. *XML Nonvalidating Parsers Available on the Internet*

Validating Parsers

Validating XML parsers are XML parsers that perform the added tasks of verifying the contents of the XML document against a DTD. This is done to ensure that all of the elements and attributes used within the XML document are used properly and testing *validity constraints* built into the XML specification. You will explore validating parsers in more depth in Chapter 8.

Parser Name	Description and Location
LT XML	LT XML is a set of XML tools including a C-based API and a developers kit. The release now available will run on UNIX and WIN32. http://www.ltg.ed.ac.uk/software/xml/
XML 4 Java	This validating XML parser is written in Java and based upon the Apache Xerces XML Parser. http://www.alphaworks.ibm.com/tech/xml4j
Microsoft XML	This validating XML parser includes support for XSLT and XPath, as well as conforming to the XML 1.0 specification requirements. This parser can be set to a nonvalidating mode. http://msdn.microsoft.com/xml/default.asp
Richard Tobin's XML Checker	This online validating XML parser checks for well-formedness and validity in your online XML documents. http://www.cogsci.ed.ac.uk/~richard/xml-check.html
STG's XML Validator	This online validating XML parser, provided by the Scholarly Technology Group, allows you to check local documents by their address, online documents, or actual XML code. http://www.stg.brown.edu/service/xmlvalid/

Table 1-2. *XML Validating Parsers Available on the Internet*

Don't Forget the DOM

The Document Object Model (DOM) is an Application Programming Interface (API). This means that the DOM provides a platform and language independent method for allowing programs and scripts to access and update the content, structure, and style sheets associated with a document. An API provides the standard model for how XML content and elements can be interacted with using scripts or other programs. The DOM Level 1 specification was completed in 1998 in two distinct parts: the Core Object Model and the HTML Object Model. XML constructs are followed in the Core Object Model.

Note *The W3C is currently previewing a candidate recommendation for DOM Level 2 and is also setting up the requirements for a DOM Level 3 specification. You can track these developments at http://www.w3.org/DOM.*

In addition to the Core Object Model constructs, XML interface objects have been added to the DOM Level 1 Core Object Model. You can implement the Core Object Model constructs without XML, but in order to implement the XML constructs you have to implement those specified in the Core Object Model. Using the DOM, you can easily apply scripts to your XML pages that will be able to show specific types of content based upon reader submissions. For example, you will be able to write JavaScript code that will read through your XML document, searching all of the `<PARTICIPANT>` tags for a `<NAME>` tag with the content "John Doe." Without the DOM this type of line-by-line or object-by-object manipulation was not possible. There is more information on using scripting based on the DOM with XML documents in Chapter 30.

Summary

As you can see, XML has a lot of pieces and parts that go into making a complete and working XML application. Each of these parts works together so that, in the end, you have a seamless application allowing you to provide information to your site visitors in any format or style that is necessary for their particular uses. Although XML is a markup language using simple text files to store vast amounts of information, it can be used to further define itself, as has been done with XML Schemas.

XML, because of its SGML foundation, is flexible enough to work for any situation that requires the formatting of structured data. Any information that can be stored in a spreadsheet or database type structure can be stored within an XML document. XML documents have very strict guidelines that must be followed in order for them to be read by the variety of parsing and validating software available for use with XML documents on the Internet. Documents that meet the requirements are termed well-formed, having followed all of the rules for creating XML documents and applications.

This quick introduction to all of the parts of XML will become clearer as you continue reading through the remaining chapters of this book. As the book progresses, you will be walked through every stage and major W3C recommendation that affects the development and implementation of XML today and its progress into the future, including its affects on HTML and sharing information on the Internet.

Chapter 2

Reviewing XML Validating and Nonvalidating Parsers

XML developers have a variety of software available that they can use to manipulate, create, edit, view, and parse XML documents. In the case of a Web browser such as Internet Explorer, Microsoft uses the MS-XML parser to parse the XML document, which in turn passes the parsed information on to the Internet Explorer 5.*x* Web browser. From the user standpoint you see none of this happening; you simply see the XML contents appear on the screen before you. As a user, you may not be highly interested in the software that is making all of this possible, but from a developer standpoint, you need to know what is happening with your document and how that process is going to affect your individual documents.

The primary type of software that you are concerned with when dealing with XML documents, since your editor can be any simple text editor available for any operating system, is the parser. There are two distinct types of parsers: nonvalidating and validating, but before you can parse your document, you must first create it.

Getting XML Documents Written

In addition to parsers, you also need to have some sort of editor for creating your XML documents. You can either use a simple text editor such as Windows Notepad or something a tad more sophisticated such as the World Wide Web Consortium's Amaya browser and editor. The World Wide Web Consortium's Amaya browser and editor is the World Wide Web Consortium's complete development environment for the majority of their standards including XML and many of its child languages.

Note *The Amaya browser is located at the World Wide Web Consortium Web site at http://www.w3.org/Amaya/User/BinDist.html. From this page you can download a copy of this browser for either the Windows or Unix operating system.*

The Amaya interface shown in Figure 2-1 provides you with line numbers that make it easier for you to find any errors that are found when your document is parsed.

If you would like to use a more advanced editor, or be able to distance yourself from the actual XML code, you should check out the editors that are available from sites such as xmlsoftware.com/editors and xmlhack.com. From these sites you can download a variety of parsers ranging from free and shareware packages to relatively spendy commercial packages. Depending upon your task, there is an editor for you. There are editors that validate your information, work with schemas, create DTDs and style sheets, and work with XSL Transformations.

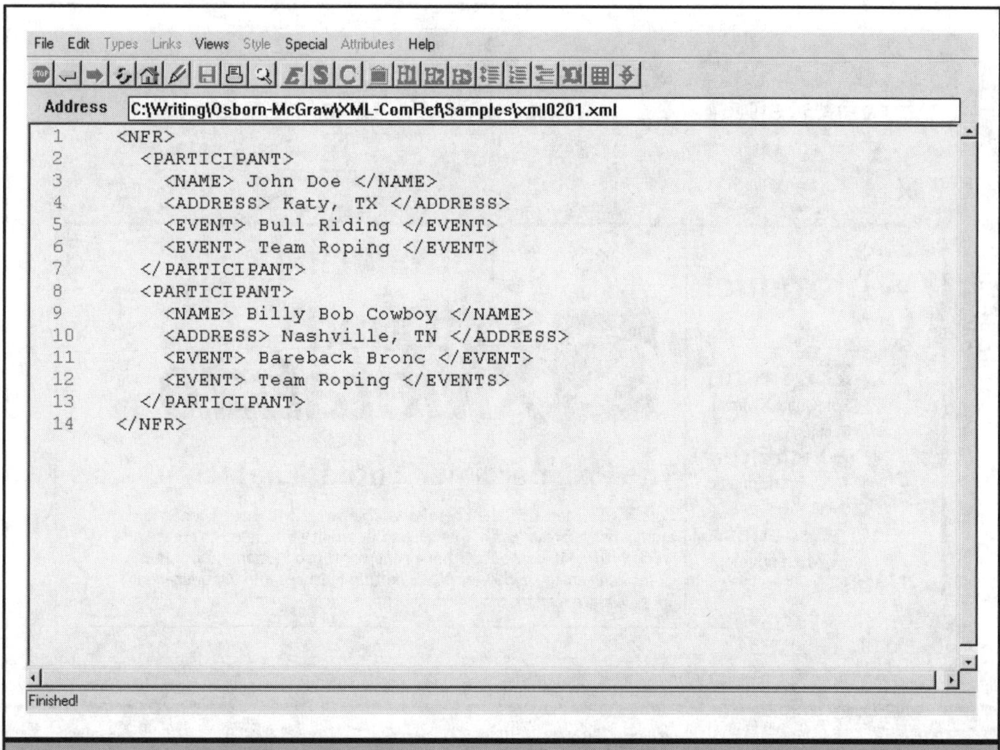
File Edit Types Links Views Style Special Attributes Help
Address C:\Writing\Osborn-McGraw\XML-ComRef\Samples\xml0201.xml
<NFR>
<PARTICIPANT>
<NAME> John Doe </NAME>
<ADDRESS> Katy, TX </ADDRESS>
<EVENT> Bull Riding </EVENT>
<EVENT> Team Roping </EVENT>
</PARTICIPANT>
<PARTICIPANT>
<NAME> Billy Bob Cowboy </NAME>
<ADDRESS> Nashville, TN </ADDRESS>
<EVENT> Bareback Bronc </EVENT>
<EVENT> Team Roping </EVENTS>
</PARTICIPANT>
</NFR>
Finished!

Figure 2-1. *The Amaya browser and editor allows you to create XML documents, but it does not check them for well-formedness.*

Note *Turbo XML 2.0 contains both XML Authority and XML Instance. You can get info about Turbo XML at www.extensibility.com/products/turboXML.*

Some of the editors that are available include

- **XMetaL by SoftQuad** (http://www. softquad.com) This software, shown in Figure 2-2, provides a complete content authoring system for your XML documents. XMetaL combines state-of-the-art XML editing features and a pleasant front end to your applications. XMetaL includes the XML support required to create both valid and well-formed XML documents. You can download a demonstration version of XMetaL from the SoftQuad Web site.
- **XML Authority by Extensibility** (http://www.extensibility.com/products/xml_authority.htm) XML Authority provides a comprehensive design environment for XML Schemas, which provides the tools for accelerating the

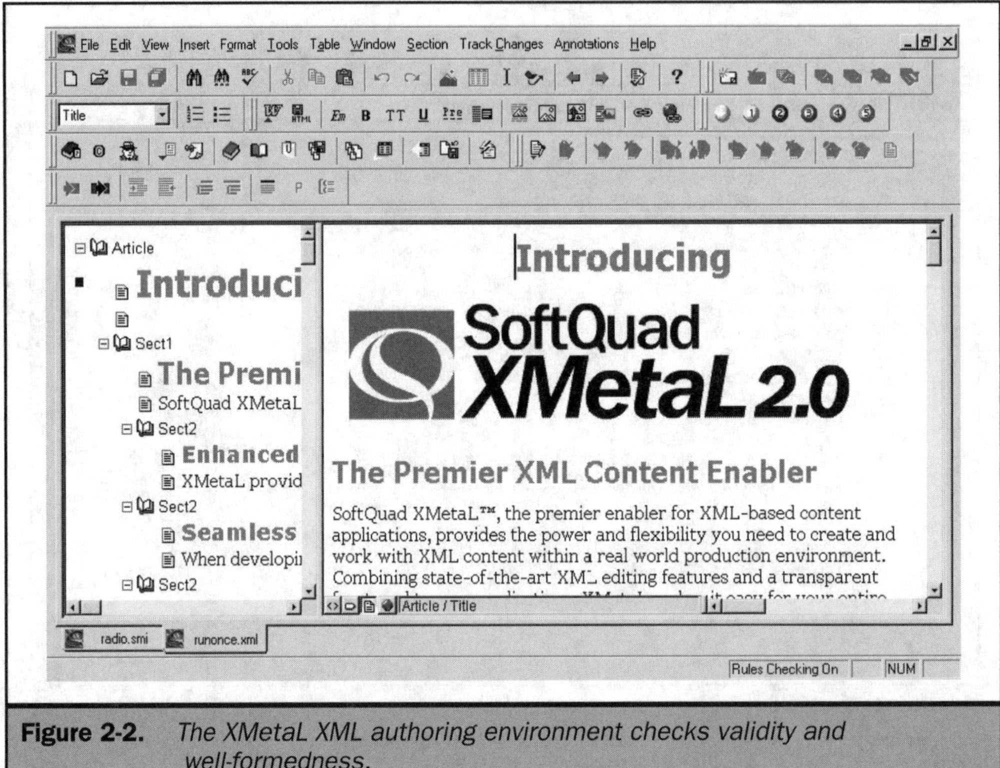

Figure 2-2. *The XMetaL XML authoring environment checks validity and well-formedness.*

creation, conversion, and management of these documents; see Figure 2-3. XML Authority supports all major and emerging schema standards including DTD, XDR, BizTalk, SOX Version 2, XML Schema DCD, DDML, and RELAX. The support of these schemas allows you to adapt your business for XML deployment with your business partners. XML Authority converts existing applications and documents into schemas, defining the basis for well-formed XML documents and enabling valid XML. The intuitive graphical user interface allows even the most complex schemas to be quickly developed and shared between groups and organizations. This product is available for a free ten-use demonstration download.

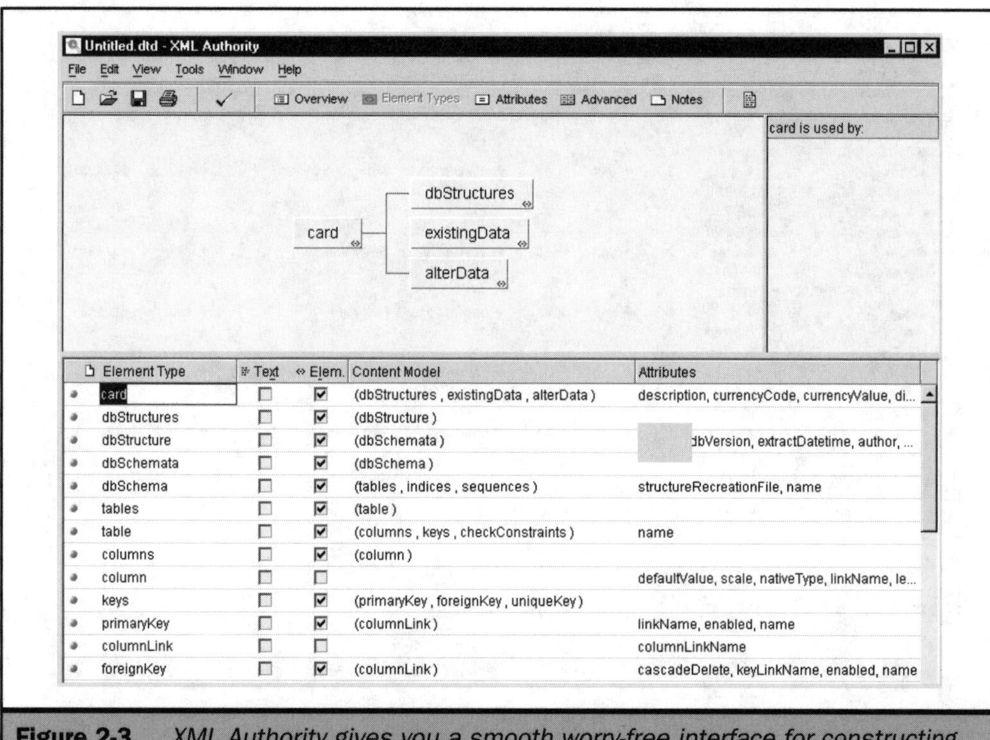

Figure 2-3. *XML Authority gives you a smooth worry-free interface for constructing XML schemas.*

- **XML Instance by Extensibility** (http://www.extensibility.com/products/xml_instance/) XML Instance, shown in Figure 2-4, is a schema-driven data-editing tool allowing you to create, edit, and manage data-oriented XML documents, messages, and configuration files. Using XML Instance you can edit and validate XML documents that conform to a DTD or XML schema using any prominent XML schema dialect, including DTD, XDR, SOX v2.0 and a subset of XML Schema. You can customize the display of internal documents to meet your needs and business processes without jeopardizing schema compliance

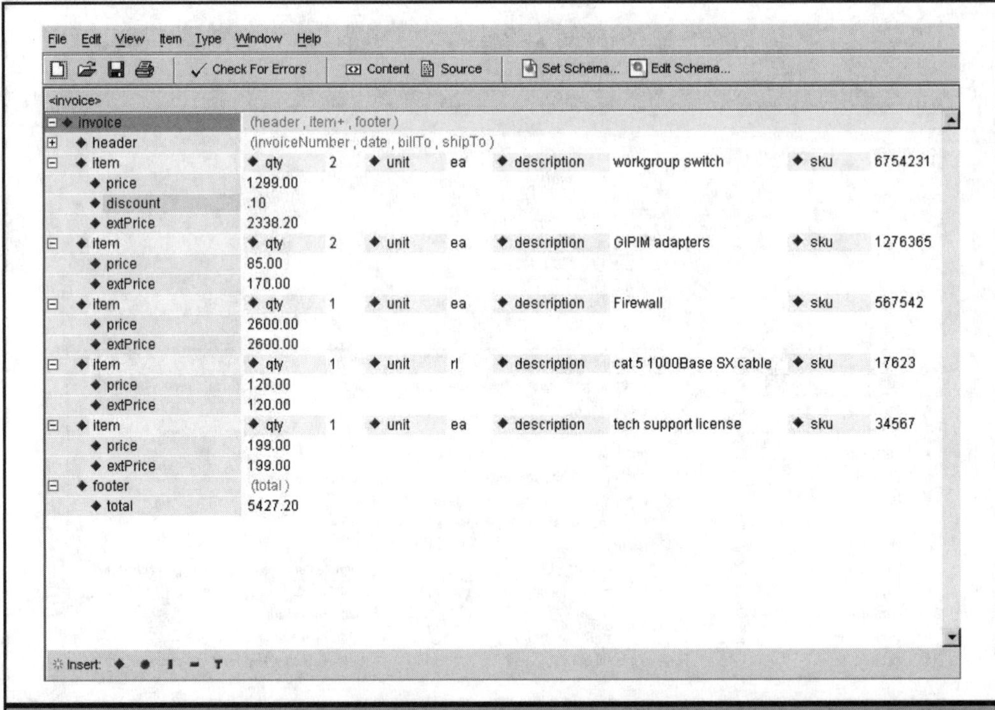

Figure 2-4. *XML Instance provides a graphical user interface for the development of DTDs, as well as XML documents for any size and scope of XML application.*

and without losing the data models. The graphical interface also facilitates easy building and navigation of long, complex XML documents. This product is available for a free ten-use demonstration download.

- **XML Spy by Icon Information Systems** (http://www.xmlspy.com) Using XML Spy (see Figure 2-5) you have a complete editing environment for XML documents, DTDs, Schemas, and XSL transformations. XML Spy has at its core a validating XML editor, which provides four views of your documents: a Grid View for structured editing, a Database/Table View for displaying repeated elements a tabular fashion, a Text View with colored syntax for low-level work,

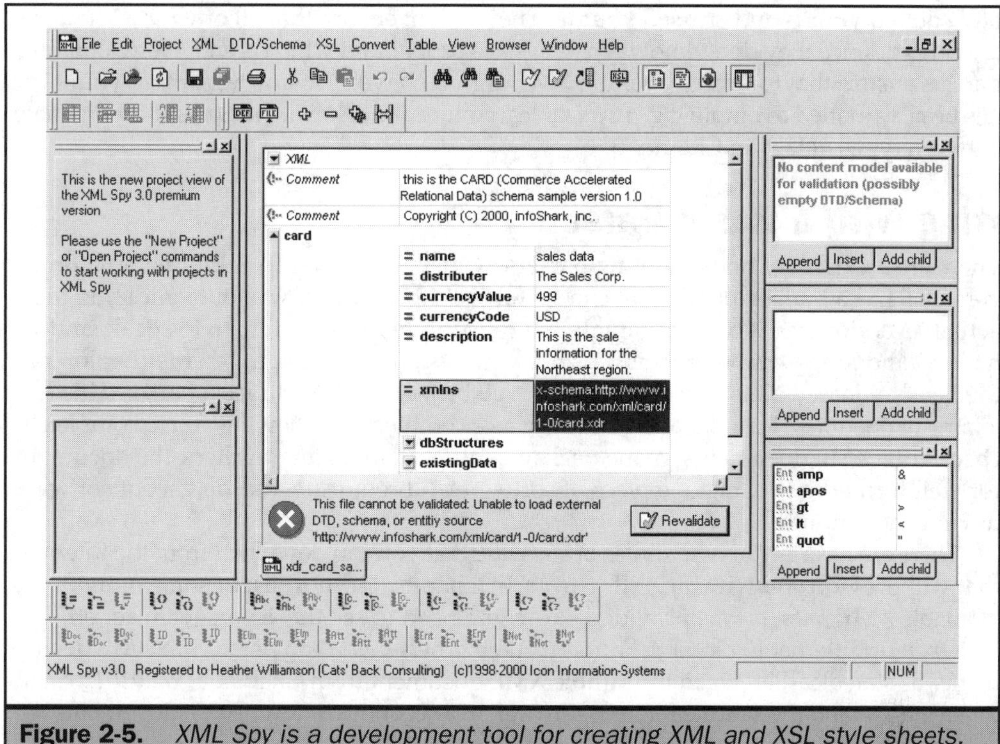

Figure 2-5. *XML Spy is a development tool for creating XML and XSL style sheets.*

and an integrated document browser that supports both CSS and XSL style sheets. You can download a 30-day demonstration version of the software from their Web site.

XML Nonvalidating Parsers

Nonvalidating parsers are the most common and are the simplest to write XML documents for. Nonvalidating parsers simply check for well-formedness within your XML document. You can think of these parsers as simply ensuring that you have dotted your *is* and crossed your *ts*. They do not ensure that all of your XML tags are proper, since they don't know what tags are proper and which aren't. Nonvalidating parsers ensure that for every opening XML tag you have a closing tag or that your tag has been formatted as empty tag. You will learn more about how to make and differentiate between types of tags in Chapter 5.

Starting with a Basic Parser

There are a variety of nonvalidating parsers available. For example, Internet Explorer version 5 has a built-in parser that checks for well-formedness without validating the actual XML document code, although you can simply flip a switch, so to speak, and have a validating version of their parser if you wish. In addition to Internet Explorer 5, the newly released Netscape Navigator 6 Web browser also includes a parser. This joining of document browser and parser is a nice combination, allowing you to completely check your XML documents in one package, rather than having to check the document for well-formedness using one piece of software and requiring a second set of software to view the output.

There are a variety of other types of software that you can download from the Internet that will provide you with an XML parser. In Chapter 1 a short list of some of the available XML parsers was provided. Now you need to see those parsers in action.

Open up Internet Explorer 5. From this Web browser you can parse your XML documents, as stated earlier. Open the sample XML document from Chapter 1, *xml0101.xml*, in one window, and the sample file, *xml0201.xml*, in a second window. These documents are exactly the same, other than one change made to the last <EVENT> element's closing tag that had caused a parsing error within the *xml0201.xml* file (as you can see in Figure 2-6).

Most parsers that don't ship as a part of a browser will display a message informing you of the type and location of the error that occurred, if an error occurred. If there were no errors in the document, then the parser will return a message letting you know that your XML document is well-formed. If the parser is shipped as part of a browser and the document has no errors, the browser will typically display the contents of the XML document.

You need to keep in mind that different parsers may produce different results when you view the documents. This is permitted by the XML 1.0 specification. For example, the expat parser used in Netscape Navigator 6 doesn't necessarily retrieve external resources, so entities (discussed in Chapter 9) may not appear, while they would have if processed, for instance, with MSXML or AElfred.

Online Parsers

There are a few nonvalidating XML parsers available online. These parsers, listed next, look at your document, either on your local machine or on another accessible Web server, and test it for well-formedness. They generally do not display the XML document; they only provide you with information about areas of the document that have errors or let you know that the document has been formatted correctly. If you are

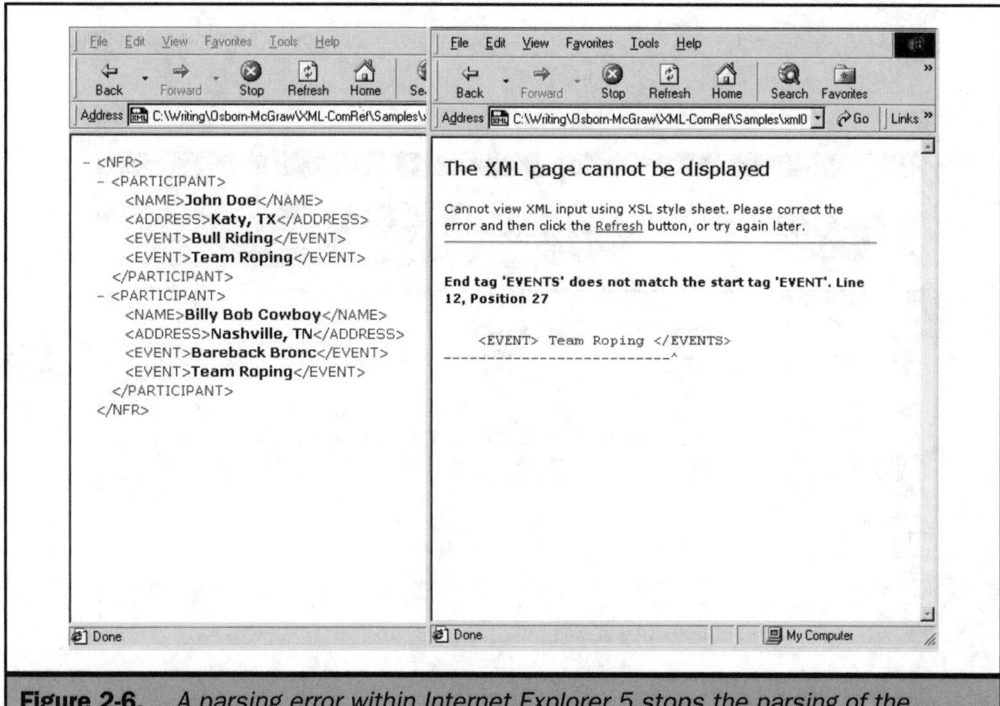

Figure 2-6. *A parsing error within Internet Explorer 5 stops the parsing of the document and forces the display of the error.*

creating a lot of XML formatted information, then you would be best served to download a local XML parser and use it for checking your documents.

- **RUWF (Are You Well-Formed)** This nonvalidating parser allows you to type in the address of any XML document, or any document for that matter, which is accessible from the Internet. The RUWF Site, found at http://xml.com/, is shown in Figure 2-7.
- **Frontier XML Syntax Checker** This Web site found at http://frontier.userland.com/stories/storyReader$1092 allows you to check any document located on the Internet with one of two different parsers. By default you will use the Frontier XML parser, but you also have the opportunity to select the *blox* parser that has been based upon the expat nonvalidating parser.

XML Validating Parsers

Validating parsers have one more job to perform than nonvalidating parsers. In addition to checking the well-formedness of your document, the validating parser verifies that your document conforms to a specific internal or external Document Type Definition (DTD). In Chapter 8, you will learn about the specific structure of a DTD and

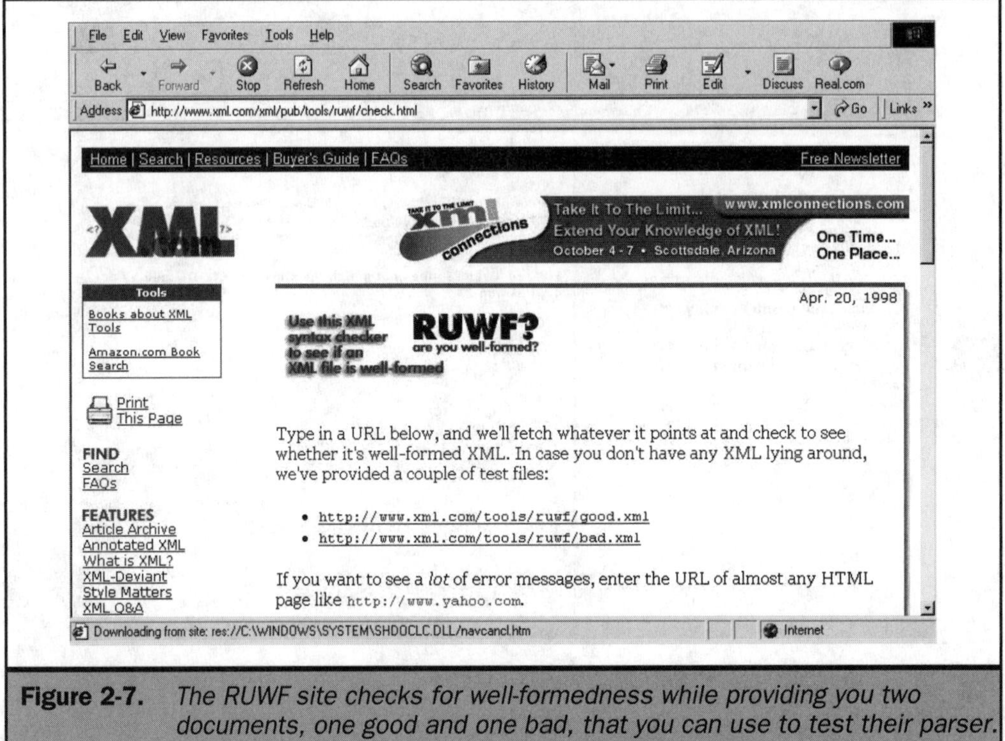

Figure 2-7. *The RUWF site checks for well-formedness while providing you two documents, one good and one bad, that you can use to test their parser.*

how to use it in conjunction with validating XML parsers to create more accurate and traceable document structures.

XML parsers generate error messages describing problems with your XML documents as they are encountered. You probably aren't going to understand the error messages until you have read through some of the rest of this book explaining how to create DTDs and normal XML elements and attributes.

Validation Requirements

When using a validating parser, such as the LT XML parser from the University of Edinburgh, you are ensuring that your documents are more than just well-formed. You are assuring the world that your document's structure itself has been documented. You are making sure that your document's structure can be read and used by any number of additional documents, by any number of organizations. The documentation of your document is included in the DTD. You can use your validating parsers to check your XML documents against any DTD, whether it is one found on a site somewhere on the Internet, is one found on your neighbor's desk, or is one you have written yourself. Since there are very few DTDs that are available for public consumption, although there are more and more being published every month, you will need to write your own DTD for your documents. If you are planning to write your own DTD, which is discussed in detail in Part 2 of this book, a validating parser is practically required.

Validating parsers go through each entry in your XML document and compares it to the DTD that has been provided with the XML code. The DTD is either included as a part of the XML document, or it is an external file that has been linked to your document. When the validating parser encounters an error in your code, it will display a message identifying the line of code that contained the error and the type of error that was encountered, as shown in Figure 2-8 on the LTG XML online parser located at http:// www.ltg.ed.ac.uk/~richard/xml-check.html.

Online Validators

If you only have a few XML documents to evaluate, use an online XML validating parser, rather than spending the time to find and check out the available parsers prior to downloading one. There are three very good online validating parsers available. Although the majority of these work only with documents accessible from the Internet, they all do a very good job of checking your document.

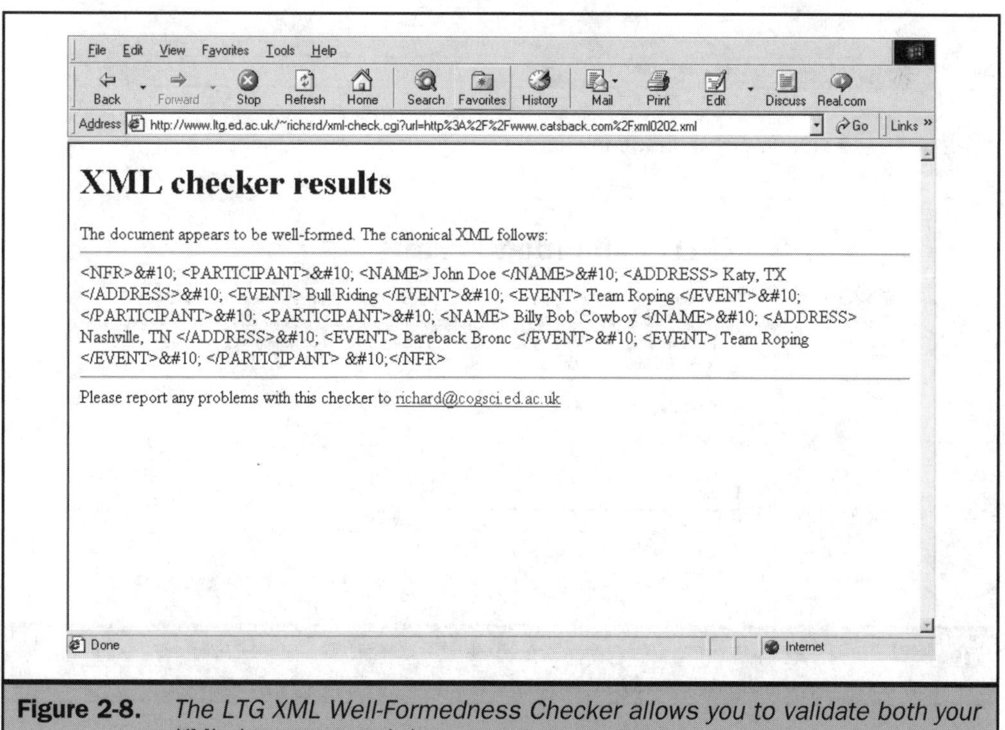

Figure 2-8. *The LTG XML Well-Formedness Checker allows you to validate both your XML document and the process namespaces.*

- **Richard Tobins Well-Formedness Checker**, found at http://www.cogsci.ed.ac.uk/~richard/xml-check.html, allows you to check any document located on an Internet-reachable computer. By default, this parser does not validate your XML documents, although it can provide that service, as well as converting your existing XML document into is canonical format. To force this parser to check the validity of your document, check the "validate?" checkbox on their Web page.
- **STG Validating Parser**, located at http://www.stg.brown.edu/service/xmlvalid/ and shown in Figure 2-9, provides you with a variety of options for checking pages. You can validate documents that are already located on the Internet or validate text that you type or paste into a form field, or you can check a document that is located on your personal computer.
- **LTG XML Well-Formedness Checker and Validator** is located at the University of Edinburgh (http://www.ltg.ed.ac.uk/~richard/xml-check.html). This validating parser also checks external entity references for all documents. This parser is based upon the LT XML, also developed by the University of Edinburgh.

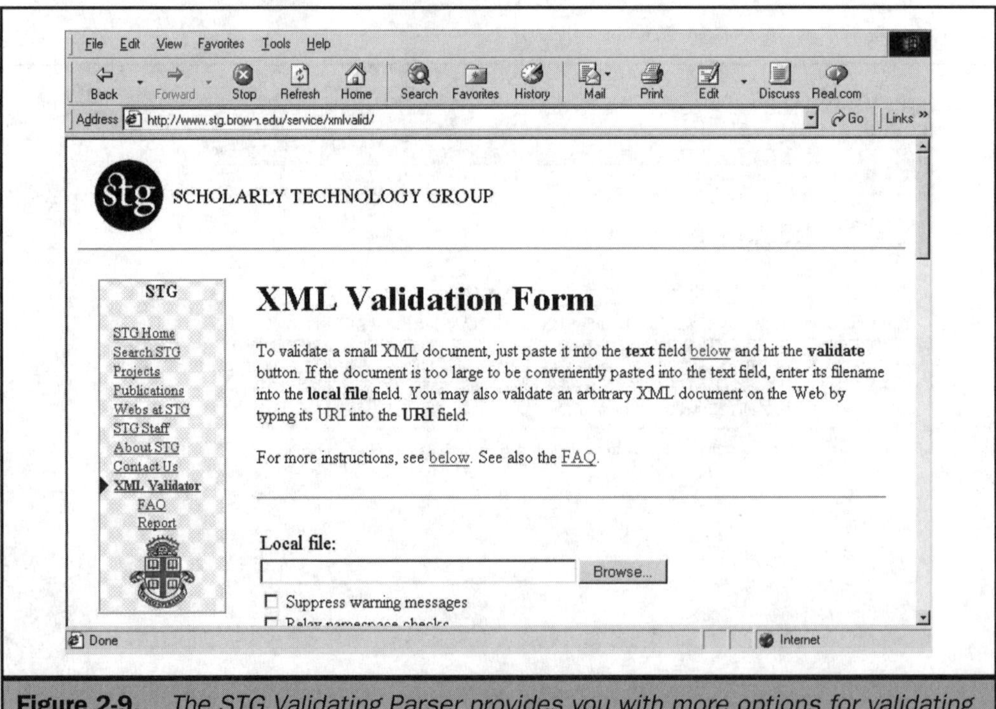

Figure 2-9. *The STG Validating Parser provides you with more options for validating your documents than any other online XML parsing site.*

Schema Checkers

In Chapter 1, XML Schemas were mentioned as being one of the new World Wide Web Consortium recommendations that will greatly enhance the usability of XML documents. Although the XML Schema specification is not yet complete, you can check out an alpha version of the World Wide Web Consortium's XML Schema Validator at http://www.w3.org/2000/09/webdata/xsv.

Summary

In this chapter you have taken a peek into XML parsers, both validating and non-validating. As you progress through this book, you will see some of these parsers at work. Parsers break out XML information in such a way that other software can use it. These parsers can check for the well-formedness of a document without validating each element name, or they can validate the use of each element against a Document Type Definition (DTD). In the following chapters, the rules of well-formedness will be defined, clarifying the task of the parsers even further.

Chapter 3

Saying “Hello World” in XML

As with any new programming or markup language, you have to learn the basics of creating a document, including its structure and valid formatting constraints, before you can begin actively to program or develop your information with that language. Traditionally you start learning a new language with some simple code that displays a rote statement such as "Hello World" or maybe "My Name is George."

No matter what the content of your first XML document, it is the structure that you need to learn. Once you understand the general structure of XML, you can then create some basic elements to contain your content and put that structure together with the elements to write your first complete XML document. After you have created your document, you have to *parse* it, or process it, so that it can be seen. Last, but definitely not least, you need to add comments to your XML document so that in six months you will know what you were doing with the document, and if you hand it down to someone else, they will know where you were going with your document. This chapter steps through a simplified development process for XML documents. You will receive more detailed information about creating advanced XML documents in the remainder of this book.

XML Structure

It is very difficult to create XML documents without understanding the structure that you are creating. Some people may wish to think of an XML document as a very long outline of information, but it would be more accurate to think of the structure as the inverted tree that was discussed in Chapter 1.

If you use the structure of this book as a model for understanding the structure of an XML document, you can easily understand the flow of your information in your document; see Figure 3-1.

This simple hierarchical structure, when placed into an XML document, would appear as follows:

```
<BOOK>XML: The Complete Reference
<PART> Part 1:
      <CHAPTER> Chapter 1
            <SECTION>Section 1</SECTION>
            <SECTION>Section 2</SECTION>
            <SECTION>Section 3</SECTION>
            <SUMMARY>Summary</SUMMARY>
      </CHAPTER>
      <CHAPTER> Chapter 2</CHAPTER>
      <CHAPTER> Chapter 3</CHAPTER>
      <CHAPTER> Chapter 4
            <SECTION>Section 1</SECTION>
            <SECTION>Section 2</SECTION>
```

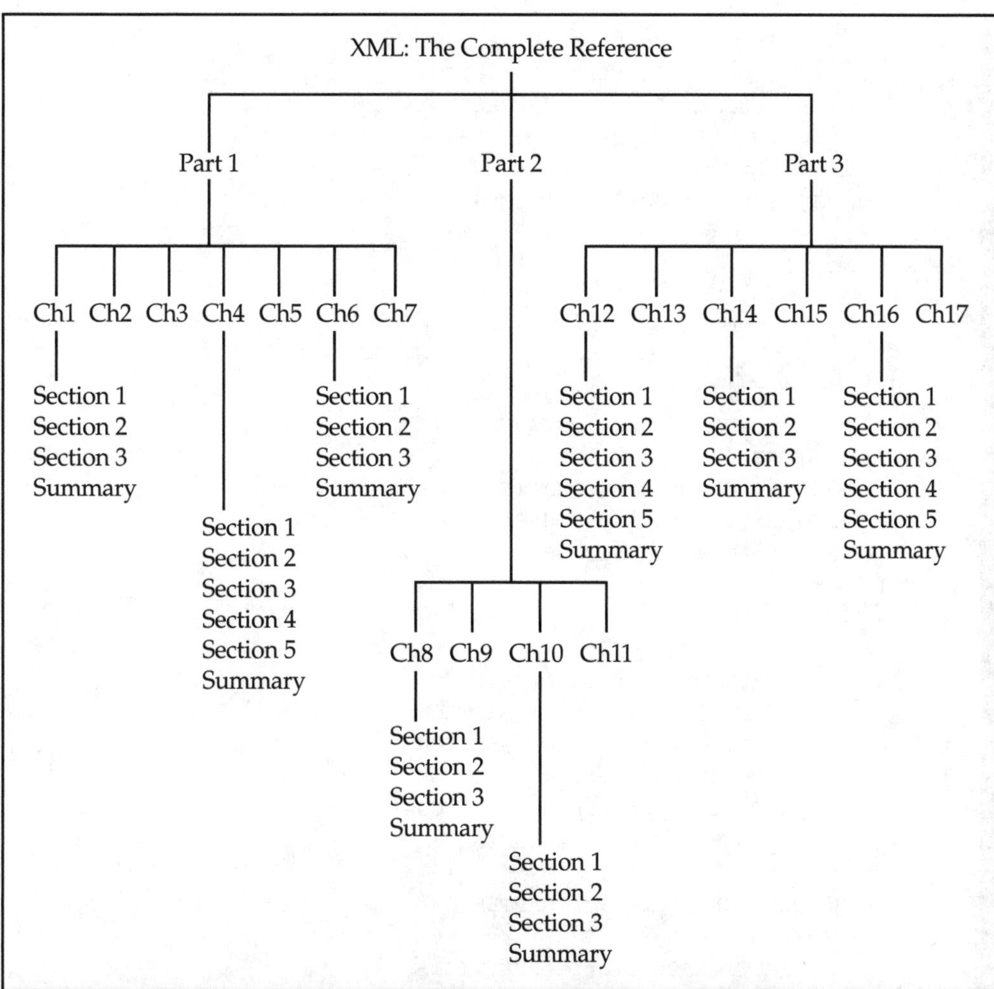

Figure 3-1. *The inverted tree structure of an XML document is similar to the structure of this book.*

```
        <SECTION>Section 3</SECTION>
        <SECTION>Section 4</SECTION>
        <SECTION>Section 5</SECTION>
        <SUMMARY>Summary</SUMMARY>
</CHAPTER>
<CHAPTER> Chapter 5 </CHAPTER>
<CHAPTER> Chapter 6
```

```
                <SECTION>Section 1</SECTION>
                <SECTION>Section 2</SECTION>
                <SECTION>Section 3</SECTION>
                <SUMMARY>Summary</SUMMARY>
        </CHAPTER>
        <CHAPTER> Chapter 7</CHAPTER>
</PART>
<PART> Part 2:
        <CHAPTER> Chapter 8
                <SECTION>Section 1</SECTION>
                <SECTION>Section 2</SECTION>
                <SECTION>Section 3</SECTION>
                <SUMMARY>Summary</SUMMARY>
        </CHAPTER>
        <CHAPTER> Chapter 9</CHAPTER>
        <CHAPTER> Chapter 10</CHAPTER>
        <CHAPTER> Chapter 11</CHAPTER>
</PART>
<PART> Part 3:
        <CHAPTER> Chapter 12
                <SECTION>Section 1</SECTION>
                <SECTION>Section 2</SECTION>
                <SECTION>Section 3</SECTION>
                <SECTION>Section 4</SECTION>
                <SECTION>Section 5</SECTION>
                <SUMMARY>Summary</SUMMARY>
        </CHAPTER>
        <CHAPTER> Chapter 13</CHAPTER>
        <CHAPTER> Chapter 14
               <SECTION>Section 1</SECTION>
                <SECTION>Section 2</SECTION>
                <SECTION>Section 3</SECTION>
                <SUMMARY>Summary</SUMMARY>
        </CHAPTER>
        <CHAPTER> Chapter 15</CHAPTER>
        <CHAPTER> Chapter 16
                <SECTION>Section 1</SECTION>
                <SECTION>Section 2</SECTION>
                <SECTION>Section 3</SECTION>
                <SECTION>Section 4</SECTION>
                <SECTION>Section 5</SECTION>
                <SUMMARY> Summary </SUMMARY>
```

```
        </CHAPTER>
        <CHAPTER> Chapter 17</CHAPTER>
    </PART>
    </BOOK>
```

Looking at this outline in conjunction with the image in Figure 3-1, you can see the simplicity of structure in XML documents. XML documents have a logical flow and progression through every part and subpart. The primary object in an XML document is referred to as the *root*. This is the object that serves as a *parent* for all of the other objects contained within the document. In this case, the root is the book title "XML: The Complete Reference." The layer of objects directly beneath the root, in this case the part headings, are the *children* of the root object, therefore making the book's title the *parent* of the part headings. Any object identified beneath another object is that object's child, and any object that is above another is a parent object. In the case of the document root, any objects identified within it are considered descendants. These objects are all contained within the global scope of the document.

With the understanding of how an XML document's structure relates to the structure of items that we handle practically every day, it is easier to understand the development of the XML elements.

XML Elements

Elements identify the type of information, or content, that is placed within a specific section of the XML document. In other words, elements can identify a book title separate from a part title or a chapter title. Elements identify what type of information is contained within that section of a document; they don't actually provide any content, just structure.

The beginning and end tags of the element provide the structure. You may see the terms element and tag used interchangeably, and for the most part that is acceptable, just a variation on the use of the terminology, but keep in mind that a tag is the specific section of the markup language that creates the element and that elements typically have two tags.

To continue with our example from the previous section, to create an XML document out of this book, we would have to start with a single root element that identifies the book: `<BOOK>`. This element has to also have a closing tag such as `</BOOK>`. Every element starts and ends with an angle bracket that frames the element's name. Everything that appears between these two XML tags provides additional content for the document. For example, you will need to identify the specific title of the book using an element such as `<BOOKTITLE></BOOKTITLE>`. To add markers for identifying part headings and chapter headings, you simply have to provide elements that identify that specific content, for example `<PARTTITLE>` or `<CHAPTITLE>`.

Writing Your First Document

Now that you have a grasp over what typical XML document structure consists of and the purpose of each element, you are ready to start writing your own XML documents. The easiest way to start creating XML is to use a text editor, such as Windows Notepad, MacIntosh BBEdit, or Linux emacs, and start typing.

Here is a very simple XML document:

```
<BOOK>
  XML: The Complete Reference
</BOOK>
```

This document is considered well-formed. Well-formedness, discussed in Chapter 2 and Chapter 5, is simply one qualification identified by the XML specifications. This is a very good, although very simple, XML document.

Once you have typed in the code, you need to be sure to save it, as seen in Figure 3-2. You must save it in a plain text format with an .xml file extension, or else it will not be legible as an XML file to your Web browser.

When saving your XML documents using Windows Notepad, be sure to select the All Files option from the Save as Type field in your Save dialog, as well as provide the full file name, such as xml0301.xml in the File name field. This will prevent Notepad from saving your file as xml0301.xml.txt.

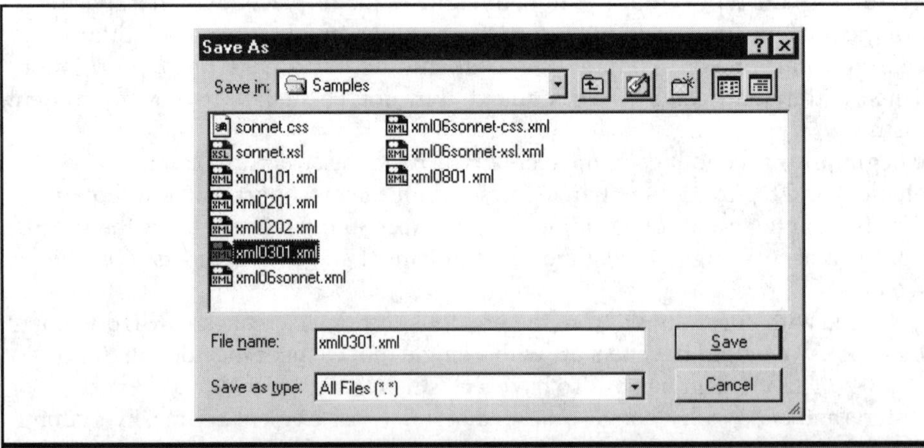

Figure 3-2. *Save your file when you create it. Watch for potential changes to your specified file extension, depending upon the editor you are using.*

Parsing Your Document

With your XML document created, you are ready to view the results. Fortunately you can quickly open your XML document in either the Internet Explorer 5.*x* or the Netscape Navigator 6.*x* (assuming you have a CSS style sheet available) Web browsers.

As with all other documents on the Internet, your results will vary in appearance between browsers.

To open your XML document in Internet Explorer 5 use the File | Open menu options to select the document you saved. When Internet Explorer views the document, as shown in Figure 3-3, you are shown everything, including the markup text. In Part 3 you will learn how to use style sheets to format your XML so that it doesn't appear as the default colored source code shown in this figure.

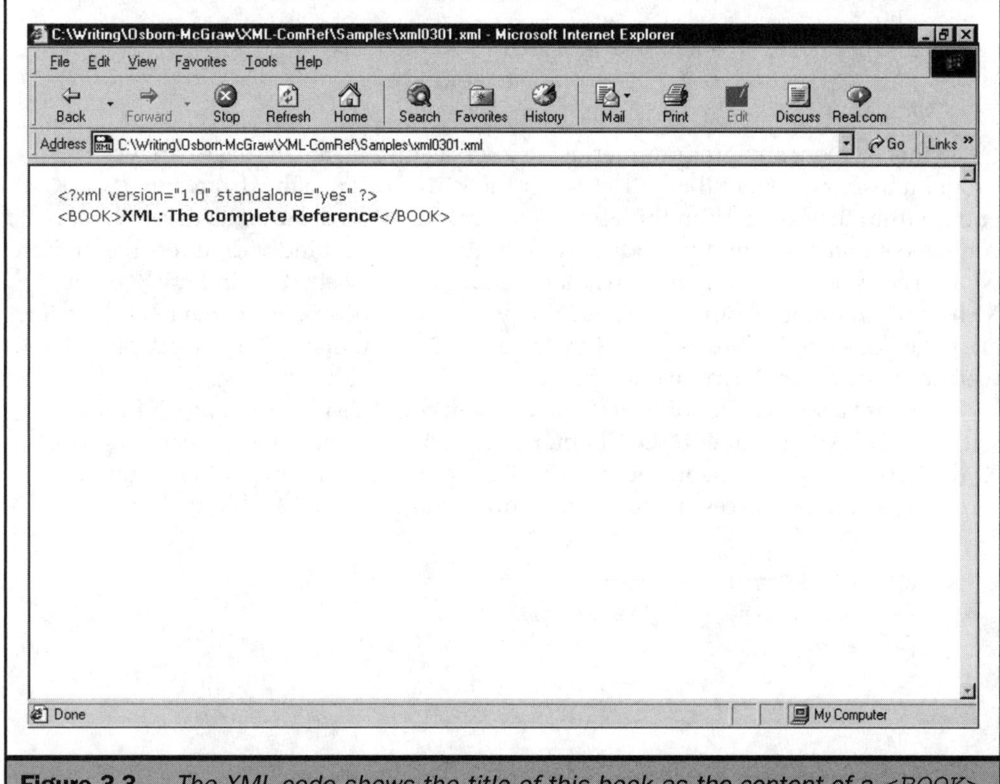

Figure 3-3. *The XML code shows the title of this book as the content of a <BOOK> element in Internet Explorer 5.*

Using Layers of Elements

XML elements can contain either character data, as seen in the previous example, or they can contain other elements, which in turn can contain either other elements, or character data, or both. If you were to take our previous example using the <BOOK> elements (under "Writing Your First Document") and wish to put additional information into it, you would have to break the document down into more parts. Take a look at the following code:

```
<BOOK>
XML: The Complete Reference
by: Heather Williamson
</BOOK>
```

In this example, there is no way to extract the title of the book separately from the author of the book. In order to be able to access each piece of information individually, you have to place the pieces of data in their own elements.

```
<BOOK>
<TITLE>XML: The Complete Reference</TITLE>
<AUTHOR>Heather Williamson</AUTHOR>
</BOOK>
```

In this fashion, any programmer using XML as their data language can write a program to extract either the <TITLE> or the <AUTHOR> name from any <BOOK> entry within their data. With this ability you can use XML documents to hold the contents of databases, and provide search utilities to extract individual records. If there were a series of <BOOK> entries in a database, and you wished to find the book on XML, a programmer would be able to take your XML document, search it, and retrieve all of the books with XML as part of their <TITLE>, no matter how many other books were located within the same document.

There are also a variety of ways in which you could display the same information within your XML document (see Chapter 4 for more information on organizing your XML data). For example, you could express the previous example in the following format and still have access to all of the information contained within the file.

```
<BOOK>
XML: The Complete Reference
<AUTHOR>Heather Williamson</AUTHOR>
</BOOK>
```

By removing the <TITLE> elements, you aren't removing the title data. The title of the book now becomes the text content of the <BOOK> element. In this example, rather than have all of the elements contain either elements or data, they are combined so the <BOOK> element has text data "XML: The Complete Reference," as well as an element <AUTHOR>. When searching this document to find the title of the books, your program would look within the <BOOK> element's text data and ignore any of the child elements within <BOOK>.

Commenting Your XML Code

Have you ever tried to start a project in the middle? When you start working on a project that someone else had previously started, you often find yourself confused and trying madly to infer where the original project coordinator was going with the project from the existing project state. Sometimes this just gets too difficult and you have to start the entire project all over again. In XML documents this should never happen—if you are a conscientious developer and use comments.

Comments within an XML document are the same as they are in person. They serve as a means of interjecting a sideline thought or direction into a program at key points, so that no one looking at the document would ever find himself or herself lost.

If you have previously developed HTML documents then you are in luck. Comments that are located within an XML document are identical to comments used within HTML documents. Comments use the <!– and the --> markers to identify the beginning and the ending of a comment, respectively. As with HTML, both the parser and the browser ignore everything contained within a comment as if it didn't exist.

Look at our short XML example with a single comment added:

```
<?xml version="1.0" standalone="yes"?>
<BOOK>
<!-- The name of the book being read. -->
  XML: The Complete Reference
</BOOK>
```

This comment provides auxiliary information to the contents of the XML file, but comments can also be used to remove segments of XML code that are not currently ready to be viewed or parsed. For example:

```
<?xml version="1.0" standalone="yes"?>
<!--
<BOOK>
  XML: The Complete Reference
</BOOK>
-->
```

In this code, the only statement that will be processed is the XML declaration located at the top of the sample. You will learn more about the specific requirements of an XML declaration statement in Chapter 5. There are a few rules that must be followed when using comments within your XML document. These rules are

- Comments may not appear before the XML declaration, which is required to be the first statement in any XML document. For example, the following XML document would be unacceptable:

```
<!-- I have added a comment here. -->
<?xml version="1.0" standalone="yes"?>
<BOOK>
  XML: The Complete Reference
</BOOK>
```

- Comments may not split XML element tags. For example, you cannot include the start tag of an element in a comment without including its ending element as well, as seen in the following code snippet:

```
<?xml version="1.0" standalone="yes"?>
<!--
<BOOK>
-->
  XML: The Complete Reference
</BOOK>
```

- You cannot include comments within XML element tags. For example, the following code would be incorrect:

```
<?xml version="1.0" standalone="yes"?>
<BOOK <!-- A comment is added here-->>
  XML: The Complete Reference
</BOOK>
```

- Comments cannot include double hyphens within its text, unless those hyphens are part of either the opening or the closing tags. This prohibits the nesting of comments as seen in the following example:

```
<?xml version="1.0" standalone="yes"?>
<BOOK>
<!-- This book is great <!-- I really liked it also.--> -->
  XML: The Complete Reference
</BOOK>
```

Data Structures and Organization

XML provides structure for your document. It also provides a sense of organization. XML forces documents to be created in such a way that both humans and computers can read them. The one trick to XML document organization is this: the order of your elements does not have to match the order of the elements when they appear in your document browser. Look at the following code for an example:

```
<BOOKLIST>
  <BOOK>
   <TITLE>XML: The Complete Reference</TITLE>
   <AUTHOR>Heather Williamson</AUTHOR>
  </BOOK>
  <BOOK>
   <TITLE>HTML: The Complete Reference</TITLE>
   <AUTHOR>A. Powell</AUTHOR>
  </BOOK>
  <BOOK>
    <TITLE>Writing your Way to Insanity</TITLE>
    <AUTHOR>Heather Williamson</AUTHOR>
  </BOOK>
</BOOKLIST>
```

Using a series of transformations (see Chapter 16) you can show all of your documents sorted by <AUTHOR> or <TITLE>, irrespective of their order within the original document. For example, you could use XSL transformations to sort and organize the previous XML document into the following structure:

```
A. Powel
      HTML: The Complete Reference
Heather Williamson
      Writing your Way to Insanity
      XML: The Complete Reference
```

Summary

In this chapter you have created a very simple XML document using a standard text editor, identified the typical structure of an XML document, were introduced to elements, and viewed your first XML document using the Internet Explorer browser and parser. As you can see from going through this entire process, it is very easy to create simple XML documents, even if you have layers of elements and text. Although in later chapters you will read about a variety of other features that can be used along with this basic implementation of XML, you already have the basics down.

As you progress through this book, you will find more detailed information about each of the steps discussed here. As you read, all of your questions will be answered about XML, well-formedness, parsers, and formatting your XML content.

The Complete Reference

Chapter 4

Organizing XML Data

How often have you tried to start a project without knowing exactly how you were going to get it done? Although "flying by the seat of your pants" is an acceptable and often worthwhile means of pursuit for many endeavors, it has a tendency to get you into trouble when you use this method to approach an XML document. Now that is not to say that XML is an unforgiving language; it is simply one best approached with a plan.

Throughout this chapter you will be taking a sales contact log and turning it into a structure that can be converted into an XML document. Even if you do not have your own sales contacts logs to convert, you can perform the same process with a standard address book listing names, addresses, and phone numbers. You can create a better-organized information tracking system or convert an already well-organized collection of information into an easily readable electronic format.

Creating Layers of Information from Your Data

All information has layers of detail that can be expounded upon. For example, people have names, addresses, and phone numbers, but they also have other details such as birthdays, anniversaries, spouse's names, children's names, and hobbies. You can track all of the information about a person in a well-structured XML document by being aware of the layers of information contained within a single person's record.

Identifying Information Importance

As you identify information about the people within your address book, you will find that some data is more important to know than other data. In today's electronic world, for example, e-mail addresses are often more important to know than fax numbers. Your purposes in tracking information may be different than someone else's. For instance the sales log of an optometrist's office may track information about eye color, while the sales log of a logging company will include the type of log truck the individual drives. The level of importance that you assign a specific characteristic is important because those levels will be used to help determine how your information will be treated when it is turned into the element and attribute structure of the XML document. In Table 4-1 you can see a sample list of the type of information and how it would be sorted as the first step to ensuring you are tracking all of the information you need in your XML document.

This may seem like a lot of information to keep track of, but it is done every day in software like Microsoft Outlook©, Act!©, and Gold Mine©. The only difference this time is that you are deciding upon your own format and structure for the information.

Primary Information	Secondary Information	Tertiary Information
Name Title Company name Address Home phone number Business phone number Fax number Cellular phone or pager number E-mail address Web address	Contact source Preferred contact method Preferred name or nickname to be called Sales log Total accumulated purchases Primary product interests A description of their business Contact information for their associate or assistant Contact information for their department manager Contact information for services such as ICQ, NetMeeting, or PowWow Sales notes and comments	Birthday Spouse's name Anniversary Children's name(s) Favorite sports teams Travel and vacation Interests

Table 4-1. *Levels of Information to Track for an Example Sales Contact Log*

Adding Detail to Your List

In addition to the list of important information that you must have, you will also find information that is directly related to just one aspect of the individual, rather than relating to them in a global fashion. To better understand this concept, think about your hobbies. In my case my hobby is riding horses. Horses, for me, are directly related to my personal life and have little or nothing to do with my professional life; therefore "horses" shouldn't be directly linked in any way to my professional title or to any company for which I may work. If your needs require tracking personal information, then you need to ensure that there is a place that the information's personal nature can be noted. For example, you do not want to confuse yourself, or other people using this XML document, by tracking the hobby of "horses" for an individual who works for

"The Lucky Horseshoe." Some people may assume it's a company that has something to do with real horses when it could be a gift shop.

Every type of database, especially one tracking people, has details (such as personal hobbies and preferences) that can be added to the information in your XML document to ensure its completeness. Look at your name, for instance: you have a title (Mr., Ms., and so on), first name, middle name, last name, and possibly a suffix (Jr., Sr., III, and so on). All of this information can be treated in the XML document as a single name, such as `<NAME> John Doe, Jr. </NAME>`, or it can be broken down into its individual parts, such as `<FIRSTNAME>John</FIRSTNAME><LASTNAME>Doe</LASTNAME><SUFFIX> Jr.</SUFFIX>`. Your decision to break information down into its detailed parts or leave it as a commonly accepted whole is to some degree directed by how you want to use your information. For example, if you wish to use the contents of your XML document to address envelopes, as well as write personalized letters to "John," then you will need to separate the name data into its individual parts. Your program can then use all of the information contained in the multiple name fields to print on the envelopes and simply grab the contents of the first name field to print on the letters. Likewise, if you only ever use this list to print envelopes, there is no need to separate the name into all five parts.

With this in mind, break down the primary information into its detailed parts in another list, as shown in Table 4-2.

Primary Information	Details to Track	Auxiliary Information
Name	Title (Mr., Ms., etc.) First Name Middle Name Last Name Suffix (Sr., Jr., III, etc.)	Sex (Male, Female) Age Group
Title		Management Level or Employment Level
Company Name		Industry
Address	Street Suite/Room Number/Floor Number City State Zip	

Table 4-2. *Your Sales Contact Primary Information*

Primary Information	Details to Track	Auxiliary Information
Home Phone Number	Area Code City Code Number	
Business Phone Number	Area Code City Code Number	
Fax Number	Area Code City Code Number	
Cellular Phone or Pager Number	Area Code City Code Number	Cellular or Pager
E-mail Address	E-mail Name Server Designator	Personal or Business
Web Address		

Table 4-2. *Your Sales Contact Primary Information* (continued)

Structuring Your Data

Now that you have some of your details broken out, you are ready to start working on the actual structure of your XML document. You do this by breaking out your details into elements and attributes. Some of this you have already done by breaking out your information into varying lists of detail and associated facts.

Identifying Your Elements

Elements, introduced in Chapter 3, provide the foundation structure of your information when put into the XML document. Because of this all-important role, you have to be sure that you have designed your document so that it can easily incorporate all of the information you have collected without restricting the addition of second or third alternatives for specific data.

When contemplating your sales-lead log using your lists of information types, sort them into a table of contents or outline-type structure. This allows you to identify which level each element will be placed in easily. Look at the example in Figure 4-1. It places business and personal information into separate areas so that you always know which type of information you are accessing.

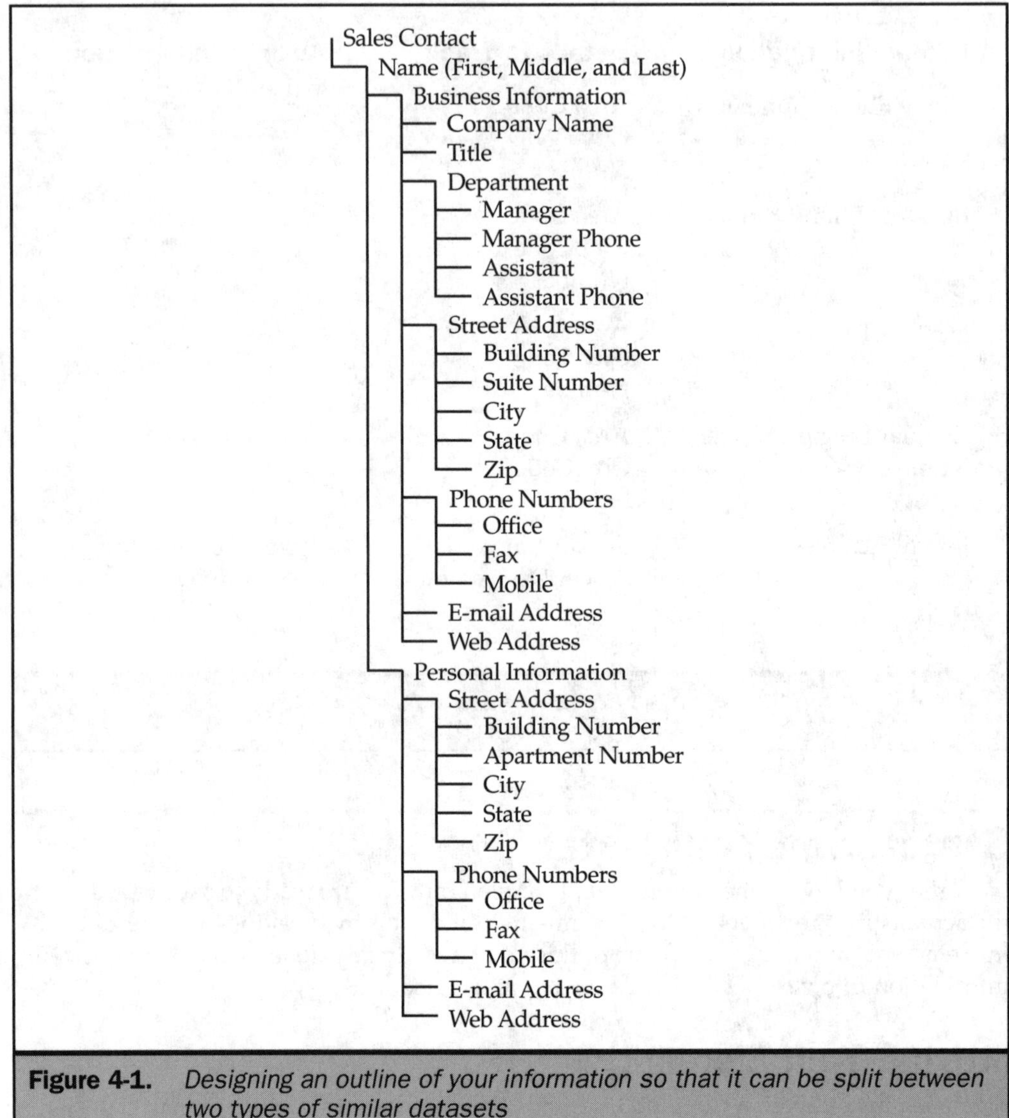

Figure 4-1. *Designing an outline of your information so that it can be split between two types of similar datasets*

This organizational diagram could be converted into an XML document with the following structure shown in the next code segment. This code uses a sales contact record broken down into name, business information, and personal information. The business and personal information is then broken down further into specific segments of information specific to that aspect of this individual. This is obviously a short example, leaving out such information as spouse, children, birthdays, and anniversaries, as well as the more necessary sales log information including repeat sales, contact dates, and logs of conversations and information requests.

```
<SALES_CONTACT>
  <NAME> </NAME>
  <BUSINESS>
    <COMPANY> </COMPANY>
    <TITLE> </TITLE>
    <DEPARTMENT>
      <DEPTNAME> </DEPTNAME>
      <MANAGER_NAME> </MANAGER_NAME>
      <MANAGER_PHONE> </MANAGER_PHONE>
      <ASSISTANT_NAME> </ASSISTANT_NAME>
      <ASSISTANT_PHONE> </ASSISTANT_PHONE>
    </DEPARTMENT>
    <ADDRESS>
      <STREET>  </STREET>
      <SUITE> </SUITE>
      <CITY> </CITY>
      <STATE> </STATE>
      <ZIP> </ZIP>
    </ADDRESS>
    <PHONES>
      <OFFICE> </OFFICE>
      <OFFICE_FAX> </OFFICE_FAX>
      <MOBILE> </MOBILE>
    </PHONES>
    <EMAIL>  </EMAIL>
    <WEB> </WEB>
  </BUSINESS>
  <PERSONAL>
    <ADDRESS>
      <STREET> </STREET>
      <APT> </APT>
      <CITY> </CITY>
      <STATE> </STATE>
      <ZIP> </ZIP>
    </ADDRESS>
    <PHONES>
      <HOUSE> </HOUSE>
      <HOUSE_FAX> </HOUSE_FAX>
      <MOBILE> </MOBILE>
    </PHONES>
    <EMAIL> </EMAIL>
    <WEB> </WEB>
  </PERSONAL>
</SALES_CONTACT>
```

XML is like anything else in this world: there isn't one right way to complete a project and represent your data, there are hundreds of ways to make your project outcome be correct. In Figure 4-2 you can see a second alternative to organizing the information contained within your sales leads log. This illustration could be expressed in XML using the following code:

```
<SALES_CONTACT>
  <NAME> </NAME>
  <ADDRESSES>
    <BUSINESS_ADDRESS>
      <COMPANY> </COMPANY>
      <TITLE> </TITLE>
      <DEPARTMENT>
        <DEPTNAME> </DEPTNAME>
        <MANAGER_NAME> </MANAGER_NAME>
        <MANAGER_PHONE> </MANAGER_PHONE>
        <ASSISTANT_NAME> </ASSISTANT_NAME>
        <ASSISTANT_PHONE> </ASSISTANT_PHONE>
      </DEPARTMENT>
      <STREET_ADDRESS>
        <STREET>  </STREET>
        <SUITE> </SUITE>
        <CITY> </CITY>
        <STATE> </STATE>
        <ZIP> </ZIP>
      </STREET_ADDRESS>
      <WORK_EMAIL>  </WORK_EMAIL>
      <WORK_WEB> </WORK_WEB>
    <BUSINESS_ADDRESS>
    <HOME_ADDRESS>
      <STREET_ADDRESS>
        <STREET> </STREET>
        <APT> </APT>
        <CITY> </CITY>
        <STATE> </STATE>
        <ZIP> </ZIP>
      </STREET_ADDRESS>
      <PERS_EMAIL> </PERS_EMAIL>
      <PERS_WEB> </PERS_WEB>
    <HOME_ADDRESS>
  </ADDRESSES>
  <PHONES>
    <OFFICE> </OFFICE>
```

```
    <OFFICE_FAX> </OFFICE_FAX>
    <BUS_MOBILE> </BUS_MOBILE>
    <HOUSE> </HOUSE>
    <HOUSE_FAX> </HOUSE_FAX>
    <PERS_MOBILE> </PERS_MOBILE>
  </PHONES>
</SALES_CONTACT>
```

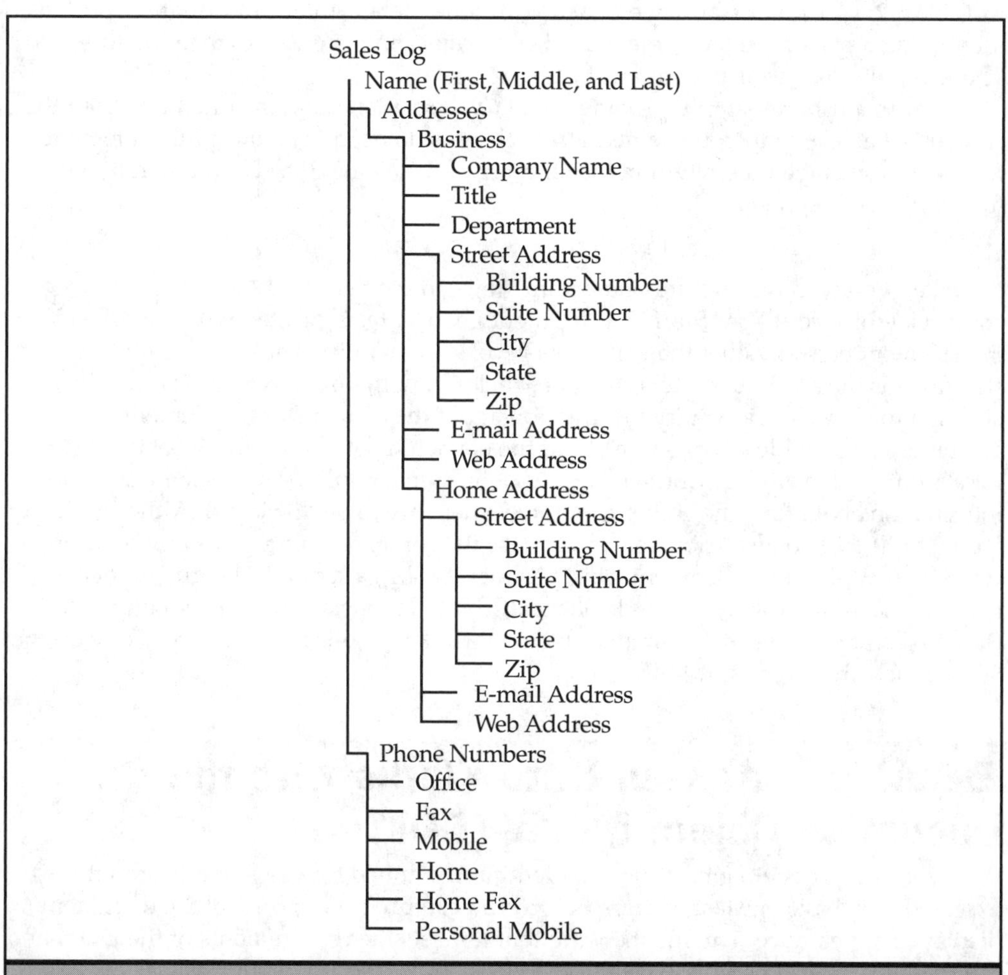

Figure 4-2. *The ability to format information into different structures allows you to work with your data in the way that is best for you.*

No matter what organizational system you use to format your information, you will want to ensure that you have it organized right the first time. There is nothing more frustrating than going back into your information and trying to reformat something that you thought you had already completed. You can find more information on creating and using elements in Chapter 5.

Identifying Your Attributes

In addition to the primary types of information that serve as your elements, you also have to specify specific types of information that are considered *attributes*. Attributes provide more information about the data content of a specific element. If you go back to Table 4-2, you will see how we added additional details to our information, such as identifying a person's management level as auxiliary information to their job title. These details work well as your attributes.

Because attributes simply provide auxiliary, or explanatory, information about the contents of an element or an element itself, there is no need to create a full statement for them. You embed them within the start tag of the element itself as shown in the following code segment:

```
<TITLE management_level="mid"> </TITLE>
```

When you read through this statement, you can see that the `TITLE` element's contents, which could be "Staff Development Lead," are associated with a midlevel management person, rather than an upper-level staff member. The `management_level` statement is the attribute that has a value, enclosed with quotations, of `"mid"`. In addition to providing auxiliary information about the contents of the element, attributes can provide information about the element itself. If you think back to HTML for a moment, the align attribute in a `<DIV>` element simply provides some additional information about how the contents of the element are to be displayed. Although XML has no built-in display attributes, you can use the contents of attributes of your own creation as well as the Document Object Model (DOM), a scripting language such as JavaScript, and the Cascading Style Sheets (CSS) or Extensible Stylesheet Language (XSL) to create completely formatted documents like the ones you see every day on the Web, which are based on HTML.

Ensuring That Your Data Works with the Document Object Model (DOM)

With your XML document's structure identified, planned, charted, and thoroughly explored, you have one last concern before you can proceed to control the document's displayed appearance. You must ensure that it meets the requirements of the DOM and can therefore be used with the common style sheet and scripting languages.

This is actually a very straightforward task if your XML documents are well-formed and properly parsed and displayed. Through the use of the already popular style sheet languages (CSS and XSL specifically) you can manipulate your XML documents using the JavaScript commands that you may already be familiar with from working with HTML pages.

Note *Check with your programmers to ensure that their programs can work with your document structures and the DOM. If their software doesn't use the DOM as an API, then you will need to format your document around the structure that they use.*

Summary

As you can see, the organization of your information is of primary importance to the actual layout of your XML document. Once you have identified the individual types of data you wish to track, you are ready to create your XML. Without this original planning stage, you can find yourself rewriting and re-editing your XML document a hundred times to add the pieces of information you forgot about or restructuring it so that it meets your needs for the future better. XML code may be very easy to create, since you are writing the language specifically for your application, but that means you have to complete your planning before you can jump in and start programming.

The Complete Reference

Chapter 5

Creating Well-Formed XML

As you have seen in previous chapters, XML document structure is very similar to HTML. This makes XML easy to learn and use for anyone who is familiar with HTML, the most common markup language in the world these days. But in one sense XML is even easier to use than HTML. Where HTML has already defined around one hundred elements, XML has less than a dozen predefined parts. When you create a document with XML, you are creating your own markup language that will define the information that you have, not the information that Joe Blow down the street has been working with. Because you are creating your own commands, you have to be concerned with the well-formedness of your document. Well-formedness encompasses a lot of constraints that control how your document is formed, which directly affects the ability of a parser, discussed in Chapter 3, to read and analyze your XML document.

This is the integral part of the extensibility of XML. Using just a few predefined elements in conjunction with the elements that you create yourself, you can create documents ranging in complexity from an extremely involved project tracking system to a very simple invitation list for a six-year-old child's birthday. With XML, no job is too big or too small.

Document Basics

HTML is used for describing the structure and visual presentation of Web pages. That has come to be an accepted fact, but we can't say the same about XML. XML doesn't care a whit about the visual presentation of information; it is focused solely on the structure and content of the document as it relates to a specific set of rules that have been defined by the World Wide Web Consortium in the XML 1.0 specification. It doesn't have just one job; it has a multitude of jobs. XML documents can be databases, they can be created on the fly by any programming language such as Perl or C, they can exist as a compilation of files and their contents, or they can exist simply as a series of instructions embedded into a program that manipulates information. You may want to think of an XML document as something as solid as the writing on a piece of paper in front of you, and that is a perfectly acceptable way of envisioning XML, but you also need to keep in mind that the simplicity of XML makes it easy to generate automatically and may therefore never be physically visible anywhere other than through your browser.

No matter how your XML document is created, it has to start with `<?xml>` *declaration* and have a *root element* in order to be well-formed.

`<?xml>` Declaration

The `<?xml>` declaration is how your software identifies an XML document. This is a statement, always appearing as the first line of your XML file, which specifies which version of XML is in use in the document.

```
<?xml version="1.0"?>
```

At this point, XML version 1.0 is the only version available. Although there is work on many other aspects of the XML implementation, such as XML Schemas and XML Queries (see Chapter 22), they do not affect the actual version of the XML specification that is being supported. In addition to specifying the version of XML that is being used within this document, you can also specify the relationship of this XML text to other files. If your XML document is completely self-sufficient and gets no information from external files such as style sheets or Document Types Definitions (DTDs) then your XML document is considered to be *standalone*. This self-sufficiency is noted in the <?xml> declaration with the use of the `standalone` attribute with a value of `"yes"`. It is interesting to note that if your XML document uses a `standalone` value of `"no"` your parser will do nothing different in regard to the processing of your document. It will continue to parse all of the information that was found within the document and all of the documents that are referenced from the XML declaration statements within your document.

```
<?xml version="1.0" standalone="yes"?>
```

The structure of XML allows the breakdown of your document into a series of *entities*, or storage units, containing information for your XML document. Think about the HTML document model for a second. Within HTML you can add sound files into your HTML document using the <EMBED> command. This joining of various types of files, in this case the binary sound file and the HTML text file, creates a single document comprised of two entities, the sound file and the HTML text code. XML works the same way. Unlike HTML, XML requires that you specify whether the document is standalone (comprised of only one part) or whether it is using additional entities to create the complete document. The use of separate entities, or additional document parts, added to your XML document is expressed through the use of the `standalone` attribute.

```
<?xml version="1.0" standalone="no"?>
```

When developing with XML, like HTML, you have the opportunity to identify the character encoding that is used for the document. The character encoding is the identification of the accepted ISO- or Unicode-based language that is used to create and mark up the document. There are two standard character encodings that you do not have to declare, but any others must be declared using the `encoding` attribute of the <?xml?> declaration statement as shown below:

```
<?xml version="1.0" encoding="UTF-8" standalone="no"?>
```

There are specific values that are acceptable in the encoding declaration. Some of these values, listed in Table 5-1, are used to specify the various registered Internet Assigned Numbers Authority (IANA) character sets that are available.

Character Encoding Name	Language	Description
US-ASCII	English	ANSI_X3.4-1968: The first 127 characters of the ASCII code.
UTF-8	Compressed Unicode	A compressed version of Unicode using one byte for ASCII characters 0–127, and three bytes for the less common characters.
UTF-16	Compressed UCS	The Universal Character System (UCS), also known as ISO 10646, uses four bytes per character (more precisely, 31 bits) to store over two billion different characters.
ISO-10646-UCS-2	Raw Unicode	The 2-octet Basic Multilingual Plane.
ISO-10646-UCS-4	Raw UCS	The full code space using 31 bit numbers (4 bytes per character).
ISO-8859-1	Latin-1, Western Europe	ASCII plus most Western European languages including characters required for Albanian, Afrikaans, Basque, Catalan, Danish, Dutch, English, Faroese, Finnish, Flemish, Galician, German, Icelandic, Irish, Italian, Norwegian, Portuguese, Spanish, and Swedish.

Table 5-1. *XML Declaration Character Encoding Values*

Character Encoding Name	Language	Description
ISO-8859-2	Latin-2, Eastern Europe	ASCII plus most Central European languages including characters required for Czech, English, German, Hungarian, Polish, Romanian, Croatian, Slovak, Slovene, and Sorbian.
ISO-8859-3	Latin-3, Southern Europe	ASCII plus most Southern European languages including characters required for English, Esperanto, German, Maltese, and Galician.
ISO-8859-4	Latin-4, Northern Europe	ASCII plus most Baltic languages characters including Latvian, Lithuanian, German, Greenlandic, and Lappish. This character encoding was superseded by ISO 8859-10, Latin-6.
ISO-8859-5	Cyrillic	ASCII plus Cyrillic characters required for Byelorussian, Bulgarian, Macedonian, Russian, Serbian, and Ukrainian.
ISO-8859-6	Arabic	ASCII plus Arabic.
ISO-8859-7	Greek	ASCII plus Greek.
ISO-8859-8	Hebrew	ASCII plus Hebrew.

Table 5-1. *XML Declaration Character Encoding Values* (continued)

Character Encoding Name	Language	Description
ISO-8859-9	Latin-5, Turkish	Latin-1 except that the Turkish letters İ, ı, Ş, ş, Ğ, and ğ replace the Icelandic letters Ý, ý, Þ, þ, Đ, and ð.
ISO-8859-10	Latin-6, ASCII plus the Nordic languages	ASCII plus most Nordic languages characters including Lithuanian, Inuit (Greenlandic Eskimo), non-Skolt Sami (Lappish), and Icelandic.
ISO-8859-11	Thai	ASCII plus Thai.
ISO-8859-13	Latin-7, ASCII plus the Baltic Rim, including Latvian	ASCII plus the Baltic Rim languages especially Latvian.
ISO-8859-14	Latin-8, Gaelic, and Welsh	ASCII plus Gaelic and Welsh.
ISO-8859-15	Latin-9, Latin-0; Western Europe	Latin-1 with a Euro sign replacing the international currency sign. Finnish characters Š, š, Z, z replacing the uncommon symbols ¦, ¨, ¸. French Œ, œ, and Ÿ characters replace the fractions ¼, ½, ¾.
ISO-2022-JP	Japanese	Uses ISO-2022 rules to select a set of Japanese characters.
Shift_JIS	Japanese, Windows	A Microsoft code extending the csHalfWidthKatakana to include kanji by adding a second byte when the value of the first byte is in the ranges 81–9F or E0–EF.

Table 5-1. *XML Declaration Character Encoding Values* (continued)

Character Encoding Name	Language	Description
EUC-JP	Japanese, Unix	Uses ISO 2022 rules to select four code sets including US-ASCII to create a full range of Japanese characters.
Big5	Chinese, Taiwan	Chinese for Taiwan multibyte set.
GB2312	Chinese, mainland China	A two-byte character set including ASCII and Kanji.
KOI6-R	Russian	A Russian character set providing for the unique characters of the Russian alphabet.
ISO-2022-KR	Korean	Uses ISO-2022 rules to select a set of Korean characters to form a complete alphabet.
EUC-KR	Korean, Unix	The characters representing those symbols in the Korean alphabet.
ISO-2022-CN	Chinese	Uses ISO-2022 rules to select a complete set of Chinese characters.

Table 5-1. *XML Declaration Character Encoding Values* (continued)

The Root Element

As discussed in Chapter 1, XML documents have a single root element that must serve as the all-inclusive base for the rest of the document. This root element, similar to the `<HTML>` element in HTML documents, provides your document's foundation. But with XML you get to identify the name of the element. In other words, if you are identifying the contents of an address book, your root element could be `<ADDRESS_BOOK>`. If you are identifying the content of a project tracking system, your root element could be `<PROJECT_TRACKER>`.

Creating and Describing Elements

As you have seen, elements are the primary structure of an XML document. You can think of elements as providing additional information about the contents of the document. In other words you can use the verbosity of XML element names to define the element's content. The well-formedness of your document is directly affected by the use of your element tags. These tags must be properly formatted and paired for the parser to work correctly. There are two types of elements that can be used in your documents: those with both opening and closing tags, and those that are considered empty elements.

Opening and Closing Element Tags

Most elements must have both an opening and a closing tag. These tags mark the location within the document where your information will be placed. If elements are written incorrectly, your document will not be well-formed. If the document is not well-formed, it can't be parsed properly. This is a well-formed element:

```
<ELEMENT_NAME> Your content here. </ELEMENT_NAME>
```

Every element has to have a name. The rules for those element names are identified later in this chapter. In addition to the actual element name, you need to ensure that every name is enclosed by angle brackets (<>). In the case of the closing element you need to precede the name of the element with the forward slash (/). This informs the XML parser and displaying software that this is the closing tag for the previous element of this name.

If you are used to programming in HTML, you will find XML is much less forgiving. In HTML you can leave off closing tags for elements such as `<BR>`, `<HR>`, and `<P>`. XML will generate fatal parser errors at this. XML requires that all elements are closed properly, using a closing tag or a properly formatted empty tag, discussed in "Empty Element Tags" later in this chapter.

Element Content

In addition to the element names and the tags themselves, you have to consider the type of content that you place within your elements. Elements can contain either references to binary data or character data. Binary data is, of course, in the form of external files such as images and other applications. On the other hand, text files contain character data that can be made up of either *entity references* or standard text characters.

Entity references are character codes that use a series of characters to instruct the XML viewer to display a character that is otherwise reserved for other aspects of your XML document. There are only five entity references, shown in Table 5-2, that are supported by XML 1.0.

Entity Command	Character
&	ampersand (&)
'	apostrophe (')
>	greater-than sign (>)
<	less-than sign (<)
"	quotation mark (“)

Table 5-2. *Valid Character Entity References in XML 1.0*

Note *The < and & characters are reserved for use with opening tags and entity references.*

Regular Character Data (CDATA) is typically anything that is not an entity reference and is not included within the markup delimiting angle brackets. Sections of text that are identified as CDATA are run through the XML parser as character information and not as markup. This allows you to display sample markup text within the visible text of your document.

Note *In Chapters 8 and 9 you will read about Parsed Character Data (PCDATA). PCDATA is not the same as CDATA (Character Data).*

A CDATA section is often identified using the <![CDATA[and]]> markup. These markup elements need to be placed around the character data being displayed so that all characters are ignored in the parser. A sample CDATA section could appear like the following code segment:

```
<![CDATA[
<?xml version="1.0" standalone="yes"?>
<PROJECT>
  Chimera Web Development Project
</PROJECT>
]]>
```

As you may have imagined, because the appearance of any]]> combination will force the closer of the CDATA section, you can’t nest CDATA sections. If you wish to create a nested appearance of CDATA sections, you will have to stack your sections carefully side by side so that you have the outward appearance of your nested data without the actual code being nested.

Empty Element Tags

Sometimes you will find that you wish to create an element that doesn't have any content. These empty elements work the same way that <BR> and <HR> elements do in HTML documents. These empty tags can contain attributes, as discussed in Chapter 6, or they can simply serve as placeholders for other information. For example, the <COMPLETED/> element can be used to insert into a project tracking record to identify the tasks within the project that have been completed.

You may have noticed that in the sample <COMPLETED/> element there is a "/" before the closing angle bracket. This symbol marks the end of the element and replaces the standard closing tag, which for this element would be </COMPLETED>. By embedding the closing slash within the opening element, the XML parser recognizes the empty element and continues looking for the next element in the document.

Naming Elements

As you lay out your XML document, you need to be aware of the various rules for naming your elements. Element names can have any combination of letters, numbers, periods, hyphens, and underscore characters. They can start with either a letter or the underscore, but numbers are reserved for later characters in the element name. You cannot have white space within your element name, as white space is used to as a separator to identify the change from and element to an attribute. The following list shows you a series of syntactically correct element names:

```
<PROJECT05>
<Project05>
<Project.05>
<_05Project>
<project05>
<Project_05>
```

The following elements have syntactically incorrect names:

```
<Project=05>
<PROJECT:05>
<Project 5>
<project%05>
<05Project>
<.Project.05>
```

While colons are legal in XML element names, they should only be used with Namespaces, as discussed in Chapter 7, as a means of providing a designator for the specific element and its source.

XML element names are case specific. This means that the elements <ADDRESS>, <Address>, and <address> will be treated as separate entities. The names of opening and closing element tags must match exactly. For example <Project05> and </Project05> will be treated as an entire element declaration, whereas <Project05> and </PROJECT05> will be treated as separate elements. XML doesn't care if you use all uppercase, mixed case, or all lowercase, but for ease of understanding, you should pick one case and stick with it for the sake of convention.

You may be thinking at this point that because XML is case sensitive and it is a long text file that can be difficult at best to type out, you may wish to shorten the element names from their more human legible <Project05> to a shorter and easier to type <P05>. Although your fingers may appreciate the shortening of the element names, it will only marginally affect the file size of your document, and can impair the documents from a human or readability standpoint. Take a look at the following XML document segment:

```
<PROJECTS_2005>
  <PROJECT_NAME> Chimera Web Development</PROJECT_NAME>
  <WEB_DEVELOPER> Heather Williamson</WEB_DEVELOPER>
  <START_DATE> May 1, 2005</START_DATE>
   <PROJECTED_END_DATE> July 31, 2005</PROJECTED_END_DATE>
   <TASK_LIST>
    <TASK>
      <TASK_NAME> Site Plan </TASK_NAME>
      <TASK_DESCRIPTION>
      Create a written copy of highly detailed descriptions of
      each stage of the development of the Web site, including
      color schemes, sample graphics, and text content.
      </TASK_DESCRIPTION>
      <COMPLETION_DATE> May 10, 2005 </COMPLETION_DATE>
    </TASK>
    <TASK>
      <TASK_NAME> Site Development Schedule </TASK_NAME>
      <TASK_DESCRIPTION>
      Create highly detailed schedule of each stage of the
      development of the Web site including the development
      of all scripts, e-commerce options, and multimedia.
      </TASK_DESCRIPTION>
      <COMPLETION_DATE> May 12, 2005 </COMPLETION_DATE>
    </TASK>
    <TASK>
      <TASK_NAME> Project Budget </TASK_NAME>
      <TASK_DESCRIPTION>
```

```
        Create task based cost estimate for the entire site.
        </TASK_DESCRIPTION>
        <COMPLETION_DATE> May 15, 2005 </COMPLETION_DATE>
      </TASK>
    </TASK_LIST>
</PROJECTS_2005>
```

You can easily identify each piece of information within this XML document because of the verbosity of the commands. In this next segment of sample code, you must know what content the XML document contains and the order of the information, because the initials <WDEV> and <SDATE> don't mean much without additional information:

```
<P2005>
  <PNAME> Chimera Web Development</PNAME>
  <WDEV> Heather Williamson</WDEV>
  <SDATE> May 1, 2005</SDATE>
   <PEDATE> July 31, 2005</PEDATE>
   <TL>
    <T>
      <TNAME> Site Plan </TNAME>
      <TDESC>
      Create a written copy of highly detailed descriptions
      of each stage of the development of the Web site,
      including color schemes, sample graphics, and text content.
      </TDESC>
      <CDATE> May 10, 2005 </CDATE>
    </T>
    <T>
      <TNAME> Site Development Schedule </TNAME>
      <TDESC>
      Create highly detailed schedule of each stage of the
      development of the Web site including the development
      of all scripts, e-commerce options, and multimedia.
      </TDESC>
      <CDATE> May 12, 2005 </CDATE>
    </T>
    <T>
      <TNAME> Project Budget </TNAME>
      <TDATE>
      Create task based cost estimate for the entire site.
      </TDATE>
      <CDATE> May 15, 2005 </CDATE>
```

```
    </T>
  </TL>
</P2005>
```

By leaving your XML elements in their verbose forms, you create a document that is self-describing. This means that anyone, with a tool as simple as a basic text-editor, can read the document and understand each piece of information with no other training or documentation. Using verbose elements allows you to know that the date `May 10, 2005` in the `<START_DATE> May 10, 2005 </START_DATE>` is without question the start date for the project.

Child Elements

As you can with HTML elements, you can nest XML elements. But unlike HTML, which allows you to nest your elements erratically, XML elements can't overlap. Well-formed XML requires that the XML element tags be stacked in an orderly fashion, as shown in the following example:

```
<?xml version="1.0" standalone="yes"?>
<PROJECT>
  <TASK> Start Car
    <STEP> 1. Find Key </STEP>
    <STEP> 2. Open Door </STEP>
  </TASK>
</PROJECT>
```

In this example the `<PROJECT>` element is the document root and the `<TASK>` element is its child. Within the `<TASK>` element are two `<STEP>` elements that provide the step-by-step instructions for the task identified by the `<TASK>` element. These child elements all complete themselves within their parents, so they are considered well-formed. An XML document that is not well-formed would have mismatched elements, as shown in this next code segment:

```
<?xml version="1.0" standalone="yes"?>
<PROJECT>
  <TASK> Start Car
    <STEP> 1. Find Key </STEP>
    <STEP> 2. Open Door </STEP>
</PROJECT>
</TASK>
```

Empty elements can appear anywhere. They can appear between other element tags within the midst of their content, for example:

```
<PROJECT> CHIMERA <BR/> Web Site Development</PROJECT>.
```

Summary

As you have gleaned from the individual parts of this chapter, in order to be well-formed an XML document must follow these rules:

- The XML declaration must be the first line of the document.
- One element, serving as the root element, contains all other elements in the document.
- Elements are required to have both opening and closing tags if they have content.
- The < and & characters are only used for opening tags and entity references.
- XML 1.0 only supports the 5 character entities `&`, `'`, `>`, `<`, and `"`.
- Elements that are empty, or without content, are closed with the /> character combination.
- Elements cannot overlap but can be nested inside other elements.

XML documents that are well-formed can be correctly parsed within any parser compatible with the version of XML that you are using. In this case, the current version of XML is 1.0 and therefore makes the parser's job easier by being the only version of XML available.

The Complete Reference

Chapter 6

Adding Attributes

Elements provide a foundation for your XML document. Attributes provide information about the foundation you are building. In other words, attributes provide metadata about the information contained within your element. With attributes you can add either additional detail or auxiliary information to your elements. Attributes can be used as a means to control the appearance of your elements in addition to style sheets. For instance, if an XML application uses a `color` attribute to provide a background color selection for displaying information on a particular type of file, then although the `color` attribute itself was provided for metadata, not formatting purposes within the document, the application can select to use the value of that attribute to control further the information that it is displaying to the document viewer.

Take a look at any HTML document on the Internet. Everywhere you look you will see attributes in action. In the simple HTML example that follows you can see a series of attributes:

```
<body bgcolor="#FFFFFF"
      background="New%20Images/mtnbkg.jpg"
      text="#000099" link="#006600"
      vlink="#0000CC" alink="#000066">
  <table border="0" width="100%">
    <tr>
      <td>
        <p align="center">
        <img src="New%20Images/outbacklogo.gif"
             width="359" height="285"></p>
        <p align="center">
        <font face="Arial, Helvetica, sans-serif" size="+2">
        <b>Horseback Vacations and Hunts<b></font><br>
        <font color="#000066">in the <br>
        Eagle Cap, Wenaha-Tucannon, <br>
        &amp; Hell's Canyon Wilderness Areas <br>
        &amp; Chesnimnus &amp; Sled Springs Units</font></p>
    </td>
    </tr>
  </table>
</body>
```

The previous code creates a very simple document with a table, an image, and some text. Within each of these objects, attributes are used. Within the <body> line of the HTML code, there are no fewer than six attributes. Each of these attributes controls the overall appearance of the document. The `bgcolor="#FFFFFF"` attribute provides a reference to the RGB (Red-Green-Blue) color that should appear in the background of the page. In this case the second attribute, `background="New%20Images/mtnbkg.jpg"`, replaces the background color with an image. The remaining attributes all control the appearance of the default text found within the HTML document. The `text="#000099"` attribute sets the color of the text itself to a dark blue. The `link="#006600"` attribute sets the color of the hot links within the document to a relatively dark green color. The `vlink="#0000CC"` and the `alink="#000066"` attributes set the color of the links when they have been visited or are actively being pressed, respectively.

As you continue to read through the remainder of this HTML code, you see more attributes performing their jobs. In the `<table>` element, the `border` and the `width` attributes provide directions that control the appearance of the table. In HTML most of the attributes are associated with instructions for controlling the display of the content or identifying document content for use in scripts. XML doesn't have to be this way. In XML documents, you can use your attributes to provide information about your elements and enhance their ability to share your information.

When to Use Attributes

Attributes can actually be used to display all of the information that would otherwise be displayed within the child elements (see Chapter 5). It is up to you to decide which information you will be placing inside attributes and which you are placing within child elements. Keep in mind that you can generally place information into an attribute if it is strictly auxiliary information that does not require the use of any specific display format in your finalized document. When deciding which information is strictly auxiliary, keep in mind these rules of elements and attributes:

- Elements allow you to store metadata as attributes.
- Elements are more easily extended in the future.
- Attributes don't hold structure.
- You have to use transformations, such as XSLT covered in Chapter 16, to display attributes in conventional browsers.

The previous convention was that "real" text was relegated to the contents of elements and attributes contained information about the markup or text. The recent influx of data-oriented programmers has altered these rules a bit, since they are not worried about the previous distinction between data and metadata.

Metadata

Although there is always some discussion about what truly makes up metadata, or information about information, attributes are one way of adding metadata to your elements. To some degree, since the element name itself already provides information about the content, the attribute then provides meta-metadata, or information about the information, which is being described in the element.

To understand the concept of metadata, look at the following example:

```
<PROJECT contact="Jim Brown (555) 555-1212">
   Chimera Web Development
</PROJECT>
```

This short example lists the name of the project with the information `"Jim Brown (555) 555-1212"` serving as metadata. It is not the information itself, which is the `Chimera Web Development` content of the `<PROJECT>` element, but it is additional information about the Chimera Web Development project. This information, of course, could be broken down into other elements:

```
<PROJECT>
   Chimera Web Development
  <CONTACT>Jim Brown</CONTACT
  <PHONE> (555) 555-1212 <PHONE>
</PROJECT>
```

By breaking down the information into its respective parts as elements, the information becomes more accessible and much more usable. Because you can use style sheets with elements, you can force the information in your elements to appear or disappear on your page, while attributes will always appear in browsers that display the full XML syntax such as Microsoft Internet Explorer.

Microsoft Internet Explorer only displays the full XML syntax if no style sheet is provided. If you use CSS (see Chapter 13), attributes will NOT be shown; if you use XSLT (see Chapter 16), you can convert attributes into elements, but only the element content of the final version will be shown.

Attributes Are Not Extensible

The other concern with using attributes is their ambiguity and lack of extensibility. In the previous example, the contact for the Chimera Web Development project is Jim Brown. But what does Jim Brown do? Is he the overall contact for the entire project? Does he work for you, or does he work for your client? Can he only discuss budgeting details or is he up on the actual development stages of the project? The simple `contact` attribute can't tell us that. It also can't tell us whether the phone number listed is a direct line to his office, voicemail, or personal or cellular number. This ambiguity can make using attributes frustrating. Of course, you have to decide when to use them and when to leave the information formatted into elements.

In Chapter 5, the Chimera Web Development project was laid out in some detail, as seen in the following code. This example uses no attributes at all in order to identify the project.

```
<?xml version="1.0" standalone="yes"?>
<PROJECTS_2005>
```

```
   <PROJECT_NAME> Chimera Web Development</PROJECT_NAME>
   <WEB_DEVELOPER> Heather Williamson</WEB_DEVELOPER>
   <START_DATE> May 1, 2005</START_DATE>
    <PROJECTED_END_DATE> July 31, 2005</PROJECTED_END_DATE>
    <TASK_LIST>
     <TASK>
       <TASK_NAME> Site Plan </TASK_NAME>
       <TASK_DESCRIPTION>
       Create a written copy of highly detailed descriptions
       of each stage of the development of the Web site,
       including color schemes, sample graphics, and text content.
       </TASK_DESCRIPTION>
       <COMPLETION_DATE> May 10, 2005 </COMPLETION_DATE>
     </TASK>
     <TASK>
       <TASK_NAME> Site Development Schedule </TASK_NAME>
       <TASK_DESCRIPTION>
       Create highly detailed schedule of each stage of the
       development of the Web site including the development
       of all scripts, e-commerce options, and multimedia.
       </TASK_DESCRIPTION>
       <COMPLETION_DATE> May 12, 2005 </COMPLETION_DATE>
     </TASK>
     <TASK>
       <TASK_NAME> Project Budget </TASK_NAME>
       <TASK_DESCRIPTION>
       Create task-based cost estimate for the entire site.
       </TASK_DESCRIPTION>
       <COMPLETION_DATE> May 15, 2005 </COMPLETION_DATE>
     </TASK>
    </TASK_LIST>
</PROJECTS_2005>
```

You can also go to the other extreme and place everything for your document within an attribute, as follows:

```
<?xml version="1.0" standalone="yes"?>
<PROJECTS_2005
    PROJECT_NAME="Chimera Web Development"
    WEB_DEVELOPER="Heather Williamson"
    START_DATE="May 1, 2005"
```

```
     PROJECTED_END_DATE="July 31, 2005">
    <TASK_LIST>
     <TASK
     TASK_NAME="Site Plan"
     TASK_DESCRIPTION="Create a written copy of highly detailed
     descriptions of each stage of the development of the Web
     site, including color schemes, sample graphics,
     and text content. "
     COMPLETION_DATE="May 10, 2005">
     </TASK>
     <TASK
      TASK_NAME="Site Development Schedule"
      TASK_DESCRIPTION="Create highly detailed schedule of each
      stage of the development of the Web site including the
      development of all scripts, e-commerce options, and
      multimedia. "
      COMPLETION_DATE="May 12, 2005"
     </TASK>
     <TASK
       TASK_NAME="Project Budget"
       TASK_DESCRIPTION="Create task-based cost estimate for
       the entire site. "
       COMPLETION_DATE="May 15, 2005"
     </TASK>
    </TASK_LIST>
</PROJECTS_2005>
```

As you can see, if you place everything in an attribute, there is no way for you to sort out easily the individual task names or the list of task names and dates for their completion. You can't use style sheets to display the name of a task without also displaying its full description. Using attributes, how would you effectively create a searchable comments field to track information about how well the project is progressing? By placing all of your information in attributes you severely limit how well your data can be used and how much data you can add to your document.

Think about that description field for a moment. It might be nice to be able to add some statistical data to that description. Using attributes you can't display images associated with a description or share marked up information. You are defeating the purpose of including metadata within your elements. By using attributes all of the time, your attributes become the content.

Because of the freedom provided with XML you neither have to swing to the extreme of all elements, nor do you have to swing to the other extreme of using all attributes. You can easily find the happy middle ground between the two that will allow you the flexibility and extensibility within your document that you need.

Using Attributes to Enhance Elements

XML attributes are not restricted to the specific set of commands that are provided with HTML. Using XML, you can create your own attribute names, just as you created your own elements. You can then program your software to interact with these attributes and elements in the manner that you require, which may be vastly different than anything currently available with HTML. This flexibility in your naming scheme allows you to greatly enhance the amount of information you can store within a single element. You are not restricted to the type of data that the element can hold.

Take a look at this sonnet by Shakespeare. In it, when displayed in traditional methods, you see only the name of the sonnet, the lines of the sonnet, and the author of the sonnet.

Sonnet XIX

Devouring Time, blunt thou the lion's paws
And make the earth devour her own sweet brood;
Pluck the keen teeth from the fierce tiger's jaws
And burn the long-liv'd phoenix in her blood;

Make glad and sorry seasons as thou fleets,
And do whate'er thou wilt, swift-footed Time,
To the wide world and all her fading sweets;
But I forbid thee one most heinous crime:

O' carve not with the hours my love's fair brow,
Nor draw no lines there with thine antique pen!
Him in they course untainted do allow
For beauty's pattern to succeeding men.
Yet do thy worst, old Time! Despite thy wrong,
My love shall in my verse ever live young.

—William Shakespeare

This pattern gives us no more information than the sonnet itself. When we use attributes, we can create a display of the sonnet that compares to our traditional methods but adds additional information so that the reader can be given a plethora of new information.

```
<?xml version="1.0" standalone="yes"?>
<SONNET>
  <TITLE written="1592" first_published="1609"
        current_source="The Kittredge-Players Edition of the
        Complete Works of William Shakespeare G. L. Kittredge;
        Grolier Inc., New York City, NY; 1958">
```

```
    Sonnet XIX
  </TITLE>
  <STANZA id="s1">
    <LINE id="s101">
      Devouring Time, blunt thou the lion's paws</LINE>
    <LINE id="s102">
      And make the earth devour her own sweet brood; </LINE>
    <LINE id="s103">
      Pluck the keen teeth from the fierce tiger's jaws</LINE>
    <LINE id="s104">
      And burn the long-liv'd phoenix in her blood; </LINE>
  </STANZA>
  <STANZA id="s2">
    <LINE id="s201">
      Make glad and sorry seasons as thou fleets, </LINE>
    <LINE id="s202">
      And do whate'er thou wilt, swift-footed Time, </LINE>
    <LINE id="s203">
      To the wide world and all her fading sweets; </LINE>
    <LINE id="s204">
      But I forbid thee one most heinous crime: </LINE>
  </STANZA>
  <STANZA id="s3">
    <LINE id="s301">
      O' carve not with the hours my love's fair brow, </LINE>
    <LINE id="s302">
      Nor draw no lines there with thine antique pen! </LINE>
    <LINE id="s303">
      Him in they course untainted do allow</LINE>
    <LINE id="s304">
      For beauty's pattern to succeeding men. </LINE>
  </STANZA>
  <REFRAIN id="r">
    <LINE id="r1">
      Yet do thy worst, old Time! Despite thy wrong, </LINE>
    <LINE id="r2">
      My love shall in my verse ever live young. </LINE>
  </REFRAIN>
  <AUTHOR birth="April, 23 1564" death="April 23, 1616">
    William Shakespeare
  </AUTHOR>
</SONNET>
```

Within this sonnet, you see the expected element markup, as well as the addition of a variety of attributes that provide some very useful, although unnecessary, additional information. In the <TITLE> element, the addition of information concerning the writing and publishing dates of this particular sonnet have no effect on your ability to read the sonnet, nor to display it in the fashion of your choice, but the information does provide you with a way of searching through your XML document in the future and displaying just the sonnets that were originally written before the 1600s, if you wish. Without this information, you would be unable to sort your completed XML document by anything other than the actual content of the elements.

Each line of the sonnet is marked with an identifier, so you could conceivably write a script that would allow you to find a specific line within the XML document and then modify its content or appearance in any fashion you see fit. This same concept works for the complete stanzas and refrains. You can select the refrain or the stanza by its identification number or number-letter combination. In addition to the line numbers and publication dates, this document has also been enhanced to show the birth and death dates of the sonnet's author. This information can be used to sort out particular sonnets by the specified authors or just those authors that are already deceased. The options are as wide as your imagination and your programming ability (or your ability to hire a programmer).

Attribute Rules

There are really no hard-and-fast rules as to which information should be placed within attributes and which should be placed as element content. A general rule of thumb is to use attributes to add additional information about the actual contents of the element that are directly related to the element. As you saw in the sonnet example, attributes can be added to the individual elements as they are most appropriate.

```
<AUTHOR birth="April, 23 1564" death="April 23, 1616">
  William Shakespeare
</AUTHOR>
```

However, even with the vast amount of freedom that you have when creating and naming your attributes, there are still a few rules that you must follow.

Naming Attributes

How do you name attributes? The simple answer is: You name them whatever you want. The more complicated answer is the same but has a few restrictions that you must follow in order for your use of attributes to be part of a well-formed document (see Chapter 5). Attributes that contain errors and don't follow these rules will "break" the XML document and will cause it to have parsing errors.

Attributes must follow these rules:

- Attribute names can contain any letters, numbers, periods, or underscore characters. (Colons can be used but are reserved for use with namespaces.)
- Attribute values must all appear within quotations.
- You can't have multiple attributes of the same name in a single element.

That is it. There really aren't very many rules, and the most important of them all may be the last: You can't have multiple attributes of the same name in a single element. This means specifically that a single `<LINE>` element can't have two `id` attributes. This statement would be wrong:

```
<LINE id="s303" id="11">
      Him in they course untainted do allow</LINE>
```

When the XML parser hits this second `id` attribute, in the same element, it will stop parsing and throw up a red flag alerting you to the problem. You can get by with this in some HTML browsers, but don't even try it with XML. It creates an error prohibiting the rest of the document from being parsed, and forcing you to edit the contents of the document to remove the erroneous `id` element.

Attribute Values

One important aspect of using attributes is identifying its value. You have a lot of options when identifying values for your attributes:

- *Values can be of a specified set.* In other words, your values can be from a preidentified list such as "sonnet, poem, ditty, prose." To force your attribute values to be restricted to a specific list, you must provide either a DTD or a document Schema providing the rules by which the XML application can validate the attribute values you are providing. You can read more about DTDs in Chapter 10. XML Schemas are introduced in Chapter 18.
- *Values can reference another file.* Think about the HTML `<IMG>` element. This element uses the `src` attribute in the form of `src="image.gif"` attribute to reference the address of an image file that will be displayed in place of that particular element. XML can do this same thing with properly loaded entities (see Chapter 11).
- *Values can be free form.* In addition to referencing a specific list or a binary object such as an image file, values can be free form. For example, the `alt` attribute of the HTML `<IMG>` element allows you to enter a string of text describing the image being displayed so those users who don't load images still know what the image was supposed to be displaying and users of nongraphical browsers can still enjoy the document. XML has the same ability.

Using Attributes to Enhance Empty Elements

So far you have seen attributes used with "normal" elements with both opening and closing markers. You can also use attributes with empty elements. Attributes may be even more important to use with empty elements, because they serve as the means of providing all of the reference and content for that element. Think about the <HR> element that draws horizontal rules in HTML documents:

```
<HR width="50%" style="style guides…">
```

The individual attributes are used to set the width of the rule and to control its appearance (style). Because the <HR> element has no content, it is strictly used as a document marker. By adding the attributes to it, you can create an element with both content and appearance controls.

Sharing Attributes

Attributes are not restricted to use with a single element. You can use attributes with any number of elements. For example, return to the Shakespearean sonnet listed in previous examples in this chapter:

```
<REFRAIN id="r">
  <LINE id="r1">
    Yet do thy worst, old Time! Despite thy wrong, </LINE>
  <LINE id="r2">
    My love shall in my verse ever live young. </LINE>
</REFRAIN>
```

As you can see from this segment, the id attribute is used with both the <REFRAIN> element and the <LINE> element to provide an identifier for each element. This is also done in HTML:

```
<BLOCKQUOTE id="r">
  <FONT id="r1" size="2">
    Yet do thy worst, old Time! Despite thy wrong, <FONT>
  <FONT id="r2" size="2">
    <I>My love shall in my verse ever live young.</I> </FONT>
</BLOCKQUOTE>
```

The use of the attributes, which provides identification for all of your elements, allows you to manipulate your information using style sheets (discussed quickly in the following section) and scripts. If you are creating a document that will go through a complete validation process, then you need to create your attributes in such a way that they can easily be documented within your XML document's DTD, discussed in Chapter 10.

Using Style Sheets with Attributes

Style sheets provide a means of configuring your XML document so that it appears the way you want. Attribute values provide an excellent way for your style sheet declarations to be joined with specific elements within your document. Without style sheets there is no way to format your information into a reasonable facsimile of a traditionally appearing document. If you view the sonnet example through Internet Explorer 5, as shown in Figure 6-1, you see all of the XML elements and attributes, as well as the information.

The addition of even the most simple style sheet can change the appearance of your document to a well-formatted sonnet that is easily readable as shown in Figure 6-2.

Adding a Style Sheet

There really isn't much of a trick to add style sheets to a document. The statement that allows XML to use style sheets is `<?xml-stylesheet?>`. This *processing instruction* informs the browsing software, as well as the parser, where to find a style sheet for use with the XML document.

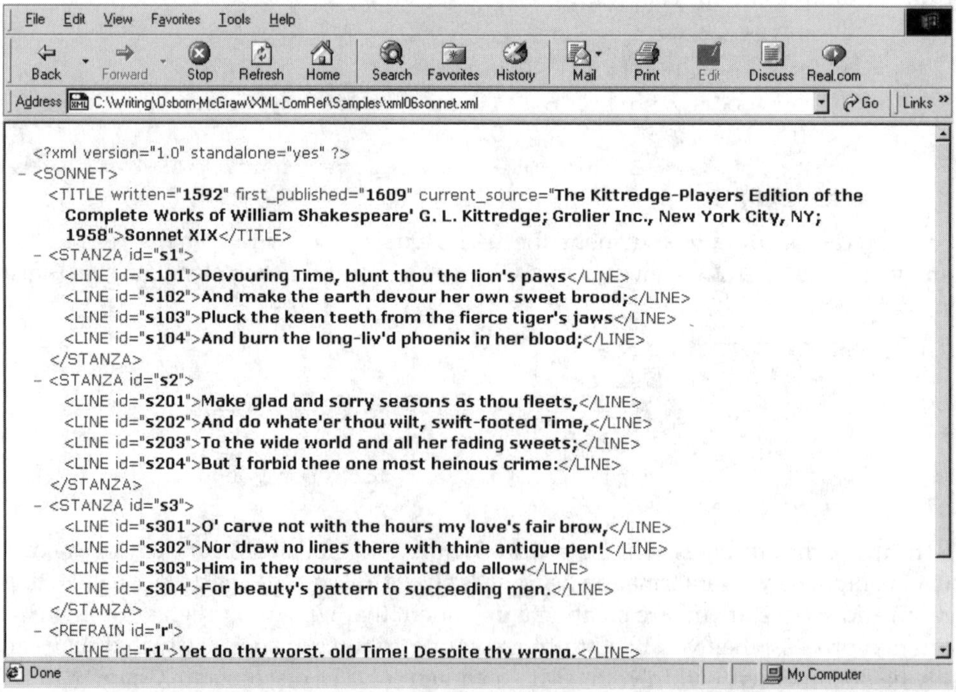

```
File  Edit  View  Favorites  Tools  Help
Back  Forward  Stop  Refresh  Home  Search  Favorites  History  Mail  Print  Edit  Discuss  Real.com
Address  C:\Writing\Osborn-McGraw\XML-ComRef\Samples\xml06sonnet.xml   Go  Links

  <?xml version="1.0" standalone="yes" ?>
- <SONNET>
    <TITLE written="1592" first_published="1609" current_source="The Kittredge-Players Edition of the
      Complete Works of William Shakespeare' G. L. Kittredge; Grolier Inc., New York City, NY;
      1958">Sonnet XIX</TITLE>
  - <STANZA id="s1">
      <LINE id="s101">Devouring Time, blunt thou the lion's paws</LINE>
      <LINE id="s102">And make the earth devour her own sweet brood;</LINE>
      <LINE id="s103">Pluck the keen teeth from the fierce tiger's jaws</LINE>
      <LINE id="s104">And burn the long-liv'd phoenix in her blood;</LINE>
    </STANZA>
  - <STANZA id="s2">
      <LINE id="s201">Make glad and sorry seasons as thou fleets,</LINE>
      <LINE id="s202">And do whate'er thou wilt, swift-footed Time,</LINE>
      <LINE id="s203">To the wide world and all her fading sweets;</LINE>
      <LINE id="s204">But I forbid thee one most heinous crime:</LINE>
    </STANZA>
  - <STANZA id="s3">
      <LINE id="s301">O' carve not with the hours my love's fair brow,</LINE>
      <LINE id="s302">Nor draw no lines there with thine antique pen!</LINE>
      <LINE id="s303">Him in they course untainted do allow</LINE>
      <LINE id="s304">For beauty's pattern to succeeding men.</LINE>
    </STANZA>
  - <REFRAIN id="r">
      <LINE id="r1">Yet do thy worst, old Time! Despite thy wrong,</LINE>
Done                                                   My Computer
```

Figure 6-1. *When displayed without a style sheet in Internet Explorer, all document elements and attributes appear.*

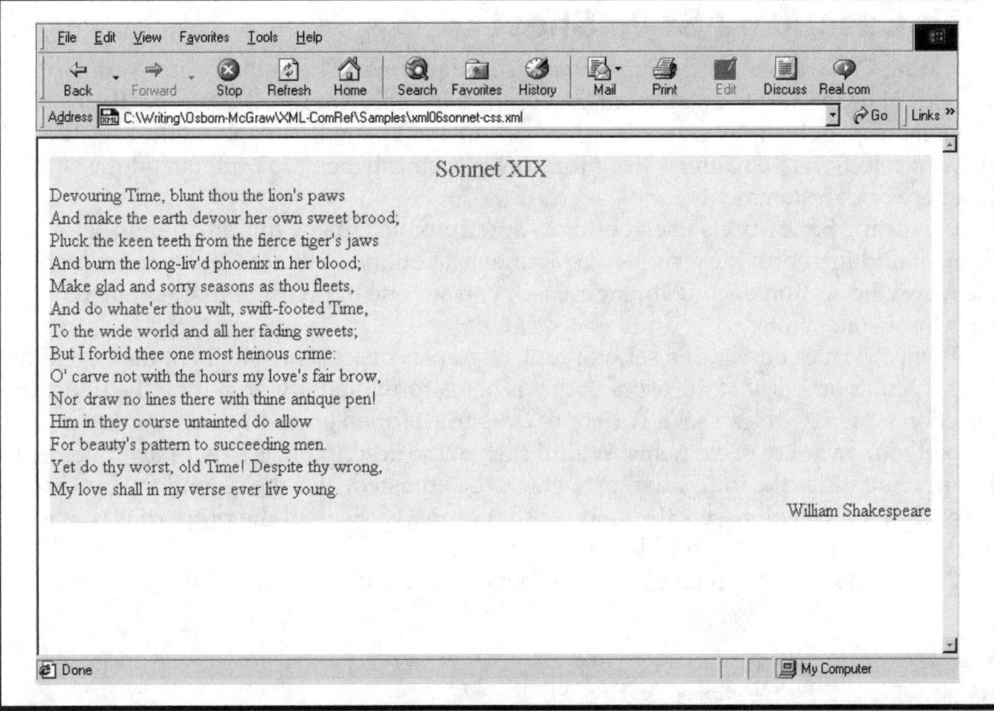

Figure 6-2. *The addition of a style sheet creates a sonnet that more closely matches the traditional experience of reading Shakespeare.*

Within this processing instruction there are two pseudoattributes. The first attribute, `type`, provides information about the specific MIME media type that is used to identify the style sheet, in this case a CSS style sheet. The second attribute, `href`, is used to identify the name and location of the style sheet that is to be used. You can see the `<?xml-stylesheet?>` processing instruction in action in the following example:

```
<?xml version="1.0" standalone="yes"?>
<?xml-stylesheet type="text/css" href="sonnet.css"?>
<SONNET>
. . . . .
```

The `<?xml-stylesheet?>` processing instruction must always follow the `<?xml?>` statement and come before the root element of your XML document. If you are using a DTD, (see Part II), the style sheet processing instruction will come before the `<!DOCTYPE>` statement. Unlike HTML documents, you can't embed style sheets within your XML documents; you can only link them. Of course, this helps promote the use of style sheets over multiple documents, which was one of its original intentions.

A Quick Cascading Style Sheet

Cascading Style Sheets (CSSs) have a very simple format. They allow you to apply individual properties to an element based upon the value of its ID attribute, the name of the element, or by its location within the document. You will learn about the specifics of element selection in Chapter 13, but for now you simply need to understand the structure of CSS statements.

Cascading Style Sheets use a selector–descriptor statement combination to select an element and then provide a series of statements about that element. Take, for example, the following section of code. In Figure 6-3, you see one of the <SONNET> element's descriptor statements.

Each CSS rule consists of a selector and a two-part descriptor statement that identifies the particular property of the element that is being formatted. By providing the two-part selection system, you can set a variety of properties for an element or set the same property for a variety of elements. Within each of the descriptors is a two-part statement. The first identifies the individual property to be adjusted, and the second, everything to the right of the colon, sets the value of that property. Each of the properties is discussed in Chapters 13 and 14 and Appendix A.

A style sheet for our Shakespearean sonnet could look as simple this:

```
SONNET  { font-size: 12pt;
          background-color: #FFFF11;
          color: blue;
          display: block;}
TITLE   { font-size: 16pt;
          color: red;
          text-align: center;
          display: block;}
STANZA  { display: block;}
REFRAIN { display: block;}
LINE    { display: block;}
AUTHOR  { display: block;
          text-align: right;
          text-style: italic;}
```

A Quick XSL Style Sheet

The Cascading Style Sheet language is probably more familiar to you than XSL, but it has its limitations. If you wish to use a style sheet that can be read by the primary Web browsers that are available, the CSS is probably your first choice, although XSL is gaining more support in the software industry with every product release. If you do decide to use an XSL style sheet, the information in Chapter 12 can help you make that decision, but for now look at the options that XSL gives you with the <SONNET> example.

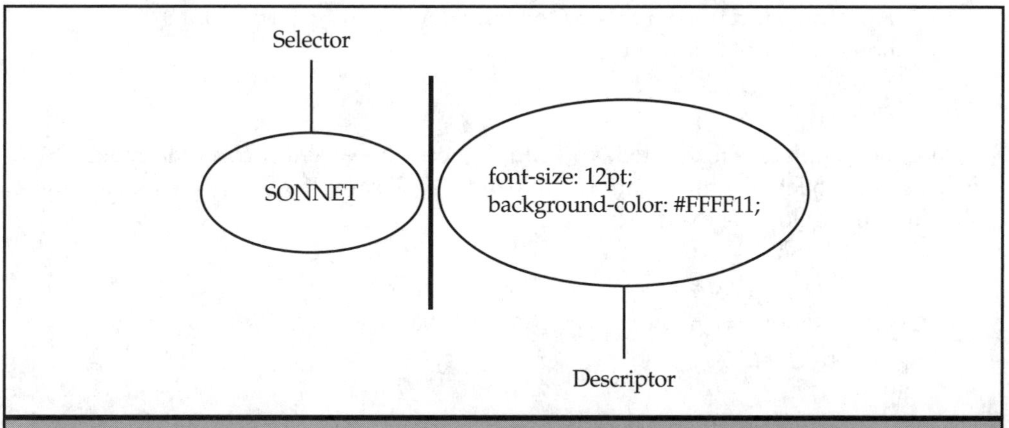

Figure 6-3. *Each CSS rule consists of a selector and a two-part descriptor statement that identifies the particular property of the element that is being formatted.*

You can add an XSL style sheet to your XML document using the same structure that you did for the CSS style sheets, but make the adjustments to your attribute values to reflect the XSL document format. For example:

```
<?xml-stylesheet type="text/xsl" href="sonnet.xsl">
```

Once you have asked the XML document to read your style sheet, you are ready to create it. XSL style sheets are based upon XML, so they have a very similar format to the XML document you are building. They also include the ability to transform the XML code into HTML code so that you can more easily display your XML document information in the exact fashion that you require.

XSL style sheets contain a template that provides you with the mechanism and format to sort information from your XML document. The structure of the template will depend upon the type of software you are using to view the XML document. For example if you are going to view your XML documents in Web browsers, then your template will be based upon HTML. If you were going to read your XML document within Adobe FrameMaker, then your XSL formatted template would include FrameMaker formatting commands. In essence your XSL template to convert an XML document to an HTML document will look something like this:

```
<HTML>
<HEAD>
  <TITLE>
    XSL instructions for collecting the title  </TITLE>
</HEAD>
<BODY>
```

```
    XSL instructions for collecting information for the
    body of the document.
  </BODY>
  </HTML>
```

Once the template is formatted, you simply need to learn how to format your XSL instructions to collect the information you need. A full sample XSL style sheet template is shown in the following example:

```
<?xml version="1.0"?>
<xsl:stylesheet xmlns:xsl="http://www.w3.org/TR/xsl">
  <xsl:template match="/">
    <HTML>
      <xsl:apply-templates />
    </HTML>
  </xsl:template>
  <xsl:template match="TITLE">
    <HEAD>
      <TITLE>
       <xsl:value-of select="." />
      </TITLE>
    </HEAD>
  </xsl:template>
  <xsl:template match="SONNET">
    <BODY>
      <P>
      <xsl:for-each select="STANZA">
        <xsl:value-of select="." />
      </xsl:for-each>
      </P>
      <P>
      <xsl:for-each select="REFRAIN">
        <xsl:value-of select="." />
      </xsl:for-each>
      </P>
      <P align="right">
      <I>
      <xsl:value-of select="AUTHOR" />
      </I>
      </P>
    </BODY>
  </xsl:template>
</xsl:stylesheet>
```

Does this seem incomprehensible? It is really much simpler than it looks. It will be described in detail in Chapter 16, but for now you can think of each XSL template as a stackable block, each one describing how the other should be inserted within itself.

Summary

Attributes have the effect of providing meta information to the elements that they are applied to. They can provide a means of identifying individual elements, as well as provide auxiliary information for the elements. All in all, attributes, although less extensible than elements, provide a very necessary method of connecting information to style sheets and enhancing the content of the elements to which they are associated.

Attributes have generally the same rules for naming as elements, but they also have the option of incorporating values. Each of these values must be found within quotation marks, or else your document will not be well-formed and will create a parsing error. Attributes must be used judiciously, so as to not incorporate information that must be displayed using the currently supported CSS style sheet properties and therefore take a lot of thought.

The Complete Reference

Chapter 7

XML Namespaces

As you work with XML there will come a time when you wish to incorporate the information contained within more than one document into another single document. You really have three choices: don't validate the document and use the well-formed XML from both documents, validate the document and rewrite the DTD for both sets of markup, or use XML Namespaces with no validation. Using XML Namespaces is a lot easier.

What Are Namespaces?

What are namespaces? You might be asking yourself this question right now, or you may be glossing over this chapter to see if there is any new information available. Since the release of the W3C "Namespaces in XML" recommendation in 1999, not a lot of new information has been made available. Unlike every other area of XML development, namespaces seem to be the one area that you can count on.

To rehash, in one sentence, what XML allows developers to do: XML allows developers to create their own markup language for their own type of projects, which can be shared with individuals working on similar projects all over the world. One specific example of this is Mathematics Markup Language (MathML). MathML is a derivative of XML that is focused on supplying a means of designing and displaying complex mathematical equations for physicists, engineers, mathematicians, teachers, and others. (MathML is discussed in detail in Chapter 31.) Besides complex mathematical equations, mathematicians and others also use information such as text, authors names, and scientific titles. To effectively provide well-formed mathematical information, as well as other forms of XML information in a single viewable document, you need to combine the references for multiple types of resources. This is where namespaces come in to play.

Take a quick look at the following example MathML code showing the simple formula for the simple equation a+b=c:

```
<?xml version="1.0"?>
<MATH>
   <MI>a</MI>
   <MO>+</MO>
   <MI>b</MI>
   <MO>=</MO>
   <MI>c</MI>
</MATH>
```

In this example code a series of predefined MathML markup has been used to identify each portion of an equation. Now add some run-of-the-mill XML elements to the document, and you end up with something like this:

```
<?xml version="1.0"?>
<MATH_ASSIGNMENT>
  <INSTRUCTIONS>Solve the following problems:</INSTRUCTIONS>
  <QUESTION id=1>
  <MATH>
   <MI>a</MI>
   <MO>+</MO>
   <MI>b</MI>
   <MO>=</MO>
   <MI>c</MI>
   <INSTRUCTIONS>
   Where A, B, and C are the sides of a right triangle
   with A=6 and B=A*2.7.
   </INSTRUCTIONS>
  </MATH>
  </QUESTION>
  <QUESTION id=2>
    If a train were driving 60 miles an hour and left point A
    at 12:00 going to point B, and a train driving 40 miles an
    hour left point B, heading to point A at 12:30, and there
    were 210 miles between point A and B, where would the
    trains meet? Show your work.
  </QUESTION>
<MATH_ASSIGNMENT>
```

As you can see from the preceding code we have mixed both XML markup with MathML code. In order for both of these chunks to be displayed, your Web browser has to be able to display both XML code and MathML code properly. It also has to be able to decipher each piece of code and identify which markup goes with the raw XML and which with the MathML.

Note *Internet Explorer 5 does not support MathML code. You can use Amaya to view the MathML code correctly, but it won't display any Cascading Style Sheet attributes that have been added to your document.*

As long as all of the commands are different, as with the previous example, your concerns are minimized. The problem arises when you have commands that use the same name. For example, the base element name in MathML is `<MATH>`. If any of the element names in my XML code was `<MATH>`, then a conflict would arise. The compiler, or user agent, would not know which of the `<MATH>` objects should be treated according to MathML instructions and which should be interpreted as straight XML markup.

You can see how this would be confusing at best for the Web browser. Now add into this picture the use of different style sheet properties for each type of `<MATH>` element, and you are proverbially "up a creek without a paddle."

In order to give documents the ability to use multiple elements of the same name within the same document, XML Namespaces was created. This system allows you to attach an URL to an element name in order to give the XML processor the ability to separate out the various elements into their correct sources. This works with both element names and attribute names, so a `font` attribute used within a standard XML formatted document, or a `font` used with MathML notation, can be interpreted separately with the correct style sheet rules applied.

Using Namespaces Within Documents

As with every programming language, whether that language is C++ or the very first version of Basic, you have a specific set of rules that must be followed to keep the language interacting with itself and its software properly. The XML Namespaces recommendation uses a series of universal names based upon approved XML notation, so that current XML 1.0 compliant software can implement this new standard today and users don't have to wait for notoriously nonpunctual software companies to provide expensive upgrades to their products. The use of Namespaces differentiates between the local names already included in your document's current DTD.

Identifying Namespaces

When you wish to declare an XML Namespace in your current document, you can use the following notation:

```
<elementname xmlns:prefix="namespaceurl">
```

This notation, when applied to MathML, would appear as follows:

```
<MATH xmlns:mm="http://www.w3.org/TR/REC-MathML">
```

This format uses a mapping system already acceptable in XML, in which you use a prefix to identify the namespace that is being associated with the element or attribute. XSL is applied this way, as you saw in the example at the end of Chapter 6. As you can see, you can specify either an element name or an attribute name after the namespace prefix used to identify the individual namespace. The namespace prefix is then used with the `xmlns` prefix to identify the source of the DTD used to identify this universal attribute fully.

You can use neither the `xml` *nor the* `xmlns` *prefix to bind a namespace to a document. The* `xml` *prefix is by default pointing to the http://www.w3.org/XML/ 1998/namespace address for the XML document itself. The* `xmlns` *prefix is used to bind elements to namespaces and therefore cannot be used as a prefix to be bound to.*

More specifically, the namespace declaration associates the specified element or attribute to the namespace prefix, or identifier, that represents the namespace located at the specified URL.

Lets look at the following example code to help us clarify this situation:

```
<?xml version="1.0"?>
<MATH_ASSIGNMENT xmlns:mdoc="http://www.catsback.com/Math/">
  <mdoc:INSTRUCTIONS>
      Solve the following problems:</mdoc:INSTRUCTIONS>
  <mdoc:QUESTION id="1">
  <MATH xmlns:mm="http://www.w3.org/TR/REC-MathML">
   <math:MI>a</math:MI>
   <math:MO>+</math:MO>
   <math:MI>b</math:MI>
   <math:MO>=</math:MO>
   <math:MI>c</math:MI>
   <mdoc:INSTRUCTIONS>
   Where A, B, and C are the sides of a right triangle
   with A=6 and B=A*2.7.
   </mdoc:INSTRUCTIONS>
  </MATH>
  </mdoc:QUESTION>
  <mdoc:QUESTION id="2">
    If a train were driving 60 miles an hour and left point A
    at 12:00 going to point B, and a train driving 40 miles an
    hour left point B, heading to point A at 12:30, and there
    were 210 miles between point A and B, where would the
    trains meet? Show your work.
  </mdoc:QUESTION>
</MATH_ASSIGNMENT>
```

In the preceding example the `<MATH_ASSIGNMENT>` and the `<MATH>` elements are using namespace declarations to identify the various XML and MathML elements that are used in the markup. Each of these declaration statements implies that all

<MATH_ASSIGNMENT> elements, attributes, and contents will be bound to the www.catsback.com/Math/Web address. The same holds true for all <MATH>elements, attributes, and contents, but in this case, the object is bound to the www.w3.org/TR/REC-MathML Web address.

It is not necessary to declare a namespace for each child element as long as the parent element has been declared. The namespace will automatically be applied to the child element and all of the attributes of those elements unless otherwise specified.

The Syntax

Qualified names are those that are a combination of the prefix and local part name, for example <mdoc:QUESTION> or <math:MI>. In each of these cases you can easily differentiate between a various elements that can appear in the specifications from both sources.

Note *The prefix is used only as a placeholder for the namespace name. If you are creating a document whose scope extends past the local document, you should use the full URL of the namespace.*

A *qualified attribute* simply applies the prefix directly to the name of the element or attribute within the markup. If an element name is being qualified, then both the opening and closing tags must have the prefix applied. If you are qualifying an attribute within an element, you only need to apply the prefix to the name of the attribute.

Note *Although the previous example is well-formed, it is not a valid document. When attempting to use multiple namespace declarations (or prefixes) within a validating processor on a single document, you will end up with errors. Many XML applications do not currently validate documents. In order for namespaces to be used with these types of processors, you must use qualified namespace declarations or make your declarations within a subset of the DTD.*

Default Namespaces

A default namespace is applied to an element where it is declared, if that element does not currently have a prefix added to it. If the URL has been left blank in an `xmlns:` namespace declaration, then that element and any of its children without an explicitly defined namespace will be considered to be in the default namespace.

Note *Default namespaces do not apply to attributes. All attributes must be explicitly defined using a namespace prefix.*

In the following example, all of the elements have inherited the default namespace defined by the `xmlns = "..."` statement because no other prefix has been defined and all of the elements are direct children of the root element without any other namespace prefix being used.

```
<?xml version="1.0"?>
<MATH_ASSIGNMENT xmlns = "http://www.catsback.com/Math/">
  <INSTRUCTIONS>Solve the following problems:</INSTRUCTIONS>
  <QUESTION id="1">
  </QUESTION>
  <QUESTION id="2">
    If a train were driving 60 miles an hour and left point A
    at 12:00 going to point B, and a train driving 40 miles an
    hour left point B, heading to point A at 12:30, and there
    were 210 miles between point A and B, where would the
    trains meet? Show your work.
  </QUESTION>
</MATH_ASSIGNMENT>
```

Adding Namespaces to DTDs

Incorporating a namespace declaration into a DTD can be both beneficial and problematic.

Because the `xmlns:prefix` declaration is treated as an attribute by the XML processor, you must define it within the DTD used by the document. This forces you to qualify all of the element names found within the XML markup in reference to their namespace. You must remember, though, that only validating parsers will read your DTD, making this a risky proposition when using your document with nonvalidating parsers. In Part IV you will see how using XML Schemas will solve many of the frustrating validation problems of using namespaces in your DTDs.

One means of defining the namespace is to use the following statement:

```
<!ATTLIST ELEMENTNAME xmlns:prefix "namespace URL" #IMPLIED>
```

This identifies the namespace declaration as an implied attribute to the specified element. If you apply this attribute to the root element of a document, then the namespace should be available to all of the root element's children and attributes.

Note *Because a namespace declaration applies to the element in which it is identified and all of that element's child elements, attributes, and contents, you may declare multiple namespaces for a single element declaration. This makes both declarations available and valid for each child element and attribute.*

In addition to using multiple namespaces in a single XML document, to merge document structure, multiple namespaces can be used to merge multiple DTDs together into one format and validate your contents simultaneously. In order to do this, you must modularize your DTD and place the declarations for those modules into your document. Look at the following DTDs. The first is for a book, the second is for a sonnet, and the third is for a play.

The DTD for the book:

```
<!ELEMENT BOOK (DIV+)>
<!ELEMENT DIV  (HEAD, DIV*, PGPH*)>
<!ELEMENT HEAD (#PCDATA)>
<!ELEMENT PGPH (#PCDATA)>
```

The DTD for the sonnet:

```
<!ELEMENT SONNET  (STANZA, STANZA, STANZA, REFRAIN)>
<!ELEMENT STANZA  (LINE, LINE, LINE, LINE)>
<!ELEMENT REFRAIN (LINE, LINE)>
<!ELEMENT VERSE   (#PCDATA)>
```

The DTD for the play:

```
<!ELEMENT PLAY     ([NARRATE]+, ACT+)>
<!ELEMENT ACT      (ACTNUM, NARRATE*, SCENE+)>
<!ELEMENT ACTNUM   (#PCDATA)>
<!ELEMENT SCENE    (SCENENUM, NARRATE*, LINE*)>
<!ELEMENT SCENENUM (#PCDATA)>
<!ELEMENT NARRATE   (#PCDATA)>
<!ELEMENT LINE     (#PCDATA)>
<!ATTLIST LINE    part (#PCDATA)>
```

Once each DTD has been developed, you need to incorporate all of them into your document by identifying them with namespaces and incorporating those into your base document declaration in the following fashion:

```
<b:BOOK xmlns:b="book.dtd"
        xmlns:s="sonnet.dtd"
        xmlns:p="play.dtd"  >
<b:DIV>
  <b:HEAD> Introduction </b:HEAD>
  <b:PGPH>
    The following divisions of this book contain a partial line
    from Act IV, Scene III of Shakespeare's King Henry the
    Fifth and Sonnet XXI.
  </b:PGPH>
</b:DIV>

<b:DIV>
  <b:HEAD>William Shakespeare's Sonnet XXI</b:HEAD>
```

```
  <s:SONNET>
    <s:STANZA id="st1">
      <s:LINE>So is it not with me as with that Muse</s:LINE>
      <s:LINE>Stirr'd by a painted beauty to his verse,
      </s:LINE>
      <s:LINE>Who heaven itself for ornament doth use
      </s:LINE>
      < s:LINE>And every fair with his fair doth rehearse.
      </s:LINE>
    </s:STANZA>
    <STANZA id="st2">
      <s:LINE>Making a couplement of proud compare</s:LINE>
      <s:LINE>With sun and moon, with earth and sea's rich
             gems, </s:LINE>
      <s:LINE>With April's first-born flowers, and all things
             rare</s:LINE>
      <s:LINE>That heaven's air in this huge rondure hems.
      </s:LINE>
    </s:STANZA>
    <s:STANZA id="st3">
      <s:LINE>O, let me, true in love, but truly write,</s:LINE>
      <s:LINE>And then believe me, my love is as fair
      </s:LINE>
      <s:LINE>As any mother's child, though not so bright
      </s:LINE>
      <s:LINE> As those gold candles fix'd in heaven's air.
      </s:LINE>
    </s:STANZA>
    <s:REFRAIN>
      <s:LINE>Let them say more that like of hearsay well,
      </s:LINE>
      <s:LINE>
         I will not praise that purpose not to sell. </s:LINE>
    </s:REFRAIN>
  </s:SONNET>
</b:DIV>

<b:DIV>
  <b:HEAD> William Shakespeare's King Henry the Fifth </b:HEAD>
  <p:PLAY>
    <p:ACT>
      <p:ACTNUM> IV </p:ACTNUM>
      <p:SCENE>
```

```
          <p:SCENENUM> III </p:SCENENUM>
          <p:NARRATE> Enter the King </p:NARRATE>
          <p:LINE part="West">
            O that we now had here but one ten thousand of those
            men in England that do no work today!
          </p:LINE>
          <p:LINE part="King">
            What's he that wishes so? My cousin Westmoreland?
            No, my fair cousin. If we are mark'd to die, we are
            enow to do our country loss; and if to live, the
            fewer men, the greater share of honor. God's will!
            I pray the wish not one man more. By Jove, I am not
            covetous for gold, nor care I who doth feed upon my
            cost; It yearns me not if men my garments wear; Such
            outward things dwell not in my desires: But if it be
            a sin to covet honor, I am the most offending soul
            alive. No, faith, my coz, wish not a man from
            England.
          </p:LINE>
        </p:SCENE>
      </p:ACT>
    </p:PLAY>
  </b:DIV>
  </BOOK>
```

Summary

You have seen how XML namespaces can be used in your document to merge information from multiple sources. XML Namespaces are used within DTDs to validate the information contained within your document. Namespaces will be more effective once the full adoption of XML Schemas has been completed, but until then you can qualify the namespace within your DTD and avoid many of the problems of using namespaces with our current DTD system. In the next part you will find out how DTDs work in more detail, and you will have a better understanding of the importance of them in the scheme of creating valid XML documents.

Part II

Working with DTD

The Complete Reference

Chapter 8

Validating Your XML Documents

XML is a markup language used for describing other languages. In addition to creating your XML document, you will also need to provide documentation and describe the markup language(s) you create. This is the job of the DTD. It provides the list of instructions or constraints that the validating parsers use as rules to check XML document elements, attributes, entities, and notations.

DTDs and Validation

DTDs are the key to validated XML documents. The constraints they provide to XML documents are used by validating XML parsers to check the document, ensure that it is well-formed, and make sure none of the elements contained within the document have been used outside of the constraints imposed by the DTD.

You can think of DTDs as a recipe. Within this recipe you tell the cook exactly when, how, and how much of every ingredient to add. If the outcome tastes good, then the dish is good enough to be served. If the outcome tastes bad, then one or more of the ingredients was wrong. The DTD is the recipe card, the XML document is the dish, and the cook is the validating parser. If the XML document follows the DTD, the validating parser will find the document well-formed and will be able to display it properly. However the catch with DTDs is their flexibility. They are designed to have a flexible enough syntax to allow you to create a rule to govern any situation you may encounter or need to restrict within your document, but that also opens up holes in the recipe for your cook to add too much of a good thing. For example you can specify that there can be only one `<TITLE>` element within a `<BOOK>`, or you can use special notation characters such as `*`, `+`, and `?` to allow zero, one, or even an infinite amount of `<TITLE>`s. As you can see, this opens a hole to add too much of one thing to your documents, and although your documents may be valid, they won't be as usable when compared to a more restrictive DTD. Thinking logically, a book really can't have more than one title and maybe a subtitle or two, so why allow someone to create a record of a book with more than one title?

Note *XML Schemas can also be used to validate XML documents, although not for 4.x and 5.x versions of any Web browsers, including Netscape Navigator and Internet Explorer and most of the XML software available in the first half of the year 2000. You can find more information on XML Schemas in Part IV. As a side note, it is worth pointing out that Netscape Navigator, Mozilla, and Opera don't use a validating parser at all, so the use of DTDs with these browsers isn't an option; they just ignore your DTD altogether.*

As has been stated before, DTDs provide a set of rules that govern the acceptable structure of an XML document. Look at the following XML document for example:

```
<PROJECT>
  <MANAGER> H. Williamson </MANAGER>
```

```
  <CLIENT> Chimera Corporation </CLIENT>
  <DESCRIPTION>
    A long elaborate description… and on, and on, and on
  </DESCRIPTION>
..<TEAM>
    <LEAD> D. Williamson </LEAD>
    <DEV> L. Corfield </DEV>
    <DEV> L. de Leon </DEV>
    <DEV> J. Harpole </DEV>
    <DEV> D. Carter </DEV>
    <GRAPHICS> A. de Leon </GRAPHICS>
  </TEAM>
  <TEAM>
    <LEAD> J. Leon </LEAD>
    <DEV> L. Miner </DEV>
    <DEV> C. de Leon </DEV>
  </TEAM>
</PROJECT>
```

A DTD that has been designed for this document may specify that within every <BOOK> element you can have exactly one <MANAGER> element, exactly one <CLIENT> element, and one or more <TEAM> elements. The DTD could further specify that within each <TEAM> element there has to be at least one <LEAD> element with any number of <DEV> elements and that it may or may not have a <GRAPHICS> element.

Note

The parser built into Internet Explorer 5 and 5.5 does not validate your XML document, nor does it work with XSL or XML Schemas. If you wish to use a validating parser with Internet Explorer, you will need to download the new MSXML3 parser from http://msdn.microsoft.com/downloads. The parser can be found under the XML subheading of the Web Development table of contents entry. If you download a beta version of this parser, you will need to have it overwrite the MSXML2 parser included with your software manually by installing it in replacement mode. You can find the instructions for this process at http://msdn.microsoft.com/xml/general/replacemode.asp.

Adding DTDs to Your Documents

There are two ways to add DTDs to your XML documents: through an external link or by imbedding the DTD internally within the XML document. No matter which choice you use to add a DTD to your document, you must use a correctly formatted *document type declaration.*

```
<!DOCTYPE root-element ...>
```

This is the basic structure of the document type declaration. This statement is used to reference either the external linked DTD or the embedded DTD. The `<!DOCTYPE` statement first informs the parser that a DTD has been provided for this document and that it has to read it as part of the processing of the document, if the parser is a validating parser. The `root-element` portion of the document type declaration identifies the name of the root element of the document for which the DTD is provided. In the case of our Web development example, this element would be `<PROJECT>`. From this point, the structure of the DTD changes, depending upon whether the DTD is embedded or linked to your XML document.

Linking to Document Type Definitions

Linking to an external DTD isn't much more difficult than linking to an image in an HTML document; you simply have to make sure the document name is spelled correctly. Take a look at the following XML document.

```
<?xml version="1.0" encoding="Latin-1" standalone="yes"?>
<!DOCTYPE PROJECT SYSTEM "project.dtd"]>
<PROJECT>
  <MANAGER> H. Williamson </MANAGER>
  <CLIENT> Chimera Corporation </CLIENT>
. . . .
</PROJECT>
```

The actual document type declaration is all on one line, and it specifies the file to use when validating this particular XML document. In this case, it is the project.dtd file, as shown below:

```
<!DOCTYPE PROJECT SYSTEM "project.dtd"]>
```

In addition to the declarative `<!DOCTYPE>` statement, the `<PROJECT>` element has been identified as the root element of the document. The `SYSTEM` declaration identifies this DTD as being part of a local, or nonpublic, selection of DTDs. A DTD can be referenced as either a `SYSTEM` or a `PUBLIC` document type definition. There is more information on these particular reference meanings in the section entitled "Public Versus System DTDs" later in this chapter. The actual name of the file is the URL, in this case a relative URL, for the actual file containing the DTD information.

Note *The URL reference for a DTD can either be relative or absolute. If the address is absolute, the entire `http://` reference for the file must be included in the document type declaration, for instance: `<!DOCTYPE PROJECT SYSTEM "http://www.dtdfactory.com/project.dtd">`. A relative URL can include as much of the reference name for the file as is needed. For instance a relative URL could include a directory designation ("`/dtds/project.dtd`") or simply the file designation ("`project.dtd`").*

There are many reasons you may wish to link your DTD to your document rather than embed it within your document text. Of these many reasons, the foremost is the ability to use a single DTD with multiple documents. Imagine for a moment that you work for a large mathematical think tank. This company wants all of their white papers to be formatted in one particular format, no matter which project or department they originate in. In this case the company would want to create one DTD specifying the structure for their documents. For example, the DTD would specify that all headings are marked with one element designator, while all of the body text is marked with another.

By using the same DTD, anyone, anywhere in the company can read the documents written by the other departments, and anyone across the world that shares that same markup plan, such as a business partner, can read and understand those documents in the form that they were intended. By using external DTDs, an entire industry can agree on a standard for documentation, thus facilitating the sharing of information between the individual corporations. Not to mention the fact that it allows you to shrink the size of your XML document by the amount of space taken up with the DTD.

Of course, if you are creating a document just for yourself, and it will most likely be the only document of its particular markup, then you may wish to include the DTD within the body of the XML document.

Note *You can use both an internal and external DTD together. This allows you to use the embedded DTD for those document elements that are specific to this one document and still be able to reference elements from a standard DTD from another location.*

Embedding Document Type Definitions

The document type declaration changes some if you are going to actually embed the DTD code within you XML document, as you can see from the following example:

```
<?xml version="1.0" encoding="Latin-1" standalone="yes"?>
<!DOCTYPE PROJECT [
  <!ELEMENT PROJECT ANY>
  ]>
<PROJECT>
  <MANAGER> H. Williamson </MANAGER>
  <CLIENT> Chimera Corporation </CLIENT>
. . . .
</PROJECT>
```

Within this XML document, there are three lines that make up the body of this DTD. These three lines, shown in the following code, include the `<!DOCTYPE` statement; the `PROJECT` root-element designation, discussed in earlier parts of this chapter; and the actual code of the DTD. When placing your DTD code within your XML document, you must wrap the DTD text within square brackets, shown here at the end of the first

line and the start of the third line. These brackets allow the parser to identify the start and stop of the DTD declarations separate from the remaining XML code and the default <!DOCTYPE statement construction.

```
<!DOCTYPE PROJECT [
  <!ELEMENT PROJECT ANY>
  ]>
```

The <!ELEMENT declaration identifies the first element of the document, in this case the root element PROJECT. You will read more about element declarations in the section of this chapter titled "Declaring Element Types."

When you embed a DTD within your XML document, you are increasing the size of the XML document. This additional text may also make the XML document that much harder for a human to read. However, whether you are embedding the DTD within the document or linking it, the actual structure of the DTD code itself doesn't change much.

PUBLIC Versus SYSTEM DTDs

As you read earlier, DTDs, in addition to being embedded within a document or linked to it, can be specified as either a PUBLIC or a SYSTEM document type definition. Although the definitions of these specific designations are not severely enforced through parsers or XML browsers, you should know when to use the PUBLIC or the SYSTEM document declaration.

A filename must be specified for either a PUBLIC or a SYSTEM declaration. In a public declaration you much include the full URL of the document being referenced as shown in the following example.:

```
"http://www.w3.org/TR/REC-html/strict.dtd"
```

In a SYSTEM declaration you can simply use a relative address for your DTD.

There is a DTD specification for each version and implementation of HTML, SMIL, SVG, and MathML. For each of these accepted languages, the DTD has been created, stored in a public location, and made available to anyone who wishes to reference it. You can create your own DTDs and make them available for anyone to reference or, at least, for other people on your local network to share. If you were sharing your DTD on the Internet, then your DTD would typically be referenced using the PUBLIC identifier, while those referencing your DTD on your local network would use the SYSTEM identifier.

Referencing SYSTEM DTDs

Private DTDs are marked by using the SYSTEM identifier. SYSTEM DTDs are typically located in the same location or on the same local networked system as the document itself. If you specify SYSTEM as the type of your DTD, then the next attribute to be specified will be the filename of the DTD being referenced:

```
<!DOCTYPE DOCUMENT SYSTEM "strict.dtd">
```

The file being referenced can either be a relative address, one not specifying the name of an actual computer location, or an absolute address using the full URI (Uniform Resource Identifier) reference for the file such as

```
"http://www.w3.org/DTD/strict.dtd"
```

Referencing PUBLIC DTDs

If you specify SYSTEM, then the next attribute to be specified will be the filename of the DTD being referenced. In the case of a PUBLIC DTD, the information following the PUBLIC statement will be the *public identifier* string as seen in this example:

```
<!DOCTYPE DOCUMENT PUBLIC "-//W3C//DTD HTML 4.0//EN"
  http://www.w3.org/TR/REC-html/strict.dtd">
```

This string, surrounded by quotation marks, is intended to be meaningful to all systems that read it. The identifier is made up of multiple parts all delineated by double forward slashes. The first part is the *owner identifier.* If the official "owner" has not been registered; this field will contain a hyphen. In this case, the second part would contain the name of the organization that developed the DTD. If the owner has been identified, the second part would contain the *text identifier.* This section specifies the public text class, such as DTD or ENTITIES, followed by the public text description, such as XML or Latin 1. The third part contains a code representing the language being used in the document, for example EN for English or FR for French. If you wish to specify a specific display version of the DTD, it can be placed as a fourth or fifth part of your public identifier. The following examples show you some of the combinations that may appear in public identifier strings:

```
"-//W3C//DTD HTML 4.0//EN"
"ISO 12083:1994//DTD Math//EN"
"-//IETF//ENTITIES Latin 1//FR"
"-//W3C//DTD HTML//EN//4.1"
```

Declaring Element Types

The basic DTD is actually quite simple. All you have to do is create a list of the elements and attributes that will be used in the file you are creating. The rules for creating this list of elements and attributes can get quite complex depending upon the particular file you are creating. Before you can start defining elements, you have to understand their structure.

A DTD is composed of individual element and attribute type declarations. Each element declaration is identified with the following basic syntax:

```
<!ELEMENT elementname content>
```

This syntax can be further explored by taking a look at its individual parts:

- ***elementname*** This is the name of the element, for example `POET`, `DOCUMENT`, or `AUTHOR`.
- ***content*** Each element has a set of allowable content. The DTD identifies the type of content that can be used with any particular element. Your options are "EMPTY", "ANY", *mixed content*, or *children*. You will discover more information about using these types of content in the following sections of this chapter. The valid content options for your elements are shown in Table 8-1.

In addition to defining the elements used in the document, the DTD must define the various entities, attributes, and notations that are also used and how these all work

Content Type	Description	Example
EMPTY	Specifies that this element can contain no content whether that content is text or child elements.	`<!ELEMENT IMAGE EMPTY>`
ANY	Specifies that this element can contain any content whether that content is text, child elements or a combination of both.	`<!ELEMENT ADDRESSBOOK ANY>`
mixed content	Allows you to specify the exact content you wish the element to contain. You can specify only text data (#PCDATA) or a combination of text and specified child elements.	`<!ELEMENT ADDRESSBOOK (NAME | NICKNAME | #PCDATA)>`
children	Specifies child element(s) that can be found within the body of the identified element. This content can't contain any character data.	`<!ELEMENT CONTACT ( NAME, STREET, CITY, PHONE)>`

Table 8-1. *Valid Types of Content for XML Elements*

together with the elements themselves. For more information on entities, attributes, and notations within DTDs, please see Chapters 9, 10, and 11, respectively, but get started with your DTD by defining your elements first.

Use the following XML document showing two address book listings as an example:

```
<ADDRESSBOOK>
  <CONTACT>
    <NAME> George Jones Sr. </NAME>
    <STREET> 1235 Nolichucky Drive </STREET>
    <SUITE-APT> Apt. 15 </SUITE-APT>
    <CITY> Houston </CITY>
    <STATE> TX </STATE>
    <ZIP> 07711 </ZIP>
    <PHONE> 555-555-1212 </PHONE>
    <FAX> 555-555-1313 </FAX>
    <CELL> 555-555-1414</CELL>
    <EMAIL> gj@nolichucky.com</EMAIL>
  </CONTACT>
  <CONTACT>
    <NAME> Jenny "Mug" Beer </NAME>
    <STREET> 4323 Natchitoches Lane</STREET>
    <SUITE-APT> Suite 4B </SUITE-APT>
    <CITY> Enterprise </CITY>
    <STATE> MS </STATE>
    <ZIP> 09988 </ZIP>
    <PHONE> 555-555-3131 </PHONE>
    <FAX> 555-555-3535 </FAX>
    <CELL> 555-555-3939</CELL>
    <EMAIL> mug@enterprise.com</EMAIL>
  </CONTACT>
</ADDRESSBOOK>
```

In this example you have a primary element called ADDRESSBOOK that serves as the root element for your document. This element must be defined in your DTD before any other elements are. The element declaration statement for ADDRESSBOOK would be

```
<!ELEMENT ADDRESSBOOK (CONTACT*)>
```

This declaration of the element ADDRESSBOOK states that this element can only contain child elements with the name CONTACT. The asterisk (*) by the name CONTACT specifies that the element can occur within ADDRESSBOOK zero or more times. You will find more information on controlling your element's content in the following section.

The declaration statement for the <CONTACT> element would appear as

```
<!ELEMENT CONTACT (NAME, STREET, SUITE, CITY, STATE, ZIP, PHONE,
  FAX, CELL)>
```

In this case, the element <CONTACT> can only contain a series of elements listed as <NAME>, <STREET>, <SUITE>, <CITY>, <STATE>, <ZIP>, <PHONE>, <FAX>, <CELL>, and <EMAIL>. Each of these elements in turn need to be defined.

```
<!ELEMENT NAME (#PCDATA)>
<!ELEMENT STREET (#PCDATA)>
<!ELEMENT SUITE (#PCDATA)>
<!ELEMENT CITY (#PCDATA)>
<!ELEMENT STATE (#PCDATA)>
<!ELEMENT ZIP (#PCDATA)>
<!ELEMENT PHONE (#PCDATA)>
<!ELEMENT FAX (#PCDATA)>
<!ELEMENT CELL (#PCDATA)>
<!ELEMENT EMAIL (#PCDATA)>
```

Each of these elements have been defined in such a way that they can contain character data (#PCDATA) but no child elements. When placed altogether within our XML document, we have a single document that can be transported anywhere in its entirety and not lose any ability be validated.

```
<?xml version="1.0" standalone="yes"?>
<!DOCTYPE ADDRESSBOOK [
  <!ELEMENT ADDRESSBOOK (CONTACT)>
 <!ELEMENT CONTACT (NAME, STREET, SUITE, CITY, STATE, ZIP, PHONE,
   FAX, CELL, EMAIL)>
 <!ELEMENT NAME (#PCDATA)>
 <!ELEMENT STREET (#PCDATA)>
 <!ELEMENT SUITE (#PCDATA)>
 <!ELEMENT CITY (#PCDATA)>
 <!ELEMENT STATE (#PCDATA)>
```

```
  <!ELEMENT ZIP (#PCDATA)>
  <!ELEMENT PHONE (#PCDATA)>
  <!ELEMENT FAX (#PCDATA)>
  <!ELEMENT CELL (#PCDATA)>
  <!ELEMENT EMAIL (#PCDATA)>
  ]>
<ADDRESSBOOK>
  <CONTACT>
    <NAME> George Jones Sr. </NAME>
    <STREET> 1235 Nolichucky Drive </STREET>
    <SUITE-APT> Apt. 15 </SUITE-APT>
    <CITY> Houston </CITY>
    <STATE> TX </STATE>
    <ZIP> 07711 </ZIP>
    <PHONE> 555-555-1212 </PHONE>
    <FAX> 555-555-1313 </FAX>
    <CELL> 555-555-1414</CELL>
    <EMAIL> gj@nolichucky.com</EMAIL>
  </CONTACT>
  <CONTACT>
    <NAME> Jenny "Mug" Beer </NAME>
    <STREET> 4323 Natchitoches Lane</STREET>
    <SUITE-APT> Suite 4B </SUITE-APT>
    <CITY> Enterprise </CITY>
    <STATE> MS </STATE>
    <ZIP> 09988 </ZIP>
    <PHONE> 555-555-3131 </PHONE>
    <FAX> 555-555-3535 </FAX>
    <CELL> 555-555-3939</CELL>
    <EMAIL> mug@enterprise.com</EMAIL>
  </CONTACT>
</ADDRESSBOOK>
```

This complete example can be validated using MSXML or any other validating XML parser. When validated using MSXML, the DTD, as shown in Figure 8-1, will not be visible.

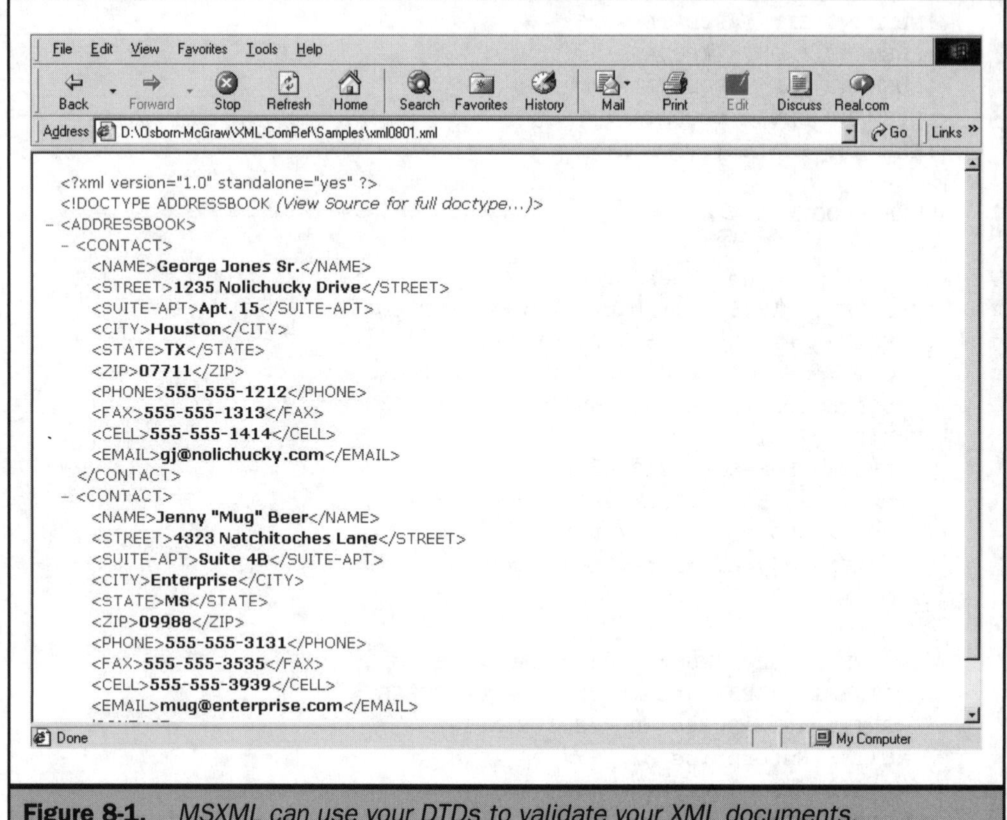

Figure 8-1. *MSXML can use your DTDs to validate your XML documents.*

Controlling Element Content

As you may have noticed in the previous example, some elements allow text content, (`ANY` or *`mixed content`*), while others don't allow any (`EMPTY`). The content model specified within the DTDs `<!ELEMENT>` statement controls the content that is allowed for each element. This identifies the valid contents of the element. The allowable content for an element is called the *content model.* An element's content model is specified with the syntax shown in Table 8-2.

Markup	Definition	Example
(. . .)	Delimits a group.	
A | *B*	Either *A* or *B* occurs, but not both. In this case the record either has a PAGER record or a CELL record but not both.	<!ELEMENT CONTACT (PAGER | CELL)
A , *B*	Both *A* and *B* occur, in that order. In this case, the CONTACT record can only have six child elements and one character data element, all of which have to occur and must occur in the order they are listed.	<!ELEMENT CONTACT (NAME, STREET, SUITE, CITY, STATE, ZIP, #PCDATA)>
A & *B*	Both *A* and *B* occur, in any order. In this case, the contact's NAME may occur before or after a selection of text.	<!ELEMENT CONTACT (NAME & #PCDATA)>
A?	*A* occurs zero or one time. In this case the element NAME has to occur either one time or not at all within the CONTACT element.	<!ELEMENT CONTACT (NAME?)>
*A**	*A* occurs zero or more times. In this case the element STREET can occur any number of times within the CONTACT element or not at all.	<!ELEMENT CONTACT (STREET*)>
A+	*A* occurs one or more times. In this case the ADDRESSBOOK must have at least one CONTACT record within it.	<!ELEMENT ADDRESSBOOK (CONTACT+)>

Table 8-2. *DTD Content Model Rules*

When you use these basic syntax structure rules, you can create very complex sets of rules to control how your document information must appear. For instance, look at the following enhanced address book model:

```
<ADDRESSBOOK>
  <CONTACT>
```

WORKING WITH DTD

```
      <NAME> George Jones Sr. </NAME>
      <ADDRESS>
       <COMPANY> DoLittles Twiddley Winks </COMPANY>
        <TITLE> Department Manager </TITLE>
        <DEPT> Plastic Processing </DEPT>
        <STREET> 1 Industrial Drive </STREET>
        <CITY> Houston </CITY>
        <STATE> TX </STATE>
        <ZIP> 07711 </ZIP>
        <PHONE> 555-555-1818 </PHONE>
        <FAX> 555-555-1919 </FAX>
        <CELL> 555-555-1010</CELL>
        <EMAIL> gj@dolittle.com</EMAIL>
      </ADDRESS>
      <ADDRESS>
        <STREET> 1235 Nolichucky Drive </STREET>
        <SUITE-APT> Apt. 15 </SUITE-APT>
        <CITY> Houston </CITY>
        <STATE> TX </STATE>
        <ZIP> 07711 </ZIP>
        <PHONE> 555-555-1212 </PHONE>
        <EMAIL> gj@nolichucky.com</EMAIL>
      </ADDRESS>
    </CONTACT>
...
</ADDRESSBOOK>
```

Using the various content model rules shown in Table 8-2, you can see that a DTD is used to enforce the order and possibility of these various elements as shown here:

```
<!DOCTYPE ADDRESSBOOK [
  <!ELEMENT ADDRESSBOOK (CONTACT)>
 <!ELEMENT CONTACT (NAME, ADDRESS+)>
 <!ELEMENT ADDRESS (COMPANY?, TITLE?, DEPT?, STREET*, SUITE*, CITY*,
   STATE*, ZIP*, PHONE*, FAX*, CELL*, EMAIL*)>
 <!ELEMENT COMPANY (#PCDATA)>
 <!ELEMENT TITLE (#PCDATA)>
 <!ELEMENT DEPT (#PCDATA)>
 <!ELEMENT NAME (#PCDATA)>
 <!ELEMENT STREET (#PCDATA)>
 <!ELEMENT SUITE (#PCDATA)>
```

```
  <!ELEMENT CITY (#PCDATA)>
  <!ELEMENT STATE (#PCDATA)>
  <!ELEMENT ZIP (#PCDATA)>
  <!ELEMENT PHONE (#PCDATA)>
  <!ELEMENT FAX (#PCDATA)>
  <!ELEMENT CELL (#PCDATA)>
<!ELEMENT EMAIL (#PCDATA)>
  ]>
```

This DTD will force the order and use of the various elements within the XML document so that they always contain the correct type of information in the correct order and occurring the right number of times within the document.

Empty Elements

Some elements do not have any content or child elements. These are referred to as *empty elements.* For these types of elements, the content model is declared using the keyword `EMPTY`.

For example, assume you wanted to add an image to the address book you are keeping for your work contacts. You could do this easily by adding a single element to each record:

```
<IMAGE src="george.jpg"/>
```

This element is an empty element. Yes, it has an attribute, but it doesn't have any content following it. You create empty elements within your XML document by closing the element tag with a forward slash. You can force the element to have no content by defining it in the DTD:

```
<!ELEMENT IMAGE EMPTY>
```

This simple statement lets the XML parser know that none of the `IMAGE` elements can have any content. This means that they will be an empty element with a single opening and closing tag (or an empty tag). You can see the addition of a few empty elements in the following segment of our `ADDRESSBOOK` example:

```
<ADDRESSBOOK>
  <CONTACT>
    <NAME> George Jones Sr. </NAME>
    <IMAGE src="george.jpg"/>
    <ADDRESS>
    <BUSINESS />
     <COMPANY> DoLittles Twiddley Winks </COMPANY>
      <TITLE> Department Manager </TITLE>
```

WORKING WITH DTD

```
      <DEPT> Plastic Processing </DEPT>
      <STREET> 1 Industrial Drive </STREET>
      <CITY> Houston </CITY>
      <STATE> TX </STATE>
      <ZIP> 07711 </ZIP>
      <PHONE> 555-555-1818 </PHONE>
      <FAX> 555-555-1919 </FAX>
      <CELL> 555-555-1010</CELL>
      <EMAIL> gj@dolittle.com</EMAIL>
    </ADDRESS>
    <ADDRESS>
      <PERSONAL />
      <STREET> 1235 Nolichucky Drive </STREET>
      <SUITE-APT> Apt. 15 </SUITE-APT>
      <CITY> Houston </CITY>
      <STATE> TX </STATE>
      <ZIP> 07711 </ZIP>
      <PHONE> 555-555-1212 </PHONE>
      <EMAIL> gj@nolichucky.com</EMAIL>
    </ADDRESS>
  </CONTACT>
...
</ADDRESSBOOK>
```

Adding Comments

Whenever you are developing a program or writing a marked-up document for consumption by other individuals, you should add notations to your document that make it easier for future developers to understand how your DTD is organized and how it works. Comments are imperative in some applications such as JavaScripts, where the document creator is doing pure programming. In other applications, such as the creation of XML documents and DTDs, it is important that you provide comments on the various sections of your text to make it easier for you or another document author to adjust the contents of the document at a later date. Comments are not required by the rules of programming, although programming convention encourages them strongly.

Comments are used to provide instructions within an XML DTD for the programmer and anyone performing follow-up maintenance. They are not interpreted by the user agent viewing the document. Comments are often used in the following situations:

- To add comments to specific sections of code found on a DTD.
- To hide code that is still being developed.

- To note changes that were made to previous versions of the document.
- To note the author and editing date of the document.

Comments can be on a single line or on multiple lines, as shown in the following example:

```
<!--This is a comment -->
<!--Comments can have multiple lines.
    If they do, they will appear like this. -->
```

Any text found between the comment markers is not visible to a site visitor when run through a good parser and browser. You shouldn't place more than two dashes in line together within a comment. In some older browsers, your comment may be truncated, and any portion of your comment past the multiple dashes will be visible to your visitors.

Summary

In this chapter you have learned about DTDs, their uses, how to incorporate them into your XML documents, and how to define elements within them. Since you can use DTDs embedded within your XML documents or as external resources, you must be sure to define your `<!DOCTYPE>` statement in such a way that it meets your needs for either a `PUBLIC` or `SYSTEM` remote DTD or to incorporate the DTD within your XML document. You need to remember that your DTD has to have an `<!ELEMENT>` statement for any element that is used on your XML document. Without this representation, your document can't be validated.

Comments can be used extensively in DTDs in order to provide additional information for the elements and the entities that are being used, as well as providing a history for the development of the DTD. Comments provide the instructions for using and modifying the DTD, whether you have put it down and not looked at it for six months or you have passed the maintenance of the document on to another person.

In the following chapters you will learn how to add entities, attributes, and notations to your DTDs to define your document further. Without the remainder of these parts defined, your document cannot be validated or can only contain elements with either child elements or text as content.

Chapter 9

Defining DTD Entities

In addition to elements, Document Type Definitions (DTDs) include *entity* declarations. Entities are used to define sets of information, providing you a shorthand way of adding large amounts of data, whether binary or text, into your XML document. The information that you are using an entity to reference may be an image, a text file, a subset of information gleaned from a database, or even a selection of text that serves as the results of a Common Gateway Interface (CGI) script. Entities can be anything, although they are typically text or chunks of XML. The XML document browser can process entities composed of text or XML data. Other entities are considered unparsed entities, which require specific knowledge about the application used to view the file before the XML document browser can work with them. Unparsed entities are discussed in Chapter 11.

Understanding Entities

So far we have been discussing XML documents as having three parts: the XML code, the DTD, and a style sheet. In all actuality, the XML document can consist of these parts, as well as a wide range of other pieces of information. Your XML documents, like HTML documents, often need images, automatically loading database content, sound tracks, or video. They may also need to use content from other XML documents. One of the common ways to incorporate this varied type of information into a single XML document is to use entities. The alternative and potentially easier method is to use XLink pointers (see Chapter 23) to link to nontextual files.

If entities still don't make sense, think about this example: You have a sales contact log of hundreds of contacts. Each of those contacts has made a purchase in the past. Each of those purchases consisted of multiple items that were ordered. Now, assuming that you have 200 sales contacts, averaging two sales per contact, with at least two items ordered per sale, you will have a minimum of 200 contacts, 400 orders, and 800 sold items to track. If you try putting all of this information into a single file, you can easily imagine the difficulty in keeping track of all of the information in a logical and error-free manner. Yes, you would only have one file to manage, but it would be a real whopper of a file. Now, if you broke off each sales contact's information into a separate file, so that for each person you track their sales and purchased items separately, you may have 201 files to keep track of, but you would lessen the chances that you would mix up individual's records. Each file representing the individual sales contact's business is an entity, as well as the XML document that combines all of the information into one easily accessible location.

A document built this way, using a series of document entities, can be validated by a validating parser that is capable of combining all the different referenced entities into a single virtual document. This parser will then pass the virtual document to the document browser or other application that will be displaying the file. Now, to be sure that this happens for both internal and external entities (discussed later in this chapter) you have to use a validating parser. Nonvalidating parsers do not have to use external entities, only internal entities.

As you can see, an entity is any source of predefined information to be used within the XML document. Typically your entities will be one of three things: a well-formed XML document, a binary file, or a selection of text. Because any single XML document can be comprised of a variety of entities, each entity has its own name. This name is used as a reference point to load and interact with the information contained within that entity. As you can imagine, without having a name to reference, the entity becomes nigh on useless for the XML developer and user.

Depending upon the type of information contained within the entity, that entity is either parsed or unparsed. Parsed entity data is comprised of well-formed XML text. This text conforms to the XML standard and can be either another XML document, a document written in any of the XML child languages, or even an XSL document. Unparsed entities contain either non-XML text such as an e-mail message or binary data such as images or audio files. At this point there aren't that many XML programs that support unparsed entities. In Chapter 11 you will find information on unparsed entities and see them in use. In this chapter you will focus on parsed entities.

There are two types of entities: internal and external. These types of entities can be used as either general entities or parameter entities; all of which are discussed in the following sections of this chapter.

Internal Entities

Internal entities are defined entirely within your document entity. For example an internal entity would have both the entity and its entire contents defined within a single well-formed XML document. Think about the HTML `<HTML>`, `<P>` and `<DIV>` tags. Each of these HTML tags is part of the document entity and doesn't inherently represent any other data. This makes them part of an internal entity.

Every XML document has at least one internal entity; the document itself. The XML document creates the document entity, which is comprised of the XML declaration, any document type declaration that is provided, and the root element of the document. In an HTML document the root element would be `<HTML>`, but in an XML document, as you saw from the earlier chapters, this element can be anything of your own making.

External Entities

External entities reference information that is contained outside of the current document entity. External entities are used to refer to images and other data that can be accessed by the use of an URL. When working with external entities, your primary XML document only includes a reference to the location of the external document source. Something that may be more familiar is the HTML `<IMG>` tag. This tag provides a reference to the location of the source file containing the image to be added to your document. In many cases, external entities are unparsed entities.

General Entities

General entities are used to add content to XML documents by substituting information for the entity reference that is used within the document. All general entities must be defined within the DTD. The format of a general entity is quite simple. It uses an ampersand (&) followed by the name of the entity and is closed with a semicolon (;):

```
&name;
```

General entities have a myriad of uses within XML, although their most common use may be as a representation of characters that fall outside of the standard ASCII character set or to provide an alternative way of representing characters that interfere with the processing of XML documents. For example; the standard abbreviation for inserting a greater-than sign (>) is `>`. There are a few standard XML entities that have been predefined within XML documents. These entities are shown in Table 9-1.

These entities are very useful for developers, but they are only the tip of the iceberg when it comes to what general entities can do for you. If you wish, you can use a general entity to add your copyright always to the bottom of a page or a heading to the top of your pages. You can use a general entity to provide headings for tables that are repeated frequently. You will see how to declare and use general entities in the rest of this chapter.

Parameter Entities

Parameter entities, like general entities, are used to insert additional information into a document, but are defined and used only in external DTDs. Parameter entities allow developers to include additional DTDs within the current DTD, merging the power of

General Entity Representation	Character Being Represented
`&`	Ampersand (&)
`'`	Apostrophe (')
`>`	Greater-than sign (>)
`<`	Less-than sign (<)
`"`	Quotation mark (")

Table 9-1. *XML Built-in General Entities*

multiple documents into a single source. This ability allows you, as the developer, to expand your DTDs more easily without having to reinvent the wheel. You could also create a series of modularized DTDs that can be merged into any configuration to meet the needs of any document you could make.

Defining General Entities

General entities are probably the most commonly used entities within XML, and they can be either internal or external entities. In the following sections you will discover how to declare both internal general entities and external general entities for use within a sales contact record-keeping system. Keep in mind that internal general entities serve the purpose of abbreviations for inserting additional text within an XML document, while external general entities provide a means of referencing information from a remote address.

Internal General Entities

The standard syntax for an internal general entity is quite simple. It simply provides an abbreviation for text:

```
<!ENTITY entity-name "entity-value">
```

This simple format allows you to create an entity that can be used to draw a specific character or something as complex as lengthy boilerplate text. The name of the entity can only contain alphanumeric characters, periods, dashes, underscores, or colon. Entity names must begin with a letter or an underscore. Colons are typically used to demark namespace prefixes, so they should be avoided for clarity's sake. The entity value can contain any valid XML formatted text and must be enclosed within quotation marks.

To create an internal general entity to be used as the payment-terms text on a sales report, you would use the following entity reference within your DTD:

```
<!ENTITY  pt "Payment Terms: ">
```

This entity would allow you to insert the payment terms heading into every document by typing fewer characters than you would if you had to insert the complete "Payment Terms: " heading each time.

The syntax to use an internal general entity is just as simple. You simply need to place the name of the entity between a leading ampersand (&) and a closing semicolon(;). For example:

```
&entity-name;
```

In order to reference our Payment Terms statement in our previous example you would use the entity reference

```
&pt;
```

You can create as many internal general entities as you wish for your documents. For example you could create a complete series of entity references for a set of payment terms to be used in addition to your heading:

```
<!ENTITY  net30 "Net 30">
<!ENTITY  dueon "Due Upon Receipt">
<!ENTITY  net15 "Net 15">
<!ENTITY  due15 "Due on the 15th">
<!ENTITY  _1per10 "1 percent discount if paid within 10 days">
```

You could then combine these entity references together within your document to create a series of easily inserted boilerplate information.

```
<PAYMENT> &pt; &net30; </PAYMENT>
```

The previous statement would print out `Payment Terms: Net 30` within the output of your XML document. You could expand these entities to include a variety of customer information messages to attach to the closing of your sales slip, such as:

```
<!ENTITY  thanks "Thank you for your patronage.
   Please come back and visit our store soon.">

<!ENTITY  pastdue "Your account has become past due.
   We are unable to do any more work for you until your
   account can be brought up to date. Thank you for your
   understanding.">

<!ENTITY  questions "This project has been completed.
   Please let us know if you have any questions.">

<!ENTITY  pastdue2 "We are sure that you have simply
   forgotten, but your account is now seriously past due.
   If payment is not received within 15 days, or if other
   payment arrangements have not been made, your account
   will be turned over to a collections agency.">
```

Within your entity reference you can include full segments of well-formed XML code. For example, if you have a company contact information block that you place at the top of all of your sales records, you could place it within an entity reference as shown below:

```
<!ENTITY company
    "<COMPANY>
        <COMPANY_NAME> Web Ravin Consulting </COMPANY_NAME>
```

```
        <ADDRESS> 555 Wilsonville Lane, Oakey, OR 99999 </ADDRESS>
        <PHONE> (555) 555-1111 </PHONE>
        <FAX> (555) 555-2222 </FAX>
        <WEB> http://www.webravin.com</WEB>
    </COMPANY>"
>
```

Note *As the contents of your entities get larger you will want to consider making them external entities to avoid confusion.*

Using Entities Within Entities

When you are working with entities you also have the option of embedding entities within other entities:

```
<!ENTITY payment "Payment of your bill is expected to
   meet the following agreed upon terms: &net30">
```

If you use embedded entity references, you must be careful not to make any of your references recursive. For example, the following code is invalid because you cannot logically embed something within itself inside of another object:

```
<!ENTITY  net30 "&pt; Net 30">
<!ENTITY  pt "Payment Terms: &net30;">
```

General Entity Restrictions

There are a few other restrictions on using entity references. The first of these prohibits you from using general entity references to refer to parts of text that will only be used within the DTD. For example the following code sample is invalid:

```
<!ENTITY elist "(PAYMENT, SUBTOTAL, TAX, SHIPPING, TOTAL)">
<!ELEMENT ORDER &elist;>
```

If you wish to merge information within the DTD, you will need to use a parameter entity, discussed later in this chapter.

The other restriction on using entities is on their value. You cannot use the ampersand (&), percent symbol (%), or the double-quotation mark (") within your entity value directly. You can include them using their character reference as another entity within your current entity. You can declare the default XML entities within your DTD if you are unsure of the support level of the XML browsers and parsers that will be viewing your document. Table 9-2 shows the general entity reference for use in your XML document, as well as the actual entity reference that will need to be placed within your DTD.

General Entity Representation	Character Being Represented	Entity Declaration
&	Ampersand (&)	<!ENTITY amp "&:#38;">
'	Apostrophe (')	<!ENTITY apos "'">
>	Greater-than (>)	<!ENTITY gt ">">
<	Less-than (<)	<!ENTITY lt "&:#60;">
"	Quotation mark (")	<!ENTITY quot """>
&perc;	Percent sign (%)	<!ENTITY perc "%">

Table 9-2. *Entity Declarations for the Predefined General Entity References*

Putting It All Together

If you put all of this information together within a single DTD and XML document, you have a relatively long document that displays the results shown in Figure 9-1.

```
<?xml version="1.0" standalone="yes"?>
<!DOCTYPE PURCHASE [
  <!ELEMENT PURCHASE (HEADER, TERMS, FOOTER)>
  <!ELEMENT HEADER (#PCDATA)>
  <!ELEMENT TERMS (#PCDATA)>
  <!ELEMENT FOOTER (#PCDATA)>
  <!ENTITY company
   "<COMPANY>
      <COMPANY_NAME> Web Ravin Consulting </COMPANY_NAME>
      <ADDRESS> 555 Wilsonville Lane, Oakey, OR 99999 </ADDRESS>
      <PHONE> (555) 555-1111 </PHONE>
      <FAX> (555) 555-2222 </FAX>
      <WEB> http://www.webravin.com </WEB>
```

```
   </COMPANY>"
  >
  <!ENTITY  pt "Payment Terms: ">
  <!ENTITY  questions "This project has been completed.
   Please let us know if you have any questions.">
]>
<PURCHASE>
    <HEADER> &company; </HEADER>
    <TERMS>&pt; Due upon Receipt </TERMS>
    <FOOTER>&questions; </FOOTER>
</PURCHASE>
```

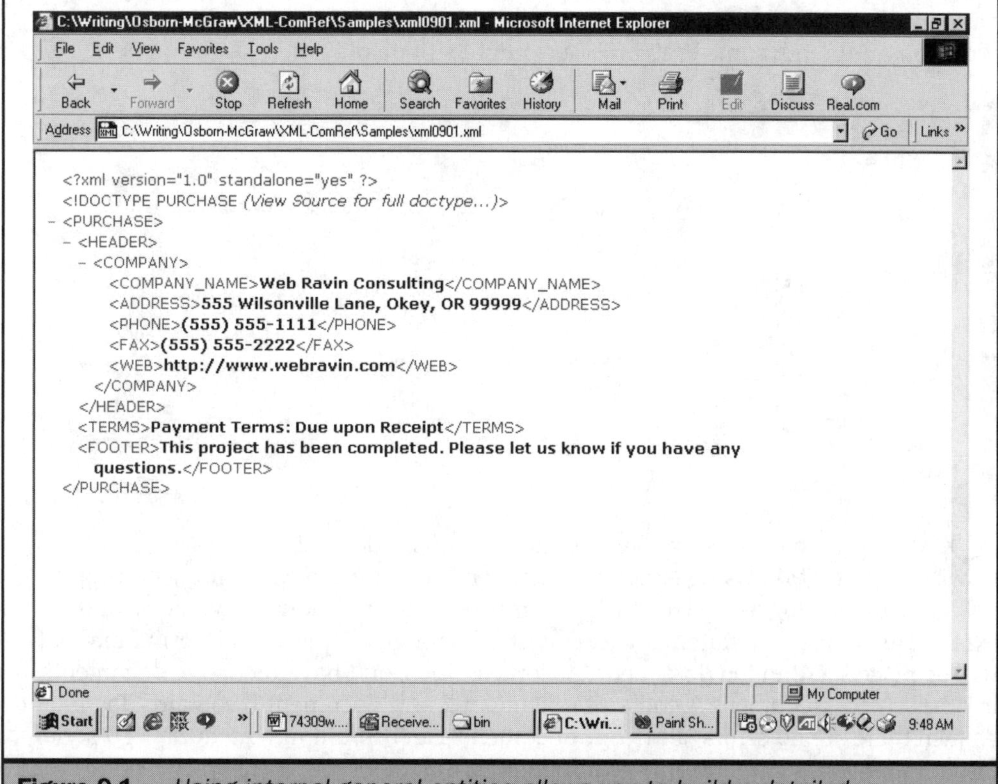

Figure 9-1. *Using internal general entities allows you to build a detailed document using extensive boilerplate text.*

External General Entities

Because external entities are data with a source outside of the current document, and general entities provide a method by which information can be used to replace a single code, external general entities provide a way that you can use external files such as images or text documents as replacement text within the current XML document. This lets you build your XML document from a variety of remote files.

Internal entities create a document in which all of the text is contained in a single file. When you use external entities, you spread your content out through multiple files. Using external entities assists you in adding dynamic information to your document by allowing the contents of your external files to change based upon search results from databases, updated images for weather reports, or even the latest radio broadcast from your favorite online radio station.

One of the largest failings of HTML is its lack of ability to merge with other HTML documents. In other words, you can't use an HTML file within an HTML file and still have a well-formed HTML file. For example, the following code would be technically erroneous, although some Web browsers might still display it:

```
<HTML>
   <HEAD>
   </HEAD>
   <BODY>
      <HTML>
         <HEAD>
         </HEAD>
         <BODY>
         </BODY>
      </HTML>
   </BODY>
</HTML>
```

XML doesn't have this problem because the DTDs don't share the same limitation found within HTML. Using external general entities, you can easily merge multiple XML documents together. The XML parser uses the instructions provided with the external general entity statements to collect and merge the pieces of information that will be placed within the document. As long as you don't have recursive documents, in other words document A contains document B and document B contains document A, then there are no errors, and your documents can be built in whatever Lego-style fashion that you want. The only requirement is that all of the documents used to create your final XML document have to be declared within your primary document's DTD in the following fashion:

```
<!ENTITY entity-name SYSTEM "entity-URI">
```

Within this syntax, the `entity-name` is the name of the entity that you will refer to in your XML document or in another entity declaration using the form `&entity-name;`. The `entity-URI` specifies the address, whether absolute or relative, of the resource providing the additional content. The following entity statements show a variety of different absolute and relative addresses:

```
<!ENTITY COMPANY
   SYSTEM "http://catsback.com/xmlfiles/company.xml">
<!ENTITY COMPANY SYSTEM "/xmlfiles/company.xml">
<!ENTITY COMPANY SYSTEM "company.xml">
```

To combine XML files using external general entities, you need first to create all of your XML documents you wish to use. These must be full-fledged, well-formed XML documents excluding the XML declaration. Below you will see three XML files that are ultimately combined within a single primary XML document.

Note *Although the content of your external entity has to be well-formed XML, it can contain additional text either before or after the root element of the document.*

This first XML document provides a listing of the information that should appear at the top of every sales invoice that is used within this particular example company:

```
<COMPANY>
   <COMPANY_NAME> Web Ravin Consulting </COMPANY_NAME>
   <ADDRESS> 555 Wilsonville Lane, Oakey, OR 99999 </ADDRESS>
   <PHONE> (555) 555-1111 </PHONE>
   <FAX> (555) 555-2222 </FAX>
   <WEB> http://www.webravin.com </WEB>
</COMPANY>
```

This document, containing only company information, will be inserted into the primary XML document using the following entity statement.

```
<!ENTITY COMPANY SYSTEM "company.xml">
```

If you wish to add a second subdocument as an external entity, such as the following sample document, you will need to create it and add its `ENTITY` declaration within your XML DTD. This document can be the output of a database or simply the contents called up from a database. For ease of representation, it will be treated like a document in this example.

```
<PRODUCTS>
   <ITEMS>
      <QUANTITY> 1 </QUANTITY>
      <DESCRIPTION>
        100 Gallons Dill Pickles - Hamburger Slices
      </DESCRIPTION>
      <AMOUNT> $50.00 </AMOUNT>
      <ITEM_TOTAL> $50.00 </ITEM_TOTAL>
   </ITEMS>
   <ITEMS>
      <QUANTITY> 2 </QUANTITY>
      <DESCRIPTION>
      Hamburger Buns - 12 bags per flat </DESCRIPTION>
      <AMOUNT> $12.95 </AMOUNT>
      <ITEM_TOTAL> $25.90 </ITEM_TOTAL>
   </ITEMS>
   <ITEMS>
      <QUANTITY> 10 </QUANTITY>
      <DESCRIPTION> Ketchup - by the gallon </DESCRIPTION>
      <AMOUNT> $5.95 </AMOUNT>
      <ITEM_TOTAL> $59.50 </ITEM_TOTAL>
   </ITEMS>
   <TAX> $1.12 </TAX>
   <SHIPPING> $9.89 </SHIPPING>
   <TOTAL> $145.41 </TOTAL>
</PRODUCTS>
```

To add this content to your document you would use the entity declaration:

```
<!ENTITY ORDER SYSTEM "order.xml">
```

Note *When using external general entities to merge XML documents, you need to be sure that the root element on the documents is not the same.*

In addition to the `<!ENTITY>` statements, you have to define all of the elements used within the subdocuments with a series of `<!ELEMENT>` statements within the primary document's DTD. The addition of the subdocument's elements within the primary document's DTD is required only if you wish to validate the document. The complete XML document shown next uses external entities to incorporate the text of the two XML files created previously, as well as declarations for those file's elements:

```
<?xml version="1.0"?>
<!DOCTYPE SALES [
  <!ELEMENT SALES (COMPANY, PRODUCTS, CLOSING)>
  <!ELEMENT COMPANY (COMPANY_NAME, ADDRESS, PHONE, FAX, WEB)>
    <!ELEMENT COMPANY_NAME (#PCDATA)>
    <!ELEMENT ADDRESS (#PCDATA)>
    <!ELEMENT PHONE (#PCDATA)>
    <!ELEMENT FAX (#PCDATA)>
    <!ELEMENT WEB (#PCDATA)>
  <!ELEMENT PRODUCTS (ITEMS*, TAX, SHIPPING, TOTAL)>
    <!ELEMENT ITEMS (QUANTITY, DESCRIPTION, AMOUNT, ITEM_TOTAL)>
       <!ELEMENT QUANTITY (#PCDATA)>
       <!ELEMENT DESCRIPTION (#PCDATA)>
       <!ELEMENT AMOUNT (#PCDATA)>
       <!ELEMENT ITEM_TOTAL (#PCDATA)>
    <!ELEMENT TAX (#PCDATA)>
    <!ELEMENT SHIPPING (#PCDATA)>
    <!ELEMENT TOTAL (#PCDATA)>
   <!ELEMENT CLOSING (#PCDATA)>
<!ENTITY COMPANY SYSTEM "company.xml">
<!ENTITY ORDER SYSTEM "order.xml">
]>
<SALES>
  &COMPANY;
  &ORDER;
  <CLOSING>
    Thank you for your order. If you have any questions
    please
call us at 1-888-555-1111.
  </CLOSING>
</SALES>
```

This complete document, shown in Figure 9-2, joins the contents of these three documents. The parser validates the sundry parts of the document and then joins them into a single virtual document using the DTD. If you were to add a style sheet to this document, you could then format each of the elements so that they would appear in a fashion suitable to give to a client as an invoice.

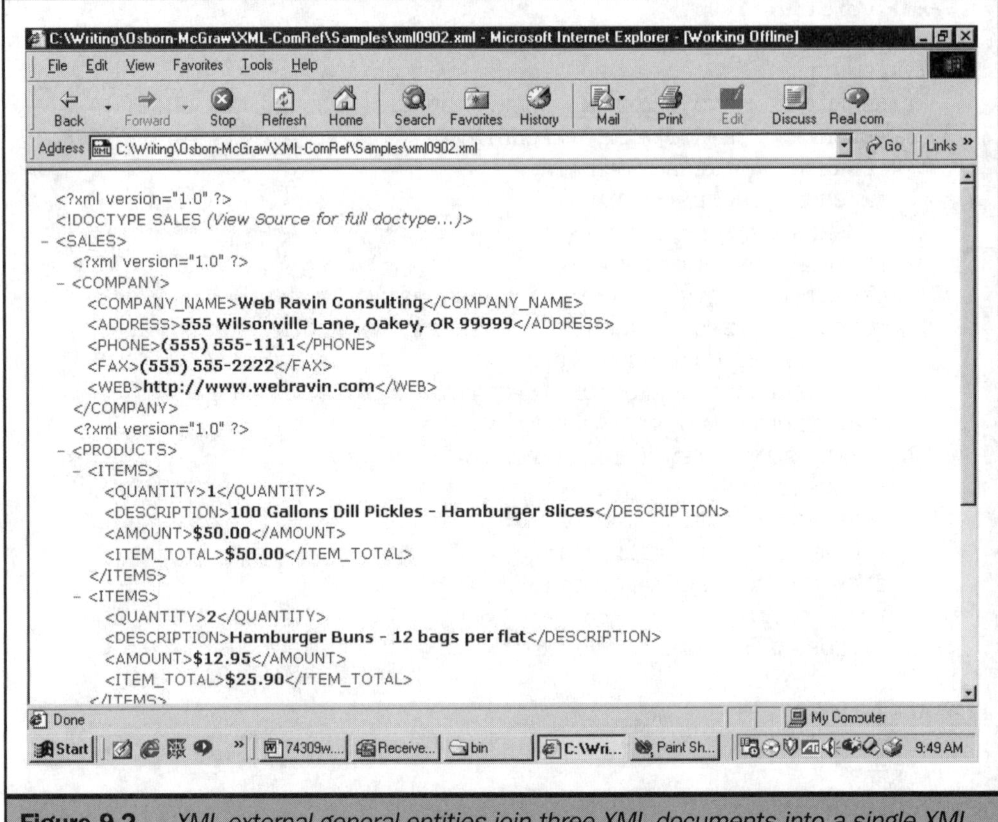

Figure 9-2. *XML external general entities join three XML documents into a single XML logical document. A style sheet was not used with this document.*

Defining Parameter Entities

Parameter entities are used strictly within DTDs and do not become a part of the resulting XML documents as do all general entities. Whereas general entities are used to reference text that will be placed within the document; parameter entities are used to declare information that will be used repeatedly within the DTD itself.

Parameter entities use a separate notation system than general entities. Whereas general entities are referenced within the document using a leading ampersand (&), a parameter entity is referenced within the DTD using a percent sign (%). Unlike general entities, parameter entities cannot appear within the XML document at all.

Parameter entities are declared within the DTD using syntax very similar to that used by general entities with the only change being the addition of a percent sign before the *entity-name*.

```
<!ENTITY % entity-name entity-definition>
```

Like general entities, parameter entities can be either internal or external. The varieties of different uses for both internal and external parameter entities are shown in the following sections.

Parameter entities can only be used in external DTDs. You cannot use parameter entities if your DTD will be included within the same file as your XML document.

Internal Parameter Entities

Internal parameter entities are perfect for creating shorthand notations for the variety of element and attribute declarations to be used within the DTD. In the DTDs that have been shown up to this point, you had to declare the list of child elements for other elements that would contain them. For example, for an <ORDER> element, you would have to make the following declaration:

```
<!ELEMENT ORDER (ITEMS+, SUBTOTAL, TAX, SHIPPING, TOTAL)>
```

If there were another element using the same set of child elements, you would have to declare them separately also.

```
<!ELEMENT CREDIT_STATEMENT
    (ITEMS+, SUBTOTAL, TAX, SHIPPING, TOTAL)>
```

This takes a lot of excess typing that is not necessary when you can use parameter entities. If you wish to save space, you can use the following entity declaration to provide access to all of the child elements, in their correct order and format, for a variety of elements.

```
<!ENTITY % elist "ITEMS+, SUBTOTAL, TAX, SHIPPING, TOTAL">
```

By using the parameter entity you can create a single entity that will be used in multiple element declarations. This allows you to refrain from reinventing the wheel. Then if you have to use additional elements other than the ones represented by the parameter entity, you can simply add them to your element in the normal fashion.

```
<!ENTITY % elist "ITEMS+, SUBTOTAL, TAX, SHIPPING, TOTAL">
<!ELEMENT ORDER (%elist;)>
<!ELEMENT CREDIT_STATEMENT (%elist;)>
<!ELEMENT STATEMENT (NAME, ADDRESS, CITY, STATE, ZIP, %elist;)>
```

As you can see, this has saved you quite a bit of typing for each of the element declarations. You will still have to declare each of the elements used within the <!ENTITY> statement, but you won't have to retype each child element list each time.

Entity statements must be defined before they can be used within an <!ELEMENT> statement. Without the entity reference being processed prior to the element declaration, the parser can't verify the element. For example the following statements result in a parser error:

```
<!ELEMENT ORDER (%elist;)>
<!ELEMENT CREDIT_STATEMENT (%elist;)>
<!ELEMENT STATEMENT (NAME, ADDRESS, CITY, STATE, ZIP, %elist;)>
<!ENTITY % elist "ITEMS+, SUBTOTAL, TAX, SHIPPING, TOTAL">
```

As you can see, this forced order for your entity and element references will encourage a specific order for the development of your DTD.

```
<!-- General entity declarations - external documents -->
<!ENTITY COMPANY SYSTEM "company.xml">
<!ENTITY ORDER SYSTEM "order.xml">

<!-- Parameter entity declarations - element subsets -->
<!ENTITY % elist "ITEMS+, SUBTOTAL, TAX, SHIPPING, TOTAL">
<!ENTITY % clist "CUST_NAME, CUST_ADDRESS, CUST_CITY, CUST_STATE, CUST_ZIP">

<!-- Root element -->
<!ELEMENT STATEMENT (CUSTOMER, SALES, CLOSING)>

<!-- Customer Information -->
<!ELEMENT CUSTOMER (%clist;)>
   <!ELEMENT CUST_NAME (#PCDATA)>
   <!ELEMENT CUST_ADDRESS (#PCDATA)>
   <!ELEMENT CUST_CITY (#PCDATA)>
   <!ELEMENT CUST_STATE(#PCDATA)>
   <!ELEMENT CUST_ZIP(#PCDATA)>

<!-- Sales Document Structure -->
<!ELEMENT SALES (COMPANY, PRODUCTS)>

<!-- Company Information -->
<!ELEMENT COMPANY (COMPANY_NAME, ADDRESS, PHONE, FAX, WEB)>
   <!ELEMENT COMPANY_NAME (#PCDATA)>
   <!ELEMENT ADDRESS (#PCDATA)>
   <!ELEMENT PHONE (#PCDATA)>
   <!ELEMENT FAX (#PCDATA)>
   <!ELEMENT WEB (#PCDATA)>
```

```
<!-- Product Order Information -->
<!ELEMENT PRODUCTS (%elist;)>
   <!ELEMENT ITEMS (QUANTITY, DESCRIPTION, AMOUNT, ITEM_TOTAL)>
      <!ELEMENT QUANTITY (#PCDATA)>
      <!ELEMENT DESCRIPTION (#PCDATA)>
      <!ELEMENT AMOUNT (#PCDATA)>
      <!ELEMENT ITEM_TOTAL (#PCDATA)>
   <!ELEMENT SUBTOTAL (#PCDATA)>
   <!ELEMENT TAX (#PCDATA)>
   <!ELEMENT SHIPPING (#PCDATA)>
   <!ELEMENT TOTAL (#PCDATA)>

<!-- Closing Statement -->
<!ELEMENT CLOSING (#PCDATA)>
```


This external DTD will be called by the primary XML document using the `DOCTYPE` statement found within your XML document. The following XML document is a well-formed and valid document that uses the DTD shown previously:

```
<?xml version="1.0"?>
<!DOCTYPE STATEMENT SYSTEM "statements.dtd">
<STATEMENT>
  <CUSTOMER>
    <CUST_NAME> Harold Brown </CUST_NAME>
    <CUST_ADDRESS> 555 Totally Bunk Road </CUST_ADDRESS>
    <CUST_CITY> Malcom </CUST_CITY>
    <CUST_STATE> TX </CUST_STATE>
    <CUST_ZIP> 77777 </CUST_ZIP>
  </CUSTOMER>
  &COMPANY;
  &ORDER;
  <CLOSING>
    Thank you for your order. If you have any questions
    please
call us at 1-888-555-1111.
  </CLOSING>
</STATEMENT>
```

External Parameter Entities

In addition to internal parameter entities, there are external parameter entities. These entities work in a fashion very similar to the external general entities, allowing you to combine external DTDs together, rather than XML document files. This allows you to create a series of smaller, more easily editable DTDs and then combine them into one larger virtual DTD for the XML documents you are creating.

By separating out your DTDs, you can have one that controls the description of a customer address and then use it for the customer statements, mass mailings, and individual contact letters. Each of these documents can be generated using a separate database of names, maintaining the same description throughout all of the instances of its use. You can use this same system of controls for describing your own company's contact information, invoice parts, headers and footers on documents, and much of the content of the document itself.

When you break apart your DTD, you only have to maintain individual DTDs for the document specific section. For instance, if you were going to create a statement of account for a sales department, you would want to include the company contact information, the customer's contact information, the textual description explaining why the statement was being sent, the invoice/accounting information that shows where the invoice had gone unpaid, and the request by the sales person for how they wish the account to be taken care of. All of the information used within this document could originate in different XML document files or databases, as well has be described using different DTDs. In the following example you will put together this document.

First you must understand the general format for creating an external parameter entity:

```
<!ENTITY % entity-name SYSTEM "entity-URI">
```

In the example being built here, you need to have two entity statements:

```
<!ENTITY % company SYSTEM "company.dtd">
<!ENTITY % customer SYSTEM "customer.dtd">
```

The company.dtd file would include the element and entity declarations used by the company records.

Parameter entities must contain complete declaration statements. You cannot include a portion of a declaration statement.

```
<!ELEMENT COMPANY (COMPANY_NAME, ADDRESS, PHONE, FAX, WEB)>
   <!ELEMENT COMPANY_NAME (#PCDATA)>
   <!ELEMENT ADDRESS (#PCDATA)>
   <!ELEMENT PHONE (#PCDATA)>
   <!ELEMENT FAX (#PCDATA)>
   <!ELEMENT WEB (#PCDATA)>
```

The customer.dtd statement needs to include the element declarations and entity references used to define the customer records.

```
<!ENTITY % clist
   "CUST_NAME, CUST_ADDRESS, CUST_CITY, CUST_STATE, CUST_ZIP">

<!-- Customer Information -->
<!ELEMENT CUSTOMER (%clist;)>
   <!ELEMENT CUST_NAME (#PCDATA)>
   <!ELEMENT CUST_ADDRESS (#PCDATA)>
   <!ELEMENT CUST_CITY (#PCDATA)>
   <!ELEMENT CUST_STATE(#PCDATA)>
   <!ELEMENT CUST_ZIP(#PCDATA)>
```

Once the company and customer DTDs are created, you can start creating the primary XML document's DTD. This DTD includes the description of the statement and how it will need to be handled, as well as the description of the invoices sent and the payments made, which will come from the accounting system. The complete DTD for this document appears as follows:

```
<!-- External Parameter entity statements -->
<!ENTITY % company SYSTEM "company.dtd">
<!ENTITY % customer SYSTEM "customer.dtd">
%customer;
%company;

<!-- Root element -->
<!ELEMENT STATEMENT
     (COMPANY, CUSTOMER, OPENING, SALES, CLOSING)>

<!-- Opening Statement -->
<!ELEMENT OPENING (#PCDATA)>

<!-- Sales and Payment List -->
<!ELEMENT SALES (INVOICE+ PAYMENTS* SUBTOTAL+ TOTAL+)>
   <!ELEMENT INVOICE (INV_NUMBER, INV_DATE, INV_TOTAL)>
      <!ELEMENT INV_NUMBER (#PCDATA)>
      <!ELEMENT INV_DATE (#PCDATA)>
      <!ELEMENT INV_TOTAL (#PCDATA)>
   <!ELEMENT SUBTOTAL (#PCDATA)>
```

```
    <!ELEMENT PAYMENTS (PAY_NUMBER, PAY_DATE, PAY_TOTAL)>
       <!ELEMENT PAY_NUMBER (#PCDATA)>
       <!ELEMENT PAY_DATE (#PCDATA)>
       <!ELEMENT PAY_TOTAL (#PCDATA)>
    <!ELEMENT TOTAL (#PCDATA)>

<!-- Closing Statement -->
<!ELEMENT CLOSING (#PCDATA)>
```

Summary

As you can see from the wide variety of options shown in this chapter, you can create vast conglomerations of documents, containing both XML and DTD information, using internal, external, general, and parameter entities. Entities are used to define sets of information, providing a shorthand method of adding large amounts of data, whether binary or text, into your XML document or DTD.

There are two types of entities that can be either internal or external: general and parameter. Internal entities create a document in which all of the text is contained within a single file. When you use external entities you spread your content out through multiple files. External entities provide a reference to a data source outside of the current document. General entities are used to add content to XML documents by substituting information for the entity reference that is used within the document. Parameter entities are also used to insert additional information into a document, but they are defined and used only in external DTDs. Parameter entities allow developers to include additional DTDs within the current DTD, merging the power of multiple documents into a single source.

Internal general entities are used to create a shortcut command that can be used to insert a specific character or something as complex as lengthy boilerplate text into the location in the XML document at which the shorthand code is placed. External general entities provide a way that you can use external files such as XML documents, images, or other text documents as replacement text within the current XML document. Internal parameter entities create shorthand notations for the variety of element and attribute declarations to be used within the DTD. External parameter entities work in a fashion very similar to the external general entities, allowing you to combine external DTDs together rather than XML document files.

In the following chapters, you will find out how to add attributes to your DTD and how they can also be used with entity references.

The Complete Reference

Chapter 10

Working with Attributes

As you read in Chapter 6, XML elements have attributes. Those attributes, just like XML elements, have to be defined within a DTD in order for the document to be validated. Since attributes provide additional information about the contents or use of an element, it is crucial that they be defined properly within the DTD. It is important to remember that attributes don't provide information for the people reading the document, but they do provide information for the computer software that is viewing the document. Your application can use attributes to identify individual elements correctly or as a means of sorting and displaying your element content. As you progress through this chapter, you will discover how to add attribute definitions to your existing DTD, improving the functionality and use of your XML document in the process.

Delving into Attributes

Attributes are nestled in the start tags and the empty tags of XML elements just as they are in HTML elements. All attributes are written in a combination of name-value pairs that provide additional meaning to the element itself. Attributes can be used as instructions for the XML application or as additional information that complements the element being used. Attributes have no one specific use in XML documents, making them the perfect tool to use for adding nonvisible information to your XML-constrained informations, as seen in the following example. You can also break tradition by displaying your attributes, using XSLT if the ability of a human reader to actually see the content of an attribute is important.

```
<PROJECT id="0511-099" language="English">
   <CONTACT type="primary"> Tom Phannon </CONTACT>
   <LOGO source="0511-099-lg.jpg"/>
</PROJECT>
```

In this code the `id` attribute of the `PROJECT` is used to provide the identification number of the project that is being described, while the `language` attribute is used to provide the primary language used for the project documentation and the project itself. The `type` attribute of the `CONTACT` field is used to specify the type of contact that this person is. The values in this attribute could be restrained so that they are only one of three strings such as "primary," "content," "graphics," or "marketing" to designate the various types of contacts you may have within a large company while working on a project. In the `LOGO` element the `source` attribute provides the address, or URL, of the image that contains the logo for that particular project. The source attribute isn't part of the content of the element, it simply points to the location where the content is stored. It requires a specially programmed browser to correctly interpret the contents of the file stored at that address and then display it.

You may have noticed in the first line of the previous example that the `PROJECT` element has two attributes, `pid` and `language`. An element can have as many attributes as is necessary to get that element's job done, but an element can only have one attribute of any given name. That means that your PROJECT element can't have two separate pid attributes. In HTML, multiple attributes are the norm rather than the exception, as you can see in the following example:

```
<IMG src="myimage.gif"
     width="100" height="150"
     alt="The company logo.">
<FONT color="red" size="+1"
     face="Arial, Helvetica"> My text here </FONT>
```

Note *All attributes will be found within the opening tags or empty tags of elements. They cannot exist within the end tags of your elements.*

After you have decided on the attributes that will be used with the elements within your document, you are ready to define them within your DTD. You must be prepared to match attributes to elements, as there is no way to define a global attribute that will work with all the elements in your document.

Attribute or Element?

When attempting to decide whether the best storehouse for your information is an element or an attribute, you have to take into account exactly where that information will be used. For instance, an ID attribute that strictly provides a unique identifier for a record is a great thing to put into an attribute since it won't typically need to be displayed to the user. When deciding whether to make information into an element or an attribute, I ask myself these three questions:

- Is this information describing a type of data I already have?
- Is this information used by the people viewing the document or only by the software reading the document?
- Is this information used to identify uniquely a set of information that is all related?

If the answer is "Yes, this information describes the type of data I have" or "Only the software is going to use the data" or "Yes, this is a unique identifier for a record" then I'm going to place that into an attribute. For example, in the case of a document discussing a project, the project identification number will go into an attribute, since it describes the project as well as uniquely identifies both the project and all of its associated records, and additionally, it is used by the software to coordinate records. Whether the user can see the project ID number is actually immaterial in relation to its use, since using XSL Transformations (XSLT) you can view any value associated with any attribute.

Defining Attributes

Attributes, like elements, have a specific format that must be used for their DTD specification. The basic structure is quite simple:

```
<!ATTLIST element_name
          attribute_name attribute_type default_value>
```

The <!ATTLIST> declaration notifies your parser that you are working with an attribute, rather than an element or entity declaration discussed in the two previous chapters. The `element_name` specifies an element that has already been declared, or is going to be declared, within the DTD. Chapter 8 provides more information on defining and using elements within DTDs. The `attribute_name` is the identifier that you use to separate this attribute from the other attributes that have been defined for this element. Attribute names have the same restrictions that element names do: they must start with a letter and can only contain letters, numbers, underscores, and colons. The colon is typically reserved for providing reference to namespaces, so it should not be used outside of a namespace prefix setup.

Take the following XML element for example:

```
<CONTACT type="primary"> Tom Phannon </CONTACT>
```

This element, `CONTACT`, has one attribute, `type`, which identifies the type of contact represented by `Tom Phannon`. This element would be declared in the following manner within the DTD for this document:

```
<!ELEMENT CONTACT (#PCDATA)>
<!ATTLIST CONTACT type CDATA "primary">
```

The element `CONTACT` is identified as containing parsed character data (`#PCDATA`). The second statement identifies an attribute "`type`," applied to the `CONTACT` element, which contains character data, represented by `CDATA` in the attribute statement, with a default value of "`primary`." The name of the element has to be specified within the <!ATTLIST> declaration for the attribute to be appropriately attached to the element for which it is meant. You can declare your attributes before or after your elements. You can declare attributes multiple times for the same element, but only the first declaration of the attribute is used. If you wish, you can also declare attributes for elements that do not exist.

In many cases, you will have the same attribute applied to many different elements. The attributes can have different default values or be of a completely different attribute type. Take the following code for example. In this example the ID attribute has been applied to two different elements and in each instance has different content:

```
<PROJECT pid="0511-099">
   <CONTACT cid="tph001"> Tom Phannon </CONTACT>
</PROJECT>
```

Within the DTD for this document you need to define both the PROJECT and CONTACT elements, as well as their respective pid and cid attributes. One possible declaration is shown in the following DTD.

```
<!ELEMENT PROJECT (CONTACT+)>
   <!ATTLIST PROJECT pid CDATA "0000-000">
<!ELEMENT CONTACT (#PCDATA)>
   <!ATTLIST CONTACT cid CDATA "AZ001">
```

Controlling Attribute Types

In addition to the various rules that govern how elements and text content can be used, you also can specify other data types to be used with the attributes. Each of the following data types are used in the attribute definitions of the DTD to identify the type of content that can be placed within the value of the attribute:

- CDATA
- ENTITY, ENTITIES
- Enumerated
- ID
- IDREF, IDREFS
- NMTOKEN, NMTOKENS
- NOTATION

CDATA Attributes

This is the most general type of attribute, allowing the attribute to contain any string of text characters. The string can contain the standard letters and numbers (A–Z, 1–0) and most punctuation characters. The only four punctuation characters excluded from attribute values of this type are: less-than (<), greater-than (>), ampersand (&), and quotation mark ("). Each of these characters can be referenced using their entity references, shown in Table 10-1.

Some samples of CDATA attributes include these:

```
<PROJECT pid="0511-099"> </PROJECT>
<OBJECT width="15.5"/>
<VIDEO source="testingimage.gif" />
<IMAGE height="10&quot;" />
```

Each of these attributes would be defined in the DTD using the following <!ATTLIST> statements:

```
<!ATTLIST PROJECT id CDATA "">
<!ATTLIST OBJECT width CDATA "1">
<!ATTLIST VIDEO source CDATA "trans.gif">
<!ATTLIST IMAGE height CDATA "1">
```

Character Being Represented	Entity Reference
Ampersand (&)	&
Greater-than (>)	>
Less-than (<)	<
Quotation mark (")	"
Single Quote/Apostrophe (')	'

Table 10-1. *Characters Only Allowed in CDATA Attribute Types When Their Entity References Are Used*

Note *You can include double quotation marks or single quotation marks within your CDATA value, if the value itself is delimited with the opposite type of quote mark. For example you can use the attribute value* `width="8.5'"` *to set a width to 8.5 feet or the inverse* `height='4"'`.

ENTITY or ENTITIES Attributes

The ENTITY attribute type enables you to link external unparsed entities that reference external binary files into your document. This attribute type can only contain the name of an entity that is defined within the DTD.

An ENTITY type attribute is typically used to insert an image or video file within the XML document. As long as the XML document browser can support the type of image or video that you are using, you can use a series of <!ELEMENT>, <!ATTLIST>, and <!ENTITY> statements to identify the entity within the document you are inserting.

```
<!ELEMENT VIDEO EMPTY>
<!ATTLIST VIDEO source ENTITY #REQUIRED>
<!ENTITY VID SYSTEM "video.rm" NDATA RM>
```

Once you have defined the DTD references, you are ready to add the video file into your XML document at your selected location using the following command:

```
<VIDEO source="VID" />
```

The ENTITIES attribute type is the same as the ENTITY type, but it allows you to reference multiple entities within your XML document. To use our previous example, you would simply add additional video options to your <!ENTITY> declarations in your DTD.

```
<!ELEMENT VIDEO EMPTY>
<!ATTLIST VIDEO source ENTITIES #REQUIRED>
<!ENTITY VID SYSTEM "video.rm" NDATA RM>
<!ENTITY VID_SM SYSTEM "video_sm.rm" NDATA RM>
<!ENTITY VID_FR SYSTEM "video_fr.rm" NDATA RM>
```

You would then be able to reference all three of these videos by using the following element statement within your XML document.

```
<VIDEO source= "VID VID_SM VID_FR" />
```

Note *Your application won't know what to do with the contents of your XML element's attributes unless it has been programmed with specific instructions for that type of attribute and its value. The parser has no information for handling various file types. For more information on embedding non-XML data within your document, see Chapter 11.*

Enumerated Attributes

Enumerated attributes are not specified by an enumerated XML keyword but are specified by a list of possible text values for the attribute. Each value must be separated by a vertical bar, or pipe symbol (|), and must follow the rules for creating valid XML names (discussed in Chapter 2). A sample attribute list for a `CITY_DESIGNATION` element that could only contain a list of local city zip codes could look like the following:

```
<!ATTLIST CITY_DESIGNATION
          zip (77123 | 77111 | 77888 | 77999 | 77011)>
```

If the DTD had this specification for the `zip` attribute of the `CITY_DESIGNATION` element, the following element designations would be valid:

```
<CITY_DESIGNATION zip="77111" />
<CITY_DESIGNATION zip="77011" />
```

This element would create a validation error within a validating parser:

```
<CITY_DESIGNATION zip="99999">
```

`ID` Attributes

When you need to use an attribute to identify a single element uniquely within your document, you will need to create an attribute with an `ID` attribute type. This type allows you to use any name that follows the XML naming conventions discussed in Chapter 2, to identify this element uniquely. The XML identifying name must start with a character or an underscore and must not contain any spaces. The nature of the `ID` attribute type prohibits the use of the same name over multiple elements. This allows you to identify individual contacts uniquely within a project or an individual project within a database of projects. If you are used to working with databases, this attribute type closely mimics that record key that you would define for identifying the database record or linking one database record to another.

You can use `ID` attribute types to create a method by which a script or other program can access the information included within the identified element. This is the same manner by which JavaScript references HTML elements. The following XML statements provide you with a sample of a DTD and XML document using an `ID` type element:

```
<?xml version="1.0" ?>
<!DOCTYPE PROJECT [
```

```
    <!ELEMENT PROJECT (CONTACT+)>
    <!ELEMENT CONTACT (#PCDATA)>
        <!ATTLIST PROJECT pid ID #REQUIRED>
        <!ATTLIST CONTACT cid ID #REQUIRED>
]>
<PROJECT pid="0511-099">
    <CONTACT cid="tph001"> Tom Phannon </CONTACT>
</PROJECT>
```

Note *A variety of default attribute values can be used with your XML attribute declarations, discussed later in this chapter. You cannot use the `#FIXED` value or a default attribute type at all with the `ID` attribute type. `#FIXED` designates a single value for an attribute, therefore negating the use of a unique identifier.*

IDREF or IDREFS Attributes

The IDREF and IDREFS attribute types simply allow you to refer to a previously used ID attribute type value. Using the example shown in the "ID Attributes" section, you would use the IDREF type to add a second attribute to the CONTACT elements to reference the project or projects (if IDREFS is used) that they are a part of.

```
<?xml version="1.0" ?>
<!DOCTYPE PROJECT [
    <!ELEMENT PROJECT (CONTACT+)>
    <!ELEMENT CONTACT (#PCDATA)>
        <!ATTLIST PROJECT pid ID #REQUIRED>
        <!ATTLST CONTACT cid ID #REQUIRED>
        <!ATTLIST CONTACT proj_id IDREF "">
]>
<PROJECT pid="0511-099">
    <CONTACT cid="tph001"
            proj_id="0511-099"> Tom Phannon </CONTACT>
</PROJECT>
```

If you wanted to include all of the projects that an individual had worked on within a single contact record, you could use the IDREFS attribute type in place of IDREF in the proj_id <!ATTLIST> statement. This would allow you to have your contact XML entry read

```
<CONTACT cid="tph001" proj_id="0511-099 0410_588 0401_001">
    Tom Phannon
</CONTACT>
```

You can use the IDREF or IDREFS type to establish relationships between the various elements used within your document. In this example you could use a script or transformation language to link the Tom Phannon contact information with all of the projects listed in the proj_id field.

This entry would not necessarily be processed by your XML application in the fashion you want, unless you use XSLT or another transformation language to format and convert the information into something that the XML application could work with.

NMTOKEN or NMTOKENS Attributes

NMTOKEN attributes are used to restrict the values of the attribute to well-formed XML names. These are text strings that start with either a letter or the underscore (_) character; contain only letters, numbers or the underscore character; and do not have any white space within them. These types of attributes work quite well for restricting the structure of the information that can be used within your attribute values without restricting their actual statement. NMTOKENs are handy for referencing functions or classes found within associated scripted programs; anything that follows the standard programming naming conventions.

As an example, imagine that you need to specify that all network login names match a specific format of all characters and numbers. You could use the NMTOKEN attribute type to do so:

```
<!ATTLIST CONTACT network_id NMTOKEN "">
```

You could use the NMTOKENS attribute type to allow you to reference multiple IDs:

```
<!ATTLIST PROJECT network_id NMTOKENS "">
```

This won't restrict you to separate login IDs, but in the case of this example that wouldn't be necessary. It will force you to only use values for network logins that use only letters, numbers, and underscores without any spaces.

NOTATION Attributes

The NOTATION attribute type works similarly to the ENTITY attribute type. It allows your attribute to reference the name of a notation that has been declared or will be declared within your XML document. Notations, discussed in Chapter 11, are used to identify the format used with non-XML information such as video, audio, and image files. They can be used to specify the application to use for working with the unparsed entities, describing the video, audio, and image files that are often added to your XML documents.

Take the following code as an example. In this code, the VIDEO element is identified as an empty element with an attribute called software. This attribute creates a software attribute of the VIDEO element with a NOTATION type. The NOTATION references the RM notation specified in the <!NOTATION> declaration. The #REQUIRED default attribute value shows that this attribute must be applied to the element. You will read more about default attribute values in the next section of this chapter.

NOTATION examples can look like this:

```
<!ELEMENT VIDEO EMPTY>
<!ATTLIST VIDEO software NOTATION (RM) #REQUIRED>
<!NOTATION RM SYSTEM "realplayer.exe">
```

You can also provide the software multiple NOTATIONS to choose from as shown in the following example. A properly programmed XML browser could interpret these options as the different type software available to view the object.

```
<!ELEMENT VIDEO EMPTY>
<!ATTLIST VIDEO software NOTATION (RM | QT | MMP) #REQUIRED>
<!NOTATION RM SYSTEM "realplayer.exe">
<!NOTATION QT SYSTEM "quicktime.exe">
<!NOTATION MMP SYSTEM "mediaplayer.exe">
```

Setting Default Values

There are times when your attributes don't have any specific value such as "primary" that need to be applied to your attribute, yet you do need to have a value provided. You can use the three default values, #REQUIRED, #IMPLIED, and #FIXED "*value*" to force the value of your attribute to be set automatically for you or force the existence of the attribute within the XML document.

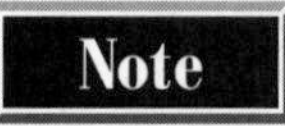

A fourth way to provide a default value for your attribute was discussed earlier in this chapter in "Defining Attributes." You can provide a default value for your attribute by adding the value, encased in quotes, after the designation of the attribute type.

#REQUIRED

I'm sure you can think of a hundred places where there is no default value for your attributes. For example, would you set the default identifier of a project to 1? How about 100? How would you make that decision?

Since in many situations you couldn't, you simply need to force the existence of the attribute within the document using the #REQUIRED value keyword. Keep in mind that this value will only be enforced if the document is read using a validating parser. In nonvalidating parsers, the attribute can be forgotten, and the document will still be considered well-formed. Take the following code into example. This code uses two required attributes for the PROJECT element. The first sets the project ID (pid), while the second provides a manner in which you can provide the name of the director of the project. The CONTACT element also has two attributes that are required. The first sets the contact ID (cid) of the individual, and the second sets the preferred method for contacting them (pref_contact).

```
<!ELEMENT PROJECT (CONTACT+)>
  <!ATTLIST PROJECT pid ID #REQUIRED>
```

```
  <!ATTLIST PROJECT director CDATA #REQUIRED>
<!ELEMENT CONTACT (EMAIL ADDRESS PHONE FAX)>
  <!ATTLST CONTACT cid ID #REQUIRED>
  <!ATTLIST CONTACT
            pref_contact (email | telephone | fax |
            in_person) #REQUIRED>
```

If you wish this document to be valid, the XML document based upon this DTD must have these attributes included within the PROJECT and CONTACT element statements.

```
<PROJECT pid="0511-099" director="Tom Phannon">
  <CONTACT cid="tph001"
          pref_contact="telephone"> Tom Phannon </CONTACT>
  <CONTACT cid="kat004"
          pref_contact="email"> Kell Attain </CONTACT>
</PROJECT>
```

#REQUIRED attributes are commonly used in the definition of images and video files that need to have a specific height and width specified. Without the height and width of a video or image file specified, the document must be reformatted as the video or image file loads. If the dimensions if the video has been specified within the element itself, the XML document browser can make adjustments for the exact dimensions of the image and format the remainder of the document text around the image insertion point.

```
<!ELEMENT VIDEO EMPTY>
  <!ATTLIST VIDEO width CDATA #REQUIRED>
  <!ATTLIST VIDEO height CDATA #REQUIRED>
```

#IMPLIED

#IMPLIED attributes are optional. They can be explicitly specified or completely ignored. The option is with the XML document author. You can use #IMPLIED attributes to allow, but not require, the existence of a particular piece of information. For example, in the case of some projects they may not currently have a specific project director assigned. If this is the case, you can't force the existence of the director's name, or else you can't enter the project in your data tracking system until after all of the project assignments have been completed.

```
<PROJECT pid="0511-099">
  <!-- Contact entries are here -->
</PROJECT>
```

The DTD that defines this document, either allowing the director attribute to exist or to be absent, is shown in the following sample of code:

```
<!ELEMENT PROJECT (CONTACT+)>
  <!ATTLIST PROJECT pid ID #REQUIRED>
  <!ATTLIST PROJECT director CDATA #IMPLIED>
```

When the validating XML parser encounters this attribute, it will process the information as normal. If it doesn't encounter the `director` attribute, it informs the processing software that an attribute value is not available nor required for that particular attribute. If the information is being written to a spreadsheet or a database, then the field that would normally contain the value of that attribute would be traditionally left blank or have a null value inserted into it. Of course, the actually ability of the software to process the information passed to it by the XML parser is completely dependent upon the instructions programmed into the processing software. There is nothing inherent in the XML DTD that provides processing instructions for the information the document contains.

#FIXED

The last of the default value keywords is `#FIXED`. When using this keyword you must set a default value for an attribute that is also the only value that is available for that attribute. This keyword literally fixes the value of the attribute so it can only be one value. In the following example, the XML document uses a value of "`WebRavin`" for the name of the consulting company working on the current project.

```
<PROJECT pid="0511-099" contractor="WebRavin">
  <!-- Contact entries are here -->
</PROJECT>
```

If this is the only contracting company that will be used for projects, it is safe to set up this attribute as a fixed value, as seen in the following DTD statements:

```
<!ELEMENT PROJECT (CONTACT+)>
  <!ATTLIST PROJECT pid ID #REQUIRED>
  <!ATTLIST PROJECT contractor CDATA #FIXED "WebRavin">
```

When a `#FIXED` attribute is used in a DTD, it forces the value of an attribute to match the specified value, or else a parser error is generated. If the attribute is not physically present within the XML document, then the value specified for that attribute in the DTD is assumed. Unlike the `#REQUIRED` attributes, `#FIXED` attributes do not have to be specified.

Defining Multiple Attributes

As you have seen from the previous sections of this chapter, elements can have multiple attributes. All of the attributes used with an element must be defined in order for the XML document to be both valid and well-formed.

If we were to expand our XML element to contain more attributes, it could appear as follows:

```
<CONTACT type="primary" pref_contact="phone" cid="tph001">
Tom Phannon
</CONTACT>
```

In this case the element `CONTACT` has three attributes: `type`, `pref_contact`, and `contact_id`. Each of these attributes will need declared within your DTD.

```
<!ELEMENT CONTACT (EMAIL ADDRESS PHONE FAX)>
  <!ATTLST CONTACT cid ID #REQUIRED>
  <!ATTLIST CONTACT
    pref_contact (email | telephone | fax | in_person) #REQUIRED>
  <!ATTLIST CONTACT
   type (primary | graphics | developer | marketing) #REQUIRED>
```

There is an alternative way of providing a list of attributes for each of your elements. This method simply saves you a bit of typing, and it may make the sorting and interpretation of your attributes easier for your human readers.

```
<!ELEMENT CONTACT (EMAIL ADDRESS PHONE FAX)>
  <!ATTLIST CONTACT cid ID #REQUIRED
    pref_contact (email | telephone | fax | in_person) #REQUIRED
    type (primary | graphics | developer | marketing) #REQUIRED>
```

This system uses a single `<!ATTLIST>` statement for each element, and it specifies multiple attributes within that statement. You can use this system of declaring attributes with any combination of attribute values, defaults, and types.

You can see both methods of applying attributes and their various values and default types in the full code of this sample project.

```
<?xml version="1.0"?>
<!DOCTYPE PROJECT_DB [
  <!ELEMENT PROJECT_DB (PROJECT+)>
  <!ELEMENT PROJECT (PROJ_NAME, CONTACT+, NOTES)>
    <!ATTLIST PROJECT pid ID #REQUIRED>
    <!ATTLIST PROJECT directory CDATA #REQUIRED>
    <!ATTLIST PROJECT type CDATA #IMPLIED>
    <!ATTLIST PROJECT start_date CDATA "getDate()" >
  <!ELEMENT PROJ_NAME (#PCDATA)>
  <!ELEMENT CONTACT (NAME, EMAIL, ADDRESS, PHONE, FAX)>
    <!ATTLIST CONTACT cid ID #REQUIRED
      pref_contact (email | telephone | fax | in_person) #REQUIRED
      type (primary | graphics | developer | marketing) #REQUIRED
      contractor CDATA #FIXED "WebRavin">
  <!ELEMENT NAME (#PCDATA)>
  <!ELEMENT EMAIL (#PCDATA)>
    <!ATTLIST EMAIL type (business | personal) "business">
  <!ELEMENT ADDRESS (#PCDATA)>
  <!ELEMENT PHONE (#PCDATA)>
    <!ATTLIST EMAIL type (business | personal) "business">
```

```
  <!ELEMENT FAX (#PCDATA)>
    <!ATTLIST EMAIL type (business | personal) "business">
  <!ELEMENT NOTES (ENTRY+)>
  <!ELEMENT ENTRY (#PCDATA)>
    <!ATTLIST ENTRY cid IDREF #REQUIRED
                    date CDATA "getDate()">
]>
<PROJECT_DB>
  <PROJECT pid="0511-001" director="Kell Attain"
           type="Web Development" start_date="11/1/05">
    <PROJ_NAME> Xray Mind Learners Web Site </PROJ_NAME>
    <CONTACT cid="kat001" contractor="WebRavin"
             pref_contact="email" type="primary">
     <NAME> Kell Attain </NAME>
      <ADDRESS>
        Web Ravin Consulting, 661 Oakey Rd, Antilles, OR 99999
      </ADDRESS>
      <PHONE type="business"> 111-555-1111 </PHONE>
      <FAX type="business"> 111-555-2222 </FAX>
      <EMAIL type="business"> kattain@webravin.com </EMAIL>
    </CONTACT>
    <CONTACT cid="fch001" contractor="WebRavin"
             pref_contact="phone" type="marketing">
     <NAME > Francis Chillington </NAME>
      <ADDRESS>
        Web Ravin Consulting, 661 Oakey Rd, Antilles, OR 99999
      </ADDRESS>
      <PHONE type="business"> 111-555-1112 </PHONE>
      <FAX type="business"> 111-555-2222 </FAX>
      <EMAIL type="business"> fchillington@webravin.com </EMAIL>
    </CONTACT>
    <CONTACT cid="lfi001" contractor="WebRavin"
             pref_contact="email" type="graphics">
     <NAME > Lara Firewalker </NAME>
      <ADDRESS>
        Web Ravin Consulting, 661 Oakey Rd, Antilles, OR 99999
      </ADDRESS>
      <PHONE type="business"> 111-555-1113 </PHONE>
      <FAX type="business"> 111-555-2222 </FAX>
      <EMAIL type="business"> lfirewalker@webravin.com </EMAIL>
    </CONTACT>
    <NOTES>
```

```
    <ENTRY date="11/03/05" contact="kta001">
    Development on the Web site has started. The primary
    graphics - logo | backgrounds | navigation system -
    should be done by 11/8/00.
    </ENTRY>
  </NOTES>
</PROJECT>
<PROJECT pid="0511-002" director="Tom Phannon"
       type="Database Development">
  <PROJ_NAME> XML Database for Site Visitors </PROJ_NAME>
  <CONTACT cid="tph001" contractor="WebRavin"
          pref_contact="telephone" type="primary">
   <NAME> Tom Phannon </NAME>
    <ADDRESS>
      Web Ravin Consulting, 661 Oakey Rd, Antilles, OR 99999
    </ADDRESS>
    <PHONE type="business"> 111-555-1122 </PHONE>
    <FAX type="business"> 111-555-2222 </FAX>
    <EMAIL type="business"> tphannon@webravin.com </EMAIL>
  </CONTACT>
  <NOTES>
    <ENTRY date="11/10/05" contact="tph001">
      Database structure is complete.
      Ready to start propagating the data.
    </ENTRY>
  </NOTES>
</PROJECT>
<PROJECT pid="0511-003" contractor="Lara Firewalker"
        type="Tech Support AI">
  <PROJ_NAME> House of Glass </PROJ_NAME>
  <CONTACT cid="swi001" contractor="WebRavin"
          pref_contact="email" type="primary">
   <NAME> Shamu Wagonride </NAME>
    <ADDRESS>
      Web Ravin Consulting, 661 Oakey Rd, Antilles, OR 99999
    </ADDRESS>
    <PHONE type="business"> 111-555-1133 </PHONE>
    <FAX type="business"> 111-555-2222 </FAX>
    <EMAIL type="personal"> shamu@wagonride.com </EMAIL>
  </CONTACT>
  <NOTES>
    <ENTRY date="11/01/05" contact="swa001">
```

```
        AI logic model software has been picked out and ordered,
        as well as the equipment required to run it. Networking
        (MIS) has been notified of the machine's arrival and
        networking needs.
        </ENTRY>
        <ENTRY date="11/11/05" contact="swa001">
        MIS has received equipment and software and is starting
        the installation. Expected date for network connection
        is 11/15/05.
        </ENTRY>
      </NOTES>
    </PROJECT>
  </PROJECT_DB>
```

Using Predefined Attributes

Within XML there are two predefined attributes. These attributes, like all others, must be declared within the DTD in order to have a valid document when the parser is processing the document. Although you do have to define the attributes, you should restrict yourself to using them in their intended fashion: `xml:space` as a descriptor for the treatment of white space in your element, and `xml:lang` as a descriptor for the language used to write the element.

xml:space

`xml:space` is used to control the white space usage within elements. If you are familiar with HTML, you may be asking yourself why white space within the XML document is so important, since white space in HTML documents is typically an insignificant concern. As you may know, the difference between a single space and two spaces in an HTML document is ignored. In XML that single additional space could be vitally important. If you think about the white space in much of the computer programming code (COBOL is one that comes to mind), the use of the white space controls the interpretation of the commands and values that are given. Even if you are displaying something as simple as haiku, the spacing within the display of the text is important to the legibility of the piece.

Unlike HTML, XML parsers preserve white space within the contents of elements. Of course, since the majority of our XML document browsers are also HTML browsers, the white space they are so nicely handed is at that point ignored. This is where the `xml:space` attribute comes in. When the `xml:space` attribute is used within an element, the XML processor can be told to keep the white space intact.

Since `xml:space` is the only way to force the retention of significant white space within an element, you must define the `xml:space` attribute for those elements. If you were defining the use of `xml:space` for a Haiku then the following `<!ATTLIST>` declaration will be used to force the preservation of the spacing in the element's content.

```
<!ATTLIST HAIKU xml:space (default | preserve) "preserve">
```

Some parsers, including MSXML, will still ignore white space in your elements, even with the `xml:space` attribute applied. Some of these parsers will have a setting that can be adjusted to force it to respect your document's white space. You will need to read the documentation on your XML parser for information on these settings.

xml:lang

The second predefined XML attribute is `xml:lang`. This attribute is used to identify the language that is being used to display the contents of the specified element. If you are familiar with HTML, this attribute performs the same function as the `lang` attribute. It uses a set of predefined codes to identify the language being used to create the content of the element the attribute is applied to. This attribute is especially useful when you are attempting to display multiple copies of text in a variety of languages. For example, both of the following statements say the same thing. The first is designated as English (`en`) by the `xml:lang` attribute; the second is designated as Spanish (`sp`).

```
<POEM xml:lang="en">
Roses are red.
Violets are blue.
I work late nights.
How about you?
</POEM>
<POEM xml:lang="sp">
Las rosas son rojas,
Las violetas, azules.
Trabajo tarde de noche,
¿Y tú?
</POEM>
```

You can program your XML processor to only display the document elements that correspond to that user's personal language setup. That means that my computer would display the English version of the poem, but my friend's computer would only show the Spanish version. This allows your software to conform a document to your requested specifications automatically. You could potentially use external entities to hold separate copies of the same document, each of which would display the information in a separate language. This would then allow you to show only that one language that is appropriate when the document is needed.

Summary

As you can see, there is a lot to think about when adding attributes to your documents, especially if you want to have the XML document validated. Just remember that all attributes must be defined using the `<!ATTLIST>` declaration. They must all be associated with an element and have their own individual name. You can't use an attribute multiple times with the same name within a single element statement.

Attributes can contain a wide variety of data that is controlled by the attribute type designator within the attribute's declaration statement in the DTD. The available attribute types are: `CDATA`, `ENTITY`, `ENTITIES`, enumerated list, `ID`, `IDREF`, `IDREFS`, `NMTOKEN`, `NMTOKENS`, and `NOTATION`. Each of these types is used to control the type of content that the attribute can have. You can also use one of three default value keywords to enforce the existence of an attribute in the element statement in the XML document or their contents. These keywords are `#REQUIRED`, `#IMPLIED`, and `#FIXED`.

In the next chapter a discussion of notations, unparsed entities, and other non-XML data will show you how to incorporate various types of information into your XML document.

Chapter 11

Adding Other Data

In addition to elements, entities, and attributes, there are other types of non-XML data that can be added to your XML document and validated through your DTD. In all actuality, most of the information in the world is probably not available in an XML-ready format. The widespread source of information formats, ranging from Microsoft Word files to Real Player video and audio formatted files, makes it imperative that XML be able to work with and incorporate information in the form that it currently exists. To incorporate these varied formats of data into your XML document, you will need to express some of these types of files as notations. In addition to notations, you also have unparsed entities and conditional statements or processing instructions that can become a part of the non-XML data found within your XML application.

Note *You can create complete XML documents without using notations, external unparsed entities, conditional statements, or even very many processing instructions. There are some individuals and organizations that do not believe that these constructs should be a part of the XML specification, although it is. It is up to you to decide whether you wish to use these constructs within your document or application. If you do decide to use them, you should also be aware that few of the XML applications will support them.*

Exploring Notations

Notations are the solution you have been looking for when attempting to identify the type of file that you are adding to your document. There is no way to identify a JPEG image separate from a GIF image by using entities, elements, or attributes. This often creates a huge mess, especially when taking into consideration the hundreds of different image formats and the thousands of different general file formats available on all the computer operating systems used every day. Without a means of telling your software what type of file it is reading, it won't be able to interpret the data included in the file correctly.

Not only do notations serve the purpose of identifying the format of your information, they also let the XML application know how to read and display the information within the file. Notations can help prevent your XML browser from attempting to display a ZIP file on your screen while the information is still in a compressed state. Notations allow you to separate the type of information contained within a file, from the file itself, allowing the XML software to properly work with the files contents.

The declaration statement used to identify a notation is similar to that used to express an external entity. You provide a name for the file type, rather than the entity, use either the `SYSTEM` or `PUBLIC` identifier, and then provide an external identifier for the file type, as seen in the sample syntax statement shown below.

```
<!NOTATION file_type (SYSTEM|PUBLIC "public id")
           "external_identifier">
```

This basic notation can be used as shown in the following example to identify a series of image types including the most basic BMP, GIF, and JPEG.

```
<!NOTATION BMP SYSTEM "image/bitmap">
<!NOTATION GIF SYSTEM "image/gif">
<!NOTATION JPEG SYSTEM "image/jpg">
```

In these statements, the MIME type of the image is used as the external identifier of the element. There are many other possibilities, including a standard URL or the use of a `PUBLIC` identifier and an URI. This type of statement requires that you be familiar with the public identifier system made available through the Internet Engineering Task Force (IETF) (www.ietf.org) and other standards organizations. The following notation identifies a JPEG image using the `PUBLIC` identifier for the JPEG standard as created by the IETF.

```
<!NOTATION JPEG PUBLIC "-//IETF//NONSGML Media Type image/
jpeg//EN" "http://www.isi.edu/in-notes/iana/assignments/
media-types/images/jpeg">
```

There has been, and probably will continue to be, a lot of debate on what makes a good identifier for a notation type. So far everything from MIME types to URLs and ISBN numbers have been used to describe a notation. Other sources have used Library of Congress catalog numbers, as well as International Standards Organization (ISO) standard identifiers. Currently there are no restrictions on the use of identifiers, but you should choose your identifier wisely. Take into account that URLs change often, so if you expect your document to last a decade, you might wish to identify it based upon a resource other than a Web URL.

In addition to identifying information that is not XML information, you can identify XML-formatable information. One good example of this is dates. How can you tell the meaning of one date from another? Take for example 05-12-01. Is this date May 12, 2001? Is it meant to represent December 1, 2005? Or maybe it is meant to be December 5, 2001? If the document doesn't have some way of specifying the format of the date, the computer and person reading the document will not be able to properly interpret the dates. Using notations you can specify any format for the dates you use, either as a standard date format such as MM-DD-YY or simply as a type of date such as Gregorian based upon ISO standard 8601. The following example uses three formats of dates that allow you to interpret the formatting of the dates found within the document properly.

Note *For more information on using Data Types in DTDs, check out the World Wide Web Consortium Site at http://www.w3.org/TR/dt4dtd.*

```
<?xml version="1.0">
<!DOCTYPE PROJECT [
  <!ELEMENT PROJECT (START_DATE, END_DATE)
  <!ELEMENT START_DATE (#PCDATA)>
    <!ATTLIST START_DATE
      system NOTATION (MM_DD_YY | DD_MM_YY | YY_MM_DD) #IMPLIED>
```

```
  <!ELEMENT END_DATE (#PCDATA)>
    <!ATTLIST END_DATE
      system NOTATION (MM_DD_YYYY | DD_MM_YY | YY_MM_DD) #IMPLIED>
  <!NOTATION MMM_DD_YYYY
            SYSTEM "http://catsback.com/dateformat/mixed.html">
  <!NOTATION SHORT
            SYSTEM "http://catsback.com/dateformat/short.html">
  <!NOTATION LONG
            SYSTEM "http://catsback.com/dateformat/long.html">
]>
<PROJECT>
   <START_DATE system="MM_DD_YYY"> 01 01 01 </START_DATE>
   <END_DATE system="YY_MM_DD"> 05 05 05 </END_DATE>
</PROJECT>
```

Note *Notations can't force document authors to display their information in the correct format, they can only remind the author of the format that they should use. You can use XML schemas, discussed in Part IV, to restrict the contents of your elements.*

Unparsed External Entities

In addition to your standard general external entities, you may also need to be able to work with unparsed external entities. By being able to declare unparsed external entities, you can work with binary information that can't be expressed in terms of XML data. Actually, XML is not prepared to deal with any information that is nontextual in nature. Images and audio files, for instance, would be very difficult to express in text. An image you might be able to draw out pixel by pixel or line by line, as is done using the Scalable Vector Graphics (SVG), but how would you explain an audio file? You can create audio effects using a voice by using syntax that would work with a speech synthesizer as shown in the following example.

```
<VOICE  volume="loud" speech-rate="slow"
        voice-family="male" pitch="x-low"
        richness="70">
   All good men must come to the aid of their country!
</VOICE>
```

Now, this works fine for speech, but how do you define a complete orchestra? Could you potentially write out the sheet music for each instrument and use timing modules or scripts to control the order in which they are played? Think about the Beethoven symphonies. Altogether those nine symphonies last over six hours when played. How many individual notes can be played in a six-hour period? By how many different instruments? If you were to write each note in XML for each instrument, you would more than likely spend more than the next three years just writing the instructions for the strings and woodwinds to play their parts.

```
<VIOLIN1 note="A" duration="1" chord="base" />
<VIOLIN2 note="C" duration="1" chord="base" />
<VIOLIN3 note="E" duration="1" chord="base" />
<VIOLA note="A#" duration="1" chord="base"  />
<CELLO note="C" duration="1" chord="base"  />
<ALTO_SAX note="A" duration="1" chord="base" />
<CLARINET note="A" duration="1" chord="base"/>
<BASSOON note="A" duration="1" chord="base" />
```

Now at first glance this seems like it could be a workable solution, if you had the time and a short enough piece of music, but it would blow the size of the music file dramatically out of proportion with the existing compressed formats for audio files. Not to mention the fact that it would be much more difficult to create the timing of the music so that it would play with the depth of feeling expressed by the heartfelt rendering of a classical orchestra. A computer may be able to play the symphony with more technical accuracy than an orchestra, but it is definitely missing the heart it takes to put real feeling into music.

Because of the difficulty in describing nontextual data with XML, it has to be able to refer to information that is already available in a binary format. Web documents are constantly playing sounds for you and are able to do so by linking to the contents of another file, not the HTML document, that contains the actual audio content. The Web browsers then know how to use the content that was provided within the HTML element and use it accordingly. These types of binary files, in XML terms, are considered external entities. They are further considered external unparsed entities because the XML parser makes no attempt whatsoever to comprehend the information they contain. Parsers will often let the XML document browser know that an external file is being referenced and what the name of the file is, but it will rarely if ever provide the XML browser with the actual content of that binary file. HTML elements use a variety of attributes to assist the Web browser in processing the information. XML browsers don't have to provide this type of processing assistance and most don't unless they are actually trying to provide compatibility within XML for the existing HTML language constructs.

XML documents work a little bit differently. XML places `ENTITY` references in the DTD to provide a link to a specific resource to be used in your XML document. The DTD then uses attributes referencing those entities to load the information, content that is intended to be a part of the XML document. As you saw in Chapter 9, a standard `ENTITY` declaration statements look like the following examples:

```
<!ENTITY entity-name SYSTEM "entity-URI">
<!ENTITY COMPANY
         SYSTEM "http://catsback.com/xmlfiles/company.xml">
<!ENTITY COMPANY SYSTEM "/xmlfiles/company.xml">
<!ENTITY COMPANY SYSTEM "company.xml">
```

WORKING WITH DTD

This system works well if you are specifying information that is, or can be, a well-formed XML document. If you are attempting to describe binary information such as images or audio files, then you need to use the NDATA keyword to specify the type of file the entity is referencing. For example, to associate a Real Audio file with the entity name SPEECH, you would need to create an ENTITY and a NOTATION declaration in your DTD similar to the following:

```
<!ENTITY SPEECH  SYSTEM "speech.ra" NDATA RA>
<!NOTATION RA SYSTEM "audio/ra">
```

As you can see the RA identifier in the ENTITY declaration refers to the RA NOTATION declaration. This combination of statements allows your browser to be able to refer to any number of files using a single RA notation and multiple ENTITY statements.

```
<!ENTITY SPEECH  SYSTEM "speech.ra" NDATA RA>
<!ENTITY BACKGROUND SYSTEM "bkgrnd.ra" NDATA RA>
<!ENTITY TRUMPETS SYSTEM "trumpet.ra" NDATA RA>
<!NOTATION RA SYSTEM "audio/ra">
```

In addition to using entity and notation declarations to incorporate your unparsed entities within your document, you need to use the entity reference as part of an attribute declaration. In Chapter 9 you saw how to embed a standard general entity within your XML document using an example similar to the following:

```
<?xml version="1.0"?>
<!DOCTYPE  ANNOUNCEMENT [
   <!ELEMENT ANNOUNCEMENT ANY>
   <!NOTATION RA SYSTEM "audio/ra">
   <!ENTITY SPEECH  SYSTEM "speech.ra" NDATA RA>
]>
<ANNOUNCEMENT>
&SPEECH;
</ANNOUNCEMENT>
```

This is an invalid way of incorporating unparsed entities within your XML. With the standard use of the &SPEECH; placeholder, you have to create an element, containing an attribute, that can serve as the container for the entity. For example, the following code incorporates an unparsed entity correctly within the XML document. It uses an AUDIO element with a source attribute, declared as an ENTITY type, to provide the name of the unparsed entity:

Note *You can include unparsed entities within either empty elements or elements with elaborate content. There are no restrictions on the type of element that can be used to display the content of unparsed external entities.*

```
<?xml version="1.0"?>
<!DOCTYPE  ANNOUNCEMENT [
```

```
    <!ELEMENT ANNOUNCEMENT ANY>
       <!ATTLIST ANNOUNCEMENT background ENTITIES #REQUIRED>
    <!ELEMENT SPEAKER (NAME, AUDIO)>
       <!ATTLIST SPEAKER image ENTITY #REQUIRED>
    <!ELMENT NAME (#PCDATA)>
    <!ELEMENT AUDIO EMPTY>
       <!ATTLIST AUDIO source ENTITY #REQUIRED>
    <!NOTATION JPG SYSTEM "image/jpg">
    <!NOTATION RA SYSTEM "audio/ra">
    <!ENTITY PHOTO SYSTEM "speaker_photo.jpg" NDATA JPG>
    <!ENTITY SPEECH  SYSTEM "speech.ra" NDATA RA>
    <!ENTITY FLAGS  SYSTEM "flag.jpg" NDATA JPG >
    <!ENTITY MOUNTAINS  SYSTEM "mtn.jpg" NDATA JPG >
    <!ENTITY BUBBLES  SYSTEM "bubble.jpg" NDATA JPG >
]>
<ANNOUNCEMENT background="BUBBLES MOUNTAINS FLAGS">
    <SPEAKER image="PHOTO">
       <NAME>Albert Einstein </NAME>
       <AUDIO source="SPEECH" />
    </SPEAKER>
</ANNOUNCEMENT>
```

With the unparsed entity included in the document this way, you have to depend upon the XML document browser to play the contents of your audio file correctly. This is not a function of the XML document itself, but lies strictly in the purview of the document browser.

Note *You can place external entities in your XML document structure by using a series of external DTD subsets and parameter entity statements. It may help you to embed a series of notations as an external DTD subset using an external parameter entity. By breaking down your DTD in this fashion, you can more easily use the same types of notations in multiple documents, without re-creating the proverbial wheel.*

Conditional Statements

There are times when you need to specify how to treat specific portions of your DTD. You may need to have specific sections be ignored while you are working on them, or maybe you need to have a section specifically included within the DTD. Conditional statements provide you with a way to ignore or include information within your DTD specifically. You can ignore some of the content of your DTD by using comments to comment out the information that is not ready to be read or that is not valid to be used in this document, but by using the IGNORE conditional statement, you can do the same thing, without risking any potential loss of information should a document processor completely ignore the commented code. The structure of the IGNORE statement is shown in the following code:

```
<![ IGNORE
   Declaration statements to be ignored
]]>
```

You can wrap as many elements, entities, notations, and attributes within the IGNORE statement as you wish. You can imbed IGNORE statements within other IGNORE statements. There is only one restriction on the use of IGNORE statements: they must include an entire declaration. They cannot be used to ignore half of a declaration statement. For example, the following use of the IGNORE statement would be invalid:

```
<![ IGNORE
   <!ELEMENT NAME
]]>
ANY >
```

You must include the complete declaration in your IGNORE statement:

```
<![ IGNORE
   <!ELEMENT NAME ANY>
]]>
```

When using IGNORE statements in your documents, you need to be conscientious about ignoring sections of your document that may be needed by other portions of the DTD. In the following example, the code is told to ignore the NOTATION declarations that are used by the declared entities:

```
<![ IGNORE
   <!NOTATION JPG SYSTEM "image/jpg">
   <!NOTATION RA SYSTEM "audio/ra">
]]>
   <!ENTITY PHOTO SYSTEM "speaker_photo.jpg" NDATA JPG>
   <!ENTITY SPEECH  SYSTEM "speech.ra" NDATA RA>
```

Note *You also need to be aware of ignoring entity declarations that are called by values of attributes within your XML document.*

In addition to the IGNORE statement you can also use the INCLUDE statement to ensure that the declarations in the DTD are read. The syntax of the INCLUDE statement is exactly like the IGNORE statement.

```
<![ INCLUDE
   Declarations to be included
]]>
```

When you are nesting INCLUDE and IGNORE statements, there are a few restrictions on action that you need to be aware of:

- An IGNORE statement within an INCLUDE statement will be ignored.
- An INCLUDE statement within an IGNORE statement will be ignored.

This may prompt you to question where an INCLUDE statement would ever be used. Basically, the INCLUDE statement allows you to use external parameter entities to create a toggle switch between ignoring blocks of declarations or including blocks of declarations within your DTD.

Define an external parameter entity using the following syntax:

```
<!ENTITY % block1 "IGNORE">
```

Include this entity within your XML document's DTD with the following statement:

```
<![ block1
   Declarations in block1
]]>
```

With the current setting for the external parameter entity, all of the declarations in block1 are ignored. By simply changing the IGNORE statement to INCLUDE in the original ENTITY declaration you can, in one step, open up an entire block of declaration statements to parsing. This is a great step to use when debugging errors within your DTD.

Adding Processing Instructions

Processing instructions provide a manner in which you can incorporate information into your document that is meant for a specific proprietary application. This is an improvement over HTML, in which it was a common practice to embed application-specific information within comment blocks. This worked great until the proprietary application either started processing information contained in actual comments of the HTML document or when some programs removed all of the comments blocks within the HTML code.

Processing instructions can provide a lot of information to the XML processor, if the processor has been programmed to understand and work with the information being displayed. Processing instructions can provide additional information about the programs required to view the contents of unparsed external entities, run external programs, and set up style sheets and other accessory documents to your XML code.

All processing instructions are found between <? and ?> brackets. The instruction itself, occurring between these brackets, must contain a valid XML formatted name, followed by the data providing the "meat" of the processing instruction. The name of the instruction can be just about anything that you wish. Many developers use the name of the application that they wish to use to view the file type they are working with, for example:

```
<?realplayer presentation="mymovie.rm"?>
<?acrobat document="xml_spec.pdf"?>
```

As you can see, these processing instructions follow the same formatting as the `<?xml ?>` declaration and the `xml-stylesheet` processing instruction. There are two restrictions on naming your processing instructions. First, your name cannot start with `xml`. This string is reserved for uses that are either currently or may be specified within the XML standard itself. Second, your name cannot start with or contain the `?>` closing delimiter. This would close your processing instruction without giving the intended application a chance to work with the instructions. The name of your processing instruction must follow the same set of rules that govern elements and attribute naming.

```
<?xml version="1.0" standalone="yes" encoding="Latin-1"?>
<?xml-stylesheet type="text/css" href="xml_spec.css"?>
```

Processing instructions formats are going to be specific to the application that they are intended for. For instance, if you were writing a processing instruction that would open a file in the old DOS Edit program, it could be formatted in the following fashion:

```
<?edit autoexec.bat?>
```

You may even want to use processing instructions to include more complex instructions for interacting with database applications when retrieving, saving, or editing information found within the document. Processing instructions are very specific to the application that they are intended to work with and, therefore, have no formatting requirements other than that required for use with the intended application. They can occur anywhere within your XML document, except for inside a tag or within a CDATA section of an attribute. They can be placed within your document prolog or within the DTD. They can even exist within the content of an element or past the closing element of your XML document.

Note *You do not need to declare processing instructions within your DTD, as they are not elements, entities, attributes, or notations, and are not used as part of the structure of the XML document itself. They are strictly provided for use by another application.*

One of the reasons that you can place your processing instructions anywhere within your XML document is that the XML parser, or processing engine, does not process them. They are simply passed on to other applications working with the XML document. This application will determine how the processing instruction should be used. If it doesn't understand the processing instruction then applications will typically ignore the instruction.

In this example, the processing instruction `<?RA realplayer.exe?>` is used to inform an application what type of program should be used to read all unparsed external entities using the `RA` designation:

```
<?xml version="1.0"?>
<!DOCTYPE  ANNOUNCEMENT [
   <!ELEMENT ANNOUNCEMENT ANY>
```

```
      <!ATTLIST ANNOUNCEMENT background ENTITIES #REQUIRED>
   <!ELEMENT SPEAKER (NAME, AUDIO)>
      <!ATTLIST SPEAKER image ENTITY #REQUIRED>
   <!ELMENT NAME (#PCDATA)>
   <!ELEMENT AUDIO EMPTY>
      <!ATTLIST AUDIO source ENTITY #REQUIRED>
   <!NOTATION JPG SYSTEM "image/jpg">
   <!NOTATION RA SYSTEM "audio/ra">
   <!ENTITY PHOTO SYSTEM "speaker_photo.jpg" NDATA JPG>
   <!ENTITY SPEECH  SYSTEM "speech.ra" NDATA RA>
   <!ENTITY FLAGS  SYSTEM "flag.jpg" NDATA JPG >
   <!ENTITY MOUNTAINS  SYSTEM "mtn.jpg" NDATA JPG >
   <!ENTITY BUBBLES  SYSTEM "bubble.jpg" NDATA JPG >
]>
<?RA realplayer.exe?>
<ANNOUNCEMENT background="BUBBLES MOUNTAINS FLAGS">
   <SPEAKER image="PHOTO">
      <NAME>Albert Einstein </NAME>
      <AUDIO source="SPEECH" />
   </SPEAKER>
</ANNOUNCEMENT>
```


Summary

In this chapter you have read about how to create notation declarations, unparsed external entities, conditional statements, and processing instructions. Notations are used to identify the format of your external binary information that you wish to include as part of your XML document. Notations also help the XML processing application know how to read and display the information within the file. Notations use identifiers to link a specific notation declaration to a specific file. So far everything from MIME types to Library of Congress catalog numbers have been used as identifiers. There are no restrictions on the use of identifiers.

Unparsed external entities allow you to work with binary information that can't be expressed in terms of XML data. They provide you a means of incorporating non-XML information into your XML document. You can include unparsed entities within either empty elements or elements with elaborate content. There are no restrictions on the type of element that can be used to display the content of unparsed external entities.

Conditional statements provide you with a way to ignore or include information within your DTD specifically. You can use conditional statements to create a toggling system between ignoring and including segments of your DTD during testing or for use with specific instances of documents. You can wrap as many elements, entities, notations, and attributes within the IGNORE statement as you wish. You can imbed IGNORE statements within other IGNORE statements, but you must include the entire declaration.

Processing instructions provide a manner in which you can incorporate information into your document that is meant for a specific proprietary application. Processing instructions are very specific to the application that they are intended to work with and, therefore, have no formatting requirements other than those required for use with the intended application. They can occur anywhere within your XML document, except for inside a tag or within a CDATA section of an attribute. They can be placed within your document prolog or within the DTD. They can even exist within the content of an element or past the closing element of your XML document.

In the next part of this book you will discover more information about incorporating CSS and XSL style sheets and transformations within your XML documents. Style sheets are the only way to control the appearance of your XML documents. Using some type of transformation language, such as XSLT, allows you to convert your XML data into a format that can be easily interpreted and manipulated by HTML and other types of document browsers.

Part III

Adding Style

Chapter 12

When to Use Style Sheets

Do you want to be able to control the appearance of your XML document when people look at it? If you do, then you want to invest the time in creating a style sheet. There are two different types of style sheets that are commonly used with XML: Cascading Style Sheets (CSS) and the Extensible Stylesheet Language (XSL). A quick introduction to both of these types of style sheets, as well as a listing of their pros and cons, is provided in this chapter.

What Are Style Sheets?

A *style sheet* is a document that allows you to alter the appearance of each item found within your XML document or series of XML documents globally. Using style sheets, you can control the size of fonts, font color, document or object backgrounds, box borders, and speech synthesizer controls, as well as many other different visual and audio effects for your XML information.

CSS allows you to format the appearance of your information using a variety of properties that can be interpreted by Web browsers and other applications. CSS works by setting property values for object appearance and also by using a set of cascading rules to decide which property values are applied and which are superseded by the Web browser and other style sheet. All of the major Web browsers, in some form or another, support CSS, including Netscape Navigator 4.5– 6, Opera 4, and Microsoft's Internet Explorer 4–5.

Note *Support for CSS in Netscape Navigator 4 is quite limited and should therefore not be considered a viable testing platform for CSS.*

XSL provides a lot more flexibility and function than CSS, although not near the amount of support. XSL is currently only supported by the Mozilla development organization (http://www.mozilla.org) and Internet Explorer 5.5 with the upgrade of Internet Explorer's MSXML parser (http://msdn.microsoft.com/xml), and neither of these supports XSL fully. XSL is broken down into two parts, the Extensible Stylesheet Language Transformations (XSLT) and the XSL Formatting Objects. XSLT convert XML document information into HTML format so that it can be easily read by Web browsers, as well as other HTML-ready applications. The XSL Formatting Objects can be used in a fashion similar to CSS by formatting the information contained within your XML document

In either CSS or XSL you can find a style sheet rule that will allow you to control the rendering of practically any stylized effect within your XML document. The key is to figure out when to use which style sheet language and then how to use it.

Where Does CSS Shine?

CSS is a style-sheet language designed to enable document authors and users to control the presentation of documents, both XML and HTML. CSS separates the presentation elements of a document from the content of that document so that document authoring and maintenance are made easier, and the jobs of XML developers are made more efficient. As a document or application developer, you can tailor the design of your document for visual display applications, aural devices, printed pages, Braille devices, TTY machines, or the television, to name a few. You can control the position of your content and the layout of tables, and you have more control over the fonts used when displaying your documents. Cascading Style Sheets 2 (CSS2), the current version of CSS that is available, has built on the previous version so that compatibility between previously conforming applications and documents designed for them still work in today's software.

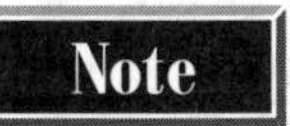

The Cascading Style Sheets 3 (CSS3) specification is currently being developed. It may not be completed until mid-2001.

The CSS1 and CSS2 specifications are based on a set of design principles that have come from both the software development world and the world of graphic design and layout. This set of principles includes the following features.

Forward and Backward Compatibility

All applications, not just CSS2-compatible ones, are able to display the content of these enhanced documents. All CSS2 compatible applications are able to display CSS1-enhanced documents.

Complementary Structure

Style sheets are designed to complement the structure of documents so that an author can change a style sheet with little to no change in the markup file. This makes the author's job more efficient and enables the XML author to update an entire suite of documents quickly in a single pass.

Independence from All Companies

Style sheets are not specific to a single vendor, platform, or device. This enables CSS formatted documents to work in all venues, although you can specify a specific style sheet to use with specific devices.

Easy Maintenance

External style sheets, linked to a document, enable XML developers to update an entire site's presentation with little or no markup changes in the XML code itself.

Simplicity

All style sheets are easily read and written by humans. CSS files are simple text files that can be read in any text editor and are identified as style sheets by their `.css` extension. Generally, there is only one way to achieve a specific effect, and most CSS properties function independently of each other. Because `.css` files affect the presentation of the information, you can often use a style sheet declaration, rather than an image or audio file, to add color or provide sound and save space on your network when downloading the information.

Rich Variety of Scripts

Along with providing document authors a way to render information on the Web in a more dynamic fashion, CSS2 provides a means for scripting languages such as JavaScript to interface with the style specifications by either retrieving or setting their values.

Accessibility

Document authors using CSS are able to delve into a variety of features that make XML documents more accessible for individuals with disabilities. You can eliminate the need to make text images to force a font to appear in the color and style of your choosing. Your readers can create their own style sheet to override the author's style sheets, giving them the power to ensure that the documents they read are legible for them. With the enhanced list of media groups, users of Braille, embossed, and TTY media devices can have information tailored specifically to the equipment they use. Individuals using speech synthesizers or other aural devices can control the voice and audio output used when reading a document.

CSS used in XML documents can come from one of three sources: the document author, the user, or the application.

- **The document author** When the author writes the XML document, he or she can specify a particular style sheet to use when displaying the document. XML requires that all style sheets be linked externally using the `<? xml-stylesheet ?>` processing instruction.
- **User style sheets** Some user agents enable the user to specify a style sheet to use when displaying documents.
- **The application** For an application to conform to the CSS specifications, it must apply a default style sheet to a document before any other style sheets. In the case of XML documents, this style sheet presents information as an extendable list of the elements and their properties. Some of the settings used in the applications style sheet might be configurable by the user. Most of the time, the user-configurable options are limited to font color, font face, background color, link colors, and default language such as English, French, German, or Spanish, for example.

As style sheets from these three sources are implemented, areas of the style sheets may overlap. The CSS cascade determines how they interact with each other by assigning a weight to each style rule. When several rules apply to a single element, the rule with the greatest weight is implemented, taking precedence over all other rules.

The cascade generally gives rules in an author's style sheet greater weight than rules in a document viewer's style sheet, although this precedence is reversed when rules marked with the `!Important` designator are used in the document viewer's style sheet. However, all document viewer and author rules have more weight than an application's style sheet rules.

You can also link CSS through other CSS. Style sheets linked in this method are also worked into the cascade and weighted according to their loading order. Each successive style sheet to be imported receives a lighter weight, so it is less likely to be implemented than the preceding style sheets.

Applications employ a specified sorting order when identifying the specific value for an element and its properties. This order has specific rules, which have been identified by the CSS2 specification and are listed here:

1. Find all the style sheet rules that are to be applied to the specific element and property for the identified media type.
2. Sort the declarations by weight and origin. For a normal declaration, the author style sheet overrides a document viewer's style sheet, which in turn overrides the application's default style sheet. For elements using the `!Important` declaration, a document viewer's style sheet overrides an author style sheet, which in turn overrides the default application style sheet. Any element in any style sheet with an `!Important` declaration overrides any normal declaration on a higher-ranking style sheet. Imported style sheets are deemed to have the same origin as the style sheet that imported them; if the application's default style sheet imports an additional style sheet, the imported style sheet is treated as coming from the application.
3. Sort the items by the level of specificity associated with a selector. This means that the more specific a style sheet is in its specifications, the more weight is applied to that particular element on the style sheet. For example, in the `font-family` CSS property, specifying a generic name is less specific than specifying a `font-family` name and would therefore have a lighter weight. Pseudo-elements and pseudo-classes are sorted in the same manner as normal elements and classes, and they are treated with no more weight than a normal element or class.
4. The final sort includes sorting by order. If two rules have the same origin, weight, and specificity, the rule that was specified last is used. In this case, rules in imported style sheets, which are read after the style sheet that imported them, are considered to occur before any rules in the style sheet itself.

This strategy of weighing elements and their properties enables authors to have greater control over the display of their information than the user does, unless, of course, the `!Important` declaration is used.

In addition to this set of principles, CSS has broken its individual style sheet rules into two main parts: a *selector* and a *declaration* (see Chapter 13 for more information on these statements). The selector identifies the XML element, such as <BOOK> or <DOCUMENT>, to which the rule is being applied. The declaration has two parts, the *property name* and the *value.* The property name identifies the aspect of the selector that you wish to change (for example, the color or width of a <TITLE> element). The value of the property identifies the specific instructions for the display of the element (for example, if the property is color, a possible value would be red, forcing the <TITLE> element to be displayed in red).

Within an XML document, you can specify a style sheet in only one way:

```
<?xml-stylesheet type="text/css" href="stylesheet.css" ?>
```

This statement uses the xml-stylesheet processing instruction to link to a style sheet that has been specified as a CSS using the type="text/css" statement, and then has the address specified through the href="" statement, which in this example is pointing to the file stylesheet.css. Take a look at the following CSS document. It uses commands, all discussed in detail in Chapter 13, to control the font appearance and font color of the text found in the head, foot, and par elements.

```
head {  font-family: "Comic Sans MS";
        font-style: italic;
        font-variant: small-caps;
        color: #3300FF}
foot {  font-family: Georgia, "Times New Roman", Times, serif;
        font-style: oblique;
        font-weight: 700;
        font-variant: normal;
        text-transform: uppercase;
        color: #FF0000;
        letter-spacing: 2em}
par {   background-color: #FFFFCC;
        border-style: inset;
        border-top-width: medium;
        border-right-width: medium;
        border-bottom-width: medium;
        border-left-width: medium}
```

If a document author is working on multiple pages of a similar design, this format of linking to style sheets in external files works best. External style sheets give developers more flexibility over their work, enabling them to alter the presentation of a series of documents without modifying the source document.

Where Does XSL Shine?

Where CSS works with the objects and elements already defined in your XML document, XSL can add content; convert your content to HTML, which is more widely supported than XML; and even sort through your information so that only the information you wish to be visible to a document viewer is visible. Unlike CSS, XSL is not a fully accepted standard. It is still considered a Working Draft from the standpoint of the World Wide Web Consortium (W3C). The full working draft of the XSL recommendation can be found at http://www.w3.org/TR/XSL/. This document is constantly being changed and updated, so you will need to refer to it repeatedly as it develops to check on continuing support for your XSL development projects.

XSL has quite a few additional features or improved features when compared to CSS2. The primary improvements follow.

Paging and Scrolling

XSL incorporates an advanced paging and scrolling system that allows you to create both scrollable documents, as well as page-based documents (such as this book), with the same type of control over formatting and alignment. Although the formatting control available in XSL does not approach the finite control over placement that most desktop publishers are used to with products such as PageMaker, there are definite improvements over those few page formatting controls that are available with CSS.

Selectors and Tree Construction

There are improved formatting commands for supporting specific patterns of selectors for identifying XML elements and applying formatting options to those selectors.

Extended Page Layout Model

XSL supports controls for identifying the exact dimensions of a page or frame and for controlling how each individual segment of XML data will be placed within those pages.

An Area Model

XSL supports an extension to the properties and values that allow you to format objects, but allows developers to control the spacing of blocks, lines, objects, and specific areas of their pages. Unlike CSS, which is actually a subset of the commands provided with XSL, the XSL area model allows you to describe the relationship and adjust the spacing between individual letters, words, lines, and blocks of information.

Internationalization and Writing Modes

Whereas CSS provides support for writing modes, such as Hebrew, where the letters are written from right to left, rather than the English practice of writing from left to right, XSL provides additional support for languages that write from top to bottom, a practice in many Far East languages.

Linking Controls

XSL provides controls to format the text of a link specifically, as well as the objects, lines, words, or letters that follow a link. XSL even provides a few methods for altering the content of the target of the link for controlling the placement of the target text on your screen or controlling the manner in which the link's target is displayed in relation to the link itself.

An early part of the XSL working draft, the XSLT recommendation, became officially recognized in November 1999. This recommendation controls the transformation of XML document information into another format, such as HTML or a format that is even more easily imported into a database or spreadsheet program. XSLT works by matching a template document to patterns of information contained within your XML document. These patterns are then inserted into the template and when the template is displayed, the resulting document appears to only contain the formatting code of the template, and the selected contents of the XML document.

An XSLT template document has two parts: the pattern matching controls and the formatting controls that allow the resulting document to be read by the document's viewer. For example if you were going to translate XML into HTML, the XSLT document would contain XSLT pattern matching statements that match up with the contents of the XML document and HTML elements that provide a recognizable structure for your Web browser to display.

Since XSLT is part of XSL, you can contain both XSLT pattern matching statements and XSL formatting statements in a single document with an `.xsl` extension.

Note *You can use XSLT with XSL, xHTML, and CSS formatting properties by incorporating a link to your CSS document within your XSLT document.*

XSL is loaded into your XML document in the same manner that CSS are loaded.

```
<?xml-stylesheet type="text/xsl" href="sonnet.xsl"?>
```

This statement uses the `xml-stylesheet` processing instruction to link to a style sheet that has been specified as a XSL style sheet using the `type="text/xsl"` statement, and then has the address specified through the `href=""` statement, which in this example is pointing to the file `sonnet.xsl`. Take a look at the following XSL document below. It uses commands, all discussed in detail in Chapters 15 and 16, to control the appearance and formatting of the content found within the XML document to which it is attached.

```
<?xml version="1.0"?>
<xsl:stylesheet xmlns:xsl="http://www.w3.org/TR/xsl">
  <xsl:template match="/">
    <HTML>
      <xsl:apply-templates />
    </HTML>
  </xsl:template>
  <xsl:template match="TITLE">
    <HEAD>
      <TITLE>
       <xsl:value-of select="." />
      </TITLE>
    </HEAD>
  </xsl:template>
  <xsl:template match="SONNET">
    <BODY>
      <P>
      <xsl:for-each select="STANZA">
        <xsl:value-of select="." />
      </xsl:for-each>
      </P>
      <P>
      <xsl:for-each select="REFRAIN">
        <xsl:value-of select="." />
      </xsl:for-each>
      </P>
      <P align="right">
      <I>
      <xsl:value-of select="AUTHOR" />
      </I>
      </P>
    </BODY>
  </xsl:template>
</xsl:stylesheet>
```

Using One or the Other

There really isn't a simple decision to be made for one or the other of these style sheets. If you are working with 4.0 browsers or wish your XML documents to be widely viewable over the Internet, then it would be best if you use CSS, since they have a broader support base than XSL. Table 12-1 will help you decide between CSS and the XSL for your projects.

Situation	Cascading Style Sheets	Extensible Stylesheet Language
Broad support in current software	*	
Flexibility for controlling object formatting		*
Control over page formatting	*	* (Extended)
Conversion to native HTML document format		*
Add information not found in XML document		*
Specifically format links.	*	*
Support for nonstandard writing directions	Left to right Right to left	Left to right Right to left Top to bottom
Pattern matching	Allows selection based upon any attribute name/value pair, element name, element hierarchy, or element position	Opens to any attribute or element value, or element content

Table 12-1. *Features and Support Between CSS and XSL*

Summary

A style sheet document allows you to alter the appearance of elements found within XML documents globally. Style sheets allow you to control the size of fonts, font color, document or object backgrounds, box borders, speech synthesizer controls, and just about everything you can modify within your XML document's data.

CSS works by setting property values that control the appearance of objects and also by using a set of cascading rules to decide which property values are used. The values identified in a CSS document can be superseded by the Web browser and/or other style sheet. All of the major Web browsers, in some form or another supports CSS, including Netscape Navigator 4.5–6, Opera 4, and Microsoft's Internet Explorer 4.x–5.

XSL can add content; convert your content to HTML, which is more widely supported than XML; and even sort through your information so that you are only displaying the information that you need. XSL works with XSLT to control the transformation of XML document information into another format, such as HTML, or even a format that is more easily imported into a database or spreadsheet program. XSLT matches a template document to patterns of information contained within your XML document. These patterns are then inserted into the template and when the template is displayed, the resulting document appears to only contain the formatting code of the template and the selected contents of the XML document.

Within an XML document, you can specify a style sheet in only one way:

```
<?xml-stylesheet type="mimetype" href="documentname" ?>
```

In the next chapters you will learn all the details you want about the specific properties and functions in both CSS and XSL/XSLT.

The Complete Reference

Chapter 13

CSS Basics

Cascading Style Sheets (CSS) are on their second iteration, and the World Wide Web Consortium (W3C) is currently developing the third. CSS is the most popular way of formatting Hypertext Markup Language (HTML) files so that they can be easily maintained and updated. CSS is also one of the most popular and well-supported methods of formatting your Extensible Markup Language (XML) document content for Web browsers. CSS allows you to separate the development of your document's format from the content of the document, working explicitly toward the goal of XML—to separate form from content.

The Basic CSS Statement

When a document author is creating a style sheet, it is important that she properly identify the specific rules and values for each element's available properties. The individual declaration for a rule must use the proper syntax shown in the following statement:

```
selector  { property: value}
```

The `selector` is the element identifier. It can be a combination of multiple elements to show a position, it can be the specific identifier of a specific element, or it can even be a class of element. `Property` is the name of one of the predefined CSS properties, all of which are identified in Appendix B, which is being set by this CSS statement. The `value` is one of the predefined value types that has been identified for that specific property. You can also create a declaration block to apply a series of attribute values to a single element. The proper syntax for using a declaration block follows:

```
selector  { property: value;
            property: value;
            property: value;
            ...
            property: value}
```

In addition to setting multiple properties for a single element, you can set either single or multiple properties for multiple elements using the following syntax:

```
selector1, selector2, selector3  { property: value}
```

Here are some examples of CSS statements used with XML documents:

```
head {  font-family: "Comic Sans MS", sans-serif;
        font-size: 16pt;
        font-style: normal}
bodytext {  font-family: "Comic Sans MS", sans-serif;
            font-size: 12pt;
            font-style: normal}
head, bodytext { color: #000000}
```

```
#specialtext {  font-family: "Comic Sans MS", sans-serif;
                font-size: 12pt;
                font-style: italic;
                color: #666633;
                background-color: #000000;
                padding: 4px 4px 4px 4px;
                border: 1px #666633 double}
rule {  color: #000000}
```

Adding CSS to Your Document

Style sheets can only be added to XML documents through the use of a processing instruction that references the external CSS file. This processing instruction, `<?xml-stylesheet?>`, can be used to add any type of style sheet that you wish to use with your XML document. It is shown here loading a CSS formatted style sheet called "`stylesheet.css`":

```
<?xml-stylesheet type="text/css" href="stylesheet.css" ?>
```

In addition to declaring the `<?xml-stylesheet?>` processing instruction to identify the style sheet, you have to create the style sheet itself. When you are defining the instructions to be used in the style sheet, you have to make decisions about which elements to change and how those elements should be selected.

CSS Selections

CSS use a system of pattern matching to determine which CSS rules are applied to which elements that are found within the document. Each of these patterns is referred to as the selector. The selector can be anything from a simple element name to a pattern

Using the `style` Attribute

When working with HTML documents you may have run across the `style` attribute. This attribute is used to incorporate style sheet elements directly into the HTML element itself. XML does not have any built-in support for the `style` attribute, although the use of a `style` attribute can be supported through the application viewing the XML document.

The syntax for implementing this attribute, when available, is

```
style="selector:value; selector:value;..."
```

incorporating element position, attribute values, and element hierarchy. When the pattern is matched, the specified values will be added to the element(s) that have been identified. Table 13-1 lists all of the available patterns in Cascading Style Sheets 2 (CSS 2). There may be more patterns available with the release of Cascading Style Sheets 3 (CSS 3). You can get more information on CSS3 by visiting the W3C at http://www.w3.org/Style/CSS.

Pattern	Description	Example
*	**Universal Selector** Matches any element	`* { font: red }`
elementname	**Type Selector** Matches any element of type *elementname*	`RULE { font: red }`
parentname childname	**Descendant Selector** Matches any element of type *childname* that is a descendant of an element of type *parentname*. A descendant does not mean a direct child. A descendant can be two or more levels beneath the parent element.	`BOOK RULE { font: red }`
parentname > childname	**Child Selector** Matches any element of type *childname* that is a direct child of an element of type *parentname*	`BOOK RULE { font: red }`

Table 13-1. *Cascading Style Sheet Selector Patterns*

Pattern	Description	Example
elementname:first-child	**:first-child pseudo-class** Matches the specified element when it is the first child element of its parent	BOOK:first-child { font: red }
elementname:link *elementname*:visited	**Link pseudo-class** Matches the element name if it is the source of a hyperlink that has either not yet been visited (:link) or has already been visited (:visited)	BOOK:link { font: Arial } BOOK:visited { font: Arial }
elementname:active *elementname*:hover *elementname*:focus	**Dynamic pseudo-class** Matches the specified element when the user is performing a specific action such loading a link (:active), moving a mouse over a link (:hover), or letting a text field or button receive the focus of either the mouse or the keyboard (:focus)	BOOK:active { font: Arial } BOOK:hover { font: Arial } BOOK:focus { font: Arial }
elementname:lang(*x*)	**:lang() pseudo-class** Matches an element if it is in the human language specified by the *x* variable	BOOK:lang(en)

Table 13-1. *Cascading Style Sheet Selector Patterns* (continued)

Pattern	Description	Example
element1 + element2	**Adjacent Selector** Matches any element of type *element2* that is immediately preceded by an element of type *element1*	`BOOK + PAGE { font: Arial }`
elementname[attribute]	**Attribute Selector** Matches any of the specified element type with an attribute of type *attribute* set, without regard to the attribute value	`BOOK[pgcnt] { font:Arial }`
elementname[attribute=value]	**Attribute Selector** Matches any of the specified element type with an attribute of type *attribute* set to the specified *value*	`BOOK[pgcnt=100] { font:Arial }`
elementname[attribute~=value]	**Attribute Selector** Matches any of the specified element types with an attribute of type *attribute* containing a space-separated list of values that has at least one exactly equal to *value*	`BOOK[author~=jones ] { font:Arial }`

Table 13-1. *Cascading Style Sheet Selector Patterns* (continued)

Pattern	Description	Example
elementname[attribute|=value]	**Attribute Selector** Matches any of the specified element types with an attribute of type *attribute* containing a hypen-separated list of values that has at least one exactly equal to *value*	`BOOK[author|=jones] { font:Arial }`
elementname#id	**ID Selector** Matches any element with an ID equal to *id*	`BOOK#fred { font:Arial }`

Table 13-1. *Cascading Style Sheet Selector Patterns* (continued)

XML, unlike HTML, is case sensitive. You must therefore be conscious of matching your text case, as well as the value itself, when matching CSS rules to their intended elements.

Selecting Elements

The most common way of applying a style to your XML document is based upon the element. Most developers, at least when they are first getting started, format all of their elements of the same name the same way and then start making exceptions. This breaks down to all book titles having the same styles applied, no matter where they are located within the XML document. Take for a moment the following code. It selects all `BOOK_TITLE` elements and writes them in a red, 12 point (12pt), fantasy font:

```
BOOK_TITLE { font: "red";
             font-size: "12pt";
             font-face: "fantasy" }
```

You can select all of the elements on your document by using the global selector: *. This selector, although not supported by many Web browsers including the 4.*x* versions of Microsoft Internet Explorer (IE) and Netscape Navigator, allows you to change the default appearance for all of the elements on your document. You can use this style selector as you would the BASE element in an HTML document. In the following sample all of the elements in an XML document are selected and changed to a blue, 12pt, Verdana font:

```
* { font: "blue";
    font-size: "12pt";
    font-face: "Verdana" }
```

If selecting all of the elements isn't what you want to do, but you do want to select more than one element, you can do so using a multiple element selector. This allows you to list the individual elements that you want to adjust the style of. The following sample selects the AUTHOR, EDITOR, and PUBLISHER elements and makes them appear in a red, 10pt, italic, Times New Roman font:

```
AUTHOR, EDITOR, PUBLISHER { font: "red";
                            font-size: "10pt";
                            font-style: "italic";
                            font-face: "Times New Roman" }
```

Selecting Classes

Unlike HTML, XML doesn't have a method of selecting elements for applying styles based upon that element's class, but you can get around this. You can create your own attribute that will allow you to group your elements for formatting in the same way that the class attribute for HTML did. As an example, while naming the attribute classy, simply define your element and attribute in the following manner and use the attribute selector in your CSS document to format the information:

```
<BOOK_TITLE classy="history">
     The Rise and Fall of the Roman Empire
</BOOK_TITLE>
<BOOK_TITLE classy="history"> How the West Was Won </BOOK_TITLE>
```

With the additional attribute added to the element, you can then use it to select and format a group of elements. In this case all BOOK_TITLE elements with the classy attribute set to history will be displayed in a brown, 16pt, Cursive text :

```
BOOK_TITLE[classy="history"] { font: "brown, 16pt, Cursive" }
```

Selecting IDs

The id attribute in XML is really an attribute that has been identified as an ID type and is used to identify the name or identifier of a particular object. The id attribute of your elements must be defined as a type ID in your XML document's Document Type Definition (DTD) (See Chapter 10 for more information on using ID type attributes in your XML documents). In this sample, the element with the id of Fred is selected, no matter what element is. In this case it is displayed with an orange font:

```
#Fred { font: "orange" }
```

Assume for a moment that you have a situation in which you want to turn a sentence orange if it has the id "Fred" and is a <BOOK_TITLE> element. If this is the case, then you can use both the element and the id together to make your selection:

```
BOOK_TITLE#Fred { font: "orange" }
```

Selecting in Context

You can make your selection of elements based upon their current location within the structure of your XML document. This is called *selecting in context*. These types of selections allow you to select elements that are either children or descendents of other known elements. For example, the following code allows you to select only the INTRO elements that are a direct child of a BOOK element. This will ignore all of the INTRO elements that are children of CHAPTER elements, even if they are also descendents of the BOOK element:

```
BOOK > INTRO { font-style="italic" }
```

On the other hand if you want to select all INTRO elements that are a descendant of a BOOK element, whether they are a direct child or not, you can use the descendant selector. The only difference between these two selectors is the placement of the greater-than symbol between the element names in the attribute selector statement above:

```
BOOK  INTRO { font-style="italic" }
```

Using Pseudo-Elements

Pseudo-elements are not included in the document source or the document tree; they only exist as a part of the format created by the use of a style sheet. These types of elements create abstractions within the document tree that cannot be specified any other way. For example, there is no other way within XML to identify the first letter or line of a paragraph. Using pseudo-elements, you can now identify these specific pieces of content and assign a style to them. Pseudo-elements are not case sensitive and may only appear directly after the subject of a style sheet selector.

:after

The :after pseudo-elements is used to insert the information specified in the content parameter after every instance of the element or elements that it is applied to. In this example, an image of a red star is placed after every book title:

```
BOOK_TITLE:after { content: url("redstar.gif") }
```

:before

The :before pseudo-elements is used to insert the information specified in the content parameter before every instance of the tag or tags that it is applied to. In this example the text string Author: is placed before every author entry:

```
AUTHOR:before { content: "Author:" }
```

:first-letter

The :first-letter pseudo-elements is used to create graphical effects such as drop caps and initial caps. In this example the first letter of the INTRO element is turned into a drop cap twice the size of the remaining text in the element:

```
INTRO:first-letter { font-size: 200%;
                     font-style: italic;
                     font-weight: bold;
```

:first-line

The :first-line pseudo-elements applies special style properties to the first line of a block-level element. It cannot be used with any other style of element such as inline or table. In this example the first line of the INTRO element is increased to 150% of the size of the normal INTRO text, is italicized, and is written in small caps:

```
INTRO:first-line { font-size: 150%;
                   font-style: italic;
                   font-variant: small-caps;"
```

:lang

The :lang pseudo-elements selects an element if the element content is written in the language specified. The following example turns all BOOK elements written in Spanish (sp) to green and all BOOK elements written in English (en) to blue:

```
BOOK:lang(sp) { font: "green" }
BOOK:lang(en) { font: "blue" }
```

Using Pseudo-Classes

A pseudo-class is similar to a normal class, but it is not included within the document tree of a document. Because some documents require formatting that cannot be based on a complete object, these types of pseudo-classes are allowed. pseudo-classes are used to classify elements based solely on their names, not their characteristics, attributes, or content.

You can use scripts to create dynamic pseudo-classes that change as a reader interacts with your document. The exception to this rule is the `:first-child` pseudo-class, which can be discovered by going through the document tree. Some of these classes can be mutually exclusive, but most can be applied simultaneously to the same element and can be placed anywhere within that element selector. When classes do conflict, the cascading order will determine which classes are rendered.

:active

The `:active` pseudo-class is applied only to objects in your XML document capable of receiving the focus of the document viewer, such as a link that is being selected by the user. The following example turns the `BOOK_INFO` lime if it is clicked on as the document users navigates a link to get more information:

```
BOOK_INFO:active {color: lime}
```

:first

The `:first` pseudo-class is applied only to the `@page` rule. Using this pseudo-class, you can apply information directly to the page layout of your document's first printed page. This rule has no effect on the document as it appears on your computer. This sample code sets the margins of the first printed page to 3cm all around:

```
@page:first {margin-top= 3cm;
             margin-bottom= 3cm;
             margin-left= 3cm;
             margin-right= 3cm }
```

:first-child

The `:first-child` pseudo-class is used to alter the first child of an element as it is mapped within the document tree. For example, this will only select the first-child element of a `LIBRARY` entry, no matter what that element might be

```
LIBRARY:first-child { font: "lime Arial 16pt" }
```

:focus

The `:focus` pseudo-class applies when an element has the focus of the reader's cursor. The following example turns the `BOOK_INFO` red when it receives the focus of the user. In order for this to happen, the `BOOK_INFO` element must be capable of receiving the focus such as a link would be

```
BOOK_INFO:focus {color: red}
```

:hover

The `:hover` pseudo-class can be applied to all active areas of the XML document, such as links, when the mouse hovers over them. A link with the `:hover` class applied becomes the specified color automatically when the mouse is dragged over it:

```
BOOK_LINK:hover {color: red}
```

:left

The `:left` pseudo-class is applied only to the `@page` rule. Using this pseudo-class, you can apply information directly to the page layout of the left-hand printed pages of your document. This sample code sets the margins of the left-hand printed page to 3cm all around:

```
@page:left { margin-top= 3cm;
             margin-bottom= 3cm;
             margin-left= 3cm;
             margin-right= 3cm }
```

:link

The `:link` pseudo-class can be applied to a link when its destination has not yet been visited. A link with the `:link` class applied becomes the specified color automatically when they are originally placed on the document and not activated:

```
BOOK_LINK:link {color: purple}
```

:right

The `:right` pseudo-class is applied only to the `@page` rule. Using this pseudo-class, you can apply information directly to the page layout of the right-hand printed pages of your document. This sample code sets the margins of the right-hand printed page to 2cm all around:

```
@page:right { margin-top= 2cm;
              margin-bottom= 2cm;
              margin-left= 2cm;
              margin-right= 2cm }
```

:visited

The `:visited` pseudo-class can be applied to a link when its destination has been visited. A link with `:visited` class applied becomes the specified color automatically when the link is activated and visited:

```
BOOK_LINK:visited {color: white}
```

Controlling Your Fonts

One of the first aspects of CSS that most people learn is the font styles. These styles allow you to control all aspects of your text appearance from font style, face, family, and variants.

Setting font-family

The `font-family` property is used to specify a prioritized list of font family names and/or generic family names that can be searched by XML document browsers to match character glyphs. Because all fonts may not contain glyphs to display all the characters in a document and because not all fonts are available on all systems, this attribute allows you to identify a specific list of fonts, generally of the same style and size, that are searched in order by the browser for a glyph for a specific character. This list is called a font set. The syntax of the `font-family` property is

```
font-family:    [[ <family-name> | <generic-family> ],]*
                [<family-name> | <generic-family>] | inherit
```

- **family-name** This is the name of the font family to use. `Font-family` names include: Bookman, Lucida, and Times New Roman. Include all font family names within quotes. If the quotation characters are omitted, any white-space characters before or after the font name are ignored. In addition, any sequence of white-space characters inside the font name is converted to a single space.
- **generic-family** Generic family names are: serif, sans-serif, cursive, fantasy, and monospace. Because they are keywords, they cannot be included within quotation marks.

The following style sheet designation identifies a variety of font family names and generic families:

```
BOOK       { font-family:  "Comic Sans";  }
INTRO      { font-family: "Times New Roman" ; }
AUTHOR     { font-family: sans-serif; }
PUBLISHER { font-family: "Helvetica"; }
SAMPLE   { font-family: serif; }
```

Setting font-size

The `font-size` property is used to identify the size of the font. The interpretation of this setting is based upon the XML browser's default `font-size` settings. The syntax of this property is

```
font-size: <absolute-size> | <relative-size> | <length> |
           <percentage> | inherit
```

- **absolute-size** If an `absolute-size` is specified (`xx-small | x-small | small | medium | large | x-large | xx-large`) there will be a scaling factor of 1.2 between each size. For example, if a `medium` font is actually 12pt, then a `large` font would be 14.4pt and a `small` font would be 10pt. This table is somewhat modifiable by the user agent to ensure the best quality and availability of characters. It will also change from one font family to another.
- **relative-size** If a `relative-size` is specified (`larger | smaller`), it is always in relation to the parent element's font size. So, if the parent element's font is medium, larger changes the size of the current element to large. In addition, when the parent element's size isn't similar to a table entry, the user agent can adjust either the table entries to match or adjust the font to fit the table.
- **length** This is used to specify a positive integer representing an absolute font size. This value is independent of the font table. You can use a specific length when you want a font size such as 38pt or 42pt.
- **percentage** This percentage value is used to identify an absolute font size in relation to the parent element's font size. You can create more robust documents and cascadable style sheets using percentages.

The following style sheet designation identifies a variety of font sizes and methods of implementing a range of sizes:

```
BOOK      { font-size: "150%"; }
INTRO     { font-size: small;  }
AUTHOR    { font-size: larger; }
PUBLISHER { font-size: "12pt"; }
SAMPLE    { font-size: medium; }
```

Setting `font-stretch`

The `font-stretch` property is used to control the kerning of your font—in other words, it controls the amount of space found between each individual character of the font. The syntax of this command is

```
font-stretch: normal | wider | narrower | ultra-condensed |
              xtra-condensed | condensed | semi-condensed |
              semi-expanded | expanded | extra-expanded |
              ultra-expanded | inherit
```

- **ultra-condensed, extra-condensed, condensed, semi-condensed, normal, semi-expanded, expanded, extra-expanded, ultra-expanded** These values are organized from most condensed to least condensed. Each of them is a small change in the horizontal spacing of your text.

- **wider** This value is relative to the parent element and expands the spacing one stop without increasing it above the `ultra-expanded level.`
- **narrower** This value is relative to the parent element and decreases the spacing one step without decreasing it below the `ultra-condensed level.`

The following style sheet designation identifies a variety of font kernings:

```
BOOK       { font-stretch: "ultra-expanded";  }
INTRO      { font-stretch: "narrower"; }
AUTHOR     { font-stretch: "expanded"; }
PUBLISHER  { font-stretch: "normal"; }
SAMPLE     { font-stretch: "wider"; }
```

Setting font-style

The `font-style` property specifies the style of font being used. You can specify normal, opaque, or italic fonts. The syntax of this attribute is

```
font-style: normal | italic | oblique | inherit
```

- **normal** No style change
- **italic** Displays with an italic or cursive slant to each character
- **oblique** Displays with an oblique, slanted, or inclined font

The following style sheet designation identifies a variety of font styles:

```
BOOK       { font-style: "oblique"; }
INTRO      { font-style: "italic"; }
SAMPLE     { font-style: "normal"; }
```

Setting font-variant

The `font-variant` property writes fonts using small caps for fonts supporting this style. Small caps are an effect that is achieved by replacing all lowercase letters with lowercase-height capital letters. The syntax for this attribute is

```
font-variant: normal | small-caps | inherit
```

- **normal** This value does not change from the standard font characters.
- **small-caps** This value specifies to use small capital letters in the place of the standard lowercase letters within the specified text.

The following style sheet changes the lower case letters in all the `BOOK_TITLES` to small caps:

```
BOOK_TITLE     { font- variant: "small-caps"; }
```

Setting `font-weight`

The `font-weight` property is used to specify the weight, or thickness, of the font used to display the specified text. The syntax of this attribute is

```
font-weight: 100 | 200 | 300 | 400 | 500 | 600 | 700 | 800 |
             900 | normal | bold | bolder | lighter | inherit
```

- **`100 to 900`** The numerical values form an ordered sequence in which each integer identifies a font weight that is at least as dark as its predecessor in all applications. In most applications, each digit will make an incremental increase in the weight of the font without using a predetermined weight.
- **`normal`** This value is typically the same as a value of 400.
- **`bold`** This value is typically the same as a value of 700.
- **`bolder`** This value is used to apply the next weight to a font that is darker than the inherited one. If the inherited value is less than 900, the value will increase by 100. If the value is 900, the value will not increase.
- **`lighter`** This value is used to apply the previous weight to a font that is lighter than the inherited one. If the inherited value is greater than 100, the value will decrease by 100. If the value is 100, the value will not decrease.

The following style sheet designation identifies a variety of font weights:

```
BOOK      { font-weight: "400";   }
INTRO     { font-weight: "lighter"; }
SAMPLE    { font-weight: "bold"; }
```

Setting `font` shorthand

This CSS attribute is used as shorthand notation for setting the attributes that affect the font used to render text on a page. These attributes include `font-style`, `font-variant`, `font-weight`, `font-size`, `line-height`, and `font-family`.

When using this attribute to set the `font` properties, they must all first be reset to their initial values, including some of the other `font` attribute values such as `caption`, `menu`, and `message-box`. Then the properties that have been given a specific value are set. The syntax of this attribute is

```
font: [ [ <'font-style'> || <'font-variant'> || <'font-weight'> ]?
      <'font-size'> [ / <'line-height'> ]? <'font-family'> ] |
      caption | icon | menu | message-box | small-caption |
      status-bar | inherit
```

- **font-style** This specifies whether the font being rendered should be displayed in a `normal`, `italic`, or `oblique` manner. `Normal` is the default.
- **font-variant** This controls whether the font is rendered in a `normal` or a `small-caps` style. `Normal` is the default.
- **font-weight** This value is used to control the thickness of the font. Valid options of this attribute are `normal`, `bold`, `bolder`, `lighter`, or a numerical value between `100` and `900`.
- **font-size** This controls the size of the font to be rendered. It can be an `absolute-size`, a `relative-size`, a `length`, or a `percentage`.
- **line-height** This attribute controls the height of the line that the font is being displayed on. It can be set to `normal`, a `number`, a `length`, or a `percentage`.
- **font-family** This attribute is used to define either the `family-name` or the `generic-family` that will be used when displaying this text.
- **caption** This is the font that is used for captioned controls such as buttons.
- **icon** This is the font that will be used to label all icons on documents.
- **menu** This font is used when rendering menus and drop-down menu lists.
- **message-box** This font is used to display text in dialog boxes.
- **small-caption** This font is used for labeling captions on small controls.
- **status-bar** This font is used when displaying messages in the status bars in user agent windows.

The following style sheet uses the shorthand `font` attribute in place of specifying each individual font-related attribute:

```
BOOK { font: italic small-caps lighter 12pt  "Comic Sans"
              "Times New Roman" "sans serif" "sans serif"
              "helvetica" "small fonts" "Festive" }
```

Setting font `color`

The `color` property identifies the foreground color for the text content of an element. The syntax of this command is

```
color: <colorname> | <RGBcolor>
```

- **colorname** This is one of the valid color names specified by the HTML 4.0 standard or, if the element is viewed with IE, one of Microsoft's identified color names.
- ***RGBcolor*** The name of the color is returned in hexadecimal format representing the Red-Green-Blue (RGB) value of the color.

The following style sheet applies color to two types of objects, using both methods of identifying color. It forces all uses of the `AUTHOR` tag to take on the RGB hex value `#FF0000`, all `into` to appear in `red`, and all `FOOTER` elements to appear in `rgb (255,0,0)`. All of these values are the same. They all force these elements to be displayed in red:

```
AUTHOR  {  font-family: Arial, Helvetica, sans-serif;
           color: #FF0000}
INTRO   {  text-decoration: underline;
           color: red}
FOOTER  {  color: rgb (255,0,0)}
```

Controlling Your Text

In addition to ensuring that each of your individual characters looks the way you want it to, you also have to format each line, paragraph, word, and space around the letters. These CSS attributes allow you to have even more control over the appearance of your document text.

Setting `letter-spacing`

The `letter-spacing` attribute is used to set the amount of space between the individual characters in an element that displays text. You can set this value in the style sheet, or you can set it using the `style` attribute within a specific command:

```
letter-spacing: normal | <length> | auto | inherit
```

- **`normal`** This is the default value, and it allows the document browser to control the space between individual characters so the user agent can justify text.
- **`length`** This value specifies a set distance between characters in the text, and it may be altered based upon the user agent's interpretation of the measurement.
- **`auto`** This value allows the text to be spaced so the complete text associated with an element can be placed on a single line.
- **`inherit`** The value for this distance is inherited from its parent elements.

The following example code shows a style sheet that sets different `letter-spacing` for various elements that could appear in a document:

```
BOOK_TITLE { letter-spacing: 2px}
AUTHOR     { letter-spacing: auto }
SAMPLE     { letter-spacing: 1mm}
INTRO      { letter-spacing: normal}
```

Setting `line-height`

The `line-height` property specifies the height of the line that either text or graphics will be displayed upon. The `line-height` property controls the amount of extra space provided for text, or it can be used to create a shadow effect with your characters. This value is interpreted differently by varying Web browsers and other XML document viewers, so test thoroughly when using this attribute:

```
line-height: normal | <number> | <length> | <percentage> | inherit
```

- **`normal`** This value informs user agents to use the computed value of the line height, based on the size of the font being used on that line. This value works the same as the `number value.`
- ***`number`*** This value is used to determine the computed line-height of your text when it is multiplied by the absolute height of the property. Negative values are not allowed.
- ***`length`*** This value is used to set the absolute height of the line. Negative values are not allowed.
- ***`percentage`*** This value allows the document author to control the height of the line by forcing the user agent to multiply this percentage to the height of the font being used. You can use negative values. For example, a value of –50% will lower the baseline of the specified element so it is now located where the midline of the next line should have been.
- **`inherit`** This value forces the element to use the `line-height` value it received from its parent elements.

The following example forces the line-height of the book title to be half again what it would naturally be due to the font selections:

```
BOOK_TITLE { color: red;
             line-height: 150%}

<BOOK>
   <BOOK_TITLE> Only the Shadow Knows!!! </BOOK_TITLE>
</BOOK>
```

Setting `text-align`

The `text-align` attribute is used to align the inline-text contents of the block element to which the attribute is applied. The syntax of this command is

```
text-align: left | right | center | justify | <string> | inherit
```

- **`left`** Left-align
- **`right`** Right-align

ADDING STYLE

- **`center`** Center text horizontally
- **`justify`** Left and right-justify text
- ***`string`*** Align against a string character

The following style sheet sets the alignment for all `BOOK_TITLE` objects to `center` and all `INTRO` objects to `justify`:

```
BOOK_TITLE { text-align: center }
INTRO      { text-align: justify }
```

Setting word-spacing

The `word-spacing` controls the amount of space used between words. The syntax of this attribute is

```
word-spacing: normal | <length> | inherit
```

- ***`length`*** This is positive integer and unit specifier identify a fixed width between each word.
- **`normal`** This setting leaves the spacing between words up to the XML browser.

The following style sheet sets the `word-spacing` for all `BOOK_TITLE` objects to `3em` and all `INTRO` objects to `normal`:

```
BOOK_TITLE { word-spacing: 3em }
INTRO      { word-spacing: normal }
```

Setting Your Alignment

Many techniques are employed to control how objects line up on a document. Most of them are based on one of two types of alignment:

- **Baseline alignment** Used to align objects with a font. The baseline of the font is the bottom edge of standard characters such as `a, e, and o` that have neither a tail nor a hat. This line serves as a means of aligning the top, bottom, or middle of an object or line of text.
- **Margin alignment** Used to align objects to the outside margins of a page. XML documents, like all others, require the ability to align objects and text on a page. You can control the alignment of your document objects by using the `valign` and the `halign` CSS properties

Using valign

`valign` works with a variety of table-related elements controlling the vertical position of information within a cell. The syntax of this command is

```
valign = top | middle | bottom | baseline
```

- **top** Information is rendered flush with the top of the cell.
- **middle** Information is centered vertically within the cell.
- **bottom** Information rendered flush with the cell bottom.
- **baseline** Information is aligned against the baseline set for other objects.

Using `halign`

`halign` works with a variety of table-related elements controlling the horizontal position of information within a cell. The syntax of this command is

```
halign = top | middle | bottom | baseline
```

- **top** Information is rendered flush with the top of the cell.
- **middle** Information is centered vertically within the cell.
- **bottom** Information rendered flush with the cell bottom.
- **baseline** Information is aligned against the baseline set for other objects.

Indenting Text

The `text-indent` property indents the first line of a paragraph. If the text in the block is a left-to-right flowing paragraph, the indent is on the left edge of the first line. If the text in the block is a right-to-left flowing paragraph, the indent is on the right edge of the first line. The syntax used to implement this property is

```
text-indent: <length> | <percentage>
```

- ***length*** The length of the indentation as a measurement such as 10px.
- ***percentage*** The indentation is a percentage of the object block's width.

The following style sheet forces the first line of all `INTRO` elements to be indented 3cm:

```
INPUT   { text-indent: 3cm }
```

Using Text Decorations

The `text-decoration` property is used to add decorative properties to element. This property can cause an element to show an overline or to blink. The syntax of this command is

```
text-decoration: none | underline | blink | overline | line-through
```

- **blink** All of the text will blink.
- **none** No decoration is applied to the text.
- **overline** A line is placed above every line of text.

- **underline** All text is underlined.
- **line-through** All text has a line midway through each character.

The following style sheet underlines all text appearing as part of a BOOK_TITLE element and makes all text appearing as part of a BEST_SELLER element blink:

```
BOOK_TITLE   { text-decoration: underline }
BEST_SELLER { text-decoration: blink }
```

Using text-shadow

The text-shadow property applies shadows to the text contents of an element. This comma-separated list of shadow effects controls the order, color, and dimensions of shadows overlaid on your text. Shadows do not extend the size of the block containing the text, but they may extend over the boundaries of the block. The stacking level of the shadows is the same as the element itself.

Each shadow effect must specify the offset of the shadow. You can optionally specify a blur radius and a shadow color. The shadow offset is specified with two length variables that identify how far out from the text the shadow extends. The first length specifies horizontal distance, while the second specifies the vertical depth of the shadow. If you apply a negative value to the shadow offsets, the shadow appears to the left and top of the text, rather than to the lower right.

The blur radius, specified as a third length property, identifies the boundary of the blur effect. The other optional value, color, controls the specific shade and tone of the shadow effect. The syntax used to implement this property is

```
text-shadow: none | [color || length length length? ,]*
             [color || length length length?] | inherit
```

- **none** No shadow effects are applied to the text.
- ***color*** This variable contains either the name or RGB value of the shadow color.
- ***length*** This value is the offset value of the horizontal, vertical, or blur shadow dimension.

The following example text applies shadows to the BOOK_TITLE element

```
BOOK_TITLE { text-shadow: "red 5px 5px 3px" }
```

Using Text Transformations

The text-transform property applies the specified capitalization style to text. The syntax of this attribute is

```
text-transform: capitalize | uppercase | lowercase | none
```

- **`capitalize`** Uses title case, in which the first letter of each word is capitalized
- **`lowercase`** Forces all characters to be lowercase
- **`uppercase`** Forces all characters to be uppercase

The following code uses the `text-transform` property to alter the text a book `BOOK_TITLE` element to have each word capitalized, no matter how it appears in a database:

```
BOOK_TITLE { text-transform: capitalize }
```

Controlling Your Object Boxes

One of the biggest problems with formatting documents, XML or otherwise, is controlling the formatting of your object boxes. Using CSS you have the option of controlling their borders, outlines, margins, and padding.

Setting Borders

All block objects have borders; you just can't always see them. You can use one of the many `border` properties to control the outline of each of these block elements. The `border` property itself is a shorthand attribute used to set the width, color, and style for all four borders of an object box. Unlike the shorthand attributes for margins and padding, discussed in the sections "Setting Margins" and "Adding Padding" later in this chapter, the `border` attribute can only set options for the box as a whole, not for its individual edges.

The syntax of `border` is

```
border = <border-width> | <border-style> | <border-color> | inherit
```

Within the shorthand border property are three other shorthand properties that can all stand on their own. These properties are discussed in the following sections. In addition to the shorthand properties for border, there are also shorthand properties for configuring the bottom, right, left, and top of the box. These properties show the following syntax:

```
border-bottom = <border-bottom-width> | <border-bottom-style> |
                <border-bottom-color> | inherit
border-right = <border-right-width> | <border-right-style> |
               <border-right-color> | inherit
border-left = <border-left-width> | <border-left-style> |
              <border-left-color> | inherit
border-top = <border-top-width> | <border-top-style> |
             <border-top-color> | inherit
```

In the following example, you can see two sample style sheet declarations that set the same borders for the `SAMPLE` and the `INTRO` elements:

```
INTRO  { border: medium red dash }
SAMPLE { border-bottom: medium red dash;
         border-left: medium red dash;
         border-right: medium red dash;
         border-top: medium red dash }
```

border-width, border-bottom-width, border-right-width, border-left-width, border-top-width

The `border-width` property is a shorthand property for setting the width of all four borders of your object box individually. The syntax for using `border-width` is

```
border-width: [medium | thin | thick | <length> ] (1,4)
```

- **medium** Displays a medium-thick line, which is roughly 1pt thick with most XML browsers. `Medium is the default value`
- **thin** Displays a width less-than-medium on most XML and Web browsers
- **thick** Displays a width greater-than-medium, generally 1 to 2pts thick
- **length** A floating-point number with either an absolute or a relative unit designator following it

The other related border width properties use the same values. Their individual syntaxes are

```
border-bottom-width: medium | thin | thick | <length>
border-left-width: medium | thin | thick | <length>
border-right-width: medium | thin | thick | <length>
border-top-width: medium | thin | thick | <length>
```

In the following example you can see two sample style sheet declarations that set the same border widths for the `SAMPLE` and the `INTRO` elements:

```
INTRO  { border-width: medium thick thin }
SAMPLE { border-bottom-width: medium;
         border-left-width: thick;
         border-right-width: thick;
         border-top-width: thin }
```

border-style, border-bottom-style, border-right-style, border-left-style, border-top-style

The `border-style` property is a shorthand property for setting the style of all four borders of your object box individually. The syntax for using `border-style` is

```
border-style: none | hidden | dotted | dashed | solid | double |
              groove | ridge | inset | outset  | inherit
```

- **`none`** No border shown for this box. This value forces the `border-width value to be zero.`
- **`hidden`** No border is shown for this element, but the width of the border is reserved.
- **`solid`** A single line
- **`groove`** The border appears engraved into the page.
- **`ridge`** The border appears to be coming out of the page.
- **`inset`** The border appears to be pressed into the document.
- **`outset`** The border appears to be extended out of the document.

The other related `border-style` properties use the same values. Their individual syntaxes are shown in the following code.

```
border-bottom-style: none | hidden | dotted | dashed | solid | double |
                     groove | ridge | inset | outset  | inherit
border-left-style: none | hidden | dotted | dashed | solid | double |
                   groove | ridge | inset | outset  | inherit
border-right-style: none | hidden | dotted | dashed | solid | double |
                    groove | ridge | inset | outset  | inherit
border-top-style: none | hidden | dotted | dashed | solid | double |
                  groove | ridge | inset | outset  | inherit
```

In the following example you can see two sample style sheet declarations that set the same border styles for the `SAMPLE` and the `INTRO` elements:

```
INTRO  { border-style: dash double none }
SAMPLE { border-bottom-style: medium;
         border-left-style: double;
         border-right-style: double;
         border-top-style: none }
```

ADDING STYLE

border-color, border-bottom-color, border-right-color, border-left-color, border-top-color

The `border-color` property is a shorthand property for setting the color of all four borders of your object box individually. You can also set this attribute to `transparent`. If this attribute is not supplied, the text color is used automatically. The syntax for using `border-color` is

```
border-color: <colorname> | <RGBcolor> | transparent
```

- ***colorname*** This is one of the valid color names specified by the HTML 4.0 standard or, if the element is viewed with IE, one of Microsoft's identified color names.
- ***RGBcolor*** The name of the color is returned in hexadecimal format representing the RGB value of the color.
- **transparent** This value sets the border to clear, but maintains its width.

The other related border-width properties use the same values. Their individual syntaxes are

```
border-bottom-color: <colorname> | <RGBcolor> | transparent
border-left-color: <colorname> | <RGBcolor> | transparent
border-right-color: <colorname> | <RGBcolor> | transparent
border-top-color: <colorname> | <RGBcolor> | transparent
```

In the following example you can see two sample style sheet declarations that set the same border styles for the `SAMPLE` and the `INTRO` elements:

```
INTRO  { border-color: red blue green }
SAMPLE { border-bottom-color: red;
         border-left-color: blue;
         border-right-color: blue;
         border-top-color: green }
```

Setting border-collapse

The `border-collapse` attribute is used to force the border of XML tables to join into a single line or to be separated as they are by default. The syntax for this attribute is

```
border-collapse: separate | collapse
```

- **separate** Forces the table borders to be detached as they appear in a standard HTML page
- **collapse** Forces the borders to collapse into a single line at the border joints

The following code uses the `border-collapse` property to collapse the edges of the border around the `BOOK_TITLE` element when it is displayed as a block element:

```
BOOK_TITLE { display: block;
             text-transform: capitalize }
```

Setting Outlines

Outlines are a new construct in CSS2 that allows you to control the appearance of the edges of each block-level element. On the surface, outlines appear to perform the same task as borders, but they differ in two primary ways:

- **Don't have to be rectangular** Outlines can conform to any shape displayed by an object.
- **Don't take up any space in your page** Unlike borders, whose width will affect the flow of a document, outlines do not take up space; therefore they have no effect on the flow of your document.

There are four outline related elements: `outline, outline-color, outline-style,` and `outline-width.`

outline

`outline` is a shorthand property that controls the appearance of the outline of each block. It sets the width, color, and style for all four edges of an object box simultaneously. Unlike the shorthand attributes for margins and padding, the `outline` attribute can only set options for the box as a whole—not for its individual edges. The syntax of `outline` is

```
outline = <outline-width> | <outline-style> | <outline-color> |
inherit
```

- **`outline-width`** Sets the box outline to a valid value for the `outline-width` property: medium, thin, thick, or a length.
- **`outline-style`** Sets the box outline to a valid value for the `outline-style` property: `none, dotted, dashed, outset, inset, groove, ridge, solid, and double.`
- **`outline-color`** Sets the box outline to a valid value for the `outline-color` property, either a valid HTML color name or the three or six hexadecimal-digit RGB representation of a color. If this attribute is not supplied, the text color will be used automatically.

The following segment of code shows how the outline property can be used in a style sheet to control the appearance of the edges of a book cover image:

```
BOOK_COVER  { outline: thin dashed red }
```

outline-color

The `outline-color` property sets the color of the left, right, top, and bottom outlines of the object box of specified elements. The syntax of this property is

```
outline-color: <colorname> | <#RGBvalue> | invert
```

- **colorname** A string value representing one of the CSS2 identified color names.
- **#RGBvalue** The three- or six-digit hexadecimal number that is used to represent the RGB value of the selected color.
- **invert** Forces the outline to invert the color of the pixels on the screen to create a visible border.

The following code shows how you can change the color of the `BOOK_TITLE, BOOK_COVER, BOOK_BACK,` and `PUB_LOGO` outlines:

```
BOOK_TITLE { outline-color: #FFCCCC black black;
             outline -style: inset;
             outline-width: thick}
BOOK_COVER { border outline-style: groove}
BOOK_BACK  { outline-color: #FF33CC #FFCCFF}
PUB_LOGO   { outline: thick #FFFF00 }
```

outline-style

The `outline-style` property controls the style of the outline being displayed for the entire box. The style sets the visual appearance of the outline. It uses the same options as the `border-style` property. The syntax for this property is

```
outline-style: none | hidden | dotted | dashed | solid | double |
               grooved | ridge | inset | outset | inherit
```

- **none** No outline shown
- **hidden** No outline shown for this element
- **dotted** A series of dots
- **dashed** A series of dashes
- **solid** A single line
- **double** Two solid lines with the clear space between the lines equal to the value of the `outline-width attribute`
- **grooved** Appears to be drawn into the page
- **ridge** Appears to rise three-dimensionally out of the page
- **inset** Appears pressed into the document
- **outset** Appears to be extended out of the document

In this example, the outline-style element is used to create a dashed border around the `BOOK_TITLE` element. It is also used to create solid borders of various types around the `BOOK_COVER` and the `BOOK_BACK` image elements:

```
BOOK_TITLE { outline-color: red;
             outline-style: dashed;
             outline-width: thick}
BOOK_COVER { outline-style: groove}
BOOK_BACK  { outline-style: double}
```

outline-width

The width of an outline actually takes up no space, but it does have an apparent width that is controlled by the `outline-width` property. This property can be controlled by one of the keyword values or by supplying a valid CSS length-value such as 1em. The syntax of this property is

```
outline-width: medium | thin | thick | <length>
```

- **medium** Displays a medium thickness line roughly 1pt thick
- **thin** Displays a width less than medium, generally .1 to .5pt. thick on most XML document browsers
- **thick** Displays a width greater than medium, generally 1.5 to 2pts thick as designed by the XML browser
- **length** A floating-point number with either an absolute or relative unit designator following it

The following example shows a variety of widths that can be used for outlines on specified property boxes.

```
BOOK_TITLE { outline-color: #FFCCCC black black;
             outline -style: inset;
             outline-width: thick}
BOOK_COVER { outline-width: 3em}
BOOK_BACK  { outline-width: thin}
PUB_LOGO   { outline-width: medium }
```

Setting Margins

Just as there are a variety of `border` properties, CSS includes many properties with the means to control the `margins` on the XML page. All of these properties can be used with all the XML block elements, as well as with the `@page` rule. CSS2-supported margin properties include `margin, margin-bottom, margin-left, margin-right,` and `margin-top`.

margin

The margin property is used as a shorthand property, allowing you to set the margin-top, margin-bottom, margin-right, and margin-left properties or block objects simultaneously. This property can have up to four margin-width values. Each of these values sets one of the margins on the block. The syntax for this command is

```
margin: <margin-width>[1,4] | inherit
```

The margin-width is a length value representing either an absolute or a relative number using a specific unit value. You can have up to four lengths listed for this value. If there is a single value assigned for margin, it is used for all the margins of the block object. If there are two values, the first is used for the top and bottom margins, and the second is used for the right and left box margins. In the case of three identified values, the first is the top, the second is the right and left margins, and the third is the bottom margin. If all four values have been set, the first is the top margin, the second is the right side, the third is the bottom, and the fourth is the left.

The value of the margin property is inherited; therefore any children of a page or box with margins set will inherit those same margin settings from its parent element. Take a look at the following groups of examples that create equal statements.

This group uses three values in the margin statement to set dimensions for all four sides of the document. As you can see, the 2cm setting is applied to both the right and left margins:

```
BOOK { margin: 1cm 2cm 3cm }
BOOK { margin-top: 1cm;
       margin-right: 2cm;
       margin-left: 2cm;
       margin-bottom: 3cm  }
```

The following group of statements uses a single setting in the margin statement to control the margins of the entire document. As you can see, the 2pc setting is applied to all the margins of the page:

```
@page { margin: 2pc }
@page { margin-top: 2pc;
        margin-right: 2pc;
        margin-left: 2pc;
        margin-bottom: 2pc }
```

The following group has two values in the margin statement that are used to set the top and bottom and the left and right margins separately for the INTRO block element. As you can see, the 1ex setting is applied to the top and bottom margins of the object, and the 2ex setting is applied to the right and left margins of the object:

```
INTRO { margin: 1ex 2ex }
```

```
INTRO { margin-top: 1ex;
margin-right: 2ex;
margin-left: 2ex;
margin-bottom: 1ex }
```

margin-bottom

The `margin-bottom` property uses the same length setting as the `margin` property, but it only sets the width of the margin for the bottom of your block element. The syntax of this property is

```
margin-bottom: <margin-width> | inherit
```

margin-left

The `margin-left` property uses the same length setting as the `margin` property, but it only sets the width of the margin for the left edge of your block element. The syntax for this property is

```
margin-left: <margin-width> | inherit
```

margin-right

The `margin-right` property uses the same length setting as the `margin` property, but it only sets the width of the margin for the right edge of your block element. The syntax for this property is

```
margin-right: <margin-width> | inherit
```

margin-top

The `margin-top` property uses the same length setting as the `margin` property, but it only sets the width of the margin for the top edge of your block element. The syntax of this property is

```
margin-top: <margin-width> | inherit
```

Adding Padding

Padding can be added to your XML elements by using the `padding` property. The `padding` property sets aside a specific amount of space between the margins of the object and the edges of the object being padded. It can be used with all the XML elements. This attribute is used as shorthand for setting the `padding-top`, `padding-bottom`, `padding-right`, and `padding-left` properties for your style sheet. The syntax for this property is

```
padding: <padding-width>[1,4] | inherit
```

`padding-width` is a length value representing either an absolute or a relative number and using a specific unit value. You can list up to four lengths for this value. If you assign a single value for `padding`, it is used for all the padding spaces of the object. If you assign two values, the first is used for the top and bottom sides of the object, and the second is used for the right and left sides. In the case of three identified values, the first is the top, the second is the right and left, and the third is the bottom. If all four values are set, the first is the top, the second is the right, the third is the bottom, and the fourth is the left.

Just like the `margin` property, padding can be inherited by its child elements. By default, objects do not have any padding. If you have applied padding to your entire page by using the `@page` element, then you cannot set the inherit value for padding individual objects in the expectation of the objects using the padding dimensions for the page itself.

The following groups of examples are equal statements. This group uses three values to set dimensions for all four sides of the `BOOK_COVER`:

```
BOOK_COVER { padding:  1cm 2 cm 3 cm }
BOOK_COVER { padding-top: 1cm;
             padding-right: 2cm;
             padding-left: 2cm;
             padding-bottom: 3cm  }
```

The following group uses a single setting to control the padding of the entire document:

```
@page { padding: 1in }
@page { padding-top: 1in;
        padding-right: 1in;
        padding-left: 1in;
        padding-bottom: 1in }
```

The following group has two values that are used to set the top and bottom padding and the left and right padding separately for a particular block element:

```
BOOK_TITLE { padding: 1em 2em }
BOOK_TITLE { padding-top: 1em;
             padding-right: 2em;
             padding-left: 2em;
             padding-bottom: 1ex }
```

padding-bottom

The `padding-bottom` property uses the same length setting as the `padding` property, but it only sets the width of the padding for the bottom of your block element. The syntax of this property is

```
padding-bottom: <padding-width> | inherit
```

padding-left

The `padding-left` property uses the same length setting as the `padding` property, but it only sets the width of the padding for the left edge of your block element. The syntax for this property is

```
padding-left: <padding-width> | inherit
```

padding-right

The padding-right property uses the same length setting as the padding property, but it only sets the width of the padding for the right edge of your block element. The syntax for this property is

```
padding-right: <padding-width> | inherit
```

padding-top

The padding-top property uses the same length setting as the padding property, but it only sets the width of the padding for the top edge of your block element. The syntax of this property is

```
padding-top: <padding-width> | inherit
```

Setting Backgrounds

In addition to controlling the formatting of your text and block objects, you also need to have control over how the background of your document and block objects appear. You can control the appearance and function of your document's background using the background-attachment, background-color, background-position, and background-repeat properties. Each of these properties controls one aspect of the background. They are all discussed in the following sections, as well as the shorthand background property that can be used to set all of these other properties simultaneously.

Using background-attachment

The background attachment property controls the scrolling of the background image (provided the image is already specified) within the document or the element to which this property has been applied. You can fix the image in relation to the viewing area of your XML browser or enable it to change as the document is read. The syntax of this attribute is

```
background-attachment: scroll | fixed | inherit
```

- **scroll** This is the default value of this property that allows the background image to scroll with the document text.
- **fixed** This property prohibits the background from scrolling as the text is scrolled.
- **inherit** This property forces the current element to use whatever setting the parent element has.

The following example code uses an image called white.gif, which is simply a white box 100 pixels by 100 pixels wide. This image is positioned at the top of the XML document with the background-position property. The remainder of the background color is red. This band is stationary when the remainder of the document is scrolled, as set by the background-attachment: fixed:

```
BOOK {background-attachment: fixed;
      background-color: red;
      background-image: url("white.gif");
      background-position: top;
      background-repeat: repeat-x;}
```

Using background-color

The background-color property provides a background color for each document or object when no background image is specified, when the background image is too small to cover the entire object and has a background-repeat property setting of no-repeat, or when the background image is unable to load. The syntax of this command is

```
background-color: <colorname> | <#RGBvalue>
```

- ***colorname*** One of the valid color names identified in the CSS document
- ***#RGBvalue*** The RGB three- or six-digit hex value representing a color on the color chart

The following sample code shows you how to use both the RGB values for a color and the color name:

```
BOOK_TITLE { background-color: red }
BOOK       { background-color: #FFFFFF } <!-- white background -->
```

Using background-image

The background-image property specifies an image to display in the background of the document or element to which it is applied. You can use the other background attributes such as background-position, background-attachment, and background-repeat to control how the image is displayed on the page. When you are using the background-image element, it is generally a good plan to include a setting for your document's background color in case the image cannot be displayed. The syntax for this command is

```
background-image: url("uri")
```

This property has only one potential value: a relative or an absolute reference to the image's URL to be displayed.

The following example code uses an image called left-edge.gif, which is simply a red box 100x100 pixels wide. This image is positioned at the top of the XML document with the background-position property. The remainder of the background color is white. This band is stationary when the remainder of the document is scrolled, as set by the `background-attachment: fixed` property. The image is repeated down the page, as specified by the `background-repeat: repeat-x` property setting:

```
BOOK {background-attachment: fixed;
      background-color: white;
      background-image: url("leftedge.gif");
      background-position: top;
      background-repeat: repeat-x;}
```

Using `background-position`

The `background-position` property controls where, within the object box or document, the background image appears. This property allows you to control both the horizontal and vertical position of the background image. The syntax for this command is

```
background-position: [ [percentage | length ]{1,2} |
                     [ [top | center | bottom] ||
                     [left | center | right] ] ] | inherit
```

- **`percentage`** A percentage value controls the position of the background image by placing the image location as a percentage of the overall containment box created by the element. For example, if you use the values 15% and 85%, the user agent displays the point 15% in from the left edge and 85% down from the top of the image into the same coordinates within the containment box.
- **`length`** This value specifies the amount of space below and to the right of the upper-left corner of the padding area in which the image should be located.
- **`top left`** and **`left top`** These values produce the same effect as using the percentages 0% and 0%.
- **`top`**, **`top center`**, and **`center top`** These values produce the same effect as using the percentages 0% and 50%.
- **`right top`** and **`top right`** These values produce the same effect as using the percentages 100% and 0%.
- **`left`**, **`left center`**, and **`center left`** These values produce the same effect as using the percentages 0% and 50%.
- **`center`** and **`center center`** These values produce the same effect as using the percentages 50% and 50%.
- **`right`**, **`right center`**, and **`center right`** These values produce the same effect as using the percentages 100% and 50%.
- **`bottom left`** and **`left bottom`** These values produce the same effect as using the percentages 0% and 100%.

- **bottom, bottom center,** and **center bottom** These values produce the same effect as using the percentages 100% and 50%.
- **bottom right** and **right bottom** These values produce the same effect as using the percentages 100% and 100%.

In the following example code, the BOOK elements background is placed in the upper-left corner of the screen, as is the BOOK_TITLE element's background. The AUTHOR and PUBLISHER elements backgrounds are placed in the lower-right corner of their object areas:

```
BOOK {background-attachment: fixed;
      background-image: url("leftedge.gif");
      background-position: top left;
      background-repeat: repeat-y ;}
BOOK_TITLE { background-attachment: fixed;
             background-image: url("toppick.gif");
             background-position: 0% 0%;
             background-repeat: repeat-x;}
AUTHOR { background-attachment: fixed;
         background-image: url("rightpic.gif");
         background-position: bottom right;
         background-repeat: no-repeat;}
PUBLISHER { background-attachment: fixed;
            background-image: url("rightpic.gif");
            background-position: 100% 100%;
            background-repeat: no-repeat;}
```

Using background-repeat

The background-repeat attribute controls how a background image is repeated over the area of your document or object box. You can select to have your background image tile, which would repeat the image both horizontally and vertically, as you would see on a typical Web page or only repeat vertically, horizontally, or not at all. The syntax is

```
background-repeat: repeat | repeat-x | repeat-y | no-repeat
```

- **repeat** This value forces the XML browser to repeat the image both horizontally and vertically. This is the default value of this property.
- **repeat-x** This value forces the XML browser to repeat the image only horizontally.
- **repeat-y** This value forces the XML browser to repeat images only vertically.

- **`no-repeat`** The image is not repeated. The original image is placed according to the positioning instructions included in the `background-position` attribute. Any space on the visual screen outside the image is displayed in the color specified by the `background-color` attribute.

In the following example code, the `PUBLISHER` element's background is placed in the lower-right corner of their object area, in a fixed position so that it does not scroll, and does not repeat itself:

```
PUBLISHER { background-attachment: fixed;
            background-image: url("rightpic.gif");
            background-position: 100% 100%;
            background-repeat: no-repeat;}
```

Using the `background` Shorthand Properties

In addition to the individual background properties, you can use the `background` property as shorthand for defining each individual background property. When the `background` property is used, the XML browser should first set every individual background property to its default. Once that is complete, the XML browser sets the individual properties that need to be adjusted to the explicit value expressed in the `background` statement. The syntax of this command is

```
background: <background-attachment> || <background-color> ||
            <background-image> || <background-position> ||
            <background-repeat> | inherit
```

Each of the properties that are reference by the shorthand background settings have been previously defined, and the values available for them with the `background` element are the same as if they were used along.

In the following code, the `background` attribute is applied to both the root `BOOK` element of the document and individual block elements such as `BOOK_TITLE` and `INTRO`:

```
BODY { background: url("bground.gif") white fixed top
                   left no-repeat }
H1 { background: red center repeat-x}
BLOCKQUOTE { background: green 75% center }
```

Putting Together a Style Sheet

Now that you have all of the pieces to format your XML document, you need to put them together with an XML document. To do that, lets use the complete XML document example from Chapter 10. This document is a valid document that includes an internal DTD. The second line, highlighted in bold text to make it easier for you to find, adds the style sheet, `project.css`, to the document.

```
<?xml version="1.0"?>
<?xml-stylesheet type="text/css" href="project.css" ?>
<!DOCTYPE PROJECT_DB SYSTEM "project.dtd">
<PROJECT_DB>
  <PROJECT pid="0511-001" director="Kell Attain"
           type="Web Development" start_date="11/1/05">
    <PROJ_NAME> Xray Mind Learners Web Site </PROJ_NAME>
    <CONTACT cid="kat001" contractor="WebRavin"
             pref_contact="email" type="primary">
     <NAME> Kell Attain </NAME>
      <ADDRESS>
         Web Ravin Consulting, 661 Oakey Rd, Antilles, OR 99999
      </ADDRESS>
      <PHONE type="business"> 111-555-1111 </PHONE>
      <FAX type="business"> 111-555-2222 </FAX>
      <EMAIL type="business"> kattain@webravin.com </EMAIL>
    </CONTACT>
    <CONTACT cid="fch001" contractor="WebRavin"
             pref_contact="phone" type="marketing">
     <NAME > Francis Chillington </NAME>
      <ADDRESS>
         Web Ravin Consulting, 661 Oakey Rd, Antilles, OR 99999
      </ADDRESS>
      <PHONE type="business"> 111-555-1112 </PHONE>
      <FAX type="business"> 111-555-2222 </FAX>
      <EMAIL type="business"> fchillington@webravin.com </EMAIL>
    </CONTACT>
    <CONTACT cid="lfi001" contractor="WebRavin"
             pref_contact="email" type="graphics">
     <NAME > Lara Firewalker </NAME>
      <ADDRESS>
        Web Ravin Consulting, 661 Oakey Rd, Antilles, OR 99999
     </ADDRESS>
      <PHONE type="business"> 111-555-1113 </PHONE>
      <FAX type="business"> 111-555-2222 </FAX>
      <EMAIL type="business"> lfirewalker@webravin.com </EMAIL>
    </CONTACT>
    <NOTES>
      <ENTRY date="11/03/05" contact="kta001">
      Development on the Web site has started. The primary
      graphics - logo | backgrounds | navigation
      system - should be done by 11/8/00.
      </ENTRY>
```

```
  </NOTES>
</PROJECT>
<PROJECT pid="0511-002" director="Tom Phannon"
         type="Database Development">
  <PROJ_NAME> XML Database for Site Visitors </PROJ_NAME>
  <CONTACT cid="tph001" contractor="WebRavin"
           pref_contact="telephone" type="primary">
   <NAME> Tom Phannon </NAME>
    <ADDRESS>
      Web Ravin Consulting, 661 Oakey Rd, Antilles, OR 99999
    </ADDRESS>
    <PHONE type="business"> 111-555-1122 </PHONE>
    <FAX type="business"> 111-555-2222 </FAX>
    <EMAIL type="business"> tphannon@webravin.com </EMAIL>
  </CONTACT>
  <NOTES>
    <ENTRY date="11/10/05" contact="tph001">
      Database structure is complete. Ready to start
      propagating the data.
    </ENTRY>
  </NOTES>
</PROJECT>
<PROJECT pid="0511-003" contractor="Lara Firewalker"
         type="Tech Support AI">
  <PROJ_NAME> House of Glass </PROJ_NAME>
  <CONTACT cid="swi001" contractor="WebRavin"
           pref_contact="email" type="primary">
   <NAME> Shamu Wagonride </NAME>
    <ADDRESS>
      Web Ravin Consulting, 661 Oakey Rd, Antilles, OR 99999
    </ADDRESS>
    <PHONE type="business"> 111-555-1133 </PHONE>
    <FAX type="business"> 111-555-2222 </FAX>
    <EMAIL type="personal"> shamu@wagonride.com </EMAIL>
  </CONTACT>
  <NOTES>
    <ENTRY date="11/01/05" contact="swa001">
    AI logic model software has been picked out and ordered,
    as well as the equipment required to run it. Networking
    (MIS) has been notified of the machine's arrival and
    networking needs.
```

```
        </ENTRY>
        <ENTRY date="11/11/05" contact="swa001">
        MIS has received equipment and software and is
        starting the installation. Expected date for network
        connection is 11/15/05.
        </ENTRY>
      </NOTES>
    </PROJECT>
  </PROJECT_DB>
```

The preceding document, when viewed without a style sheet, appears as a simple listing of the information that is contained within the document, as seen in Figure 13-1.

The following is the style sheet for the <PROJECT_DB> document in the previous code example. It only uses the style properties discussed in this chapter. Each of the styles is written in the order that the element first appears in the document. This is

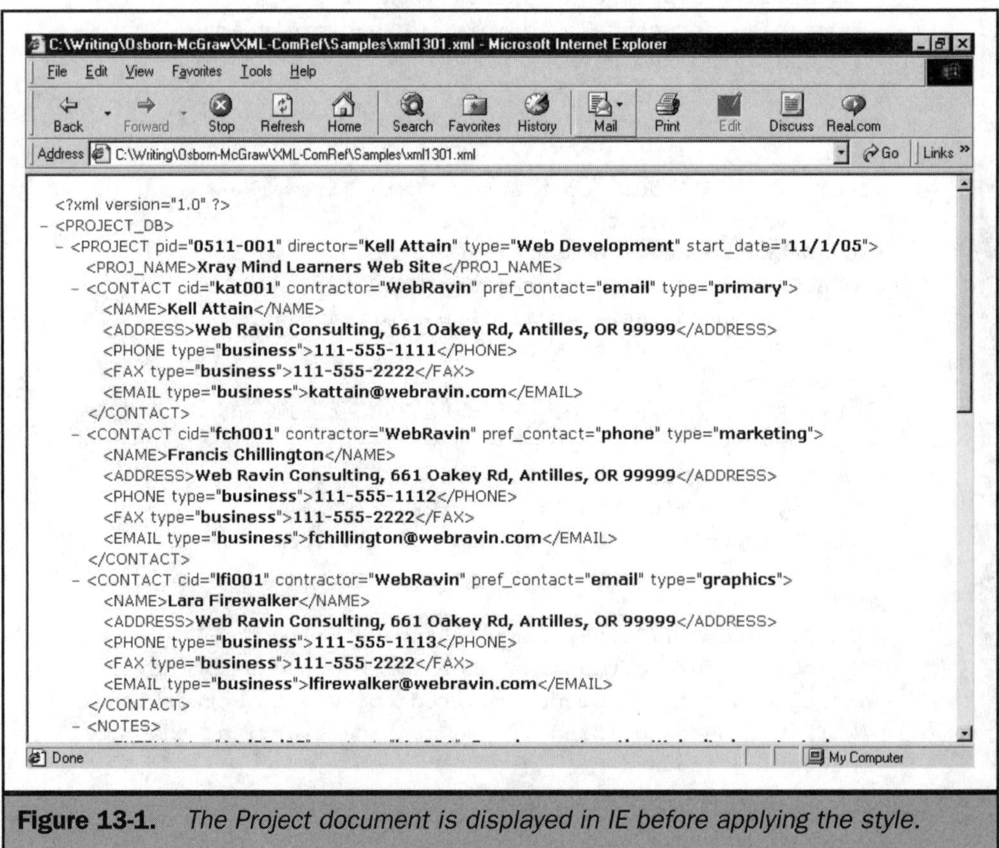

Figure 13-1. *The Project document is displayed in IE before applying the style.*

simply one way to make your style sheets easier to follow and is by no means necessary for creating a usable style sheet:

```
PROJECT_DB { font-style: normal;
             color: 000000 }
PROJECT    { display: block;
             background: blue;
             font-family: sans-serif;
             margin: 1cm }
PROJ_NAME  { display: block;
             background: #FF0000;
             font-size: larger;
             font-weight: bold;
             word-spacing: 2em;
             color: white ;
             font-family: Arial, Helvetica, sans-serif;
             border: #FF0000;
             border-style: double;
             border-top-width: medium;
             border-right-width: medium;
             border-bottom-width: medium;
             border-left-width: medium}
CONTACT    { display: block;
             padding: 5pt;
             text-indent: 1cm }
NAME       { display: block;
             font-variant: small-caps;
             font-size: medium;
             font-weight: bold;
             color: red;
             text-decoration: overline;}
ADDRESS    { display: block;
             font-style: italic;
             font-size: smaller;
             color: white}
PHONE      { display: block;
             font-weight: bold;
             font-size: smaller;
             color: white}
FAX        { display: block;
             font-weight: bold;
             font-size: smaller;
             color: white}
```

```
EMAIL      { display: block;
             font-weight: bold;
             font-style: italic;
             color: white}
NOTES      { display: block;
             font-weight: bold;
             font-style: italic;
             color: white;
             padding: 3em}
ENTRY      { display: block;}
```

Once the style sheet has been applied to the XML document, the pages start to look like formatted information that has important information to share, rather than rows of garbled text. You can see this document formatted with the style sheet in Figure 13-2.

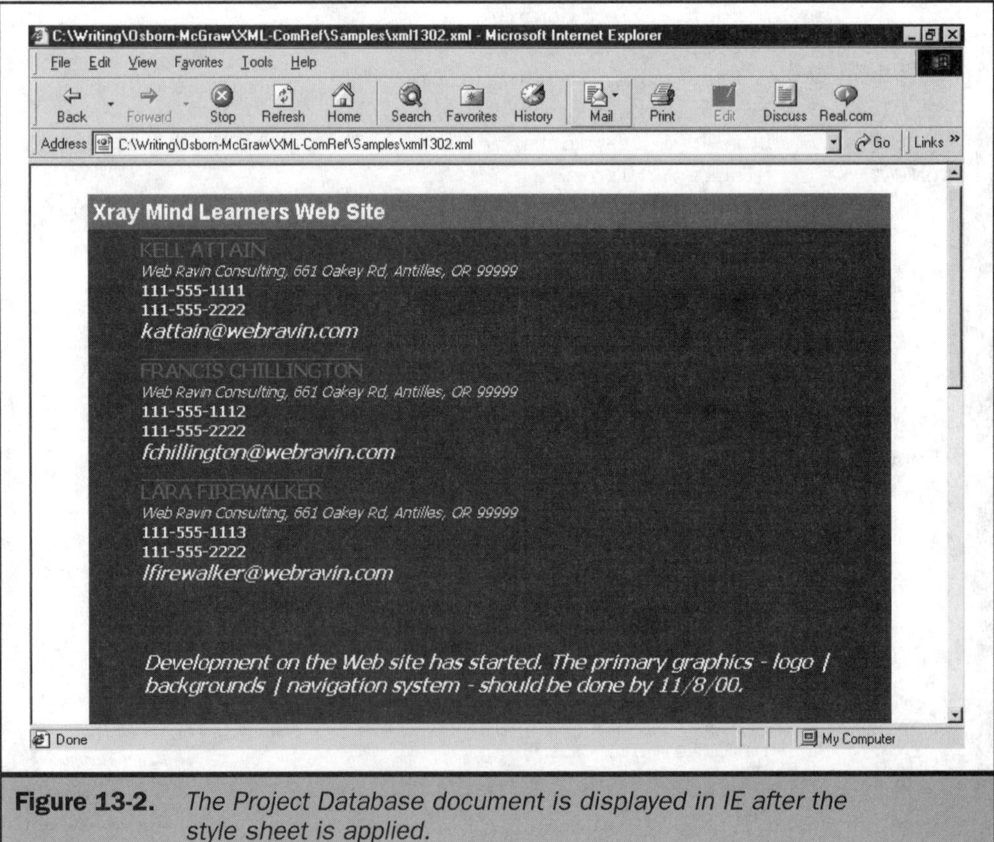

Figure 13-2. *The Project Database document is displayed in IE after the style sheet is applied.*

Summary

As you can see from this chapter, there are a lot of different properties for controlling the appearance of your XML documents using CSS. These properties include styles for controlling the appearance of your fonts, text, background images, background colors, document and object margins, document padding, and object outlines. All of these properties work together to create well-formatted documents to be used on the Internet or your corporate intranet.

The next chapter takes a deeper look at the more complicated formatting issues of using CSS to format your XML documents, including how elements are displayed and positioned on both your screen and printed page.

Chapter 14

CSS: The Next Step

CSS provide a wide variety of ways to modify your documents automatically and format them in such a way that all Web browsers or other XML software that support either Cascading Style Sheets 1 (CSS1) or Cascading Style Sheets 2 (CSS2) can display your documents. These modification and formatting effects include

- Adding content to your document
- Using pseudo-classes and pseudo-elements to affect parts of element content that are not referencable in any other way
- Controlling the visual formatting of your elements
- Personalizing your cursors
- Exploring the different types of media and creating style sheets for each type

Adding Content

CSS2 enables you to generate some content automatically as part of the formatting of your XML document. For instance, you can use the style sheet to create outlines that are properly indented with different numbering systems for each level of the outline. You can create automatically generated object counters, add line numbering systems, and add graphical list markers. By the incorporation of CSS2's content property, document authors have been given the ability to force applications to create information on the fly as the document is being rendered. Because the automatic numbering systems are created while the document is being drawn, line numbers can be recalculated on the fly whenever a document changes, rather than having to be inserted painstakingly by hand.

There are a variety of properties and parameters, listed next, that are used to provide the ability to automatically insert information into your document.

- **`:before`** Inserts content before the current object
- **`:after`** Inserts content after the current object
- **`content`** Specifies the content to add to the document
- **`counter`** Adds an automatic number to an object
- **`counter-increment`** Increments the number used with the counter property
- **`counter-reset`** Resets the counter to zero or any other preset value

Adding `:before`

`:before` is a pseudo-element that is used to insert the information specified in the `content` parameter before every instance of the tag or tags that the `:before` selector has been applied to. `:before` uses a single parameter value: `content`. The `content` parameter is used to identify either the string of text or the Uniform Resource Locator (URL) of the file that will be inserted into your document.

The following example contains two files. The first is the CSS document that inserts a small blue ball, created with the blueball.gif file, before the start of every PROJECTTITLE element:

```
PROJECTTITLE:before {content: url("blueball.gif")}
```

After you save your CSS document as project.css, you are ready to create your XML document. This document, shown in the following example, needs to incorporate the project.css file, as well as include the <PROJECTTITLE> elements that will be used as the markers for inserting the small blue bullets in the images.

```
<?xml version="1.0" encoding="UTF-8"?>
<?xml-stylesheet type="text/css" href="project.css"?>
<!DOCTYPE PROJECTDB "projects.dtd">
<PROJECTDB>
  <PROJECT>
    <PROJECTTITLE> WebRavin Web site </PROJECTTITLE>
    <DEVELOPER> H. de Leon </DEVELOPER>
  </PROJECT>
  <PROJECT>
    <PROJECTTITLE> Moonlight Chronicles Web site </PROJECTTITLE>
    <DEVELOPER> L. de Leon </DEVELOPER>
  </PROJECT>
</PROJECTDB>
```

The above code displays the text and images shown in Figure 14-1.

The :before *is not supported by Microsoft Internet Explorer 5 but is supported by Netscape Navigator 6.*

ADDING STYLE

Adding :after

:after is a pseudo-element that is used to insert the information specified in the content parameter after every instance of the tag or tags that it has been applied to. It uses a single parameter value: content. The content parameter itself is used to identify either the string of text or the URL of the file that will be inserted into your document.

The following example contains two files. The first is the CSS document that inserts a small blue ball, created with the blueball.gif file, after the end of every <DEVELOPER> element:

```
DEVELOPER:after {content: url("blueball.gif")}
```

After you save your CSS document as project.css, you are ready to create you're your second document shown in the following code. This XML document needs to incorporate the project.css file, as well as include the <DEVELOPER> elements that will be used as the markers for inserting the small blue bullets in the text.

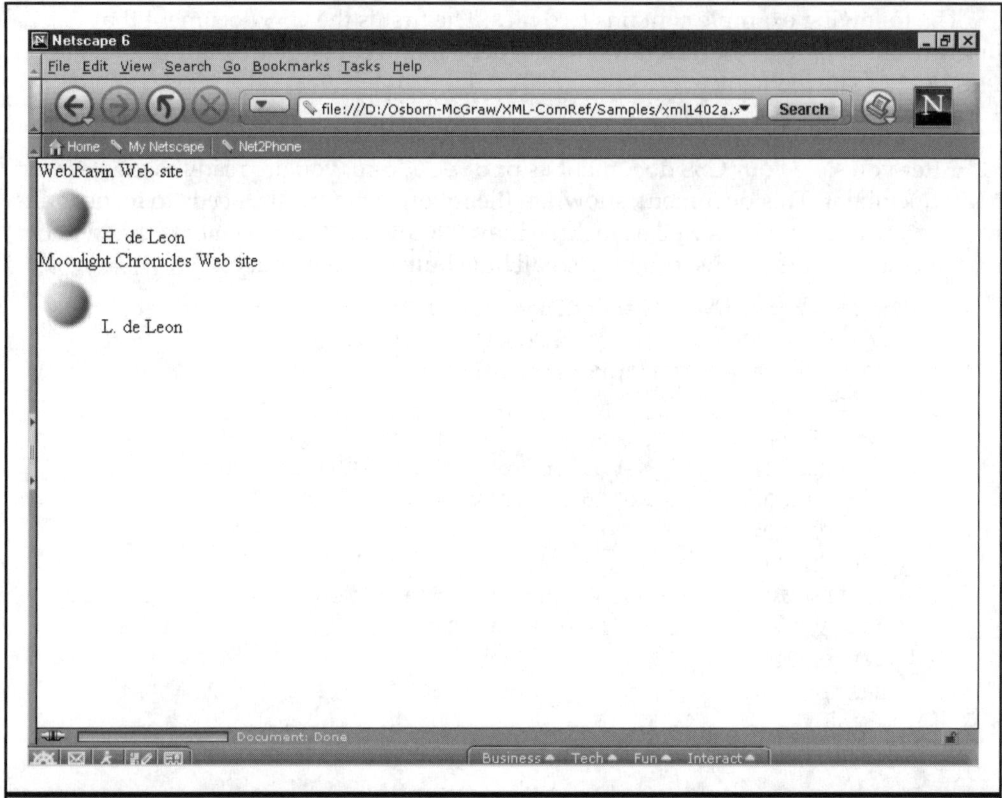

Figure 14-1. *The results of using* `:before` *to add an image before each developer's name are shown in Netscape 6.*

```
<?xml version="1.0" encoding="UTF-8"?>
<?xml-stylesheet type="text/css" href="project.css"?>
<!DOCTYPE PROJECTDB "projects.dtd">
<PROJECTDB>
  <PROJECT>
    <PROJECTTITLE> WebRavin Web site </PROJECTTITLE>
    <DEVELOPER> H. de Leon </DEVELOPER>
  </PROJECT>
  <PROJECT>
    <PROJECTTITLE> Moonlight Chronicles Web site </PROJECTTITLE>
    <DEVELOPER> L. de Leon </DEVELOPER>
  </PROJECT>
</PROJECTDB>
```

The previous code displays the text and images shown in Figure 14-2.

The `:after` *property is not supported by Microsoft Internet Explorer 5 but is supported by Netscape Navigator 6.*

Creating Counters and Automatic Numbering

The `counter`, `counter-increment`, and `counter-reset` properties all work together to create an automatic numbering system within your document. You can create a wide variety of numbering systems—everything from outline styled numbers to roman numerals to combination part numbers such as 5.1 to represent page 1 of part 5.

The `content` property inserts the current value of a named counter by using either the `counter(id)` or `counter(id, list-style-type)` functions as values. The `counter-increment` property adds one to the value of the counter. Finally, the `counter-reset` property sets the counter back to 0 or another predetermined value.

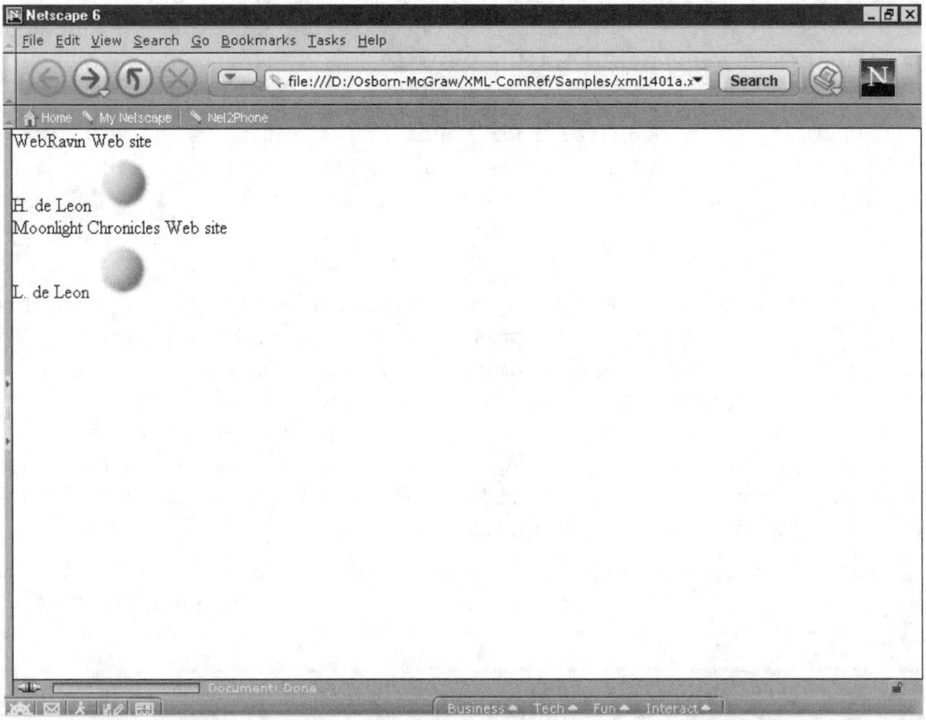

Figure 14-2. *The results of using* `:after` *to add an image after each developer's name are shown in Netscape 6.*

For example, let's suppose you want to number each PROJECT in a list of consulting projects starting from 1, but you want to reset the counting in each new TOPICAREA. You can do that with the following rules:

```
PROJECT          {counter-increment: proj-num}
TOPICAREA        {counter-reset: proj-num}
PROJECT:before {content: counter(proj-num) }
```

You can reset back to a number other than 0 by specifying the integer to reset to after the counter name in `counter-reset`. For example, to reset the counter to 10 use the `counter-reset` property in the following fasion:

```
TOPICAREA          {counter-reset: proj-num 10}
```

You can also increment by an integer other than 1 by specifying it in `counter-increment` after the counter name. For example, the following code increments the counter by 2 every time the PROJECT element is found:

```
PROJECT          {counter-increment: proj-num +2}
```

Finally, the `content` property can have more than one counter and additional content as well as counters. For instance, the following style sheet rules, or statements, number the projects in the form 1.1, 1.2, 1.3, and 2.1, 2.2, 2.3, and so on, where the first number indicates the TOPICAREA and the second the PROJECT:

```
PROJECT          {counter-increment: proj-num}
TOPICAREA        {counter-reset: proj-num}
TOPICAREA        {counter-increment: topic-num}
PROJECT:before {content:
                    counter(topic-num) "." counter(proj-num) }
```

Although these examples use Latin numerals, you can use any of the options that are available with list bullets. You can pass a second argument to the `counter()` function to specify a different number format. Available formats include `disc`, `circle`, `square`, `decimal`, `decimal-leading-zero`, `lower-roman`, `upper-roman`, `lower-greek`, `lower-alpha`, `lower-latin`, `upper-alpha`, `upper-latin`, `hebrew`, `armenian`, `georgian`, `cjk-ideographic`, `hiragana`, `katakana`, `hiragana-iroha`, and `katakana-iroha`. For example, to number the projects using Japanese numerals in hiragana, you would write

```
PROJECT:before {content: counter(topic-num, hiragana)
                       "." counter(proj-num, hiragana) }
```

Using CSS Pseudo-Classes and Pseudo-Elements

Pseudo-class selectors select elements based on aspects other than the name, attributes, or content of the element. For example, a pseudo-class may be based on the position of the mouse, the object that has the focus, or the status of a link. A pseudo-element allows you to access content within your document that is only identifiable by its position within an object.

An element may repeatedly change its pseudo-classes as the reader interacts with the document. Some pseudo-classes are mutually exclusive, but most can be applied simultaneously to the same element and can be placed anywhere within an element selector. When pseudo-classes do conflict, the cascading order determines which rules are activated.

Pseudo-elements, on the other hand, tend towards maintaining the same relationship within a document. For example, you can use pseudo-elements to mark the first letter of a paragraph or the first line of a paragraph.

The `first-child`, `:first-line`, and `:first-letter` pseudo-class and pseudo-elements are discussed in the following sections.

Working with `:first-child`

The `:first-child` pseudo-class selects the first child element of the specified element, regardless of its type. For example, in the following sample, the first element following a `TOPICAREA` element, would be designated by this style sheet rule and have any characters it contains in bold:

```
TOPICAREA:first-child {font-style: bold}
```

You can also specify that the first child element of a specific series is the element to be selected. For instance, in the following example, the first element following a `PROJECT` child of `TOPICAREA` element is selected:

```
TOPICAREA>PROJECT:first-child {font-style: bold}
```

Working with `:first-line`

The `:first-line` pseudo-element applies special style properties to the first line of a block element, such as the first line of a paragraph. It cannot be used with any other style of element such as a table or inline string of text.

This pseudo-element works similarly to inline elements, but because it isn't an actual element itself, it has some restrictions on the other CSS properties that can be used with it. The only properties that can be applied to the `:first-line` element are listed in Table 14-1.

The following code forces the first line of the `PROJECTTITLE` to appear in 14 point* (pt), aqua, Arial text, small caps:

```
PROJECTTITLE:first-line { font-size: 14pt;
                          line-height: 16pt;
                          font-color= aqua;
                          font-style="Arial";
                          font-variant= small-caps}
```

<table>
<tr><th>CSS Property</th><th>Property Syntax</th></tr>
<tr><td>background</td><td>background-attachment: scroll | fixed | inherit</td></tr>
<tr><td></td><td>background-color: <<i>color-name</i>> | <<i>color-RGB</i>> | transparent | inherit</td></tr>
<tr><td></td><td>background-image: <<i>uri</i>> | none | inherit</td></tr>
<tr><td></td><td>background-position: [[<<i>percentage</i>> | <<i>length</i>>]{1,2} | [top | center | bottom] | [left | center | right]] | inherit</td></tr>
<tr><td></td><td>background-repeat: repeat | repeat-x | repeat-y | no-repeat | inherit</td></tr>
<tr><td>clear</td><td>clear: none | left | right | both | inherit</td></tr>
<tr><td>color</td><td>color: <<i>color-name</i>> | <<i>color-RGB</i>> | inherit</td></tr>
<tr><td>font</td><td>font-family : <<i>family-name</i>> | <<i>generic-family</i>> | inherit</td></tr>
<tr><td></td><td>font-size: integer | +(1 to 9) | -(1 to 9)</td></tr>
<tr><td></td><td>font-style: normal | italic | oblique | inherit</td></tr>
<tr><td></td><td>font-variant: normal | small-caps | inherit</td></tr>
<tr><td></td><td>font-weight: normal | bold | bolder | lighter | 100 | 200 | 300 | 400 | 500 | 600 | 700 | 800 | 900 | inherit</td></tr>
<tr><td>letter-spacing</td><td>letter-spacing: normal | <<i>length</i>> | auto | inherit</td></tr>
<tr><td>text-decoration</td><td>text-decoration: none | [underline || overline || line-through || blink] | inherit</td></tr>
<tr><td>text-transform</td><td>text-transform: capitalize | uppercase | lowercase | none | inherit</td></tr>
<tr><td>vertical-align (only if float is none)</td><td>vertical-align: baseline | sub | super | top | text-top | middle | bottom | text-bottom | <<i>percentage</i>> | <<i>length</i>> | inherit</td></tr>
<tr><td>word-spacing</td><td>word-spacing: normal | <<i>length</i>> | inherit</td></tr>
</table>

Table 14-1. *CSS Properties Supported by* :first-line

The previous style sheet code would be saved in the style sheet file `projects.dtd`, which is added to the XML document using the `<?xml-stylesheet?>` instruction. The style sheet rules in `projects.dtd` forces each of the project title first lines to appear in 14 pt, aqua, Arial text:

```
<?xml version="1.0" encoding="UTF-8"?>
<?xml-stylesheet type="text/css" href="project.css"?>
<!DOCTYPE PROJECTDB "projects.dtd">
<PROJECTDB>
  <PROJECT>
    <PROJECTTITLE> WebRavin Web site - Covering SMIL, XML, XHTML</PROJECTTITLE>
    <DEVELOPER> H. de Leon </DEVELOPER>
  </PROJECT>
  <PROJECT>
    <PROJECTTITLE> Moonlight Chronicles Web site </PROJECTTITLE>
    <DEVELOPER> L. de Leon </DEVELOPER>
  </PROJECT>
</PROJECTDB>
```

The `:first-line` pseudoelement is not supported in Internet Explorer 5 but is supported by Netscape Navigator 6.

Working with `:first-letter`

The `:first-letter` pseudo-element is most commonly used to create graphical effects, such as drop caps and initial caps, in text. These effects can be either inline or floating, depending upon the status of the float attribute of `:first-letter`.

The CSS2 specification, which identifies which characters, such as quotation marks, are a part of the first letter, creates the rules that will be used when deciding upon how an initial letter is outlined. Quotation marks are generally considered to be part of the first letter of a paragraph, while parentheses and ellipses are ignored if they occur in the position of a first letter; this is because they are not considered general characters. Some languages have specific rules that control how special letter combinations are dealt with. Languages that have special two-letter sound combinations, such as *Æ*, are treated as a single character, and both are contained within the `:first-letter` pseudo-element.

Table 14-2 lists the properties that can be applied to the `:first-letter` pseudo-elements.

CSS Property	Property Syntax
background	background-attachment: scroll | fixed | inherit
	background-color: *<color-name>* | *<color-RGB>* | transparent | inherit
	background-image: *<uri>* | none | inherit
	background-position: [[*<percentage>* | *<length>*]{1,2} | [top | center | bottom] | [left | center | right]] | inherit
	background-repeat: repeat | repeat-x | repeat-y | no-repeat | inherit
border	border-bottom-width: thin | medium | thick | *<length>* | inherit
	border-left-width: thin | medium | thick | *<length>* | inherit
	border-right-width: thin | medium | thick | *<length>* | inherit
	border-top-width: thin | medium | thick | *<length>* | inherit
	border-width: [thin | medium | thick | *<length>*]{1,4} | inherit
clear	clear: none | left | right | both | inherit
color	color: *<color-name>* | *<color-RGB>* | inherit
float	float: left | right | none | inherit
font	font-family : *<family-name>* | *<generic-family>* | inherit
	font-size: integer | +(1 to 9) | -(1 to 9)
	font-style: normal | italic | oblique | inherit
	font-variant: normal | small-caps | inherit

Table 14-2. *CCS Properties That Can Be Applied to* :first-letter (continued)

CSS Property	Property Syntax
	`font-weight: normal | bold | bolder | lighter | 100 | 200 | 300 | 400 | 500 | 600 | 700 | 800 | 900 | inherit`
`line-height`	line-height: normal | *<number>* | *<length>* | *<percentage>* | inherit
`margin`	margin: : [*<length>* | *<percentage>*] {1,4} | inherit
	margin-bottom: [*<length>* | *<percentage>*] | inherit
	margin-left: [*<length>* | *<percentage>*] | inherit
	margin-right: [*<length>* | *<percentage>* | inherit
	margin-top: [*<length>* | *<percentage>*] | inherit
`padding`	padding: : [*<length>* | *<percentage>*] {1,4} | inherit
	padding-bottom: [*<length>* | *<percentage>*] | inherit
	padding-left: [*<length>* | *<percentage>*] | inherit
	padding-right: [*<length>* | *<percentage>*] | inherit
	padding-top: [*<length>* | *<percentage>*] | inherit
`text-decoration`	text-decoration: none | [underline || overline || line-through || blink] | inherit
`text-transform`	text-transform: capitalize | uppercase | lowercase | none | inherit

Table 14-2. *CCS Properties That Can Be Applied to* `:first-letter` (continued)

CSS Property	Property Syntax
vertical-align (only if float is none)	vertical-align: baseline | sub | super | top | text-top | middle | bottom | text-bottom | <*percentage*> | <*length*> | inherit

Table 14-2. *CCS Properties That Can Be Applied to* :first-letter (continued)

The following example will make a drop-cap initial letter on each project name that spans two lines. The first statement sets the default size of the PROJECTTITLE element to 12pts on a 12pt line. The second statement sets the first letter of each PROJECTTITLE element to 200%, or twice the size, of the default paragraph and has it displayed in italicized bold font:

```
PROJECTTITLE { font-size: 12pt; line-height: 12pt }
PROJECTTITLE:first-letter { font-size: 200%;
                              font-style: italic;
                              font-weight: bold;
                              float: left }
```

The :first-letter *pseudo-element is not supported in Internet Explorer 5 but is supported by Netscape Navigator 6.*

Visually Formatting Your Objects

CSS2 adds many new features for formatting that provide more control over the visual layout of your XML document. The display property has many new values that expand on the basic block and inline types of CSS1. You can control the height and width of all object boxes. CSS2 also gives you the ability to modify your document objects' visibility, clip size, color, and alignment and control how an object's contents are dealt with if overflow should occur. The cursor property, introduced in CSS2, enables you to identify the style of cursor displayed over your XML document objects.

display Property

The display property was originally designed to provide control over the layout appearance of objects in XML and Hypertext Markup Language (HTML) documents. It was used to control the manner in which other CSS properties would interact with each other on the same object and to control how objects would interact with each other on a page. The expansion of the `display` property in CSS2 provides more complete layout options, most notably in tables. In CSS2, there are 17 possible values of the `display` property:

- `inline`
- `block`
- `list-item`
- `run-in`
- `compact`
- `marker`
- `table`
- `inline-table`
- `table-row-group`
- `table-header-group`
- `table-footer-group`
- `table-row`
- `table-column-group`
- `table-column`
- `table-cell`
- `table-caption`
- `none`

Each of these values will be described in more detail in the following sections.

`block` elements are drawn by breaking out space around the objects, forcing a buffer of space around their contents. `inline` elements work without setting aside separate space. `inline` elements are like string of beads. If one bead is green and the others are black, as you slide the beads back and forth, the green bead will always stay in the same position in relation to the black beads, but will change position in relation to the ends of the string. `table` elements are various parts of a grid. A `table` is a grid in which everything is static in its position. `block` objects are fixed, and, move up and down but not left and right as content is added before and after them. `block` items include such items as tables, lists, and list items. Most display types are just modifications of the main `block` or `inline` types.

`inline` Objects

`inline` object boxes are laid horizontally in a wrapping row starting from the top of the document or a `block` object box. You can think of this as how you build with LEGOs. Between these boxes, the variety of horizontal margins, borders, and padding spaces are implemented. You can also align these types of boxes against each other vertically in a variety of ways including character baselines, box bottoms, or box tops. In HTML, a `<span>` element is your typical inline object. It creates boundaries around information so that the information can be formatted without adjusting the visual appearance of the information.

In CSS1, the `block` *value was the default display type of all objects, but that has changed in CSS2. Elements are now automatically displayed as* `inline` *unless otherwise designated.*

In the following example the style sheet designates DEVELOPER as an inline object:

```
DEVELOPER {display: inline;}
```

block Objects

block objects are laid out vertically, one on top of the other. The first block is laid flush in the upper-left corner of the containing block, then the second block is placed below it, also flush against the left edge of the containing block. The vertical distance between each block is defined by the individual block's margin and padding properties. For example, the following style sheet rule identifies the PROJECT, TOPICAREA, and PROJECTTITLE elements as individual blocks

```
PROJECT, TOPICAREA, PROJECTTITLE  { display: block }
```

Figure 14-3 shows a sample PROJECTDB document when this rule (and only this rule) is applied.

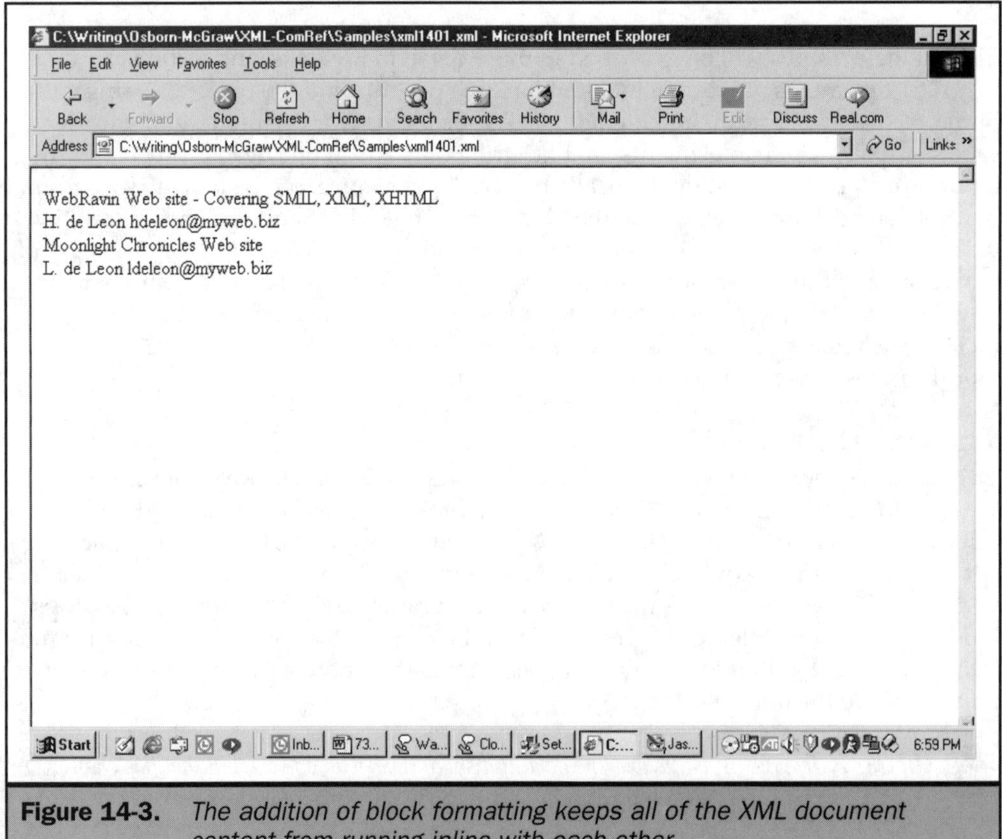

Figure 14-3. *The addition of block formatting keeps all of the XML document content from running inline with each other.*

The DEVELOPER *and the* CONTACT *information are shown on the same line in Figure 14-1 because they are inline by default; however, when a block element follows an inline element, a line break is required before and after the block element.*

The following is the code for the document displayed in Figure 14-3:

```
<?xml version="1.0" encoding="UTF-8"?>
<?xml-stylesheet type="text/css" href="xml1401.css"?>
<PROJECTDB>
  <PROJECT>
    <PROJECTTITLE> WebRavin Web site - Covering SMIL, XML, XHTML</PROJECTTITLE>
    <DEVELOPER> H. de Leon </DEVELOPER>
    <CONTACT> hdeleon@myweb.biz</CONTACT>
  </PROJECT>
  <PROJECT>
    <PROJECTTITLE> Moonlight Chronicles Web site </PROJECTTITLE>
    <DEVELOPER> L. de Leon </DEVELOPER>
    <CONTACT> ldeleon@myweb.biz</CONTACT>
  </PROJECT>
</PROJECTDB>
```


none

The value of `none` forces the element to generate no visible display effect of any kind for formatting the content of the element. When `display = none`, the box is not just invisible, it doesn't exist. Elements with a `display` value of `none` will not have any effect on the layout of the document. Even the child and descendant elements of an object with a `display` value of `none` don't generate boxes, even if the `display` property is set for them.

compact and run-in Values

A `display` value of `compact` and `run-in` values can identify either a block or an inline element, depending on the context that element is used in. Depending upon the final rendered status of the element, some CSS properties will not be available.

If it will fit, a `compact` box is placed in the margin of the block box that follows it. If the box that follows it is not a `block` box, or if the `compact` box will not fit in the margin, then it is rendered simply as another `block` box.

The `run-in` value enables you to format normal `block` elements as the first inline block of the next `block` element in the code. If the next element is not a `block` element, then the `run-in` element is formatted as a `block` element.

marker Value

Setting the `display` property to the `marker` value identifies a block that's formed by content generated with the `:before` and `:after` pseudo-elements in the style sheet, rather than copied in from the XML document. The `marker` value can only be used with block-level elements.

Table Display Values

One of the most important new features in CSS2, especially for XML developers who often create tabular structures with tags that look nothing like HTML's table tags, is support for table layout of elements. CSS2 adds support for styling elements as parts of tables using these ten values of the `display` property:

- **inline-table** Creates an inline table, not the standard block table
- **table** Creates a standard HTML formatted block table
- **table-caption** Creates a caption formatted to rest near one edge of a table
- **table-cell** Formats text within the confines of a table cell, requiring that the element be within another element displayed in table format
- **table-column** Identifies a single column in a table
- **table-column-group** Identifies a group of columns in a table
- **table-footer-group** Identifies a group of `table-footer` elements
- **table-header-group** Identifies a group of `table-header` elements
- **table-row** Identifies a single row in a table
- **table-row-group** Identifies a group of rows in a table

For example, setting the `display` property to `table` indicates that the selected element is a block-level container for various smaller children that will be arranged in a grid. The `inline-table` value forces the table to function as an inline object, enabling text to float along its side and enabling multiple tables to be placed side by side. The `table-caption` value formats an element as a table caption. The `table-row-group`, `table-header-group`, and `table-footer-group` values create groups of data cells that work as a single row, as if it was defined using the `table-row` value. The `table-column-group` creates a group of data cells that work as a single column that was defined using the `table-column` value. XML elements that appear in table cells have, naturally enough, a `display` property with the value `table-cell`.

For example, if you were to configure a project in a table-like structure, you might set each `PROJECT` element as a table, with each `DEVELOPER` as a table row and the contact and name information in table cells. The style sheet to create this effect might include these three rules:

```
PROJECT   { display: table }
DEVELOPER { display: table-row }
CONTACT   { display: table-cell }
NAME      { display: table-cell }
```

Setting Object Position

CSS2 provides the document author with control over the position of individual objects within a document. You can place objects in layers and move them independently of each other. All of this position manipulation is done with one of these four values of the `position` property:

- **`relative`** Objects are offset from their static positions.
- **`absolute`** Objects are placed at a specific position relative to the box they're contained in.
- **`static`** This is the default layout.
- **`fixed`** Objects are placed at a specific point in the window or on the page.

Relative Positioning

Relative positioning allows document objects to follow the natural flow of a document layout. As documents are created, the developer places items in the document according to the normal flow of the objects and text and his or her idea for the ultimate appearance of the document. In XML, the relative layout of a document is the series of element contents strung together as inline elements. This is essentially the default formatting of objects used by many XML creators who don't wish to display their information through a Web browser.

Developers often wish to provide more control over their document; formatting, even over their relatively positioned objects, is often necessary. The steps involved in relatively positioning objects include the original rendering of the various XML objects on the document in the browser. After the rendering is complete, the objects may be shifted relative to their current position using the various CSS positioning attributes affected by the `position` CSS property value. This adjustment in an object's position is known as *relative positioning*. By using relative positioning, altering the position of an object has no effect on the objects following it; thus boxes can overlap, since relatively positioned boxes retain all of their normal flow sizes and spacing.

You can generate a relatively positioned object by setting the `position` property to `relative`. Its *offset*, or distance it will be moved from its originally intended position, is controlled by the `bottom`, `left`, `right`, and `top` properties. By changing these properties in a scripting language such as JavaScript, you can even move objects in your document, including images or text, just by adjusting the offset values of the relatively positioned object. For example, the following rule moves the `PROJECTTITLE` element 50 pixels up and 65 pixels to the left from where it would normally be. By having a script that looks for a particular `PROJECTTITLE` element, this object could be moved within your screen while the document is actually being viewed and not just drawn:

```
PROJECTTITLE { display: inline;
               position: relative;
               top: 50px;
               left: 65px}
```

ADDING STYLE

For more information on using XML with JavaScript see Chapter 27.

Absolute Positioning

Absolute positioning is a rigid, although convenient, way to format your document content. An absolutely positioned element is fixed within the space of your document. For example, if you position a `block` object 50 pixels down and over from the top of your XML document, that object is always exactly 50 pixels from the upper-left corner of your document, no matter how big or small the document window or how far down the document you scroll. Absolutely positioned objects scroll up and down with the rest of the document, maintaining their relationship to the top of the document itself, not to the document window.

An absolutely positioned element is placed in reference to the block that contains it. This is often the XML document itself, but it could be an object within the document. Absolutely positioned elements have no impact on the flow of their following siblings, so elements that follow an absolutely positioned one act as if it were not there and as if they were floating above the remainder of the document.

Whenever you place an image, or other object, in an absolute position, you always know exactly where it's located, but you may have problems with the other information on your page if that information isn't also absolutely positioned. Absolutely positioned elements are outside of the natural flow of your XML page and can, therefore, sometimes obscure the information in the regular flow of your page. For example, the following style sheet rule puts the upper-left corner of the `PROJECT` element 60 pixels down and 140 pixels to the right of the upper-left corner of the document window or other box that it's contained in:

```
PROJECT    { display: block;
             position: absolute;
             top: 60px;
             left: 140px }
```

Fixed Positioning

Fixed positioning is a variation on absolute positioning. With fixed positioning, you don't position your object in relation to the document, you position it in relation to the browser window. So instead of scrolling with the rest of the document, the information contained within a fixed positioned object always appears at a specific location in the presentation window without regard to what the rest of the presentation is doing. This enables you to create a constant footer at the bottom of your screen, a constant header at the top of your screen, or any of many other effects.

Elements with fixed position are placed at coordinates relative to the window or page on which they're displayed. If you are viewing a document composed of continuous media, as is standard on a computer screen, the fixed box will not move when the document is scrolled. If the fixed box is located on paged media, such as a book, it will always appear at the same location in relation to the page. This could be in the upper-left corner of a page, smack dab in the middle of a page, or along one edge, for example.

The following CSS example places the upper-left corner of the TOPICAREA element box 30 pixels down and 30 pixels to the right of the upper-left corner of the window it's displayed in or the page it's printed on:

```
TOPICAREA  { display: block;
             position: fixed;
             top: 300px;
             left: 140px}
```

Stacking Elements with the z-index Property

The z-index property controls the stacking order of positioned block boxes. By default the z-index value of every object is placed in order in which the objects appear on the XML document. You adjust the vertical stacking order of your objects by adjusting the value of their z-index property. Objects with larger z-index values are placed on top of objects with smaller z-index values. Whether the objects on the bottom show through is a function of the background properties of the object(s) on top of them. If the backgrounds of the upper-level objects are transparent, at least some of what's below will be visible.

The following style sheet uses absolute positioning with specified z-index values to create a multipart overlay of the project database:

```
TOPICAREA { position: absolute;
            top: 20px;
            left:20px;
            height: 550px;
            width:700px;
            border=1;
            background=yellow;
            z-index: 2}
PROJECT   { position: absolute;
            top: 100px;
            left:50px;
            height: 400px;
            width:600px;
            border=1;
            background=white;
            z-index: 3}
PROJECTTITLE { position: absolute;
               top: 150px;
               left:100px;
               height: 100px;
               width:300px;
               border=1;
               background=pink;
               z-index: 5}
```

The result of the above style sheet is shown in Figure 14-4. The screen shown in Figure 14-4 is created from the following XML document:

```
<?xml version="1.0" encoding="UTF-8"?>
<?xml-stylesheet type="text/css" href="xml1402.css"?>
<PROJECTDB>
  <TOPICAREA>
  <PROJECT>
    <PROJECTTITLE> WebRavin Web site - Covering SMIL, XML, XHTML</PROJECTTITLE>
    <DEVELOPER> H. de Leon </DEVELOPER>
    <CONTACT> hdeleon@myweb.biz</CONTACT>
  </PROJECT>
  </TOPICAREA>
</PROJECTDB>
```

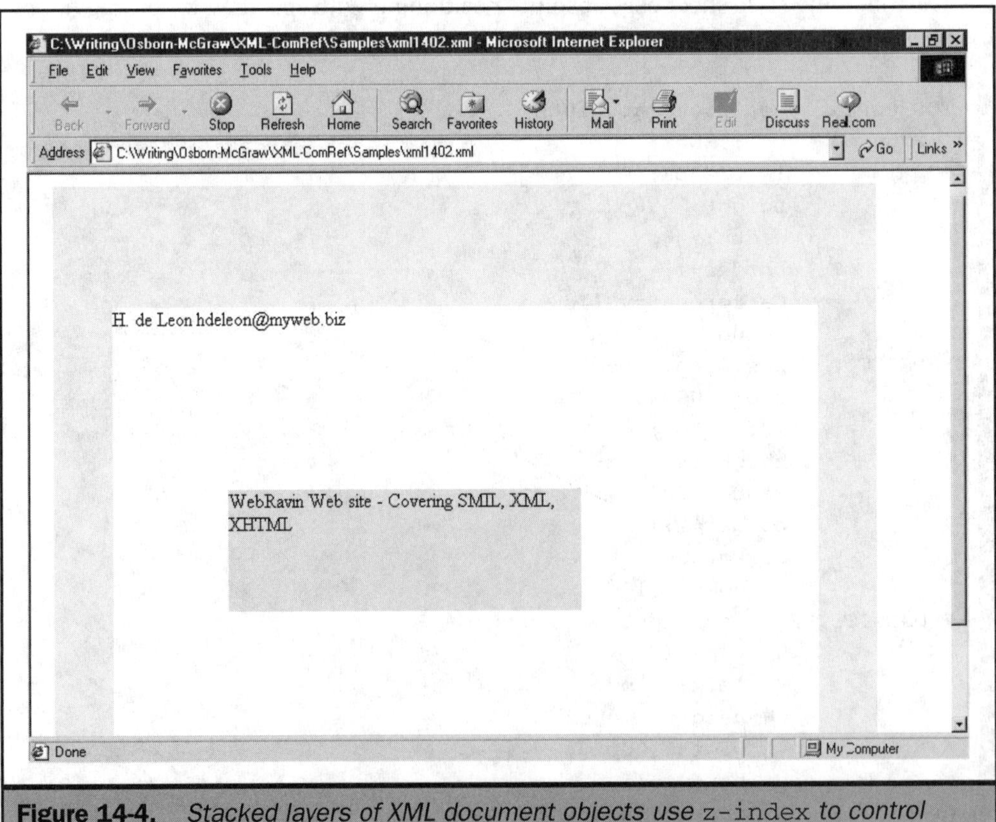

Figure 14-4. *Stacked layers of XML document objects use* `z-index` *to control their vertical stacking order.*

Using `top`

The `top` CSS attribute specifies the distance between the top edge of an object's containing block and the top of the object itself. The syntax of this property is

```
top=length | percentage | auto
```

The property above sets the amount of space from the top of the containment block, which is the offset distance as described in pixels, the percentage of the total height of the current objects containing block, or the value of `top` can be calculated automatically.

The following sample sets the top of the `TOPICAREA` object 20 pixels from the top of the object area that contains it, such as the document, or another element:

```
TOPICAREA { position: absolute;
            top: 20px }
```

Using `left`

The `left` CSS attribute specifies the distance between the interior left edge of an object's containing block and the left edge of the object itself. The syntax of this property is

```
Left = length | percentage | auto
```

The property above allows you to set the amount of space between the left edge of the current object and the left edge of the containing block, which is the offset distance as described in pixels, the percentage of the total height of the current objects containing block, or they can be calculated automatically.

The following sample sets the left edge of the `TOPICAREA` object 20 pixels from the left edge of the element, or document, that contains it:

```
TOPICAREA { position: absolute;
            top: 20px;
            left: 20px }
```

Using `right`

The `right` CSS attribute specifies the distance between the interior right edge of an object's containing block and the right edge of the object itself. The syntax of this property is

```
right=length | percentage | auto
```

The property above sets the amount of space from the right of the containment block, which is the offset distance as described in pixels, the percentage of the total height of the current objects containing block, or the value of `right` can be calculated automatically.

The following sample sets the right of the `PROJECT` object 100 pixels from the top of the object area that contains it, such as the document, or another element:

```
PROJECT { position: absolute;
          top: 20px;
          left: 20px;
          right: 100px }
```

Using bottom

The `bottom` CSS attribute specifies the distance between the interior bottom edge of an object's containing block and the bottom edge of the object itself. The syntax of this property is

```
bottom=length | percentage | auto
```

The property above sets the amount of space from the bottom of the containment block, which is the offset distance as described in pixels, the percentage of the total height of the current objects containing block, or the value of `bottom` can be calculated automatically. The following sample sets the top of the `PROJECT` object 100 pixels above the bottom of the object area that contains it, such as the document, or another element:

```
PROJECT { position: absolute;
          top: 20px;
          left: 20px;
          right: 100px;
          bottom: 100px }
```

Setting Object Size

The default height of a box in which each element appears is calculated from the combined height of the element's contents. The default width of each element's box is calculated from the combined width of the element's contents or the width of the viewable area on the page or screen. Inline elements and table elements that contain text always have these automatically calculated dimensions. However, CSS properties can be used to alter these defaults for block-level elements and replace inline elements by specifying values for any of these six properties:

- **`min-width`** Sets the minimum width that an object can use up
- **`max-width`** Sets the maximum width for the specified object
- **`min-height`** Sets the minimum height that an object can be
- **`max-height`** Sets the maximum height for the selected object
- **`height`** Sets a specific height for the current object
- **`width`** Sets a specific width for the selected object

The `min-height` and `min-width` properties specify the smallest dimensions that the object can be displayed with. The `max-height` and `max-width` properties set a maximum size that an object, regardless of the total size of its contents, can take up on your document. The XML document browser is free to adjust the size of the object's box within these limits. However, if `height` and `width` are set, then they determine exactly the size of the box.

The following style sheet declaration for the PROJECT element sets the minimum width and height of all PROJECT boxes to 75 pixels. It also sets the maximum width and height of the PROJECT boxes to 550 pixels:

```
PROJECT { min-width: 75px;
          max-width: 550px;
          min-height: 75px;
          max-height: 550px }
```

Of all of the object-size controlling properties, the most commonly used are width and height, which are both detailed in the following sections.

Using height

The height of each element's containment block is automatically calculated based on the inherited height of the element's contents. This inherited height is computed based upon three things: the inherited height of each object within the XML document, the width of the screen and its effect on text wrapping, and the specified heights of objects contained within the XML object. Each of these properties can be overridden with the use of the height CSS and HTML attributes.

The height attribute is used to override the inherit height of an element's contents, and it is available to work with practically every type of element that can be affected by CSS. The height attribute specifies the height of the containment block of the element being discussed, and its effect varies greatly, based upon the display value of the object to which it is applied. The syntax of the command is

```
height= length | percentage
```

The length value, as it is associated with height, is any number followed by a unit identifier to specify either a relative or absolute height for the element. Valid values for this attribute include such measurements as 3px, 1cm, 5ex, and so on. The height of your objects can also be expressed as a percentage of the object's original containing block.

Using width

The width property works very similar to the height property. The syntax of the command is

```
width: length | percentage | auto |
```

As with the height property the length value is any number followed by a unit of measurement identifier specifying either a relative or absolute height for the element. Values for this property include a variety of measurements such as 3px, 1cm, 5ex, and so on. Object width can also be expressed as a percentage of the object's original containing block. In addition to the measurement options of the height property, the auto value allows the object's width to be based upon the values of the other properties associated with it, such as height.

Controlling Object Visibility

You can control whether the contents of an element are seen within your XML browser by using the `visibility` property. Using this property allows you to show only the objects that you wish to show and then manipulate their visibility using JavaScript or another scripting language. You can read more about using JavaScript with XML in Chapter 30. The four possible values of this property are

- **`visible`** The contents of the box, including all borders are shown
- **`hidden`** The box's contents and borders are not seen, but they will still take up space on the document. Setting `visibility: hidden` is not the same as setting `display: none`.
- **`collapse`** The same as `hidden` for any object, except a table row or column. However, for table rows and columns, it completely hides (as with `display: none`) the row or column so that no space is taken up by these collapsed elements.
- **`inherit`** The same visibility setting as its parent element is used.

In the following set of style sheet descriptors, the visibility of the `CONTACT` information is set to hidden, while the `PROJECT` itself remains visible:

```
PROJECT { visibility: visible }
CONTACT { visibility: hidden }
```

Controlling Object `overflow` and `clip` Properties

When the size of a box is precisely specified using the `width` and `height` properties, it's entirely possible that its contents may take up more area than the box actually has. The `overflow` property controls how the excess content is dealt with. This property can be set to one of four values:

- **`auto`** Scroll bars are added, if necessary, to enable the user to see excess content.
- **`hidden`** The excess content is simply truncated.
- **`scroll`** Scroll bars are added whether there's overflow or not.
- **`visible`** The complete contents are shown, if necessary, by overriding the size constraints that were placed on the box.

The following example CSS statement creates a `PROJECT` whose `overflow` property is set to `scroll`. This results in the scroll bars being visible all of the time in most CSS2-compatible browsers:

```
PROJECT { width: 75px;
          height: 75px;
          overflow:  scroll }
```

In addition to the `overflow` property, you will typically need to control the `clip` property. These two properties most often work together to control the contents of each individual layer of your document. The `clip` property identifies the portion of an object's content that will be visible when rendered by the XML browser. Generally the clipping region will match the outside borders of the element's box, but using the `clip` property alters this region.

Note *The* `clip` *property applies only to elements with an* `overflow` *attribute that is set to a value other than* `visible`.

In CSS2, you can only clip to rectangular regions. Set the `clip` property to `rect(top, bottom, left, right)` where *top, bottom, left,* and *right* are the offsets on each side. If the clipped object still exceeds the viewable area of the browser's window; the contents will be further clipped to fit in the window. The following rule uses the `clip` property with a `PROJECT` block element:

```
PROJECT { clip: rect(5px, 5px, 5px, 5px);
          overflow: auto }
```

Controlling Your Cursors

The cursor is the arrow/hand/insertion bar/other icon that indicates the position of the mouse pointer on the screen. A cursor is the visible representation of your mouse's logical position that is displayed on the viewable area of your computer monitor. The `cursor` property specifies the cursor the user's software should display when a reader moves the mouse over a particular object. CSS2 allows these 16 cursor values:

- **auto** The browser chooses a cursor based on the current context; the default value
- **crosshair** A simple crosshair cursor
- **default** The platform-dependent default cursor, usually an arrow
- **e-resize** East-pointing arrow (up is north)
- **hand** A hand
- **help** A question mark
- **move** A set of crossed arrows indicating something to be moved
- **ne-resize** A northeast-pointing arrow
- **n-resize** A north-pointing arrow
- **nw-resize** A northwest-pointing arrow
- **se-resize** A southeast-pointing arrow
- **s-resize** A south-pointing arrow

- **sw-resize** A southwest-pointing arrow
- **text** An I-beam
- **wait** A stop watch, spinning beach ball, hourglass, or other icon indicating the passage of time
- **w-resize** A west-pointing arrow

The following style sheet descriptor uses the `cursor` property to force the hand cursor to appear whenever a mouse pointer is over a `CONTACT` element:

```
CONTACT  { cursor: hand }
```

If you wish, you can create a custom cursor and load it from an image file by providing an URL for the image. Generally you'll provide cursors in several formats in a comma-separated list, the last of which is the name of a generic cursor. For example:

```
CONTACT { cursor: url("project.cur"), url("project.gif"), text }
```

The above example provides a `.cur` file for a Web browser to attempt first. If this cursor file isn't supported, or can't be found, then the `.gif` file is used. If that `.gif` file is not supported or can't be found, then the default `text`-styled cursor is used.

Setting Object Importance

CSS developers can add implied importance to various specified styles by using the `!important` declaration. The default result, when working with both author and user style sheets, is for the author style sheet to override the users. By declaring a property `!important`, you will add more force to the specification, making it harder to be overwritten by a viewer's software. This declaration will override any normal ruling specified in a reader's user agent software. An `!important` declaration in the viewer's software will override a `normal` declaration in the documents. If a user's style has been declared `!important`, it will override an `!important` declaration in the author's document. By declaring a property `!important`, you are declaring all of that property's subproperties important also.

When using the following code in your style sheet, every piece of text tagged `CONTACT` will be displayed in a maroon, Verdana font even if the reader has specified that all text be black and Times New Roman (unless that user has a style sheet with the same rule marked `!important`). On systems that don't have the Verdana font, Helvetica will be used

```
CONTACT { color: "maroon !important";
          font-family: "Verdana, Helvetica !important";
          font-style: "bold"}
```

Using Media Types

You can apply different style sheets to different types of media using the @media rule created in CSS2. This rule defines the type of media that is affected by the set of elements and classes defined in the code block following this rule designator. You can have as many @media rules in a document as you have media types to specify. An alternative to using @media, if you are only specifying a single style sheet, is to use the @import command.

Using @media

Many types of media are used to impart information to readers, and each media type is best presented in a specific fashion. CSS allows you to specify a particular presentation style for each identified media type. For example, text is easier to read on the screen if it uses a sans serif font, while text on paper is generally easiest to read if it is written in a serif font. The property that controls this feature is font-family, and it can be used for both print and screen media. You will often require a larger font on screen than you will on paper. The font-size property controls this feature.

In order to define a specific style sheet for each of the media, use multiple @media rules, as shown in the following example:

```
@media print {
  CONTACT { font-size: 11pt;
            font-family: times new roman }
  PROJECT { font-family: comic sans}}
@media screen {
  CONTACT { font-size: 12pt;
            font-family: arial }
  PROJECT { font-family: comic sans}}
@media screen, print {
  PROJECTDB { line-height: 1.2 }}
```

In the preceding example, the first two declaration blocks provide information specific to an individual media type—in this case, print and screen individually. The third style sheet declaration block provides style sheet instructions for both of these media types simultaneously. To designate style sheet instructions for multiple media types in the same command, list them following the @media rule designator with commas between them.

Some properties are only available with specific media. One example of this is the cue-after property, discussed in the "A Look at Aural Style Sheets" section later in this chapter, that is available only with aural style sheets. CSS2 does not specify a definitive list of media types (listed in Table 14-3), although it does provide a list of CSS2-defined values for the @media rule. These values are not case sensitive.

Media Type	Description
All	This value designates that the following style sheet is suitable for all devices.
Aural	This value designates that the following style sheet is to be used with speech synthesizers.
Braille	This value designates that the following style sheet is to be used with Braille tactile feedback devices.
Embossed	This value designates that the following style sheet is to be used with paged Braille printers.
Handheld	This value designates that the following style sheet is to be used with handheld devices such as Windows CE palmtops, monochromatic monitors, and Palm Pilots.
Print	This value designates that the following style sheet is to be used with all printed material and opaque material and for documents that are viewed on screen in print preview mode.
Projection	This value designates that the following style sheet is to be used with projected presentations. The presentation can be either on a digital projector or have been printed to transparencies.
Screen	This value designates that the following style sheet is to be used primarily for color computer screens.
TTY	This value designates that the following style sheet is to be used for teletypes and terminals that use a fixed-pitch character grid. Document developers should avoid using pixel units with the TeleType (TTY) media type.
TV	This value designates that the following style sheet is to be used with color television-type devices using a low resolution with a limited ability to scroll.

Table 14-3. *CSS Media Types*

Using the `@import` Alternative

The `@import` rule allows you to import an additional external style sheet into your XML document. These style sheets use a `.css` extension, and they must be readable by the XML browser used by the viewer. The `@import` rule can be used to limit the types of style sheets to be imported.

When you use the `@import` rule you are essentially embedding a style sheet import command within an `@media` rule. This prevents your XML browser from retrieving resources for media types that are unsupported. The following examples show how the `@import` command can be used. You can only have one `@import` rule in any document.

If no media type has been specified, the `@import` rule is considered unconditional, and it will be used for all media types.

The following code imports the specified CSS file to be used only in print media:

```
@import url (printmedia.css) print;
```

The following code imports the specified CSS file to be used for both of the TV and screen media types. With this designation, the style sheet will be used when information is being displayed upon your PC or terminal screen:

```
@import url (continuous.css) tv, screen;
```

The following code imports the specified Aural Cascading Style Sheet file to be used on systems that actively support speech synthesizers:

```
@import url (voices.css) aural;
```


A Look at Aural Style Sheets

With the constant growth of impaired communities' use of the Web, the World Wide Web Consortium (W3C) decided that a style sheet should be devoted to the blind and print-impaired communities. When you attempt to render a printed document aurally, you combine speech-synthesis technology with a variety of audio icons. Often, in order to synthesize the text, you have to convert the document to a straight text file and then feed that text through a screen reader. This type of rendering results in a less-informative document, because the structure of the document is lost. The W3C intends that this collection of Aural style sheet properties will enable both aural and visual rendering of a document to maintain a document's full meaning.

In addition to the most obvious uses of aural style sheets for the visually disabled, they can also be used for in-car readings of information, assisting illiterate users, industrial or corporate documentation systems, home entertainment, and more.

All of the Aural style sheet attributes supported by CSS2 are listed in Table 14-4.

<table>
<tr><th>Attribute</th><th>Syntax</th><th>Description</th></tr>
<tr><td>azimuth</td><td>azimuth=<<i>angle</i>> | [[left-side | far-left | left | center-left | center | center-right | right | far-right | right-side] || behind] | leftwards | rightwards | inherit</td><td>This attribute defines the angle of approach that a speaker's voice appears to be coming from. This attribute is used with elevation to provide a range of voices to a multipart document.</td></tr>
<tr><td>cue</td><td>cue=[<cue-before> || < cue-after>] | inherit</td><td>This attribute is shorthand for setting both the cue-before and cue-after attributes. When two values are supplied, the first applies to cue-before and the second applies to cue-after. When only one value is given, it applies to both properties.</td></tr>
<tr><td>cue-after</td><td>cue-after=<<i>uri</i>> | none | inherit</td><td>This attribute specifies the sound that plays after a speaker utters an element's contents.</td></tr>
<tr><td>cue-before</td><td>cue-before=<<i>uri</i>> | none | inherit</td><td>This attribute specifies the sound that plays before a speaker utters an element's contents.</td></tr>
</table>

Table 14-4. *The Aural Style Sheet Attributes Supported by CSS2*

<table>
<tr><th>Attribute</th><th>Syntax</th><th>Description</th></tr>
<tr><td>elevation</td><td>elevation=<<i>angle</i>> | below | level | above | higher | lower | inherit</td><td>This attribute controls the height from which the sound of the speaker's voice appears to be coming at you.</td></tr>
<tr><td>pause</td><td>pause=[[<<i>time</i>> | <<i>percentage</i>>]{1,2}] | inherit</td><td>This attribute is shorthand for setting both the pause-before and pause-after attributes. When two values are supplied, the first applies to pause-before and the second applies to pause-after. When only one value is given, it applies to both properties.</td></tr>
<tr><td>pause-after</td><td>pause-after=<<i>time</i>> | <<i>percentage</i>> | inherit</td><td>This attribute specifies the length of time that a pause is in effect after a speaker utters an element's contents.</td></tr>
<tr><td>pause-before</td><td>pause-before=<<i>time</i>> | <<i>percentage</i>> | inherit</td><td>This attribute specifies the length of time that a pause is in effect before a speaker utters an element's contents.</td></tr>
<tr><td>pitch</td><td>pitch=<<i>frequency</i>> | x-low | low | medium | high | x-high | inherit</td><td>This attribute controls the average pitch and speaking range of the voice.</td></tr>
<tr><td>pitch-range</td><td>pitch-range=<<i>number</i>> | inherit</td><td>This attribute specifies the acceptable variations in the speaker's average pitch.</td></tr>
</table>

Table 14-4. *The Aural Style Sheet Attributes Supported by CSS2* (continued)

Attribute	Syntax	Description
play-during	play-during=<*uri*> | mix? repeat? | auto | none | inherit	Similar to cue-before and cue-after, this attribute specifies a sound to play in the background while an element's content is spoken.
richness	richness=<*number*> | inherit	This attribute controls the richness of the speaking voice.
speak	speak= normal | none | spell-out | inherit	This attribute specifies whether text is rendered aurally and, if so, how.
speak-numeral	speak-numeral=digits | continuous | none | inherit	This attribute controls how numerals are spoken.
speak-punctuation	speak-punctuation: code | none | inherit	This attribute controls how punctuation is spoken.
speech-rate	speech-rate=<number> | x-slow | slow | medium | fast | x-fast | faster | slower | inherit	This attribute specifies the speaking rate of the speech synthesizer.
stress	stress=<number> | inherit	This attribute specifies the level of assertiveness or emphasis (stress) in the speaking voice. When using this attribute with languages such as English, which uses vocal stress based upon on sentence position to add meaning to your sentence, you can select primary, secondary, or tertiary stress points. The points control the style of inflection applied to these areas of the sentence.

Table 14-4. *The Aural Style Sheet Attributes Supported by CSS2* (continued)

Attribute	Syntax	Description
voice-family	voice-family=[[<*specific-voice*> | <*generic-voice*>],]* [<*specific-voice*> | <*generic-voice*>] | inherit	This comma-separated, prioritized list of voice family names controls the voices used when reading the text of the document.
volume	volume=<*number*> | <*percentage*> | silent | x-soft | soft | medium | loud | x-loud | inherit	This attribute controls the median volume of the waveform. In other words, it adjusts the dynamic range over which a voice inflects during a speech-synthesized readout of a document.

Table 14-4. *The Aural Style Sheet Attributes Supported by CSS2* (continued)

The following example style sheet creates an aural style sheet identifying only the aural attributes for a variety of objects found in a PROJECT-based XML document:

```
/* Aural Style Sheets  */
PROJECTTITLE TOPICAREA {
       voice-family: men;
       stress: 20;
       richness: 90;
       cue-before: url("ping.au") }
NAME { pause: 20ms;
       cue-before: url("pop.au");
       cue-after: url("pop.au");
       azimuth: 30deg;
       elevation: above }
CONTACT { pause: 30ms 40ms } /* pause-before: 30ms; pause-after: 40ms */
EMAIL   { pause-after: 10ms }
PROJECTTITLE { cue-before: url("bell.aiff");
               cue-after: url("dong.wav") }
```

Summary

As you have seen in this chapter, CSS provides developers with ways to modify and format XML documents so that all Web browsers or other XML software that supports Cascading Style Sheets can display them. This chapter covered the more advanced functions of CSS2, including

- Adding content to your document in the form of automatic numbering systems, additional images or text, and line counters
- Using pseudo-classes and pseudo-elements to affect parts of elements, without other designations, such as adding drop caps and altering the appearance of the first line of text within an object
- Using the `display` property to control the layout appearance of objects in your documents so that you can more easily moderate the interactions of each object and control how objects interact with each other within documents
- Controlling the visual formatting of your elements including their `size`, `position`, `visibility`, `overflow`, and `clip` values
- Exploring the different types of media and creating style sheets for each type so that you can have your documents appear in the best format possible for each of the various types of media supported by CSS
- Creating Aural style sheets so that documents can be read in their most effective manner through speech synthesizers

The Complete Reference

Chapter 15

XSL Basics

XSL is the umbrella term for two standards published by the World Wide Web Consortium (W3C). Taken together, these standards enable XML developers and document authors to expand the use of XML documents further. Specifically, the XSL standards provide a framework for converting XML documents to other forms of structured text (such as well-formed Hypertext Markup Language [HTML] and other XML vocabularies) and for styling XML documents for output to various media, including print and electronic media.

Background

The XSL standard actually comprises two separate specifications. Each is itself an XML vocabulary, including reserved element and attribute names, as well as structural requirements. The first, XSL Transformations (XSLT), lays out a means of transforming XML documents to other and perhaps non-XML forms. The second, XSL Formatting Objects (XSL-FO), consists of a comprehensive set of markup that works much like Cascading Style Sheets (CSS) (covered in Chapter 13 and 14) to render XML documents for display, print, and other media.

The Need for XSL

Why do we need another style sheet language? After all, we already have CSS. What does XSL do that CSS cannot do?

At one level, the answer is syntactic: CSS syntax is not XML compatible. Not only is the punctuation and other syntactic characteristics different between the two style-sheet languages, thereby requiring separate skill sets for developers and designers, but CSS also requires different software—particularly parsers—to support it. If style sheets can be constructed using the rules of at least well-formed XML, they can be processed by the same tools that process documents in any other XML vocabulary.

At another level, the answer is structural. A CSS rule set is a simple stream of directives expressing how to render one element as opposed to a second, third, and so on. This is analogous to a flat-file database: all the information is there, one record at a time, but a given record stands in isolation with little if any relationship to other records in the set. At the other end of the spectrum, stands an XSL style sheet—itself an XML document with an inherent tree of relationships between and among elements, attributes, and miscellaneous content such as comments and processing instructions [PIs]. By its very nature, implicit in an XSL style sheet is the sense that given any data point, you can locate any other simply by examining this chain of relationships to locate ancestor data, descendant data, and sibling data—even siblings-of-ancestors, children-of-siblings, and so on.

Finally, there is simply much that CSS cannot do (or can do only with great difficulty) that XSL excels at:

- CSS cannot change the order of appearance of content within a document. Content can appear in the output only in the order in which it appears in the source document, and only as many times as it appears there. For example, you cannot display a copyright date at the bottom of a page if it appears as the text content of an element at the top of the document. Given a `<BOOK_TITLE>` element in a document, you cannot display its contents both at the top of the document, in a large heading-style font, and also at the bottom with the book purchasing information (ISBN, price, and so on).

- CSS cannot display attribute values, even though you can use attributes as selectors in CSS rules—if the copyright date is in an attribute value, rather than an element's content, it might as well not be in the document at all. Similarly, comments and PIs are inaccessible to processing by a CSS.
- CSS doesn't address the ongoing need for formatting documents in print, even though its history makes it quite suitable for rendering content in a Web browser or similar output form (such as a screen reader for aural style sheets).

In short, while building on CSS's successes, the authors of the two XSL standards wanted to construct a document-styling environment that both leveraged the strengths of XML itself and plugged the holes in CSK's capabilities.

XSL History and Status

As with all things, XSL started out in the mind of a group of developers who saw a need for a more complete and more easily manipulated style sheet language. This need eventually developed into the XSLT and XSL-FO languages that you see today.

Beginnings

From the start of the XML movement, with its strict emphasis on the separation of presentation and content, it was obvious that a styling mechanism would be required if XML documents were to have standing as anything other than inert repositories of document contents and data. Accordingly, the original working draft of the XSL specification was published by the World Wide Web Consortium (W3C) in mid-1998, just months after the XML 1.0 Recommendation itself.

This working draft put forth several principles that would be critical in all later incarnations.

The first of these principles was that in order to display or otherwise render an XML document—which, by definition, should be presentation-neutral—you must effectively transform it to something other than pure XML.

The second principle was that of XML-based *flow objects*. Each flow object would consist of one or more XML elements, attributes, and so on, whose only purpose and meaning would be the rendering of content. Flow objects could be hierarchically nested within one another in the usual manner of an XML document; for example, an element corresponding to a physical page could be considered to consist of elements representing a header, a block of text, and a footer, with the block of text further broken down into elements for paragraphs and other text blocks (such as callouts), inline units of text, tables, figures, and so on.

This original version of the XSL standard was not created from scratch. Rather, it was an adaptation of a widely used standard for styling Standard Generalized Markup Language (SGML) documents, called (accurately, if verbosely) the Document Style Semantics and Specification Language (DSSSL, pronounced to rhyme with *whistle*). DSSSL did not use SGML-like notation for its styling and transformational instructions, but you can see from the following example how the analogous markup form might be represented:

```
(element para
     (make paragraph
          font-size: 12pt
          font-weight: bold
          line-spacing: 12pt
          (process-children}))
```

The preceding instruction says that when the DSSSL processor finds a `para` element in an SGML source document, it is to construct as output the contents of that element rendered in paragraph form with particular font and line-spacing characteristics. The `process-children` directive tells the DSSSL processor to iterate then through all immediate descendants of the `para` element (including, perhaps, other `para` elements) and attempt to match and render them, as well.

The most obvious similarity to CSS in this example is that the DSSSL properties such as `font-size` have direct counterparts in the list of available CSS properties. However, the example also demonstrates how the grammar of DSSSL added another layer to CSS's functionality. CSS essentially consists of adjectives that are to be applied to nouns (XML elements); DSSSL added verbs (such as `make paragraph` and `process-children`) to the mix.

Splitting Transformations from Formatting

Besides providing for conversion of XML content to flow objects, the first working draft of the XSL standard also permitted its conversion to HTML. The general approach, as it had been with DSSSL, was that the style sheet would lay out a series of *template rules*, each consisting of a match pattern and a template to be created in the output when matching content was found in the source document. (The commonly accepted way to express this is to say that the template *instantiates*—creates an instance of—a particular result.)

Here is the mid-1998 XSL equivalent of the above DSSSL instruction:

```
<xsl:template match="para">
     <fo:block
          font-size="12pt"
          font-weight="bold"
          line-spacing="12pt">
          <xsl:process-children/>
     </fo:block>
</xsl:template>
```

As you can see, this is basically the DSSSL code straightforwardly transcribed to XML format, replacing the parentheses used as delimiters with entire element names (using < and > angle brackets) and formatting properties with attribute-value pairs. Also note the use of the namespace prefixes `xsl:` and `fo:` to ensure that a given element name belongs to the XSL instruction or flow-object namespace, respectively.

It wasn't long before the XSL standard's authors and others observed that the requirement to instantiate XSL flow objects or HTML elements in the result was entirely arbitrary—you could use XSL template rules to instantiate virtually any text or markup. This meant that you could use XSL to transform an XML document into one based on a different version of the same vocabulary, into a document based on a completely different vocabulary, into a comma-separated values (CSV) flat file, into plain text, and so on.

Accordingly, later versions of the standard split it into two: one vocabulary for conducting transformations and one for rendering document content. These are known, respectively, as XSLT and XSL itself. What had been called flow objects are now referred to as *formatting objects*, and what is officially still called XSL is now more commonly called XSL-FO. The term *XSL* in common use therefore refers to the two separate standards taken together (even though they have little to do with one another any longer).

Current Status

Through 1998 and 1999, the XSLT standard went through a number of intermediate working drafts, finally becoming a full-fledged W3C Recommendation in November 1999. It remains at version 1.0 as of this writing.

The XSL-FO standard, by contrast, has only recently (November, 2000) become a W3C Candidate Recommendation. This means that although the authors and editors of the standard believe it to be stable, complete, consistent, and ready for Recommendation status, it is still in fact tentative. A decision as to its next change in status is currently scheduled for early Spring, 2001.

XSL Basics

XSLT will be covered in detail in Chapter 16, and XSL-FO will be covered in Chapter 17. This section of Chapter 15 introduces you to the general concepts of both, using simple examples.

Styling Through Transformation: XSLT

As mentioned previously, the easiest way to make XML presentable is to turn it into something else: a Web page, a print catalog, a Scalable Vector Graphics (SVG) illustration, or other.

An XSLT style sheet accomplishes this transformation using a series of one or more template rules; together with the source document to be transformed, these template rules are fed into an XSLT processor, which performs the desired transformation(s), placing the results into an output file or (as in the case of a Web page) directly onto a display device such as a user's monitor.

Linking an XSLT Style Sheet to an XML Document

In order to associate an XSLT style sheet with an XML document, most processors require that the document include at the top a special PI, whose format is as follows:

```
<?xml-stylesheet type="text/xsl" href="uri"?>
```

where *uri* is the Uniform Resource Identifier (URI), such as a Web address, where the style sheet is located.

For example, consider the following simple XML document:

```
<?xml version="1.0"?>
<BOOK>
     <BOOK_TITLE>A Journal of the Plague Year</BOOK_TITLE>
     <AUTHOR>Defoe, Daniel</AUTHOR>
</BOOK>
```

To assert that the preceding document be transformed according to the template rules laid out in an XSLT style sheet named book.xsl (located on the same path as the XML document itself), we'd add the following line to the document, immediately following the XML declaration and before the <BOOK> start tag:

```
<?xml-stylesheet type="text/xsl" href="book.xsl"?>
```

Note that this PI is identical to the one described in Chapter 13 for linking a CSS to the document, except for the value of the type pseudo-attribute.

XSLT Style Sheet Structure

The root element of a typical XSLT style sheet is the xsl:stylesheet element.

The XSLT standard also allows the root element of the style sheet to be called xsl:transform; however, most style sheet authors use the xsl:stylesheet name. Also note that the namespace prefix xsl: is entirely arbitrary—you can use any namespace prefix you wish, as long as it follows the rules for XML names and is associated with the proper namespace URI; however, again by convention, xsl: is the most common prefix.

Some of the elements that may be contained within the scope of this element's start and end tags are called *top-level* elements; these must be immediate children of the xsl:stylesheet element (that is, one step immediately below xsl:stylesheet in the hierarchy of the style sheet's content). The most common top-level element in a typical XSLT style sheet is a template rule—an xsl:template element, consisting of two parts:

- A *match expression* indicating which portion(s) of the source document will be processed by this template rule
- The *template* proper, meaning something to be instantiated or some action(s) to take place when a matching portion of the source document is found

Assume that we want to process the simple XML document presented above by transforming it to an HTML document; specifically, the book's title will be transformed to a level-1 heading, and the author's name will be transformed to a level-2 heading. The following style sheet will accomplish this objective:

```
<xsl:stylesheet version="1.0"
    xmlns:xsl="http://www.w3.org/1999/XSL/Transform"
    xmlns="http://www.w3.org/TR/REC-html40">
    <!-- Template rule to suppress all default text processing -->
    <xsl:template match="text()"/>
    <!-- Template rule for processing BOOK element -->
    <xsl:template match="BOOK">
        <html>
            <head><title>Book Information</title></head>
            <body>
                <h1><xsl:value-of select="BOOK_TITLE"/></h1>
                <h2>by <xsl:value-of select="AUTHOR"/></h2>
            </body>
        </html>
    </xsl:template>
</xsl:stylesheet>
```

In general, note that an XSLT style sheet must be a well-formed XML document. This includes not only the XSLT code, but also markup of any other kind (HTML, in this example).

The result of passing this style sheet through an XSLT processor, given the above XML document, will be the following HTML document:

```
<html>
    <head><title>Book Information</title></head>
    <body>
        <h1>A Journal of the Plague Year</h1>
        <h2>by Defoe, Daniel</h2>
    </body>
</html>
```

For more details about the various components of XSLT style sheets, consult Chapter 16.

CSS via XML: XSL-FO

Unlike either CSS or XSLT style sheets, XSL-FO style sheets cannot be linked directly to an XML document. That's because the XSL-FO vocabulary is not meant to style another document's content; it styles its own document's content. The trick is that all its own content comes from an XSLT style sheet—transferred to it either from a source XML document or as literal text from the XSLT style sheet's templates. For this reason, you will seldom create or manipulate an XSL-FO style sheet as a standalone, static document.

Instead, its structure and content will be implicit in an XSLT style sheet, and it may be output from the latter's transformations either virtually (in the case of on-the-fly transformations) or physically as a document whose sole purpose is to be piped into some downstream process such as creation of a PDF document.

The HTML vocabulary, as you know, consists of elements and attributes representing a combination of content and presentation. XSL-FO's vocabulary, on the other hand, represents nothing but presentation. In essence, it's an enhanced CSS, coded in an XML-native format.

As you will see in Chapter 17 (and in Appendix C), the XSL-FO specification defines a quite large number of elements and attributes. These markup components describe a set of nested and sequential containers—so-called area trees—of content, with each container to be represented using various traits. Within each area tree (such as a Web page or a physical page of a print document) are any number of formatting objects, representing text sequences, images, tables, and so on. This model provides for a complete range of complex layouts.

Going back to the simple XML BOOK document used in the previous section of this chapter, we could use XSLT to transform the document to XSL-FO instead of HTML. A style sheet to do so would, however, be considerably more complex:

```
<xsl:stylesheet version="1.0"
     xmlns:xsl="http://www.w3.org/1999/XSL/Transform"
     xmlns:fo="http://www.w3.org/1999/XSL/Format">
     <!-- Template rule to suppress all default text processing -->
     <xsl:template match="text()"/>
     <!-- Template rule for processing BOOK element -->
     <xsl:template match="BOOK">
          <fo:root xmlns:fo="http://www.w3.org/1999/XSL/Format">
               <fo:layout-master-set>
                    <fo:simple-page-master page-master-name="main"
                         margin-top="72pt" margin-bottom="72pt"
                         margin-left="72pt" margin-right="72pt">
                         <fo:region-body margin-bottom="72pt"/>
                    </fo:simple-page-master>
               </fo:layout-master-set>
               <fo:page-sequence>
                    <fo:sequence-specification>
                         <fo:sequence-specifier-alternating
                              page-master-first="main" page-master-odd="main"
page-master-even="main"/>
                    </fo:sequence-specification>
                    <fo:flow flow-name="xsl-region-body">
                         <fo:block font-size="24pt" line-height="27pt"
font-weight="bold">
                              <xsl:value-of select="BOOK_TITLE"/>
```

```
                        </fo:block>
                        <fo:block font-size="18pt" line-height="21pt"
font-weight="bold">
                            by <xsl:value-of select="AUTHOR"/>
                        </fo:block>
                    </fo:flow>
                </fo:page-sequence>
            </fo:root>
        </xsl:template>
</xsl:stylesheet>
```

As before, this style sheet contains only a single functional template rule: the one for the document's root `BOOK` element. There are several notable differences, though; the most obvious of them is attributable to the fact that none of the formatting characteristics we want to specify are built in. With the HTML output, we could rely on certain browser defaults, such as that headings are rendered in a large, boldface font.

Specifically, working down through the style sheet, here is what the code does:

- The `xsl:stylesheet` element is very similar to the one in the earlier (HTML-generating) style sheet; the difference is that we now have a namespace declaration for the `fo:` prefix.
- The XSL-FO equivalent to HTML's `html` element is the `fo:root` element, within which the entire body of the result is contained. Although the `fo:` namespace declaration is implicitly inherited from the `xsl:stylesheet` element, we want to ensure that it gets copied to the result, so it's explicitly added to the `fo:root` element.
- Within `fo:root`, the first thing the result specifies (in `fo:layout-master-set`) is a page master—that is, the overall layout of the page to be created. It's given a name of `main`, and assigned margins of about an inch on all four sides. The `fo:region-body` element is where the bulk (in this case, all) of the page's content will reside.
- The `fo:page-sequence` element lays out what will appear on this page. For long documents, you can specify different layouts for the first-, odd-, and even-numbered pages; in this case, we're simply making them all the same (since there is, after all, only one page to be output).
- Finally, the `fo:flow` element specifies (in its `fo:block` children) that on this page, within the main text area (`flow-name="xsl-region-body"`) appear two text blocks, one for `BOOK_TITLE` and one for `AUTHOR`.

Of course, this results in a considerably longer and more complex style sheet than the one provided earlier. It may help to put the different lengths in perspective if you imagine that the earlier XSLT style sheet had also generated in the result an HTML style element, complete with CSS specifications for everything to be displayed.

The result of transforming the BOOK XML document is the following XSL-FO style sheet:

```
<fo:root xmlns:fo="http://www.w3.org/1999/XSL/Format">
     <fo:layout-master-set>
          <fo:simple-page-master page-master-name="main"
               margin-top="72pt" margin-bottom="72pt"
               margin-left="72pt" margin-right="72pt">
               <fo:region-body margin-bottom="72pt"/>
          </fo:simple-page-master>
     </fo:layout-master-set>
     <fo:page-sequence>
          <fo:sequence-specification>
               <fo:sequence-specifier-alternating
                    page-master-first="main" page-master-odd="main" page-master-
even="main"/>
          </fo:sequence-specification>
          <fo:flow flow-name="xsl-region-body">
               <fo:block font-size="24pt" line-height="27pt" font-weight="bold">
                    A Journal of the Plague Year
               </fo:block>
               <fo:block font-size="18pt" line-height="21pt" font-weight="bold">
                    by Defoe, Daniel
               </fo:block>
          </fo:flow>
     </fo:page-sequence>
</fo:root>
```

XSL Software and XSLT Software

In this section, we will look at brief examples of software for processing (editing/authoring, transforming, and displaying) both XSLT and XSL-FO. Remember that this overview barely scratches the surface of tools currently available, especially for XSLT style sheets. For a more complete and up-to-date listing, consult James Tauber's Web site http://www.xmlsoftware.com.

Editors/Authoring Tools

As with XML itself, you don't need any special software to edit/author an XSLT style sheet. Any simple text editor such as Windows Notepad or Unix vi/emacs will suffice.

However, to ensure typo-free data entry, it always helps to use software that knows something about the type of data being edited. At a minimum, you'll want an editing package that allows you to select from the range of acceptable element and attribute names at a given point in the style sheet.

XML Spy

XML Spy, from Icon Information-Systems, is an editing package that allows you to select from the range of acceptable element and attribute names at a given point in the style sheet. XML Spy is available only for Microsoft Windows platforms; a 30-day trial version is available, or you can purchase a single-user registered copy for $149.

Figure 15-1 shows the complete XML Spy interface when working on an XML document and accompanying XSLT style sheet. The XML document and style sheet appear in the large central portion of the window. Documents and style sheets may be viewed in a number of different ways; here, the XML document is displayed (and may be edited) as plain text, while the style sheet is displayed in an expandable/collapsible tree of document content. Additional elements and attributes may be added using various Graphical User Interface (GUI) techniques, such as double-clicking and dragging-and-dropping.

Along the top and bottom edges of the window are arrayed a dizzying assortment of toolbar buttons. To the left in this screen shot are two subwindows showing the

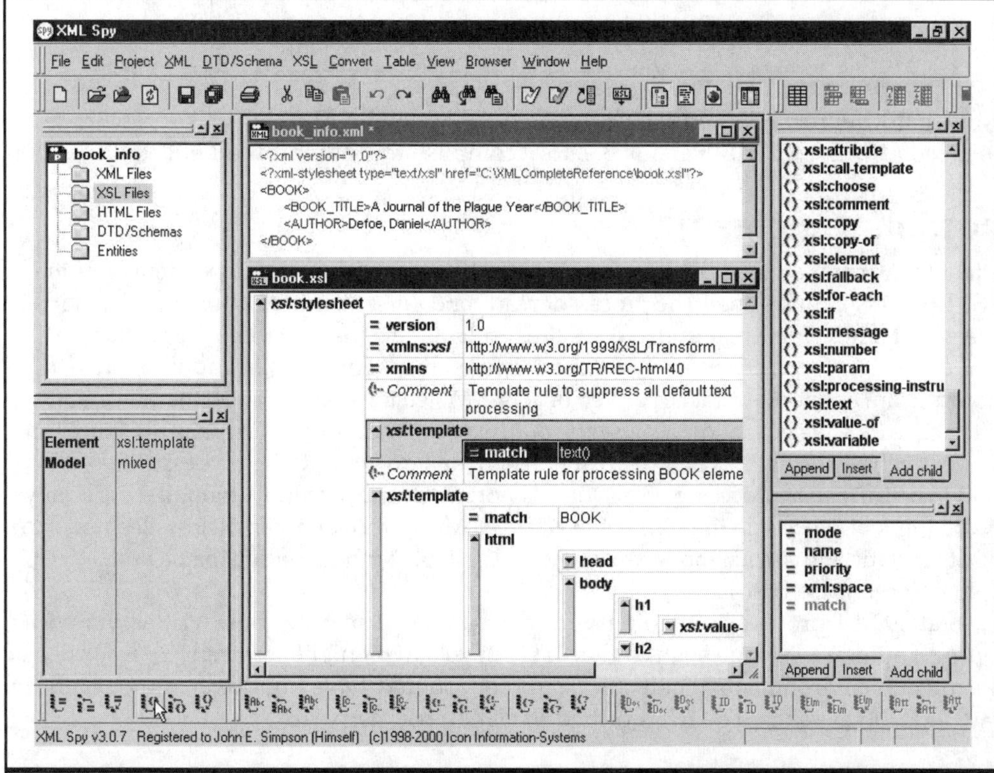

Figure 15-1. *The XML Spy GUI allows you to add elements, attributes, PIs, comments, and text easily to both your XML document and your style sheet.*

directory structure of the current project (a collection of XML, XSLT, and other files) and information about the currently selected element (`xsl:template`, in this case). To the right are two subwindows showing you the list of available child elements (top) and attributes (bottom), based on the currently selected element. Notice that in the top listing (alphabetically ordered here), the `xsl:template` element does not appear; this is because an `xsl:template` element (like the one currently selected) may not contain another `xsl:template` element.

If the transformation in question is a conversion from XML to HTML, you can apply the transformation to the XML document with XML Spy and view the result in a miniature browser window superimposed on the editing area:

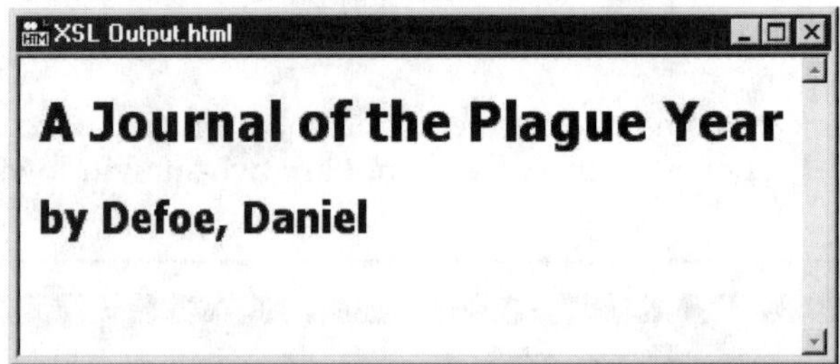

Note that XML Spy relies on the presence of the Microsoft XML/XSLT processor, Microsoft XML [MSXML] version 3.0, to accomplish this minibrowser effect.

Processors (Engines)

Other than an editor, the XSLT processing software you will be most dependent on is the XSLT processor (or engine). The processor reads and parses the XML source and style sheet, and if no errors are found, creates the result of the transformation. This result may be in the form of a file or a virtual document delivered by a server or other application to a downstream application such as a Web browser. When the result is a file, the processor is often called a *static* processor because the output of the transformation is simply held in a static (unchanging) file. When the result is a virtual document, the processor may be said to be a *dynamic* processor. (This term is not necessarily accurate, though—especially if you think of *dynamic* in the sense of *interactive*.) Most processors can be installed and run in either static or dynamic mode, making them suitable for both offline/batch and online/server-based uses.

Static XSLT processors are often command-line-driven programs, written in Java or a programming language such as C++. This makes them highly efficient tools for use in production environments where, for example, you may have hundreds or thousands of raw XML documents to be transformed to HTML counterparts.

Saxon

One of the most popular XSLT processors is Saxon, a free tool developed by Michael Kay of ICL. Saxon is written in Java, so it is fully platform independent and can be run in command-line mode or as a servlet for Web use. For the Windows platform, there is a special easy-to-install and -run executable called Instant Saxon.

The command-line for running Saxon is simple:

```
saxon [options] source-doc style-doc
```

source-doc is the path/name of the XML source document and *style-doc* is the path/name of the XSLT style sheet. Various options can be supplied in place of [*options*]; the most common is probably the `-o output-doc` option, which specifies the name of a file to hold the result of the transformation. (The default is simply to pass the result to the system's standard output device, such as the console.)

In Figure 15-2, you see the result of running Saxon using our simple XML document and XSLT style sheet. The output does not print each element separated by new lines from adjacent ones, which makes the document more difficult to read for humans. This is immaterial in most cases, since a Web browser will display the output correctly, regardless of this white space. If you wish your document to be printed in a more attractive format, you can control Saxon's output using various XSLT techniques as described in Chapter 16.

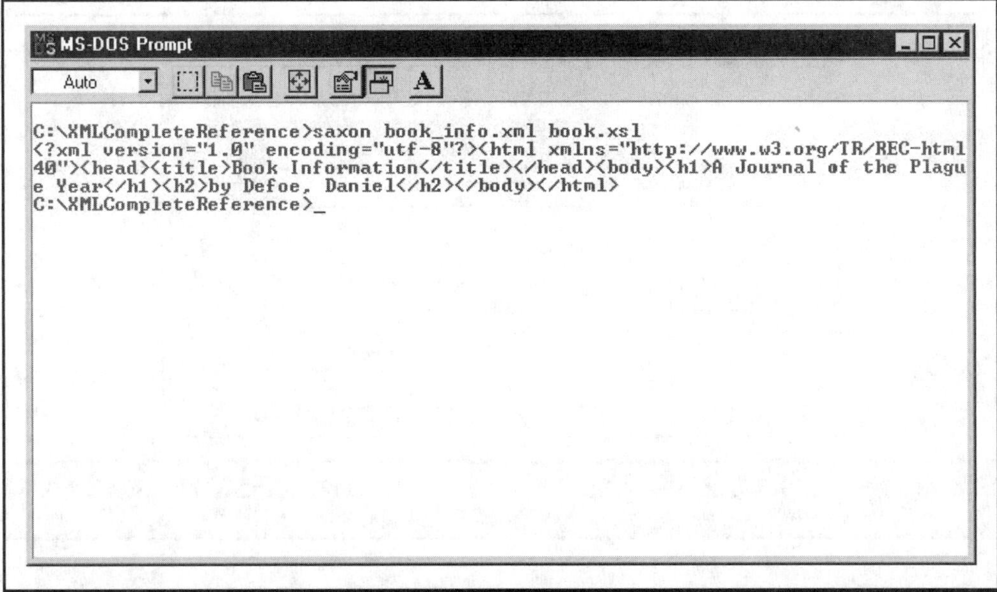

Figure 15-2. *With Saxon, the default association between an XML document and its style sheet is made in command-line arguments.*

MSXML

Although not always a supporter of open standards in the past, Microsoft has delivered a fully compliant XSLT processor as part of its MSXML processor. Since MSXML is integrated into the Microsoft Internet Explorer (IE) browser, this promises to make both XML and XSLT acceptable to a large number of Web users.

MSXML cannot easily be made to produce static result documents; it really is intended for use only within IE. Thus, unlike Saxon, MSXML typically produces only virtual documents and thus might be classified as a dynamic XSLT processor.

MSXML comes with a built-in style sheet. If an XML document is not linked to an XSLT style sheet with an `<?xml-stylesheet?>` PI, it displays as an expandable/collapsible tree using proprietary Microsoft dynamic HTML techniques. The results are shown in Figure 15-3 in IE version 5 and up. Portions of the document tree can be hidden by clicking the – (minus) signs, such as the one at the left of the `BOOK_TITLE` element. When the tree is collapsed this way, the – signs change to + (plus) signs, which when clicked, expand the corresponding portion of the tree.

By contrast, when the document is associated with a style sheet, MSXML runs the transformation and displays the result in the browser window. Thus, if the result is HTML, the XML document's contents display in a way familiar to browser users, as in Figure 15-4.

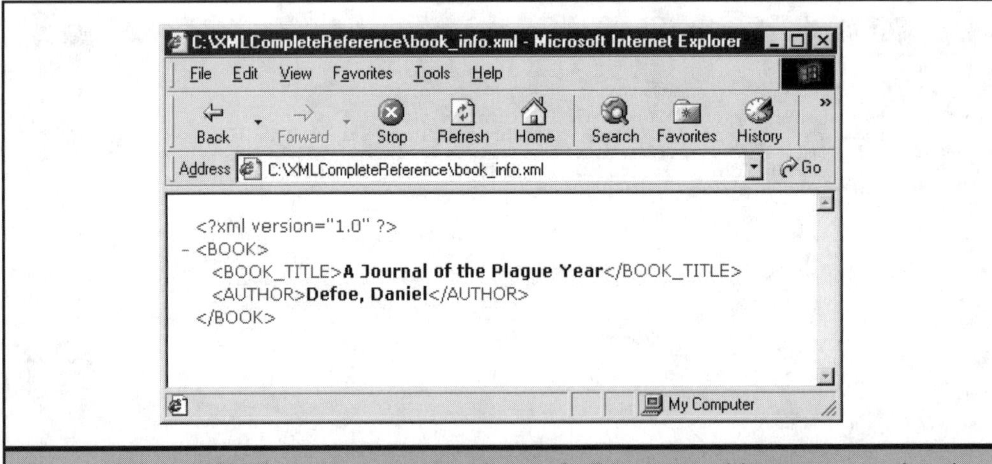

Figure 15-3. *MSXML as shown in the Microsoft IE browser without an associated style sheet.*

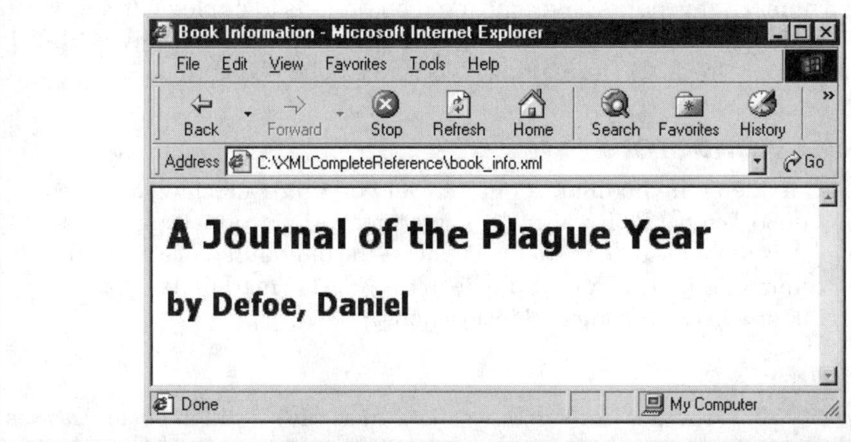

Figure 15-4. *MSXML displays the XML document with its associated XSLT style sheet.*

XSL-FO Software

For three reasons, software to support the XSL-FO standard has lagged behind that for XSLT:

- First, the XSL-FO standard itself has not yet been finalized. This makes software developers and vendors naturally reluctant to devote resources to what may turn out to be a quite different set of requirements.
- Second, the XSL-FO standard is large and complex. Hundreds of elements and attributes must be supported by software in order to comply with the current prefinal version of the specification.
- Finally, and perhaps most important, there has been relatively little pressure from potential users. Web developers are primarily interested in transforming XML to HTML (and question how much they'll ever need presentation capabilities other than those provided by CSS); database and document interchange industries are primarily interested in transforming XML to other forms of structured text, different XML vocabularies, or otherwise. Both of these goals can be accomplished using XML and XSLT alone. The one user community potentially most interested in XSL-FO is the publishing industry, which has already invested much time, effort, and human resources in using special-purpose packages such as FrameMaker, Quark, and so on.

That said, a number of vendors have embarked on projects to implement XSL-FO in a variety of ways. In general, these projects might be classified as either native XSL-FO renderers or converters from XSL formatting objects to Adobe PDF format.

Native XSL-FO Renderers

A native XSL-FO renderer, if you think about it, would do pretty much what a Web browser or the Adobe Acrobat PDF reader does: interpret various formatting commands in order to display content in some predefined ways—the only difference being that the formatting commands in question would be in the XSL-FO markup language, rather than HTML or a PDF file's internal instructions.

XSL Formatter

Antenna House's XSL Formatter (for Windows platforms only) is still in beta release as of this writing, but it already promises to be a very interesting demonstration of how a native formatting object renderer might work.

When you first open Antenna House's XSL Formatter, the main window is empty. Select Open from the File menu, and you're prompted to enter the location and name of both the XML source document and the XSLT style sheet used to transform the source to XSL formatting objects. Given our sample `book_info.xml` and `book.xfo` files from above, as you can see here, some of the kinks are not entirely worked out of XSL Formatter yet:

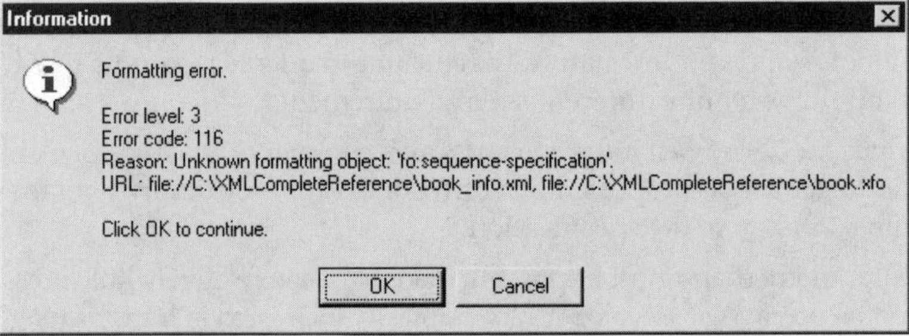

Evidently the software has not (as of this beta version) caught up with the XSL-FO specification yet. (This is just one of several similar messages issued from our particular XSLT style sheet.)

Removing the offending unknown elements and attributes enables the transformation to complete. The large blank area is now replaced with a fully rendered version of the resulting XSL formatting objects, as you can see in Figure 15-5.

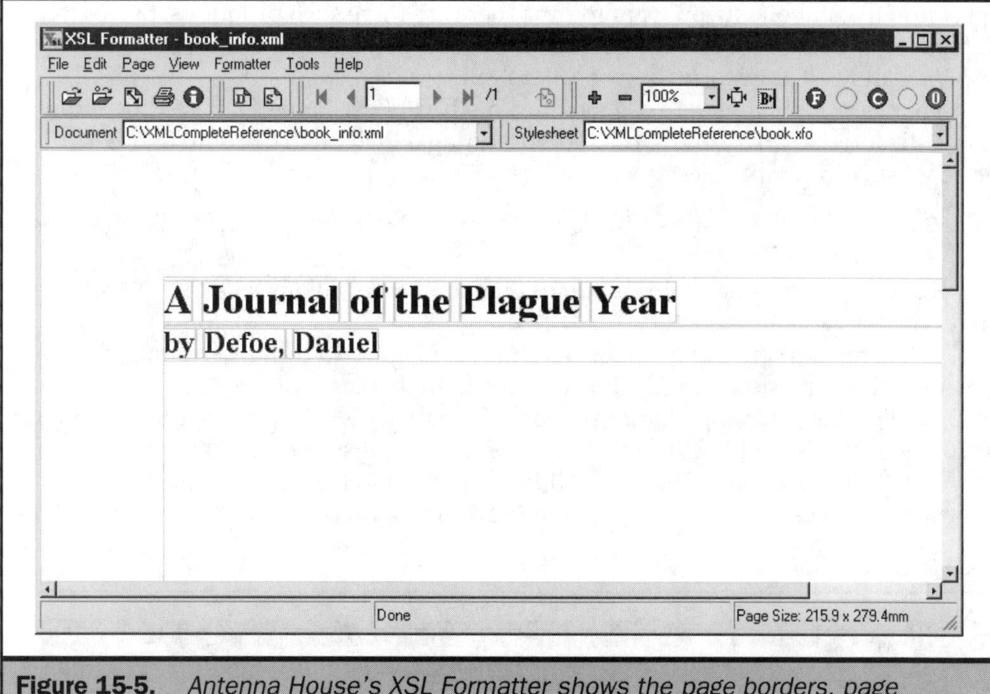

Figure 15-5. *Antenna House's XSL Formatter shows the page borders, page margins, and margins around the various flow objects on the page.*

Formatting Objects-to-PDF Converters

A number of efforts have concentrated, not on rendering XSL formatting objects per se, but on converting them to their counterparts in the widely supported Adobe PDF format. Because Adobe offers the cross-platform Acrobat Reader program free for the download, this is an attractive option—you can be fairly confident that the resulting documents can be viewed and printed exactly as desired.

Formatting Objects to PDF (FOP)

FOP is one component in the Cocoon Web publishing suite currently maintained by the open-source Apache Project. It's a Java-based package, so it runs in a wide variety of environments both on- and offline.

When run offline, FOP (like Saxon, covered in the "Processors/Engines" section) is run from the command line. You invoke the Java interpreter, passing it the name of the specific FOP component you want to run. There are three such programs, two of which depend on the existence of a complete XSL-FO-only document—that is, the result of applying an XSLT transformation of XSL to XSL-FO.

In our case, we're going to use the third method of executing FOP, feeding it the raw XML and the XSLT style sheet and outputting a PDF file. The command line to do so, given our sample files, is

```
java org.apache.fop.apps.XalanCommandLine book_info.xml book.
xfo book_info.pdf
```

Note that this command line assumes that you have set your Java `CLASSPATH` environment variable correctly.

FOP displays a series of messages as shown in Figure 15-6 and, assuming no errors, generates the requested PDF file (book_info.pdf, in this case).

Note that the "warning" message shown in Figure 15-6, despite the presence in our XSLT style sheet's templates of the `flow-name` attribute to the `fo:flow` element.

Having produced the book_info.pdf file requested in Figure 15-6, you can then view it in Adobe Acrobat. The results are shown in Figure 15-7.

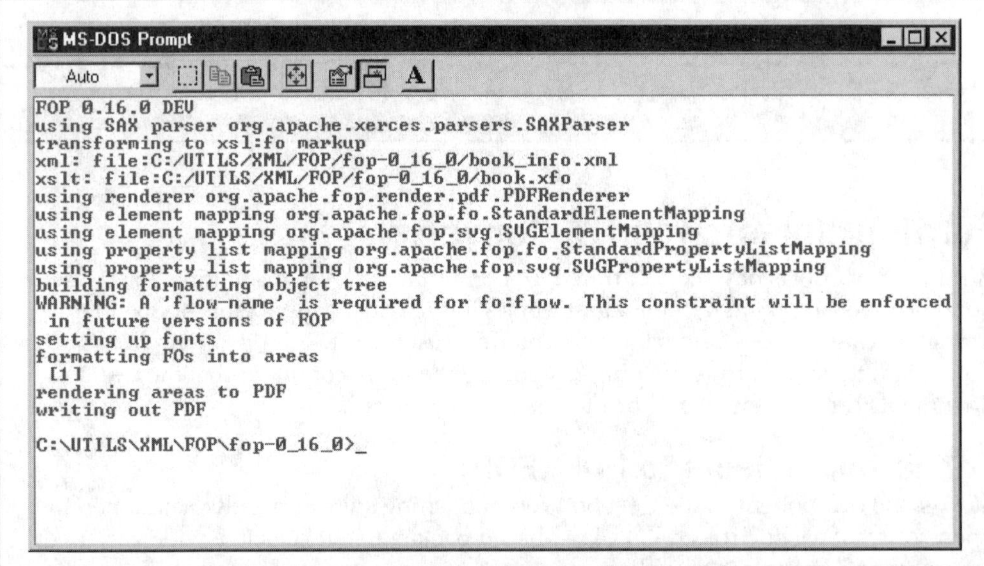

Figure 15-6. *FOP is generating a PDF file from XML source and an XSLT style sheet that transforms it to XSL formatting objects.*

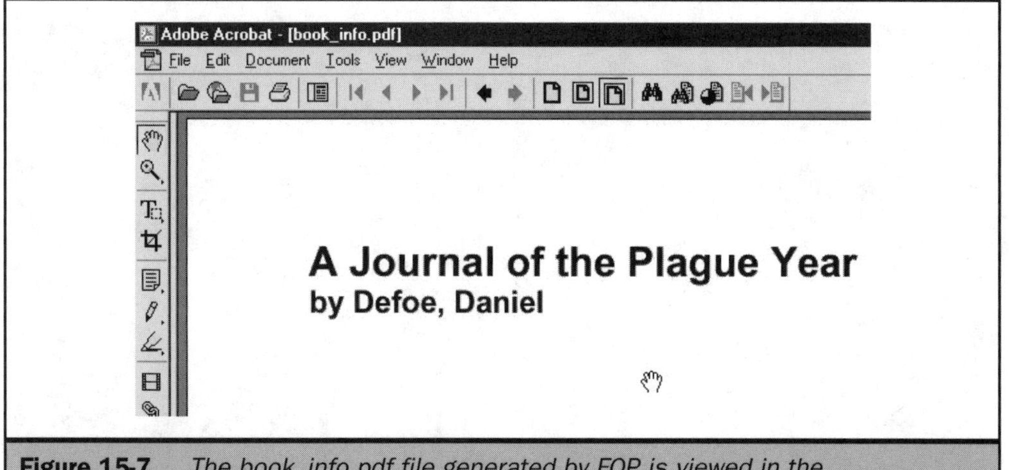

Figure 15-7. *The book_info.pdf file generated by FOP is viewed in the Adobe Acrobat Reader program.*

Summary

In this chapter you learned why CSS (or CSS alone) may not be sufficient for rendering XML documents in presentable form. We covered some of the history of the XML-based transformation and styling specification, we covered XSL, and we covered why what was originally a single XSL standard has split into two: one for transforming XML documents to other forms of structured text (XSLT) and one for directly styling text content (XSL-FO). Finally, the chapter presented brief overviews of selected XSLT and XSL-FO processing software.

The next chapter examines XSLT (including the closely related XPath specification) in detail. The XSL-FO specification is more fully covered in Chapter 17.

Chapter 16

XSL Transformations

An XML document's content often needs to assume some other form in order to be most useful. Perhaps you need to load the content into a Web page or into a newsletter or other print publication; maybe the document needs to be upgraded to a newer version of the Document Type Definition (DTD) to which it conforms or be transferred to a business partner using some other XML vocabulary; or maybe the data needs to be made available for loading into an XML-unaware spreadsheet or legacy database. The most popular standard for effecting all these varieties of changes to the form of XML-based content is Extensible Stylesheet Language Transformations (XSLT). XSLT, in concert with the XML Path Language (XPath) standard for locating specific portions of an XML document, enables you to easily repurpose your documents' content for just about any target environment.

XSLT Concepts

To understand how to make XSLT work for you, you need to understand a few of the primary concepts associated with the using XSL to transform your documents into another language, such as HTML, that can be read by other types of document browsers.

Source and Result Trees

The most important concept you need to understand when first exposed to XSLT is the transformation of one structure into another; each of these structures is called a *tree.* The XSLT specification defines two such trees: the *source tree* and the *result tree.* An XSLT transformation turns a source tree into a result tree.

Consider the following simple XML document:

```
<?xml version="1.0"?>
<?xml-stylesheet type="text/xsl" href="emp.xsl"?>
<EMP_INFO>
    <EMPLOYEE>
        <EMP_NAME empID="id73519">
            <GIVEN>Raoul</GIVEN>
            <SURNAME>Oaks</SURNAME>
        </EMP_NAME>
    </EMPLOYEE>
</EMP_INFO>
```

Even without the new lines and other white space added to the document for legibility, this markup and text represents a document tree that might be depicted as shown in Figure 16-1.

Although an XML document contains all of the data within its scope, as in Figure 16-1, not all of those contents contribute to the structure of the tree—only the elements (and, to a lesser extent, the text) contribute to the structure of the tree. Attributes and text

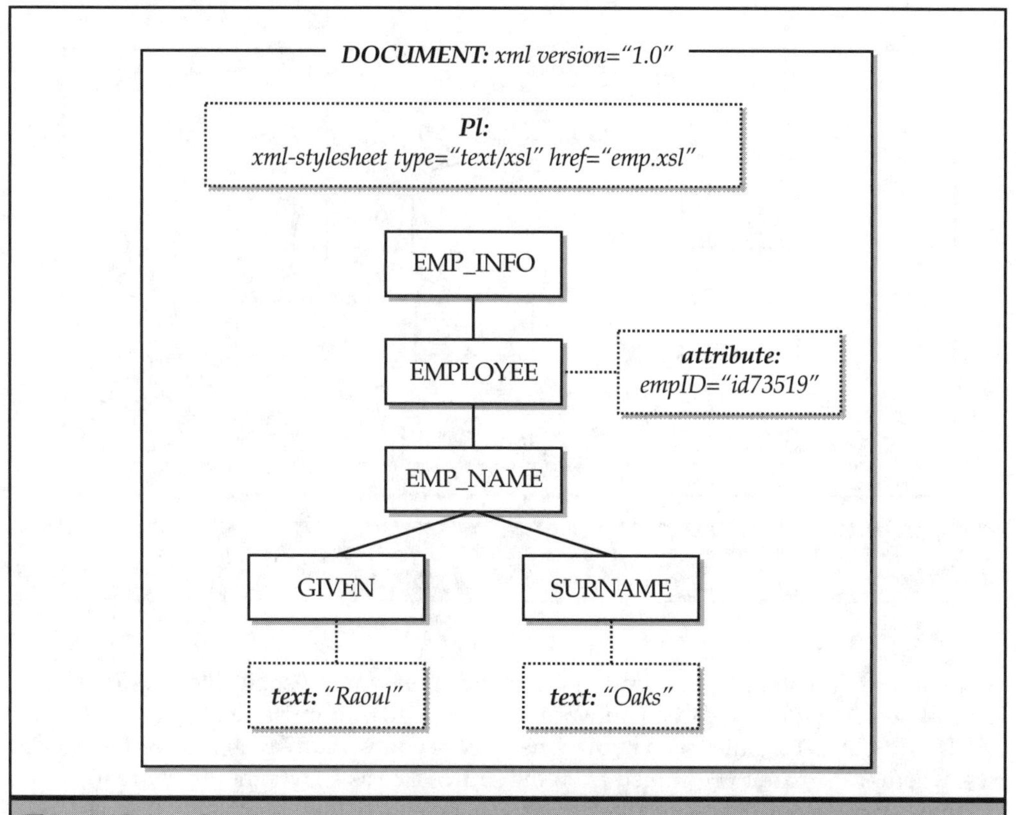

Figure 16-1. *This is a simple tree of XML-based content: note the resemblance to a family tree or bloodline showing how one element is descended from another*

belong to their containing elements. A processing instruction (PI) may or may not be logically contained by an element, but it will always be somewhat apart from what its container represents (since a PI, by definition, is directed to the attention of some application downstream from the parser itself).

Our objective in XSLT transformations will nearly always be to take content from a source tree, such as that shown in Figure 16-1, and place it into a differently structured result tree. For instance, maybe we want to transform our simple document into HTML for display on a Web page; the result tree might look like Figure 16-2.

As you can see, the content from our source tree has been retained, but it is restructured into a form that bears little resemblance to the original. Notice also that there is not necessarily a one-to-one correspondence between the source tree's and result tree's content: the result tree, for example, has a few additional pieces of text added to it, and the `empID` attribute's value is presented in a form that truncates the leading `id` characters.

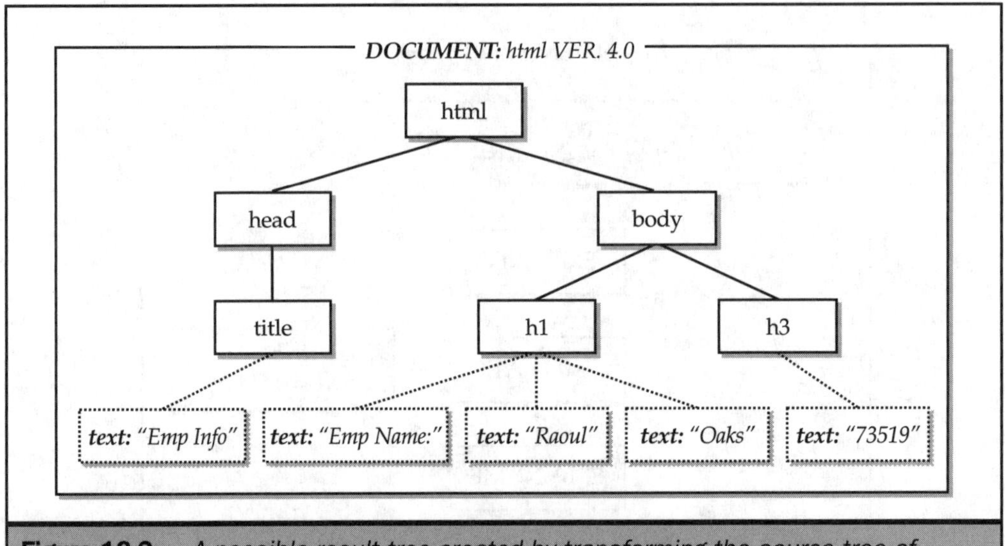

Figure 16-2. *A possible result tree created by transforming the source tree of Figure 16-1 from XML version 1.0 to HTML version 4.0.*

In order to accomplish this kind of transformation, you must be able to understand what pieces of your source tree you want to retain, and you must identify them in your XSLT style sheet. You must also know what pieces you want to appear in your result tree, whether they are to be copied from the source tree as is, whether they are to be modified from the form in which they appear in the source tree, or whether they should be created anew strictly for the result tree's purposes. All of these pieces are known as *nodes*.

Nodes and Node Types

A node is a discrete logical component of an XML document, equivalent to each of the boxes depicted earlier in Figure 16-1. Some nodes may contain other nodes, of the same or different node type, within their scope. XSLT identifies the following node types:

- **Root node** The root node is the document entity itself, which contains all other nodes.
- **Element nodes** Element nodes are the principle containers in any XML document. An XML document with no element nodes is not possible.
- **Attribute nodes** Attribute nodes always belong to some element, never stand alone, and do not contain any other nodes.
- **Text nodes** Strings of text are always associated with some containing element. Using a variety of techniques, text nodes can be further broken down into

substrings, but for the most part, such substrings do not necessarily constitute text nodes in their own right.

- **PI nodes** Like all the rest of a document's content, PI nodes are always contained by the root node. They may or may not also be within the scope of some element as well. (The `xml-stylesheet` PI node in our sample *employee-information* document is not contained by any element.) Although PI nodes usually contain information that looks like attribute-value pairs in addition to the PI target, these pseudo-attributes are not accorded a node type.
- **Comment nodes** Like PIs, comment nodes may be located anywhere in the root node, contained by an element or not. Also like PIs, their content (the text making up the body of the comment) has no special node type associate with it.
- **Namespace nodes** For each namespace declared in a document, an element within the scope of the declaring element has an associated namespace node. Since our sample document does not declare any namespaces, it has no namespace nodes.

Taken together, these seven node types comprise everything within any possible XML document. Given a source tree, if you can locate a node, with XSLT you can transfer it, unchanged, to a node in the result tree; transfer it with changes; or not transfer it at all.

The first and most important question is "How do you locate a node in the first place?" The (deceptively simple) answer to this question is "Use XPath expressions."

The XPath Standard

The World Wide Web Consortium (W3C) has issued the XPath specification as a means of locating any single unit of content—any node—within an XML document. The need to isolate given nodes is critically important not only to XSLT, but also to the XML Pointer Language (XPointer) specification covered in Chapter 24; thus, the need to isolate given nodes is addressed by a separate standard rather than by XSLT itself.

Nodes are located using a construct called an XPath expression, which can often be further decomposed into subordinate expressions. The XPath expression language itself is not an XML vocabulary; rather, it defines a mechanism for using specially formatted text strings as values assigned to specific attributes (in the case of XSLT) or added to Uniform Resource Identifiers (URIs) (in the case of XPointer).

A full XPath expression is coded as a *location path*, consisting of one or more *location steps* delimited as necessary by forward slashes (/ characters). A simple location path therefore resembles a path to a specific file located on some file system, such as a server or workstation. For instance, the following location path locates the `SURNAME` element node in the simple XML document introduced earlier:

```
/EMP_INFO/EMPLOYEE/NAME/SURNAME
```

The leading slash (/) orients the search to the root of the document—the root node—in the same way that a leading slash starts a file-system search at its root directory. Each succeeding location step (reading from left to right) repositions the search deeper into the document's tree of content.

Such simple location paths are often suited best to locating content in simply structured XML documents, such as the *employee-information document* introduced earlier. For example, in that document each element type occurs only once, elements containing text nodes never contain other elements, nor are there any namespaces to deal with. More complex XML structures, such as the following example, will require more sophisticated XPath expressions. We will use a more complete employee-information document as a basis for the XSLT code presented throughout this chapter:

```
<?xml version="1.0"?>
<!DOCTYPE EMP_INFO [
<!ENTITY umlaut "&#252;">
]>
<?xml-stylesheet type="text/xsl" href="emp.xsl"?>
<EMP_INFO
     xmlns="http://foo.com/empinfo" >
     <EMPLOYEE empID="id73519">
          <NAME>
               <GIVEN>Raoul</GIVEN>
               <SURNAME>Oak</SURNAME>
          </NAME>
          <HIRE_DATE>1995-12-01</HIRE_DATE>
          <JOB posID="pos00769">
               <TITLE>President</TITLE>
               <HIRE_DATE>1996-10-12</HIRE_DATE>
               <SUPERVISOR empID="id43298"/>
          </JOB>
          <REVIEW date="2000-09-30">
               <RATING>4.75</RATING>
               <REMARKS>Exceptional job again this year. Job
               performance could not be better. Employee morale
               high.<BREAK/>One suggestion, however: PLEASE buy
               at least a second suit.</REMARKS>
          </REVIEW>
          <SALARY units="usd">
               <BASE>84000</BASE>
               <BONUS>12000</BONUS>
          </SALARY>
     </EMPLOYEE>
```

```
<EMPLOYEE empID="id43298">
     <NAME>
          <GIVEN>Marcia</GIVEN>
          <SURNAME>Elm</SURNAME>
     </NAME>
     <HIRE_DATE></HIRE_DATE>
     <JOB posID="pos00083">
          <TITLE>Chair/Chief Executive Officer</TITLE>
          <HIRE_DATE>1994-03-15</HIRE_DATE>
          <SUPERVISOR/>
     </JOB>
     <REVIEW date="">
          <RATING>N/A</RATING>
          <REMARKS></REMARKS>
     </REVIEW>
     <SALARY units="usd">
          <BASE>175000</BASE>
          <BONUS>12000</BONUS>
     </SALARY>
</EMPLOYEE>
<EMPLOYEE empID="id88822">
     <NAME>
          <GIVEN>Jakob</GIVEN>
          <SURNAME>Pine</SURNAME>
     </NAME>
     <HIRE_DATE>1997-03-15</HIRE_DATE>
     <JOB posID="pos09031">
          <TITLE>Marketing, East Coast</TITLE>
          <HIRE_DATE></HIRE_DATE>
          <SUPERVISOR empID="id98023"/>
          <CURR_PROJ projID="MURG"/>
     </JOB>
     <REVIEW date="2000-09-30">
          <RATING>2.75</RATING>
          <REMARKS>Outstanding effort on the Murgatroyd
          contract led to the division successfully
          meeting overall targets this year. Both parties
          agreed that Jakob's contribution was invaluable,
          especially in negotiating the difficult parking
          issue.<BREAK/>On the other hand, seemed to be
          asleep at the wheel in planning Customer NitFest
          2000 expo, at which attendance fell to 17 this
```

```
            year from last year's record 8,706.<BREAK/>
            Consider reassignment to Kazakhstan field office.
            </REMARKS>
        </REVIEW>
        <SALARY units="usd">
            <BASE>56000</BASE>
            <BONUS>4500</BONUS>
        </SALARY>
    </EMPLOYEE>
    <EMPLOYEE empID="id98023">
        <NAME>
            <GIVEN>I-Ping</GIVEN>
            <SURNAME>Yew</SURNAME>
        </NAME>
        <HIRE_DATE>1996-01-01</HIRE_DATE>
        <JOB posID="pos00021">
            <TITLE>Marketing Director</TITLE>
            <HIRE_DATE>2000-09-30</HIRE_DATE>
            <SUPERVISOR empID="id73519"/>
        </JOB>
        <REVIEW date="">
            <RATING>N/A</RATING>
            <REMARKS>No review; new in position.</REMARKS>
        </REVIEW>
        <SALARY units="eu">
            <BASE>73429.14</BASE>
            <BONUS>6000</BONUS>
        </SALARY>
    </EMPLOYEE>
    <EMPLOYEE empID="id04332">
        <NAME>
            <GIVEN>G&umlaut;nnar</GIVEN>
            <SURNAME>Ash</SURNAME>
        </NAME>
        <HIRE_DATE>1998-11-10</HIRE_DATE>
        <JOB posID="pos50988">
            <TITLE>Marketing, West Coast</TITLE>
            <HIRE_DATE></HIRE_DATE>
            <SUPERVISOR empID="id98023"/>
            <CURR_PROJ projID="RADIO GOVT NONPROF"/>
        </JOB>
        <REVIEW date="2000-09-30">
            <RATING>3.5</RATING>
```

```
                <REMARKS>Although G&umlaut;nnar at times takes
                excessive advantage of the Company's generous
                cell-phone privileges (his monthly bill exceeded
                that of the marketing director), there is no denying
                his enthusiasm and his ingenuity.<BREAK/>This was
                most in evidence in his successful organization of
                the annual company-client volleyball game, for
                which he arranged an appearance by the Dallas
                Cowboys cheerleaders.</REMARKS>
            </REVIEW>
            <SALARY units="usd">
                <BASE>48000</BASE>
                <BONUS>2000</BONUS>
            </SALARY>
        </EMPLOYEE>
    </EMP_INFO>
```


Context

As an XPath-aware processor (like an XSLT processor) works its way through a location path, each location step is considered in the context of the one(s) preceding it. For instance,

```
/EMP_INFO
```

considers the `EMP_INFO` element in the context of the document root node (`/`). One of the differences between XPath as used in XSLT, as opposed to the way it is used in an XPointer, is that the context in the former is continually shifting, requiring the use of relative location steps rather than the absolute location steps leading from the root node. For example,

```
HIRE_DATE
```

is a legitimate location step whose meaning depends on the context in which it is encountered in the style sheet. If in the context of an `EMPLOYEE` element node it means one thing; if in the context of a `JOB` element node, it means quite another.

The node that establishes the context in which an XPath expression is evaluated is called, reasonably enough, the *context node*.

Location Step Syntax

Each location step in a location path is itself an XPath expression. A location step consists of up to three components: an axis; a node test; and a predicate. The general format of a location step containing all three components is as follows:

```
axis::nodetest[predicate]
```

If an axis is present, the double colon (::) is required; similarly, if a predicate is present, it must be enclosed in square brackets ([and]). Whether or not a given location step contains an axis or a predicate, it will always have a node test component.

The purpose of these three components is to select a node (or set of nodes, called a *node-set*) which bears some relationship to the context node. This will be clearer as we examine each of the three components in detail in the following sections and, especially, when we start putting them altogether into complete location steps.

The Axis

The axis tells the processor which direction to look from the context node. The XPath specification defines 13 axes, identified by keywords. Depending on the context node, a given axis enables the processor to see a node-set consisting of one node, several nodes, or no nodes at all. The following are the axes supported by XPath-aware processors:

- **`self`** Locates the context node itself; thus, if using the `self` axis, one and only one node will be visible to the processor.
- **`attribute`** Locates an attribute of the context node. Since only elements may have attributes, if the context node is anything other than an element, the resulting node-set will always be empty.
- **`child`** Locates a node immediately descended from the context node. For instance, if the context node is the root node in our sample document, there is only one node on the child axis: the root element `EMP_INFO`. If the context node is any `NAME` element, looking along the child axis will locate a node-set of two nodes: a `GIVEN` element and a `SURNAME` element. Note that attributes, PIs, and comments are never considered when looking along the `child` axis, even though those node types may (and in the case of attributes, will) belong to an element. If the axis is omitted from an XPath expression, the child axis is the default. It locates the node immediately above the context node in the hierarchy established by the document tree. Only the root node and element nodes will be found along the parent axis, and any given context node will always have one and only one parent. As mentioned in the description of the child node, attributes, PIs, and comments are never considered children of their containing elements; however, if the context node is an attribute, PI, or comment, it will still have a parent. The parent of the `xml-stylesheet` PI in our sample document is the root node of a `posID` attribute, also the `JOB` element to which it applies; the root node has nothing along its parent axis.
- **`descendant`** Extends the notion of the child axis to locate all nodes descended from the context node and at any level of the hierarchy. Since only the root node and element nodes may have child nodes, only they can have descendants as

well. Every node in the document is a descendant of the root node (except of course the root node itself). If the context node is an `EMPLOYEE` element, its descendants are the corresponding `NAME`, `GIVEN`, `SURNAME`, `HIRE_DATE`, `JOB`, `TITLE`, and so on.

- **`descendant-or-self`** Locates all descendants of the context node, as well as the context node itself.
- **`ancestor`** Extends the notion of the parent axis to locate all elements (and the root node) in a direct line above the context node in the document tree—that is, to locate the context node's parent, the parent's parent, and so on. The root node is an ancestor of every other node in the document. The ancestors of a given `NAME` element include the `EMPLOYEE` element directly above it, the `EMP_INFO` element, and the root node. The `xml-stylesheet` PI has only one ancestor, the root node.
- **`ancestor-or-self`** Locates all ancestors of the context node, as well as the context node itself.
- **`preceding`** Locates all nodes that appear in their entirety before the context node and in document order. For any given `EMPLOYEE` element, for example, the `preceding` axis locates not only all the `EMPLOYEE` elements before it (if there are any), but also all descendants of those `EMPLOYEE` elements.
- **`preceding-sibling`** Locates all preceding nodes that share the same parent as the context node. If the context node is a `REMARKS` element, it has only one node along the `preceding-sibling` axis: the corresponding `RATING` element. The root `EMP_INFO` element likewise has a single preceding-sibling: the `xml-stylesheet` PI.
- **`following`** Locates all nodes that appear in their entirety after the context node, in document order. For any given `EMPLOYEE` element, for example, the `following` axis locates not only all the `EMPLOYEE` elements after it (if there are any), but also all descendants of those `EMPLOYEE` elements.
- **`following-sibling`** Locates all following nodes that share the same parent as the context node. If the context node is a `REMARKS` element, it has no nodes at all along the `following-sibling` axis. If the context node is the `xml-stylesheet` PI, it has a single `following-sibling`: the root `EMP_INFO` element.
- **`namespace`** Locates all namespace nodes in effect for the context node. The root node has nothing along the `namespace` axis, since namespace declarations aren't in effect until some element has established them. For any element in our sample document, only one namespace is in effect—the one corresponding to the Uniform Resource Identifier (URI) http://foo.com/empinfo.

Axis Short cuts Several of the axes have shortcut forms, obviating the need to use the full axis name. When you use a shortcut, you do not use the double colon (`::`) that accompanies the equivalent full name. These shortcut forms are

- `.` (single period) is the shortcut for the `self` axis when using the `node()` node test. (This node test is covered next.) The following two expressions both locate the context node:

  ```
  self::node()
  .
  ```

  As mentioned earlier, the child axis is the default; thus, both of the following shortcuts locate all children of the context node that satisfy the node test criterion:

  ```
  child::nodetest

  nodetest
  ```

- `..` (two succeeding periods) locate the parent of the context node. The following two expressions (the first of which uses the node() node test, which is covered in the following section) are equivalent:

  ```
  parent::node()
  ..
  ```

- `@` (at sign) is the short cut for the attribute axis; thus, the following two expressions are equivalent:

  ```
  attribute::nodetest
  @nodetest
  ```

- `//` (two succeeding slashes) is the short cut for the descendant-or-self axis when using the `node()` node test; therefore, the following two expressions are equivalent, both locating all nodes that lay along the descendant-or-self axis from the context node:

  ```
  descendant-or-self::node()
  //
  ```

The Node Test

The node test portion of an XPath expression or location step narrows the view of all the nodes available along the given axis to just a subset of them—that is, it produces a set of *candidate nodes* located by that expression or step.

The node test can take any of three possible forms: a node type, a name, or a specific PI.

- **Node type** If you want to search along the specified axis for nodes of a particular type, you have four choices: the keywords `node()`, `text()`, `comment()`, or `processing-instruction()`. If the node type is `node()`, then all nodes along the indicated axis are located; if the node type is `text()`, then only the text nodes are located; if the node type is `comment()`, then only the comment nodes are located; and if the node type is `processing-instruction()`, then only the PI nodes are located.
- **Name** This is almost certainly the node test you will use or encounter most often. You can test for a specific name; thus, if the context node is a `NAME` element in our sample document, the expression `child::GIVEN` locates the corresponding `GIVEN` element. You can also test using an asterisk (*) as a wildcard. In other words, a wildcard character says: match all named nodes along the axis, regardless of their specific name; therefore, if the context node is a `NAME` element, `child::*` locates a node-set consisting of both the corresponding `GIVEN` and `SURNAME` elements.

Note *Since the child axis is the default, the proceeding two `NAME` expressions could also be represented simply as `GIVEN` or `*`, respectively (assuming the same context node).*

- **Specific PI** If the document contains more than one PI, you can locate it along the indicated axis using the following form:

  ```
  processing-instruction(target)
  ```

  where *`target`*, of course, is the target of the specified PI. If the context node in our sample document is the root node, both the generic node-type test `descendant::processing-instruction()` and the specific `descendant::processing-instruction("xml-stylesheet")` locate the same PI.

Note that each axis has what is called a *principal node type* in effect if none of these specific keywords are used. For most axes, the principal node type is element, but for the attribute axis, is it (obviously) attribute, and for the namespace node it is (also obviously) namespace. Assume that the context node is the root EMP_INFO and that we use this XPath expression to search our sample document:

```
preceding-sibling::node()
```

This locates the PI that precedes the root element

The following XPath expression

```
preceding-sibling::*
```

locates an empty node-set because there are no elements (the preceding-sibling's principal node type) along that axis from the same context node.

The Predicate

The optional predicate portion of an XPath expression further refines the set of candidate nodes established by the axis and node test. What goes between the predicate's square brackets is a *logical test*, yielding a true or false value; only those candidate nodes for which the result of the test is true will be located.

Most commonly, the logical test is in the following form:

```
node operator value
```

where node is itself an XPath expression, operator is a logical operator (to be discussed in the following section) and value is some value to be compared to that of the node.

Operators in a predicate are one of the following:

=	Tests whether the node equals the value
>	Tests whether the node is greater than the value
<	Tests whether the node is less than the value
>=	Tests whether the node is greater than or equal to the value
<=	Tests whether the node is less than or equal to the value
!=	Tests whether the node is not equal to the value

Remember that the node is always evaluated in the context of whatever node is being examined at that point. For example, consider the following expression:

```
JOB[TITLE = "Marketing Director"]
```

The TITLE element being tested here is the TITLE child of whatever JOB element is being evaluated. This might be clearer if we consider how the expression might be alternatively coded using the explicit form of the child axis:

```
JOB[child::TITLE = "Marketing Director"]
```

Compound Predicates A predicate is not constrained to testing a single value; it may establish several conditions, all of which are tested. These multiple conditions are separated from one another using the `and` and `or` keywords, and they are grouped as needed using parentheses.

For example, the following location step locates a `JOB` child of the context node only if the corresponding `TITLE` element is either Marketing Director or President:

```
JOB[TITLE = "Marketing Director" or TITLE="President"]
```

The following location step locates a `JOB` child of the context node only if the corresponding `TITLE` element is Marketing Director or the `TITLE` is President and the `empID` of the corresponding `EMPLOYEE` element is id73519:

```
JOB[TITLE = "Marketing Director" or (TITLE = "President" and empID="id73519")]
```

Note the grouping with parentheses that forces the second and third condition to be evaluated as a single group of conditions that independently returns a true or false value.

Testing for a Node's Existence A predicate can consist of simply a node without the operator and value components. A simple node form of the predicate simply tests whether the indicated node exists.

In the following location step, a `REMARKS` child of the context node is selected only if it contains at least one `BREAK` child:

```
REMARKS[BREAK]
```

As you look back over our sample document, notice that in some cases certain attributes (such as `date`) and elements (such as `HIRE_DATE`) have a value and in other cases they are empty. Testing for a node's empty value is not the same as testing for its existence. To select a `REVIEW` element only if its `date` attribute were specified at all, you'd use a location step such as the following:

```
REVIEW[@date]
```

On the other hand, to select a `REVIEW` element only if its `date` attribute had a nonempty value, you'd use a location step such as the following:

```
REVIEW[@date != ""]
```

This form of the predicate also requires that a `date` attribute be present. If the attribute is completely missing, its value will not be an empty (or any other) string.

XPath Location Path Examples

The following list shows some examples of XPath expressions that can be applied to our sample employee-information XML document. For convenience, rather than change the context node for each example, all of the following examples use absolute rather than relative location paths by using a leading slash to set the context node to the root node.

- Locate all SURNAME elements:

  ```
  /descendant-or-self::SURNAME
  ```

  Note that the preceding example can use the short-cut form of the descendant-or-self axis just as well:

  ```
  //SURNAME
  ```

- Locate all date attributes of REVIEW elements:

  ```
  //REVIEW/attribute::date
  ```

  This could be abbreviated, using the shortcut form of the attribute axis:

  ```
  //REVIEW/@date
  ```

- Locate all date attributes of REVIEW elements, but only if the date is 2001-09-30:

  ```
  //REVIEW/@date[.="2001-09-30"]
  ```

- Locate all REVIEW elements that have a date attribute of 2001-09-30:

  ```
  //REVIEW[@date="2001-09-30"]
  ```

  Note the difference between the example just preceding this one (which locates the elements which have such an attribute) and this one (which locates all occurrences of the attribute itself). Locate all EMPLOYEE elements representing employees reporting to the supervisor whose employee ID is id98023—that is, all EMPLOYEE elements with a descendant SUPERVISOR element whose empID attribute has that value:

  ```
  //EMPLOYEE[descendant::SUPERVISOR/@empID = "id98023"]
  ```

- Locate the surname of the employee responsible for the MURG project:

  ```
  //SURNAME[../following-sibling::JOB/CURR_PROJ/projID="MURG"]
  ```

  The predicate in this expression moves up to the parent of each SURNAME element (..), finds that parent's following-sibling named JOB, moves down to the CURR_PROJ child of that JOB element, and then checks the projID attribute of that CURR_PROJ element for the desired value.

- Locate every RATING element for each REVIEW element with a date attribute of 2000-09-30:

  ```
  //REVIEW[@date="2000-09-30"]/RATING
  ```

- In this example, note that the predicate is applied to an intermediate location step, not to the final one, as in preceding examples. The same result could be achieved by navigating directly to the RATING element, then testing the date attribute of its parent, as follows:

  ```
  //RATING[../@date="2000-09-30"]
  ```

As you can see, location paths can be quite complex—even more so when using relative instead of absolute location paths as in the preceding example. Although complex, such location paths satisfy the need for XPath expressions to locate any given node from any other as the context changes, often in more than one way.

Node Values

In addition to its position in the document tree, every result returned by an XPath expression has a value. This value can be of several data types, as follows:

- **Node-set** The result is an unordered list of one or more nodes.
- **String** The result is a text string.
- **Numeric** The result is a floating-point number.
- **Boolean** The result is a true or false value.

The result of evaluating an XPath location step is always a node-set. A predicate always evaluates to a Boolean value. For text nodes, the data type is string. The number data type has meaning only in terms of XPath functions, which will be covered in the next section.

In addition—and this is important for most applications—a node-set itself has a value. If the node-set consists of a single node, the value is a string consisting of all the text nodes descended from that node. If the node-set comprises more than one node, the value is the same as if the location path had located only the first node in the node-set—that is, a single string consisting of all the text nodes descended from the first node. Consider the following location path:

```
/EMP_INFO/EMPLOYEE/NAME[../empID="id98023"]
```

The path walks down the document to each NAME element, then tests the empID attribute of that NAME element's parent. If the empID attribute has a value of id98023, the NAME element is added to the resulting node-set. Since there is only one NAME element matching this condition, the value of the resulting node-set is the concatenated string values of all text nodes descended from that NAME element, which in this case is I-PingYew. (Note that there is no white space between the concatenated values.)

Now consider the effect of the same location path, without the predicate:

```
/EMP_INFO/EMPLOYEE/NAME
```

Because the resulting node-set consists of all the NAME elements in the document, the value of the node-set is the value of only the first node-set's descendants, which in this case is RaoulOak.

XPath Functions

Although location paths, simple or complex, provide an extraordinary range of possibilities for locating document content, the XPath specification's authors went a step further: they defined a rich set of functions for manipulating content in various ways, thereby returning subsets of the nodes selected by the location paths alone.

As in most programming languages, an XPath function takes the following form:

```
functionname(arg1...)
```

where *functionname* is the name of the function and *arg1...* is a comma-delimited list of arguments, values are passed into the function for evaluation or manipulation in some way. Most functions require a specific number of arguments to be passed into them, and some require no arguments at all. If no arguments at all are required, the parentheses must still be present. (Because arguments can be passed an XPath-aware application to distinguish between a call to the function and a node whose name just happens to be functionname.)

A function (using the arguments passed to it, if any) returns a value to the XPath location step referencing the function. The value effectively replaces the function call in the location step, just as if it were hard coded there.

Functions are classified based on the type of data they return and/or operate on. The next four sections describe each function's purpose and provide examples of each in the context of a full location path. Arguments are identified by their types and are appended with a question mark if they are optional.

Node-Set Functions

This class of function operates on a node-set, returning a value of either string, numeric, or node-set data type.

- **last()** Returns a numeric value representing the number of nodes in the current context. (Also see the count() function, later in this list.) The following example

```
//*[last()=2]
```

returns a node-set consisting of all nodes with exactly two children.

- **`position()`** Returns a numeric value representing the relative position of the current node within a node-set. When used in a predicate with the equality operator (=), the `position()` function call and the operator can be omitted, leaving only the numeric value of the position you want to check for. The following example

  ```
  //EMPLOYEE[position()=2]
  ```

  locates the second `EMPLOYEE` element in the document. This could also be coded more simply by taking advantage of the abbreviated form, as follows:

  ```
  //EMPLOYEE[2]
  ```

- **`count(`*`node-set`*`)`** Returns a numeric value representing the number of nodes in the argument. Note the similarity between this and the `last()` function; the latter, which takes no arguments, always operates on the node-set that is current at the time of the function call. The following example

  ```
  count(//processing-instruction())
  ```

  returns the number 1—the number of PIs in the document.

- **`id(`*`object`*`)`** Returns the element whose ID-type attribute has the string value of object, where object can be either a literal string or a node-set. In the latter case, the value of the node-set is determined using the rules described previously under "Node Values." The following example (assuming `posID` to be an ID-type attribute of the JOB element)

  ```
  id("pos50988")
  ```

  returns the `JOB` element for Günnar Ash (the one whose `TITLE` child is "Marketing, West Coast").

- **`local-name(`*`node-set`*`?)`** Returns as a string the local portion of the expanded name of the first node (in document order) in the node-set passed to the function. If the node-set argument is omitted, the function operates on the context node. The following example

  ```
  local-name(/node()[2])
  ```

  returns the string `EMP_INFO`—the unprefixed name of the second child of the root node. (The first child of the root node is the `xml-stylesheet` PI, which has no namespace association at all.)

- **`namespace-uri(`*`node-set?`*`)`** Returns as a string the URI associated with the namespace of the first node in the passed node-set. If no node-set argument is passed, the function operates on the context node. The following example

  ```
  namespace-uri(/node()[2])
  ```

  returns the string `http://foo.com/empinfo`, or the namespace URI associated with the name of the second child of the root node (the `EMP_INFO` element).

- **`name(`*`node-set?`*`)`** Returns a string representing the fully expanded name, including the namespace URI and local name, of the first node in the node-set passed to the function. If the node-set argument is omitted, the function operates on the context node. The following example

  ```
  name(/node()[2])
  ```

  returns the string `http://foo.com/empinfo:EMP_INFO`—the qualified name (including namespace URI and local-name portions) of the second child of the root node.

String Functions

This set of powerful functions enables you to perform simple to complex operations on values of the string data type. These functions return string, Boolean, or numeric values, as shown.

- **`string(`*`object?`*`)`** Returns the value of object converted to a string. If object is omitted, the function converts the context node to its string value. Otherwise, if object is a
  - **Node-set** The function returns the string value of the first node in the node-set.
  - **Number** The function returns the string value of the number (for example, the number 2 is returned as the string 2). Note that some values that are supposed to be numbers may not actually be so at a given point. For example, if the `SALARY` element were empty or contained alphabetic characters, its numeric value would be a special XPath value called `NaN` (for "not a number"). Passing such a value to the `string()` function results in the string `NaN`.
  - **Boolean** The function returns the string true or false, depending on the value of the Boolean passed to it.
  - **String** The result is the same as if object were simply used by itself without calling the `string()` function.

The following example

```
string(//BONUS)
```

returns the string 12000, which is the string value of the first node in the node-set consisting of all `BONUS` elements.

And the example

```
string(//BONUS[1] = 5000)
```

returns the string `false`, because the result of evaluating the expression inside the parentheses (testing whether the value of the first `BONUS` element equals 5000) is Boolean false.

- **`concat(`*`string1, string2...`*`)`** Returns a string value: the result of concatenating the value of `string2` to `string1`. Note that `string2` can be followed by as many comma-delimited strings as desired, with the result being the concatenation of all arguments.

  The following example

  ```
  concat(//SURNAME[2], ", ", //GIVEN[2])
  ```

  returns the string `Elm, Marcia` (note embedded "," string), and the example

  ```
  concat("Position #", //JOB[2]/@posID, " - " , //JOB[2]/TITLE)
  ```

  returns the string "Position #pos00083 - Chair/Chief Executive Office" (some leading literal text, followed by the value of the second `JOB` element's `posID` attribute, followed by the value of the second `JOB` element's `TITLE` child).

- **`starts-with(`*`string1, string2`*`)`** Returns a Boolean value true if `string1` begins with `string2`; returns a Boolean value false otherwise. The following example

  ```
  starts-with(//JOB/@posID, "pos")
  ```

  returns the Boolean value true. The location path passed as the first argument locates a node-set consisting of all `posID` attributes of all `JOB` elements; the node-set is converted to a string by using the string value of the first node in the node-set (`pos00769`), which does start with the value of the second argument, `pos`, and the example

  ```
  //EMPLOYEE[starts-with(HIRE_DATE, "1995")]
  ```

locates a node-set consisting of all `EMPLOYEE` elements whose `HIRE_DATE` children begin with the string 1995. There is only one such `EMPLOYEE` element, the one corresponding to the employee named Raoul Oak, so the node-set will contain just that one node.

- **`contains(`*`string1, string2`*`)`** Returns a Boolean value true if `string1` contains `string2`; returns a Boolean value false otherwise. The following example

```
//SURNAME[contains(../../JOB/TITLE, "Marketing")]
```

  locates the `SURNAME` element for all employees in the marketing department.

- **`substring-before(`*`string1, string2`*`)`** Returns a string value: that portion of *`string1`* that appears before the value of *`string2`*. The following example

```
substring-before(//NAME[3], //SURNAME[3])
```

  is a rather roundabout way of obtaining the value of the third `GIVEN` element in the document, or Jakob. Note that the value of *`string1`* is the value of the third `NAME` element—the concatenated value of all text nodes descended from that element, or JakobPine.

- **`substring-after(`*`string1, string2`*`)`** Returns a string value: that portion of *`string1`* that appears after the value of *`string2`*. The following example

```
substring-after("text/xsl ", /processing-instruction())
```

  returns the string `href='emp.xsl'`: the portion of the `xml-stylesheet` PI's value that appears after the `type` pseudo-attribute and its value.

- **`substring(`*`string, number1, number2?`*`)`** Returns a string value: that portion of `string` starting at the character position *`number1`* and, if *`number2`* is included as an argument, for the number of characters expressed in *`number2`*. If *`number2`* is not included, the function simply returns the rightmost characters, beginning with number plus 1. The following example

```
substring(//REVIEW[3]/@date, 1, 4)
```

  returns `2000`—the first four characters in the document's third `REVIEW` element's `date` attribute. And the example

```
substring(//TITLE[starts-with(., "Marketing, ", 11)][1]
```

  returns the string `East Coast`, or the value of the first `TITLE` element in the document that starts with the string `Marketing`, beginning at character 12 and continuing through the end of the `TITLE` element's value. (Note the double predicate here: the first selects all applicable `TITLE` elements, and the second selects a specific one of those located by the first.)

- **`string-length(`*`string?`*`)`** Returns a numeric value, the length in characters of *`string1`*. The following example

  ```
  //EMPLOYEE[string-length(HIRE_DATE) = 0]
  ```

  locates all `EMPLOYEE` elements with an empty `HIRE_DATE` child element (that is, the `EMPLOYEE` element for Marcia Elm).

- **`normalize-space(`*`string?`*`)`** Returns a string value equivalent to *`string`*, except that all leading and trailing white space has been stripped, and each occurrence of multiple white space within string is replaced by a single occurrence. This is often an important function to use when comparing two strings to see if they're equal, as sometimes strings (especially in manually created documents) acquire stray blank characters, new lines, and so on. The following example

  ```
  normalize-space("   String with leading and   embedded space")
  ```

  returns the string `String with leading and embedded space` (for example, the same string but with all extraneous white space removed).

- **`translate(`*`string1, string2, string3`*`)`** Returns a string value, the result of replacing each character in *`string2`* that appears within *`string1`* by the corresponding character in *`string3`*. This is often used to force a string to upper- or lowercase, as in the following example

  ```
  translate(//SURNAME[1], "abcdefghijklmnopqrstuvwxyz",
        "ABCDEFGHIJKLMNOPQRSTUVWXYZ")
  ```

  which returns the uppercased value of the document's first `SURNAME` element by substituting capital *A* for each lowercase *a*, capital *B* for each lowercase *b*, and so on. The result is the string `OAK`.

Boolean Functions

These functions all return Boolean true or false values. This makes them particularly suitable for use in the predicate portion of a location step.

- **`boolean(`*`object`*`)`** Converts the *`object`* argument to a `true` or `false` value, depending on its data type. If *`object`* is a number, the function returns `true` only if it is nonzero and not the special `NaN` value; if a node-set, only if it is nonempty; and if a string, only if the length of the string is greater than 0. The following example

  ```
  boolean(//BONUS[3])
  ```

returns true because the value of the document's third BONUS element (4500) is a number. The example

```
boolean(//XYZ)
```

returns false because there is no element in this document named XYZ. And the example

```
boolean(//JOB[last()]/HIRE_DATE)
```

returns false because the value of the last JOB element's HIRE_DATE child is an empty string.

- **not(*boolean*)** Returns the Boolean opposite of whatever value is passed as the argument. That is, if boolean is true, not (*boolean*) returns false; if boolean is false, not (boolean) returns true. Note that if boolean is anything other than a native Boolean value, it is first converted as if using the boolean() function (see boolean(object) at the beginning of this section); if it is a number, for instance, not(boolean) will return true if the number is zero or NaN, and false otherwise. The following example

  ```
  //EMPLOYEE[not(substring(HIRE_DATE, 1, 4) = "1995")]
  ```

  returns a node-set consisting of all EMPLOYEE elements except the first—all EMPLOYEE elements representing employees hired sometime other than in 1995. Note that this returns Marcia Elm's EMPLOYEE element, even though it the corresponding HIRE_DATE is empty, because (since it is empty) it does not indicate a hire year of 1995.

- **true()** Always returns a Boolean true value. This is not particularly useful in its own right, except perhaps to explicitly document that you're testing for a true value; however, it can be useful when using XSLT to pass a parameter to a template. (See the discussion of the xsl:with-param element in "Using Parameters with Named Elements" for an example.)

- **false()** Always returns a Boolean false value. This is not particularly useful in its own right, except perhaps to explicitly document that you're testing for a true value; however, it can be useful when using XSLT to pass a parameter to a template. (See the discussion of the xsl:with-param element in "Using Parameters with Named Elements" for an example.)

- **lang(*string*)** Tests whether the context node is in the language denoted by the string argument as determined by any xml:lang attributes in effect at that point. Our sample document doesn't make use of the xml:lang attribute; suppose, however, that the context node in some document looked like the following:

  ```
  <QUESTION xml:lang="DE">Sprechen Sie Englisch?</QUESTION>
  ```

In this case, this call to the `lang()` function

```
lang("DE")
```

would return true, while

```
lang("EN")
```

would return false.

Numeric Functions

Each of these five functions returns a numeric value, based on the value of the argument passed to it.

- **`number(`*`object?`*`)`** Converts the optional object argument to its numeric value for use in performing arithmetic operations or in other contexts in which a number is required. The object can be of any data type. If it is a string and begins with optional white space, followed by an optional minus sign, followed by a legitimate string representation of a number (for example, with no embedded commas or any other punctuation except a single decimal point), it is converted to that number; any other string is converted to the special `NaN` value. If it is a Boolean `true`, the function returns the number 1, or if it is a Boolean false, the function returns the number 0. If it is a node-set, it is first converted to a string using the rules applied by the `string()` function (see "String Functions" earlier in this chapter) and then handled as if it were itself a string value. Usually, you don't need to convert a value to a number explicitly in order to use it as a number; however, in a location step's predicate (especially when testing a node's position in a node-set), it may be critical to do so. The reason for this is that the position must be numeric—any other data type returns a Boolean true or false, or 1 or 0, respectively. Consider the following example:

  ```
  //EMPLOYEE["5"]
  ```

  Because the value of the predicate (an abbreviated way of saying `position()='5'` in this case) is a string, the predicate (which must always be Boolean) is true, or 1. This will produce quite different results from the following which looks for the information as a numerical value, not a string or Boolean value:

  ```
  //EMPLOYEE[number("5")]
  ```

- **`sum(`*`node-set`*`)`** Returns the sum of the string values (converted to numbers) of all the nodes in the *`node-set`* argument. The following example

  ```
  sum(//BONUS)
  ```

  returns the sum of all `BONUS` elements' values—36500.

- **`floor(`*`number`*`)`** Returns the largest integer that is less than or equal to the argument. The following example

  ```
  floor(//RATING[1])
  ```

  returns the number 4—the largest integer less than or equal to Raoul Oak's `RATING` (4.75).

- **`ceiling(`*`number`*`)`** Returns the smallest integer that is greater than or equal to the argument. The following example

  ```
  ceiling(//RATING[1])
  ```

  returns the number 5—the smallest integer that is greater than or equal to Raoul Oak's `RATING` (4.75).

- **`round(`*`number`*`)`** Returns the integer closest in value to the argument; if there are two such numbers (that is, if the decimal portion of *`number`* equals .5), the larger of the two numbers is returned. The following example

  ```
  round(//RATING[1])
  ```

  returns the number 5—the closest integer to Raoul Oak's `RATING` of 4.75.

Numeric Operators Technically speaking, numeric operators are not XPath functions—no argument is passed to them, but it is important that you understand how to use numeric operators for performing arithmetic calculations.

Most of these operators will be familiar to you from non-XPath contexts. Addition, subtraction, and multiplication are performed using the + (plus), - (minus), and * (asterisk) characters, respectively, and the order in which operations are performed in a single statement can be controlled by grouping with parentheses; however, there are some exceptions to the order in which operations are performed.

First, division is performed using the special operator `div`. This is necessary because the more conventional division operator, a forward slash (/), has special meaning as a step delimiter in an XPath expression.

Second, the modulus (remainder) operation is performed using the special operator `mod`.

Third, you must be careful with white space when using the arithmetic minus (-) operator. Because hyphens are permitted in XML names, an expression such as

```
value1-value2
```

will be interpreted by the application—almost certainly incorrectly—as a node named `"value1-value2"` rather than as the result of subtracting `value2` from `value1`. Written correctly, this expression would be

```
value1 - value2
```

An example of a common arithmetic operation is the calculation of an average. We could calculate the sum of the average salary plus the average bonus using an expression such as this:

```
(sum(//SALARY) div count(//SALARY)) + (sum(//BONUS) div count(//BONUS))
```

The calls to the `count()` function return the number of `SALARY` and `BONUS` elements in the document, each of which is divided into the corresponding sum for the respective averages and then added together using the arithmetic + operator.

Transforming XML with XSLT

Armed with basic concepts already introduced in Chapter 15 and early in this chapter, and with a detailed knowledge of XPath, you're ready to embark on understanding and using XSLT itself.

Style Sheet Structure

An XSLT style sheet is, of course, itself an XML document. This means that at a gross level, it may contain a prologue (the XML declaration, the document-type declaration, and perhaps some comments and PIs), it must contain a root element, and it may contain an epilogue following the root element's end tag. Most commonly, though, a style sheet will consist of the root element only, perhaps preceded by the XML declaration and a comment or two.

Note *Almost no XSLT style sheet will include a document type declaration or, at least, not one requiring validation. Remember that a typical style sheet will, by definition, commingle XSLT markup with result-tree markup and will use namespaces to ensure that the two markup vocabularies do not clash. As discussed in Chapter 7, using namespaces in a document virtually guarantees that you cannot validate it.*

The other significant (and occasionally problematic) implication of an XSLT style sheet being an XML document is that it must be well-formed:

- Special characters such as < and & must be escaped using entities (perhaps declared in an internal DTD subset in the style sheet's prologue) or CDATA sections.
- If the result tree will consist of markup, all its nonempty elements must be delimited by balanced start and end tags—balanced not only in the result tree, but also within the overall framework of the style sheet itself.

- Empty elements must be represented using either the empty start-end tag pair construct or using the special XML <element_name/> syntax.
- All element and attribute names are case sensitive. (All XSLT element and attribute names must be in lowercase, and result-tree names must be in whatever case is appropriate for the target vocabulary.)

The `xsl:stylesheet` Element

The root element in any XSLT stylesheet is the `xsl:stylesheet` element. (Alternatively, you may use a root element of `xsl:transform`, which is a straightforward synonym. Either element is acceptable, but in this chapter we will use the more commonly accepted alternative, `xsl:stylesheet`.)

`xsl:stylesheet` typically declares any namespaces in use throughout the document, and it may perform certain other functions as well. The following is the general syntax of the `xsl:stylesheet` element's start tag:

```
<xsl:stylesheet version="number"
     xmlns:xsl="http://www.w3.org/1999/XSL/Transform"
     [other namespace declarations]
     id="id"
     extension-element-prefixes="tokenizedprefixes"
     exclude-result-prefixes="tokenizedprefixes">
```

Note *The `<xsl:stylesheet>` root element declares an association between the `xsl:` namespace prefix and a particular URI, http://www.w3.org/1999/XSL/Transform. This namespace URI is required by version 1.0 of the XSLT specification. (The prefix itself can be anything, but by convention is almost always `xsl`.)*

Each of the other attributes of your `<xsl:stylesheet>` element are described next.

`version` This attribute, which (like the `xmlns:xsl` namespace declaration) is required, declares the version of the XML specification to which the style sheet conforms. Currently, the only allowable value for this is 1.0.

`[other namespace declarations]` Typically, a style sheet will represent a mix of elements from the XSLT namespace and from the namespace of the result tree. The former is identified by the required namespace declaration described in "The `xsl:stylesheet` Element "above, and the latter must be included, depending on the requirements of the XSLT processor (and perhaps of the result-tree processor itself). Remember that even if the result tree's element names are unprefixed, you must still declare a default namespace for them with an `xmlns` attribute.

The following are some namespace declarations you may see or use

- **xmlns="http://www.w3.org/TR/REC-html40"** Used when the result tree will consist of (unprefixed) elements in the HTML 4.0 namespace
- **xmlns="http://www.w3.org/1999/xhtml"** Used when creating result trees to conform to the XHTML 1.0 specification
- **xmlns:svg="http://www.w3.org/2000/svg"** Used for transforming to a Scalable Vector Graphics (SVG) result tree
- **xmlns:wml="http://www.wapforum.org/xmlns/wml"** Used for transforming XML to the Wireless Markup Language (WML). (The prefix may also be *wap*, declared as xmlns:wap="http://www.wapforum.org/xmlns/wml".)

id This optional attribute is useful when your XSLT style sheet is embedded in the document it is meant to transform, as shown in the following example. The value of the id attribute is presumably unique, and it is used as the value of the href pseudo-attribute in the xml-stylesheet PI that links the document to the internal style sheet.

```
<?xml-stylesheet type="text/xsl" href="#transform_here"?>
<root_elem>
     [etc.]
     <xsl:stylesheet id="transform_here"
          version="1.0"
          xmlns:xsl="http://www.w3.org/1999/XSL/Transform">
          [etc.]
     </xsl:stylesheet>
     [etc.]
</root_elem>
```

extension-element-prefixes This optional attribute declares the namespace prefix(es) that will be used for vendor- or processor-specific elements that extend the XSLT vocabulary in some way. For instance, the Saxon XSLT processor (discussed in Chapter 15) supports a number of such elements; a style sheet making use of these elements (and, of course, intended for processing by Saxon!) might include an xsl:stylesheet start tag such as the following:

```
<xsl:stylesheet version="1.0"
     xmlns:xsl="http://www.w3.org/1999/XSL/Transform"
     xmlns:saxon="http://icl.com/saxon"
     xmlns="http://www.w3.org/TR/REC-html40"
     extension-element-prefixes="saxon">
```

The `saxon` *extension prefix is simply referenced by the* `extension-element-prefixes` *attribute shown in the following example, but declared by its own* `xmlns:saxon` *attribute. If there are more than one such prefix in use in the style sheet, the attribute's value must present them as a tokenized (white space–delimited) list.*

```
extension-element-prefixes="saxon msxml xt"
```

`exclude-result-prefixes` One occasionally disconcerting effect of applying an XSLT transformation to a source tree is that the result tree contains what may be superfluous namespace nodes. (An important word there is *may;* this effect may or may not cause problems downstream.) To ensure that these namespace nodes are not copied to the result tree, use the optional `exclude-result-prefixes` attribute, whose value is a white space–delimited list of the prefixes associated with the namespace nodes that you do not want to be copied.

Consider a hypothetical transformation from some XML vocabulary to one whose associated namespace URI is `http://www.foo.com/myvocab`. The XSLT style sheet might begin as follows:

```
<xsl:stylesheet version="1.0"
     xmlns:xsl="http://www.w3.org/1999/XSL/Transform"
     xmlns:target_vocab="http://www.foo.com/myvocab">
```

Throughout the style sheet, there would be a mix of element names prefixed `xsl:` and also those prefixed `target_vocab:`. The XSLT processor does not know anything about the uses to which the result tree's downstream application will put the names prefixed `target_vocab:`, so, to be safe, it will copy all the namespace nodes (except for the one associated with the `xsl:` prefix itself) to the result tree, just in case they're needed by this downstream program.

Again, this may or may not be a problem (depending particularly on the downstream program's sensitivity to namespaces). An HTML processor (Web browser) is one example of an application that doesn't notice namespaces. If those namespace nodes are indeed superfluous and/or undesired, you can suppress them using the following example attribute:

```
exclude-result-prefixes="target_vocab"
```

There is no way to exclude a default namespace (for example, one declared with a simple `xmlns` *attribute). Also note that despite its name, the* `exclude-result-prefixes` *attribute does not do anything like strip the prefixes from element names—it simply excludes from the result tree the namespace nodes associated with the prefixes.*

Top-Level Elements

XSLT elements that are allowed to appear only as immediate children of the `xsl:stylesheet` element are known as *top-level* elements. Among the top-level elements are several whose role is to establish conditions that will hold true throughout the style sheet's processing. For instance, the `xsl:output` element tells the XSLT processor that the result tree from this transformation should be considered XML, HTML, or plain text. This information lets the processor make various assumptions about its preferred behavior. All the top-level elements will be documented in "Template Rules" later in this chapter.

Arguably the most important single element type in an XSLT style sheet is `xsl:template`. Within each `xsl:template` element—or *template rule*—is where a transformation from source to result tree is specified, and it's hard (to say the least) to imagine an XSLT style sheet that specifies no transformations. For more information on the `xsl:template` element, consult the section "Template Rules" later in the chapter.

Other Elements

Aside from the root `xsl:stylesheet` and its top-level element children, including all the `xsl:template` template rules, an XSLT style sheet may contain a variety of other element types. Many of these will be from the XSLT namespace (and, accordingly, include the `xsl:` prefix in their names) and, depending on the specific element type, may appear as lower-level elements only or as either top- or lower-level elements.

The result trees output from most XSLT transformations are in the form of well-formed documents in a markup language: either HTML or some other XML vocabulary. The non-XSLT elements in these result trees typically appear in the form of *literal result elements*—that is, simply placed as markup in whatever template rule(s) will be instantiating them—in the style sheet mixed among the XSLT elements.

In Chapter 15, we saw an example of an XSLT style sheet containing a single template rule. That template rule was as follows:

```
<xsl:template match="BOOK">
     <html>
          <head><title>Book Information</title></head>
          <body>
               <h1><xsl:value-of select="BOOK_TITLE"/></h1>
               <h2>by <xsl:value-of select="AUTHOR"/></h2>
          </body>
     </html>
</xsl:template>
```

In this template rule, all the markup between the `xsl:template` element's start and end tags, except the two `xsl:value-of` elements, consists of literal result elements from the HTML namespace: `html`, `head`, `body`, `h1`, and `h2`.

Note *In some circumstances, using literal result elements is not possible. For instance, the name of the result element may not be known until runtime, depending on conditions in the source tree. In these cases, the element can be instantiated in the result tree using the special* `xsl:element` *element. There is also an* `xsl:attribute` *element for instantiating computed attributes to result-tree elements, whether the latter are literal or created with* `xsl:element`. *Both* `xsl:element` *and* `xsl:attribute` *are covered later in this chapter in "Creating Elements with* `xsl:element`*" and "Creating Attributes with* `xsl:attribute`*".*

Text

All text that appears in a style sheet between an element's start and end tags, whether the element is from the XSLT or another namespace, is considered to be part of the result tree. (Note, though, that the `xsl:stylesheet` element itself may not directly contain any text nodes, except for white space–only ones such as new lines, tabs, and blank spaces. The latter are assumed to be present only for the style sheet's legibility to human readers and not passed to the result tree.)

A special case is that of white space–only text nodes (blank spaces, tabs, and new lines) that you want to appear in the result tree. An XSLT processor assumes that such white space appears in the style sheet strictly for legibility and will not pass it to the result tree, effectively stripping it as though it had not been included in the first place.

There are a number of ways of overriding this default behavior, the primary way is to use the `xsl:text` element. The following is the general syntax of the `xsl:text` element:

```
<xsl:text disable-output-escaping="yes_or_no">textcontent</xsl:text>
```

To create a white space–only text node, simply enter the desired white space in place of *`textcontent`*. The white space can be entered literally or, if necessary, in the form of an entity reference. For example, the following might appear in an XSLT stylesheet intended to transform the source tree to HTML:

```
<td><xsl:text>&#x20;</xsl:text></td>
```

This forces the table cell (represented by the `td` element) to contain a single nonbreaking space. (It therefore solves a problem with some browsers, which interpret empty `td` elements as though they did not exist at all.)

The optional `disable-output-escaping` attribute of the `xsl:text` element is used to control whether markup-significant characters, such as < and `&`, are *escaped* when placed into the result tree. (The attribute takes a value of either `yes` or `no`, with the latter as the default if the attribute is not provided.) Normally, when an XSLT style sheet is generating a markup-based result tree (such as HTML or XML), you'll want these special characters to be escaped (for example, output in their entity-reference form such as `&` for an ampersand or `<` for a less-than/left-angle-bracket character). In some cases, though, the output must appear in its literal form. For instance, perhaps the style sheet is transforming the source tree to an HTML result tree that includes embedded JavaScript code that needs to do Boolean comparisons:

```
if numVar < 10
```

You can simply enter your `if` statement into a suitable template rule that be passed to the result tree, using any of the following examples (among others):

```
if numVar &lt; 10
```

or

```
if numVar &#60; 10
if numVar <!CDATA[[<]]> 10
```

Regardless of which approach you take, you still need to escape the < character in your style sheet, without which the style sheet would not be well-formed XML.

Whichever method you use, the XSLT processor will output the result tree in its escaped form:

```
if numVar &lt; 10
```

Of course, your style sheet may also use any of the other approaches to escaping the < character, and the result tree will still comply with XML well-formedness requirements. The problem is that the JavaScript will not work correctly with the escaped values. To override this behavior, you need to do something like the following in the style sheet, instead of simply entering the text of the script:

```
<xsl:text disable-output-escaping="yes">
     if numVar &lt; 10</xsl:text>
```

More information about outputting special kinds of text, including white space, is provided in the "Special Result Tree Output" section later in this chapter.

Comments and PIs

As with any other XML document, an XSLT style sheet may contain comments and PIs at any point in the document (except, of course, within a tag, comment, or PI). Comments serve to document the purpose of a given template rule or other markup for human readers of the style sheet. PIs might be required by some XSLT processors to control the behavior of the PIs at specific points during the transformation.

In a style sheet, though, an extra problem arises: "How do we put a comment or PI into the result tree?" Consider the following fragment of a style sheet:

```
<xsl:template ...>
     <BOOK_INFO>
          <!Here is a PI for use by the XYZ application that
          processes the BOOK_INFO element: -->
          <?somePI pseudo-attrib="somevalue"?>
          ...
     </BOOK_INFO>
</xsl:template>
```

The purpose of this template rule is to instantiate a `BOOK_INFO` element in the result tree, within which will appear a comment and the PI that the comment describes; however, if we examine the result tree from the previous example template rule, it looks like the following:

```
<BOOK_INFO>
     ...
</BOOK_INFO>
```

What happened to our comment and PI?

What happened was that the comment and PI were considered to be part of the style sheet itself, not part of the result tree. If comments and PIs were associated with namespaces, we'd be able to disambiguate their purposes in a mixed-vocabulary context. Since that isn't the case, we need a means of explicitly telling the XSLT processor to instantiate a comment or PI in the result tree. XSLT provides two elements to accomplish this: `xsl:comment` and `xsl:processing-instruction`.

`xsl:comment` Using `xsl:comment` is simple. Wherever you'd like the comment to be placed in the result tree, insert an `xsl:comment` element. `xsl:comment` can only contain a text string. In the result tree the content of your `xml:comment` element will appear within the standard `<!– and –> comment` delimiters. The following code places this comment in the same example code from the previous section:

```
<xsl:comment>Here is a PI for use by the XYZ application that
processes the BOOK_INFO element:</xsl:comment>
```

Note *To avoid confusing downstream processors of the result tree, do not include two or more succeeding hyphens (for example, "`--`" or "`---`") in the comment text. The hyphens will not present any special problems for the XSLT processor itself, since they're simply part of a PCDATA text string; however, the result tree will include the hyphens within the comment's `<!– and –>` delimiters, making the comment (and the result-tree document itself) not well-formed.*

xsl:processing-instruction To place a PI into the result tree you just use the `xsl:processing-instruction` element. You can learn more about processing instructions in Chapter 11. The following is the syntax:

```
<xsl:processing-instruction name="target">pi_content</xsl:processing-instruction>
```

For *target*, provide the value to be used as the PI's target. For *pi_content*, provide all the information that you want to appear in the resulting PI between the target and the closing `?> delimiter.`

For instance, the PI in the preceding style-sheet fragment could be placed into the result tree (rather than just skipped over as a PI that the XSLT processor probably does not understand) in the following manner:

```
<xsl:processing-instruction name="somePI">pseudo-
     attrib="somevalue"</xsl:processing-instruction>
```

Template Rules

Easily the most numerous component of a typical XSLT style sheet are its *template rules*. Each template rule is embodied by an `xsl:template` element consisting of the following:

- **Match condition** Locates a portion of the source tree to which this template rule applies
- **Template proper** Instantiates something in the result tree for each matching portion of the source tree

The match condition is specified by the `match` attribute of the `xsl:template` element. The template itself consists of a mix of literal result elements, subordinate XSLT elements, and/or plain text.

The following is the syntax of the `xsl:template` element's start tag:

```
<xsl:template match="xpathpattern"
     name="name"
     priority="priority"
     mode="mode">
```

All attributes are optional; however, there must be either a `match` or a `name` attribute present.

At this point, we will cover the `match` attribute, which is the one you are likely to see and use most often. For more information about the `name` attribute, see the "Using Parameters with Named Templates" section later in this chapter. For more information about the `priority` attribute, see the "Conflict Resolution" section later in this chapter. For more information about the `mode` attribute, see the "Template Rule Modes" section later in this chapter.

To return to our discussion of template rules, we will assume that the following simple XML document is to be transformed to a simple HTML document:

```
<?xml version="1.0"?>
<?xml-stylesheet type="text/xsl" href="temprule_demo.xsl"?>
<BOOKS>
     <BOOK pubyear="1929">
          <BOOK_TITLE>Look Homeward, Angel</BOOK_TITLE>
          <AUTHOR>Wolfe, Thomas</AUTHOR>
     </BOOK>
     <BOOK pubyear="1973">
          <BOOK_TITLE>Gravity's Rainbow</BOOK_TITLE>
          <AUTHOR>Pynchon, Thomas</AUTHOR>
     </BOOK>
     <BOOK pubyear="1977">
          <BOOK_TITLE>Cards as Weapons</BOOK_TITLE>
          <AUTHOR>Jay, Ricky</AUTHOR>
     </BOOK>
     <BOOK pubyear="2001">
          <BOOK_TITLE>XML: The Complete Reference</BOOK_TITLE>
          <AUTHOR>Williamson, Heather</AUTHOR>
     </BOOK>
</BOOKS>
```

The `temprule_demo.xsl` style sheet to which this document is linked might start out containing just an empty `xsl:stylesheet` element such as the following:

```
<xsl:stylesheet version="1.0"
     xmlns:xsl="http://www.w3.org/1999/XSL/Transform"
     xmlns="http://www.w3.org/TR/REC-html40">
</xsl:stylesheet>
```

If you actually apply this style sheet to the previous document, using a conformant XSLT processor such as Saxon, you get a result tree that looks something like the following:

```
Look Homeward, Angel
Wolfe, Thomas


Gravity's Rainbow
Pynchon, Thomas
```

```
Cards as Weapons
Jay, Ricky


XML: The Complete Reference
Williamson, Heather
```

While this is not necessarily wrong output, it depends what we really want the result tree to look like; this output certainly won't display in a Web browser in a useful form. Remember that Web browsers collapse each occurrence of contiguous white space (such as the new lines and blank spaces in the preceding result tree) into a single blank space; therefore, the preceding list would display as a single string of text:

```
Look Homeward, Angel Wolfe, Thomas Gravity's Rainbow Pynchon,
Thomas Cards as Weapons Jay, Ricky XML: The Complete Reference
Williamson, Heather
```

Where did this result tree come from?

Built-in Template Rules

The preceding result tree was created from the template rules built into any conformant XSLT processor. These built-in template rules are the default for any nodes in the source tree that are unmatched by specific template rules. Each node type possible in the source tree (elements, text, attributes, and so on) has its own built-in rule; however, in general, the effect of the built-in template rules is to transfer only the text nodes (and all the text nodes) found in the source tree to the result tree. Any or all of the built-in rules can be overridden, as we will see, by coding an explicit template rule that matches the same types of nodes as those matched by a given built-in rule.

Built-in Template Rule for the Root and All Element Nodes The root node and all element nodes in the source tree are by default processed by a template rule that looks like the following:

```
<xsl:template match="*|/">
     <xsl:apply-templates/>
</xsl:template>
```

The `match` portion of this template rule states that the rule applies either to all element nodes, regardless of their names (note the asterisk in the `match` attribute's value), or (symbolized by the pipe symbol, |) to the root node (symbolized by the forward slash, /).

As for the template portion of the rule, because it contains only the empty `xsl:apply-templates` element, it does one thing only: instructs the XSLT processor to look for and apply all template rules for any children of the current node in the node-set located by the match expression.

Therefore, considering this built-in template rule only, the XSLT processor starts reading the source tree by looking for a root node. It finds one (since all source trees have a root node) and then looks for any template rule (built-in or explicit) for the root node's children. From the discussion of the XPath child axis in "The XPath Standard" earlier in this chapter, we know that there are two node types that can be located as children: text and element nodes. The root node has no text children, but it has an element node child, the `BOOKS` element. And where in this style sheet so far is there a template rule that matches the `BOOKS` element? The answer: Only in this same built-in template rule. So the `BOOKS` element is then processed by the built-in rule, by processing all its children, which locates the four `BOOK` elements, and so on, recursively, down the document tree.

Text and Attribute Nodes Text and attribute nodes in the source tree are, by default, processed according to a built-in template rule that looks like the following:

```
<xsl:template match="text()|@*">
     <xsl:value-of select="."/>
</xsl:template>
```

This is the template rule that is primarily responsible for the result we've gotten from our (so-far) empty style sheet. Translated, the match expression says that this template rule applies to any node in the source tree that is either a text-type node (note the `text()` node-type test in the XPath expression) or (symbolized by the pipe, `|`) an attribute node of any name (the `@*`, which is an abbreviated form of the XPath location step `attribute::*`).

The template portion of this built-in rule says to instantiate in the result tree, for each matching portion of the source, its value. (Recall that a single period, `.`, is an abbreviated form of the `self::node()` location step.)

At this point, we've got a style sheet that is not truly empty but includes two implicit (built-in) template rules and looks like the following:

```
<xsl:stylesheet version="1.0"
     xmlns:xsl="http://www.w3.org/1999/XSL/Transform"
     xmlns="http://www.w3.org/TR/REC-html40">

     <xsl:template match="*|/">
          <xsl:apply-templates/>
     </xsl:template>

     <xsl:template match="text()|@*">
          <xsl:value-of select="."/>
     </xsl:template>

</xsl:stylesheet>
```

The first built-in rule causes the tree of root and element nodes to be walked recursively, looking for any child nodes and processing them according to this or other template rules in the style sheet. The second rule is fired whenever a text or attribute node is encountered through the recursive walk of the tree effected by the first rule.

The second built-in rule is the source of all the text in our result tree. The values of all the text nodes—children of the `BOOK_TITLE` and `AUTHOR` elements—are copied unchanged to the result tree. But why didn't the `pubyear` attributes' values likewise get copied?

The answer is that an element's attributes are invisible when looking along the child axis. Although the match expression in this second built-in rule itself looks along the attribute axis, this template rule is fired only within the context of a higher-level template rule that says "process all children."

If we really want each attribute's values (as well as the text nodes) to be dumped to the result tree, we need to override the first built-in template rule by supplying another that explicitly does something different when encountering the same match pattern. Something like the following would serve this purpose:

```
<xsl:template match="*|/">
     <xsl:apply-templates select="*|text()|@*"/>
</xsl:template>
```

Note that here we've supplied an explicit select attribute for the `xsl:apply-templates` element. By default, `xsl:apply-templates` element processes all children of the context node. The optional `select` attribute's value is an XPath expression whose value is evaluated relative to the context in which the `xsl:apply-templates` element occurs. This `select` attribute, which appears in the context of processing the root and all element nodes, says to process all child elements, regardless of their name (the asterisk in the attribute value), regardless of all text nodes (the `text()`), and regardless of all nodes visible along the attribute axis from the current node.

Now, whenever a root or element node is encountered in the source tree, not just that node's children (elements or text) but also any nodes visible along the attribute axis from that node will be processed by other template rules (built-in or explicit) in the style sheet. The result tree from our transformation now looks like the following:

```
1929
     Look Homeward, Angel
     Wolfe, Thomas

1973
     Gravity's Rainbow
     Pynchon, Thomas

1977
     Cards as Weapons
```

ADDING STYLE

```
     Jay, Ricky

2001
     XML: The Complete Reference
     Williamson, Heather
```

Note the addition of the pubyear attributes' values to the result tree.

Processing Instruction and Comment Nodes By default, all PIs and comments in the source tree are processed by a built-in template rule that puts nothing into the result tree for each match. This built-in rule looks like the following:

```
<xsl:template match="processing-instruction()|comment()"/>
```

As you can see, the match portion of the template rule matches any PI or comment node. Because the xsl:template element is empty, it contains only a match pattern, no template proper, and hence instantiates nothing in the result tree.

Explicit Template Rules

The built-in template rules, unless overridden, will handle all of the source tree not explicitly handled by explicit template rules for specific nodes or node types. You can provide as many of these explicit template rules as you want or need.

Returning to our sample XML document and remembering that we'd like to transform it to HTML, we could code an explicit template rule for the root BOOKS element that looks something like this:

```
<xsl:template match="BOOKS">
     <html>
          <head>
               <title>Influential Books</title>
          </head>
          <body>
               <table border="1">
                    <tr>
                         <th>Title</th>
                         <th>Author</th>
                    </tr>
                    <xsl:apply-templates/>
               </table>
          </body>
     </html>
</xsl:template>
```

Reading down through the preceding template rule, it performs the following steps:

- Matches the root BOOKS element.
- Instantiates html, head, title, and body elements in the result tree.
- Sets up a table in the result tree, the first row of which consists of two table header (th) cells.
- Still within the bounds of the result tree's table element, instructs the XSLT processor to process all children of the BOOKS element (xsl:apply-templates with no select attribute specified).

When applied to the sample document by the Saxon XSLT processor, this stylesheet produces the following result tree:

```
<html xmlns="http://www.w3.org/TR/REC-html40">
     <head>
          <title>Influential Books</title>
     </head>
     <body>
          <table border="1">
               <tr>
                    <th>Title</th>
                    <th>Author</th>
               </tr>

               Look Homeward, Angel
               Wolfe, Thomas


               Gravity's Rainbow
               Pynchon, Thomas


               Cards as Weapons
               Jay, Ricky


               XML: The Complete Reference
               Williamson, Heather

          </table>
     </body>
</html>
```

When viewed in the browser (Microsoft Internet Explorer 5.5 in this case), the preceding HTML document appears as in Figure 16-3.

Netscape 6 and Opera 4 display the HTML document slightly differently than in Figure 16-3. Regardless of the browser used, though, the results are definitely not what we want. More likely, what we want is to have a separate table row for each BOOK element in the document. So let's add a second explicit template rule to the style sheet:

```
<xsl:template match="BOOK">
     <tr>
          <td><xsl:value-of select="BOOK_TITLE"/></td>
          <td><xsl:value-of select="AUTHOR"/></td>
     </tr>
</xsl:template>
```

This template rule says that whenever you encounter a BOOK element in the source tree, instantiate a table row (tr element) in the result; and, within each such table row, instantiate two table cells whose contents are the value of the BOOK_TITLE and AUTHOR elements, respectively.

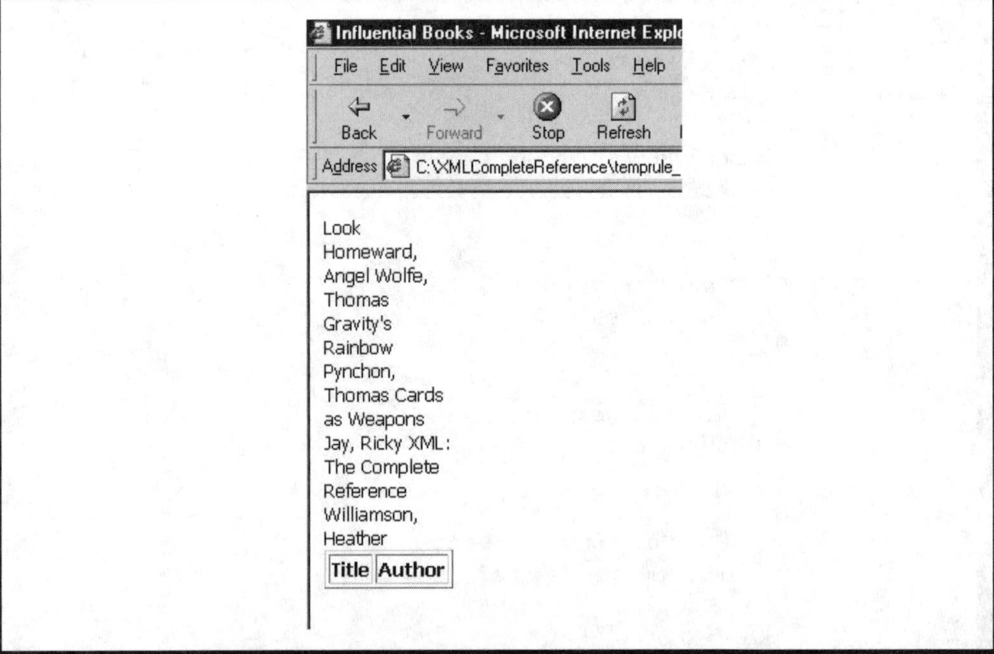

Figure 16-3. *This HTML document is a result of applying a single explicit template rule to the book-information XML document (`temprule_demo.xml`).*

Note *It is important that the values of the two* `xsl:value-of` *elements'* `select` *attributes are* relative *XPath expressions. The values of the* `select` *attributes do not specify that the processor should begin at the top of the source tree to obtain the correct* `BOOK_TITLE` *and* `AUTHOR` *elements; this would be extremely complicated to code and also extremely inefficient. Rather, they say to locate the children (remember: the child axis is the default) of the* `BOOK` *element whose names are* `BOOK_TITLE` *and* `AUTHOR`*. The template rule's match pattern (*`match="BOOK"`*) establishes a context within which the relative XPath expressions are evaluated.*

Now the following is the complete result tree:

```
<html xmlns="http://www.w3.org/TR/REC-html40">
     <head>
          <title>Influential Books</title>
     </head>
     <body>
          <table border="1">
               <tr>
                    <th>Title</th>
                    <th>Author</th>
               </tr>
               <tr>
                    <td>Look Homeward, Angel</td>
                    <td>Wolfe, Thomas</td>
               </tr>
               <tr>
                    <td>Gravity's Rainbow</td>
                    <td>Pynchon, Thomas</td>
               </tr>
               <tr>
                    <td>Cards as Weapons</td>
                    <td>Jay, Ricky</td>
               </tr>
               <tr>
                    <td>XML: The Complete Reference</td>
                    <td>Williamson, Heather</td>
               </tr>
          </table>
     </body>
</html>
```

When viewed in IE 5.5, this HTML document looks much more like what we're after, as you can see in Figure 16-4.

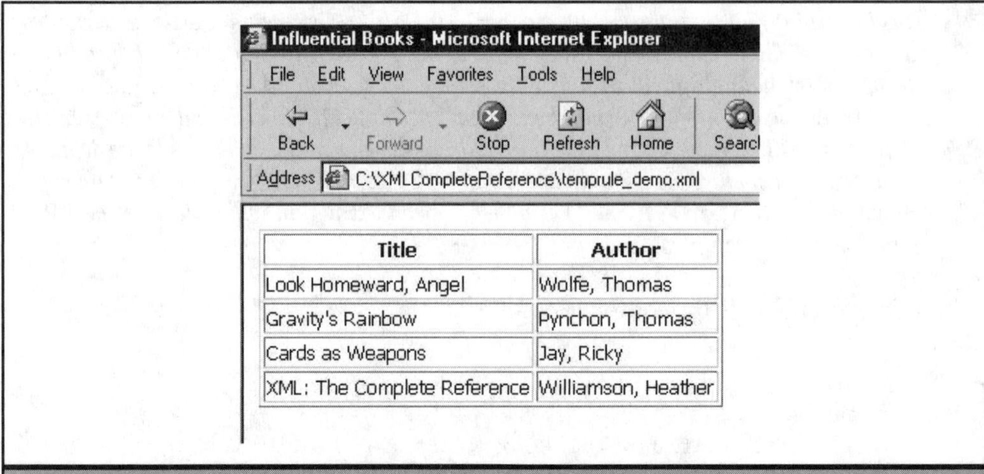

Figure 16-4. *Element and text nodes from the source document are transformed to an HTML table in the result tree and viewed in a browser*

At this point, the only text we're viewing from the document comes from the text nodes that make up various elements' content. We could also include the text making up the `pubyear` attributes' values by modifying the template rule for the `BOOK` element as follows:

```
<xsl:template match="BOOK">
     <tr>
          <td><xsl:value-of select="BOOK_TITLE"/></td>
          <td><xsl:value-of select="AUTHOR"/></td>
          <td><xsl:value-of select="@pubyear"/></td>
     </tr>
</xsl:template>
```

Take note of the addition of the third table cell in the row. This will also require an additional table header cell in the template rule for the `BOOKS` element. When the additional header row has been added, the resulting HTML document finally contains all the content that was in our original source document, as depicted in Figure 16-5. The source tree's `xml-stylesheet` PI is part of that document's content, but we haven't bothered copying the PI to the result tree because Web browsers ignore PIs.

Template Rule Processing Sequence

The designers of the XSLT specification created the standard with the intention that no template rule could interfere with or otherwise affect the processing of any other template rule. This goal has the useful effect of enabling each template rule to stand on its own

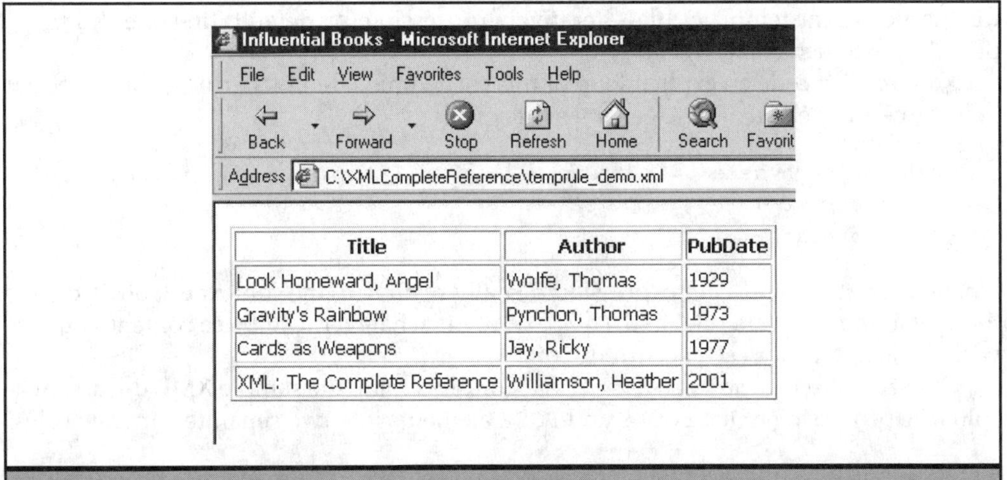

Title	Author	PubDate
Look Homeward, Angel	Wolfe, Thomas	1929
Gravity's Rainbow	Pynchon, Thomas	1973
Cards as Weapons	Jay, Ricky	1977
XML: The Complete Reference	Williamson, Heather	2001

Figure 16-5. *Result of completely transforming the source document to an HTML result tree, is viewed in IE 5.5*

without us having to worry whether some other template rule might be superseding it or changing the context in which it operates; however, this so-called side-effect-free processing model can lead to some surprising conclusions, especially if you are used to using procedural programming languages. In such languages, one statement that follows another is generally executed after it. In the XSLT world, however, there is no telling in what order the processor will actually fire any template rules. The only thing that you can be sure of is that the structure of the source tree will probably influence the processing order.

Note *The operational word in the preceding sentence is probably. No XSLT processor is required to fire template rules in any particular order; firing them in the order that their source tree matches are found is simply one practical approach that a processor's developer may take.*

While this can be confusing, one beneficial effect is that you can group template rules in any order that makes sense for your purposes, which means any order that makes sense for other human readers or users of your style sheets.

Looping Within a Template Rule

As described in "Built-in Template Rule for the Root and All Element Nodes", a template rule's `xsl:apply-templates` descendant will cause all (or selected) nodes along the child or other axis to be processed. Since there are often multiple nodes along a given axis from any other node in the document, this results in a sort of implicit looping within that portion of the template rule—iteratively processing (by default) first one child, then the next, then the next, and so on.

You can also code an explicit loop of this sort within a template rule, using a special `xsl:for-each` element. The general syntax is

```
<xsl:for-each select="pattern">
     [template]
</xsl:for-each>
```

where *`pattern`* is an XPath expression (usually relative to the context established by the containing template rule) and *`[template]`* is whatever result tree content you wish to instantiate for each occurrence of *`pattern`*.

Our style sheet (`temrule_demo.xsl`) for processing the sample XML document splits the processing of the `BOOKS` and `BOOK` elements into two separate template rules:

```
<xsl:template match="BOOKS">
     <html>
          <head>
               <title>Influential Books</title>
          </head>
          <body>
               <table border="1">
                    <tr>
                         <th>Title</th>
                         <th>Author</th>
                         <th>Pub Date</th>
                    </tr>
                    <xsl:apply-templates/>
               </table>
          </body>
     </html>
</xsl:template>

<xsl:template match="BOOK">
     <tr>
          <td><xsl:value-of select="BOOK_TITLE"/></td>
          <td><xsl:value-of select="AUTHOR"/></td>
          <td><xsl:value-of select="@pubyear"/></td>
     </tr>
</xsl:template>
```

These two template rules could be combined into one by extracting the BOOK element's template and adding it to that of the BOOKS element, which is in an xsl:for-each loop that replaces the latter's xsl:apply-templates element:

```
<xsl:template match="BOOKS">
     <html>
          <head>
               <title>Influential Books</title>
          </head>
          <body>
               <table border="1">
                    <tr>
                         <th>Title</th>
                         <th>Author</th>
                         <th>Pub Date</th>
                    </tr>
                    <xsl:for-each select="BOOK">
                         <tr>
                              <td><xsl:value-of select="BOOK_TITLE"/></td>
                              <td><xsl:value-of select="AUTHOR"/></td>
                              <td><xsl:value-of select="@pubyear"/></td>
                         </tr>
                    </xsl:for-each>
               </table>
          </body>
     </html>
</xsl:template>
```

This behaves exactly as the two separate template rules did. Which you use is often a matter of choice, but sometimes you will need to use one or the other, depending on the structure of the source tree and, especially, the nature of the result tree to which you're transforming it.

Conflict Resolution

What happens when a given portion of the source tree is matched by more than one template rule? Which template rule applies?

How to resolve this kind of conflict is defined by the XSLT standard in a series of tie-breaking tests, which work something like the conflict resolution rules in Cascading Style Sheets (CSS). In general, the template rule that most specifically matches is the one that wins the tie and will be applied to the portion of the source tree that is causing the conflict.

To be specific, the conflict resolution is handled by a conformant XSLT processor as follows:

1. Any matching template rules with a lower import precedence are eliminated from consideration. (See Chapter 12 for more information on importing and including style sheets.)
2. If there is still a conflict, the processor computes a priority for each conflicting template rule. This priority is assigned in the following way:
   - If the match pattern contains a pipe symbol (|) separating alternative match patterns, it is treated as if it were a set of independent template rules, one per alternative pattern.
   - If the pattern consists of a specific element name or is of the form `processing-instruction (name)`, the priority is 0.
   - If the pattern uses a wild card asterisk as the node test, optionally preceded by an axis, the priority is –0.25.
   - If the pattern consists of a simple node test preceded by an axis, the priority is –0.5.
   - Otherwise, the priority is 0.5.

Note *The general effect here is to assign a priority of 0 to the most common match pattern—which is typically a pattern that locates a node by its specific name. Because the more general cases (locating using the wild card or using a simple node-type test) are assigned lower priorities, anything more specific than a pattern locating a node by name will* fall through *to be given a priority of 0.5.*

3. Only the template rule(s) with the highest priority are retained. If there is still a conflict, the XSLT processor may either flag it as an error or accept the conflicting template rule that occurs last in the style sheet.

Let's look at a simple XML document (`priority.xml`) and some match patterns that refer to it:

```
<?xml version="1.0"?>
<ROOT_ELEM>
     <SUBORD_ELEM>Some content</SUBORD_ELEM>
     <SUBORD_ELEM>Some more content</SUBORD_ELEM>
</ROOT_ELEM>
```

Assume that a style sheet to process this document contains a number of template rules (`xsl:template` elements), including five whose start tags are as follows:

```
<!-- Template rule #1 -->
<xsl:template match="*">...</xsl:template>
<!-- Template rule #2 -->
<xsl:template match="SUBORD_ELEM">...</xsl:template>
<!-- Template rule #3 -->
<xsl:template match="SUBORD_ELEM[2]">...</xsl:template>
<!-- Template rule #4 -->
<xsl:template match="node()">...</xsl:template>
<!-- Template rule #5 -->
<xsl:template match="SUBORD_ELEM[position()!=1]">...</xsl:template>
```

We have a conflict in the making here: all five template rules potentially apply to the second `SUBORD_ELEM` element. The following are the priorities that the XSLT processor will assign to these template rules and the rules it will therefore select

- Template rule #1 uses the wildcard syntax for locating an element, regardless of its name; therefore, the priority assigned to this rule is –0.25.
- Template rule #2 is a bit more specific, matching all element nodes named `SUBORD_ELEM`. This fits the most-common-pattern situation and is therefore assigned a priority of 0.
- Template rule #3's match pattern not only locates an element with the name `SUBORD_ELEM`, it also specifically locates the second node in the node-set of all `SUBORD_ELEM` elements. This is a fall-through case and receives a priority of 0.5.
- Template rule #4 applies to all nodes on the child axis, regardless of their type or name. This gets the –0.5 priority.
- Template rule #5 locates a node-set consisting of all `SUBORD_ELEM` nodes other than the first. Since this document has only two such nodes, this match pattern locates the second `SUBORD_ELEM`, and since the pattern is not structured according to one of the other forms, it falls through to the 0.5 priority.

Thus, the highest priority assigned is 0.5, meaning that template rules 3 and 5 are still in conflict. The XSLT processor might opt to flag this as an error, or it might simply accept rule #5 without comment. (As a practical matter, most XSLT processors can be expected to follow the latter course of action.)

Conditional Processing

Often, you will want to instantiate content in your style sheet's result tree depending on some condition(s) inherent in the source. This can be accomplished using either an `xsl:if` element if there is only one condition and a corresponding result tree, or an `xsl:choose` structure if there is more than one.

The `xsl:if` Element: Single Conditions, Single Results

The `xsl:if` element places content into the result tree only if its condition is met. The general syntax is

```
<xsl:if test="condition">
     [template]
</xsl:if>
```

where *condition* is a logical test resulting in a Boolean true or false value, and *[template]* is whatever content you want to instantiate in the result tree if the value of *condition* is true.

In our sample XML document, take note of the values of the various `pubyear` attributes. One of the books was first published in 1929, two were first published in the 1970s, and one was first published in 2001. Suppose we wanted to highlight the titles of the books published during the 1970s by adding an asterisk to the titles. We might use the following template for the `BOOK` element:

```
<xsl:template match="BOOK">
     <tr>
          <td>
               <xsl:value-of select="BOOK_TITLE"/>
               <xsl:if test="starts-with(@pubyear, '197')"> *</xsl:if>
          </td>
          <td><xsl:value-of select="AUTHOR"/></td>
          <td><xsl:value-of select="@pubyear"/></td>
     </tr>
</xsl:template>
```

The `xsl:if` element here tests to see if the current `BOOK` element's `pubyear` attribute starts with the string `197`, and if so, a space and an asterisk are appended to the value of the `BOOK_TITLE` element. To see the result as viewed in IE, see Figure 16-6. The test for when each book was published is handled by an `xsl:if` element.

The `xsl:choose` Structure: Multiple Conditions, Multiple Results

While the `xsl:if` element is useful, it works only for testing conditions (and instantiating templates) one at a time. More useful and concise for most purposes is the `xsl:choose` structure, which permits testing as many conditions (and instantiating as many different templates) as you need. The following is the general form of this structure of elements and attributes:

```
<xsl:choose>
     <xsl:when test="condition1">[template1]</xsl:when>
     <xsl:when test="condition2">[template2]</xsl:when>
```

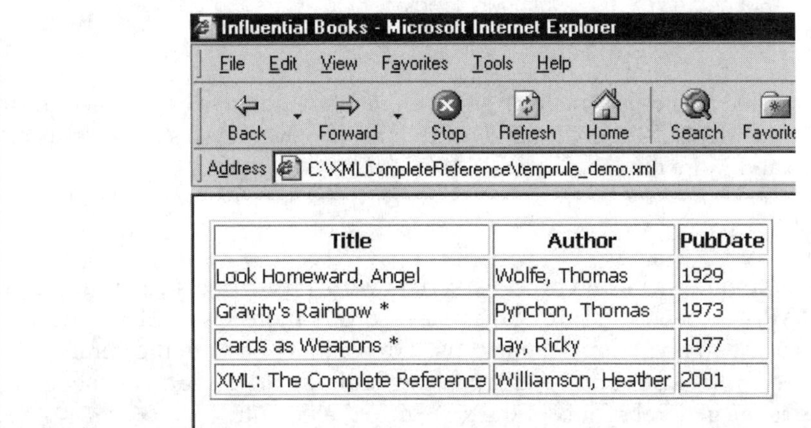

Title	Author	PubDate
Look Homeward, Angel	Wolfe, Thomas	1929
Gravity's Rainbow *	Pynchon, Thomas	1973
Cards as Weapons *	Jay, Ricky	1977
XML: The Complete Reference	Williamson, Heather	2001

Figure 16-6. *Book information document is shown with titles of all books published in the 1970s marked with an asterisk.*


```
    ....
    <xsl:when test= "conditionn">[templaten]</xsl:when>
    <xsl:otherwise>[fallthrough_template]</xsl:otherwise>
</xsl:choose>
```

Here, each of the various conditions (1 through n) is paired with a corresponding template of its own. If none of the conditions are true, the `[fallthrough_template]` associated with the `xsl:otherwise` element is instantiated.

Note `xsl:otherwise` *is optional. If it is omitted, and none of the* `xsl:when` *conditions are met, then nothing is instantiated in the result tree at the point of the* `xsl:choose`.

Whether you're using `xsl:if` or a series of `xsl:when` elements in an `xsl:choose` block, the `condition` evaluated by the `test` attribute can be a compound condition: multiple tests, separated from one another by *and* and/or *or* keywords and, optionally, grouped as necessary using parentheses. For example, consider the following template rule (which does not apply to the sample XML document we've been using up to this point):

```
<xsl:template match="REGION">
     <xsl:choose>
          <xsl:when test="REG_NAME='NORTH AMERICA' or REG_NAME='EUROPE'
               or REG_NAME='SOUTH AMERICA' or REG_NAME='CENTRAL AMERICA'">
               <h2>Western Hemisphere</h2>
          </xsl:when>
          <xsl:when test="REG_NAME='ASIA' or REG_NAME='AUSTRALIA' ">
               <h2>Eastern Hemisphere</h2>
          </xsl:when>
```

```
            <xsl:otherwise><h2>(Unknown Region)</h2></xsl:otherwise>
        </xsl:choose>
    </xsl:template>
```

Each of the six expected values for the REG_NAME element could have been tested for in its own xsl:when element. Using compound conditions, however, makes the style sheet both more concise and more readable.

Sorting

One of the most common tasks when processing data with a recurring structure—such as the data in an XML document—is sorting the data on one or more keys. XSLT provides this function by way of an xsl:sort element used in conjunction with the iterative processing afforded by the xsl:apply-templates and xsl:for-each elements.

The following is the general syntax of the xsl:sort element:

```
<xsl:sort
      select="xpathexp"
      lang="languagecode"
      data-type="text_number_name"
      order="ascending_descending"
      case-order="upper-first_lower-first" />
```

All the attributes are optional. The purpose of each attribute and the kinds of values it may take are as follows:

- **select** Identifies the key on which the data will be sorted. Takes as its value a string representing an XPath expression evaluated relative to the context in which the xsl:sort element appears. The default value is simply . (the XPath abbreviated syntax for self::node()), meaning that the sort will be on the string value of the current node-set.
- **lang** This identifies the language of the document, using a string value that may be any of the language codes supported by the xml:lang attribute. There is no express default value; if not supplied, the default is simply determined by the processor from the system environment. The language in which the sort key appears is important because different languages sort the same sequences of characters differently.
- **data-type** The datatype is specified by the string designators "text" or "number", or by a name representing some other data type (although the XSLT standard explicitly says that processor behavior when using such other data types is "not specified"). The default value is text. You should consider using the value number if the key on which you are sorting is truly numeric, as this can affect the final ordering. Consider the following data values:

```
1
2212
```

```
101
35
```

Sorted as text, these values would appear in the order 1, 101, 2212, 35 because lexically speaking, the sort examines the characters in the data from left to right. The single character 1 is lexically less than the string 101, which in turn is less than the string 2212, which is less than the string 35. Sorted numerically, the order is more likely to be as expected: 1, 35, 101, 2212.

- **order** This controls the sort order of the nodes. Its values ascending (the default) or descending; the order in which the nodes are to be sorted.
- **case-order** This controls the sort order of the document in reference to the letter-case of the document content. Allowable values upper-first or lower-first with the default dependent on the value of the `lang` attribute (if explicit in the document or as inferred from the system environment). The idea here is that you may need to be concerned with (for example) sorting the string abc either before or after the string Abc. To make abc sort ahead of Abc, assign a `case-order` of lower-first; otherwise, use "upper-first."

Sorting on Multiple Keys

If you need to sort your data on more than one value, simply specify multiple `xsl:sort` elements, one after another. Each succeeding `xsl:sort` will be interpreted as less important than the one(s) preceding it. For instance, consider an employee-information document whose data we want to appear sorted, in its transformed state, first by surname (ascending order), then by given name (ascending order), then by birth date (descending order). We could use a set of `xsl:sort` elements such as the following to accomplish this:

```
<xsl:sort select="SURNAME"/>
<xsl:sort select="GIVEN"/>
<xsl:sort select="BIRTH_DATE" order="ascending"/>
```

Sorting with xsl:apply-templates

One way you can use `xsl:sort` is as a child of the (normally empty) `xsl:apply-templates` element. For example, our current XSLT style sheet (`temprule_demo.xsl`) for the book-information document currently contains two template rules, one for processing the root `BOOKS` element and one for the subordinate `BOOK` element; the latter is invoked by an `xsl:apply-templates` element within the former:

```
<xsl:template match="BOOKS">
     <html>
          <head>
               <title>Influential Books</title>
          </head>
          <body>
```

```
                <table border="1">
                     <tr>
                          <th>Title</th>
                          <th>Author</th>
                          <th>Pub Date</th>
                     </tr>
                     <xsl:apply-templates/>
                </table>
           </body>
      </html>
</xsl:template>

<xsl:template match="BOOK">
      <tr>
           <td>
                <xsl:value-of select="BOOK_TITLE"/>
                <xsl:if test="starts-with(@pubyear, '197')"> *</xsl:if>
           </td>
           <td><xsl:value-of select="AUTHOR"/></td>
           <td><xsl:value-of select="@pubyear"/></td>
      </tr>
</xsl:template>
```

We can specify that the children of BOOKS (that is, the four BOOK elements) are to be sorted by the author's name by replacing the xsl:apply-templates element with the following:

```
<xsl:apply-templates>
     <xsl:sort select="AUTHOR"/>
</xsl:apply-templates>
```

Note that the XPath expression used as the value of the select attribute is not BOOK/AUTHOR, but simply AUTHOR. This attribute's value has already been pushed down to the level of the BOOKS element's children (that is, the BOOK elements) by virtue of being embedded in an xsl:apply-templates element.

Sorting with xsl:for-each

Unlike the xsl:apply-templates element, xsl:for-each generally is not empty; it contains a template to be instantiated in the result tree for each of the selected nodes. For xsl:sort elements to be used with xsl:for-each, they must be the first children of the xsl:for-each and ahead of any other content (including text as well as markup).

Our sample XSLT style sheet does not include an `xsl:for-each` element, but as mentioned in "The `xsl:choose` Structure: Multiple Conditions, Multiple Results", we could easily combine the two template rules into a single one using `xsl:for-each` instead of xsl:apply-templates. Within the `xsl:for-each` element described in that section, we could sort the book information by publication date with the following template rule:

```
<xsl:template match="BOOKS">
     <html>
          <head>
               <title>Influential Books</title>
          </head>
          <body>
               <table border="1">
                    <tr>
                         <th>Title</th>
                         <th>Author</th>
                         <th>Pub Date</th>
                    </tr>
                    <xsl:for-each select="BOOK">
                         <xsl:sort select="@pubyear"/>
                         <tr>
                              <td><xsl:value-of select="BOOK_TITLE"/></td>
                              <td><xsl:value-of select="AUTHOR"/></td>
                              <td><xsl:value-of select="@pubyear"/></td>
                         </tr>
                    </xsl:for-each>
               </table>
          </body>
     </html>
</xsl:template>
```

Effects of Sorting on Node Position

Aside from knowing how to sort the nodes in a node-set, you need to understand how sorting nodes affects their position.

When nodes are processed normally (without an `xsl:sort`) by an `xsl:apply-templates` or `xsl:for-each` element, the value of the XPath `position()` function for a given node indicates its position in that node-set *in document order*.

Sorting changes this default; now the `position()` function returns a given node's position *in sorted order*.

So nodes C, D, B, and A may appear in the document in that order, with C in position 1, D in position 2, and so on, and that is the order in which the `xsl:apply-templates` or `xsl:for-each` loop will process them. When processed within a sorted `xsl:apply-templates` or `xsl:for-each`, though, A will be in position 1 (and processed first), B in position 2 (processed second), and so on.

Generating Content in the Result Tree

Probably the most common ways of instantiating content in a style sheet's result tree are by placing literal result elements and/or the `xsl:value-of` element at the desired point in your template.

Those are not the only ways, however, and in some cases they may not work at all. Such cases are those in which a result-tree element or attribute's name cannot be known in advance, but must be computed at runtime, and those in which a result-tree attribute's value must be computed at runtime.

Creating Elements with `xsl:element`

Look back at our sample book-information XML document. It contains data on four books. Suppose as an exercise you want to display each book's title as an HTML heading element, with the size of the heading dependent on the position of the `BOOK` element, for instance the first title will be displayed as an `h1` element, the second as an `h2`, and so on.

You can do this using literal result elements, but the XSLT coding required to do so is rather clumsy and, depending on how many `BOOK` elements there are, may not work for all of them. The following code creates a document with various levels of heading elements based upon the position of the book title within the document:

```
<xsl:template match="BOOK">
     <xsl:choose>
          <xsl:when test="position()=1">
               <h1><xsl:value-of select="BOOK_TITLE"/></h1>
          </xsl:when>
          <xsl:when test="position()=2">
               <h2><xsl:value-of select="BOOK_TITLE"/></h2>
          </xsl:when>
          <xsl:when test="position()=3">
               <h3><xsl:value-of select="BOOK_TITLE"/></h3>
          </xsl:when>
          [etc., perhaps to infinity]
          <xsl:otherwise>(Too many book titles!)</xsl:otherwise>
     </xsl:choose>
</xsl:template>
```

Note the relationship between the `BOOK` element's position and the name of the corresponding HTML heading element. Basically, you must hardcode this relationship for as many `BOOK` elements as you can imagine a document having.

XSLT provides a special element, `xsl:element`, whose purpose is the creation of result-tree elements when literal result elements cannot be made to work easily (or at all). The following is its syntax:

```
<xsl:element
     name="name"
     namespace="uri"
     use-attribute-sets="setnames">
     [content]
</xsl:element>
```

The attributes and their values are as follows:

- **name** This required attribute specifies the name of the element that will be created in the result tree. Its value can be an XPath expression, an attribute value template (as shown in the following example), or a combination of the two.
- **namespace** This attribute, which is optional, specifies the namespace URI to be associated with the generated element name. If omitted, the generated element will be associated with whatever namespace the same element would have if it were represented as a literal result element.
- **use-attribute-sets** This optional attribute's value is a white space–delimited list of names of named attribute sets (as shown in the following example) to be associated with this generated element.

Using the name attribute alone, we could solve our theoretical heading-size problem with an `xsl:element` element, as in the following code:

```
<xsl:template match="BOOK">
     <xsl:element name="concat('h', position())">
          <xsl:value-of select="BOOK_TITLE"/>
     </xsl:element>
</xsl:template>
```

The name of the HTML heading element is created dynamically, at runtime, by concatenating the letter *h* with the value of the given BOOK element's position in the current node-set. The corresponding portion of the result tree looks like this:

```
<h1>Look Homeward, Angel</h1>
<h2>Gravity's Rainbow</h2>
<h3>Cards as Weapons</h3>
<h4>XML: The Complete Reference</h4>
```

Creating Attributes with `xsl:attribute`

The `xsl:attribute` element serves two roles. First, it can be used in the same way as `xsl:element`—in this case, to create an attribute whose name is not known until runtime. Second, it must be used if the element to which the attribute will be assigned is instantiated with `xsl:element` statement, rather than as a literal result element.

The following is the general syntax of the `xsl:attribute` element:

```
<xsl:attribute
     name="attribname"
     namespace="uri">
     [attrib_value]
</xsl:attribute>
```

The attributes and their values are as follows:

- **name** This is the name of the attribute to be instantiated in the result tree. Its value, *attribname*, can be a simple string, an XPath expression, or an attribute value template (see the following example). The `name` attribute is required.
- **namespace** This optional attribute's value is a URI to be associated with the generated attribute's name. If the `namespace` attribute is not provided, its value is undefined.
- ***[attrib_value]:*** This is the text that the generated attribute will take as its value.

Whether used to create an attribute for a literal result element or to create an attribute for an element generated with `xsl:element`, the `xsl:attribute` element must appear as a child of that literal result element or `xsl:element` immediately following the start tag (for example, before any actual content).

In the discussion of the `xsl:element` element, located in the previous section "Creating Elements with `xsl:element`", we saw how to use that element to assign heading sizes based on the position within a node-set of selected source-tree nodes. We could assign a `class` attribute to those heading elements using the `xsl:attribute` element discussed in " Creating Attributes with `xsl:attribute`", enabling them to be styled in a particular way with a CSS style sheet, as in the following example:

```
<xsl:template match="BOOK">
     <xsl:element name="concat('h', position())">
          <xsl:attribute name="class">book-title</xsl:attribute>
          <xsl:value-of select="BOOK_TITLE"/>
     </xsl:element>
</xsl:template>
```

The corresponding portion of the result tree will now look like this:

```
<h1 class="book-title">Look Homeward, Angel</h1>
<h2 class="book-title">Gravity's Rainbow</h2>
<h3 class="book-title">Cards as Weapons</h3>
<h4 class="book-title">XML: The Complete Reference</h4>
```

Named Attribute Sets A very useful feature of XSLT is the use of *named attribute sets* to group together often-referenced attributes and their values, obviating the need to repeat identical `xsl:attribute` definitions across many elements. The following is its syntax:

```
<xsl:attribute-set
     name="attribsetname"
     use-attribute-sets="setnames">
     [xsl:attribute elements]
</xsl:attribute-set>
```

The attributes and their values are as follows:

- **`name`** This required attribute assigns a name to the attribute set; this name can then be used in the value of a `use-attribute-sets` attribute of any `xsl:element`, `xsl:attribute`, or `xsl:copy` element. (The `xsl:copy` element is covered later in this chapter in the section titled "Copying Nodes from Source to Result Tree.")
- **`use-attribute-sets`** This optional attribute permits the use of named attribute sets by other named attribute sets. The value of the attribute is a white space–delimited list of names corresponding to the values of the `name` attributes of other named attribute sets.
- ***`[xsl:attribute elements]`*** These types of attributes are simply a list of `xsl:attribute` elements that you want to group together under the umbrella of this named attribute set.

One instance in which these attributes are useful when transforming to HTML is the creation of tables and, in particular, of table cells. Frequently, all of the `td` elements (and sometimes the `th` elements as well) in a table or table column share the same attributes and values: `align` and `valign`, cell width, and perhaps height, background, style, as well as other HTML attributes. A named attribute set per this description might look like the following:

```
<xsl:attribute-set
     name="col-attribs">
     <xsl:attribute name="align">left</xsl:attribute>
     <xsl:attribute name="valign">top</xsl:attribute>
     <xsl:attribute name="width">25%</xsl:attribute>
     <xsl:attribute name="class">special-data</xsl:attribute>
</xsl:attribute-set>
```

A template rule could then make use of this named attribute set as follows:

```
<tr>
     <xsl:element name="td" use-attribute-sets="col-attribs">
          value1
     </xsl:element>
```

```
        <xsl:element name="td" use-attribute-sets="col-attribs">
             value2
        </xsl:element>
        <xsl:element name="td" use-attribute-sets="col-attribs">
             value3
        </xsl:element>
        <xsl:element name="td" use-attribute-sets="col-attribs">
             value4
        </xsl:element>
</tr>
```

This creates a table row comprising four table cells (`td` elements), each of them having the identical attributes as established by the `col-attribs` named attribute set. The result tree from this template will appear like this:

```
<tr>
     <td align="left" valign="top" width="25%" class="special-data">
          value1
     </td>
     <td align="left" valign="top" width="25%" class="special-data">
          value2
     </td>
     <td align="left" valign="top" width="25%" class="special-data">
          value3
     </td>
     <td align="left" valign="top" width="25%" class="special-data">
          value4
     </td>
</tr>
```

Note *Using named attribute sets not only can make your style sheet more concise and readable. It can also greatly simplify maintenance because you simply need to change an* `xsl:attribute` *element's value once to have the change propagate out to all elements that reference that named attribute set.*

Attribute Value Templates

It is often useful to generate an attribute's value at the time of transformation and based upon, but not necessarily exactly equal, to something in the source tree; furthermore, sometimes we'd like to be able to use source-tree content in the attributes of elements from the XSLT namespace. Both of these situations can be handled using what are called *attribute value templates*.

An attribute value template (AVT) is used as all or part of some attribute's value. The word *template* in the term refers to the use of an XPath expression that grabs something from the source tree and inserts it into the attribute value, perhaps intermingled with literal text. The template portion of the AVT is enclosed in curly braces ({}), and the whole thing is enclosed within the quotation marks or apostrophes that surround (as usual) the given attribute's value.

For instance, in "Creating Elements with `xsl:element`", found earlier in this chapter, we used an `xsl:element` element to create an HTML heading element whose size correlated to a given node's position in a node-set. The name of the generated element was computed using the XPath `concat()` string function:

```
<xsl:element name="concat('h', position()">...</xsl:element>
```

The same thing could have been accomplished using an AVT:

```
<xsl:element name="h{position()}">...</xsl:element>
```

AVTs are a very common solution to a very common question: "How do I create an HTML link (`a` element) from my XML document, which stores the URIs as element content?" For example, the XML document in question may look something like the following:

```
<?xml version="1.0"?>
<?xml-stylesheet type="text/xsl" href="avt_demo.xsl"?>
<LINKBASE>
     <LINK>
          <LINK_TEXT>CNN</LINK_TEXT>
          <LINK_URI>http://www.cnn.com</LINK_URI>
     </LINK>
     <LINK>
          <LINK_TEXT>Osborne-McGrawHill</LINK_TEXT>
          <LINK_URI>http://www.osborne.com/</LINK_URI>
     </LINK>
     <LINK>
          <LINK_TEXT>World Wide Web Consortium</LINK_TEXT>
          <LINK_URI>http://www.w3.org</LINK_URI>
     </LINK>
     <LINK>
          <LINK_TEXT>Internal Revenue Service</LINK_TEXT>
          <LINK_URI>http://www.irs.gov</LINK_URI>
     </LINK>
</LINKBASE>
```

We could transform this to an unordered list of HTML hyperlinks using a style sheet (avt_demo.xsl) such as the following:

```
<xsl:stylesheet version="1.0"
     xmlns:xsl="http://www.w3.org/1999/XSL/Transform"
```

```
     xmlns="http://www.w3.org/TR/REC-html40">

<xsl:template match="LINKBASE">
     <html>
          <head>
               <title>My Linkbase</title>
          </head>
          <body>
               <h2>Favorite Links</h2>
               <ul>
                    <xsl:apply-templates/>
               </ul>
          </body>
     </html>
</xsl:template>

<xsl:template match="LINK">
     <li>
          <a href="{LINK_URI}"><xsl:value-of select="LINK_TEXT"/></a>
     </li>
</xsl:template>

</xsl:stylesheet>
```

Take note of the AVT in the template rule for the `LINK` elements.

Restrictions on Using Attribute Value Templates An AVT can be used in the attribute value for any literal result element (such as the `a` element in the preceding example). It may also be used in attribute values for some XSLT elements, except the following:

- Attributes whose value is an XPath expression/pattern, such as the `match` attribute of the `xsl:template` element
- Attributes for top-level elements
- Attributes that refer to named XSLT objects, such as a named attribute set
- Attributes that declare a namespace, such as `xmlns` and `xmlns:html`

For the complete list of which attributes of which XSLT elements may contain attribute value templates, consult the XSLT specification at http://www.w3.org/Style/XSL.

Variables and Parameters

Most programming languages provide a means of setting aside named areas of storage into which values can be placed during program execution. These values can then be retrieved simply by referring to the corresponding name of that area of storage.

Similarly, most programming languages include some convention for passing data back and forth among discrete units of program code. Even though one unit cannot see what is going on inside another, it may still be able to see, and use, shared data values.

Strictly speaking, XSLT is not a programming language; nonetheless, the standard does include both variables and parameters.

Variables

Using variables in your style sheets can accomplish a couple of goals. First, they offer a convenient shorthand way of referring to complex code or XPath expressions that you need to use more than once. Second, even if you need to use the code/expression just once, the name of the variable can afford a convenient way to document the variable's purpose.

Note *An XSLT variable is not like variables in other languages in one very important respect: once its value is assigned during a given transformation, it never changes. The term variable refers simply to the fact that its value is unknown until runtime, and it may in a different runtime session assume a totally different value. In practice, XSLT variables are more like constants than like traditional variables!*

In XSLT, a variable is assigned a value using the `xsl:variable` element. This element, which can be a top-level element or included within a template rule, has the following general syntax:

```
<xsl:variable
     name="varname"
     select="expression">
     [content]
</xsl:variable>
```

The attributes of the `xsl:variable` element are as follows:

- **name** This required attribute provides a name by which the variable can be referred to. Elsewhere in the style sheet, references to a variable always take the form `$varname`; in the `name` attribute's value, the leading `$` is omitted.

- **select** This optional attribute can assign to the variable some portion of the source tree, using an XPath expression or a string value. Note that if you want to assign a literal string value to the variable in this way, you must enclose the `select` attribute's value in internal quotation marks as well. For example:

  ```
  <xsl:variable name="alpha_chars" select="'abcd'"/>
  ```

  If the internal quotation marks were not included, the XSLT processor would assume that the select attribute intended to assign to the variable the value of the XPath expression abcd—that is, the value of the node-set containing all `abcd` elements.

- ***[content]*** An `xsl:variable` element may be empty or may have content, which is a template just like those that appear in a template rule. (If a `select` attribute is used, the element must be empty.) This template will then be the value of the variable whenever it is referred to in the style sheet. The data type of this value is neither string, numeric, Boolean, nor node-set, but a new type called a *result tree fragment*. More information on result tree fragments is provided later in the chapter in the section titled, "Result Tree Fragments."

Here's a template rule that we might include in a style sheet intended to process the sample book-information XML document we've been using throughout this chapter:

```
<xsl:template match="BOOK">
    <tr>
        <td>
            <xsl:value-of select="BOOK_TITLE"/>
            <xsl:if test="starts-with(@pubyear, '197')"> *</xsl:if>
        </td>
        <xsl:variable name="auth_sur" select="substring-before(AUTHOR, ', ')"/>
        <xsl:variable name="auth_given" select="substring-after(AUTHOR, ', ')"/>
        <td><xsl:value-of select="concat($auth_given, ' ', $auth_sur)"/></td>
        <td><xsl:value-of select="@pubyear"/></td>
    </tr>
</xsl:template>
```

Within the template rule, two variables are declared—`$auth_sur` and `$auth_given`—representing the author's surname and given name, respectively. They're assigned values extracted from the `AUTHOR` element's content, keying on the fact that this content is always structured the same way, as "surname, givenname" (with a comma and space between the two). These two variables are then used to fill in the second table cell (`td` element), instead of the value as it appeared in the source tree's `AUTHOR` element.

We haven't changed the template rule for the `BOOKS` element at this point; the template still sorts the `BOOK` elements by the `AUTHOR` element's value. Thus, the output from the style sheet at this point appears in IE as in Figure 16-7.

Variable Scope An XSLT variable has meaning only within the element in which the `xsl:variable` appears—that is, its value is visible only there (and in subordinate elements, if any).

In the previous example, we saw how one template rule could sort on the value of the `AUTHOR` element, even though the value actually displayed was the concatenation of two substrings of that element, each substring being declared as a variable. What we could not do would be to sort in the first template rule using as a sort key the variables declared in the second. That is, the following would be illegal:

```
<xsl:apply-templates>
     <xsl:sort select="concat($auth_given, ' ', $auth_sur)"/>
</xsl:apply-templates>
```

This would be illegal not because the select attribute's value is malformed—this is a perfectly acceptable sort key—but because the first template rule cannot see the variables declared in the second.

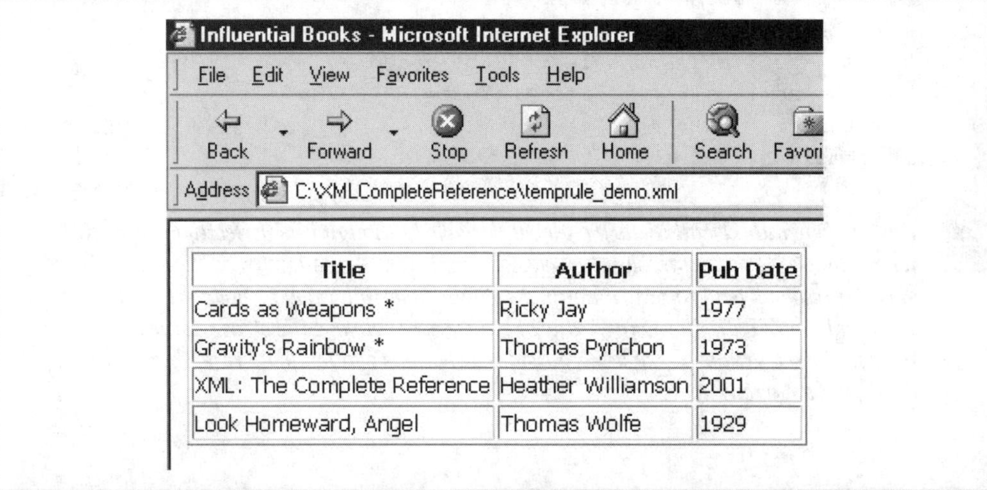

Figure 16-7. *Result of sorting by `AUTHOR` in "surname, givenname" form, but actually displaying the name in natural "givenname surname" form using variables looks like this.*

Global Variables The `xsl:variable` element does not have to appear in a template rule; it can be a top-level element(a child of `xsl:stylesheet`) that makes its value accessible to any template rule that needs it. However, this kind of variable is most commonly used for simple boilerplate text that you want to instantiate more than once in the result tree.

For example, a style sheet might need to create multiple tables, each with the same table headings (`th` elements). You could put this heading code into a top-level `xsl:variable` element such as the following:

```
<xsl:variable name="tbl_head">
     <tr>
          <th>Emp ID</th>
          <th>Emp Name</th>
          <th>SSN</th>
          <th>Salary</th>
     </tr>
</xsl:variable>
```

Then, any template rule in the style sheet could include these table headings in its template simply by referencing the variable `$tbl_head`:

```
<xsl:template match="EMPLOYEES">
     <table>
          <xsl:value-of select="$tbl_head"/>
          <xsl:apply-templates select="EMPLOYEE"/>
     </table>
</xsl:template>
```

Note

It is not generally useful in such a global variable (although it is perfectly legal in XSLT terms) to use XPath expressions to select content from the source tree. The reason is that such expressions tend to return not just a single node, but a whole node-set, and according to the rules of XPath, the string value of a node-set is always the string value of the first node in the set. At the global level, outside the bounds of a template rule, there is no real concept of a current node.

Result Tree Fragments When an `xsl:variable` uses the `select` attribute to assign the variable's value, the data type of the value depends on the data type returned by the XPath or string expression in that attribute; however, when an `xsl:variable`'s value is assigned by way of a template, the value has a data type of result tree fragment.

A result tree fragment is something like a node-set that has a single root node. The result tree fragment contains one or more element nodes, perhaps some attributes and text, and so on—in short, it contains whatever a regular template might include. However, there are only two things you can do with a result tree fragment: you can treat it as a string, or you can copy it to the result tree. Most important, you cannot walk through its structure as you can with a node-set. This is something of a crippling limitation.

For example, it would be nice to be able to define a variable whose contents consisted of a mixture of text and a subtree of the source tree. Then we could simply walk through that variable's tree of nodes whenever we needed to, which would be more concise, more legible, more convenient, and quite possibly more efficient than repeatedly constructing the same subtree for each template rule that needed it.

Most XSLT processors come with an extension function—`prefix:node-set()`—whose purpose is to convert a result tree fragment into a node-set for performing exactly such operations. You pass the function the name of the variable in question, and, in return you get to process it just as if it were a true tree of content. For instance, consider the following global variable declaration:

```
<xsl:variable name="bookinfo">
     <xsl:value-of select="(BOOK_TITLE | AUTHOR)[starts-with
   (../@pubyear, '197')]"/>
</xsl:variable>
```

When this variable is applied to our sample book-information XML document, it assumes as its value a result tree fragment that looks like the following:

```
<BOOK_TITLE>Gravity's Rainbow</BOOK_TITLE>
<AUTHOR>Pynchon, Thomas</AUTHOR>
<BOOK_TITLE>Cards as Weapons</BOOK_TITLE>
<AUTHOR>Jay, Ricky</AUTHOR>
```

A result tree fragment needn't be a well-formed XML document in its own right when there is no single root element.

ADDING STYLE

To process the AUTHOR nodes in this variable, we could use the node-set() extension function of our favorite XSLT processor (Saxon, in this case) in something like the following manner:

```
<xsl:template match="saxon:node-set($bookinfo)/AUTHOR">
     [etc.]
</xsl:template>
```

Parameters

Very similar to variables, *parameters* are used to pass information back and forth among templates and even (using *global parameters*) from the operating environment to the style sheet.

Parameters are declared using the following syntax:

```
<xsl:param
     name="paramname"
     select="expression">
     [content]
</xsl:param>
```

The attributes and *[content]* take the same values and perform as they do when used in an xsl:variable element; in addition, you refer to a parameter just as you do a variable, using its name prefixed with a leading dollar sign ($). The difference is that the value of a parameter as established by the xsl:param element is only its default value. The style sheet may set other values for it at different points and (if it is a global parameter) so may the operating environment. If the xsl:param element is a top-level element, it identifies a global parameter; if used within a template, its effects are visible only within that template.

Using Parameters with Named Templates The most common use of local (for example, nonglobal) parameters is to pass information to *named templates*. A named template is a boilerplate template consisting for the most part of what you'd normally see in a template: literal result elements, text, xsl:element and/or xsl:attribute elements, but (optionally) also data that may be filled in by the template that invokes the named template. The syntax for a named template requires a top-level xsl:template element with a name attribute and no match attribute:

```
<xsl:template name="templatename">
     [template]
</xsl:template>
```

Here, of course, *templatename* is used as the name of the template—the referenceable name used by other templates in the style sheet. This invocation takes the following form:

```
<xsl:call-template name="templatename"/>
```

When an `xsl:call-template` element as shown in the previous example is encountered, the information included in the named template's *[template]* is copied to the result tree at that point in the invoking template. So far, the function performed by a named template is identical to that performed by a global variable, as described in the paragraphs above the previous example.

The difference becomes plain when you use a named template with an embedded `xsl:param` element. The following is a simple example:

```
<xsl:template name="book_hdg">
     <xsl:param name="book_title" select="(No Title)"/>
     <h1>Title: <xsl:value-of select="$book_title"/></h1>
</xsl:template>
```

Here, the value of the parameter `$book_title` is inserted into a level-1 heading. The value of the parameter, as set by the `xsl:param` element, is by default the string `(No Title)`; therefore, under normal circumstances, whenever the processor encounters

```
<xsl:call-template name="book_hdg"/>
```

it will instantiate in the result tree the same boilerplate:

```
<h1>(No Title)</h1>
```

However, the XSLT standard provides a way for invoking templates to override the parameter's default value: the `xsl:with-param` element. This element (which must be a child of the `xsl:call-template` element in question) takes the following syntax:

```
<xsl:with-param
     name="paramname"
     select="expression">
     [value]
</xsl:with-param>
```

As with both the `xsl:variable` and `xsl:param` elements, you can assign a value to the `xsl:with-param` element using either the `select` attribute (in which case the element will be otherwise empty) or by providing some content in place of *[value]* (in which case there will be no `select` attribute). In either case, the value of the `xsl:with-param` element will override the default value of the indicated parameter in the named template.

Thus, assuming the preceding named template, book_hdg, we could do something like the following:

```
<xsl:template match="BOOK[1]">
     <xsl:call-template name="book_hdg">
          <xsl:with-param name="book_title" select="BOOK_TITLE"/>
     </xsl:call-template>
```

```
        <h2>by <xsl:value-of select="AUTHOR"/></h2>
</xsl:template>
```

The value of the first BOOK element's BOOK_TITLE child will be passed to the named template, overriding the default value of the $book_title parameter; thus, the result tree from this template rule (assuming no sorting of the BOOK elements) would be the following:

```
<h1>Title: Look Homeward, Angel</h1>
<h2>by Wolfe, Thomas</h2>
```

Global Parameters A *global parameter* is defined by any top-level xsl:param element. Such a parameter may have a default value, but whether it does or not, the value of the parameter can be changed only by the environment in which the XSLT processor is operating, not by a template in the style sheet that contains an xsl:with-param element. Exactly how the operating environment does this depends on both the operating system and the XSLT processor; it's not uncommon, though, for the overriding value to be supplied via a command-line argument.

Suppose we wanted to add a processing date to our result tree. Of course this information is not available within the source tree or, for that matter, within the style sheet itself, but we could pass the current date in from the command line to a global parameter and then reference that parameter where desired; thus, the style sheet might look in part like the following:

```
<xsl:param name="rundate">(No Date Supplied)</xsl:param>

<xsl:template match="BOOKS">
     <html>
          <head>
               <title>Influential Books</title>
          </head>
          <body>
               <table border="1">
                    <tr>
                         <th>Title</th>
                         <th>Author</th>
                         <th>Pub Date</th>
                    </tr>
                    <xsl:apply-templates>
                         <xsl:sort select="AUTHOR"/>
                    </xsl:apply-templates>
               </table>
          <p><i>As of: <xsl:value-of select="$rundate"/></i></p>
          </body>
```

```
    </html>
</xsl:template>
```

The reference to the `$rundate` *parameter in the template rule's template inserts a date-stamp below the table serving as a footer to the result tree.*

If the operating environment passes nothing at all to override the default value of `$rundate`, the relevant portion of the result tree will be the following:

```
<p><i>As of: (No Date Supplied)</i></p>
```

If we're processing this style sheet with Saxon, from the command line we can supply parameters and their values using a simple name=value form. For example:

```
saxon -o temprule_demo.html temprule_demo.xml temprule_demo.xsl
    rundate="2001-08-15"
```

The date-stamp footer portion of the result tree now looks like this:

```
<p><i>As of: 2001-08-15</i></p>
```

Remember that there are restrictions on where you can use variable and parameter references. Particularly, you cannot use them as the value of `match` *or* `select` *attributes. For example, this means that you cannot pass into a style sheet a particular XPath expression and expect to be able to use it to locate a portion of the source tree.*

Importing and Including Style Sheets

The authors of the XSLT standard recognized not only that large documents would typically require large style sheets, but also that much of the code in those style sheets would benefit from being made *modular*. (By *modular*, we mean that whole chunks of style sheet code can be extracted out into sub–style sheets. This makes these blocks of code easier to maintain and also makes them usable by more than one style sheet.)

XSLT provides two facilities, including and importing, for bringing into a given style sheet the code from another. Each method comes with its unique advantages.

Including Code with `xsl:include`

The most straightforward way of bringing XSLT code from one style sheet into another is using the top-level `xsl:include` element. The following is the syntax

```
<xsl:include href="uri"/>
```

where *`uri`* is the URI of the style sheet whose code you want to include in this one. That external style sheet must itself be a legitimate XSLT style sheet with its own `xsl:stylesheet` element, all necessary namespace declarations, and so on. The children of the external style sheet are copied directly into the invoking style sheet, logically replacing the xsl:include element.

For example, we could remove the second template rule from our temprule_demo.xsl style sheet and put it into its own style sheet. This style sheet—call it temprule_BOOK.xsl—would now look like the following:

```
<xsl:stylesheet version="1.0"
     xmlns:xsl="http://www.w3.org/1999/XSL/Transform"
     xmlns="http://www.w3.org/TR/REC-html40">

<xsl:template match="BOOK">
     <tr>
          <td>
               <xsl:value-of select="BOOK_TITLE"/>
               <xsl:if test="starts-with(@pubyear, '197')"> *</xsl:if>
          </td>
          <xsl:variable name="auth_sur"
             select="substring-before(AUTHOR, ', ')"/>
          <xsl:variable name="auth_given"
             select="substring-after(AUTHOR, ', ')"/>
          <td><xsl:value-of
              select="concat($auth_given, ' ', $auth_sur)"/>
          </td>
          <td><xsl:value-of select="@pubyear"/></td>
     </tr>
</xsl:template>

</xsl:stylesheet>
```

Then, back in the original temprule_demo.xsl style sheet, add the following line:

```
<xsl:include href="temprule_BOOK.xsl" />
```

Note the following effects:

- Applying the original temprule_demo.xsl style sheet to our XML document produces exactly the same result tree as before.
- The temprule_demo.xsl style sheet is now significantly shorter than it had been.
- The code in the new temprule_BOOK.xsl style sheet is now available for use, if desired, by other style sheets. Changing this code will immediately propagate the identical change(s) out to all style sheets that include this one.

Importing Code with xsl:import

As an alternative to the simple xsl:include, the XSLT standard offers an xsl:import element as well. The syntax is identical:

```
<xsl:import href="uri"/>
```

Like xsl:include, xsl:import must be a top-level element, and the style sheet whose contents are to be imported must itself be a legitimate style sheet with a root xsl:stylesheet element.

There are some differences, however, in how the xsl:import is used and, especially, in terms of its effects.

- All xsl:import elements must be the first top-level elements in the importing style sheet.
- Imported style sheets will have a lower import precedence than a style sheet that imports them. This is important for purposes of conflict resolution. In effect, it enables you to override a template rule appearing in the imported style sheet, simply by including a template rule, in the style sheet performing the import, whose match pattern for the same portion of the result tree is identical to that which is being imported.
- You can actually combine the effects of conflicting template rules using a special xsl:apply-imports element.

Assume a simple XML document, as follows:

```
<?xml version="1.0"?>
<?xml-stylesheet type="text/xsl" href="topics.xsl"?>
<MAIN_TOPIC>
     <DESCR>This is the main topic</DESCR>
     <SUB_TOPIC>Subtopic #1</SUB_TOPIC>
     <SUB_TOPIC>Subtopic #2</SUB_TOPIC>
     <SUB_TOPIC>Subtopic #3</SUB_TOPIC>
     <SUB_TOPIC>Subtopic #4</SUB_TOPIC>
     <SUB_TOPIC>Subtopic #5</SUB_TOPIC>
     <SUB_TOPIC>Subtopic #6</SUB_TOPIC>
</MAIN_TOPIC>
```

And now assume a style sheet (topics.xsl) to process this document:

```
<xsl:stylesheet version="1.0"
     xmlns:xsl="http://www.w3.org/1999/XSL/Transform"
     xmlns="http://www.w3.org/TR/REC-html40">

<xsl:template match="MAIN_TOPIC">
     <html>
          <head><title>Topics</title></head>
          <body>
               <h2><xsl:value-of select="DESCR"/></h2>
```

```
                <xsl:apply-templates select="SUB_TOPIC"/>
            </body>
        </html>
    </xsl:template>

    <xsl:template match="SUB_TOPIC">
        <h3><xsl:value-of select="."/></h3>
    </xsl:template>

    </xsl:stylesheet>
```

As you might expect, the result tree from this transformation appears as follows:

```
<html>
     <head><title>Topics</title></head>
     <body>
          <h2>This is the main topic</h2>
          <h3>Subtopic #1</h3>
          <h3>Subtopic #2</h3>
          <h3>Subtopic #3</h3>
          <h3>Subtopic #4</h3>
          <h3>Subtopic #5</h3>
          <h3>Subtopic #6</h3>
     </body>
</html>
```

Now we're going to import another style sheet called sub_top.xsl. To do so, we'll add the following line to `topics.xsl` as the first child of its `xsl:stylesheet` element:

```
<xsl:import href="sub_top.xsl"/>
```

And finally, here is sub_top.xsl:

```
<xsl:stylesheet version="1.0"
     xmlns:xsl="http://www.w3.org/1999/XSL/Transform"
     xmlns="http://www.w3.org/TR/REC-html40">

<xsl:template match="SUB_TOPIC">
     <i><xsl:value-of select="."/></i>
</xsl:template>

</xsl:stylesheet>
```

As you can see, the only template rule in this style sheet matches the SUB_TOPIC elements already accounted for in the main topics.xsl style sheet, except that, on its own terms, this imported style sheet will display the SUB_TOPIC elements' contents in simple italic text rather than as a heading. Because this template rule conflicts with one in the main style sheet, the XSLT rules for conflict resolution kick in; since an imported template rule has a lower precedence than a conflicting one in the importing style sheet, sub_top.xsl is ignored completely, and the result tree from the transformation is identical to topics.xsl.

Now we're going to make a slight change in the importing style sheet, topics.xsl, in the template rule that processes the SUB_TOPIC elements:

```
<xsl:template match="SUB_TOPIC">
     <h3><xsl:apply-imports/></h3>
</xsl:template>
```

All we've done is replaced the `xsl:value-of` element with a simple empty `xsl:apply-imports`. The effects of this substitution imports into the main style sheet—at the point of the `xsl:apply-imports` element—the template from the (otherwise conflicting) template rule in sub_top.xsl. That is, this substitution forces this `xsl:template` element in topics.xsl to behave as if it were coded as follows:

```
<xsl:template match="SUB_TOPIC">
     <h3><i><xsl:value-of select="."/></i></h3>
</xsl:template>
```

The result tree from the transformation now looks like this:

```
<html>
     <head><title>Topics</title></head>
     <body>
          <h2>This is the main topic</h2>
          <h3><i>Subtopic #1</i></h3>
          <h3><i>Subtopic #2</i></h3>
          <h3><i>Subtopic #3</i></h3>
          <h3><i>Subtopic #4</i></h3>
          <h3><i>Subtopic #5</i></h3>
          <h3><i>Subtopic #6</i></h3>
     </body>
</html>
```

That is, the level-3 headings for the six subtopics are now all italicized.

Special Result Tree Output

Under normal circumstances, XSLT does a straight XML-to-XML transformation from source to result tree. The result tree may be in a different vocabulary and/or different structure than the source, but both would still be XML.

This doesn't always lead to the most desirable outcome, though. Some common examples of why result trees don't always turn out the same are:

- Web browsers vary widely in how well they interpret HTML elements that are presented in their pure XML form. This is especially true in regard to empty elements. A browser might not recognize a break tag (<br/>) at all, for example, but if you use the alternative empty-element syntax (
</br>), the browser might interpret it as two succeeding breaks.
- If you want to transform your XML document to something like a comma-separated-values (CSV) flat file, you will quickly become frustrated if there are many occurrences of special markup characters such as <, &, and > in the output. The XSLT processor will stubbornly insist on presenting these characters, such as entity references, in escaped form, on the assumption that if you're outputting markup then you want them to be escaped.
- Most XSLT processors will try to help you by including in the output all relevant namespace declarations, even if they are useless in your specific case.
- When transforming from XML to XML, you often want to be able to control the form of the result tree's XML and document-type declarations. Unfortunately, there's no way to output such content directly; if you enter into a template something such as <?xml version="1.0" ?> (for an XML declaration), the XSLT processor will output it that way—not in its literal (and necessary, in this case) form of <?xml version="1.0"?>.

There are ways to work around some of these problems that may be more or less effective for a quick-and-dirty solution in a particular case. For example, a common way to work around the fact that many Web browsers don't understand empty XML elements is to take advantage of a peculiar foible of those browsers: they read the empty tag just fine if you insert an extra space before the trailing / in the tag. That is, use <br /> instead of the closed-up, more XML-conventional <br/>.

Much cleaner and more effective over the long run is to tell the XSLT processor what kind of result tree you're transforming your source to; the means of doing so is the top-level, empty xsl:output element. The following is its complete syntax:

```
<xsl:output
     method="outputtype"
     version="versionnum"
     encoding="encodingtype"
     omit-xml-declaration="yesorno"
     standalone="yesorno"
```

```
doctype-public="publicID"
doctype-system="systemURI"
cdata-section-elements="elemnames"
indent="yesorno"
media-type="mediatype" />
```

There are a lot of attributes which affect the results of your XSL Transformation. Each of them is discussed in the following sections.

The method Attribute

Valid values of the `method` attribute are `xml`, `html`, and `text`. This attribute provides hints to the XSLT processor about how it should output the result tree for each of those sorts of content. For instance, if `method="html"`, the processor will output an empty `<br/>` tag in the less problematic (if ill-formed) form that Web browsers handle correctly: `<br>`.

The text value is very useful for getting around the problems related to putting markup characters in the result in their literal form rather than escaped using entities or some other mechanism. The default value for the method attribute is `xml`.

The version, encoding, omit-xml-declaration, standalone, doctype-public, and doctype-system Attributes

All of these attributes are relevant only when the value of the `method` attribute (explicit or by default) is `xml`. They are used to control the form of important parts of the result document's prologue: its XML and document-type declarations.

Values for these attributes are what you would expect. For instance, the following `xsl:output` element will cause both an XML declaration and a document-type declaration to be added to the output's prologue:

```
<xsl:output omit-xml-declaration="no" encoding="utf-8"
     standalone="no" version="1.0"
     doctype-system="http://www.foo.com/dtds/myxml.dtd"/>
```

The resulting prologue will look like the following (with `rootelem` replaced by the name of the result tree's root element node):

```
<?xml version="1.0" encoding="utf-8" standalone="no"?>
<!DOCTYPE rootelem SYSTEM="http://www.foo.com/dtds/myxml.dtd"/>
```

The cdata-section-elements Attribute

This attribute takes as its value a white space–separated list of result tree element names. The XSLT processor will place the content of each instance of each of these element types in a CDATA section wrapper.

For example, if the `xsl:output` element looked like this,

```
<xsl:output cdata-section-elements="SOME_TEXT"/>
```

and the style sheet contained the following code as part of a template,

```
<SOME_TEXT>Special characters such as &amp; and &gt;</SOME_TEXT>
```

then the result tree would contain the following:

```
<SOME_TEXT><![CDATA[Special characters such as & and >]]></SOME_TEXT>
```

The `indent` Attribute

This attribute specifies whether the XSLT processor should include additional white space in the result tree for purposes of making it more legible and understandable to human readers; allowable values of the `indent` attribute are `yes` or `no` (the default).

The XSLT standard does not explicitly say what kind or how much white space is to be added if `indent="yes";` the processor is supposed to use some kind of reasonable algorithm to determine this. Adding indents can be a bit tricky to put into practice; for example, the processor has to be careful not to add any white space to a text node, lest it change the content of the node.

Nevertheless, in general, you will find that setting the indent attribute to yes will help make your output more accessible to the human eye. Note that this is important only if the result tree is meant to be read by the human eye; if it's simply being passed to a downstream application, like a Web browser, the readability is irrelevant.

The `media-type` Attribute

This attribute takes as its value a Multipurpose Internet Mail Extensions (MIME) type such as `text/xml` (which is the default value) to be applied to the output file. The XSLT standard does not specify how a processor is to apply this MIME type or how (or even whether) applying it will affect the content; nonetheless, it may be important for some applications. For example, if serving the result tree in a stream to be sent out from a server to a client, the server may need to know how to serve it—as `text/xml`, `text/html`, `application/xml`, or some other MIME type declaration. In this case, specifying a `media-type` attribute may make the difference between the client failing or succeeding to recognize the content type.

Copying Nodes from Source to Result Tree

If all you ever use XSLT for is transforming XML to HTML, you might naturally conclude that copying content from source to result tree is always a matter of using the `xsl:value-of` element within templates to copy text from one tree to the other.

With the source and result trees consist of nodes from two different markup vocabularies; there'd be little if any point to copying elements, attributes, PIs, and so on, as well as text.

However, when you're transforming from a source tree in one vocabulary to a result in the same or similar one, you need to transfer some or all of the markup and the text. XSLT provides two facilities for doing so: the `xsl:copy` and `xsl:copy-of` elements.

Copying the Current Node Only with `xsl:copy`

The `xsl:copy` element, which always appears as part of a template, is used to copy the current node to the result tree. If the current node is an element, the `xsl:copy` element copies only the element node itself, not any descendants of the current node including the element's children or attributes. If the current node is a comment or PI, its content will be copied (otherwise the result tree would end up with an empty comment or PI, which would not be useful in most cases). If the current node is an attribute, a copy of that attribute is instantiated (including both name and value) in the result tree. The following is the general syntax:

```
<xsl:copy
     use-attribute-sets="name">
     [optional content]
</xsl:copy>
```

The value of the optional `use-attribute-sets` attribute is a white space–delimited list of tokens, each of which maps onto a named attribute set in the style sheet. (See the discussion of named attribute sets in "Named Attribute Sets" earlier in this chapter.) The *[optional content]* may appear only if the current node is an element, in which case that content is considered to be the resulting element's content. If the current node is not an element, then the `xsl:copy` element must be empty.

If you need to copy entire branches of the source tree to the result, it is generally easier to use the `xsl:copy-of` element (discussed in the next section) than `xsl:copy`; however, the latter provides a finer degree of control over which portions of the branch are to be copied. For instance, consider a source document such as the following:

```
<A attribA="valueA">
     <B>...</B>
     <B>...</B>
     <B>
          <C attribC="valueC"/>
          <D attribD="valueD">...</D>
     </B>
</A>
```

If you want to copy everything except the `D` element from the source tree to the result tree, you could not use `xsl:copy-of` applied to the `A` element because it copies an entire branch indiscriminately; however, you could copy everything other than one elment using `xsl:copy` within a template rule that effectively calls itself, as shown in the following example:

```
<xsl:template match="A | B | C | @*">
     <xsl:copy>
          <xsl:apply-templates select="A | B | C | @* | text()"/>
     </xsl:copy>
</xsl:template>
```

Here, the `xsl:apply-templates` element invokes this same template rule for every `A`, `B`, or `C` element, as well as any attribute nodes. The `text()` portion of the select attribute's value simply enables the built-in rule for text nodes to be invoked for any such nodes that are children of any of the `A`, `B`, or `C` elements.

Applying this style sheet to the source document with Saxon produces the following result tree, which is exactly the effect intended:

```
<A attribA="valueA">
     <B>...</B>
     <B>...</B>
     <B>
          <C attribC="valueC"/>
     </B>
</A>
```

Copying Entire Branches of the Source Tree with `xsl:copy-of`

Unlike `xsl:copy`, the `xsl:copy-of` element copies complete selected branches of the source tree. This can be a powerful ally when transforming from one XML vocabulary to a slightly different one (or a different version of the same one). The following is the general syntax:

```
<xsl:copy-of
     select="expression" />
```

where *`expression`* is an XPath expression (typically relative to the context node) that selects some portion of the source tree to be copied. The entire node-set, including the element nodes, any attributes, text, PIs, comments, namespaces, and any descendants, is copied.

One interesting use of `xsl:copy-of` is to copy result tree fragments (created by using nonempty `xsl:variable` elements) to the result tree. A result tree fragment is treated just as if it were a source tree node-set, which allows for many more possibilities than available just from the source tree itself.

Consider the case of the simple XML document used throughout this chapter. For convenience, here it is again:

```
<?xml version="1.0"?>
<BOOKS>
     <BOOK pubyear="1929">
          <BOOK_TITLE>Look Homeward, Angel</BOOK_TITLE>
          <AUTHOR>Wolfe, Thomas</AUTHOR>
     </BOOK>
     <BOOK pubyear="1973">
          <BOOK_TITLE>Gravity's Rainbow</BOOK_TITLE>
          <AUTHOR>Pynchon, Thomas</AUTHOR>
     </BOOK>
     <BOOK pubyear="1977">
          <BOOK_TITLE>Cards as Weapons</BOOK_TITLE>
          <AUTHOR>Jay, Ricky</AUTHOR>
     </BOOK>
     <BOOK pubyear="2001">
          <BOOK_TITLE>XML: The Complete Reference</BOOK_TITLE>
          <AUTHOR>Williamson, Heather</AUTHOR>
     </BOOK>
</BOOKS>
```

We can easily use the `xsl:copy-of` element to create from this document one that contains only the books published in the 1970s, using a style sheet such as the following:

```
<xsl:stylesheet version="1.0"
     xmlns:xsl="http://www.w3.org/1999/XSL/Transform">

<!-- Suppress text nodes unless specifically requested -->
<xsl:template match="text()"/>

<!-- Copy the root BOOKS element itself -->
<xsl:template match="BOOKS">
     <xsl:copy>
          <xsl:apply-templates/>
     </xsl:copy>
</xsl:template>

<xsl:template match="BOOK[starts-with(@pubyear,'197')]">
     <xsl:copy-of select="."/>
</xsl:template>

</xsl:stylesheet>
```

Note *The final template rule does not need to include an `xsl:apply-templates` or `xsl:for-each` loop to process each descendant element, attribute, and so on; this recursive loop is implicit in the `xsl:copy-of`.*

Applied to the sample document, the preceding style sheet produces the following result tree:

```
<BOOKS>
     <BOOK pubyear="1973">
          <BOOK_TITLE>Gravity's Rainbow</BOOK_TITLE>
          <AUTHOR>Pynchon, Thomas</AUTHOR>
     </BOOK>
     <BOOK pubyear="1977">
          <BOOK_TITLE>Cards as Weapons</BOOK_TITLE>
          <AUTHOR>Jay, Ricky</AUTHOR>
     </BOOK>
</BOOKS>
```

Template Rule Modes

When you need to do one kind of transformation for a given node in one circumstance and a completely different transformation for the same node in a different circumstance, you need two separate template rules that match on the same node. The problem of course is that if you stop there, then only one of the template rules will apply because of the XSLT rules for resolving match conflicts.

The solution to this problem is to make use of the special `mode` attribute. This attribute is applied to an `xsl:apply-templates` element and to a corresponding `xsl:template` element. The `xsl:apply-templates` says, in effect, "apply the template rule whose `mode` attribute is *`[value]`* at this point, but not any other template rule that might conceivably be used here."

As a simple case, consider a source document such as the following:

```
<?xml version="1.0"?>
<?xml-stylesheet type="text/xsl" href="modes.xsl"?>
<BOOK>
     <TITLE>Look Homeward, Angel</TITLE>
     <AUTHOR>Thomas Wolfe</AUTHOR>
     <PART>
          <NUMBER>One</NUMBER>
          <EPIGRAPH>...a stone, a leaf, an unfound door...
          </EPIGRAPH>
          <CHAPTER>
           A destiny that leads the English to the Dutch...
          </CHAPTER>
          <CHAPTER>Oliver married Elizabeth in May...</CHAPTER>
     </PART>
</BOOK>
```

It often happens when transforming such a document that you want to use different portions of it more than once. For example, you might want to generate a table of contents at the beginning of the result tree, followed by the contents themselves, and followed by an index. Each part and chapter number or title would thus appear in the result tree three times, with each appearance styled differently; therefore, each form of the content that is to be reused requires its own template rule.

To distinguish among the uses to which a given portion of content is put at a given point in the result tree, you use `mode` attributes as in the following example:

```
<xsl:stylesheet version="1.0"
     xmlns:xsl="http://www.w3.org/1999/XSL/Transform">

<xsl:template match="/">
     <book>
          <title><xsl:value-of select="BOOK/TITLE"/></title>
          <author><xsl:value-of select="BOOK/AUTHOR"/></author>
          <xsl:apply-templates select="BOOK" mode="contents"/>
          <xsl:apply-templates select="BOOK" mode="body"/>
     </book>
</xsl:template>

<xsl:template match="BOOK" mode="contents">
     <toc>
         <xsl:apply-templates select="PART/CHAPTER" mode="toc"/>
     </toc>
</xsl:template>

<xsl:template match="BOOK" mode="body">
     <text>
          <xsl:apply-templates select="PART" mode="body"/>
     </text>
</xsl:template>

<xsl:template match="PART/CHAPTER" mode="toc">
     <chap>
       <num><xsl:value-of select="position()"/></num>
       <open><xsl:value-of select="substring(., 1, 15)"/></open>
     </chap>
</xsl:template>

<xsl:template match="PART" mode="body">
     <epi><xsl:value-of select="EPIGRAPH"/></epi>
```

```
          <xsl:for-each select="CHAPTER">
             <chapter>
              <chap_num><xsl:value-of select="position()"/></chap_num>
              <xsl:apply-templates/>
             </chapter>
          </xsl:for-each>
     </xsl:template>

     </xsl:stylesheet>
```

The goal is to build a result document consisting of a table of contents and the text proper from the source document. Within the table of contents, each chapter will be represented by its chapter number and the opening 15 characters of its text. Within the result tree's `text` element, each part is transcribed (with some changes to element names and so on) directly to the result.

Note that the `BOOK` element is processed twice in the root node's template rule, once using a contents mode and once using a body mode; furthermore, modes are used to process portions of the source tree further down as well.

Note *It is important to recognize that the specific values of the* `mode` *attributes do not matter except for human readability of your style sheet. You could use values such as* `mode="dZq"` *just as easily as the ones used in the preceding style sheet. For purposes of the style sheet's processing, all that matters is that a select expression and mode in an* `xsl:apply-templates` *correspond to the match expression and mode in an* `xsl:template`.

The result tree from the preceding transformation looks like this:

```
<book>
     <title>Look Homeward, Angel</title>
     <author>Thomas Wolfe</author>
     <toc>
          <chap>
               <num>1</num>
               <open>A destiny that </open>
          </chap>
          <chap>
               <num>2</num>
               <open>Oliver married </open>
          </chap>
     </toc>
```

```
        <text>
            <epi>...a stone, a leaf, an unfound door...</epi>
            <chapter>
                <chap_num>1</chap_num>
                A destiny that leads the English to the Dutch...
            </chapter>
            <chapter>
                <chap_num>2</chap_num>
                Oliver married Elizabeth in May...
            </chapter>
        </text>
    </book>
```

Issuing Messages from Style Sheets

So you've put all this work into building a full style sheet to process documents of a particular kind, and you make the style sheet available to authors of those documents. Because you've tested the style sheet with a variety of source documents, you know that most conditions that the XSLT document is likely to encounter will result in acceptable result trees. Errors in the source documents' structures, such as well-formedness and the like, will be trapped by the built-in processing of the parser being used.

The problem is that the general rules of XML documents, such as the balancing of tags and so on, are often not the only (and perhaps not even the most important) kinds of correctness you need to test for. You might need to ensure that a particular element's content is numeric or that it falls between a range of acceptable values or that it has a hyphen in the fourth position and so on.

A special XSLT element, `xsl:message`, can be used to alert document authors and users to these kinds of content problems. The following is its general syntax:

```
<xsl:message
    terminate="yesorno">
    [template]
</xsl:message>
```

The optional `terminate` attribute, whose value may be yes or no (the default), instructs the XSLT processor to halt or not to halt processing, respectively. The *[template]* is the content of the message that is issued at that point.

The following is an example of how you might use the `xsl:message` element. It assumes a simple XML stock-quote document:

```
<?xml version="1.0"?>
<?xml-stylesheet type="text/xsl" href="message.xsl"?>
<STOCKS>
```

```
        <STOCK>
            <SYMBOL>IBM</SYMBOL>
            <VALUE>The Washington Monument</VALUE>
        </STOCK>
        <STOCK>
            <SYMBOL>T</SYMBOL>
            <VALUE>12000</VALUE>
        </STOCK>
    </STOCKS>
```

We'd like to verify that the value of each stock is numeric and, if so, that the value is less than or equal to 500. The following is a simple style sheet consisting of a single template rule that will give us this information:

```
<xsl:stylesheet version="1.0"
    xmlns:xsl="http://www.w3.org/1999/XSL/Transform">

<xsl:template match="STOCK">
    <xsl:choose>
        <xsl:when test="string(number(VALUE))='NaN'">
            <xsl:message>
                For stock "<xsl:value-of select="SYMBOL"/>":
                VALUE element's value
                (<xsl:value-of select="VALUE"/>)
                is not a number.
            </xsl:message>
        </xsl:when>
        <xsl:when test="number(VALUE) > 500">
            <xsl:message>
                For stock "<xsl:value-of select="SYMBOL"/>":
                VALUE element's value
                (<xsl:value-of select="VALUE"/>)
                is greater than 500.
            </xsl:message>
        </xsl:when>
    </xsl:choose>
</xsl:template>

</xsl:stylesheet>
```

Applied to the above document using Saxon, this style sheet displays the following result:

```
For stock "IBM":
VALUE element's value
(The Washington Monument)
is not a number.

For stock "T":
VALUE element's value
(12000)
is greater than 500.
```

This may seem fairly pointless, since you can get the same result simply by putting the contents of the message into a regular template. The difference is that the content of an `xsl:message` element does not go to the result tree, it goes directly to the operating environment's standard error display.

By sending the contents of the `xsl:message` element to the software and not the screen means that using a product such as IE will not display the resulting messages. IE displays the result tree and has no standard error display. If you need to display error messages such as these for IE users or authors, you'll need to put the messages into the result tree. In this case, of course, there is no option to terminate processing.

XSLT Functions

Because XSLT makes heavy use of XPath expressions, you can use any XPath functions in a context that calls for such an expression; however, these aren't the only functions available to you in a style sheet.

The `document()` Function

This function takes the following general form:

```
document(uri, ?node-set)
```

The first argument is (or is converted to) a string expression, which is assumed to be a standard URI. The optional (and seldom-used) second argument is used for establishing a base URI for the first argument.

The result of a call to the `document()` function is always a node-set. This node-set can be processed by the style sheet just like node-sets in the source tree. The `document()` function, therefore, provides a simple means of processing multiple source trees. For example, these multiple source trees may be used to in a document merge.

Suppose we've got information about books in two separate XML documents. One document contains the book titles, the other contains the books' authors. Books are uniquely identified in both documents by their ISBNs. Simple versions of these two documents might look something like the following

```
<?xml version="1.0"?>
<?xml-stylesheet type="text/xsl" href="document.xsl"?>
<BOOKS>
  <BOOK isbn="0684804433">
    <BOOK_TITLE>Look Homeward, Angel</BOOK_TITLE>
  </BOOK>
  <BOOK isbn="0140188592">
    <BOOK_TITLE>Gravity's Rainbow</BOOK_TITLE>
  </BOOK>
</BOOKS>
```

and

```
<?xml version="1.0"?>
<BOOKS>
     <BOOK isbn="0684804433">
          <AUTHOR>Thomas Wolfe</AUTHOR>
     </BOOK>
     <BOOK isbn="0140188592">
          <AUTHOR>Thomas Pynchon</AUTHOR>
     </BOOK>
</BOOKS>
```

Please note that the first document (with the titles) links to the style sheet document.xsl. That style sheet can produce a result tree containing content from both documents in the following manner; pay particular attention to the match expression in the template rule for the `BOOK` element:

```
<xsl:stylesheet version="1.0"
  xmlns:xsl="http://www.w3.org/1999/XSL/Transform">

<xsl:template match="BOOKS">
  <html>
    <head><title>Books and Their Authors</title></head>
    <body>
      <xsl:apply-templates/>
    </body>
  </html>
```

```
</xsl:template>

<xsl:template match="BOOK">
   <xsl:variable name="titleisbn" select="@isbn"/>
   <h2>Title: <xsl:value-of select="BOOK_TITLE"/></h2>
   <h3>by: <xsl:value-of
select="document('authors.xml')//BOOK[@isbn=$titleisbn]/AUTHOR"/></h3>
</xsl:template>

</xsl:stylesheet>
```

In the BOOK element's template rule, the code first establishes a variable, `$titleisbn`, whose value is the ISBN from the current node—that is, from the current BOOK element in the document of book titles. The `xsl:value-of` element in this template rule matches the ISBN from the BOOK element in the document of authors against `$titleisbn`. When it finds a match, it places that AUTHOR element's content into the result tree.

The following is the result tree from this transformation:

```
<html>
      <head>
            <title>Books and Their Authors</title>
      </head>
      <body>
            <h2>Title: Look Homeward, Angel</h2>
            <h3>by: Thomas Wolfe</h3>
            <h2>Title: Gravity's Rainbow</h2>
            <h3>by: Thomas Pynchon</h3>
      </body>
</html>
```

Keys

The XPath `id()` function is a convenient way to locate the one element in a document whose ID-type attribute matches the value passed to the function. There are a few drawbacks to using the `id()` function, however:

- In order to use `id()`, the source-tree document must be validated against a DTD. Only a DTD can declare that an attribute is of the ID type, and, therefore, a merely well-formed source document cannot take advantage of the `id()` function.
- Because the values of an ID-type attribute must by definition be unique in a given document instance, the `id()` function can locate at most one element node. It would be very convenient to have some kind of nonunique indexing available as well.

- An ID-type attribute's value must be in the form of a legitimate XML name. For instance, it cannot begin with a digit and it cannot contain embedded white space.
- Often, source tree content may be uniquely identified by text nodes rather than attribute values.

For these and other reasons, the XSLT standard's authors specified a means to access source tree content using *keys* quickly and conveniently.

A key is declared using the top-level `xsl:key` element, which associates a key of a given name with a particular node-set in the source tree. The node(s) in this node-set can then be located all at once using the XSLT `key()` function.

The `xsl:key` Element To define a key for use in the style sheet, include a top-level `xsl:key` element of the following form:

```
<xsl:key
      name="keyname"
      match="pattern"
      use="expression" />
```

The attributes for the `xsl:key` element are

- **`name`** Gives the key a name, which may later be used by the `key()` function to retrieve all nodes associated with the name
- **`match`** Identifies the portion of the source tree that can be located, collectively, by a single reference to the `name` attribute's value
- **`use`** Assigns the key's value, which may be the same for all nodes selected by the `match` attribute or (more typically) may be different for each node

The `key()` Function The XSLT `key()` function works exactly like the XPath `id()` function: it returns a node-set matching certain key values. The difference is that the `id()` function will return at most one element node; the `key()` function may return a node-set of many nodes.

The general form of a call to the `key()` function is

```
key(keyname, object)
```

where

- *`keyname`* is the name of the key associated with the desired node-set
- *`object`* is the key value that you want to locate

Note *`object` can itself be a node-set instead of a string. If this is the case, the `key()` function behaves as if it were called multiple times and as if it passed the string value of another member in the node-set in each call.*

To see how you could use the `xsl:key` element and `key()` function together, consider the following XML document:

```
<?xml-stylesheet type="text/xsl" href="key.xsl"?>
<COUNTRIES>
      <COUNTRY>
            <NAME>Canada</NAME>
            <CURRENCY>Dollar</CURRENCY>
      </COUNTRY>
      <COUNTRY>
            <NAME>United Kingdom</NAME>
            <CURRENCY>Pound</CURRENCY>
      </COUNTRY>
      <COUNTRY>
            <NAME>Singapore</NAME>
            <CURRENCY>Dollar</CURRENCY>
      </COUNTRY>
      <COUNTRY>
            <NAME>Japan</NAME>
            <CURRENCY>Yen</CURRENCY>
      </COUNTRY>
      <COUNTRY>
            <NAME>United States</NAME>
            <CURRENCY>Dollar</CURRENCY>
      </COUNTRY>
      <COUNTRY>
            <NAME>Russia</NAME>
            <CURRENCY>Ruble</CURRENCY>
      </COUNTRY>
      <COUNTRY>
            <NAME>Burundi</NAME>
            <CURRENCY>Franc</CURRENCY>
      </COUNTRY>
</COUNTRIES>
```

As you can see, each country name in this document is paired with a currency denomination.

We're going to process this document with a style sheet that uses two keys. The following is the style sheet:

```
<xsl:stylesheet version="1.0"
      xmlns:xsl="http://www.w3.org/1999/XSL/Transform"
      xmlns="http://www.w3.org/TR/REC-html40">
```

```
<!-- Suppress all output not otherwise requested -->
<xsl:template match="node()"/>

<xsl:key name="CName" match="COUNTRY" use="NAME"/>
<xsl:key name="CCurr" match="COUNTRY" use="CURRENCY"/>

<xsl:template match="/">
     <html>
          <head><title>Keys</title></head>
          <body>
               <xsl:for-each select="key('CName', 'Canada')">
                    <h1>Canadian currency is:
                    <xsl:value-of select="CURRENCY"/></h1>
               </xsl:for-each>
               <xsl:for-each select="key('CCurr', 'Dollar')">
                    Country name: <xsl:value-of select="NAME"/> -
                    Currency: <xsl:value-of select="CURRENCY"/><br
/>
               </xsl:for-each>
          </body>
     </html>
</xsl:template>

</xsl:stylesheet>
```

The first key declared is named `Cname` and is a unique value. For each `COUNTRY` element, there's a key whose value is the name of the country in question. In this document, since each country has a different name, each `CName` key is different as well.

The second key declared, `CCurr`, is a *nonunique* key. Its value is defined as the value of a given country's `CURRENCY` element, which may be duplicated multiple times in a document.

In the style sheet's lone template rule are two `xsl:for-each` loops. The first `xsl:for-each` loop processes all members of the `CName` set of elements for which that key's value is the string `Canada`. The second `xsl:for-each` loop processes all members of the `CCurr` set of elements for which that key's value is `Dollar`.

The following is the result tree from this transformation:

```
<html>
     <head><title>Keys</title></head>
     <body>
          <h1>Canadian currency is: Dollar</h1>
          Country name: Canada - Currency: Dollar<br/>
          Country name: Singapore - Currency: Dollar<br/>
```

```
            Country name: United States - Currency: Dollar<br/>
        </body>
    </html>
```

The effect of using keys can be duplicated in simple cases (such as the preceding example) using XPath expression predicates instead of keys; however, this becomes very inefficient when the need arises to process matching nodes many times. Remember that the principal problem addressed by the use of keys is efficiency through indexing, and you will see that the value of keys rises dramatically with each succeeding access of a given node. The start-up processing of a given keyed document will be greater than its nonkeyed form because of the time required by the processor to build the index. Once the index is built, however, getting to any given keyed node, or any set of them, is much quicker.

Numbering and Number Formatting

Generating numbers and controlling their formats with XSLT is the province of a special XSLT element used singly, or of a function and element designed to be used together. We will examine these number generators in the following sections.

The `xsl:number` Element Many XML source documents contain a collection of data about similar things: books, employees, varieties of coffee, and so on. For such documents, it is fairly simple to transform the source tree to an HTML ordered-list (`ol`) element and its subordinate `li` elements (list item) to produce a numbered list of the objects in the collection.

The HTML ordered-list construct doesn't solve all problems associated with numbering such lists, however. The following pose a particular problem:

- Controlling the list's starting value and style (such as lowercase alphabetic versus uppercase Roman numerals and so on) requires use of the now-deprecated `type` and `start` attributes. In order to control those features in HTML ordered lists without relying on these deprecated attributes, you must use CSS.
- Even if CSS solves your problems for generating numbered lists in HTML, it will not do so for transformations to non-HTML markup vocabularies, in which the need for numbering may be just as great.

To solve the problems created by using CSS and list elements, you need to work with the `xsl:number` element. It always appears within a template, because it is used to place a number in the result tree. The `xsl:number` element takes a fairly large number of attributes, as you can see in its general format:

```
<xsl:number
     level="single_multiple_any"
     count="pattern"
     from="pattern"
     value="number"
```

```
format="formatstring"
lang="langcode"
letter-value="alphabetic_traditional"
grouping-separator="char"
grouping-size="number" />
```

All of these attributes are optional. The last five (`format` through `grouping-size`) are interpreted as attribute value templates; this means that their values can be computed, rather than interpreted literally, by enclosing the values in curly braces (`{}`). The following are the attributes and their values:

- **`level`** Allowable values for the `level` attribute are single (the default), multiple, or any. This attribute reflects the nature of the collection of objects you're numbering. If all the objects are peers—that is, they share the same level in a hierarchy—then use the single value. The multiple value is used when you want the generated number to reflect some sort of hierarchic relationship, for instance, when the chapters, sections, and pages in a reference manual might be numbered 1.1.2, 1.1.2, 1.2.1, and so on. A value of any is most commonly used when you simply want the numbering to be sequential.
- **`count`** The allowable value for the `count` attribute is an XPath expression that instructs the XSLT processor exactly what is to be counted. If no value is supplied, the default is to count all nodes of the same type as the current node (element, attribute, PI, and so on.), and if the current node has a name, the default is to count only nodes of the same type that have the same name.
- **`from`** The value of the `from` attribute is an XPath expression that identifies the node or level in the hierarchy at which numbering is to start over. The default is a pattern that matches no nodes—that is, the numbering of objects in this collection will never be restarted.
- **`value`** The value of the `value` attribute is a number (explicit or implied) that will be used instead of some number that depends on the current node's position in a node-set.
- **`format`** Valid values for the `format` attribute includes a string of characters that establishes a template of sorts for all numbers generated by the `xsl:number` element. Each portion of the generated number, if using the hierarchic number form such as chapters, sections, and pages, is separated from others by some punctuation mark such as a period or hyphen, and the string as a whole might include leading and trailing punctuation such as square brackets or parentheses. The following are the literal values that may be used in the format string:
  - The digit 1 says to output a digit at this position in the generated number. This format suppresses leading zeroes.
  - The digit 0 also says to output a digit at this position, but it forces a leading zero not to be suppressed. A format string of `001` will always result in a number of at least three digits, including one or two leading zeroes if necessary.

- Lower- and uppercase *a* and *A* generate alphabetic sequences, running from *a* through *z* and then moving on into *aa*, *ab*, and so on, or the equivalent uppercase sequence respectively.
- Lower- and uppercase *i* and *I* generate Roman-numeral sequences in lower- and uppercase form, respectively.
- Any other Unicode digit or letter that can be used to make the generated numbers or letters start with that digit or letter and go up.

Note *This enables the list to consist of non-Arabic or Roman numbers or letters.*

- **lang** A two- or three-character language code, such as `en` or `de`, indicating the language whose conventions for alphabetization will be used.
- **letter-value** Allowable values are alphabetic or traditional. The goal is that in a format attribute, a given letter of the alphabet may indicate either "start the sequence with this letter of the alphabet" or "use a special sequencing system known to processors familiar with this language." The classic case is the letter *i* or *I* which you can use to indicate that Roman numerals are to be used, but how do you start a sequence of alphabetic characters with that letter (for example, *i*, *j*, *k*, and so on)? To start the sequence with a specific letter, literally, and not as some kind of generic use-this-alternate-numbering-system indicator, set the `letter-value` attribute's value to `alphabetic`; otherwise, set it to `traditional`.
- **grouping-separator** You can generate numbers that are broken up internally into groups of numbers, for legibility, to indicate thousands or to meet some format requirements. This attribute specifies the character that is to be used to separate one group from those adjacent to it. See the following `grouping-size` attribute for more information.
- **grouping-size** The number of digits or letters in each group which will be separated from those on either side by the value of the grouping-separator attribute; thus, if `grouping-separator` is a hyphen and `grouping-size` is 2, the number 123456 would be represented as 12-34-56. If you specify only the `grouping-separator` or the `grouping-size`, but not the other, the value you specify is ignored,—that is, your generated numbers will not be grouped at all; the numeric value for one thousand will be represented as 1000, and so on.

Given the number and variety of possible combinations of these attributes, demonstrating them all with a single example would be quite difficult. But let's look at an example that shows some simple possibilities.

Consider the following XML document:

```
<?xml version="1.0"?>
<?xml-stylesheet type="text/xsl" href="numbering.xsl"?>
```

ADDING STYLE

```
<BOOK>
     <CHAPTER>
          <FOOTNOTE>#1 (#1 in CHAPTER 1)</FOOTNOTE>
          <FOOTNOTE>#2 (#2 in CHAPTER 1)</FOOTNOTE>
     </CHAPTER>
     <CHAPTER>
          <FOOTNOTE>#3 (#1 in CHAPTER 2)</FOOTNOTE>
          <FOOTNOTE>#4 (#2 in CHAPTER 2)</FOOTNOTE>
          <FOOTNOTE>#5 (#3 in CHAPTER 2)</FOOTNOTE>
     </CHAPTER>
     <CHAPTER>
          <FOOTNOTE>#6 (#1 in CHAPTER 3)</FOOTNOTE>
     </CHAPTER>
     <CHAPTER>
          <FOOTNOTE>#7 (#1 in CHAPTER 4)</FOOTNOTE>
          <FOOTNOTE>#8 (#2 in CHAPTER 4)</FOOTNOTE>
     </CHAPTER>
     <CHAPTER>
          <FOOTNOTE>#9 (#1 in CHAPTER 5)</FOOTNOTE>
          <FOOTNOTE>#10 (#2 in CHAPTER 5)</FOOTNOTE>
          <FOOTNOTE>#11 (#3 in CHAPTER 5)</FOOTNOTE>
          <FOOTNOTE>#12 (#4 in CHAPTER 5)</FOOTNOTE>
     </CHAPTER>
     <CHAPTER>
          <FOOTNOTE>#13 (#1 in CHAPTER 6)</FOOTNOTE>
          <FOOTNOTE>#14 (#2 in CHAPTER 6)</FOOTNOTE>
     </CHAPTER>
</BOOK>
```

In general, this document represents the structure of a book consisting of six chapters, each of which has one or more footnotes.

To this document, we'll apply the transformations laid out in the following style sheet. Pay special attention to the template rule for processing `FOOTNOTE` elements; this is where the `xsl:number` element is used:

```
<xsl:stylesheet version="1.0"
     xmlns:xsl="http://www.w3.org/1999/XSL/Transform"
     xmlns="http://www.w3.org/TR/REC-html40">

<xsl:template match="BOOK">
     <html>
          <head><title>Numbering</title></head>
```

```
        <body>
            <xsl:apply-templates/>
        </body>
    </html>
</xsl:template>

<xsl:template match="CHAPTER">
    <h3>Chapter <xsl:number/></h3>
    <table border="1">
        <tr>
            <th>Note Desc</th>
            <th>Single (alpha)</th>
            <th>Multiple (ch-note)</th>
            <th>Any (Roman)</th>
        </tr>
        <xsl:apply-templates/>
    </table>
</xsl:template>

<xsl:template match="FOOTNOTE">
    <tr>
        <td><xsl:value-of select="."/></td>
        <td align="center"><xsl:number level="single"
            format="A"/></td>
        <td align="center"><xsl:number level="multiple"
            count="CHAPTER | FOOTNOTE"
            from="BOOK"
            format="1-1 "/></td>
        <td align="center"><xsl:number level="any"
            format="I"/></td>
    </tr>
</xsl:template>

</xsl:stylesheet>
```


Note that the CHAPTER template rule uses a simple xsl:number element, with no attributes at all, within the level-3 heading for each CHAPTER. This will cause the chapter numbers to be displayed and numbered from the beginning of the document. In this context, note that using xsl:number alone produces results identical to what you'd get if you used an xsl:value-of element whose select attribute had a value of position().

In the final template rule, table cells are constructed so that they contain the following, respectively:

- The value of the `FOOTNOTE` element's text node
- A generated single-level number using the *A* format (uppercase letters)
- A generated multilevel number using the 1-1 format
- A generated any-level number using the *I* format (capital Roman numerals)

The single-level number will not number the footnotes consecutively from the beginning of the document to the end. Why not? Because the numbering occurs in a template rule for the `FOOTNOTE` element that is invoked by the `xsl:apply-templates` in the template rule for the `CHAPTER` element; thus, the set of peers used to construct this single-level number will be the set of all footnotes for this chapter.

The `count` attribute for the multilevel number specifies that what are counted at various portions of the generated number are all `CHAPTER` and `FOOTNOTE` elements. The `from` attribute, whose value is `BOOK`, says that we'll consider all `CHAPTER` and `FOOTNOTE` elements within a given `BOOK` element as a single numbering sequence. The `format` attribute for this `xsl:number` element specifies that the two levels in the numbered hierarchy will be represented in chapter-note form with each number separated by a hyphen.

Finally, the any-level number simply spells out the numbering format. Since none of the other attributes are specified, this `xsl:number` generates a new number for `FOOTNOTE` elements found at any level of the hierarchy, irrespective of their grouping within chapters.

When viewed in IE, this transformation displays as shown in Figure 16-8. The any level corresponds to the number of the footnote within the entire document, while the single and multiple levels cause the footnote to be numbered consecutively within the corresponding chapter.

The `format-number()` Function The purpose of this function is to convert a numeric value into a string using specified patterns that control the number of leading zeroes, separator between thousands, and so on. The general syntax of a call to the function is

```
format-number(number, pattern, formatname?)
```

where

- *`number`* is the numeric value to be converted.
- *`pattern`* is a string that lays out the general representation of a number. Each character in the string represents either a digit from *`number`* or some special punctuation such as a comma or minus sign.

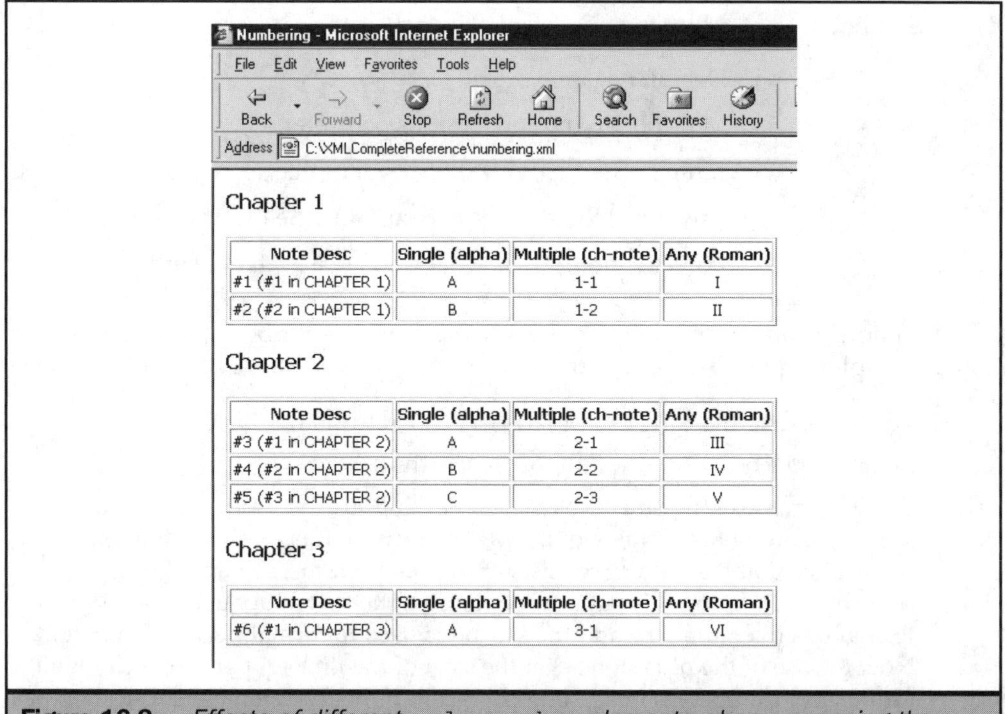

Figure 16-8. *Effects of different `xsl: number` elements when processing the same nodes, shown in IE.*

- *`formatname?`* (optional) is the name of a format declared by an `xsl:decimal-format` element. If *`formatname?`* is not supplied in the call to `format-number()`, the default format is used.

The default format used when the *`formatname?`* argument is omitted is taken from the Java Development Kit (JDK) 1.1 specification of the DecimalFormat class. This format uses the following characters and their meanings:

Symbol	Meaning
0	A digit.
#	A digit, zero shows as absent.
. (period)	Placeholder for decimal separator.
,	Placeholder for grouping separator.
;	Separate formats.

Symbol	Meaning
-	Default negative prefix.
%	Multiply by 100 and show as percentage.
‰	Multiply by 1000 and show as per mille.
X	Any other characters can be used in the prefix or suffix.
'	Used to quote special characters in a prefix or suffix.

The following are some examples of using the `format-number()` function with patterns employing these default characters:

- `format-number(123456, "#,##0.00")` returns 123,456.00
- `format-number(0, "#,##0.00")` returns 0.00
- `format-number(number (NET), "+#,##0.0;- #,##0.0")` returns a string according to the value of the `NET` element that is a child of the context node. Note that the pattern consists of two subpatterns, separated by a semicolon (`;`). Using this pattern convention, the first subpattern is used to format positive numbers, and the second is used to format negative numbers. Note the use of the plus sign (+) at the start of the first subpattern; the default for positive numbers is no leading character. If the `NET` element in question has a value of `123.4`, this call to `format-number()` returns the string +123.4; if `NET` has a value of `-1234.5`, it returns the string -1,234.5.

The `xsl:decimal-format` Element This top-level element is used to declare the characteristics of a named format for numbers. Once named, the format may be used by the `format-number()` function as described above. Note that the format declared by `xsl:decimal-format` doesn't get applied directly to the *value* of a number; rather, it declares the `symbols` to be used in formatting patterns.

The following is the general syntax of the `xsl:decimal-format` element:

```
<xsl:decimal-format
     name="formatname"
     decimal-separator="dec_char"
     grouping-separator="grp_char"
     infinity="string"
     minus-sign="char"
     NaN="string"
     percent="pct_char"
     per-mille="pm_char"
     zero-digit="zero_char"
     digit="dig_char"
     pattern-separator="patt_char" />
```

All attributes are optional. The following are the attributes and their values that work with the `xsl:decimal` element:

- **`name`** The name by which this pattern can be referred to in calls to the `format-number()` function
- **`decimal-separator`** The character used to separate the integer portion of a number from the fractional portion
- **`grouping-separator`** The character used to separate subgroups of numbers (typically thousands) for greater legibility
- **`infinity`** The string to be used if the value of the number is infinity. The default is the string `Infinity`.
- **`minus-sign`** The character to be used to prefix negative numbers
- **`NaN`** The string to be used if the value of the first argument to the `format-number()` function is nonnumeric. The default is the string `NaN`.
- **`percent`** The character to be used to prefix percentages
- **`per-mille`** The character to be used to prefix parts-per-thousand numbers
- **`zero-digit`** The character to be used to represent the digit 0
- **`digit`** The character to be used to represent any digit
- **`pattern-separator`** The character used to break up the pattern string into subpatterns for positive and negative numbers

Additional Functions

The XSLT standard also defines several miscellaneous functions that cannot be grouped with others.

Getting the Current Node: The `current()` Function In nearly all cases in an XPath expression, the current node and the context node are identical. Where this generalization sometimes breaks down is within the predicate portion of a location step, especially when you're trying to establish some kind of cross-reference from one portion of the source tree to another. The `current()` function always returns a node-set consisting of a single node: the one currently being processed, regardless of the context node that may be in effect at a given moment. Note that the XPath expression `.` (the abbreviated form of `self::node()`) and this function's value will be different in such cases; the former is the node that is current at the point of the expression, while the latter is the node that is current at the time the expression starts to be evaluated.

Consider the following XML document:

```
<?xml version="1.0"?>
<?xml-stylesheet type="text/xsl" href="current.xsl"?>
```

```
<BOOK>
     <CHAPTER id="chap001">
          <TITLE>The First Chapter</TITLE>
          <XREF>chap003</XREF>
     </CHAPTER>
     <CHAPTER id="chap002">
          <TITLE>The Second Chapter</TITLE>
          <XREF>chap004</XREF>
     </CHAPTER>
     <CHAPTER id="chap003">
          <TITLE>The Third Chapter</TITLE>
          <XREF>chap001</XREF>
     </CHAPTER>
     <CHAPTER id="chap004">
          <TITLE>The Fourth Chapter</TITLE>
          <XREF>chap002</XREF>
     </CHAPTER>
</BOOK>
```

Each chapter in this book cross-references one other chapter. In order to establish this cross-reference, we have to use the `current()` function as in the following style sheet:

```
<xsl:stylesheet version="1.0"
     xmlns:xsl="http://www.w3.org/1999/XSL/Transform"
     xmlns="http://www.w3.org/TR/REC-html40">

<xsl:template match="BOOK">
     <html>
          <head><title>Current vs. Context Node</title></head>
          <body>
               <xsl:apply-templates/>
          </body>
     </html>
</xsl:template>

<xsl:template match="CHAPTER">
     <p>
          <xsl:value-of select="TITLE"/>
          (id=<xsl:value-of select="@id"/>)
          cross-references (via its XREF,
          <xsl:value-of select="XREF"/>) the chapter titled
```

```
            "<xsl:value-of select="//CHAPTER[@id=current()/XREF]/TITLE"/>"
      </p>
</xsl:template>

</xsl:stylesheet>
```

Be aware of the use of the `current()` function in the predicate of the final `xsl:value-of` element's `select` attribute. That attribute says "locate the one chapter in the document whose `id` attribute equals the value of the `XREF` element of the current chapter, and display that chapter's title." If you didn't use the `current()` function here, the test within the predicate would locate a chapter whose `id` attribute equals its own `XREF` element, which would return an empty node-set (since none of the chapters cross- reference themselves).

The IE browser displays the results of this transformation as shown in Figure 16-9.

Getting to Non-XML Content: The `unparsed-entity-uri()` Function

Using XPath alone, you can locate any XML content in a document, one way or another. However, the XML specification permits documents to reference non-XML content as well by using unparsed entities declared in a DTD; while such content cannot be physically incorporated in a document, it might with some justification be considered a logical part of the document.

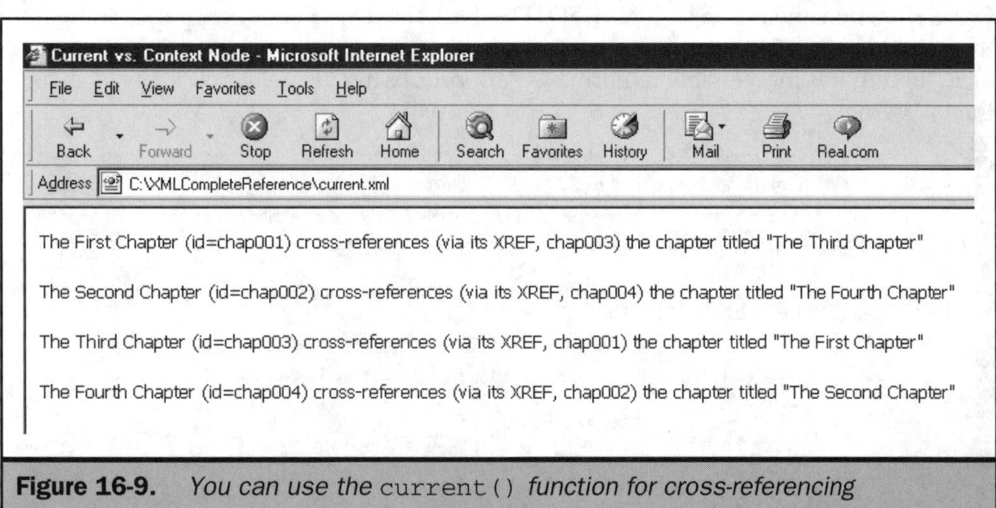

Figure 16-9. *You can use the `current()` function for cross-referencing*

The `unparsed-entity-uri()` function enables you to access unparsed entities for possible XSLT transformation to result environments that can incorporate them in ways that XML itself cannot. Its general syntax is

```
unparsed-entity-uri(entname)
```

where *entname* is the name of the unparsed entity whose URI you wish to retrieve.

The most obvious case where something like this might be useful is in processing images defined in a DTD in such a way that they can be included in an HTML result tree. Consider the following document:

```
<?xml version="1.0"?>
<!DOCTYPE LOGOPAGE [
<!NOTATION image_gif
     SYSTEM "http://www.isi.edu/in-notes/iana/
assignments/media-types/image/gif">
<!ENTITY omhlogo SYSTEM "osborne_logo.gif" NDATA image_gif>
]>
<?xml-stylesheet type="text/xsl" href="unparsed_ent.xsl"?>
<LOGOPAGE/>
```

This document is completely empty in the sense that its root element, LOGOPAGE, is itself an empty element, lacking even an attribute that might be located using an XPath expression; nonetheless, in its internal DTD subset, the document does specify something that might be considered content: a .gif image. We can display this image on a Web page, even though it is inaccessible to normal XPath processing, using a style sheet such as the following:

```
<xsl:stylesheet version="1.0"
     xmlns:xsl="http://www.w3.org/1999/XSL/Transform"
     xmlns="http://www.w3.org/TR/REC-html40">

<xsl:template match="LOGOPAGE">
     <html>
          <head><title>Unparsed Entities</title></head>
          <body>
               <img src="{unparsed-entity-uri('omhlogo')}" />
          </body>
     </html>
</xsl:template>

</xsl:stylesheet>
```

In the call to the `unparsed-entity-uri()` function, we've passed as an argument the name of the entity, `omhlogo`, that we're interested in. The value returned by the function is assigned to the img element's `src` attribute in an attribute value template. When we view the result of this transformation in IE, it appears as shown in Figure 16-10.

Getting the Processor to Identify a Node Uniquely: `generate-id()` Function

In the preceding section, "Getting to Non-XML Content: The `unparsed-entity-uri()` Function", we pointed out that the use of ID-type attributes has certain drawbacks that keys are designed to get around; nonetheless, there is no denying that having a unique identifier for a given node can be quite handy, even indispensable, and that in some cases there will be no value intrinsic to the document's content that can serve as a unique key.

The XSLT `generate-id()` function provides a convenient way to assign a unique identifier (let's call it an ID for convenience) to every node in the document, if so desired, without worrying about the potential for duplicates. A call to the function follows this general syntax:

```
generate-id(node-set?)
```

The optional argument *`node-set?`* identifies the node-set that you want to identify uniquely; the ID is assigned to the first node in the node-set. If no `node-set?` argument is passed, the function assigns the ID to the context node.

The XSLT standard does not specify how a conforming processor is to arrive at a unique ID; it specifies only that the ID will always be the same for a given node in a given document in a given transformation and that each node will have one and only one unique ID. There is no guarantee that XSLT processor A will assign the same ID to a given node that processor B does, or that processor A will assign the same ID to the node during one transformation that it does during another.

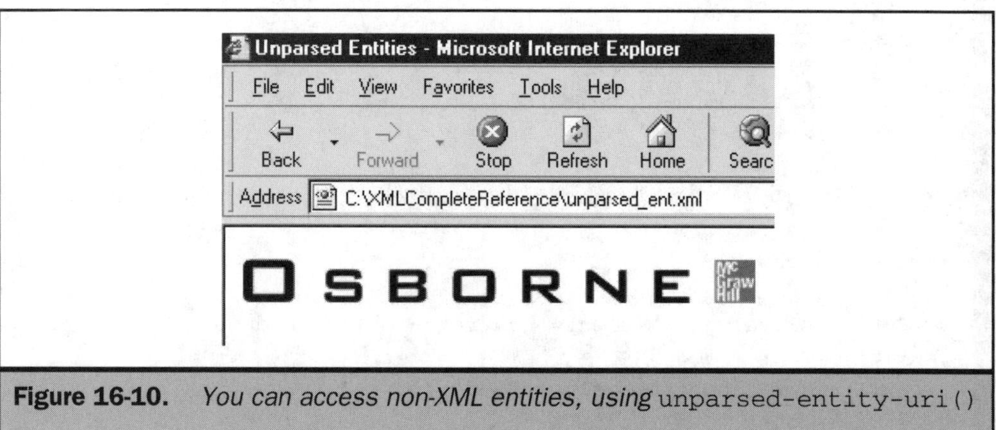

Figure 16-10. *You can access non-XML entities, using* `unparsed-entity-uri()`

Determining what these generated IDs look like for a given processor is simple. You can use a style sheet such as the following (gen_id.xsl), applied to any XML document, including itself, as you can see from the `xml-stylesheet` PI:

```
<?xml-stylesheet type="text/xsl" href="gen_id.xsl"?>
<xsl:stylesheet version="1.0"
    xmlns:xsl="http://www.w3.org/1999/XSL/Transform"
    xmlns="http://www.w3.org/TR/REC-html40">

<xsl:template match="/">
   <html>
    <head><title>Generating IDs</title></head>
    <body>
     <table border="1">
        <tr>
         <th style="background-color: #CECECE">
          Node Name or [Value]</th>
         <th style="background-color: #CECECE">Generated ID</th>
        </tr>
        <xsl:apply-templates select="node()"/>
     </table>
    </body>
   </html>
</xsl:template>

<xsl:template match="node()">
   <tr>
    <td>
     <xsl:choose>
        <xsl:when test="name(.)=''">
         [<xsl:value-of select="."/>]
        </xsl:when>
        <xsl:otherwise>
         <xsl:value-of select="name(.)"/>
        </xsl:otherwise>
     </xsl:choose>
    </td>
    <td><xsl:value-of select="generate-id()"/></td>
   </tr>
   <xsl:apply-templates select="node()"/>
</xsl:template>

</xsl:stylesheet>
```

The style sheet displays a table. In the first column is either the name of the visited node or (if it has no name) its string value, enclosed in square brackets. In the second column is the value of the `generate-id()` function for that node. We're going to apply the style sheet to itself to see the IDs as computed using the Microsoft XML (MSXML) processor built into IE and using Saxon.

Note *As presented in the preceding section, "The* `indent` *Attribute," in readable form, this document will display stray text nodes for each block of contiguous white space. For purposes of the following demonstration, we'll strip out all extraneous white space in the style sheet, including new lines; this white space–less version of the style sheet is called gen_id_no_space.xsl.*

Figure 16-11 shows how the result tree displays when viewed directly in IE. Compare this with Figure 16-12, which is the document created using Saxon to

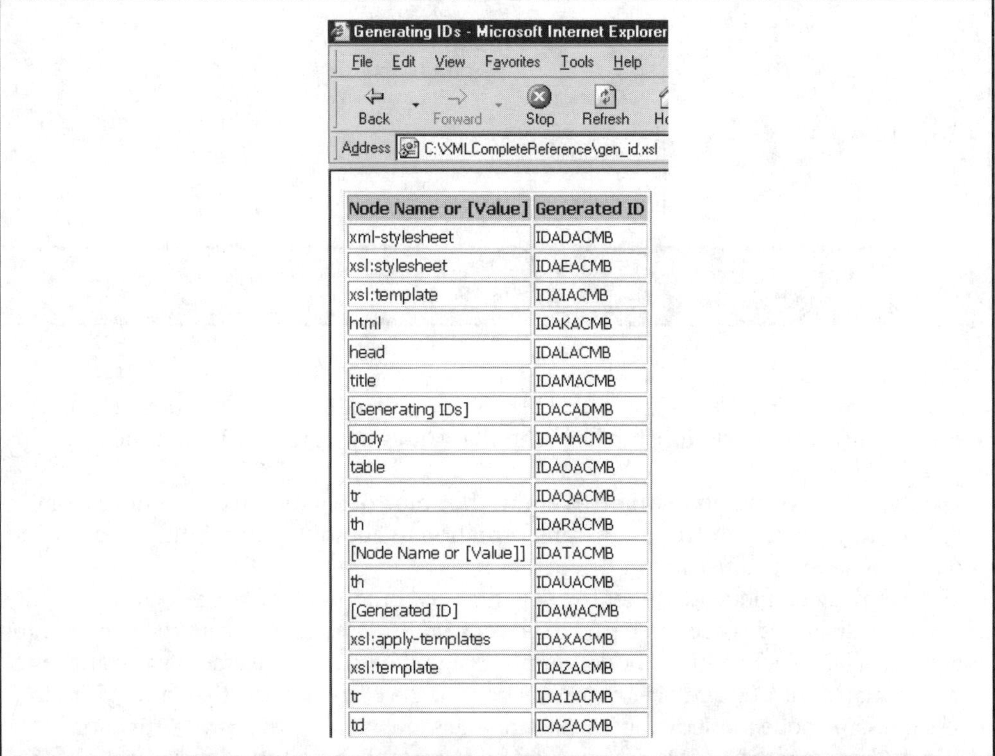

Generating IDs - Microsoft Internet Explorer
File Edit View Favorites Tools Help
Back Forward Stop Refresh
Address C:\XMLCompleteReference\gen_id.xsl
Node Name or [Value] | Generated ID
xml-stylesheet | IDADACMB
xsl:stylesheet | IDAEACMB
xsl:template | IDAIACMB
html | IDAKACMB
head | IDALACMB
title | IDAMACMB
[Generating IDs] | IDACADMB
body | IDANACMB
table | IDAOACMB
tr | IDAQACMB
th | IDARACMB
[Node Name or [Value]] | IDATACMB
th | IDAUACMB
[Generated ID] | IDAWACMB
xsl:apply-templates | IDAXACMB
xsl:template | IDAZACMB
tr | IDA1ACMB
td | IDA2ACMB

Figure 16-11. *An XSLT style sheet with computed IDs for each PI, element, and text node provided by the MSXML XSLT processor is shown in IE.*

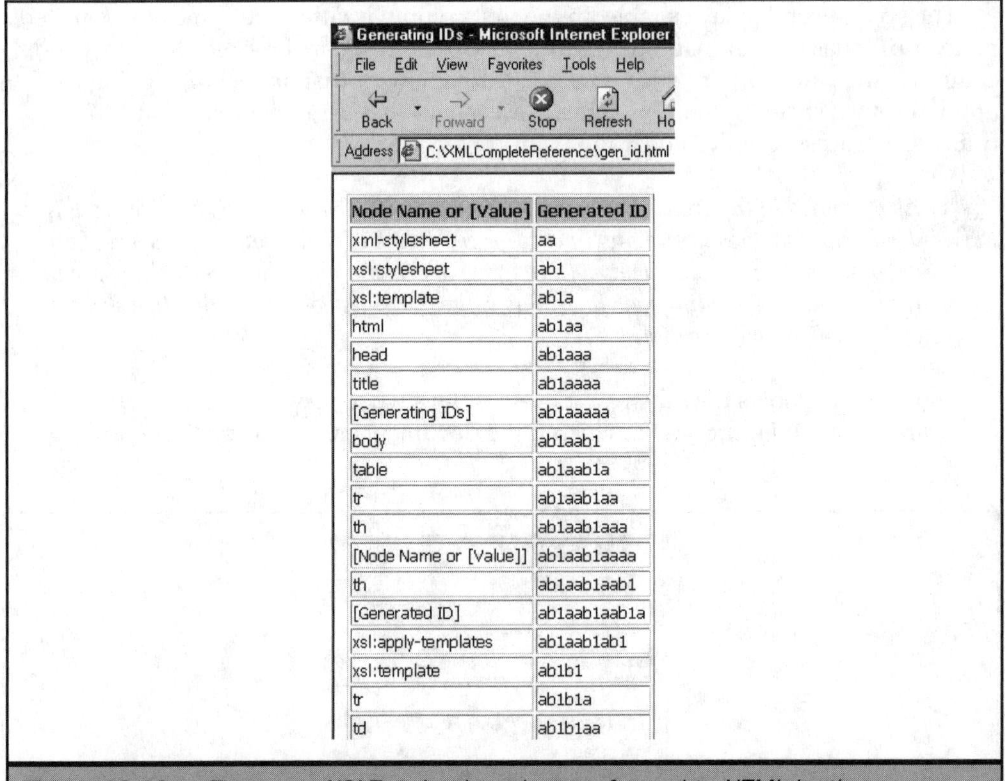

Node Name or [Value]	Generated ID
xml-stylesheet	aa
xsl:stylesheet	ab1
xsl:template	ab1a
html	ab1aa
head	ab1aaa
title	ab1aaaa
[Generating IDs]	ab1aaaaa
body	ab1aab1
table	ab1aab1a
tr	ab1aab1aa
th	ab1aab1aaa
[Node Name or [Value]]	ab1aab1aaaa
th	ab1aab1aab1
[Generated ID]	ab1aab1aab1a
xsl:apply-templates	ab1aab1ab1
xsl:template	ab1b1
tr	ab1b1a
td	ab1b1aa

Figure 16-12. *The same XSLT style sheet is transformed to HTML by the Saxon XSLT processor*

transform the original style sheet to HTML. Saxon calculates the IDs and checks that there's no discernible relationship between the values in Figure 16-12 and those in Figure 16-11.

So then, if there are no guarantees about the value of a generated ID, either from processor to processor or from one transformation to another, you might wonder what good the generated values are.

First, having a unique identifier can speed up the processing of large documents quite a bit, especially if nodes need to be accessed repeatedly. When there is no certainly unique data value available for a given node, simply assign the `xsl:key` element's use attribute a value equal to the `generate-id()` function for the current node; thereafter you can access the same node immediately by passing the same value to the `key()` function.

Second, the generated IDs are very useful for establishing intradocument links in the result tree document in the same way that a true `ID-IDREF` combination works. Again, the actual value of the key is immaterial in this case; all that matters is that there is one and only one node that corresponds to a given value (whatever it is).

Consider the case of an XML-based quotations database. A simple version of such a database might look like the following:

```
<?xml version="1.0"?>
<?xml-stylesheet type="text/xsl" href="gen_id_links.xsl"?>
<QUOTES>
     <QUOTE>Books, the children of the brain.
     <AUTHOR>Jonathan Swift</AUTHOR></QUOTE>
     <QUOTE>'Tis very warm weather when one's in bed.
     <AUTHOR>Jonathan Swift</AUTHOR></QUOTE>
     <QUOTE>Look homeward, Angel, now, and melt with truth.
     <AUTHOR>John Milton</AUTHOR></QUOTE>
     <QUOTE>The covers of this book are too far apart.
     <AUTHOR>Ambrose Bierce</AUTHOR></QUOTE>
     <QUOTE>A nice man is a man of nasty ideas.
     <AUTHOR>Jonathan Swift</AUTHOR></QUOTE>
     <QUOTE>All hell broke loose.<
     AUTHOR>John Milton</AUTHOR></QUOTE>
     <AUTHORS>
          <AUTHOR>
               <NAME>Jonathan Swift</NAME>
               <DATES>1667-1745</DATES>
          </AUTHOR>
          <AUTHOR>
               <NAME>Ambrose Bierce</NAME>
               <DATES>1842-c.1914</DATES>
          </AUTHOR>
          <AUTHOR>
               <NAME>John Milton</NAME>
               <DATES>1608-1674</DATES>
          </AUTHOR>
     </AUTHORS>
</QUOTES>
```

We'd like to display the quotations and the biographical information about their authors in two separate HTML tables with a link from each of the quotes to the corresponding information about its author. An XSLT style sheet to accomplish this might look as follows:

```
<?xml-stylesheet type="text/xsl" href="gen_id.xsl"?>
<xsl:stylesheet version="1.0"
    xmlns:xsl="http://www.w3.org/1999/XSL/Transform"
```

```
    xmlns="http://www.w3.org/TR/REC-html40">

<xsl:template match="QUOTES">
    <html>
       <head><title>Intra-Document Links</title></head>
       <body>
          <table border="1">
              <tr>
                 <th>Quotation</th>
                 <th>Author</th>
              </tr>
              <xsl:apply-templates select="QUOTE"/>
          </table>
          <table border="1">
              <tr>
                 <th>Author</th>
                 <th>Lived</th>
              </tr>
              <xsl:apply-templates select="AUTHORS"/>
          </table>
       </body>
    </html>
</xsl:template>

<xsl:template match="QUOTE">
  <tr>
    <td><xsl:value-of select="text()"/></td>
    <td align="center">
    [<a href="#{generate-id(//AUTHOR[NAME=current()/AUTHOR])}">
    <xsl:value-of select="position()"/></a>]</td>
  </tr>
</xsl:template>

<xsl:template match="AUTHORS">
  <xsl:for-each select="AUTHOR">
     <tr>
        <td>
        <a name="{generate-id()}"/><xsl:value-of select="NAME"/>
        </td>
        <td><xsl:value-of select="DATES"/></td>
     </tr>
  </xsl:for-each>
```

```
</xsl:template>

</xsl:stylesheet>
```

There are two calls to the `generate-id()` function:

- The first occurs within the template rule for the `QUOTE` element in the construction of the second table cell. The value of the HTML a element's `href` attribute is set to a # sign, followed by the generated ID for the `AUTHOR` node whose `NAME` child matches the `AUTHOR` child of the `QUOTE` itself.
- The second occurs when processing the template rule for the `AUTHORS` element in the `xsl:for-each` that processes each individual `AUTHOR`. Here, the generated ID is simply assigned to an a element's `name` attribute.

Applying this style sheet to the document produces the following result tree in Saxon:

```
<html xmlns="http://www.w3.org/TR/REC-html40">
   <head><title>Intra-Document Links</title></head>
   <body>
    <table border="1">
     <tr>
        <th>Quotation</th>
        <th>Author</th>
     </tr>
     <tr>
        <td>Books, the children of the brain.</td>
        <td align="center">[<a href="#ab1c13b1">1</a>]</td>
     </tr>
     <tr>
        <td>'Tis very warm weather when one's in bed.</td>
        <td align="center">[<a href="#ab1c13b1">2</a>]</td>
     </tr>
     <tr>
        <td>Look homeward, Angel, now, and melt with truth.</td>
        <td align="center">[<a href="#ab1c13b5">3</a>]</td>
     </tr>
     <tr>
        <td>The covers of this book are too far apart.</td>
        <td align="center">[<a href="#ab1c13b3">4</a>]</td>
     </tr>
     <tr>
```

```
          <td>A nice man is a man of nasty ideas.</td>
          <td align="center">[<a href="#ab1c13b1">5</a>]</td>
       </tr>
       <tr>
          <td>All hell broke loose.</td>
          <td align="center">[<a href="#ab1c13b5">6</a>]</td>
       </tr>
      </table>
      <table border="1">
       <tr>
          <th>Author</th>
          <th>Lived</th>
       </tr>
       <tr>
          <td><a name="ab1c13b1"/>Jonathan Swift</td>
          <td>1667-1745</td>
       </tr>
       <tr>
          <td><a name="ab1c13b3"/>Ambrose Bierce</td>
          <td>1842-c.1914</td>
       </tr>
       <tr>
          <td><a name="ab1c13b5"/>John Milton</td>
          <td>1608-1674</td>
       </tr>
      </table>
    </body>
</html>
```

Note *The generated IDs for the target nodes are unique, even though each may be referred to multiple times in the table of quotes.*

Learning about the XSLT Processor: `system-property()` The `system-property()` function retrieves information, which may or may not be important, from the XSLT processing environment, making it available for use in your style sheet. The general syntax of a call to the `system-property()` function is

```
system-property(propertyname)
```

where *propertyname* is a string with one of the following three values:

- **xsl:version** Returns the version of the XSLT standard supported by the processor (currently 1.0 for all conforming processors)
- **xsl:vendor** Returns a string identifying the vendor or developer of the processor
- **xsl:vendor-url** Returns the URL associated with the vendor (generally, the vendor's home page)

You could use the system-property() function to create a note, for documentation purposes, describing the product and vendor responsible for this particular transformation. A style sheet to create such a note might include the following template rule:

```
<xsl:template match="/">
     ...
     <i>XSLT version <xsl:value-of select="system-property('xsl:version')"/>
     transformation courtesy of <a
     href="{system-property('xsl:vendor-url')}"><xsl:value-of
     select="system-property('xsl:vendor')"/></a>.</i>
</xsl:template>
```

This would add to the foot of the result tree the following code (assuming use of the Saxon 5.5 processor):

```
<i>XSLT version 1
     transformation courtesy of
     <a href="http://users.iclway.co.uk/mhkay/saxon/index.html">
     SAXON 5.5 from Michael Kay of ICL</a>.</i>
```

Summary

This chapter provided you with information about the XPath standard for locating content in an XML document and the XSLT standard for transforming XML content located via XPath.

An XSLT style sheet is, of course, itself an XML document. The XSLT specification defines two trees: the *source tree* and the *result tree*. An XSLT transformation turns a source tree, and XML document, into a result tree, often an HTML document. A node is a discrete logical component of an XML document.

The World Wide Web Consortium (W3C) has issued the XPath specification as a means of locating any single unit of content—any node—in an XML document. Nodes are located using a construct called an XPath expression, which can often be further decomposed into subordinate expressions. The XPath expression language itself is not an XML vocabulary; rather, it defines a mechanism for using specially formatted text strings as values assigned to specific attributes (in the case of XSLT) or added to Uniform Resource Identifiers (URIs) (in the case of XPointer).

Chapter 17 provides you with basic information about XSL Formatting Objects, an as-yet-unfinished specification for creating units of displayable text and other content in an XML framework.

The Complete Reference

Chapter 17

XSL: Completing Your Application

Sometimes, laying out your content for display on the Web is not good enough; sometimes, even in the Internet age, you simply must optimize your presentation for print media. That is where XSL Formatting Objects (XSL-FOs) come in. While the XSL-FO standard is not (as of this writing) yet in a final form, this chapter introduces you to its basic concepts and practice. (We will not cover the XSL-FO vocabulary in this chapter. To learn about the XSL-FO vocabulary, see Appendix C.)

XSL-FO Document Structure

Like any other XML document, an XSL-FO document contains a single root element. In XSL-FO's case, that root element is `fo:root`.

Note *As with any other namespace prefix, the `fo:` prefix for XSL-FO element names is by convention and is not a requirement. The same is true of the filename extension to most XSL-FO documents, generally `.fo`, `.fob`, or `.xfo` (the latter stands for "XSL formatting objects").*

The `fo:root` element takes a single attribute, which is the `xmlns:fo` attribute declaring the XSL-FO vocabulary's namespace. The value of this attribute, according to the XSL-FO standard, must be `http://www.w3.org/1999/XSL/Format` in order for an XSL-FO processor to recognize the document's elements and attributes.

In this order, the following element sets appear in the `fo:root` element:

- **Layout master set** This is a set of elements and attributes (contained in a single `fo:layout-master-set` element) whose purpose is to specify the overall layout and sequence of pages in the document. Each layout in the master set is defined by an `fo:simple-page-master` element, and each sequence is defined by an `fo:page-sequence-master` element. It is important to recognize that the layouts represent types of pages, not specific individual pages. Actual content will be poured into the forms established by these layouts later, creating the individual pages.
- **Declarations** This optional portion of the XSL-FO document declares color profiles that may be used anywhere throughout the document. (A color profile is basically a specification of a particular color or group of colors that may be used in a platform-independent way by any number of color-rendering hardware devices.) The element in which all these declarations appear is called (not surprisingly) `fo:declarations`, and each color profile is defined by the attributes of an empty `fo:color-profile` element.
- **Page sequences** The document contains one or more page sequences in which the document's actual content appears, laid out according to the specifications provided in the layout master set. Each page sequence consists of a single `fo:page-sequence` element, within which may appear an optional

title, one or more optional static pieces of content (such as page headers and footers appearing on every page of this kind), and the actual content itself, contained in a single `xsl:flow` object and its descendants.

Thus, a typical XSL-FO document might have the following structure:

```
<fo:root xmlns:fo="http://www.w3.org/1999/XSL/Format">

  <fo:layout-master-set>
    <fo:simple-page-master...>...</fo:simple-page-master>
    <fo:page-sequence-master...>...</fo:page-sequence-master>
    [etc.]
  </fo:layout-master-set>

  <!-- Use the fo:declarations element if your document requires
    cross-platform control of color representation. -->
   <fo:declarations>
    <fo:color-profile.../>
    [etc.]
  </fo:declarations>

  <fo:page-sequence...>...</fo:page-sequence>
  <fo:page-sequence...>...</fo:page-sequence>
  [etc.]

</fo:root>
```


Creating an XSL-FO Document

As explained in Chapter 15, XSL-FO documents are not likely to be created by hand. Instead, they will be generated by XSL Transformations (XSLT) style sheets, transforming XML source to XSL-FO result trees. While this chapter will present examples of XSL-FO elements and attributes in isolation, understand that in all cases these will have been created as part of an XSL transformation's result tree rather than from scratch.

Layout Master Sets: Page Layouts and Sequences

XSL-FO works by building a rendered document from the outside in. Within the XSL-FO document as a whole, the first two things you need to build is a description of the kinds of pages that the document contains and the order in which these pages appear. This description appears within the XSL-FO document's single `fo:layout-master-set` element.

Page Layouts

Most professionally printed works include a number of different page layouts. For instance, all of a book's front matter has one set of margin dimensions; the table of contents will have a different margin, with perhaps its own page header; the body of the book will have slightly different layouts for right and left pages and slightly different layouts for the first pages of chapters and sections or parts; and the index will be laid out not only within particular margins with special page headers, but also in columnar format unlike anything else in the book. Even a simple report from a database program may have a report header and footer whose page layouts are dramatically different from the layout of the report.

Each of these general kinds of layouts or formats will require its own `fo:simple-page-master` element (within the `fo:layout-master-set`) that describes the geometry of the page and the relationships among various portions of it. A simple example that defines two layouts—one for left pages and one for right pages—might look like the following:

```
<fo:layout-master-set>
     <fo:simple-page-master master-name="lefthand"
          margin-bottom="1in"
          margin-left=".75in"
          margin-right="1.25in"
          margin-top="1in"
          page-height="9in"
          page-width="6in">
     </fo:simple-page-master>
     <fo:simple-page-master master-name="righthand"
          margin-bottom="1in"
          margin-left="1.25in"
          margin-right=".75in"
          margin-top="1in"
          page-height="9in"
          page-width="6in">
     </fo:simple-page-master>
     [page-sequencing information]
</fo:layout-master-set>
```

The only difference between left and right pages in this layout would be in the left and right margins, offset appropriately to allow for stapling or other binding.

Within each `fo:simple-page-master` element are elements defining the distinct *regions* within that page's layout. These regions define the areas in which text may be printed on the page. Up to five regions may be specified, each with its corresponding element:

- **`fo:region-body`** Required region, corresponding to the area in which the bulk of the page's content will typically appear
- **`fo:region-before`** Optional region, corresponding to the area used for the header of a page in a book printed in Western top-to-bottom, left-to-right orientation
- **`fo:region-after`** Optional region, corresponding to the area used for the footer of a page in a book printed in Western top-to-bottom, left-to-right orientation
- **`fo:region-start`** Optional region, corresponding to the left printable side of a page in a book printed in Western top-to-bottom, left-to-right orientation
- **`fo:region-end`** Optional region, corresponding to the right printable side of a page in a book printed in Western top-to-bottom, left-to-right orientation

Note *The XSL-FO specification provides many features in support of internationalization, including, for example, text running form top to bottom, bottom to top. or right to left, rather than English's normal left-to-right writing style. All of these possibilities are the reason why XSL-FO tends to favor words like start and end, rather than left and right, and before and after, rather than top and bottom.*

To visualize how all five regions might be used in a `fo:simple-page-master`, imagine a technical reference book whose main pages contain not only body copy, figures, and so on—all of which appear in the region-body—but also headers, footers, an innermost area (closest to the page's bound edge) in which cross-references to other chapters will appear, and an outermost area (furthest from the page's bound edge) in which callouts from the text, important notes, and so on, will appear. Right pages in such a book might be laid out schematically as shown in Figure 17-1. This figure shows the layout of a right page consisting of five printable regions.

The layout depicted in Figure 17-1 could be described in an `fo:simple-page-master` element as shown in the following example. Note that the

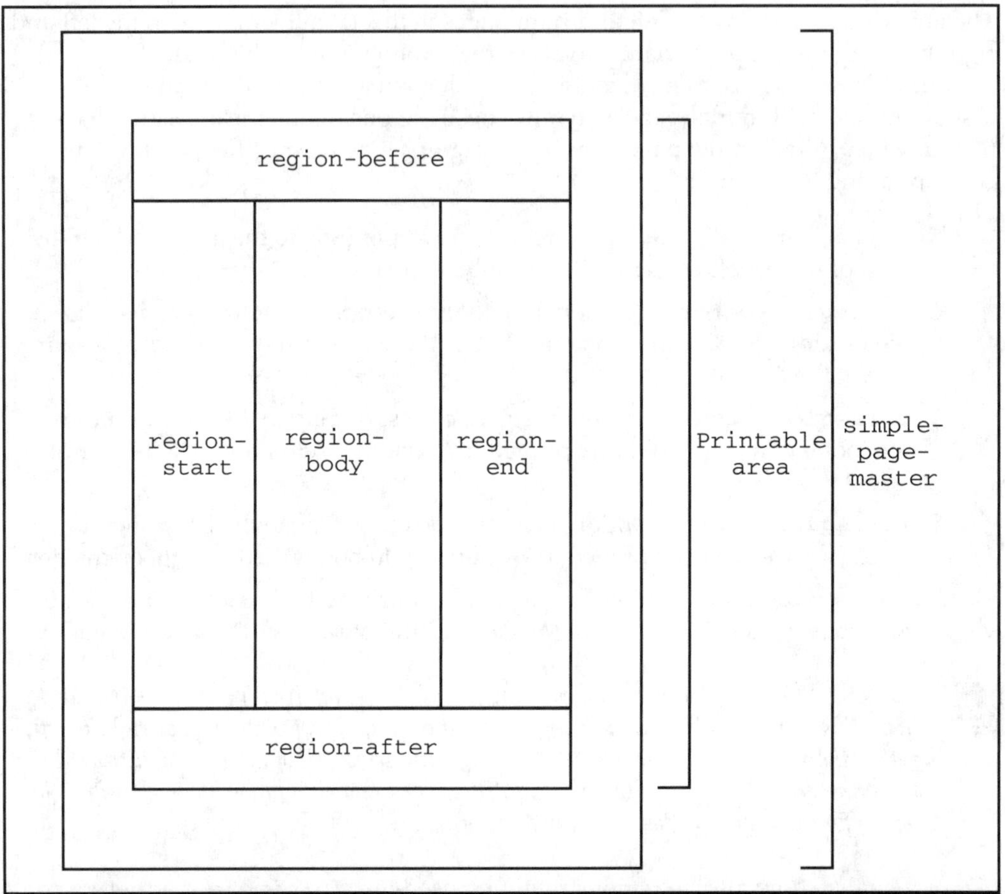

Figure 17-1. *The area outside the prinable portion of the page is defined by the* `fo:simple-page-master` *element's various margin attributes (for example,* `margin-left`, `margin-bottom`*).*

left and right margins of the overall page master itself are exaggerated here, moving the edge of the printable area to within only a quarter inch of the right edge of the page:

```
<fo:simple-page-master master-name="contents_r"
    margin-bottom="1in" margin-left="1.25in"
    margin-right=".25in" margin-top="1in"
    page-height="9in" page-width="6in">
  <!-- Note that the page's printable area, see page-width,
       is 6 inches (the page width) minus 1.5 inches (for
```

```
    the left/right margins) wide, by 9 inches (the page
    height) minus 2 inches (for the top/bottom margins)
    high, or 4.5x7 inches. -->

  <fo:region-before region-name="xsl-region-before"
       extent="1in"
       margin-left="0in" margin-right="0in"
       margin-top=".5in" margin-bottom="1in"/>

  <fo:region-body region-name="body"
       margin-left="0in" margin-right="0in"
       margin-top="1.25in"/>

  <fo:region-after region-name="xsl-region-after"
       extent="1in"/>

  <!-- FOP v. 0.16.0 does not support the region-start and
       region-end regions, so the corresponding elements
       below are commented out. If using another XSL-FO
       processor, or a later version of FOP, you may be
       able to specify those regions as well. -->
  <!-- fo:region-start region-name="xsl-region-start"
       extent="1.25in"/-->
  <!--fo:region-end region-name="xsl-region-end"
       extent=".5in"/-->
  <!-- Because the extents for the region-start and -end add
       up to 1.75 inches, the width of the region-body will
       be the printable width minus this sum, i.e. 4 inches
       minus 1.75, or 2.25 inches. -->

</fo:simple-page-master>
```

As you might have observed from the preceding example, the size of the `region-body` is not specified directly, but it may be calculated relative to the size of the printable area of the page, less the values of the extent attributes on any of the regions above, below, and to either side of the `region-body`. (If any of those regions are missing from a given `fo:simple-page-master`, their extents are assumed to be 0.)

Each of the five regions is treated as if it were a separate, potentially printable area in its own right. That is, each region may also have its own margin settings. If a margin setting is omitted, it is assumed to be a setting of 0.

Page Sequences

Within the `fo:layout-master-set`, you specify not only the kinds of layouts to be used throughout the resulting document, but also the order in which they are to appear. This is done using an `fo:page-sequence-master` element with one or more of the following child elements:

- **`fo:single-page-master-reference`** Used to indicated that the corresponding page master will appear once in the result. You might use a sequence like this for a book's cover, for example.
- **`fo:repeatable-page-master-reference`** Used when the same page master layout is to be repeated over and over until all corresponding content is exhausted.
- **`fo:repeatable-page-master-alternatives`** Used when one layout is in effect on certain pages and a different layout is in effect on others. Typical examples might be a layout used only for the first page of a document, versus all pages, and a document with different layouts for the left and right pages.

Remember that a given page sequence points back to a page layout (as specified by a fo:`simple-page-master` element). This linkage is accomplished by a `master-name` attribute on the appropriate descendants of the `fo:page-sequence-master` element. For instance, a `fo:page-sequence-master` and its descendants might look like the following:

```
<fo:page-sequence-master master-name="mainpage">
     <fo:repeatable-page-master-alternatives>
          <fo:conditional-page-master-reference
               master-name="contents_l"
               odd-or-even="even"/>
          <fo:conditional-page-master-reference
               master-name="contents_r"
               odd-or-even="odd"/>
     </fo:repeatable-page-master-alternatives>
</fo:page-sequence-master>
```

Note *The* `master-name` *attributes of the* `fo:conditional-page-master-reference` *elements correspond to the values of name attributes of* `fo:single-page-master` *elements already defined in the document, or* `contents_l` *and* `contents_r` *in the preceding case. This page sequence master therefore tells the XSL-FO processor that all even-numbered pages (*`odd-or-even="even"`*) are to be structured according to the layout called "*`contents_l`*", and all odd-numbered pages according to the one called "*`contents_r.`*"*

Adding Content: Page Sequences

Up until this point, no output has actually been rendered on the chosen device. We have several page formats specified and an order in which they will be generated, but those all remain like theoretical constructs with no actual reference to the real world of document content.

To embed content in a document to be rendered according to XSL formatting objects, normally you would run an XSLT transformation against an XML document, instantiating in its result tree a mixture of contents and XSL-FO elements and attributes. We will demonstrate this using the following XML document, whose content and element names indicate where on the rendered page the content will go:

```
<?xml version="1.0"?>
<?xml-stylesheet type="text/xsl" href="xml_to_fo.xsl"?>
<book>
     <title>Book Title Appears in Page Header</title>
     <chapter>
          <title>Chapter Title Appears in Page Footer</title>
          <page>Odd page... bound edge at left &lt;--- </page>
          <page>Even page... bound edge at right ---&gt;</page>
     </chapter>
</book>
```

The XSLT style sheet that will transform this content to XSL formatting objects begins with a template rule for the root node. This is a long but fairly simple template rule; essentially it instantiates the `fo:root`, `fo:layout-master-set` (and its child page masters and page sequence). Here is that opening template rule with comments and blank lines removed for brevity:

```
<xsl:template match="/">
   <fo:root xmlns:fo="http://www.w3.org/1999/XSL/Format">
    <fo:layout-master-set>
     <fo:simple-page-master master-name="contents_l"
        margin-bottom="1in"
        margin-left=".25in"
        margin-right="1.25in"
        margin-top="1in"
        page-height="9in"
        page-width="6in">
        <fo:region-before region-name="xsl-region-before"
         extent="1in"
         margin-top=".5in"
         margin-bottom="1in"/>
        <fo:region-body region-name="body"
```

```
        margin-top="1.25in"/>
       <fo:region-after region-name="xsl-region-after"
        extent="1in"/>
    </fo:simple-page-master>
    <fo:simple-page-master master-name="contents_r"
       margin-bottom="1in"
       margin-left="1.25in"
       margin-right=".25in"
       margin-top="1in"
       page-height="9in"
       page-width="6in">
       <fo:region-before region-name="xsl-region-before"
        extent="1in"
        margin-top=".5in"
        margin-bottom="1in"/>
       <fo:region-body region-name="body"
        margin-top="1.25in"/>
       <fo:region-after region-name="xsl-region-after"
        extent="1in"/>
    </fo:simple-page-master>
    <fo:page-sequence-master master-name="mainpage">
       <fo:repeatable-page-master-alternatives>
        <fo:conditional-page-master-reference
         master-name="contents_l"
         odd-or-even="even"/>
        <fo:conditional-page-master-reference
         master-name="contents_r"
         odd-or-even="odd"/>
       </fo:repeatable-page-master-alternatives>
    </fo:page-sequence-master>
   </fo:layout-master-set>
   <xsl:apply-templates/>
  </fo:root>
</xsl:template>
```

Note *The template rule instantiates all the general page-formatting XSL-FO markup but does not actually introduce any content from the source tree.*

That missing component—adding content from the source tree—is the function of what the XSL-FO standard refers to as *page sequences*. (Don't let yourself be confused here. The order in which pages appear is defined by page sequence *masters*; the word *master* is always used in XSL-FO to refer to a general class of some object, rather than to an instance of the object.) As you might guess, the XSL-FO element that instantiates a page sequence is called `fo:page-sequence`. This element has one required attribute, `master-name`, whose value equals the name of some page sequence master set up in the "XSL-FO Document Structure" earlier in the XSL-FO document.

In this case, we've established only a single page sequence master, the one named `"mainpage."` So now, within a template rule for processing the source tree's chapter element, we'll instantiate the `fo:page-sequence` element:

```
<xsl:template match="chapter">
   <xsl:for-each select="page">
     <xsl:variable name="align">
        <xsl:choose>
          <!-- If this is an even-numbered page element, set the
             variable's value to "start", otherwise to "end" -->
          <xsl:when test="position() mod 2 = 0">start</xsl:when>
          <xsl:otherwise>end</xsl:otherwise>
        </xsl:choose>
     </xsl:variable>
     <fo:page-sequence master-name="mainpage">
        ...
     </fo:page-sequence>
   </xsl:for-each>
</xsl:template>
```

Remember that this XSLT template rule (`fo:page-sequence`) is doing some other things as well:

First, it is instantiating a page sequence for each page element in the source tree, not for each chapter element. (If there were a single page sequence for the whole chapter, the content of the two page elements would simply flow one after the other in the resulting document. The general rule of thumb is that each XSL-FO page sequence starts on a new page; within a continuous page sequence, with no page breaks except what naturally occurs as a page fills up.)

Second, the template rule declares a variable, `$align`, whose value will differ depending on the position of the current `page-element` node within the parent chapter element. For even-numbered page elements, `$align` will have a value of `start`, and for odd ones, the value will be end. (This variable will be used to align text on each page and to highlight the effects of how the left and right pages are processed differently.)

Within a page sequence, content is transferred to the result tree in the form of two XSL-FO elements: `fo:static-content` and `fo:flow`. Before getting into the details of those elements, though, we need to look at the two main classes of formatting provided by XSL-FO.

Block Versus Inline Formatting

XSL-FO makes explicit a distinction between block and inline formatting that is largely implicit in Hypertext Markup Language (HTML) formatting.

Block formatting applies to whole contiguous chunks of content and is handled by the XSL-FO `fo:block` element. The analogous HTML element is `div`. In general, in an HTML document (particularly one styled with Cascading Style Sheets [CSS]) you treat whole groups of contiguous paragraphs and/or tables and/or images as separate `div` elements. That is also what the `fo:block` element is for. Each block starts on a new line.

Inline formatting occurs within a block. Probably the best parallel in HTML would be the `i` and `b` elements for italicizing and boldfacing text, respectively; those elements most commonly appear within a line of text contained by some larger unit, such as a paragraph, heading, or `div` element. The `fo:inline` element typically is used in the same way, to turn on and off some characteristic within a line of text, such as its background color or font characteristics.

Both the `fo:block` and `fo:inline` elements can take a host of attributes that style their contents in various ways. Most of these attributes' names and allowable values are taken directly from CSS properties and their values. For instance, you might style a block of text in the following way:

```
<fo:block font-family="Times" font-size="14pt">Some 14-point
    <fo:inline font-style="italic" font-weight="bold">bold and
    italicized</fo:inline> text.</fo:block>
```

Certain kinds of formatted content, such as tables and images, have their own styling characteristics. We will take a look at them later in this chapter. For now, though, you should understand that most of the content you're placing in almost any XSL-FO document will be contained within `fo:block` and/or `fo:inline` elements.

Fixed Content within a Page Sequence

When you want the same content to appear in a given region of the instantiated page, use the `fo:static-content` element. By *the same content* we mean either literal text or text that may vary according to some condition inherent in the content. Its content is always a block-level element, such as `fo:block` or `fo:table`.

Given our sample XML document, suppose that we'd like to put the book's title in every page-header. We could do this with an `fo:static-content` element such as the one shown here, placed into the XSLT style sheet's template rule for processing each page element within each chapter:

```
<fo:page-sequence master-name="mainpage">
    <fo:static-content flow-name="xsl-region-before">
        <fo:block
            font-family="Helvetica"
            font-size="14pt"
            font-style="italic"
            font-weight="bold"
```

```
                text-align="{$align}">
                <xsl:value-of select="../../title"/>
            </fo:block>
        </fo:static-content>
        ...
    </fo:page-sequence
```

This fo:static-content element instructs the formatting processor to instantiate a block-level element in the region whose name is xsl-region-before (note the value of the flow-name attribute). The contents of the block-level element will be the title element belonging to the page element's parent's parent (../../title)— that is, the title of the book (as opposed to the chapter). Also note that the text will be aligned according to the value of the $align variable previously assigned.

Note *The* text-align *attribute may take a number of values, such as "*left*" and "*right*,*" in addition to the values "*start*" and "*end*" assigned in this style sheet; however, the latter are more acceptable in contexts where internationalization is important. (Also, Formatting Objects to PDF [FOP] 0.16.0 complains that the values "*left*" and "*right*" are illegal. Presumably this will be fixed in later versions.)*

We can also add an fo:static-content element for the page footer. With the following fo:static-content example, we'll display, on every page, the chapter title and page number (still within the same page sequence):

```
<fo:page-sequence master-name="mainpage">
   ...
   <fo:static-content flow-name="xsl-region-after">
     <fo:block
        font-family="Times"
        font-size="14pt"
        font-weight="bold"
        text-align="{$align}">
        <xsl:value-of select="../title"/>
       (page <fo:page-number/>)
     </fo:block>
   </fo:static-content>
   ...
</fo:page-sequence
```

As you can see, this static content includes some text from the source tree (the chapter title), some literal text (the word *page* and the enclosing parentheses), and a special XSL-FO element, fo:page-number, that is replaced in the result by the given page number.

Note *The* fo:page-number *element's value is not inserted into the result tree by the XSLT transformation. It will be generated only at the time the resulting XSL-FO document is actually rendered for display, since this is a runtime item whose value is unknown at the time of the transformation.*

Content That Varies from Page to Page

In almost any print publication generated from XSL formatting objects, the bulk of the material that appears on a given page will be contained within an `fo:flow` element. In the case of our simple document, this might appear as follows, to conclude our single page sequence:

```
<fo:page-sequence master-name="mainpage">
     ...
     <fo:flow flow-name="body">
          <fo:block
               font-family="Courier"
               font-size="12pt"
               text-align="{$align}">
               <xsl:value-of select="text()"/>
          </fo:block>
     </fo:flow>
</fo:page-sequence>
```

Viewing the Resulting Document

Our XSLT style sheet is now complete and contains the following characteristics:

- It establishes two `simple-page-master` layouts, one for left and one for right pages.
- It defines a single alternating `fo:page-sequence-master`, which displays even- and odd-numbered pages according to the left and right layouts, respectively.
- It fills the page header and footer within this `fo:page-sequence-master` with the book and chapter titles, respectively, as well as some supporting text.
- It flows the content of each page element in the source tree into a separate page sequence.

We now run FOP (described in Chapter 15) to transform the XML document into an XSL-FO document and to convert the XSL formatting objects to their Portable Document Format (PDF) equivalents. FOP shows the following messages:

```
FOP 0.16.0 DEV
using SAX parser org.apache.xerces.parsers.SAXParser
transforming to xsl:fo markup
xml: file:C:/XMLCompleteReference/xml_to_fo.xml
xslt: file:C:/XMLCompleteReference/xml_to_fo.xsl
using renderer org.apache.fop.render.pdf.PDFRenderer
using element mapping org.apache.fop.fo.StandardElementMapping
using element mapping org.apache.fop.svg.SVGElementMapping
```

```
using property list mapping
org.apache.fop.fo.StandardPropertyListMapping
using property list mapping
org.apache.fop.svg.SVGPropertyListMapping
building formatting object tree
setting up fonts
formatting FOs into areas
 [1]
 [2]
rendering areas to PDF
writing out PDF
```

The output [1] and [2] indicate that two pages are being rendered. If page 1 had rendered successfully, but there was a problem with page 2, only the [1] would show.

The resulting PDF document looks like Figure 17-2 when viewed in Adobe Acrobat. Acrobat's grid display has been turned on to demonstrate the effects of the various regions' margins relative to those for the page as a whole.

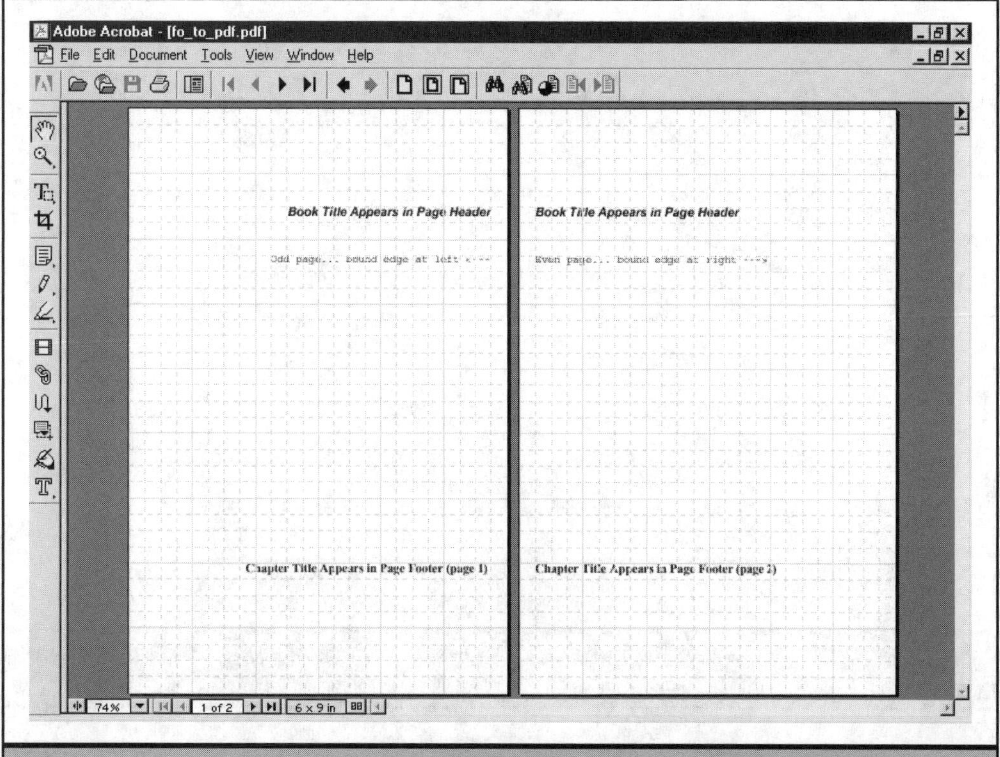

Figure 17-2. *This PDF document is created by FOP from the sample XML document and XSLT style sheet (by way of XSL formatting objects)*

Compare this with Figure 17-3, which uses Antenna House's XSL Formatter to display the various regions' boundaries.

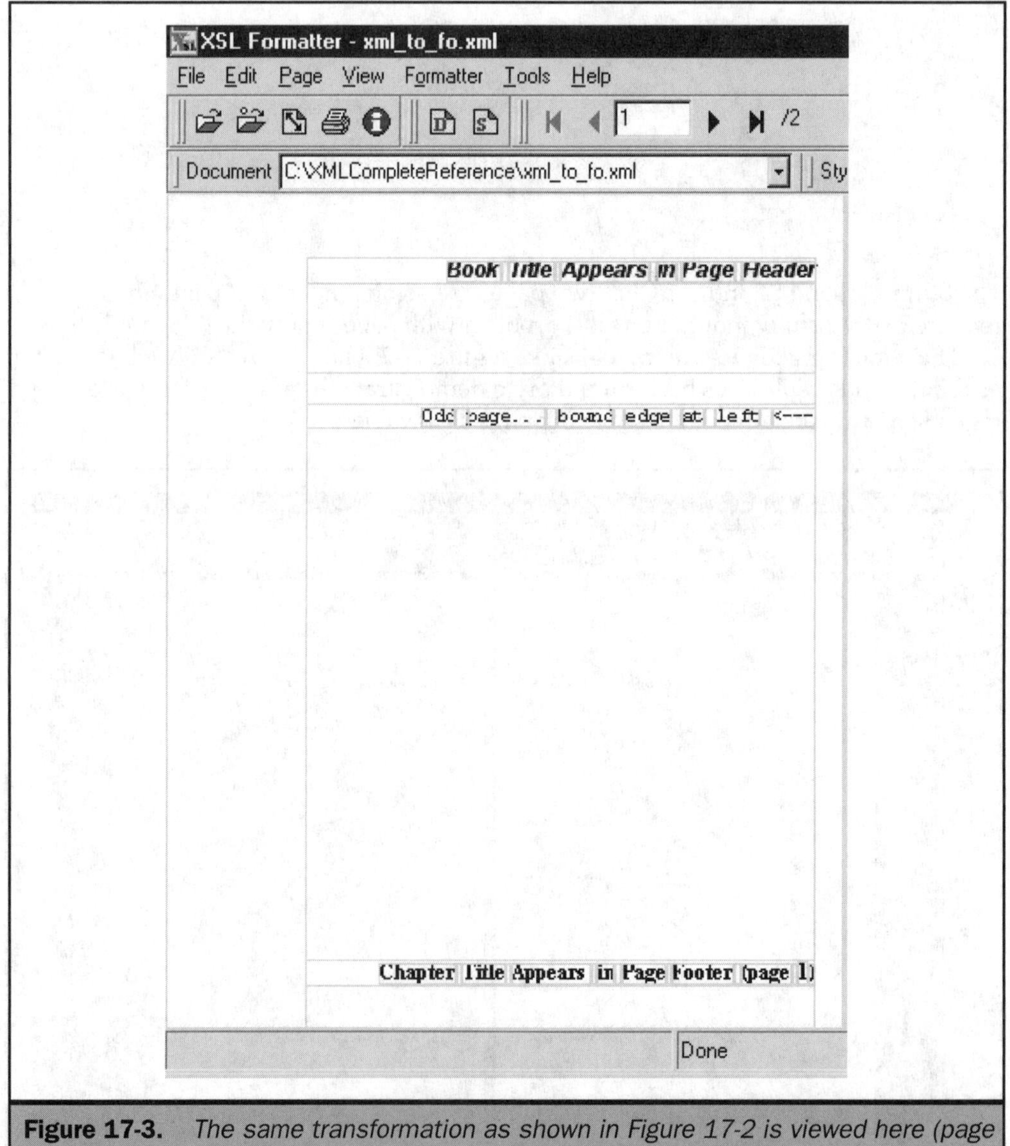

Figure 17-3. *The same transformation as shown in Figure 17-2 is viewed here (page 1 only) in Antenna House's XSL Formatter application*

Modifying a Region's Display Properties

Altering the look of a region is simply a matter of altering the look of the corresponding `fo:static-content` or `fo:flow` element using any of a number of attributes based on CSS properties.

For instance, we can change the look of our sample document's header and footer by adding a silver background to the former and adding a black top-and-bottom border to the latter by changing the corresponding portions of the XSLT style sheet's template rule for the chapter element:

```
<fo:page-sequence master-name="mainpage">
    <fo:static-content flow-name="xsl-region-before">
       <fo:block
          font-family="Helvetica"
          font-size="14pt"
          font-style="italic"
          font-weight="bold"
          align="{$align}"
          background-color="silver">
          <xsl:value-of select="../../title"/>
       </fo:block>
  </fo:static-content>
  <fo:static-content flow-name="xsl-region-after">
     <fo:block
            font-family="Times"
            font-size="14pt"
            font-weight="bold"
            text-align="{$align}"
            border-top-style="solid"
            border-bottom-style="solid"
            border-top-width="2pt"
            border-bottom-width="2pt">
       <xsl:value-of select="../title"/> (page <fo:page-number/>)
     </fo:block>
  </fo:static-content>
    ...
</fo:page-sequence>
```

The PDF generated from the resulting XSL-FO document now appears as in Figure 17-4.

In Figure 17-4 the borders and background colors span the entire region from margin to margin and not simply the text content included in the region.

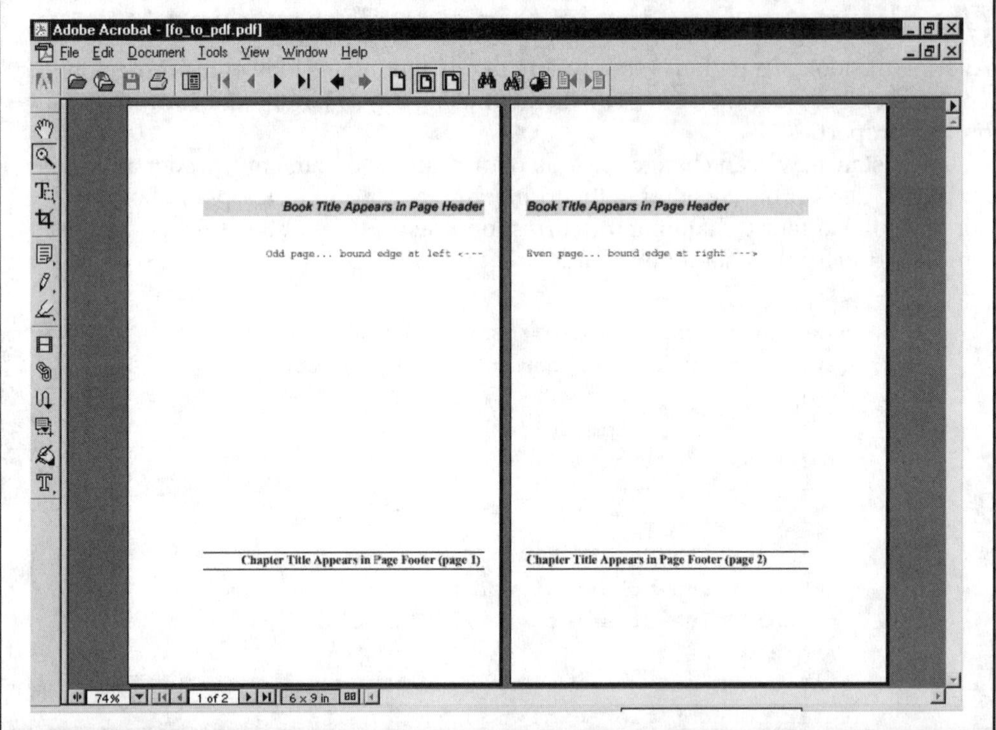

Figure 17-4. *This sample document is shown with background color and borders added to the before and after regions, respectively*

Inserting Images

In HTML, you insert an image into the displayed page using the `img` element (whose `src` attribute is the Uniform Resource Identifier [URI] of the image to be inserted). The XSLT-FO counterpart is the `fo:external-graphic` element. This element on its own is considered to be an inline formatting object; however, you can make it block-level by including it in a block-level formatting object (such as `fo:block`).

The `fo:external-graphic` element comes with an `src` attribute, which serves the same purpose as its HTML counterpart; thus, we could insert a logo into our sample document using code such as the following:

```
<fo:external-graphic src="osborne_logo.gif" />
```

FOP 0.16.0 only supports absolute URIs as the value for the `src` *attribute; thus, if using this version of FOP, the preceding code would have to include the protocol and other portions of the full URI, such as* `http://www.foo.bar/imgs/osborne_logo.gif`.

If `fo:external-graphic` of an XSLT transformation's result tree is added to the body region in our sample XSL-FO document, we see results as in Figure 17-5.

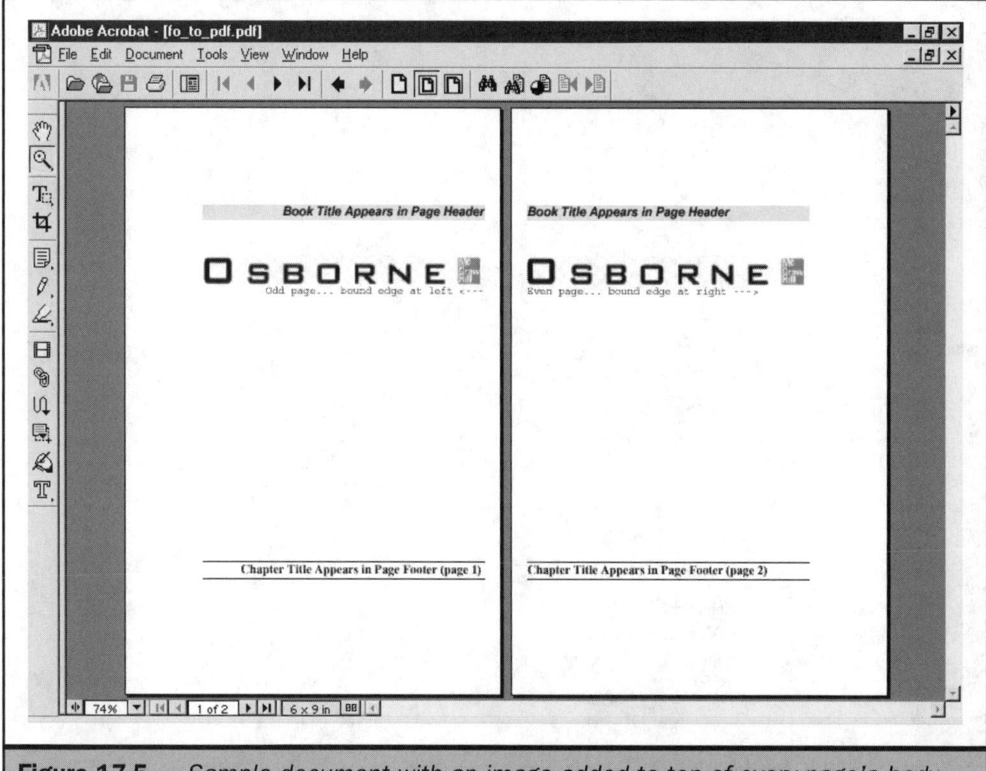

Figure 17-5. *Sample document with an image added to top of every page's body region is viewed in Adobe Acrobat*

XSL-FO Tables

Tabular output in XSL-FO is a complete topic all to itself in a number of ways—the most significant being that tables are themselves block-level formatting objects.

In this section we will use a different XML source document than the one we've employed so far in this chapter. The new source document will be more amenable to demonstrating tabular layouts:

```
<?xml version="1.0"?>
<CALENDAR>
    <YEAR>
        <YEARNUM>2000</YEARNUM>
        <MONTH>
            <NAME>December</NAME>
            <WEEK>
                <DAY></DAY>
                <DAY></DAY>
```

```
    <DAY></DAY>
    <DAY></DAY>
    <DAY></DAY>
    <DAY>1</DAY>
    <DAY>2</DAY>
</WEEK>
<WEEK>
    <DAY>3</DAY>
    <DAY>4</DAY>
    <DAY>5</DAY>
    <DAY>6</DAY>
    <DAY>7</DAY>
    <DAY>8</DAY>
    <DAY>9</DAY>
</WEEK>
<WEEK>
    <DAY>10</DAY>
    <DAY>11</DAY>
    <DAY>12</DAY>
    <DAY>13</DAY>
    <DAY>14</DAY>
    <DAY>15</DAY>
    <DAY>16</DAY>
</WEEK>
<WEEK>
    <DAY>17</DAY>
    <DAY>18</DAY>
    <DAY>19</DAY>
    <DAY>20</DAY>
    <DAY>21</DAY>
    <DAY>22</DAY>
    <DAY>23</DAY>
</WEEK>
<WEEK>
    <DAY>24</DAY>
    <DAY>25</DAY>
    <DAY>26</DAY>
```

```
            <DAY>27</DAY>
            <DAY>28</DAY>
            <DAY>29</DAY>
            <DAY>30</DAY>
        </WEEK>
        <WEEK>
            <DAY>31</DAY>
            <DAY></DAY>
            <DAY></DAY>
            <DAY></DAY>
            <DAY></DAY>
            <DAY></DAY>
            <DAY></DAY>
        </WEEK>
    </MONTH>
  </YEAR>
</CALENDAR>
```


The general idea in formatting this document for print is that we'd like to produce a page in a calendar—a table in which each row represents a week and each column represents a day of the week. Some cells will be empty when there is no date that corresponds to that row/column intersection. Within each nonempty cell will be a number representing the day of the month.

We'll start by defining two regions in the rendered document: a `region-before`, in which the month and year will appear, and a `region-body` holding the table representing the main body of the calendar. These two region definitions will be instantiated in the result tree for the source tree's root node:

```
<fo:root xmlns:fo="http://www.w3.org/1999/XSL/Format">
    <fo:layout-master-set>
        <fo:simple-page-master master-name="calendar"
            page-height="11in"
            page-width="11in"
            margin-left=".25in"
            margin-right=".25in"
            margin-top=".25in"
```

```
            margin-bottom=".25in">
            <!-- Region for the month/year header -->
            <fo:region-before region-name="calendar_page_head"
               extent="48pt"/>
            <!-- Region for the main calendar page body -->
            <fo:region-body region-name="calendar_page_body"
                margin-top="48pt"/>
       </fo:simple-page-master>
      <!-- Page sequence pointing back to the simple-page-master
            defined above. (Note master-name="calendar" in the
            repeatable-page- master element.)
       <fo:page-sequence-master master-name="calendar_page">
         <fo:repeatable-page-master-reference
                             master-name="calendar"/>
       </fo:page-sequence-master>
    </fo:layout-master-set>
    <xsl:apply-templates/>
</fo:root>
```

The `xsl:apply-templates` element in the preceding fragment simply says to process any templates established for children of the root node, which, in this case, is the root `YEAR` element. The template rule for processing the `YEAR` node simply contains another `xsl:apply-templates`, which will cause the template rule for any `MONTH` element(s) to be invoked.

When encountering a `MONTH` element in the source tree, what do we want to appear in the result tree? Two things: First, we want a page-sequence to begin (since each month goes on its own page), at the top of which will be a running header containing the month name and year. Second, below the header (which is an `fo:static-content` element), we want the body of the calendar to appear wrapped in an `fo:flow` element. The latter includes column headings for each day of the week. The following is the template rule in question:

```
<xsl:template match="MONTH">
    <fo:page-sequence master-name="calendar_page">
       <fo:static-content flow-name="calendar_page_head">
          <fo:block
              font-family="Helvetica"
              font-size="36pt"
              font-style="italic"
```

```
        font-weight="bold"
        background-color="silver">
        <xsl:value-of select="NAME"/>,
        <xsl:value-of select="../YEARNUM"/>
    </fo:block>
</fo:static-content>
<fo:flow flow-name="calendar_page_body">
    <fo:table>
        <fo:table-column column-width="1.5in"/>
        <fo:table-column column-width="1.5in"/>
        <fo:table-column column-width="1.5in"/>
        <fo:table-column column-width="1.5in"/>
        <fo:table-column column-width="1.5in"/>
        <fo:table-column column-width="1.5in"/>
        <fo:table-column column-width="1.5in"/>
        <fo:table-body>
            <fo:table-row>
                <fo:table-cell>
                    <xsl:element name="fo:block"
                        use-attribute-sets="day-name">
                        Sunday
                    </xsl:element>
                </fo:table-cell>
                <fo:table-cell>
                    <xsl:element name="fo:block"
                        use-attribute-sets="day-name">
                        Monday
                    </xsl:element>
                </fo:table-cell>
                <fo:table-cell>
                    <xsl:element name="fo:block"
                        use-attribute-sets="day-name">
                        Tuesday
                    </xsl:element>
                </fo:table-cell>
                <fo:table-cell>
                    <xsl:element name="fo:block"
                        use-attribute-sets="day-name">
                        Wednesday
                    </xsl:element>
```

```
                    </fo:table-cell>
                    <fo:table-cell>
                        <xsl:element name="fo:block"
                          use-attribute-sets="day-name">
                          Thursday
                        </xsl:element>
                    </fo:table-cell>
                    <fo:table-cell>
                        <xsl:element name="fo:block"
                          use-attribute-sets="day-name">
                          Friday
                        </xsl:element>
                    </fo:table-cell>
                    <fo:table-cell>
                        <xsl:element name="fo:block"
                          use-attribute-sets="day-name">
                          Saturday
                        </xsl:element>
                    </fo:table-cell>
                  </fo:table-row>
                  <xsl:apply-templates select="WEEK"/>
                </fo:table-body>
            </fo:table>
        </fo:flow>
    </fo:page-sequence>
</xsl:template>
```

Most of this template rule consists of flow objects instantiated in the result tree. The following are the primary things to note about the previous example:

- The `fo:static-content` element's `flow-name` attribute points back to the previously defined region called `calendar_page_head`. This region is the `region-before` element in the page layout.
- The `flow-name` attribute of the `fo:flow` element is tied to the `region-body` region of the page layout by way of its `calendar_page_body` value.
- This version (0.16.0) of the FOP processor requires that each column in the table (as defined by an `fo:table-column` element) include a `column-width` attribute.

- Since the table header cells are to be formatted identically, this is a convenient place to use named attribute sets, which were discussed in Chapter 16. The attribute set in question, called day-name, is declared earlier in the style sheet and looks like the following:

```
<xsl:attribute-set name="day-name">
  <xsl:attribute name="background-color">silver</xsl:attribute>
  <xsl:attribute name="border-style">solid</xsl:attribute>
  <xsl:attribute name="border-width">2pt</xsl:attribute>
  <xsl:attribute name="text-align">center</xsl:attribute>
  <xsl:attribute name="font-size">18pt</xsl:attribute>
</xsl:attribute-set>
```

So far, then, we have a page layout consisting of a static-content header region, in which the month and year appear, and a body region consisting of a table seven columns wide. The first row of the table is set up with literal text (the day of the week) in each cell, shaded in such a way as to represent a table header cell.

Constructing the balance of the table is the work of two template rules, one for processing the WEEK elements (instantiating a table row for each week) and one for processing each DAY element within that WEEK:


```
<xsl:template match="WEEK">
    <fo:table-row>
       <xsl:apply-templates select="DAY"/>
    </fo:table-row>
</xsl:template>

<xsl:template match="DAY">
    <fo:table-cell>
       <fo:block
          border-style="solid"
          border-width="1pt"
          font-size="24pt"
          font-weight="bold"
          background-color="white"
          padding-bottom="80pt">
          <xsl:choose>
              <xsl:when test="text()">
                 <xsl:value-of select="."/>
              </xsl:when>
```

```
                <xsl:otherwise> </xsl:otherwise>
            </xsl:choose>
        </fo:block>
    </fo:table-cell>
</xsl:template>
```

It is important to note two things about the preceding portion of the XSLT style sheet:

- The `padding-bottom` attribute of the `fo:block` element is not, in theory and per the XSL-FO standard, necessary. It should be possible to simply specify the height of a table cell or row, with the height attribute applied to the `fo:table-row` or `fo:table-cell` element, respectively. In practice, though, FOP 0.16.0 seems not to honor this attribute if the actual cell contents are shorter than the specified height. After experimenting with possible values for the `padding-bottom` attribute, it was determined that a setting of 80 points produced acceptable results.
- The `xsl:choose` block actually fills in the cell with the value of that `DAY` element's text node. Note that some `DAY` elements at the beginning and end of the `MONTH` are empty; in these cases, simply filling in the cell produces a table cell that is too short by one line, so the `xsl:otherwise` branch fills in the cell with a nonbreaking space if the element has no text node.

Passing the XML document name and XSLT style sheet name to FOP produces the following command-line messages:

```
FOP 0.16.0 DEV
using SAX parser org.apache.xerces.parsers.SAXParser
transforming to xsl:fo markup
xml: file:C:/XMLCompleteReference/calendar.xml
xslt: file:C:/XMLCompleteReference/calendar.xsl
using renderer org.apache.fop.render.pdf.PDFRenderer
using element mapping org.apache.fop.fo.StandardElementMapping
using element mapping org.apache.fop.svg.SVGElementMapping
using property list mapping
        org.apache.fop.fo.StandardPropertyListMapping
using property list mapping
        org.apache.fop.svg.SVGPropertyListMapping
building formatting object tree
setting up fonts
formatting FOs into areas
```

```
 [1]
rendering areas to PDF
writing out PDF
```

The PDF document produced as a result appears as in Figure 17-6 when viewed in Adobe Acrobat Reader. This PDF document was generated by the FOP open-sourcew FO-to-PDF processor, which exhibits certain interesting foibles and requires a little help at various points along the way (as explained in the text).

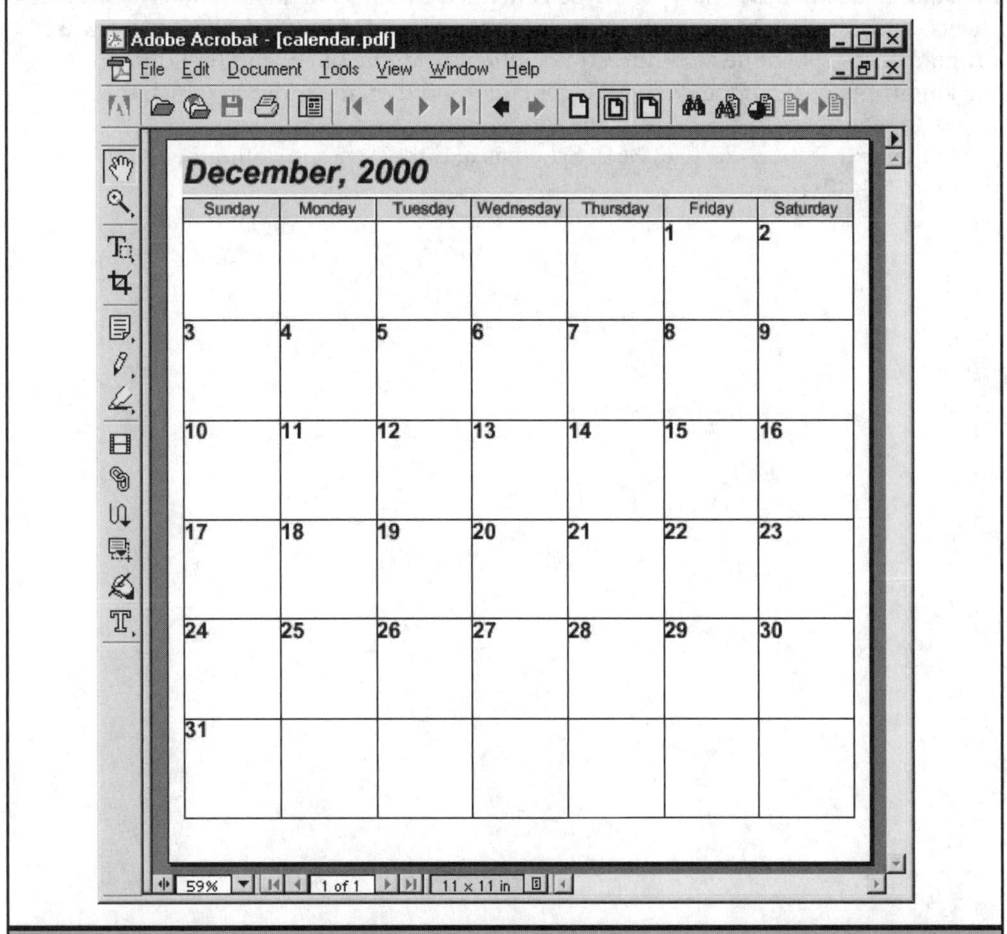

Figure 17-6. *A monthly calendar, rendered as a PDF document by way of XSL-FO table-related elements and attributes is shown in Acrobat*

Summary

This chapter provided an overview of key features of the XSL-FO specification. Although that specification is not yet in final form, we saw how XSLT style sheets can transform XML content into XSL formatting objects that can then be converted, as needed, to Adobe Acrobat PDF format for final rendering to print.

XSL-FO documents contain a single root element. In XSL-FO's case, that root element is `fo:root`. The `fo:root` element takes a single attribute, which is the `xmlns:fo` attribute declaring the XSL-FO vocabulary's namespace: `"http://www.w3.org/1999/XSL/Format"`. XSL-FO documents are not likely to be created by hand. Instead, they will typically be generated by XSL Transformations (XSLT) style sheets, transforming XML source to XSL-FO result trees through the use of software programs. XSL-FO builds a rendered document from the outside in first describing the kinds of pages that the document contains, and then the order in which the pages appear.

In the next section, Part IV, XML Schemas and their uses in validating XML documents is discussed.

Part IV

Using Schemas

The Complete Reference

Chapter 18

Introducing Schemas

XML Schemas provides a means of creating a set of rules that your computer can use to identify document rules governing the validity of the XML documents that you create. Schemas provide a means of defining the structure, content, and semantics of XML documents that can be shared between many different types of computers and documents.

XML Schemas are based on XML, so, like XML, they can be created in a simple text editor or by one of the available schema development programs that are available through the Internet. XML Schemas became a Candidate Recommendation of the World Wide Web Consortium (W3C) in October 2000 and should be a full recommendation soon, if not already by the time you read this book.

Note *Schemas have the potential of changing substantially through the next few years as XML and all of its subsidiary languages change and the Internet is slowly "upgraded" to new formats of storing and validating information. For the latest news on Schemas check out the W3C at http://www.w3.org and be sure to read the articles on XML Schemas, including the development of alternative systems such as RELAX and TREX at the XMLHack site located at http://www.xmlhack.com*

What Are Schemas?

The XML Schema candidate recommendation is based on the XML 1.0 recommendation. XML 1.0 defined one way to describe the content of an XML document using Document Type Definitions (DTDs), discussed in Part II. DTDs are the original way to validate an XML document, and the entire definition of a valid XML document is based upon its conformance to a specified DTD. As the development of XML Namespaces (discussed in Chapter 7) and other XML child languages such as the Synchronized Multimedia Integration Language (SMIL, Chapter 29) and the Mathematical Markup Language (MathML, Chapter 31) progressed, it became increasingly obvious that the DTD form of specifying constraints for XML document content was not a flexible enough system to work with the wide variety of applications to which XML was being applied.

So it was in 1999 that the W3C began developing the XML Schema definition language (XSD). XML Schema uses the core of XML to create an extremely powerful, yet flexible document definition language that can provide controls over not only element and attribute existence, content, and order, but over specific data types, when elements can be used, how attributes can be used, and the content of attribute based on the attribute's element's position within the document hierarchy.

Schemas are used to test the information in a document after it has been parsed, entities have been expanded, and default attribute values have been loaded. When a schema has been used to evaluate an XML document you receive a list of any violations of the schema constraints, as well as the resulting enhanced information set, which will often include information about the contents and markup of the XML document.

You will often see an XML document that conforms to a specific Schema called an *instance document*. This term is not meant to imply that either the XML data or the Schema itself must be a document, since either the Schema or the XML document can exist simply as a string of data being sent between two applications, a collection of information items, or the contents of a database record. Table 18-1 provides a list of how XML Schemas can work with your XML document markup.

XML Document Markup	XML Schema Effects
Elements	XML Schemas can be created to control which elements can be used in a particular context. This can be done by identifying which elements an element can constrain or by setting up a series of complex types to control element and element content.
Element content	XML Schemas can be created to control values allowed in a particular context. The context is based on the current element type and its ancestor types.
Attributes	W3C XML Schemas can be created to control attributes and attribute values, including which attributes are allowed in a particular context.
Attribute values	XML Schemas can be created to control the available attribute values based upon a particular situation in the document. The context is based on the current type and its ancestor types.
Entities	Entities are not constrained by schemas.
Notations	Notations are not constrained by schemas.
Comments	Comments are not constrained by schemas.
Processing Instructions (PIs)	PIs are not constrained by schemas.
`<?xml ?>`	Not constrained. Because the `standalone` and `encoding` declarations are not part of the core information set of an entity, XML Schemas provide no support for constraining them.
XML namespaces	Not constrained.

Table 18-1. *Schema Elements*

Comparing DTDs and Schemas

DTDs are focused on providing simple datatyping on attributes and elements that is sufficient to most of your document needs. XML Schemas provide a systematic datatyping capability. Whereas XML DTDs provide a basic macro facility using parameter entities, XML Schemas allow you to re-create these effects using a system of high-level built-in features which are listed in Table 18-2.

XML Declarations	XML Schemas Effects
`DOCTYPE`	Schemas have no equivalent to this document header declaration because they have no conception of "document." Schemas operate on elements and attributes whether those elements and attributes are in namespaces or an XML instance document.
Internal and external subset	Although there is no equivalent declaration for identifying internal and external subsets with Schemas. However, a schema can be placed within the document that uses it. Schemas can also `<include>`, `<import>`, and `<redefine>` other schemas that exist outside of the XML document.
`ELEMENT`	Elements in schemas are declared with the `<element>` declaration, which creates a link between an element name (with or without a namespace) and its attributes, content models and annotations. Schemas differ from DTD's in their lack of a one-to-one correspondence between an element name and its type. For example, you can create a complex type to define local types of elements that have precedence over global declarations of elements with the same name.
`#PCDATA` element content	This type of declaration requires the use of the `mixed=true` attribute in the Schema element declaration, as long as it is contained within a complex type declaration. If you only wish to have an element used text data you can use the type string. If at any future point you wish your string element to contain sub-elements you will need to update your schema and define the element as a complex type.

Table 18-2. *XML Schema Part and DTD Part Comparison*

XML Declarations	XML Schemas Effects
ANY element content	Schemas support the ANY DTD keyword as the <any> statement. This statement has different wildcards to support a richer range of possibilities than were available with the DTD. There is also an <anyAttribute> element available allowing wildcards on the possible attributes.
EMPTY element content	EMPTY elements are created by declaring a complex type with a mixed="false" attribute and not allowing any child elements.
Content model	Schemas support the content model through the creation of <complexType> elements. Schemas maintain XML's model of mixed content, either allowing character data anywhere inside an element or nowhere.
, (Sequence connector)	The syntax to provide an alternative in your sequence; is supported through the <sequence> grouping element.
| (Alternative connector)	The syntax to provide an alternative in your choices; is supported through the <choice> grouping element.
? (Optional)	The syntax to provide optional occurrences is supported through maxOccurs and minOccurs attributes on elements, wildcards, and groups.
+ (required and repeatable)	The syntax to provide required and repeatable occurrences is supported through maxOccurs and minOccurs attributes on elements, wildcards, and groups.
* (optional and repeatable)	The syntax to provide optional and repeatable occurrences is supported through maxOccurs and minOccurs attributes on elements, wildcards, and groups.
( ) (groups)	The group syntax is supported through the <group> element
ATTLIST	Attributes are defined using the <attribute> declaration and can be grouped into <attributeGroup> declarations.

Table 18-2. *XML Schema Part and DTD Part Comparison* (continued)

USING SCHEMAS

XML Declarations	XML Schemas Effects
Multiple ATTLIST declarations	<attribute> declarations cannot contain more than one attribute per each <attribute> statement. All attribute declarations for a complex type are typically declared in one place; however, you can define them in an <attributegroup>.
CDATA attribute type	CDTA attribute types in schemas are expressed using a built-in simple type with a pattern attribute with regular expressions.
ID attribute type	The ID attribute type is part of the *simple type*. XML Schemas uses the <unique> element, allowing the testing of uniqueness and multipart IDs based upon the XPath recommendation.
IDREF IDREFS attribute types	Both of the IDREF and IDREFS attribute types are included as a *simple type* in the Schema recommendation. XML Schemas adds to the capability of DTD IDREF and IDREFS statements with the <key> and <keyref> elements, which allow the testing of references and multipart keys based upon the XPath recommendation.
NOTATION attribute type	Notations in schemas are expressed using a built-in simple type with a pattern attribute.
NMTOKEN NMTOKENS attribute types	The XML Schema expresses NMTOKEN and NMTOKENS using a built-in simple type with a pattern attribute.
ENTITY ENTITIES attribute types	The XML Schema expresses ENTITY and ENTITIES using a built-in simple type with a pattern attribute containing regular expressions.
Enumerations	Schemas support Enumerations in elements and attributes.
Attribute defaults	Schemas support default attribute values with the attribute use="default" using an attribute default of type string.
#FIXED attributes	Schemas support FIXED attribute values with the attribute use="default" using an attribute fixed of type string.

Table 18-2. *XML Schema Part and DTD Part Comparison* (continued)

XML Declarations	XML Schemas Effects
#REQUIRED and #IMPLIED	Schemas support the #REQUIRED and #IMPLIED attribute types t through the use of the use="prohibited",use="optional", or use="required" attributes.
ENTITY	Schemas do not support ENTITY declarations.
ENTITY % Parameter entity declaration	Schemas do not support parameter entity references. Other portions of the Schema recommendation have adapted much of the functionality of parameter entities. Because parameter entities provide a low-level mechanism useful for many different purposes, the Schema developers have tried to support some of the most important, including Separation of <element> and <complexType> Support for attribute groups Support for named model groups Support for the type extension and restriction mechanisms Creation of the <import>, <include> and <redefine> mechanism for composing schemas The element equivalence class mechanism allowing redefinition of element names
IGNORE/INCLUDE marked sections	The IGNORE and INCLUDE statements are not supported in XML Schemas. In the event that this functionality is required as part of the markup XML DTDs should be used.
NOTATION Declaration	Schemas use the same markup for supporting NOTATION declarations as were discussed in Chapter 11 for DTDs.
Comments in DTDs	XML Schemas use the <documentation> child element of the <annotation> element to provide comments, although standard comments can still be used. The content of <documentation> elements are available to users of the Schema, whereas traditional comments are not part of the information set of a document and therefore will be unavailable to the user.

Table 18-2. *XML Schema Part and DTD Part Comparison* (continued)

XML Declarations	XML Schemas Effects
Processing instructions in DTDs	Schemas use the <appinfo> child element of the <annotation> element to provide Processing Instruction (PI) functionality; although traditional DTD formatted PIs can still be used.

Table 18-2. *XML Schema Part and DTD Part Comparison* (continued)

Writing a Basic Schema

Writing a basic schema isn't much different than writing your XML document. The syntax and punctuation is very similar, but you are working with XML elements that describe the XML elements found within your document. Use the following XML document describing a series of business contacts as the foundation document for our schema example.

```
<?xml version="1.0" encoding="utf-8"?>
<company idcode="CBCC">

 <owner>Heather Williamson</owner>
 <organization>S. Corp</organization>
 <department>
  <director>Luis de Leon</director>
  <assistant>Victoria Rivera</assistant>
  <review-date>2005-10-04</review-date>
  <role-description>
    Training staff for technical support.
  </role-description>
 </department>
 <department>
  <director>Ann Williamson</director>
  <review-date>1966-08-22</review-date>
  <role-description>
    customer service to all end user customers
  </role-description>
 </department>
</company>
```

There are many ways to create a schema based upon this document. Two different approaches will be shown in the following text. No matter which style you wish to use to record your schema, you will need to open with an `xsd:schema` element following your <?xml?> declaration.

```
<?xml version="1.0" encoding="utf-8"?>
<xsd:schema xmlns:xsd="http://www.w3.org/2000/10/XMLSchema">
```

The following two sections define a schema for the previous company example document, but the schemas follow two different structures.

A Hierarchical Schema

This first example writes out the schema in the same order that the document itself was displayed. In this system the schema element opens the schema, holding the name of the root element of the XML document. This opening schema element could also define the target namespace and several default options for the entire schema.

To match the start tag for the company element, we define an element named `"company"`. This element has attributes and non-text children and is therefore considered a `<complexType>` (since the other datatype, `<simpleType>`, is reserved for datatypes holding only values and no elements or attributes). Both complex and simple types are discussed in Chapter 19. The `<sequence>` element contains the list of child elements of the document root.

```
<xsd:element name="company">
 <xsd:complexType>
  <xsd:sequence>
```

Note *The* `xsd:` *namespace prefix is used with all of the Schema element statements to identify the origin of the elements, when the schema is included within the XML document's text itself.*

The use of the `<sequence>` element defines the order of the child elements. Other elements, called *compositors*, which can be used to control the order of elements include `<choice>` and `<all>`, which are also detailed in Chapter 19.

With the company element defined as an element of a complex type, you need to define the remainder of its child elements. In the following code, the owner and the organization elements are defined as elements with a datatype of string.

Note *The type* (`xsd:string`) *is prefixed by the Schema namespace, indicating a predefined XML Schema datatype. This process goes beyond the implications made in the XML Namespaces recommendation. You can read more about namespaces in Chapter 7.*

```
<xsd:element name="owner" type="xsd:string"/>
<xsd:element name="organization" type="xsd:string"/>
```

You then add in the department element as another complex datatype. Since this element can occur many times or not at all you must use the minOccurs and the maxOccurs schema attributes to identify an acceptable number of department child elements of the company element.

```
<xsd:element name="department"
    minOccurs="0" maxOccurs="unbounded">
 <xsd:complexType>
  <xsd:sequence>
```

You can then specify the list of all the department element's children elements in the same manner as the office and organization elements. You also need to close the <sequence> element for both the department and the company elements, the <element> statement identifying the department element, and the <complexType> element identifying the child elements of the department element.

```
   <xsd:element name="director" type="xsd:string"/>
   <xsd:element name="assistant" type="xsd:string"
       minOccurs="0" maxOccurs="unbounded"/>
   <xsd:element name="review-date" type="xsd:date"/>
   <xsd:element name="role-description" type="xsd:string"/>
  </xsd:sequence>
 </xsd:complexType>
</xsd:element>
</xsd:sequence>
```

Note *You don't want to close the* <complexType> *element of the document's root company element until you have applied all of the attributes to the element. At that point you can also close the original* <element> *statement identifying the company element.*

The following statement declares the attribute of the company element. The company element and its <complexType> declaration are also closed. Once the root element is closed, then you need to close the schema itself using the </xsd:schema> element.

```
   <xsd:attribute name="idcode" type="xsd:string"/>
  </xsd:complexType>
 </xsd:element>
</xsd:schema>
```

Note *Attribute definitions must always follow the element definitions. This is a rule imposed by the W3C Schema Working Group, who found that it was simpler to impose an order to the definitions of listed element and attributes within a* <complexType> *element. It is also easier to define attributes for elements that you have already defined.*

The following code puts together all of the pieces discussed for our original schema to make it easier for you to read. This system of designing the schema in the order of the XML document allows you to define each element and attribute in its document context.

```
<?xml version="1.0" encoding="utf-8"?>
<xsd:schema xmlns:xsd="http://www.w3.org/2000/10/XMLSchema">
<xsd:element name="company">
 <xsd:complexType>
  <xsd:sequence>
   <xsd:element name="owner" type="xsd:string"/>
   <xsd:element name="organization" type="xsd:string"/>
   <xsd:element name="department"
        minOccurs="0" maxOccurs="unbounded">
    <xsd:complexType>
     <xsd:sequence>
      <xsd:element name="director" type="xsd:string"/>
      <xsd:element name="assistant" type="xsd:string"
          minOccurs="0" maxOccurs="unbounded"/>
      <xsd:element name="review-date" type="xsd:date"/>
      <xsd:element name="role-description" type="xsd:string"/>
     </xsd:sequence>
    </xsd:complexType>
   </xsd:element>
</xsd:sequence>
<xsd:attribute name="idcode" type="xsd:string"/>
  </xsd:complexType>
 </xsd:element>
</xsd:schema>
```

Flat Catalog of Schema Elements

You can also organize your element definitions into groups to make them easier to read for people, although it will have no effect on the software working with your schema. By grouping element definitions, you can avoid the deeply embedded elements, which are often created using the hierarchical structure of developing your schemas.

A flat catalog design allows you to describe each of the elements in the document and all of their child elements and attributes in more easily understood groupings. In order to group your elements and attributes in this fashion, you have to use references to point to where child elements and attributes are for `<complexType>` elements. These references are in boldface in the following schema. You can read more about the `ref` attribute in Chapter 20.

```
<?xml version="1.0" encoding="utf-8"?>

xsd:schema xmlns:xsd="http://www.w3.org/2000/10/XMLSchema">
<!-- definition of simple type elements -->
   <xsd:element name="ownwer" type="xsd:string"/>
  <xsd:element name="organization" type="xsd:string"/>
```

USING SCHEMAS

```
    <xsd:element name="director" type="xsd:string"/>
    <xsd:element name="assitant" type="xsd:string"/>
    <xsd:element name="review-date" type="xsd:date"/>
   <xsd:element name="role-description" type="xsd:string"/>
 !-- definition of attributes -->
   <xsd:attribute name="idcode" type="xsd:string"/>
 <!-- definition of complex type elements -->
   <xsd:element name="department">
    <xsd:complexType>
      <xsd:sequence>
       <!-- the simple type elements are referenced using
        the "ref" attribute  -->
       <xsd:element ref="director"/>
       <!-- the definition of the cardinality is done
         when the elements are referenced    -->
      <xsd:element ref="assistant"
            minOccurs="0" maxOccurs="unbounded"/>
       <xsd:element ref="review-date"/>
       <xsd:element ref="role-description"/>
   </xsd:sequence>
  </xsd:complexType>
 </xsd:element>
 <xsd:element name="company">
  <xsd:complexType>
   <xsd:sequence>
    <xsd:element ref="owner"/>
    <xsd:element ref="orgnaization"/>
    <xsd:element ref="department"
         minOccurs="0" maxOccurs="unbounded"/>
   </xsd:sequence>
   <xsd:attribute ref="idcode"/>
  </xsd:complexType>
 </xsd:element>
 </xsd:schema>
```

By using the `ref` attribute to reference an element or attribute that has been created previously, you are, in one sense, cloning that previous element or attribute. You are not redefining it, because the name and type are only being specified once, but you can reference it multiple times and apply various other attributes to the element as needed.

What Software Is Available?

There is a small selection of editors and parsers available for Schemas, and as the Schema recommendation becomes more mature and supported in all of our primary Web and document browsers, more editors and parsers will become available. The following sections show you a few of the more mature programs that can be used to work with Schemas and are available for the October 2000 XML Schema Candidate Recommendation.

Schema Editors

Editors for schemas work much like editors for any other types of document. Some of them even allow you to convert your XML document's DTD into a schema; an increasingly important feature as Schema takes over the definition of documents.

XML Spy

XML Spy, available for download from http://www.xmlspy.com, supports both editing and schema validation of

- XML Schema Definition (XSD) Candidate Recommendation (October 2000)
- Document Type Definitions (DTDs)
- Document Content Descriptions (DCDs)
- XML-Data Reduced (XDR)
- BizTalk

XML Spy can validate your XML instance document against any or all of the primary types of schemas used, as shown in this list.

Because XML Spy can create your schema for you from a sample XML document, you can simply use an existing or new XML document and have your schema created from it, saving yourself an immeasurable amount of time, work, headache, frustration, and hair pulling. Of course this schema won't be perfect if your documents don't show all of various situations that can be used for different elements and attributes. You will also have make sure that all of your elements and attribute content values match your intentions, not the interpretation of the software, but this is easily done through XML Spy's grid view, shown in Figure 18-1, which allows you to edit the structure of the schema directly.

Turbo XML

Turbo XML, available through Tibco Extensibility at http://www.extensibility.com, provides you with a collection of software focused on helping you create XML documents, schemas, and DTDs while validating and parsing them for you to ensure

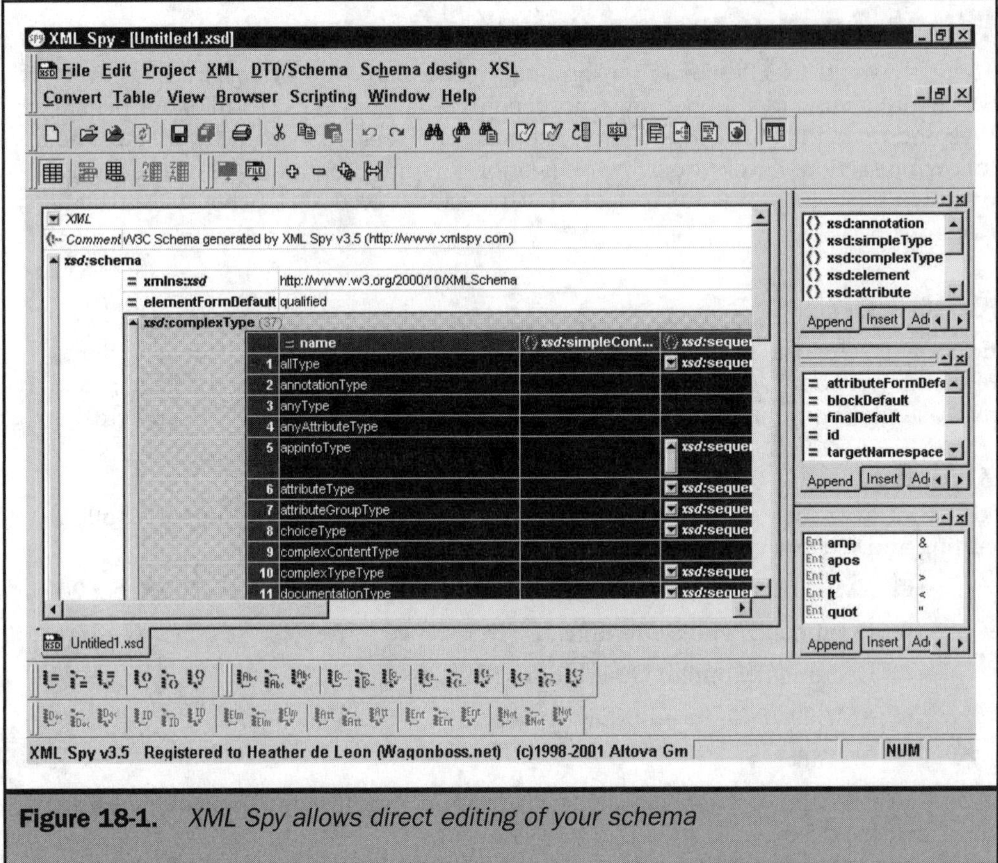

Figure 18-1. *XML Spy allows direct editing of your schema*

that your documents are always well-formed. The software packages included in Turbo XML (see Figure 18-2) are

- **XML Authority** The primary job of XML Authority is the creation, conversion, and management of DTDs and XML schemas.
- **XML Instance** XML Instance provides a developing environment for the creation, editing, and management of data-oriented XML documents, messages, and configuration files.
- **XML Console** XML Console is a complete desktop XML development environment allowing for the centralized documentation management, validation, and conversion of schemas and XML business documents within a network environment.

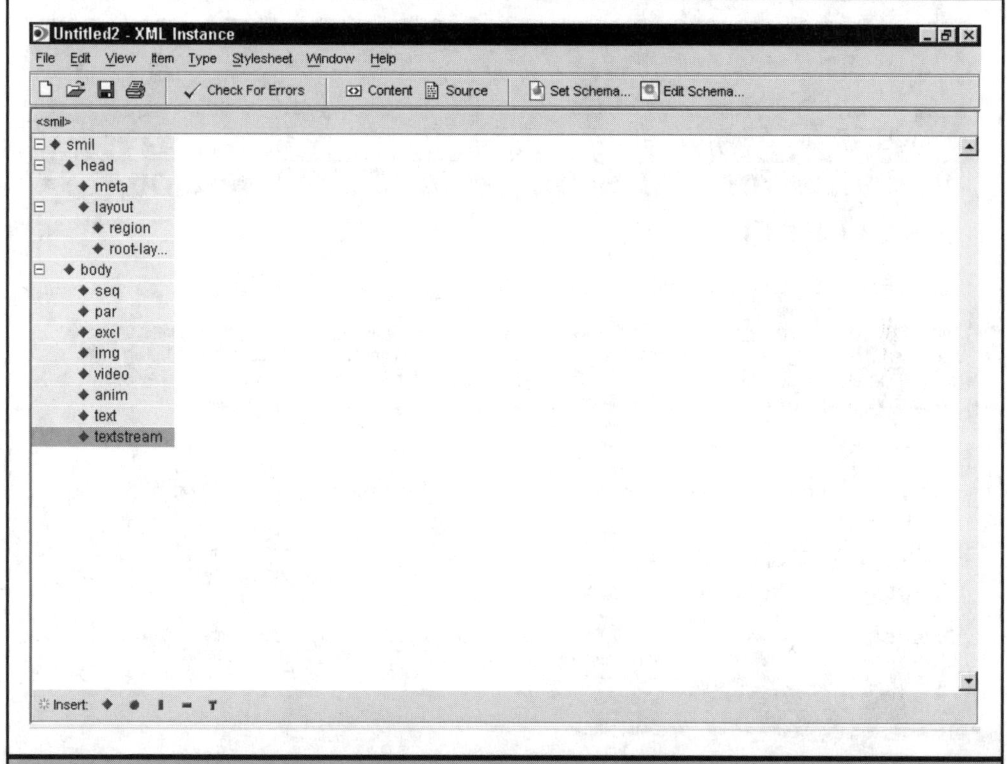

Figure 18-2. *Turbo XML creates Schemas, XML instance documents, and DTDs, making sure that all of your applications are well-formed.*

Schema Validators and Parsers

Schema validators and parsers provide a way to check the XML and Schema documents that you have created. They can run either on your local machine, as does Xerces Java, or on the Internet, as you can see with the W3C's Validator, both of which are discussed in the following sections.

W3C Validator for XML Schema

The World Wide Web Consortium has made available an online schema validator at http://www.w3.org/2000/09/webdata/xsv. This validator/parser is currently still being tested. When completed, it will allow you to test any document or schema accessible through the Internet. Simply provide the address of the document in the screen shown in Figure 18-3 and receive a report listing all of the warnings, errors, and problems encountered with both the XML document and the schema.

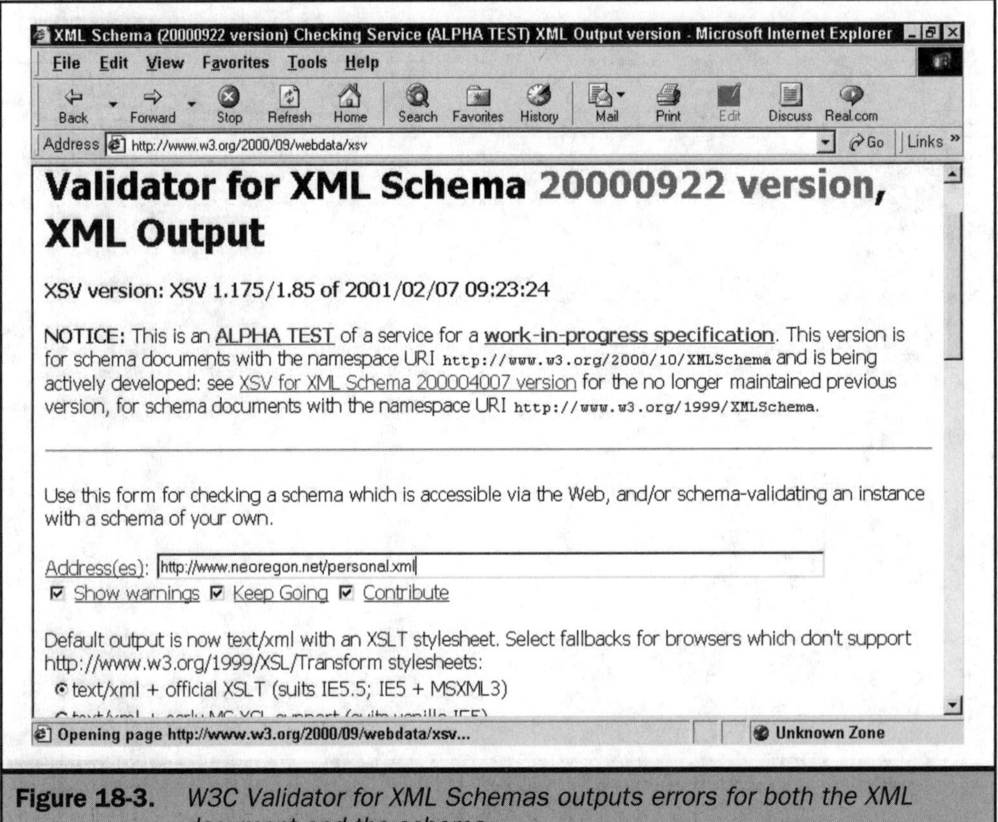

Figure 18-3. *W3C Validator for XML Schemas outputs errors for both the XML document and the schema*

Xerces Java

Xerces Java is a java based XML parser developed by the Apache XML Project located at http://xml.apache.org/xerces-j/. It provides support for the XML Schema Candidate Recommendation released in October 2000. Xerces Java provides support for declaring Schema elements and attributes, groups, attribute groups, simple and complex type definitions, as well as wildcard elements and identity constraints. It doesn't support notation declarations or annotation elements as they are defined in the Schema Candidate Recommendation. You can use Xerces Java to check simple types, regular expressions, binary information, and constraints in your Schema documents. The one datatype that is not supported by Xerces is date/time.

Summary

Schemas create a set of rules allowing your computer to identify document rules governing the validity of the documents that you create. Schemas provide a means of defining the structure, content, and semantics of XML documents that can be shared between many different types of computers and documents.

Schemas are based on XML. They are used to create a powerful, yet flexible document definition language providing control over element and attribute existence, content, and order, as well as over specific data types, when elements can be used, how attributes can be used, and the content of attribute based upon the attribute's element's position within the document hierarchy. Schemas test information contained in a document after it has been parsed, had its entities expanded, and default attribute values loaded.

XML documents that conform to a specific Schema are often called *instance documents*. This term implies neither the XML data nor the Schema itself be a document, but implies the possible existence of both of these resources simply as a string of data being sent between two applications, a collection of information items, or the contents of a database record.

Chapter 19

Schema Elements, Types, and Groups

XML Schemas have a set of predefined elements that are used to lay out the rules governing the organizational structure of your XML documents. These elements are all discussed in this chapter, as well as some of the rules that enable you to use these elements to properly implement your XML document with a schema.

All of the elements in your schema start with the prefix `xsd:`, which has been associated with the Schema namespace by the XML Namespace declaration: `xmlns:xsd="http://www.w3.org/2000/10/XMLSchema"`. This namespace declaration is often applied to the root `<schema>` element and is used throughout the schema to identify the elements and attributes that are part of the Schema, not the actual XML document. The `xsd:` prefix will also be used with simple types to associate those types with the predefined types used with the XML Schema language, rather than enable them to be associated with a specific vocabulary created by the document. Although the `xsd:` prefix is not required, I suggest using it for readability.

Because the XML Schema recommendation is not complete and may change repeatedly before it is officially a recommendation, you should check with the World Wide Web Consortium (W3C) Web site at http://www.w3.org for the latest on XML Schema developments.

Schema Element Descriptions

Schemas provide a specific set of elements that provide the syntax for describing your documents. Because Schemas themselves are based upon XML, as soon as you learn the elements, their attributes, and the syntax for schemas, you can start developing your own. There are 36 elements described in the October 2000 XML Schema Candidate Recommendation. Many changes are not expected in this list, but before developing schema for all of your documents, you need to check with the W3C to ensure that these elements are still valid in any future releases of the Schema specification. You can find the latest information at http://www.w3.org/TR. All of the elements available with XML Schemas are described in Table 19-1.

Element	Syntax	Description
`all`	`<all id="ID" maxOccurs="1:1" minOccurs="1:1"...> (annotation? , element*) </all>`	In a `complexType` element, makes all of the elements, no matter what their order, valid

Table 19-1. *XML Schema Elements*

<table>
<tr><th>Element</th><th>Syntax</th><th>Description</th></tr>
<tr><td>annotation</td><td><annotation>
(appinfo |
documentation)*
</annotation></td><td>Provides comments in the Schema</td></tr>
<tr><td>any</td><td><any id="ID"
minOccurs="0|Unbounded"
maxOccurs="1"
namespace="namespace"
...>
(annotation?)
</any></td><td>Represents a wildcard element inside the XML document</td></tr>
<tr><td>anyAttribute</td><td><anyAttribute id="ID"
namespace="namespace"
processContents = (skip
| lax | strict)...>
(annotation?)
</anyAttribute></td><td>Represents a wildcard attribute inside the elements of the XML document</td></tr>
<tr><td>appInfo</td><td><appInfo source=URI>
({any})*
</appInfo></td><td>Provides information on the application</td></tr>
<tr><td>attribute</td><td><attribute
form = (qualified |
unqualified)
id = ID name = NCName
ref = QName type =
QName
use = (prohibited |
optional | required |
default | fixed)
value = string. . .>
(annotation? ,
(simpleType?))
</attribute></td><td>Creates an attribute in your element's <code>complexType</code> declaration</td></tr>
<tr><td>attributeGroup</td><td><attributeGroup
id = ID
ref = QName
. . .>
(annotation?)
</attributeGroup></td><td>Creates a group of attributes to use within a <code>complexType</code> element</td></tr>
</table>

Table 19-1. *XML Schema Elements* (continued)

<table>
<tr><th>Element</th><th>Syntax</th><th>Description</th></tr>
<tr><td>choice</td><td><choice id="ID"
minOccurs="0:Unbounded"
maxOccurs="0:1" ...>
(annotation? , (element |
group | choice | sequence
| any)*)
</choice></td><td>In a <complexType> element, forces a choice to be made</td></tr>
<tr><td>complexContent</td><td><complexContent
  id = ID
  mixed = boolean . . .>
(annotation? ,
(restriction |
extension))
</complexContent></td><td>Enables the combination of element and data values in the content of your XML document elements</td></tr>
<tr><td>complexType</td><td><complexType
  abstract = boolean
  block = (#all | List
of (extension |
restriction))
  final = (#all | List
of (extension |
restriction))
  id = ID
  mixed = boolean
  name = NCName . . .>
(annotation? ,
simpleContent |
complexContent | ((group
| all | choice |
sequence)? , ((attribute
| attributeGroup)* ,
anyAttribute?))))
</complexType></td><td>Creates an element that contains both child elements and attributes, in addition to other content</td></tr>
<tr><td>documentation</td><td><documentation
source=URI
xml:lang=language>
({any})*
</documentation></td><td>Provides accessible comments about the XML Schema document</td></tr>
</table>

Table 19-1. *XML Schema Elements* (continued)

Element	Syntax	Description
`element`	`<element` `abstract = boolean` `block = (#all	List of (substitution | extension | restriction))` `default = string` `final = (#all	List of (extension | restriction))` `fixed = string` `form = (qualified | unqualified)` `id = ID` `maxOccurs = (nonNegativeInteger | unbounded)` `minOccurs = nonNegativeInteger` `name = NCName` `nullable = boolean` `ref = QName` `substitutionGroup = QName` `type = QName . . . >` `(annotation? , ((simpleType | complexType)? , (key | keyref | unique)*))` `</element>`	Identifies the elements used in a document you are preparing to validate

`extension`	`<extension`
	`base = QName`
	`id = ID . . .>`
	`(annotation? , ((attribute | attributeGroup)* , anyAttribute?))`
	`</extension>`
		Enables you to create new attributes for elements with `complexContent`

Table 19-1. *XML Schema Elements* (continued)

Element	Syntax	Description
field	`<field id = ID xpath = An XPath expression . . .> (annotation?) </field>`	Holds XML Path Language (XPath) content and comments as part of a choice being made in your element selections
group	`<group id = ID maxOccurs = (nonNegativeInteger | unbounded) minOccurs = nonNegativeInteger name = NCName ref = QName . . .> (annotation? , (all | choice | sequence)?) </group>`	Creates groups of elements for use with <all>, <sequence> and <choice>
import	`<import id = ID namespace = URI schemalocation=URI. . > (annotation?) </import>`	Identifies a namespace and associates that namespace to be imported into your existing schema document
include	`<include id = ID schemalocation=URI. . > (annotation?) </include>`	Incorporates the definitions and declarations contained in another schema file, making them available as part of the importing schema namespace. When using `include`, the target namespace of the included components must be the same as the target namespace of the including schema.
key	`<key id = ID name = NCName . . > (annotation? , (selector , field+)) </key>`	Forces the values of designated elements to be unique and not nullable and allows the `key` to be referenced from elsewhere

Table 19-1. *XML Schema Elements* (continued)

Element	Syntax	Description
keyRef	<keyRef id = ID name = NCName refer=QName. . > (annotation? , (selector , field+)) </keyRef>	References a key element
list	<list id = ID itemtype= QName. . > (annotation? , (simpletype?)) </list>	Enables the creation of new list types by derivation from existing atomic types.
notation	<notation id = ID name = NCName public = PUBLIC identifier system = uriReference. . > (annotation?) </notation>	Creates the Schema-enabled version of an XML DTD NOTATION
pattern	<pattern value = string />	Provides a pattern that must be matched using the <restriction> element
redefine	<redefine schemaLocation = uriReference. . > (annotation | (attributeGroup | complexType | group | simpleType))* </redefine>	Enables you to redefine simple and complex types, groups, and attribute groups that are obtained from external schema files. This element requires that the external components be in the same target namespace as the redefining schema, although external components from schemas that have no namespace can also be redefined.

Table 19-1. *XML Schema Elements* (continued)

Element	Syntax	Description
restriction	`<restriction base = QName id = ID ...> (annotation? , (simpleType? , (duration | encoding | enumeration | length | maxExclusive | maxInclusive | maxLength | minExclusive | minInclusive | minLength | pattern | period | precision | scale | whiteSpace)*)? , ((attribute | attributeGroup)* , anyAttribute?)) </restriction>`	Indicates the existing (base) type and identifies the facets that constrain the range of values
schema	`<schema attributeFormDefault = (qualified | unqualified) blockDefault = (#all | List of (substitution | extension | restriction)) elementFormDefault = (qualified | unqualified) finalDefault = (#all | List of (extension | restriction)) id = ID targetNamespace = uriReference version = string . . .> ((include | import | redefine | annotation)* , ((attribute | attributeGroup | complexType | element | group | notation | simpleType) , annotation*)*) </schema>`	The root element of an XML Schema document. This element must be located at the opening and closing of every schema. You must use the `xmlns` namespace attribute to declare the namespace of the Schema.

Table 19-1. *XML Schema Elements* (continued)

<table>
<tr><th>Element</th><th>Syntax</th><th>Description</th></tr>
<tr><td>selector</td><td><selector id = ID
xpath = An XPath expression . . .>
(annotation?)
</selector></td><td>Enables you to select all of the elements meeting specific criteria and works with the <field> element to ensure that the criteria meets specific base requirements</td></tr>
<tr><td>sequence</td><td><sequence
id="ID"
minOccurs="0:Unbounded"
maxOccurs="0:1" ...>
(annotation? , (element | group | choice | sequence | any)*)
</sequence></td><td>In a <complexType> element, forces the elements listed in the content of this element to occur in this order in the XML document</td></tr>
<tr><td>simpleContent</td><td><simpleContent
id = ID . . .>
(annotation? ,
(restriction | extension))
</simpleContent></td><td>Indicates that the content model of the new type contains only character data and no elements</td></tr>
<tr><td>simpleType</td><td><simpleType id = ID
name = NCName . . .>
(annotation? , ((list | restriction | union)))
</simpleType></td><td>Defines and names the new simple type</td></tr>
<tr><td>union</td><td><union id = ID
membertypes=Qname List. . >
(annotation? ,
(simpletype?))
</union></td><td>Enables an element or attribute value to be one or more instances of one type drawn from the union of multiple atomic and list types</td></tr>
<tr><td>unique</td><td><unique id = ID
name = NCName . . >
(annotation? ,
(selector , field+))
</unique></td><td>Indicates that one particular attribute or element value is unique</td></tr>
</table>

Table 19-1. *XML Schema Elements* (continued)

Element Types

Schemas break your XML document elements down into two main types: simple and complex. The basic difference between complex types and simple types is that complex types enable elements as part of their content and may have attributes, while simple types can have neither element content nor attributes.

Complex Types

Complex types of elements, which enable attributes and elements in their content, are created using the <complexType> schema element declaration. The complete <complexType> element declaration typically contains information for referencing and declaring elements and attributes. This declaration is in the <element> schema element declaration, which names the complex element, as you can see in the following code:

```
<xsd:element name="project">
  <xsd:complexType …>
  </xsd:complexType>
</xsd:element>
```

Elements are declared using the <element> element, and attributes are declared using the <attribute> element. The following example uses the <complexType> to define the elements and attributes in an address book record:

```
<xsd:element name="ContactRecord">
  <xsd:complexType>
   <xsd:sequence>
    <xsd:element name="Name">
     <xsd:complexType>
      <xsd:sequence>
       <xsd:element name="FirstName" type="xsd:string" />
       <xsd:element name="LastName" type="xsd:string" />
      </xsd:sequence>
      <xsd:attribute name="Title" type="xsd:string" />
     </xsd:complexType>
    </element>
    <xsd:element name="Street" type="xsd:string" />
    <xsd:element name="City" type="xsd:string" />
    <xsd:element name="State" type="xsd:string" />
    <xsd:element name="Zip" type="xsd:decimal" />
   </xsd:sequence>
  </xsd:complexType>
</xsd:element>
```

This code forces any element that has been named "ContactRecord" to contain in order a Name element composed of a FirstName and LastName element and a Title attribute, as well as Street, City, State, and Zip elements.

The preceding code example defines an element, of complexType named ContactRecord. You also have the option of define a complexType named ContactRecord that will work like an NMTOKEN, so that you can apply the type ContactRecord to any element and have that element take on the definition of the ContactRecord including all of its child elements and attributes:

```
<xsd:complexType name="ContactRecord">
 <xsd:sequence>
   ... Remainder of element declarations for the contact record...
  </xsd:sequence>
</xsd:complexType>
```

To create an element of complexType ContactRecord, now you simply need to create an element of type="ContactRecord" as shown in the following statement:

```
<element name="address" type="ContactRecord" />
```

Once you have created a series of basic element layouts, such as ContactRecord, that work for a variety of different situations, you can use a single type reference to assign that type to any number of other elements. Take the following Projects example into account. Both its ProjHead and ProjOwner address records have been designated as ContactRecord types, which enables you to designate a format for addresses only one time, while enabling you to use them throughout your document multiple times. As you can see, each project record has also been created as a complexType, enabling you to create a document containing multiple types of project records:

```
<xsd:complexType name="Projects">
  <xsd:sequence>
    <element name="ProjHead" type="ContactRecord" />
    <element name="ProjOwner" type="ContactRecord" />
    <element name="Description" type="xsd:string" />
  </xsd:sequence>
  <attribute name="start" type="xsd:date" />
  <attribute name="stop" type="xsd:date" />
</xsd:complexType>
```

The preceding schema is defining an XML document with the format shown in the following code:

```
<Project start="01/01/10" stop="01/01/20">
  <ProjHead>
    <Name title="Project Head Title">
```

```
      <FirstName>  </FirstName>
      <LastName>   </LastName>
    </Name>
    <Street>   </Street>
    <City>   </City>
    <State>   </State>
    <Zip>    </Zip>
  </ProjHead>
  <ProjOwner>
    <Name title="Owner Title">
      <FirstName>  </FirstName>
      <LastName>   </LastName>
    </Name>
    <Street>   </Street>
    <City>   </City>
    <State>   </State>
    <Zip>    </Zip>
  </ProjOwner>
  <Description>  </Description>
</Project>
```

Note *When you are defining your elements and* `complexTypes`, *you may run into instances in which your items have the same name. The results you see in your document depend upon what items are sharing a name. For instance, if you have two elements with the same name, a conflict will result. If you have an element and a* `complexType` *with the same name, there will be no conflict. If you have both a* `simpleType` *and a* `complexType` *defined with the same name, a conflict will result and your document will not be parsed correctly. If you have two elements with the same name that are part of different complex types, you will not have any problems with errors.*

Simple Types

There are a variety of simple types that have been defined within XML Schemas in Chapter 18. These types enable you to control the type of content that is used within your elements and attributes. The selection of types included with the XML Schema specification is listed in Table19-2.

You can create your own datatypes by using *facets*. Facets are instances of values that are used to define what is considered valid markup for your document. Facets serve as the basis for creating new simple datatypes by specifying which values or value ranges can be used within the simple type.

Type	Example	Description
binary	#FFF	Represents arbitrary binary data in either Hex or Base-64 notation
boolean	true	Forces the value of an element to be either true or false
byte	-128 ,127, 5	Forces a single byte of space to be used to represent an integer between –128 and 127
CDATA	"my string"	Creates white-spaced normalized strings. CDATA is the set of strings that do not contain the carriage-return (#xD), line-feed (#xA), or tab (#x9) characters.
century	20	Period of time that starts at midnight the first day of the century and ends at the midnight the last day of the century as set by the Gregorian calendar. Specifically, it is a set of one-century-long, nonperiodic instances, for example, literal 20 to represent the whole of the twenty-second century.
date	2005-07-31	Period of time that starts at midnight the specified day and lasts until midnight the following day as set by the Gregorian calendar. Specifically, a set of one-day-long, nonperiodic instances, for example, lexical 2005-7-31 to represent the whole day of July 31, 2005, with the total number of hours in that day being irrelevant.
decimal	-10, -1.56, 0.55, 23.5	Arbitrary precision decimal number
double	-INF, -1E4, -0, 0, 12.78E-2, 12, INF, NaN	Double-precision 64-bit floating-point type number consisting of the values $m \times 2^e$, where m is an integer whose absolute value is less than 2^{53}, and e is an integer between 1075 and 970, inclusive

Table 19-2. *XML Schema Simple Types*

Type	Example	Description
ENTITIES	>	XML 1.0 ENTITIES attribute type, see Chapter 10. This is a space-separated list of ENTITY items.
ENTITY	< &	XML 1.0 ENTITY attribute type, see Chapter 10
float	-INF, -1E4, -0, 0, 12.78E-2, 12, INF, NaN	Single-precision 32-bit floating point. NaN stands for "not a number."
ID	r1c1	XML 1.0 ID attribute type, see Chapter 10
IDREF	item="r1c1"	XML 1.0 IDREF attribute type, see Chapter 10
IDREFS	r1c1, r3c9, pg10	XML 1.0 IDREFS attribute type, see Chapter 10. This is a space-separated list of IDREFS items.
int	--2147483648 to 2147483647	Long integer
integer	-126789 to 126789	Any whole number
language	en-GB, fr	Any valid value for the xml:lang attribute as defined in XML 1.0
long	-9223372036854775808 to 9223372036854775807	Long integer
month	2005-07	Period of time starting at midnight the first day of the month and lasting until midnight the last day of the month as set by the Gregorian calendar. Specifically, it is a set of one-month-long, nonperiodic instances, for example, 2005-07 to represent the whole month of July in 2005, independent of how many days this month has.
Name	Any string of characters	Represents any XML valid name
NCName	Any string of characters other than the colon	Represents XML "non-colonized" Names
negativeInteger	-126789 to -1	Standard integer that can't have a positive or zero value

Table 19-2. *XML Schema Simple Types* (continued)

Type	Example	Description
NMTOKEN	Any name token valid in XML 1.0	XML 1.0 NMTOKEN attribute type, see Chapter 10
NMTOKENS	Any name token valid in XML 1.0	XML 1.0 NMTOKENS attribute type, see Chapter 10. This is a space-separated list of NMTOKEN items.
nonNegativeInteger	0 to 126789	Integer that is restricted from having any value less than 0
nonPositiveInteger	-126789 to 0	Integer that is restricted from having any value greater than 0
NOTATION	XML-compliant character string	XML 1.0 NOTATION attribute type, see Chapter 10
positiveInteger	1 to 126789	Integer restricted from having any value less than 1
Qname	XML-compliant character string	Namespace-qualified XML-compliant name
recurringDate	--07-31	Recurring date, specifically a single day of the year such as the thirty-first of July. Arbitrary recurring dates are not supported by this datatype.
recurringDay	----31	Recurring day, specifically a day of the month such as the 31st of the month. Arbitrary recurring days are not supported by this datatype.
recurringDuration	--05-31T13:20:00	Represents a period of time that recurs at a specified frequency. This value is interpreted as the point in time when the recurrence begins.
short	-32768 to 32767	Short integer value in a specified range
string	String of characters	Represents the ASCII character set
time	13:20:00.000, 13:20:00.000-05:00	Represents an instant of time that recurs every day

Table 19-2. *XML Schema Simple Types* (continued)

Type	Example	Description
`timeDuration`	`P1Y2M3DT10H30M12.3S`	Represents a specific duration of time. The value designate the Gregorian year, month, day, hour, minute, and second.
`timeInstant`	`2005-07-31T13:20:00.000-08:00`	Represents a specific instant in time on the Gregorian calendar, for example, July 31st 2005 at 1:20 P.M. Pacific Standard Time, which is eight hours behind Coordinated Universal Time (UTC)
`timePeriod`	`2005-07-31T13:20`	Represents a specific period of time with a given start and end
`token`	All character data	Set of strings that do not contain the line-feed `(#xA)` or tab `(#x9)` characters, have no leading or trailing spaces `(#x20)`, and have no internal sequences of two or more spaces
`unsignedByte`	0 to `255`	Positive integer value
`unsignedInt`	0 to `4294967295`	Positive integer value
`unsignedLong`	0 to `18446744073709551615`	Positive integer value
`unsignedShort`	0 to `65535`	Positive integer value
`uriReference`	`http://www.mysite.com` `http://www.mysite.com/index.html#test`	Any Internet or intranet address
`year`	`2005`	Period in time starting at midnight the first day of the year and ending at midnight the last day of the year set by the Gregorian calendar

Table 19-2. *XML Schema Simple Types* (continued)

Note *To maintain 100 percent compatibility between XML Schemas and XML 1.0 Document Type Definitions (DTDs), you should only use the simple types:* `ID`, `IDREF`, `IDREFS`, `ENTITY`, `ENTITIES`, `NOTATION`, `NMTOKEN`, `NMTOKENS` *in attributes.*

Defining Your Own Simple Types

In addition to using the simple types predefined by XML Schemas, you can create your own simple types based upon the existing types. The <simpleType> element is used to define new simple types that place more restrictions upon the existing simple types. The use of the <restriction> element enables you to specify the existing simple type you are basing your new type upon, as well as identify the different areas of that simple type that you are going to be restricting.

One of the most common reasons to create a new type is the restriction of an integer or decimal value. For instance, assume that you wish to restrict the values of a mailing ZIP code to a number between 0 and 99999. You would need to create a new simple type called ZipCode as shown in the following statements:

```
<xsd:simpleType name="ZipCode">
  <xsd:restriction base="xsd:integer">
    <xsd:minInclusive value="0"/>
    <xsd:maxInclusive value="99999"/>
  </xsd:restriction>
</xsd:simpleType>
```

First you specify the <simpleType> element and give it the name="ZipCode". This creates the simple type, but it has no form. The inclusion of the <restriction> element uses the base attribute to identify the foundation Schema type of xsd:integer for the new simple type being created. In order to restrict the standard integer type further, the <minInclusive> and <maxInclusive> elements are applied with the new values for the allowable integer range.

The preceding ZipCode example is quite simple using only the <minInclusive> and <maxInclusive> values to restrict the allowable value range of the element content. You can use the <pattern> element to restrict the values of your new type further as shown in the following sample, which specifies that an e-mail address must be formatted correctly with an indefinite number of characters preceding an at-symbol and an indefinite number of characters following it:

```
<xsd:simpleType name="email">  <xsd:restriction
base="xsd:string">
    <xsd:pattern value=".*@.*"/>
  </xsd:restriction>
</xsd:simpleType>
```

Selecting the proper pattern is often difficult. Table 19-3, taken from the W3C's XML Schema Candidate Recommendation (http://www.w3.org/TR/xmlschema-0/#regexAppendix), should provide more insight into what can be done using regular expressions to create pattern matching in your simple types.

Expression	Match(s)
`Chapter \d`	Chapter 0, Chapter 1, Chapter 2 . . .
`Chapter\s\d`	Chapter, followed by a single white space character (space, tab, new line, and so on), followed by a single digit
`Chapter\s\w`	Chapter, followed by a single white space character (space, tab, new line, and so on), followed by a word character
`Espanñola`	Española
`\p{Lu}`	Uppercase characters. The value of \p{} (for example, "Lu") is defined by UNICODE.
`\p{IsGreek}`	Greek characters. The *Is* construction may be applied to any block name (for example, "Greek") as defined by UNICODE
`\P{IsGreek}`	Non-Greek characters. The *Is* construction may be applied to any block name (for example, "Greek") as defined by UNICODE.
`a*x`	x, ax, aax, aaax . . .
`a?x`	ax, x
`a+x`	ax, aax, aaax . . .
`(a|b)+x`	ax, bx, aax, abx, bax, bbx, aaax, aabx, abax, abbx, baax, babx, bbax, bbbx, aaaax . . .
`[abcde]x`	ax, bx, cx, dx, ex
`[a-e]x`	ax, bx, cx, dx, ex
`[-ae]x`	-x, ax, ex
`[ae-]x`	ax, ex, -x
`[a-e-[bd]]x`	ax, cx, ex
`[^0-9]x`	Nondigit character followed by the character *x*
`\Dx`	Nondigit character followed by the character *x*

Table 19-3. *XML Schema Table of Regular Expressions for Pattern Matching*

Expression	Match(s)
`.x`	Character followed by the character *x*
`.*abc.*`	1x2abc, abc1x2, z3456abchooray . . .
`ab{2}x`	abbx
`ab{2,4}x`	abbx, abbbx, abbbbx
`ab{2,}x`	abbx, abbbx, abbbbx . . .
`(ab){2}x`	ababx

Table 19-3. *XML Schema Table of Regular Expressions for Pattern Matching* (continued)

In addition to performing pattern matching, you can use a list of enumerated types, through the `<enumeration>` element, to force your new simple types to be restricted to a specific list of values such as all of the city and ZIP code combinations for a large city such as Houston, Texas:

```
<xsd:simpleType name="HoustonZip">
  <xsd:restriction base="xsd:string">
    <xsd:enumeration value="77011"/>
    <xsd:enumeration value="77045"/>
    <xsd:enumeration value="77050"/>
    <!-- and the list goes on ... -->
  </xsd:restriction>
</xsd:simpleType>
```

Note *This type of enumeration list is commonly used for specifying all of the states and provinces in North America or for providing a list of contact names at a company.*

Using Groups of Elements

Just as you can create your own `<complexTypes>` and `<simpleTypes>`, you can create your own groups of elements. These groups can be used simply to aid in corralling your elements and attributes into more easily interpreted categories, or you can use them as a means of providing a shorthand notation for groups of elements that are applied to multiple <complexTypes>. The following group of elements, created using the <group> element, enables you to create a grouping out of the standard contact record information for use in multiple places in your XML Schema:

```
<xsd:group name="AddressEntry">
 <xsd:sequence>
   <xsd:element name="Name">
    <xsd:complexType>
     <xsd:sequence>
      <xsd:element name="FirstName" type="xsd:string" />
      <xsd:element name="LastName" type="xsd:string" />
     </xsd:sequence>
     <xsd:attribute name="Title" type="xsd:string" />
    </xsd:complexType>
   </element>
   <xsd:element name="Street" type="xsd:string" />
   <xsd:element name="City" type="xsd:string" />
   <xsd:element name="State" type="xsd:string" />
   <xsd:element name="Zip" type="xsd:decimal" />
  </xsd:sequence>
</group>
```

Groups do not define datatypes; they define containers holding sets of elements or/and attributes to be used to describe complex types.

Element Content

Schemas must be able to define elements with element content and with text content, and to define attributes with no content and with mixed content (attributes, child elements, and text). There are multiple variations on the makeup of your element's content, and each of them can be addressed within your XML schema.

Attributes and Simple Values

Assigning both an attribute value and a simple value to your elements is quite easy. Take, for instance, the following <name> element. It uses an attribute to provide salutation information and simple string content to provide the actual name of the person being discussed:

```
<name salutation="Mr."> Luis de Leon </name>
```

To define this element in your schema, you can start with the basic name element, as shown in the following statement:

```
<xsd:element name="name" type="xsd:string" />
```

To expand this element, you have to expand the simple type into a complex type, as shown in the following example code:

```
<xsd:element name="name">
<xsd:complexType>
 <xsd:simpleContent>
  <xsd:extension base="xsd:string">
   <xsd:attribute name="salutation" type="xsd:string" />
  </xsd:extension>
 </xsd:simpleContent>
</xsd:complexType>
</xsd:element>
```

In the preceding example, the <complexType> element was used to create a new anonymous type definition. That type was modified by the <simpleContent> element indicating that the content model of the new type created contains only character data and no child elements. The <extension> element expands the original string type by enabling a standard <attribute> declaration statement that is used to define the salutation used with this contact.

Mixed Content

Many times in your XML documents, you will have both character content and element content in your elements. The schema, used to define the following XML element statement, must provide both element and character content for your company element:

```
<company> The Crystal Company:
 <comp-id> 001 </comp-id>
 <owner> George J. Leon </owner>
</company>
```

The following XML Schema defines the company element with both character content and two child elements, <comp-id> and <owner>:

```
<xsd:element name="company">
 <xsd:complexType mixed="true">
  <xsd:sequence>
    <xsd:element name="comp-id" type="xsd:string" />
    <xsd:element name="owner" type="xsd:string"/>
  </xsd:sequence>
 </xsd:complexType>
</xsd:element>
```

Empty Content

One of the easiest elements to define is one with no content at all, only attributes. Take for instance a company contact record in which all of the information is stored within attributes of the element itself, as shown in the following XML element statement:

```
<company name="The Crystal Company"
         owner="George J. Leon"
         location="Houston, Texas" />
```

To restrict this element to having no content, you need to jump through a hoop. You define an element whose content model only allows elements—no character data—and then not declare any elements in its content. This setup, as shown in the following code, forces the element's content model to be empty, other than any applied attributes:

```
<xsd:element name="company">
 <xsd:complexType>
    <xsd:attribute name="name"     type="xsd:string"/>
    <xsd:attribute name="owner"    type="xsd:string"/>
    <xsd:attribute name="location" type="xsd:string"/>
 </xsd:complexType>
</xsd:element>
```

Summary

XML Schemas use a set of predefined elements to lay out the rules governing the organizational structure of your XML documents. All of the elements in your schema start with the `xsd:` prefix associated with the Schema namespace `xmlns:xsd="http://www.w3.org/2000/08/XMLSchema"`. This namespace declaration is always applied to the root <schema> element. The `xsd:` prefix is also applied to simple types to associate those types with the XML Schema language, rather than enables them to be associated with a specific vocabulary created by the document author.

There are 36 XML Schema elements defined that provide the structure for your schema documents:

- `all`
- `annotation`
- `any`
- `anyAttribute`
- `appInfo`
- `attribute`
- `attributeGroup`
- `choice`
- `complexContent`
- `complexType`
- `documentation`
- `element`
- `enumeration`
- `extension`
- `field`
- `group`
- `import`
- `include`
- `key`
- `keyRef`
- `length`
- `list`
- `maxInclusive`
- `maxLength`
- `minInclusive`
- `minLength`
- `pattern`
- `redefine`
- `restriction`
- `schema`
- `selector`
- `sequence`
- `simpleContent`
- `simpleType`
- `union`
- `unique`

Complex types of elements, which enable attributes and elements in their content, are created using the `<complexType>` schema element declaration. The `<simpleType>` element enables you to control the type of content that is used within your elements and attributes. Each of these types depends upon the use of attributes, discussed in Chapter 20, to complete the descriptions and restrictions in your schema.

Chapter 20

Defining Schema Attributes

XML schemas use a wide variety of attributes, in addition to the elements discussed in Chapter 19. In Chapter 19 you were actually introduced to a few of the major Schema attributes that must be used to define elements in your documents. These attributes use a set of preconfigured values or values that fall within a specific range to describe each XML document element or attribute that the XML schema is describing.

Schema Attributes Descriptions

Just as XML documents depend on attributes to define the elements in the XML document further, XML Schemas use attributes to provide specific information about the XML elements and attributes being described by the schema. Each schema attribute has a specific role in the declaration of your XML elements. Table 20-1 lists all of the schema attributes used to describe the elements and attributes in the XML document the Schema is being used with.

Attribute	Values	Description
`abstract`	`true | false`	Forces an abstract element or attribute to be created. An abstract element or attribute cannot physically exist within an XML document.
`attributeForm Default`	`unqualified | qualified`	Indicates whether or not locally declared attributes must be unqualified.
`base`	A simple type from the XML Schema Datatypes recommendation	Indicates the base type of an element or attribute being modified with the `<restriction>` element.
`block`	`restrictions | #all | extensions`	This attribute allows you to block specific types of elements or attributes from use in the current element.
`blockDefault`	`restrictions | #all | extensions`	The effect of specifying the `blockDefault` attribute is equivalent to specifying a `block` attribute on every type definition and element declaration in the schema.

Table 20-1. *XML Schema Attributes*

Attribute	Values	Description
elementForm Default	unqualified | qualified	Indicates whether or not locally declared element must be unqualified.
final	restrictions | #all | extensions	This attribute allows you to block specific types of elements or attributes from use within the current element.
finalDefault	restrictions | #all | extensions	The effect of specifying the `finalDefault` attribute is equivalent to specifying a `final` attribute on every type definition and element declaration in the schema.
fixed	true | false	When a simple type is defined, the `fixed` attribute may be applied to any of its facets to prevent a derivation of that type from modifying the value of the fixed facets.
form	unqualified | qualified	Controls element qualifications on a declaration-by-declaration basis
itemType	A type reference for a previously created type	References a custom type or simple type from which to create a new item.
memberTypes	A type reference for a previously created type	A list of all the types in the `<union>` element.
maxOccurs	*nonNegative Integer* | unbounded	Maximum number of times an element can occur.
minOccurs	*nonNegative Integer* | unbounded	The maximum number of times an element may appear
mixed	true | false	Allows both text and element content within an element.
name	text string	Identifies the reference name for the element or attribute being defined.

Table 20-1. *XML Schema Attributes* (continued)

Attribute	Values	Description
namespace	##any | ##local | ##other | "*URI*"	Identifies the namespace of the element being described.
noNameSpace Location	http://www.w3. org/2000/10/XML Schema-instance	Provides hints for the locations of schema documents that do not have target namespaces
xsi:null	true | false	If set to `true`, represents that the element has a null value in the XML instance document. This is applied in the XML document.
nullable	true | false	Allows the XML element to be set null in the XML document.
process Contents	strict | lax	If set to `strict`, an XML processor is obliged to obtain the schema associated with the required namespace and validate the HTML. If set to `lax`, It will validate elements and attributes for which it can obtain schema information, but it will not signal errors for those it cannot obtain schema information.
ref	The name of a previously defined element	References an existing element.
schemaLocation	*URL*	Contains pairs of values: The first member of each pair is the namespace for which the second member is the hint describing where to find to an appropriate schema document.
xsi:schema Location	*URL*	Provides hints from the author to a processor regarding the location of schema documents.

Table 20-1. *XML Schema Attributes* (continued)

Attribute	Values	Description
substitution Group	Name of existing group	Used to specify a group of elements to replace a single defined element.
targetName space	*URL*	Identifies the namespace of the target document.
type	A simple type, or a custom type identifier	Identifies the type of content that can be contained within the element or attribute.
xsi:type	A simple type, or a custom type identifier	Identifies the type of content that can be contained within the element or attribute.
use	*prohibited* | *optional* | *required* | *default* | *fixed*	Used in attribute declarations to indicate whether the attribute is required, optional, prohibited, fixed, or default.
value	*string*	Provides any value needed for the attribute being declared.
xpath	An XPath expression	Provides an XPath expression for finding a destination resource for the attribute.

Table 20-1. *XML Schema Attributes* (continued)

Note *Before counting on these attributes to work exactly as expressed here, please refer to the latest schema recommendation located at http://www.w3.org/TR. Because XML Schemas is a constantly changing world, you should habitually check for any changes in the specifications and the support provided by your chosen software.*

Attribute Groups

You can create groups of attributes to be used with multiple elements. By grouping your attributes, as you grouped your elements in Chapter 19, you can apply a group of attributes to as many elements as you require, much as you did with parameter entities in DTDs, so that you don't have to redefine the attribute used in your document continually.

The following example creates a group of attributes that are used in both the `InvoiceLineItem` and an `InventoryEntry` element declarations that follow the attribute group.

Note *Both the individual attribute declarations and attribute group references must appear at the end of complex type definitions.*

```
<!-- Attribute group declaration -->
<xsd:attributeGroup name="ItemDesc">
  <xsd:attribute name="itemNum" type="xsd:short"/>
  <xsd:attribute name="weight"  type="xsd:decimal"/>
  <xsd:attribute name="location">
    <xsd:simpleType>
     <xsd:restriction base="xsd:string">
      <xsd:enumeration value="warehouse"/>
      <xsd:enumeration value="drop-ship"/>
      <xsd:enumeration value="production"/>
     </xsd:restriction>
    </xsd:simpleType>
  </xsd:attribute>
  <xsd:attribute name="in-stock"  type="xsd:boolean"/>
  <xsd:attribute name="cost"  type="xsd:decimal"/>
  <xsd:attribute name="sales-price"  type="xsd:decimal"/>
  <xsd:attribute name="availability"  type="xsd:byte"/>
</xsd:attributeGroup>

<!-- Element declarations using the previously
     declared attribute group -->
<xsd:element name="invoiceLineItem"
             minOccurs="0" maxOccurs="unbounded">
 <xsd:complexType>
  <xsd:sequence>
   <xsd:element name="itemName" type="xsd:string"/>
   <xsd:element name="itemDescription" type="xsd:string" />
  </xsd:sequence>
  <!-- attributeGroup replaces individual declarations -->
  <xsd:attributeGroup ref="ItemDesc"/>
 </xsd:complexType>
</xsd:element>
<xsd:element name="inventoryEntry"
             minOccurs="0" maxOccurs="unbounded">
<xsd:complexType>
```

```
    <xsd:attributeGroup ref="ItemDesc"/>
    <xsd:attribute name="numOnHand"
                   type="xsd:nonNegativeInteger"/>
  </xsd:complexType>
  </xsd:element>
```

Using attribute groups can improve the readability of a schema and makes it easier to update the schema because all of the attributes in the group can be defined and edited in one location while updating multiple element definitions.

Note *Attribute groups may contain other attribute groups.*

Using Schema Annotations

In XML schemas, annotations expand on the role of XML DTD comments. Whereas comment statements, which are formatted the same for both DTDs and schemas, can be used only to provide information to the human reader of a document and are inaccessible by the document application software, Schema annotations can be used by the XML parser or viewing application.

XML Schema provides three elements for annotating schemas for the benefit of both humans and applications. These elements are: `annotation`, `documentation`, and `appInfo`, which are all discussed here:

- **`annotation`** Container for both the `documentation` and `appInfo` elements.
- **`documentation`** Primarily used for human-readable comments, such as a description of the schema and its copyright information.
- **`appInfo`** Primarily used for applications providing information on style sheets, tools, and other application-specific information.

The following example shows how you can use the `annotation` element to provide information for both human readers and applications using the `documentation` and `appInfo` elements. This code provides a description and copyright for a schema describing an invoice, as well as descriptions of where the style sheet for the document is located.

```
<xsd:schema>
  <xsd:annotation>
    <xsd:documentation>
      Schema document describing the format of invoices for
      WebRavin sales and service department.
    </xsd:documentation>
    <xsd:documentation>
```

```
        Copyright (c) 2005 WebRavin Inc. All rights reserved.
      </xsd:documentation>
      <xsd:appInfo source="http://www.mysite.com/stylesheet.css">
         Download CSS style sheet
      </xsd:appInfo>
    </xsd:annotation>
</xsd:schema>
```

Using Constraints

In the process of creating `complexTypes` of elements you can add a series of *constraints* to your statements. Using constraints in your schema controls the occurrence of individual elements, or groups of elements, in the XML document. These constraints mirror those available in XML 1.0, although there are some additional restrictions that can be implemented.

There are three primary constraints that are used on your groups of elements. These constraints are

- **<choice>** Elements are constrained so that only one of the elements may appear in that position in the document.
- **<sequence>** Elements are constrained to appear in the same order (sequence) as they are declared.
- **<all>** Elements can occur in any order and in any combination.

Note *Each of these compositors can use the* `minOccurs` *and* `maxOccurs` *attributes to define the use of the elements themselves.*

Making a <choice>

The `<choice>` compositor describes a choice between several possible elements or groups of elements that can appear in your XML Instance document. You can use compositors together, allowing you to create a set of complex criteria for your XML document to follow. The basic structure of a `<choice>` compositor is shown in the following code:

```
<xsd:choice>
    <xsd:element name="name" .../>
    <xsd:element name="name1" .../>
    <xsd:element name="name2" .../>
</xsd:choice>
```

This code simply forces an XML instance document to use one of these elements, but not more than that.

You can also force a choice to be made between individual elements and groups of elements, as shown in the following code example. In this example, your XML instance document will be able to have an invoice, purchase order, or mailing label set of elements used.

```
<xsd:choice>
     <xsd:element ref="invoice" />
     <xsd:element ref="purchaseOrder" />
     <xsd:element ref="mailingLabel" />
</xsd:choice>
```

Note *Each of the groups used in a* `<choice>` *statement must be defined in the schema document prior to the choice being made.*

You can use compositors in groups, complex types or other compositors. For instance, the following example will accept either a single `"phone"` element or a sequence of `"homePhone,"` a `"busPhone,"` and an optional `"mobilePhone"` element.

```
<xsd:group name="phoneList">
  <xsd:choice>
    <xsd:element name="phone" type="xsd:string" />
    <xsd:sequence>
      <xsd:element name="homePhone" type="xsd:string" />
      <xsd:element name="busPhone" type="xsd:string" />
      <xsd:element name="mobilePhone" type="xsd:string" minOccurs="0"/>
    </xsd:sequence>
  </xsd:choice>
</xsd:group>
```

Creating a <sequence>

The `<sequence>` compositor you were introduced to in Chapter 19 works much like the `<choice>` compositor, but instead of forcing a choice, it forces an order to your elements. In other words, the order of the element declarations in your schema, becomes the order that the elements must appear in your XML document.

Take the following example into account. It uses a single `<complexType>` element that forces all of its child elements to appear within the same `<sequence>`. This `<sequence>` contains the `itemNum`, `weight`, `location`, `cost`, `sales-price`, and `availability` elements. The location element is an empty element with a single attribute, `stored`, that has one of three enumerated values: `warehouse`, `drop-ship`, or `production`.

```
<xsd:element name="ItemDesc">
  <xsd:complexType>
   <sequence>
    <xsd:element name="itemNum" type="xsd:short"/>
    <xsd:element name="weight"  type="xsd:decimal"/>
    <xsd:element name="location">
      <xsd:complexType>
        <attribute name="stored">
          <xsd:restriction base="xsd:string">
            <xsd:enumeration value="warehouse"/>
            <xsd:enumeration value="drop-ship"/>
            <xsd:enumeration value="production"/>
          </xsd:restriction>
        </attribute>
      </xsd:complexType>
    </xsd:element>
    <xsd:element name="cost"  type="xsd:decimal"/>
    <xsd:element name="sales-price"  type="xsd:decimal"/>
    <xsd:element name="availability"  type="xsd:byte"/>
   </sequence>
  </xsd:complexType>
</xsd:element>
```

Using <all>

The <all> compositor defines an unordered set of elements. All the elements in the group may appear once or not at all, and they may appear in any order. The use of <all> is limited to the top level of any content model. In addition to this restriction, the group's children must all be individual elements and may appear only once in the content model. The following complex type definition allows the elements describing an invoice to appear in any order:

```
<xsd:complexType name="invoiceLineItem">
  <xsd:all>
    <xsd:element name="itemNum" type="xsd:short"/>
    <xsd:element name="weight"  type="xsd:decimal"/>
    <xsd:element name="location">
      <xsd:complexType>
        <attribute name="stored">
          <xsd:restriction base="xsd:string">
            <xsd:enumeration value="warehouse"/>
            <xsd:enumeration value="drop-ship"/>
```

```
          <xsd:enumeration value="production"/>
        </xsd:restriction>
      </attribute>
    </xsd:complexType>
  </xsd:element>
  <xsd:element name="cost"  type="xsd:decimal"/>
  <xsd:element name="sales-price"  type="xsd:decimal"/>
  <xsd:element name="availability"  type="xsd:byte"/>
</xsd:all>
<xsd:attribute name="isbn" type="isbnType" use="required"/>
</xsd:complexType>
```

In order to avoid combinations that could become ambiguous or too complex to be solved by W3C XML Schema tools, a set of restrictions has been added to the <all> compositor.

- They can appear only as a unique child at the top of a content model.
- Their children can be only <element> definitions or references and cannot have a cardinality greater than 1.

Creating Unique Elements and Attributes

You can use XML schema to indicate that an attribute or element value must be unique within a specific document. The <unique> element is used to identify a set of elements, and then to identify the attribute or element "field" relative to each selected element that has to be unique. The basic syntax for the <unique> element is shown in the following schema statements:

```
<unique>
   <selector xpath="element identifier" />
    <field xpath="attribute identifier" />
</unique>
```

When applied to a specific application, such as an inventory list, you can use the <unique> element to identify the `item` as a unique element of the `inventory` element by specifying it as the value of the `xpath` attribute in the field element. The value of the <field> element, in this case the `itemId` attribute, must have a unique value.

```
<unique>
   <selector xpath="inventory/item" />
    <field xpath="@itemId" />
</unique>
```

Note *The XPath expression limits the scope of what must be unique. For instance, the* `itemNum` *element must have a unique* `itemId` *value, but* `itemId` *can be applied to a different element and does not have to be unique.*

Schemas and Namespaces

Schemas allow you to control the contents and structure of XML documents, but they also allow you to control the contents of merged XML and HTML documents through the use of XML namespaces. Using schemas and namespaces, you can describe a flexible mechanism enabling content models to be extended by any elements and/or attributes belonging to specified namespaces. The easiest way to show this is through example. In the following XMLS document, a combination of XML and HTML is used to create an inventory list.

```
<?xml standalone="yes" ?>
<inventory xmlns="http://www.myserver.com/inventory"
           lastupdate="06/06/05"
           nextshipment="07/01/05" >
  <item itemID="1234-56">
    <table xmlns="http://www.w3.org/1999/xhtml">
      <tr>
        <td> Name </td>
        <td> Description </td>
        <td> Cost </td>
        <td> Sales Price </td>
        <td> Weight </td>
        <td> In Stock </td>
      </tr>
      <tr>
        <td> Great Big Widgets </td>
        <td> Gigantic Widgets ready for any job. </td>
        <td> $12.00 </td>
        <td> $20.00 </td>
        <td> 12 </td>
        <td> 145 </td>
      </tr>
    </table>
  </item>
  <!-- More items should be added here -->
</inventory>
```

With the HTML code mixed in with the XML code it now becomes necessary to inform the XML schema that it will be parsing not only XML, but HTML also. The schema uses a namespace, creating a complex type element out of the items element and declaring that <any> elements can be used from the specified namespace.

```
<?xml version="1.0" encoding="utf-8"?>
<xsd:schema xmlns:xsd="http://www.w3.org/2000/10/XMLSchema">
 <element name="inventory">
 <complexType>
  <sequence>
   <element name="item">
    <complexType>
     <sequence>
      <any namespace="http://www.w3.org/1999/xhtml"
           minOccurs="1" maxOccurs="unbounded"
           processContents="skip"/>
     </sequence>
    </complexType>
  </element>
  </sequence>
  <attribute name="itemID" type="xsd:string"/>
 </complexType>
</element>
```

Namespaces may be used to permit and forbid element content in various ways, depending upon the value of the nameSpace attribute, as shown in Table 20-2

Namespace Attribute Value	Allowed Element Content
##any	Any well-formed XML from any namespace (default).
##local	Any well-formed XML that is not qualified, (not declared to be in a namespace).
##other	Any well-formed XML that is not from the target namespace of the type being defined.
"http://www.w3.org/1999/xhtml *##target*"	Any well-formed XML belonging to any namespace in the (whitespace-separated) list; *##target* is shorthand for the target namespace of the type being defined.

Table 20-2. *Namespace Attribute Values Used in Schemas*

Using Entities

Schemas don't provide the same syntax for describing entities as were provided with XML 1.0 DTDs, although there are two ways to provide entity values in Schemas. The first option is to declare the entity as an element with a fixed value. For instance assume you are replacing the caret (`⁁`) shown in bold in the following example, using a DTD with a schema statement.

```
<?xml version="1.0" ?>
<!DOCTYPE Letter [
<!ENTITY caret "#905">
]>
<letter xmlns="http://www.mysite.com/letter" >
 <!-- etc -->
  <equation>Heather &caret; Ann</equation>
 <!-- etc -->
</letter>
```

in order to replace this DTD entity declaration with a schema statement such as

```
<xsd:element name="caret" type="xsd:token" fixed="^"/>
```

This element can be used in an XML document using the following code:

```
<?xml version="1.0" ?>
<letter xmlns="http://www.mysite.com/letter"
        xmlns:char="http://www.mysite.com/characters.xsd">
 <!-- etc -->
  <equation>Heather <caret/> Ann</equation>
 <!-- etc -->
</letter>
```

Summary

XML Schema attributes use a set of preconfigured values or values that fall within a specific range to describe each XML document element or attribute that the XML schema is describing. Each schema attribute has a specific role in the declaration of your XML elements. Schema attributes include the following:

```
abstract                    fixed
attributeFormDefault        form
base                        itemType
block                       memberTypes
blockDefault                maxOccurs
elementFormDefault          minOccurs
final                       mixed
finalDefault                name
```

```
nameSpace                       substitutionGroup
noNamespaceSchemaLocation       targetNamespace
xsi:null                        type
nullable                        xsi:type
processContents                 use
ref                             value
schemaLocation                  xpath
xsi:schemaLocation
```

Attribute groups allow you to use sets of attributes with multiple elements much as you did with parameter entities in DTDs, so that you don't have to continually redefine the attribute used in your document. Comment statements, which are formatted the same for both DTDs and schemas, can be used only to provide information to the human reader of a document and are inaccessible by the document application software. Schema annotations can be used by the XML parser or viewing application to provide additional information to the application.

Using constraints in your schema controls the occurrence of individual elements, or groups of elements, in the XML document. There are three primary constraints that are used on your groups of elements. These constraints are `<choice>`, `<sequence>`, and `<all>`.

The `<unique>` element is used to identify a set of elements and then to identify the attribute or element "field" relative to each selected element that has to be unique. XPath statements are used to define the selections and fields used to control the unique aspect of the elements.

Using schemas and namespaces, you can describe a flexible mechanism enabling content models to be extended by any elements and attributes belonging to specified namespaces. When using schemas, you exchange your entity reference for an element with a fixed value.

In the next chapter you will see how to put together some of the more complex aspects of XML Schemas.

Chapter 21

Advanced Concepts with Schemas

XML schemas can be used in a wide variety of situations, replacing DTDs while providing more control over the contents and structure of the document being worked with. As was discussed in Chapters 18–20, XML schemas use XML structure so that you can easily develop schemas for each of the types of documents you work with. This chapter covers some of the more theoretical details associated with using schemas.

Target Namespaces and Schemas

A schema can be viewed as a collection (vocabulary) of type definitions and element declarations whose names belong to a particular target namespace. The target namespace enables you to distinguish between definitions and declarations used in your document that originate in different document vocabularies. For example, target namespaces would enable us to distinguish between the declaration for an element in the XML Schema language vocabulary and a declaration for an element of the same name in another document vocabulary.

When we want to check that an instance document conforms to one or more schemas (through a process called schema validation), we need to identify which element and attribute declarations and type definitions in the schemas should be used to check which elements and attributes in the instance document. The target namespace plays an important role in the identification process.

As the author of a schema, you have several options that have an effect on how the identities of elements and attributes are used in your XML documents. As the author, you have the ability to decide whether locally declared elements and attributes are qualified by a namespace, use an explicit prefix, or are implicitly identified using the default namespace. The use of the target namespace allows you to define elements that are defined in your XML schema and nowhere else. Using a target namespace, you can specify that locally defined elements and attributes are unqualified. If qualification of your local elements and attributes is required, you can qualify them using the `elementFormDefault` and the `attributeFormDefault` attributes applied to the `<schema>` element. These attribute values can be set to either `unqualified` or `qualified` to indicate whether or not a locally declared element or attribute must be qualified. In the following example, the `elementFormDefault` and the `attributeFormDefault` attributes have been applied to the `<schema>` element, ensuring that the individual element declarations do not need to be qualified.

```
<schema xmlns=http://www.w3.org/2000/08/XMLSchema
        xmlns:inv="http://www.myexample.com/Invoice"
        targetNamespace=http://www.myexample.com/Invoice
        elementFormDefault="unqualified"
        attributeFormDefault="unqualified">
```

```
<xsd:element name="invoice">
 <xsd:complexType>

 <!— Attribute group declaration —>
<xsd:attributeGroup name="ItemDesc">
  <xsd:attribute name="itemNum" type="xsd:short"/>
  <xsd:attribute name="weight"  type="xsd:decimal"/>
  <xsd:attribute name="location">
    <xsd:simpleType>
     <xsd:restriction base="xsd:string">
      <xsd:enumeration value="warehouse"/>
      <xsd:enumeration value="drop-ship"/>
      <xsd:enumeration value="production"/>
     </xsd:restriction>
    </xsd:simpleType>
  </xsd:attribute>
  <xsd:attribute name="in-stock"  type="xsd:boolean"/>
  <xsd:attribute name="cost"  type="xsd:decimal"/>
  <xsd:attribute name="sales-price"  type="xsd:decimal"/>
  <xsd:attribute name="availability"  type="xsd:byte"/>
</xsd:attributeGroup>

<!— Element declarations using the previously
     declared attribute group —>

 <xsd:element name="invoiceLineItem"
            minOccurs="0" maxOccurs="unbounded">
  <xsd:complexType>
   <xsd:sequence>
    <xsd:element name="itemName" type="xsd:string"/>
    <xsd:element name="itemDescription" type="xsd:string" />
   </xsd:sequence>
<!— attributeGroup replaces individual declarations —>
   <xsd:attributeGroup ref="ItemDesc"/>
  </xsd:complexType>
 </xsd:element>

 <xsd:element name="inventoryEntry"
             minOccurs="0" maxOccurs="unbounded">
 <xsd:complexType>
   <xsd:attributeGroup ref="ItemDesc"/>
   <xsd:attribute name="numOnHand" type="xsd:nonNegativeInteger" />
 </xsd:complexType>
```

```
  </xsd:element>
  <!— etc —>
  </xsd:complexType>
  </xsd:element>
</schema>
```

By allowing none of your elements to be qualified, your XML document looks like this:

```
<?xml version="1.0"?>
<invoice>
  <invoiceLineItem itemNum="12345" weight="13lb"
                   location="drop-ship" in-stock="true"
                   cost="15.00" sales-price="25.00"
                   availability="1" >
    <itemName> Professional Widgets </itemName>
    <itemDescription> Widgets for all professional purposes,
       but not at a professional price. </itemDescription>
  </invoiceLineItem>
</invoice>
```

There may be times when you need to qualify your local element and attribute declarations independently. In that case, the `elementFormDefault` and the `attributeFormDefault` attributes applied to the `<schema>` element should be equal to "`qualified`".

```
<schema xmlns=http://www.w3.org/2000/08/XMLSchema
        xmlns:inv="http://www.myexample.com/Invoice"
        targetNamespace=http://www.myexample.com/Invoice
        elementFormDefault="qualified"
        attributeFormDefault="unqualified">
```

By forcing the elements to be qualified specifically, your XML document looks like this:

```
<?xml version="1.0"?>
<inv:invoice>
  <inv:invoiceLineItem itemNum="12345" weight="13lb"
                       location="drop-ship" in-stock="true"
                       cost="15.00" sales-price="25.00"
                       availability="1" >
    <inv:itemName> Professional Widgets </inv:itemName>
    <inv:itemDescription> Widgets for all professional purposes,
       but not at a professional price. </inv:itemDescription>
  </inv:invoiceLineItem>
</inv:invoice>
```

Undeclared Target Namespaces

You do not have to specify a target namespace for your document. Most of the documents in the examples in Chapters 18–20 do not have a target namespace declared. When a `targetNamespace` is not explicitly defined, the types that you create are not qualified using a namespace. Because you are not defining a namespace, there is no default namespace that is used in its stead.

When you declare elements in your XML schema that have not target namespace, you are validating elements in your instance document that have been left unqualified and have no concrete relationship to any other elements contained in the document outside of those relationships specified by the schema itself. So, to validate a traditional XML 1.0 document that does not use namespaces at all, you must provide a schema with no target namespace. Of course, there are many XML 1.0 documents that do not use namespaces, so there will be many schema documents written without target namespaces; you must be sure to give to your processor a schema document that corresponds to the document language you are validating.

Schema Constraints Versus ID Attributes

When you create an XML document that provides unique `ID` attributes for the elements included in the document, you are providing a means to identify each element in the document. These unique identifiers need to be expressed in the XML Schema. By using the `ID`, `IDREF`, and `IDREFS` simple types in your XML schema, you can emulate the use of the `ID`, `IDREF`, and `IDREFS` usage in an XML 1.0 DTD.

The system used by XML Schemas is much more flexible than that used by DTDs. DTDs can only use the `ID`, `IDREF`, and `IDREFS` types on attributes, whereas the mechanism used by Schemas can be used for both element and attribute content, regardless of the type of element or attribute being used. Schemas further enable you to specify the scope within which uniqueness of the value applies, while the scope of a DTD ID is fixed to the entire document. In addition to all of this, schemas enable you to create a `key` or a `keyRef` from combinations of element and attribute content, which is a function that can't be re-created at all using DTDs.

Note *Rumor has it that `key` and `keyRef` may be removed from future versions of XML Schemas. Be sure to check the W3C site before implementing these values in your Schemas.*

Global Versus Local Declarations

You have two options for defining elements in your document. You can make them either global or local. Global elements emulate DTDs, in that each element is required to have a unique name. When you are using a variety of local elements, you can have multiple elements of the same name, but they must occur with different types and as children of different elements.

The following example uses global elements entirely. This allows you to omit the `elementFormDefault` and `attributeFormDefault` attributes associated with the `<schema>` element. None of these elements have duplicate names, and they are all included in the target namespace identified by the `targetNamespace` attribute.

```
<schema xmlns=http://www.w3.org/2000/08/XMLSchema
        xmlns:inv="http://www.myexample.com/Invoice"
        targetNamespace="http://www.myexample.com/Invoice">

 <xsd:element name="invoice">
  <xsd:complexType>

 <!— Attribute group declaration —>
<xsd:attributeGroup name="ItemDesc">
  <xsd:attribute name="itemNum" type="xsd:short"/>
  <xsd:attribute name="weight"  type="xsd:decimal"/>
  <xsd:attribute name="location">
    <xsd:simpleType>
     <xsd:restriction base="xsd:string">
      <xsd:enumeration value="warehouse"/>
      <xsd:enumeration value="drop-ship"/>
      <xsd:enumeration value="production"/>
     </xsd:restriction>
    </xsd:simpleType>
  </xsd:attribute>
  <xsd:attribute name="in-stock"  type="xsd:boolean"/>
  <xsd:attribute name="cost"  type="xsd:decimal"/>
  <xsd:attribute name="sales-price"  type="xsd:decimal"/>
  <xsd:attribute name="availability"  type="xsd:byte"/>
</xsd:attributeGroup>

<!— Element declarations using the previously
     declared attribute group —>

 <xsd:element name="invoiceLineItem"
            minOccurs="0" maxOccurs="unbounded">
  <xsd:complexType>
   <xsd:sequence>
    <xsd:element name="itemName" type="xsd:string"/>
    <xsd:element name="itemDescription" type="xsd:string" />
```

```
    </xsd:sequence>
  <!— attributeGroup replaces individual declarations —>
    <xsd:attributeGroup ref="ItemDesc"/>
   </xsd:complexType>
  </xsd:element>

  <xsd:element name="inventoryEntry"
              minOccurs="0" maxOccurs="unbounded">
  <xsd:complexType>
    <xsd:attributeGroup ref="ItemDesc"/>
    <xsd:attribute name="numOnHand" type="xsd:nonNegativeInteger" />
  </xsd:complexType>
  </xsd:element>

  <!— etc —>
  </xsd:complexType>
  </xsd:element>
</schema>
```

When all elements are declared globally, it is not possible to take advantage of local names. For example, you can only declare one global element called `<name>`, but, you can declare one local element called `<name>` that has a `complexType` and is a child element of `<ContactRecord>`. Within the same schema (target namespace) you can declare a second element also called "`name`" that is an enumeration of the values `"Widget Do-dad Cog"` and is a child element of `<invoice>`, as shown in the following example.

```
<schema xmlns=http://www.w3.org/2000/08/XMLSchema
        xmlns:inv="http://www.myexample.com/Invoice"
        targetNamespace="http://www.myexample.com/Invoice">

 <xsd:element name="invoice">
   <xsd:simpleType>
     <xsd:restriction base="xsd:string">
      <xsd:enumeration value="Widget"/>
      <xsd:enumeration value="Do-dad"/>
      <xsd:enumeration value="Cog"/>
     </xsd:restriction>
   </xsd:simpleType>
 </xsd:element>
<xsd:element name="ContactRecord">
```

```
    <xsd:complexType>
     <xsd:sequence>
      <xsd:element name="Name">
       <xsd:complexType>
        <xsd:sequence>
         <xsd:element name="FirstName" type="xsd:string" />
         <xsd:element name="LastName" type="xsd:string" />
        </xsd:sequence>
        <xsd:attribute name="Title" type="xsd:string" />
       </xsd:complexType>
      </element>
      <xsd:element name="Street" type="xsd:string" />
      <xsd:element name="City" type="xsd:string" />
      <xsd:element name="State" type="xsd:string" />
      <xsd:element name="Zip" type="xsd:decimal" />
     </xsd:sequence>
    </xsd:complexType>
  </xsd:element>
```

Using Schemas as Multiple Documents

As schemas increase in size, it is often necessary to divide their content among several schema documents. This makes them easier to maintain and control access to them, and it improves their readability. For these reasons, you can separate the schema into separate files, each of which discusses one applicable area of the document being described. In the following example, you can see how the <include> element is used to include the contents of another schema document within the current document.

```
<schema targetNamespace="http://www.example.com/Invoice"
        xmlns="http://www.w3.org/2000/08/XMLSchema"
        xmlns:ipo="http://www.myexample.com/Invoice">

 <!— include item constructs —>
 <include
  schemaLocation="http://www.myexample.com/schemas/iteminfo.xsd"/>

<!— other schema element and attribute definitions —>
</schema>
```

The various invoice information and item information are contained in two schema files. The effect of this <include> element is to bring in the definitions and declarations contained in iteminfo.xsd and make them available as part of the primary document's schema target namespace.

When using `<include>`, the target namespace of the included components must be the same as the target namespace of the including schema.

Substitution Groups

XML Schemas provides a mechanism, called substitution groups, which allows elements to be substituted for other elements. Substitution groups allow elements to be assigned to a special group of elements, which can be substituted for another specified element called the *head element.*

The head element must be declared as a global element.

In the following example, you can see how the declaration of two elements called `<firstName>` and `<lastName>` that are assigned to a substitution group whose head element is `<name>`. This declaration allows `<firstName>` and `<lastName>` to be used any place that you can use `<name>`. The only concern for using substitution groups is that the elements in the group must have either the same type as the head element or a type that has been derived from the head element's type. To declare these two new elements and make them substitutable for the `<name>` element, we use the following syntax:

```
<element name="name" type="string" />
<element name="firstName" type="string"
   substitutionGroup="name" />
<element name="lastName" type="string"
   substitutionGroup="name" />
```

When these declarations are added to a simple address book schema, `name` can be substituted for in the instance document, for example the bold lines in the following code show how either the `<name>` or the `<firstName>` and `<lastName>` elements can be used interchangeably.

```
....
 <address>
   <name>Fred de Leon </name>
     <city>Houston</city>
     <state>TX</state>
     <zip>99.95</zip>
</address>
<address>
   <firstName>Fred </firstName>
  <lastName> de Leon </lastName>
     <city>Houston</city>
     <state>TX</state>
```

USING SCHEMAS

```
        <zip>99.95</zip>
    </address>
    ....
```

Abstract Elements and Types

XML Schemas provide you with a mechanism allowing you to create abstract elements. Abstract elements don't exist in the same fashion as other elements. Abstract elements can't exist in an XML instance document themselves, so they must be substituted by another element. Think back to our name example in the previous section. If you were to define <name> as an abstract element, then either <firstName> or <lastName>, or both, would have to be used for the current document to be considered a valid document. To declare the <name> element abstract, we modify its original declaration in the previous section's schema, to match the following:

```
<element name="name" type="string" abstract="true"/>
<element name="firstName" type="string"
    substitutionGroup="name" />
<element name="lastName" type="string"
    substitutionGroup="name" />
```

Summary

In this chapter you studied some of the more advanced topics of XML Schemas. There are many more to be learned from the World Wide Web Consortium Web site located at http://www.w3.org/. Here are some of the specific items to keep in mind:

- The target namespace enables you to distinguish between definitions and declarations used in your document that originate in different document vocabularies.
- When a `targetNamespace` is not explicitly defined, the types that you create are not qualified using a namespace.
- By using the `ID`, `IDREF`, and `IDREFS` simple types in your XML Schema, you can emulate the use of the `ID`, `IDREF`, and `IDREFS` usage in an XML 1.0 DTD. The mechanism used by Schemas can be used for both element and attribute content, regardless of the type of element or attribute being used.
- Global elements emulate DTDs, in that each element is required to have a unique name. Local elements allow you to have multiple elements of the same name, but they must occur with different types and as children of different elements.

- You can separate the schema into separate files using the `<include schemaLocation="http://www.myexample.com/schemas/iteminfo.xsd"/>` syntax.

Substitution groups allow elements to be assigned to a special group of elements, which can be substituted for another specified element called the head element.

In the next part, you will find out about the myriad of options you have using XML and its child languages to expand the quality of your XML documents.

Part V

Using XML Query

Chapter 22

Introducing XML Query

XML Query is a series of specifications, still at Working Draft stage, that primarily include the XML Query Requirements, XML Query Data Model, and XML Query Algebra. Each of these specifications identifies a specific aspect of the XML Query language. In addition to these three working drafts (released February, 2001) is the XML Query Use Cases working draft, which provides extensive examples of how and where XML Queries can be used. The XML Query Requirements, XML Query Data Model, and XML Query Algebra working drafts are discussed in the following sections.

XML Query Requirements

The XML Query Working Group has three goals which are expressed in the XML Query Requirements working draft: to produce a data model for XML documents, to produce a set of query operators on that data model, and to produce a query language based on these query operators. The data model being developed for XML Queries is based on the W3C XML Infoset, which is located at http://www.w3.org/TR/xml-Infoset.

XML Queries work with a single document or with a fixed collection of documents. The primary function of a Query is to select either a whole or subtree of a document based upon the content and structure of that document. Once a Query finds the information it is looking for, it then writes that information to a new document.

In order to make this search-and-rewrite operation work best, XML Queries have a variety of requirements that the language must meet in order to fulfill all of its expectations. The following are some of the requirements:

- XML Queries must be readable and writable by humans.
- XML Queries must be written in valid XML syntax.
- XML Queries must be defined independently of any protocols that it might be used with. In other words, XML Queries can't be dependent upon SQL or another query language to provide their functionality.
- XML Queries must return errors that occur while a query is being processed.
- The XML Query language must be expandable so that future versions and implementations can add further capability to Queries.
- XML Queries support a finite number of data instances. In other words, you can have your Query return the first five records that match your query or all of them.
- XML Queries must support namespaces.
- XML Queries must support XML 1.0 data, as well as XML Schema complex and simple types.
- XML Queries must support references between XML documents, as well as references within a single XML document.
- XML Queries must work correctly, whether or not an XML Schema or DTD is available.

- XML Queries must support operations on all the data types created in the XML Query Data Model.
- XML Queries must be able to work with simple text conditions, including those that span the boundaries of elements.
- XML Queries must support operations on specified document hierarchies and sequences of elements.
- XML Queries must be able to create summary information from groups of related elements across multiple documents.
- XML Queries must be able to sort the results of queries.
- XML Queries must be able to perform operations on element names, attribute names, and processing instructions included in your XML documents.
- XML Queries should be able to provide access to the XML Schema or DTD provided with a document, including potentially mapping a DTD to a schema if necessary.
- XML Queries must be able to access information provided from the environment in which the query is run, not just from a document. This type of environmental information includes such things as user ID, software ID, date and time, location, and time zone.

Although this appears to be quite a long list, there are more requirements for XML Queries specified in the XML Query Requirements specification located at http://www.w3.org/TR/xmlquery-req.

XML Query Data Model

The XML Query Data Model working draft provides a formal definition for types of information and data that can be accessed using the XML Query language. The XML Query Data Model is based upon the XML Information Set (http://www.w3.org/TR/2001/WD-xml-infoset-20010202/), which defines an abstract data set used to provide a consistent set of definitions for use in other specifications that need to refer to the information in a well-formed XML document.

The current XML Query Data Model working draft can be located at http://www.w3.org/TR/query-datamodel. This draft provides a precise and formal definition of how values in the XML Query Data Model are constructed and accessed. The definitions of these operators provide the foundation of the XML Query Algebra (http://www.w3.org/TR/query-algebra). A document containing the XML Query Data Model is used to represent one or more complete XML documents or parts of those documents. The XML Query Data Model identifies which information in a document is accessible, and it identifies this information without specifying the programming language used to access the information. This allows you to use XML Queries in a multitude of situations without being required to use only one type of database and interface language.

The XML Query Data Model assumes that the information in an XML document is static for the duration of the evaluation of the query, so that the contents of the query will not change while the query is being performed.

The XML Query Data Model uses a node-based tree representation and the concept of node identity. The addition of node identity simplifies the representation of XML reference values such as IDREF, XML Pointer Language (XPointer), and Uniform Resource Identifier (URI) values. The contents of the XML Query Algebra working draft, discussed in the following section, provide you with a sample of how the XML Query Data Model and the XML Query Algebra work together in your document.

XML Query Algebra

The XML Query Algebra working draft provides a formal basis for an XML query language. An XML Query Algebra expression is parsed and type-checked before the value of the expression is evaluated, and then, once the evaluation is complete, it is reduced to a value that can be displayed to the document viewer as the results of the query. This method of querying data is based on the long-standing traditions of the database community and has been particularly influenced by systems such as SQL.

When working with databases, most query languages are translated into an algebraic format. This is done for two reasons: First, an algebraic system is easy to provide rules and semantics for. Second, it is easy to define and test for rules governing the interactions of algebraic mathematics in a way that is difficult to do for text-based requests. The algebraic math used with XML Queries captures the semantics of several XML query languages, including XML-QL and XQL.

The XML Query language uses DTDs and XML Schemas in order to detect errors at the time the query is run and to support query optimization. Knowing the type of input values, the query applied to those values, and the expected type of the query's output value, the XML Query Algebra's type-system can detect at query runtime if the query's output value matches what is expected.

DTDs and XML Schemas provide types for XML. The XML Query Algebra uses a simple type-system based on XML Schema Part 1. XML Query Algebra is statically typed, or checked, against the output of a document after the schema has been applied. This saves you the time and difficulty involved in querying a document and validating the schema simultaneously. When attempting to validate and query simultaneously, there is no guarantee that the query will succeed.

The following sections introduce you to the primary features of XML Query Algebra, using examples based on accessing a database of contact records. All of these sections use the following example document as their source data:

```
<addressbook>
  <contact type="business" lastchecked="02/10/2005">
```

```
    <name> George Jones Sr. </name>
    <street> 1235 Nolichucky Drive </street>
    <suite-apt> Apt. 15 </suite-apt>
    <city> Houston </city>
    <state> TX </state>
    <zip> 07711 </zip>
    <phone> 555-555-1212 </phone>
    <fax> 555-555-1313 </fax>
    <email> gj@nolichucky.com</email>
  </contact>
  <contact type="personal" lastchecked="01/01/2005">
    <name> Jenny "Mug" Beer </name>
    <street> 4323 Natchitoches Lane</street>
    <city> Enterprise </city>
    <state> MS </state>
    <zip> 09988 </zip>
    <phone> 555-555-3131 </phone>
    <cell> 555-555-3939</cell>
    <email> mug@enterprise.com</email>
  </contact>
</addressbook>
```

The following XML Schema describes the contact records shown in the previous example code:

```
<xsd:schema>
  <xsd:element name="contact">
    <xsd:complexType>
      <xsd:sequence>
        <xsd:element name="name" type="xsd:string" />
        <xsd:element name="street" type="xsd:string" />
        <xsd:element name="suite_apt" type="xsd:string"
                     minOccurs="0" maxOccurs="unbounded"/>
        <xsd:element name="city" type="xsd:string" />
        <xsd:element name="state" type="xsd:string" />
        <xsd:element name="zip" type="xsd:string" />
        <xsd:element name="phone" type="xsd:string" />
        <xsd:element name="fax" type="xsd:string" />
        <xsd:element name="cell" type="xsd:string" />
        <xsd:element name="email" type="xsd:string" />
      </xsd:sequence>
```

```
        <xsd:attribute name="type" type="xsd:string" />
        <xsd:attribute name="lastchecked" type="xsd:date" />
      </xsd:complexType>
    </xsd:element>
    <xsd:element name="addressbook">
      <xsd:complexType>
        <xsd:group ref="contact"
                   minOccurs="0" maxOccurs="unbounded"/>
      </xsd:complexType>
    </xsd:element>
  </xsd:schema>
```

Note *There are many more forms of queries that can be created using the XML Query Algebra than are listed here. Let the queries in the following sections provide you a basic guide for future research. These example query statements may change as the XML Query Algebra working draft is expanded and finalized into a full W3C recommendation.*

Data and Types

The basic representation of data and types in XML Query Algebra is quite easy to follow. Each type represents a complex type in the Schema, where the individual data is represented as a value of an element designator. The following example shows the basic algebra for representing all of the data and types included in our `addressbook` example:

```
type addressbook=
  addressbook [ contact{0, *} ]
type contact =
  contact [
    @type    [ String ] &
    @lastchecked [ Date ],
    name     [ String ],
    street   [ String ],
    suite_apt [ String ] {0,1),
    city     [ String ],
    state    [ String ],
    zip      [ String ],
    phone    [ String ],
    fax      [ String ] {0,1),
    cell     [ String ] {0,1),
    email    [ String ] {0,*),
  ]
```

```
let address0 : addressbook =
addressbook [
    contact [
      @type [ "business" ],
      @lastchecked [ 02/10/2005 ],
      name  [ "George Jones Sr." ],
      street [ "1235 Nolichucky Drive" ],
      suite-apt  [ "Apt. 15" ],
      city [ "Houston" ],
      state [ "TX" ],
      zip [ "07711" ]
      phone [ "555-555-1212" ],
      fax [ "555-555-1313" ],
      email [ "gj@nolichucky.com" ]
    ],
    contact [
      @type [ "personal" ],
      @lastchecked [ 01/01/2005 ],
      name  [ "Jenny 'Mug' Beer" ],
      street [ "4323 Natchitoches Lane" ],
      city [ "Enterprise" ],
      state [ "MS" ],
      zip [ "09988" ]
      phone [ "555-555-3131" ],
      cell [ "555-555-3939" ],
      email [ "mug@enterprise.com" ]          ]
  ]
```

The preceding expression defines two types, `addressbook` and `contact`, and defines one global variable, `address0`.

The `addressbook` type corresponds to a single addressbook element, which contains a *forest* of zero or more `contact` elements. *Forest* is the term used by the creators of the XML Query specification to represent a selection of zero or more attributes and elements associated with a type. The `contact` type corresponds to a single `contact` element, which also contains a forest of zero or more attributes and elements. From the algebra, you can tell that the contact type contains two attributes, `type` and `lastchecked`, which can occur in any order, as noted by the *interleave operator* (&) occurring between the two attributes names, which are identified by their preceding at (@) symbol. The `type` attribute contains a `String`, while the `lastchecked` attribute contains `Date` type information. The `contact` type contains one `name`, `address`, `city`, `state`, `zip`, and `phone` element, and these are interspersed with either zero or one `suite-apt`, `fax`, and `cell` elements—all of which are followed by one or more email elements. All of the elements in the example will contain string values as noted by the [String] identifier in the algebra.

The let expression in the previous algebra example statement binds the variable address0 to a literal XML value, which is the data model representation of the XML document. The variable address0 is a global variable that allows the data model of the XML document to appear in any other expression in the query. A global variable is defined once and cannot be defined again without an error resulting. XML Query Algebra also provides a let expression for binding local variables. The value of both global and local variables cannot be changed once their value is defined. In the previous example, the value of address0 is an addressbook element that contains two contact elements, and the value of address0 cannot be modified.

There are multitudes of ways that you can define the information in your XML document, breaking it down into global and local variables that can be then accessed by other Queries. For more information on creating global and local variables using XML Query Algebra on your XML document, read the XML Query Algebra working draft located at http://www.w3.org/TR/query-algebra.

Projection

One of the most basic operations of the XML Query Algebra is *projection*. Projection simply finds the XML document entries that match the information being looked for in the query statement. XML Query Algebra uses a notation similar in syntax and meaning to path navigation in XML Path Language (XPath). The following expression returns all name elements contained in name elements contained in address0:

```
address0/contact/name
```

The preceding code creates the following results:

```
name [ "George Jones Sr." ],
name [ "Jenny 'Mug' Beer" ],
```

The following is the type of expression that supports the findings of the projection:

```
:   name [ String ] {0,*}
```

Atomic Data

You can access atomic data (strings, integers, or Boolean values) using the data() function. In the following example, all of the contact names, rather than the contact elements, are selected:

```
address0/contact/name/data()
```

The preceding code creates the following results:

```
"George Jones Sr."
"Jenny 'Mug' Beer"
```

The following is the type of expression that supports the findings of the projection:

```
String {1,*}
```

Iteration

An iteration allows you to select elements in a document and transform them into newly formatted information. In this example, each contact entry is processed and lists just the `name` and `email` address, ignoring all of the other content of the `contact` record:

```
for c in address0/contact do
contact [ c/name, c/email ]
```

The preceding code creates the following results:

```
contact [
      name [ "George Jones Sr." ],
      email [ "gj@nolichucky.com" ],
    ],
    contact [
      name [ "Jenny 'Mug' Beer" ],
      email  [ "mug@enterprise.com" ]
    ]
```

The following is the type of expression that supports the findings of the projection:

```
contact [
      name[ String ]{1, *},
      email[ String ]
]{0, *}
```

The `for` expression iterates over all `contact` elements in `address0` and binds the variable `c` to each such element. For each element bound to `c`, the inner expression constructs a new contact element containing only the `contact`'s `name` followed by their `email` address. The transformed elements appear in the same order as they occur in `address0`.

Selection

You can also use XML Query Algebra to select elements based upon their values. The following example selects all the `contact` elements in `address0` that have a `lastchecked` date prior to `02/01/2005`:

```
for c in address0/contact do
  where c/@lastchecked/data() <= 02/01/2005 do
   c
```

The preceding code creates the following results:

```
contact [
      @lastchecked [ 01/01/2005 ],
```

```
            email [ "gj@nolichucky.com" ],
            name  [ "Jenny 'Mug' Beer" ],
            street [ "4323 Natchitoches Lane" ],
            city [ "Enterprise" ],
            state [ "MS" ],
            zip [ "09988" ]
            phone [ "555-555-3131" ],
            cell [ "555-555-3939" ],
            email [ "mug@enterprise.com" ]
      ]
```

The following is the type of expression that supports the findings of the projection:

```
contact {0, *}
```

In general, the expression "`where c/@lastchecked/data() <= 02/01/2005 do c`" follows the basic format:

```
where exp1 do exp2
```

is converted to the form

```
if exp1 then exp2 else ()
```

where *exp1* and *exp2* are expressions.

In the `if-then-else` statement, () is an expression representing the empty sequence: a forest that contains no attributes or elements. We also write () for the type of the empty sequence. According to this example, the expression in the preceding example translates to

```
for c in address0/contact do
  if c/@lastchecked/data() <= 02/01/2005 then c else ()
```

and has the same value and type as the example preceding this latest expression.

Quantification

Quantification allows your Query to find only the records that have specific content. For instance, the following expression selects all `contact` elements in `address0` for a `contact` named "`George Jones Sr.`":

```
for c in address0/contact do
  for a in c/name/data() do
    where a = "George Jones Sr." do
      c
```

The preceding code creates the following results:

```
contact [
        @type [ "business" ],
        @lastchecked [ 02/10/2005 ],
        name  [ "George Jones Sr." ],
```

```
        street [ "1235 Nolichucky Drive" ],
        suite-apt  [ "Apt. 15" ],
        city [ "Houston" ],
        state [ "TX" ],
        zip [ "07711" ]
        phone [ "555-555-1212" ],
        fax [ "555-555-1313" ],
        email [ "gj@nolichucky.com" ]
      ]
```

The following is the type of expression that supports the findings of the projection:

```
contact{0, *}
```

Join

When you need to combine, or join, values from multiple documents, you use the algebra shown in the following example. This will allow you to collect all of the information about a specific person. For instance, in the following example, a join is formed between our contact records and those individuals project records. The project record document is not shown here:

```
for c in address0/contact do
  for p in project0/contact do
    where c/name/data() = p/name/data() do
      contact [ c/name, c/email, p/projecttitle ]
```

The preceding code creates a joining of the following information:

```
contact [
  name  [ "George Jones Sr." ],
  email [ "gj@nolichucky.com" ],
  projecttitle [ "WebRavin Web Site." ]
],
contact [
  name  [ "Jenny 'Mug' Beer" ],
  email [ "mug@enterprise.com" ],
  projecttitle [ "WagonBoss.Net Web Site" ]
]
```

The following type of expression supports the results of this query:

```
contact [
      name [ String ],
      email [ String ] {0, *},
      projecttitle [ String ]
      ] {0, *}
```

Sorting

One of the most common jobs for a query is the sorting of information in a document. The following expression sorts all of the `contact` records in `address0` and sorts them by `city`:

```
sort c in address0/contact by c/city
```

The preceding code creates the following results:

```
contact [
      @lastchecked [ 01/01/2005 ],
      email [ "gj@nolichucky.com" ],
      name  [ "Jenny 'Mug' Beer" ],
      street [ "4323 Natchitoches Lane" ],
      city [ "Enterprise" ],
      state [ "MS" ],
      zip [ "09988" ]
      phone [ "555-555-3131" ],
      cell [ "555-555-3939" ],
      email [ "mug@enterprise.com" ]
],
contact [
          @type [ "business" ],
          @lastchecked [ 02/10/2005 ],
          name  [ "George Jones Sr." ],
          street [ "1235 Nolichucky Drive" ],
          suite-apt  [ "Apt. 15" ],
          city [ "Houston" ],
          state [ "TX" ],
          zip [ "07711" ]
          phone [ "555-555-1212" ],
          fax [ "555-555-1313" ],
          email [ "gj@nolichucky.com" ]
        ]
```

Utilizing XML Query

Taking into account the following algebra examples, it would be nice to see how XML Query will actually be implemented. Using the same document which served as the foundation for the previous XML Algebra examples, shown next, you will see how different query statements can work with that information.

```
<addressbook>
  <contact type="business" lastchecked="02/10/2005">
```

```
        <name> George Jones Sr. </name>
        <street> 1235 Nolichucky Drive </street>
        <suite-apt> Apt. 15 </suite-apt>
        <city> Houston </city>
        <state> TX </state>
        <zip> 07711 </zip>
        <phone> 555-555-1212 </phone>
        <fax> 555-555-1313 </fax>
        <email> gj@nolichucky.com</email>
    </contact>
    <contact type="personal" lastchecked="01/01/2005">
        <name> Jenny "Mug" Beer </name>
        <street> 4323 Natchitoches Lane</street>
        <city> Enterprise </city>
        <state> MS </state>
        <zip> 09988 </zip>
        <phone> 555-555-3131 </phone>
        <cell> 555-555-3939 </cell>
        <email> mug@enterprise.com</email>
    </contact>
</addressbook>
```

An Algebra statement that finds all of the business contact entries would appear as follows:

```
<addressbook>
   FOR $b IN
document("http://www.myexample.com")/addressbook/contact
   WHERE $b/@type = "business"
   RETURN
      <contact type = $b/@type>
         $b/name
      </contact>
</addressbook>
```

This would give you the following results:

```
<addressbook>
    <contact type="business">
        <name> George Jones Sr. </name>
```

```
    </contact>
</addressbook>
```

If you wanted to find all of the `contacts` in the document and return the `contact` name and `email` address, you would find them using the following XQuery statement:

```
<results>
   FOR $b IN
document("http://www.myexample.com")/addressbook/contact
   RETURN
      <result>
         $b/name,
         $b/email
      </result>
</results>
```

This would give you the following results:

```
<results>
    <result>
        <name> George Jones Sr.</name>
        <email> gj@nolichucky.com </email>
    </result>

    <result>
        <name> Jenny "Mug" Beer </name>
        <email>mug@enterprise.com</email>
    </result>
</results>
```

There are many other options and queries that can be created with XQuery, but due to the instability of the current working drafts, you will need to check the W3C Web site at http://www.w3.org/TR/XQuery for more up-to-date information.

Summary

The XML Query Working Group has three goals: to produce a data model for XML documents, to produce a set of query operators on that data model, and to produce a query language based on these query operators. XML Queries work with a single document or with a fixed collection of documents. The primary function of a query is to select either a whole or subtree of a document, based upon the content and structure of that document.

The XML Query Data Model working draft, based on the XML Information Set, provides a formal definition for types of information and data that can be accessed using the XML Query language. The XML Query Data Model working draft provides a precise and formal definition of how values in the XML Query Data Model are constructed and accessed, while providing the foundation of the XML Query Algebra.

The XML Query Algebra provides a formal basis for an XML query language. The XML Query language uses the DTDs and Schemas to detect errors at the time the query is run and to support query optimization. XML Query Algebra supports all of the primary types of queries that can be performed in traditional SQL systems, including sorting, quantifying data, and joining data.

In Chapter 23, you will learn about the XML Linking Language (XLink) and its use in linking together resources from multiple XML documents and resources.

Chapter 23

XLinks

The XML Linking Language (XLink) allows XML elements to be created that describe traversable relationships between documents, images, and files on the Internet or other networks. The XLink standard, developed by the World Wide Web Consortium (W3C) and a proposed recommendation in December 2000, provides a framework for creating both basic unidirectional links and more complex linking structures. XLink allows XML documents to

- Create a relationship of links between multiple documents
- Add information about the link (metadata) to a link
- Create and describe links to documents in a myriad of locations

The development process of XLink has been primarily focused toward the development of a vast system of interconnected documents using hyperlinks such as the Hypertext Markup Language (HTML) `<a>` element. The `<a>` element in HTML is essentially a unidirectional link, allowing you to traverse from one document to another in one direction. XLink expands on this model by creating a linking system that is more flexible and more capable of being scaled to work with complex data structures, alternative linking mechanisms, and potentially, a variety of different rendering effects. The XLink recommendation is just the first step in creating a fully functional hypermedia system that will allow for the linking of not only text and images, as is done currently in HTML, but also for will create timing-based links within videos, and other types of media with their own intrinsic time.

Understanding XLink

XLink has one job: to create and define relationships between documents and other resources on the Internet through a system of hypertext links. The XLink specification, available from the W3C at http://www.w3.org/TR/xlink, uses XML syntax to create sets of instructions that describe links between resources. XLinks can be used to define every type of link from a simple `<a>` link within an HTML document to a more sophisticated link allowing you to select between different documents, based upon everything from language support in your XML browsing software to the current playing time of a video file.

The XLink specification defines specific relationships between various complete resources or portions of those resources. Think for a moment of the `<area>` element in HTML. It provides links from a portion of an image to another document or to a specific point within either the current document or another document. XLink takes this process one step farther.

XLink's entire linking system is based upon the concept of resources. Resources are obviously not new to the Web, since we have always had resources in the case of HTML documents, images, video files, audio files, programs, and automatically generated database query results. XLink takes a slightly different perspective on the concept of resources though. As far as the XLink specification is concerned, a resource is any item, whether a full document or part of one, that can be referenced by a Uniform Resource Identifier (URI). You can already link to complete resources with HTML documents, but, until now, you haven't been able to link to portions of other types of objects. For example, if you link to a point in a document, you would most likely have that document scrolled down to the point you selected. If you linked to a point in a video, you would be able to force the video to start playing at the point that you selected.

In addition to being able to link to specific areas in a document or points inside of some type of continuous media, you can also provide a series of resources for a link to consider. Although XLinks are forced to appear within an XML document, they don't have to just refer to objects or files that can be used in that XML document. They don't even have to appear on an actual written document. They can be the results of a database query, simply existing for that instant in the memory of a computer.

XLink brings with it the introduction of some new vocabulary: *traversal*, *arc*, and *behavior*. A traversal is any interaction with a link. Even though you can provide any number of resources within a link, you can only traverse between two at a time. The nature of a link is that you can only go from one location to another; XLink just provides you more options than HTML links do for selecting your destination. An arc defines the link that you are traversing. The arc is the information that lets you know how you are traveling from your source to your destination and how the software will interact with the link as it is being traversed. The software that is viewing your XML document governs the behavior of a link. You can have a link that simply clicks directly over to the new document or one that causes a fade-in transition to take place.

The XLink specification uses six different components to define and describe a link between resources in an XML document. Of these six, only two do the linking; the rest are auxiliary elements that define the link in more detail. All of the syntax for working with XLink is discussed in the following section.

XLink Syntax

XLink, like all other constructs in XML, has a rigid format and structure that must be supplied to the markup language used to create the links. The markup of XLink is important, not only for clarity between applications, but for cross-applications support. At this point Internet Explorer 5.5, Netscape Navigator 6, and most other Web-based browsers support the new XLink specification. In order to be able to test XLink properly, you have to have an XML application that properly recognizes and reliably handles the XLink markup. At this point the XLink specification uses XML Namespaces, discussed in Chapter 7, as its mechanism for integrating XLink into current XML documents.

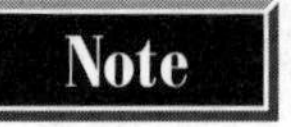

You can find a copy of the XLink namespace definition at http:/www.w3.org/1999/xlink. This specification might not be used in the future as the XLink specification and XML continue to expand and grow.

The XLink Namespace

The XML Namespace specification controls how declarations of other standardized documents or document-defining elements and attributes used within an XML document must be referenced. It does the same for the use of XLink elements and attributes. For example, the following XML Namespace declaration assigns a prefix `xlink` to the XLink namespace definition and makes it available to all attributes and elements found within the `PROJECT` element:

```
<PROJECT
 xmlns:xlink="http://www.w3.org/1999/xlink">
</PROJECT>
```

The `xlink` prefix, although by no means a requirement, is the standard method of referring to the XLink namespace in XML documents. Because this convention is adopted by the W3C and all of its member organizations, you should use it also. It not only helps applications identify `xlink` attributes, it also makes the link more readable for humans.

XLink defines global attributes that are used to create XLinks. These attributes include

- **type** Specifies the type of link to be created
- **href** Specifies the address (URI) of the link destination
- **role** Specifies the type of resource that defines the destination of this link
- **arcrole** Specifies the type resource that defines the source of the link
- **title** Describes the meaning of a link
- **show** Specifies how the destination resource should be displayed
- **actuate** Specifies when the link should be traversed
- **label** Specifies an identifiable name for the link

- **from** References a label of a link to use as a reference point in the traversal of the current link
- **to** References a label of a link to use as a destination reference point in the traversal of the current link

These attributes are used to convert your document's XML elements into links based upon the XLink Namespace. The following example uses a simple CONTACTLIST element and converts it into a link to an XML document containing what you expect to be a list of people associated with the current project:

```
<CONTACTLIST
  xmlns:xlink="http://www.w3.org/1999/xlink"
  xlink:type="simple"
  xlink:href="contacts.xml"
  xlink:role="developerlist"
  xlink:title="Developer List"
  xlink:show="new"
  xlink:actuate="onRequest">
List of Project Developers
</CONTACTLIST>
```

Note *You must use namespace prefixes on global attributes.*

The XLink Attributes

XLink uses a variety of attributes to create links that are embedded within your existing XML elements. These attributes are used to create one of the two different types of links offered by the XLink specification:

- **Extended links** Offers the full range of functionality that has been designed into the XLink specification. This functionality includes in- and outbound arcs, and links with multiple resources. These are the most complex types of links to create and will often contain instructions for local resources, traversal-rules, and human-readable information about the link.
- **Simple links** Offers a shorthand syntax for creating the most common kind of links: those that you see in HTML documents and that are a single outbound link with only two resources—the source document and the link destination.

Simple links are essentially a subset of the features provided with extended links, but they also differ in their syntax as you will see in the following discussions about XLink attributes.

The `type` Attribute

The primary attribute used with XLink is `type`. This attribute provides the foundation upon which all other attribute values are interpreted and defines the type of link element being created.

Note *There is some confusion here between* elements *and* attributes *when discussing XLink elements. You create XLink link types and attribute relationships to an XLink element by applying a* `type` *attribute to your existing XML elements.* `type` *specifies the kind of link to be created out of this particular XML element. The link is created by simply having XLink attributes associated with it.*

Although XLink attributes are considered global when used with the XLink namespace, they can only appear in a specific combination, depending upon the value of the `type` attribute. The `type` attribute has seven available values:

- Simple
- Locator
- Resource
- None
- Extended
- Arc
- Title

Each of these types of links works with the other XLink attributes to create and define the XML link element you are creating. Table 23-1 shows each type of link element, and it tells you the attributes that they can be used with and whether those attributes are optional, required, or not used.

Note *If* `type="none"` *the element does not serve as a link between documents, and the values of other XLink attributes will be ignored.*

The following example applies the `xlink:type` attribute to a `CONTACT` element in a Document Type Definition (DTD). This `ATTLIST` statement forces this element to always serve as a simple link element:

```
<!ATTLIST CONTACT
  xlink:type  (simple)  #REQUIRED
  ...>
```

Link Type	Required Attributes	Optional Attributes	Not Used
Simple	type	actuate arcrole href role title show	from label title to
Extended	type	role title	actuate arcrole from href label show to
Locator	type href	label role title	actuate arcrole from show to
Arc	type	actuate arcrole from role show title to	href label
Resource	type	label role title	actuate arcrole from href show to
Title	type	role	actuate arcrole from href label show to

Table 23-1. *XLink Link Type and Attribute Relationships*

The href Attribute

The href attribute supplies the URL of the destination resource of the links, just as it does in HTML links. The URI specified in this attribute can be either a relative or absolute address referencing either a remote or local resource. If the value of href is empty (""), then it is assumed to reference the resource that the href element currently exists within.

When specifying the URI for your link, you need to be aware that non-ASCII characters are not allowed in the URL address.

The following DTD example applies an IMPLIED xlink:href attribute to the CONTACT element previously described:

```
<!ATTLIST CONTACT
  xlink:type  (simple) #REQUIRED
  xlink:href   CDATA   #IMPLIED
  ...>
```

The role, arcrole, and title Attributes

The role, arcrole, and title attributes are used to define the meaning of the various resources that are part of the linking process. Both the role and arcrole attributes contain URI values that reference a resource that can be used to describe the sources associated in the link. The title attribute simply describes the link resource in terms that are readable by humans. The use of the title attribute is dependent upon the type of work that is being performed. In some software applications, the information is used to provide information about the links to visually impaired users, to create a table of links, or to provide help-styled text to users of your XML documents.

The following sample provides a look at the DTD statements used to add the XLink role and title attributes to a simple linking element:

```
<!ATTLIST CONTACT
  xlink:type  (simple) #REQUIRED
  xlink:href   CDATA   #IMPLIED
  xlink:role   CDATA   #IMPLIED
  xlink:title  CDATA   #IMPLIED
  ...>
```

The arcrole attribute is used primarily with the arc type link. The following example creates the DTD statements that create an arc link in your XML document:

```
<!ATTLIST CONTACT
  xlink:type  (arc) #REQUIRED
  xlink:href   CDATA   #IMPLIED
  xlink:arcrole   CDATA             #IMPLIED
```

```
   xlink:title      CDATA              #IMPLIED
   ...>
```

The `show` and `actuate` Attributes

The `show` and `actuate` attributes control the behavior of your links. These attributes are only used with the `simple` and `arc` elements, as shown in Table 23-1. When they are used with a `simple` link, they control the behavior associated with the traversal of the link to its destination. When used with an `arc` element they control the behaviors associated with whichever local or remote ending resource. Although neither of the `show` or `actuate` attributes is required for any link, they should be properly interpreted and acted upon when they are used.

The `show` attribute is in charge of identifying where the destination resource should appear. The `show` attribute can have the following values:

- **`new`** This value loads the destination resource in a new window, frame, pane, or other presentation area.
- **`replace`** This value loads the resource in the source resource's window, frame, pane, or other presentation area.
- **`embed`** This value loads the ending resource in place of the source resource, such as what happens with an image loading in place of an `<img>` HTML element.
- **`other`** Although the current XLink specification provides no set behavior for this value, the XML application should look for application specific instructions for navigating the link.
- **`none`** This value has no specified behavior as far as the XLink specification is concerned, but it does restrict the XML application from looking for other markup to determine a behavior for the link.

The function of the `actuate` attribute is to control the timing associated with the traversal of the link. The `actuate` attribute can have the following values:

- **`onLoad`** The link is traveled as soon as the document containing the source resource is loaded, a process similar to what happens with images in HTML documents in which the image is immediately loaded in place of the `<img>` tag.
- **`onRequest`** The link should be traveled only when a request is made. For instance, a link will be traveled when a user clicks a mouse or when a program within the XML document requests that the link be activated.
- **`other`** This value forces the XML application to interpret the behavior of the link based upon application-specific information embedded within the document.
- **`none`** This value forces the XML application to ignore not only this link, but any other elements that attempt to affect the behavior of the link.

- The following DTD example shows the description of the `xlink:show` and `xlink:actuate` attributes as they are applied to a simple link element:

```
<!ATTLIST CONTACT
  xlink:type   (simple) #REQUIRED
  xlink:href    CDATA   #IMPLIED
  xlink:show    (new|replace|embed|other|none)  #IMPLIED
  xlink:actuate (onLoad|onRequest|other|none)   #IMPLIED
  ...>
```

XML applications containing `arc` elements with behavior attributes must treat those attributes with the values `show="none"` and `actuate="onLoad"`, no matter what other attribute values were specified.

The `label`, `from`, and `to` Attributes

The `label`, `from`, and `to` attributes provide information defining the traversal to take place within the link. The `label` attribute is used to define the name of either a `locator` or a `resource` link. The `from` and `to` attributes are used with `arc` links to identify the `locator` and `resource` label associated with that link, as they are used within the `extended`-type link elements.

The following DTD example shows the description of the `xlink:label` as it is applied to a locator link element:

```
<!ATTLIST CONTACT
  xlink:type   (locator) #REQUIRED
  xlink:href    CDATA    #IMPLIED
  xlink:label   CDATA    #IMPLIED
  ...>
```

Types of Links

There are two types of links that can be created using an XLink: `simple` and `extended.` `simple` links provide shorthand syntax for creating the common types of links, such as you see in HTML documents. `extended` links provide complex linking relationships among multiple resources including both inbound and outbound arcs.

The following information defines the various types of links that are available with the XLink specificatoin.

`simple` Links

`simple` links associate just two resources: the local source and the destination resource. `simple` links are always outbound, in other words, they always point out from the current link location to another location. `simple` links combine the basic functions of `extended`, `locator`, `arc`, and `resource` link elements, performing all of the tasks of these types of links in one step.

Take the following example XML document, which uses a simple link to connect the name of a contact with its actual record document:

```
<CONTACT xlink:href="jim.xml"> Jim Hall Jr. </CONTACT>
```

This same link, if expanded to an extended link, could include all of the following information:

```
<CONTACT xlink:type="extended">
  <resource xlink:type="resource"
    xlink:label="local">Jim Hall Jr.</resource>
<locator xlink:type="locator"
    xlink:href="jim.xml"
    xlink:label="remote"
    xlink:role="..." />
    xlink:title="..."
  <go xlink:type="arc"
    xlink:from="local"
    xlink:to="remote"
    xlink:arcrole="..."
    xlink:show="..."
    xlink:actuate="..." />
</CONTACT>
```

The simple link element uses the locator link elements href, role, and title attributes, and the show, arcrole, and actuate attributes from the arc link element in order to create a simple link with only one required attribute, href, which specifies the destination resource of the link.

The simple link combines most of the above extended links features into one single step. The only features missing from a simple links are

- Multiple local and remote resources
- Creation of a link from the remote resource to the local resource
- Addition of a title associated with the link and its individual arcs

simple link elements may also have any type of content you wish, whether it is text, an image, or a portion of a video. The code creating the link and all of the content of the link are referred to globally as the link. You can also use simple links without content, although this is typically only useful if there is a script or other program that will activate the link without user interaction directly with the link.

Note simple *link elements do not have to have an* href *attribute value. The lack of an* href *attribute prohibits the link from being traversed, but can be useful as a means of providing a label or resource name with the links contents.*

The following is a sample DTD declaration that can be added to your existing XML document in order to turn a CONTACT element into a simple link:

```
<!ELEMENT CONTACT ANY>
<!ATTLIST  CONTACT
  xlink:type    (simple)  #FIXED "simple"
  xlink:href    CDATA     #IMPLIED
  xlink:role    NMTOKEN   #FIXED "http://www.mylist.com/contacts"
  xlink:arcrole    CDATA  #IMPLIED
  xlink:title      CDATA  #IMPLIED
  xlink:show       (new|replace|embed|other|none)  #IMPLIED
  xlink:actuate    (onLoad|onRequest|other|none)   #IMPLIED>
```

If you wish to use a CONTACT link with the previous DTD definition, it could be used in your XML document in a manner similar to the following:

```
... The project manager for your new web site will be <CONTACT
xlink:href="jim.xml"> Jim Hall Jr. </CONTACT> who will be
assisted by...
```

extended Links

extended links provide the only way to associate an arbitrary number of resources together in any combination of local and remote associations. Although most situations will find the old standby simple link sufficient, when you are developing documents and applications that use multimedia resources, you will often need more advanced ways of associating your information. This is where extended links shine.

extended links are a combination of locator, arc, title, and resource links. Each of these other types of links are embedded within a parent element or has been designated as an extended link, as shown in the following example:

```
 <CONTACT xlink:type="extended">
  <resource xlink:type="resource"
    xlink:label="local">Jim Hall Jr.</resource>
<locator xlink:type="locator"
    xlink:href="jim.xml"
    xlink:label="remote"
    xlink:role="..." />
    xlink:title="..."
  <go xlink:type="arc"
    xlink:from="local"
    xlink:to="remote"
    xlink:arcrole="..."
    xlink:show="..."
    xlink:actuate="..." />
</CONTACT>
```

Using `extended` links, you can create an association between resources with information in multiple documents, where even their reference links are located in multiple documents. Without using the ability of XLink `extended` links, the resources would appear, and typically be used, as completely unrelated information. By using a set of `locator` and `arc` rules, links on one page can direct the activity of links on other resources. The content of an `extended` element can contain any of the following:

- `locator` link elements for addressing the remote resources participating in the link
- `arc` link elements providing traversal rules for the link's resources
- `title` link elements providing human-readable link labels
- `resource` link elements supplying local resources that are part of the link

`extended` links can associate with no resources, one resource, or as many resources as is applicable in the situation. If the link is associated with less than two resources, the link simply becomes untraversable. Links with fewer than two resources allow you to associate link-related properties with a single resource, or provide placeholders for information to be used by links later.

Note `locator`, `arc`, *or* `resource` *link elements that are not direct children of an extended link element have no XLink-specified relationship to the parent link, and therefore, they can not be used to complete a linking action.*

The following code shows a sample DTD that defines an `extended` element, `CONTACT`, of which there were three parts, a `locator link`, `title link`, and `arc link`. Be aware that `type` attribute, as well as others, are provided with default values in the DTD in order to highlight the attributes that are changing on a per-instance basis:

```
<!ELEMENT CONTACT ((EMAIL|NAME|IMAGE)*)>
<!ATTLIST CONTACT
  xmlns:xlink      CDATA      #FIXED "http://www.w3.org/1999/xlink"
  xlink:type       (extended) #FIXED "extended"
  xlink:role       CDATA      #IMPLIED
  xlink:title      CDATA      #IMPLIED>

<!ELEMENT NAME ANY>
<!ATTLIST NAME
  xlink:type       (title)    #FIXED "title"
  xml:lang         CDATA      #IMPLIED>

<!ELEMENT EMAIL EMPTY>
<!ATTLIST EMAIL
  xlink:type       (locator)  #FIXED "locator"
  xlink:href       CDATA      #REQUIRED
```

```
  xlink:role      CDATA       #IMPLIED
  xlink:title     CDATA       #IMPLIED
  xlink:label     NMTOKEN     #IMPLIED>

<!ELEMENT IMAGE EMPTY>
<!ATTLIST IMAGE
  xlink:type      (arc)     #FIXED "arc"
  xlink:arcrole   CDATA     #IMPLIED
  xlink:title     CDATA     #IMPLIED
  xlink:show      (new|replace|embed|other|none)  #IMPLIED
  xlink:actuate   (onLoad|onRequest|other|none)   #IMPLIED
  xlink:from      NMTOKEN  #IMPLIED
  xlink:to        NMTOKEN  #IMPLIED>
```

The following is how XML elements using these declarations might look, since you can adjust your links, and the attributes used to describe them in any way you wish:

```
<CONTACT xlink:title="Course Load for Pat Jones">
  <NAME
    xlink:href="contacts/jimhall.xml"
    xlink:label="jimhall"
    xlink:role="http://www.mysite.com/contacts"
    xlink:title="Jim Hall" />
  <EMAIL
    xlink:href="mailto:jimhall@mysite.com"
    xlink:label="jimemail"
    xlink:title="Jim Email" />
  <!-- more remote resources for other contacts -->
<IMAGE
    xlink:from="jimhall"
    xlink:to="jimhallpic"
    xlink:show="new"
    xlink:actuate="onLoad"
    xlink:title="Jim Hall Mug Shot" />
</CONTACT>
```

`locator` Links

`locator` links are used by extended links to provide the addresses for remote resources that the extended link will be linking to. You can create `locator` elements out of an XML element, as long as that element has an `xlink:type="locator"` attribute associated with it. `locator` elements can contain their own content, which can be any type of text or image that you, the XML developer, wish to use; you have to be sure to also associate an `xlink:href` attribute with the locator element. In this instance `href` can't be blank, as it could with a simple link. Inside of a `locator` link element, you must provide an address for the remote resource.

`locator` link elements must be contained within extended link elements if they are to be treated as links. Just because they may have an `href` attribute does not mean that there is a linking association being made, which does happen in simple link elements.

The following statements are excerpts from a DTD that provide an `EMAIL` element as a `locator` element serving as part of the overall `CONTACT` extended element:

```
<!ELEMENT EMAIL EMPTY>
<!ATTLIST EMAIL
  xlink:type      (locator)       #FIXED "locator"
  xlink:href      CDATA           #REQUIRED
  xlink:role      CDATA           #IMPLIED
  xlink:title     CDATA           #IMPLIED
  xlink:label     NMTOKEN         #IMPLIED>
```

Here is now an XML element using this declaration might look:

```
<EMAIL   xlink:href="mailto:jimhall@mysite.com"
         xlink:label="jimhalljr"
         xlink:role="http://www.mysite.com/contacts"
         xlink:title="Jim Hall Jr." />
```

arc Links

`arc` links are used by extended links to set the rules used for traversing the link between the various resources. Although you can create an extended link without using the `arc` link elements, they do provide assistance when working with multiple resources and multiple link destinations.

The `arc` link element, just as both simple and extended links, can have content of any type, allowing you to work with images, videos, or text equally as easily. The `arc` link element uses the `from` and `to` attributes, discussed earlier in this chapter, to define the direction of the desired traversal between the different pairs of resources. The resources, previously identified by `label` values, which are a part of this link, use the `from` attribute identifying the link's starting point and the `to` attribute identifying the link's destination.

Multiple `arc` values are often used for a single link because a link can have a different relationship, depending upon the point of view from which the link is approached. For instance, think of your address book. Within your address book is your Uncle Floyd's address. From your standpoint he is your uncle during family outings, but when you are at work he is your boss. In other words, your two resources, you and Floyd, have a different relationship dependant upon the outlook of the source.

Note *Since a single resource can serve as a starting point for multiple arcs, the traversal of the link isn't governed by the XLink specification. It is conceivable, though, that the software viewing the XLink-enabled document could provide a pop-up menu of linking options from the link title attributes associated with that content.*

Using the following code as an example, it creates a link from a single destination to multiple locations:

```
<go xlink:type="arc" xlink:from="A" xlink:to="B" />
<go xlink:type="arc" xlink:from="A" xlink:to="C" />
```

This actual resource that is eventually loaded is not decided upon by the XLink specification, but by the XML software viewing the document.

Note *You can't duplicate an arc. In other words, you can't have an arc associated with the same extended element that has the same* `from` *and* `to` *values.*

The following DTD statements provide a sample of an `arc` link associated with an `IMAGE` element:

```
<!ELEMENT IMAGE EMPTY>
<!ATTLIST IMAGE
  xlink:type       (arc)              #FIXED "arc"
  xlink:arcrole    CDATA              #IMPLIED
  xlink:title      CDATA              #IMPLIED
  xlink:show       (new |replace|embed|other|none)     #IMPLIED
  xlink:actuate    (onLoad|onRequest|other|none)       #IMPLIED
  xlink:from       NMTOKEN            #IMPLIED
  xlink:to         NMTOKEN            #IMPLIED>
```

Here is how an XML element using the previous DTD declaration might look:

```
<IMAGE
    xlink:from="jimhall"
    xlink:to="jimhallpic"
    xlink:show="new"
    xlink:actuate="onLoad"
    xlink:title="Jim Hall Mug Shot" />
```

`resource` Links

`resource` links are used within extended links to identify the local resources used by the link. They may have no content, but they provide the addresses (URI) of the resources used within the link's traversal process.

The following DTD statement defines the attributes for the `RAISE` element, as they would be stated to create a `resource` link:

```
<!ELEMENT RAISE ANY>
<!ATTLIST RAISE
 xlink:type     (resource)  #FIXED "resource"
  xlink:role    CDATA       #FIXED "http://www.mysite.com/raises
  xlink:title   CDATA       #IMPLIED
  xlink:label   NMTOKEN
```

You can see the previous DTD declaration at work in the following XML document statement:

```
<RAISE xlink:label="JimHallRaise">3.5%</RAISE>
```

`title` Links

`extended`, `locator`, and `arc` linking elements may use the `title` attribute, but they may also use a series of one or more `title` link elements. These elements provide a human-readable label providing further information about the linking element. Title links are often used to provide information for internationalization and localization of your XML documents.

The following example DTD statements describe a `title` linking element:

```
<!ELEMENT NAME (PCDATA)>
<!ATTLIST NAME
  xlink:type   (title)   #FIXED "title"
  xml:lang     CDATA     #IMPLIED>

Following is how XML elements using these declarations might look.
<CONTACT xlink:href="contacts/jimhall.xml" ...>
    <NAME xml:lang="en">Jim Hall Jr. </NAME>
</CONTACT>
```

A Glance at XBase

XLink defines XML 1.0 constructs to describe links between resources. One of the stated requirements of XLink is to support HTML 4.01 linking constructs in a generic way, as is done in HTML files with the `<base>` element. The XLink Working Group has delved into the development of an `xml:base` attribute, which is defined in detail in the XML Base (XBase) specification. You can find more on this specification at http://www.w3.org/TR/2000/CR-xmlbase-20000908/.

The XBase specification allows authors to explicitly specify a document's base URI for the purpose of resolving relative URIs found in links to external resources, such as images, applets, form-processing programs, style sheets, and others. Because XBase is being developed concurrently with the XLink attribute, any programs that support

XLink will also support XBase. The only additional attribute not covered in the XLink specification is the `xml:base` attribute itself.

The `xml:base` attribute is primarily used to specify a base URI other than the base URI of the XML document, or external entity, itself. This attribute must be a standard URI reference including the protocol used to reference the type of connection to make to the document (`http:`, `ftp:`, `mailto:`); the name of the computer containing the files (`www.mysite.com`); and the location and specific name of the resource (`/contacts/myfile.xml`).

Note *Although `xml:base` is more obviously recognized and interpreted by XML namespace aware applications, XBase can be still used by non-namespace-aware processors. For more information on XML Namespaces, see Chapter 7.*

An example of `xml:base` follows. XLink often references XBase for interpretation of relative URI references in `xlink:href` attributes:

```
<?xml version="1.0"?>
<PROJECT xml:base="http://mysite.com/projects/"
       xmlns:xlink="http://www.w3.org/1999/xlink">
  <CONTACT>
    <NAME>Developer:
      <link xlink:type="simple" xlink:href="jhall.xml">Jim Hall</link>
    </NAME>
    <LIST xml:base="/JHall/">
      <EMAIL> Email Address:
        <link xlink:type="simple" xlink:href="mailto:jhall@mysite.com">
        jhall@mysite.com</link>
      </EMAIL>
      <WEB> Web Address:
        <link xlink:type="simple"
              xlink:href="http://mysite.com/contacts/jhall.htm">
        mysite.com/contacts/jhall.htm </link>
      </WEB>
    </LIST>
  </CONTACT>
</PROJECT>
```

Summary

This chapter expresses the current status of the XLink specification and its usage. There are many ways an XLink can be used to link to resources both locally and remotely using the URI of the destination resource. You can be kept apprised of the status of the XLink specification on the W3C's Web site located at http://www.w3.org/TR/xlink/.

XLink allows linking elements to be created within XML documents using your existing XML elements, to traverse the arc between the source and the destination resource. The XLink specification creates the framework for creating both basic one-directional links and more complex linking structures by allowing XML documents to

- Create a relationship of links between multiple documents
- Add information about the link (metadata) to a link
- Create and describe links to documents in a myriad of locations

With the development of the XLink specification, there is finally a way to create links from native XML documents without first using XSLT to tranform your XML document into an HTML document to be read by your typical HTML-based Web browser.

Chapter 24

Using XPointer

The XML Pointer Language (XPointer) allows you to identify fragments of XML documents, which can be used by any Uniform Resource Identifier (URI) reference to locate Internet media resource types such as text, images, or applications. XPointer can be used to identify the specific strings and content of a document, as well as provide links to that content from other locations and other documents.

Understanding XPointer

XPointer provides you with a way to identify portions of an XML document uniquely for linking purposes. The XPointer specification provides a mechanism for addressing XML documents based upon their internal structure, allowing for the examination of the hierarchical structures of XML documents while also allowing the choosing of its internal parts such as the elements, attribute values, character content, and relative position. In other words, XPointer allows you to reference a specific element in your XML document based upon the contents of that element. For instance, using XPointer, you can identify each of these following statements separately:

```
<NAME> Heather Williamson</NAME>
<NAME> Heather de Leon </NAME>
```

Once an object has been identified in a document that uses XPointer, that particular object can then be used as part of a link or for any other purpose that is supported by the application viewing the document. For instance, while a Web browser may use the XPointer simply as a destination for a link, an indexable value, or the key to starting some other type of software, an application may use the locations that have been identified by XPointer in any fashion it wishes. There are no constraints placed upon the application by the XPointer specification.

XPointer is layered on top of the XML Path Language (XPath). XPath is the primary method used for creating links and traversals in XSL Transformations (XSLT). You can find more discussion of XPath in Chapter 16. The XPointer extension to XPath allows it to

- Address points, ranges, and nodes
- Use string matching to locate information
- Use addressing expressions in URI references as identifiers of fragments

Now that you can see what XPointer is supposed to do, you are ready to find out how it accomplishes its task using a specific set of testing schemes and property syntax.

XPointer Schemes

XPointer uses a set of schemes to identify the format used to describe the information found within your XML document and, in turn, it identifies the type of information that is usable within your XPointer statements. The XPointer 1.0 specification identifies the schemes that can be used with XPointer syntax: `xpointer` and `xmlns`. In addition to identifying these schemes specifically, XPointer also reserves all other possibilities when you are working with a document identified as any one of the following MIME types: `text/xml`, `application/xml`, `text/xml-external-parsed-entity`, or `application/xml-external-parsed-entity`.

The default scheme to use with XPointer is `xpointer`. This scheme incorporates all of the options discussed in this chapter. It provides access to all of the elements, attributes, and contents of your document without regard to the type of document it is (in the examples in this chapter, we will use XPointer in reference to XML documents). The use of the `xmlns` scheme requires that you reference an XML Namespace that contains the instructions for using that particular document.

You can also create your own MIME type to reference personal files that will support XPointer. For instance if you want to define your own Dbase+xml media type, you can create and use an XPointer scheme that directly supports that media type in addition to the default `xpointer` scheme. No matter which route you choose to take, whether it is through the creation of a new media type, through the use of the `xmlns` identifier, or through the `xpointer` scheme, there are the minimal conformance requirements that must be met.

The minimal conformance requirements of XPointer follow many of the cascade-related standards you may already be familiar with from using Cascading Style Sheets (CSS) (discussed in Chapter 13). These are the minimal requirements:

- XPointer statements can identify multiple schemes with which the process can be evaluated.
- If an XPointer statement fails its evaluation for any reason from the scheme being unknown to it not referencing a proper resource document, the next XPointer statement will be evaluated.

Note *An XPointer statement that uses the* `xmlns` *scheme never returns a valid resource document and, thus, always fails. However, its evaluation has a potential effect on later XPointer statements. See Chapter 7 for more information on XML Namespaces.*

The following XPointer statement uses the `xpointer` scheme to find the specific element within your XML document that has an `ID` attribute with a value of `"haw"`:

```
xpointer(id("haw"))
```

If the XML document that uses the previous XPointer statement has a DTD that recognizes attributes of a specific `ID` attribute type, then this statement will work as it is. If the XML document does not have a Document Type Definition (DTD) to identify the types of each attribute used in the document, another statement will need to be added to this one as shown in the following example. The second statement does not look for an attribute of type `ID`, but it looks for an attribute with the name `id`.

```
xpointer(id("haw")) xpointer(//*[@id="haw"])
```

Although the second statement only approximates the first, it may be the exact approximation that you intended in the first place. An XPointer statement, such as this two-part evaluation, is first evaluated for the original `xpointer(id("haw"))` statement, and when or if that statement is found erroneous, the second half of the complete XPointer statement is evaluated, searching for an attribute with the name `id` and `value` "haw".

XPointer Syntax

XPointer uses a series of string instructions to identify the specific portions of a document it is working with. XPointer, like all other document description languages, has specific syntax rules that must be followed. These rules include

- An XPointer string must conform to the syntax requirements imposed by the specification. The specification does not require that a string actually point to a resource or subresource.
- XPointer strings work on a hierarchy of elements so that once you find your first selection from a pointer, you can make a second selection. For example, you can have XPointer first select all of the `<NAME>` elements and then from those select the element with the content `"heather"`.
- Application software must recognize `xpointer` statements that are suitably escaped and appear as the fragment identifier of a URI reference used to locate a resource with a media type such as `"text/xml"` or `"application/xml"`. It must also correctly interpret fragment identifiers.

XPointer addresses objects within your XML documents in one of three forms: full form, bare names, and child sequences. While both the bare names and the child sequences forms of XPointer statements are shorthand versions of the full form, your application does not need to convert your shorthand to the full form to be worked with. This in and of itself will save you time when developing complexly linked XML applications.

The Full Form

All XPointer statements have the same basic internal structure. This structure, shown in the following list, provides for the identification of the specific portion of the XML dataset being referenced:

- The sequence of child elements that the XPointer will be searching. For instance you can specify any `<NAME>` element that is one level down from the root of the document and differentiate it from <NAME> elements that are located five levels down from the root of the document.

- The scheme and test value that will be used to assist in the selection of your specified element. This can be based upon a string value, the value of an attribute, or the number of characters within a string from an identifiable point within the XML document.

The full form of an XPointer consists of one or more parts that are separated by an optional white space, as you saw previously in this chapter in the section titled "XPointer Schemes." XPointer Schemes start with a scheme name, by default `xpointer`, and are followed by an expression to be evaluated in parenthesis.

Note *To make your applications using XPointer compatible with future versions of the XPointer language, you should always use the full form for your pointers.*

The full form of XPointer statements requires that all of the parts of the statement be explicitly specified. For instance, a full-form XPointer statement would read as follows:

```
documentname#xpointer(task(childsequence || task_value))
```

By uniquely identifying all of the parts of the XPointer statement, your application will not be affected by changes in the XPointer language, and documents using full-form pointers will be more easily read by other types of applications. For instance the following `xpointer` statement uses a `string-range` type to identify a specific string of text, in this case `"clean house"`, within a document called `work.xml`, where that string is located within a <TODO> element:

```
work.xml#xpointer(string-range(//TODO,"clean house"))
```

Bare Names

The first short form is called bare names. This shorthand form provides a way of using a single name to represent the value of the assumed `id()` function that searches for an attribute of type `ID` with the specified value. If you want to create an `xpointer` statement referencing an element with an `ID` type `attribute` with a value of `"todolist"`, then both of these statements are correct:

```
todolist
xpointer(id("todolist"))
```

The bare names shorthand is provided mainly for two reasons:

- To encourage usage of `ID` type attributes with all XML elements, because this type of reference is most likely to survive document changes.
- To provide a method of referencing XML document resources in a markup that is similar to the commonly known and understood HTML.

Child Sequence

The second shorthand form created by the XPointer specification is the child sequence. This sequence is used to locate elements within your XML document by performing a hierarchical navigation of your document using a sequence of name or numerical values separated by slashes (/). Each integer *n* will locate the *n*th child element of a previously located element.

For instance assume you wish to find the first child element of the root element of the document with the ID value `work`. To do this you would use either of the following `xpointer` statements. The first is the shorthand version of the full-form version expressed in the second statement:

```
WORK/1
xpointer(work/1)
```

XPointer Escaping

XPointer works on the complete set of information contained in your XML document. This set of information, also commonly referred to as a data set, is comprised of all the elements, attributes, and contents of your XML document. The expressions used with XPointer allow you to select specific portions of the XML document or dataset.

When you are using Xpointer, you have the option of selecting a singular item based upon a variety of characteristics. Take a moment and look at the following code. Using XPointers, for instance, you can select all of the `<NAME>` elements, then the elements with a `sex="f"` attribute, and finally the one with the content of `Franny`.

```
<NAME sex="f"> Georgia</NAME>
<NAME sex="m"> Fred</NAME>
<NAME sex="m"> George</NAME>
<NAME sex="f"> Franny</NAME>
```

This entire process of sorting through a complete XML dataset for the specific piece of information you are looking for is based upon the use of *axis*, *predicates*, and *functions*. An axis is used to identify the specific object that is being searched for, while predicates test those objects for matches to the specified characteristics. Once a match has been found, functions will either generate a new list of candidates to be found or perform another task, such as activating a link or loading an image, specified by the application software.

XPointer is used to reference the context of URI references. Because these complex addresses use characters with specific meanings in XML documents and the use of these characters within the XPointer process themselves, specific escape sequences must be used to reference these types of special characters. In order to perform its tasks, XPointer therefore uses a series of character-escaping codes in order to be able to search for information within the XML dataset. These types of escaping sequences include

- Specific XPointer characters
- URI characters
- XML text

Escaping XPointer Specific Characters

The XPointer syntax uses a lot of parentheses and carets, so all uses of parenthesis and carets must be escaped. You can do this by simply placing an additional caret in front of the parenthesis or caret that is part of the test and not the actual XPointer syntax. For instance, if you want to place a left parenthesis in your XPointer syntax, you write it as "^(". To add a caret into your syntax, you would simply use "^^".

Escaping Characters in URIs

URIs come in two flavors. Your standard run-of-the-mill URI that uses a standard ASCII character-based address, and the Internationalized URI (IURI) that uses UNICODE characters. When working with either of these types of addresses, characters such as percent marks (%) and brackets ([]) may appear in your addresses. In order to use special characters, such as % and [] in your XPointer statements, you need to use the actual UNICODE reference for them. The UNICODE representations for these characters are shown in the following table.

XPointer Character	UNICODE Representation
%	%25
[	%5B
]	%5D

Escaping Characters for Use in XML Text

XPointer and XML use the same character set, which can obviously create problems when the characters in XML collide with those required by XPointer functionality. When your characters collide, the XML characters begin referenced must be escaped (or set off) in some fashion for the XPointer process to work with that character. Without that escape sequence, it would be impossible for the XPointer process ever to complete the work it was intended to do correctly.

In order to work with these otherwise disallowed characters, they must be broken down into their proper UTF-8 UNICODE-based character representation. The list of characters that must be treated in this fashion includes all non-ASCII characters, as well as the pound sign (#), percent sign (%), and square bracket ([]) characters. Table 24-1 provides a short list of some of the more commonly used UNICODE representations.

XPointer Character	UNICODE Representation	XML Entity Reference
<space>	%20	
" (double quotation)	%22	"
^ (caret)	%5E	
% (percent)	%25	%perc;
[(left bracket)	%5B	
] (right bracket)	%5D	
> (greater than)	%	>
< (less than)	%	<
& (ampersand)	%	&

Table 24-1. *UNICODE Representations of Common XML and XPointer Characters*

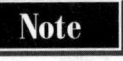

Note *If you wish to see all of the 16 million UNICODE character representations, you will need to read the "UTF-8, a transformation format of ISO 10646," which is the IETF RFC 2279 located at http://www.ietf.org/rfc/rfc2279.txt.*

When a character is escaped, the UNICODE value is can be used to replace the problematic character. For instance, the following statements are the same. The first statement is the initial human-readable format for the XPointer. The second statement converts the problematic XPointer characters into UNICODE, creating an escaped version of the same pointer:

```
xpointer(string-range(/NAME,"Fred ^ and Ginger"))
xpointer(string-range(/NAME,%22Fred%20%e5%20and%20Ginger%22))
```

When your XML application encounters an XPointer *fragment identifier*, which is an escaped XPointer statement, the application must resolve the encoding and escaping in reverse order. In other words, the XML application must convert the UNICODE characters back to their original ASCII characters as the XML application processes the XPointer information.

XPointer Functions

The XPointer 1.0 specification defines a series of functions that extend the XPath specification and allow you to find specific subsets of data within your XML document. These functions include

- Three location types: `location-set`, `point`, and `range`, which correspond to Document Object Model (DOM) positions and ranges that can be evaluated in your XML documents
- The `string-range` function for identifying ranges based on content
- The `range-to` function for identifying a starting and ending point for a range based upon the number of characters you wish to find in the range
- The `here` and `origin` functions for finding data in a relative position to the location of the XPointer expression itself
- The `start-point` and `end-point` functions that are used to set the beginning and ending locations that are used to demarcate a range

Each of these functions are discussed in the following sections.

Identifying a `location-set`

Because XPointer must be able to identify portions of a document that are not specific nodes, or elements, in the document itself, there must be some way of identifying ranges of information contained within that document. This is where the `location-set` identification comes in to play. In order to accomplish the identification of individual points in a XML document, XPointer defines locations as a concept of an XPath node, point, or range. Therefore XPointer defines `location-set` as a concept of the XPath node set or an XPointer point or range. You can read more about XPath in Chapter 16.

A `location-set` can be described using a variety of options including a specific location, starting position, size, and namespace declaration. In the following table, the `location-set` for a variety of common data sets are shown in bold within the code examples.

`location-set` Type	**Example**
ID-type attribute	`xpointer(id("name")...)`
Position/point within document	`xpointer(`**`/1/6/5...`**`)`
Using a namespace	`xmlns(`**`x=http://mysite.com/someplace`**`)` `xpointer(`**`//x:a`**`)`
Using an attribute with the name "id"	`xpointer(`**`//*[@id("name)]`**`...)`

Point Location Type

A point, according to the XPointer 1.0 specification, is defined by specifying a node, in many cases an element, from which to count out an index value, which is a nonnegative integer. The index can represent two values: a child node or a character point. In order for the index value to represent a child node, the original element that was selected must contain child elements. If child elements are found, then the point value of 4, for example, identifies the fourth child node contained within the originally selected node/element. If a selected node does not have any children and only character content, then the index value references the specific number of characters from the opening element of the node to the point at which your range should start.

The following example shows a selection of a point. Both of these statements are equivalent, assuming that `name` is the ID attribute value of the element, or node, that is the fifth child element of the third element in the XML document:

```
name/6/6
/1/3/5/6/6
```

Range Location Type

The range location type is defined by a starting and ending point, allowing the range to be representative of all the XML content and structure between those two points. In order for a range to be valid, both the starting and ending points must be in the same document, and the `start-point` must not appear after the `end-point` in the document order. For example, you can't have a `start-point` at position 150 with an `end-point` at position 100. Ranges must proceed forward through your document; they cannot be specified in such a way that they select a range in a backward fashion.

It is possible to create a collapsed range by specifying an equal `start-point` and `end-point`. Collapsed ranges allow you to identify a single location in a document, without any relationship to actual content. Most ranges that are identified will be coverage ranges that encompass the contents of the selected area completely.

The following example shows a selection of a range using the `start-point` and `end-point` functions discussed later in this chapter. The `start-point` function identifies that the start of the range should be the first child element of the first element in the document. The `end-point` function identifies the end of the range as the third child element of the first element in the document. The first element of a document is commonly the document root:

```
range(start-point(/1/1) end-point(/1/3))
```

`string-range` Function

XPointer provides a series of functions allowing you to select a string of characters based upon their location in the document and the number of times that the string has appeared within the document. The following syntax shows how the `string-range` function is used:

```
location-set string-range(location-set , string, number?, number? )
```

After identifying the original location that will be used, such as the entire XML document, the `string-range` function would be evaluated. First the `location` of the string you are looking for is examined. In most cases this will be a specific node, such as an ID type attribute with a specific value or a specific element name. Second, the `string` itself will be provided. Once the string has been identified, the first number following the string value identifies the character position prior to the located node that will be included in the selected range. The default value for this is 1, which identifies the start of the range as the position directly preceding the identified string. The second numerical value identifes the number of characters that should be included within the range, which by default is the entire selected string.

In this first example, the `string-range` to be selected will start characters before the string `Fred` is found within a <NAME> element, and it will end `17` characters after the starting point:

```
string-range(//NAME "Fred" 6, 17)
```

If this `string-range` function were used on the following document, it would select the bold text. Notice that the selection area includes both the opening and closing tags that surround the name `Fred`:

```
<ACTOR>
  <NAME>Wilma</NAME>
  <NAME>Fred</NAME>
</ACTOR>
```

You can also select a `string-range` based upon the number of iterations that has occurred within a document. For instance, the following function would select the third iteration of a <NAME> element with the contents of `Fred`:

```
string-range(//NAME "Fred" 6, 17)[3]
```

Note *When found, the identified location will contain a range for each nonoverlaping match of the string. Any empty string will be considered a match before each character of the string value and after the final character of the string. The white space in a string will be matched literally.*

Because a `string-range` can select both a string of characters and any document structure that it includes, you can even search for strings that have additional markup within them. For instance, if you were to attempt to find the third iteration of `Fred` in a

<NAME> element in the following document, it would still be found properly, since the markup is ignored during the search for a string:

```
<NAME>Fred</NAME>
<NAME>Fred</NAME>
<NAME>F<B>r</B>ed</NAME>
```

You would still be able to select the entire `Fred` string, including both `<B></B>` tags with the following `string-range` function. The only difference between this selection and the selection made in the previous example is that the start and end index points have been removed from the statement:

```
string-range(//NAME "Fred")[3]
```

In addition to selecting elements, you can use the `string-range` function to locate any range from a single character to an attribute, processing instruction, or comment found within your XML document. The following function statement selects the third exclamation mark in any text node in the document:

```
string-range(/,"!")[3]
```

range-to Function

Once you have identified a specific location, you may find that you want to extend the range being selected. The `range-to` function works perfectly for this. `range-to` works by locating the specified point in the document that follows the starting point of the originally selected location. The syntax of the range-to statement is shown here:

```
location-set range-to(expression)
```

Take the following statement for an example. In this statement the XPointer is using the element with the ID value of `"Fred"` as the original location of the first selected range. It then expands that range until it finds an element with an ID value of `"Wilma"`:

```
xpointer(id("Fred")/range-to(id("Wilma")))
```

For another example, let's suppose that a document is using empty elements (such as `<OUTSTART/> and <OUTEND/>`) to mark the boundaries of a specific section of an outline. In this case, the following XPointer statement would select, for each outline section, a range starting at the beginning of the <OUTSTART> element and ending at the end of the next <OUTEND> element:

```
xpointer(descendant::OUTSTART/range-to(following::OUTEND[1]))
```

here Function

The `here` function will return a location set with a single member by locating the element, or node, directly containing the XPointer being evaluated. This node type will probably be text, an attribute, or a processing instruction. The location that is returned for an XPointer appearing in the element content will not have a node type of element because the XPointer is in a text node located inside of the element.The defualt syntax for the here function is

```
location-set here()
```

Using the `here` *function can result in a syntax error if the resource that contains the XPointer statement is not formulated in well-formed XML.*

`origin` Function

The `origin` function allows you to address relative locations that are not inline with the existing document. This is how the XLink Specification works. (XLink is discussed in Chapter 23.) The `origin` function enables XPointer to be used in applications to express relative locations if links do not reside directly at one of their endpoints. These relative links work by returning a `location-set` for the referenced address, identifying the specific element from which the user or application will begin the link traversal process. The default syntax for this function is

```
location-set origin()
```

`start-point` Function

The `start-point` function provides a point type of location identifier that signifies the beginning of a range selection. Because you can refer to a point, range, element, or text value as a `start-point`, you need to be aware of the exact point you are specifying with your `start-point` value.

- If your `start-point` is a true point, then the point specified is the start of your range.
- If your `start-point` is a range, then the point interpreted as the start of your range is the first point of the specified range.
- If your `start-point` is a document root or an element, then the actual selected `start-point` is the beginning of the content of the first child of the specified element.
- If your `start-point` is a text string, XML comment, or processing instruction, then the start of the range being selected is the first character of the comment or processing instruction or the physical location of the first character of the specified text string or character.

Note

You cannot specify an attribute or a namespace as a `start-point`. *This will create a syntax error.*

The syntax for creating a `start-point` is

```
start-point(location-set)
```

In the following example, the `start-point` of the selected range is the fourth child element of the document root:

```
start-point(/1/4))
```

You can also select a `start-point` using the results of another function, such as `string-range`. For instance, the following statement selects the third exclamation point in the document as the `start-point` of your range:

```
start-point(string-range(/,"!")[3])
```

end-point Function

The `end-point` function provides a point type of location identifier that signifies the end of a selected range. Because you can refer to both a point and a range value as an `end-point`, you need to be aware of the exact point you are specifying with your `end-point` value.

- If your `end-point` is a true point, then the point specified is the end of your range.
- If your `end-point` is a range, then the point interpreted as the end of your range is the `end-point` of the specified range.
- If your `end-point` is a document root or an element, then the actual selected end-point is the end of the last content of the last child of the specified element.
- If your `end-point` is a text string, XML comment, or processing instruction, then the end of the range being selected is the end of the comment or processing instruction, or the physical location of the specified text string or character.

Note *You cannot specify an attribute or a namespace as an* `end-point`*. This will create a syntax error.*

The syntax for creating an `end-point` is

```
end-point(location-set)
```

In the following example, the `end-point` of the selected range is the third child element of the document root:

```
end-point(/1/3))
```

You can also select an `end-point` using the results of another function. For instance, the following statement selects the third exclamation point in the document as the `end-point` of your range:

```
end-point(string-range(/,"!")[3])
```

Summary

XPointer provides you with a way to identify uniquely portions of an XML document for linking purposes. The XPointer specification provides a mechanism for addressing XML documents based upon their internal structure, allowing for the examination of the hierarchal structures of XML documents while also allowing the choosing of its internal parts such as your elements, attribute values, character content, and relative position.

XPointer uses a set of schemes to identify the format used to describe the information found within your XML document, and in turn it identifies what type of information is therefore usable within your XPointer statements. XPointer uses both the `xpointer` and the `xmlns` schemes, as well as the `text/xml` and `applications/xml` media types.

The process XPointer uses to sort through a complete XML dataset for a specific piece of information is based upon the use of axis, predicates, and functions. An axis is used to identify the specific object being searched for, while predicates test those objects for matches to the specified characteristics. Once a match has been found, functions will either generate a new list of candidates to be found or perform another task, such as activating a link or loading an image, specified by the application software.

The XPointer 1.0 specification defines a series of functions that extend the XPath specification and allows you to find specific subsets of data within your XML document. These functions include

- Three location types: `location-set`, `point`, and `range`, which correspond to DOM positions and ranges that can be found within your XML documents
- The `string-range` functions for identifying ranges based on content
- The `range-to` function for identifying a `start-point` and `end-point` for a range based upon the number of characters you wish to find in the range
- The `here` and `origin` functions for finding data in a relative position to the location of the XPointer expression itself
- The `start-point` and `end-point` functions for setting the beginning and ending locations that are used to demarcate a range

Chapter 25

Resource Description Framework

XML uses a system of identifying information about the information contained within an XML document or application. This system is called the Resource Description Framework (RDF).

RDF is an infrastructure that enables structured metadata to be encoded, exchanged, and reused through multiple documents. RDF is an application of XML. It enables document authors to publish both human-readable and machine-processable vocabularies relating to the description of information contained within any XML application for any industry. The rigid structure that RDF imposes supports a standardized meta data system, providing for the exchange of metadata that has been defined by different resource communities.

What Is the RDF and the RDF Schema?

RDF is the primary framework that has been defined as a means of standardizing metadata. The RDF data model provides no mechanism for declaring the properties of your metadata, nor does it provide for the definition of relationships between metadata properties and other resources—that is the role of RDF Schema. The RDF Schema describes how RDF should be used to describe RDF vocabularies.

RDF

RDF is an XML-derived structure that enables organizations or individuals to encode, exchange, and reuse structured metadata, or information about the information contained within your XML documents. RDF provides instantaneous access to a globally supported method of sharing information about the vast number of documents available across the Internet. Although metadata is typically customized to each application, RDF creates a series of conventions that control how the semantics, syntax, and structure of metadata are formed.

The World Wide Web Consortium (W3C) adopted the RDF specification in February of 1999. This move opened the door to the definition of both machine- and human-readable data, which can be used in a variety of industries. RDF has found uses in current systems such as implementing site maps, setting preferences for documents, providing collaborative services, and adding information verification to electronic commerce shopping carts.

RDF is simply a system in which you can take a format developed for defining information from one industry, merge it with a format from a second industry, and apply that information to a third industry without losing any of the abilities of the original formats and while adding to their functionality.

Note *RDF uses many of the ideas expressed in the Dublin Core for describing metadata. The Dublin Core metadata was designed to help researchers store data in electronic resources in a manner similar to the creation of a library card catalog. You will find references to the Dublin Core used throughout the examples in this chapter.*

RDF is a system wherein a resource is described through a series of related properties. Each property description is comprised of a statement, which is composed of a property type, a value, and the resource identifier to which the property is applied. Using this model, any resource that has a Uniform Resource Identifier (URI) can be described using RDF.

RDF Schema

There is a need to be able to describe the various documents and resources that are available on the Internet. Since the RDF specification doesn't provide any means of describing the data sets to use, you need a new tool. This tool is the RDF Schema. The RDF Schema enables you to declare the document structure of the properties, which you want to track for your metadata. An RDF Schema defines not only the properties of a resource, for instance title and author, but it may also define the kinds of resources being described, such as a book, magazine, training document, or Web page.

RDF Schemas are best thought of as a slight twist implemented on XML Document Type Definitions (DTDs) (see Part II) and XML Schemas (see Part IV). An RDF Schema does not describe the structure of an XML document, as is done in DTDs and XML Schemas, it provides information about how the various statements used to define the metadata should be interpreted.

The RDF Schema doesn't specify a vocabulary of descriptive elements; it instead identifies the mechanisms needed to define elements. In addition, the RDF Schema defines the classes of resources that elements may be used with, restricts the number of possible combinations of classes and relationships, and detects any violations of those restrictions. As you can see, the RDF Schema defines a schema specification language. More succinctly, the RDF Schema mechanism provides a basic type system for use in RDF models. It defines resources and properties used in specifying application-specific schemas.

The RDF Schema became a candidate recommendation in March 2000, and, as of February 2001, it has not received full recommendation status.

Implementing the RDF Basic Model

The RDF model uses namespace declarations to identify the resources used in the markup of a document. The following is the namespace for RDF:

```
<RDF xmlns="http://www.w3.org/TR/REC-rdf-syntax#">
```

The use of namespaces within the RDF model enables you to point your document to multiple resources including the Dublin Core:

```
<xmlns:DC="http://www.purl.org/DC#">
```

An RDF description is composed of resources, properties, and statements. Each portion of the RDF construct is discussed in the following sections.

Resources

RDF descriptors describe resources. A resource might be an entire Web page (http://www.w3.org/index.htm), parts of a Web page (a specific HTML or XML element), a database, or even a simple image that may or may not be associated to a Web page at all. All resources have a Uniform Resource Identifier (URI) and an optional anchor identifier that can be used to describe it. Any type of object can have an URI, as well as items that aren't really objects per se. For example, URI can point to anything, nothing, or even a set of data that may be created in the future.

Properties

A property is a specific characteristic, attribute, or relationship that can be used to describe a resource. A perfect example of a property is your name. It is used to describe you. Each property has a specific meaning that can be identified by a value associated with the property's name. The RDF Schema provides the controls that are associated with each property. An RDF Schema defines the values or value ranges that are permitted for use with the property and the types of resources that the property can be used to describe. The RDF Schema also defines the property's relationships with other properties.

The RDF Schema proposal identifies a series of classes, properties, and constraints that are used to identify the who, what, where, and how of the RDF information defined by the document. The RDF Schema is based on the XML Schema syntax discussed in Part IV.

Statements

When a property and its value for a resource join together, an RDF statement is born. Statements have three parts that are called, respectively, the subject, the predicate, and the object. The subject is the item that the statements are referencing. The predicate is the role of that subject in reference to the resource. The object is the value of the property and can be either another resource or a literal. If it is another resource, it will contain a URI. A literal can be any content that is XML markup but is not evaluated further by the RDF processor.

Lets look at a standard human-readable statement:

```
Heather Williamson is the developer of http://catsback.com/.
```

If you were to break this statement down into its component parts and place it into a table, we would end up with something like this:

Statement Part	Value
Subject (Resource)	`http://catsback.com/`
Predicate (Property)	`developer`
Object (Literal)	`Heather Williamson`

The following is the previous statement written in RDF:

```
<RDF xmlns="http://www.w3.org/TR/REC-rdf-syntax#">
  <DEVELOPER about="http://catsback.com/">
    Heather Williamson
  </DEVELOPER>
</RDF>
```

RDF Basic Syntax

Within the RDF specification are two types of XML syntax used for encoding an RDF data model: serialization syntax and abbreviated syntax. The serialization syntax expresses the data in full fashion and makes the data available to be read on screen by XML-compliant browsers. The abbreviated syntax uses attribute-styled constructs to provide a more compact representation of the data. RDF compliant applications should be able to read both models of syntax, enabling you to use them together within a single RDF data block.

Serialized

Serialized statements break each property into child elements with the child element's contents representing the value of that property. The <RDF> statement provides the opening and closing root of the RDF resource. The <DESCRIPTION> element is the primary container for storing information about a single RDF resource.

The basic RDF block using serialized syntax will look similar to the following code:

```
<RDF [namespacedeclaration(s)]>
  <rdf:DESCRIPTION [id= name] | [about=URL]>
    <PROPERTY> value </PROPERTY>
    <!-- Add as many properties as you have values for -->
    <PROPERTY resourceAttr="URL" />
  </rdf:DESCRIPTION>
</RDF>
```

The <RDF> element provides a boundary between the XML or HTML document and the content mapped to the RDF data model.

The <RDF> element does not need to be stated if it is obvious from the application context where the RDF block begins and ends.

Look at some statements and the RDF blocks that would re-create them. In this first example, a simple RDF block identifies the document address (http://www.catsback.com) and the name of the developer (Heather Williamson), as shown in the following descriptive statement:

```
Heather Williamson developed the document located at
http://www.catsback.com.
```

```
<RDF xmlns="http://www.w3.org/TR/REC-rdf-syntax#">
  <Description about="http://www.catsback.com/">
    <Developer>Heather Williamson</Developer>
  </Description>
</RDF>
```

The following example uses a more complicated joining of structures from both the RDF schematic and the Dublin Core. The text description shown next provides multiple pieces of information about the Wallowa County Chamber Site.

```
Heather Williamson, whose contact e-mail address is
webmaster@wallowacountychamber.com, created the "The Wallowa
County Chamber of Commerce Page" located at
http://www.wallowacountychamber.com/index.html on July 5, 2000.
```

The statement above is described using RDF syntax in the following code:

```
<RDF xmlns="http://www.w3.org/TR/REC-rdf-syntax#"
     xmlns:DC="http://www.purl.org/DC#">
  <Description about="http://www.wallowacountychamber.com/">
    <DC:Creator> Heather Williamson </DC:Creator>
    <DC:Title> The Wallowa County Chamber of Commerce Page</DC:Title>
    <DC:Contact> webmaster@wallowacountychamber.com </DC:Contact>
    <DC:Date> July 5, 2000</DC:Date>
  </Description>
</RDF>
```

Abbreviated

Abbreviated syntax is not as clear or as widely usable as serialized syntax, although it does enable you to provide RDF data in a compact format. This RDF syntax enables documents that use well-structured XML DTDs to be directly interpreted as RDF models.

The primary form of abbreviation for the original basic serialization syntax enables you to use unique properties within the `Description` element to define your RDF information. The following is the syntax for the `Description` element:

```
<RDF [namespacedeclaration(s)]>
  <rdf:Description [id= name] | [about=URL]
       property1=value
       property2=value
       property3=value .../>
</RDF>
```

Note *Because the* `Description` *element no longer has a variety of child elements, it does not need a closing tag and is written using normal empty element syntax.*

The first example from the "Serialized" section, earlier in this chapter, can be rewritten using abbreviated syntax. The original statement is shown here, with the abbreviated RDF syntax following it.

```
Heather Williamson developed the document located at
http://www.catsback.com.

<RDF xmlns="http://www.w3.org/TR/REC-rdf-syntax#">
  <Description about="http://www.catsback.com/"
    developer=Heather Williamson />
</RDF>
```

The second example in the "Serialized" section can also be expressed in abbreviated format. The complex statement providing information on the Wallowa County Chamber of commerce is shown here, with the abbreviated RDF syntax following:

```
Heather Williamson, whose contact e-mail address is
webmaster@wallowacountychamber.com, created the "The Wallowa
County Chamber of Commerce Pages" located at
http://www.wallowacountychamber.com/index.html on July 5, 2000.

<RDF xmlns="http://www.w3.org/TR/REC-rdf-syntax#"
     xmlns:DC="http://www.purl.org/DC#">
  <Description about="http://www.wallowacountychamber.com/">
    DC:Creator="Heather Williamson"
    DC:Title="The Wallowa County Chamber of Commerce Pages "
    DC:Contact="webmaster@wallowacountychamber.com"
    DC:Date=" July 5, 2000" />
</RDF>
```

Using RDF Containers

When you are using RDF to describe a collection of resources, for example, to say that a document was written by a group of individuals or to list the available resources for downloading a software package, you will need to use a *container*. A container is simply a construct that has been defined to hold lists of either literals or resources.

When a resource has multiple statements that need to use the same property, as in the case of a document with a group of authors, you have two options for displaying the resource information: you can use a container and place the contents in a bag, or you can use multiple properties with different values. If you are using the abbreviated format for your RDF declaration you will need to use a bag, or one of the alternatives shown in the previous section.

RDF Container Syntax

The following is the basic syntax for a container within the RDF:

```
<RDF [namespacedeclaration(s)]>
  <rdf:DESCRIPTION [id= name] | [about=URL]>
    <rdf:Set|Bag|Alt [id= name]>
      <PROPERTY>
        <!-- One of the following list options is available -->
        <rdf:li [resource="URL"]/>
        <rdf:li> value </rdf:li>
      </PROPERTY>
    </rdf:Set|Bag|Alt>
  </rdf:DESCRIPTION>
</RDF>
```

Note *RDF uses the familiar* `li` *element from HTML as a convenience to avoid having to explicitly number each member of the list. This element assigns the properties a number in the form of _1, as necessary.*

Container Objects

The RDF defines three separate types of container objects: a bag, a sequence, and an alternative.

Bag

A bag is an unordered list of resources or literals that have been combined in no particular order of importance. The use of a bag enables you to declare a property that has more than one value, for instance, a series of authors for a document, a series of committee members, or a list of part numbers for a computer where processing order is not important. Because bags serve as a "catch-all" way of grouping information it is possible for duplicate values to be identified.

The following sentence model provides a foundation for the RDF bag statement that follows it.

```
The Wallowa County Chamber of Commerce Pages were written by Tom,
George, and Ernie.
```

This sentence is written using a bag, shown in bold text in the following RDF statements:

```
<RDF xmlns:rdf="http://www.w3.org/TR/REC-rdf-syntax#"
     xmlns:DC="http://www.purl.org/DC#"
```

```
     xmlns:bcard="http://www.wallowacountychamber.com/bcard#">
<rdf:Description about="http://www.wallowacountychamber.com/"
  <DC:Title>The Wallowa County Chamber of Commerce Page</DC:Title>
  <DC:Creator>
    <rdf:Bag>
      <rdf:li resource="http:// wallowacountychamber.com/staff/tom" />
      <rdf:li resource="http:// wallowacountychamber.com/staff/george" />
      <rdf:li resource="http:// wallowacountychamber.com/staff/Ernie"/>
    </rdf:Bag>
  </DC:Creator>
</rdf:Description>
</rdf:RDF>
```

Sequence

Lists of resources or literals that must be used in a specific order are displayed in a sequenced list. Sequences keep lists with alphabetic ordering that must be maintained or lists of numerical values that must be run in succession and in the proper order. Sequenced lists also enable you to have duplicate values.

Using the sentence model we previously created

```
The Wallowa County Chamber of Commerce Pages were written by Tom,
George, and Ernie.
```

you can use the following sequence, shown in bold text, to force the names to be written in alphabetical order:

```
<RDF xmlns:rdf="http://www.w3.org/TR/REC-rdf-syntax#"
     xmlns:DC="http://www.purl.org/DC#"
     xmlns:bcard="http://www.wallowavalley.com/bcard#">
<rdf:Description about="http://www.wallowacountychamber.com/"
  <DC:Title>The Wallowa County Chamber of Commerce Page</DC:Title>
  <DC:Creator>
    <rdf:Seq>
      <rdf:li resource="http://wallowavalley.com/staff/ernie"/>
      <rdf:li resource="http://wallowavalley.com/staff/george" />
      <rdf:li resource="http://wallowavalley.com/staff/tom"/>
    </rdf:Seq>
  </DC:Creator>
</rdf:Description>
</rdf:RDF>
```

Alternative

RDF statements enable you to provide a list of resources or literals, which represent a series of alternatives for a single value of a property, by using an alternative (`Alt`) list. You can use an alternative list to provide a list of alternative contact people for a project or to provide a list of locations that carry the merchandise you are looking for in your area. Applications that are RDF compliant know that they can choose any of the values in the list that are appropriate for its needs.

Look, at the following sample sentence. It offers you three addresses to which you can mail your information:

```
You can reach the Wallowa County Chamber of Commerce
through these e-mail addresses: wallowa@eoni.com,
chamber@wallowacountychamber.com, and webmaster@neoregon.net.
```

The previous statement, written using an RDF alternative list in bold, would appear like the following:

```
<RDF xmlns:rdf="http://www.w3.org/TR/REC-rdf-syntax#"
     xmlns:s="http://www.schema.org#" />
<rdf:Description about="Wallowa County Chamber of Commerce" >
  <s:EmailAddys>
    <rdf:Alt>
      <rdf:li resource="wallowa@eoni.com"/>
      <rdf:li resource="chamber@wallowacountychamber.com"/>
      <rdf:li resource="webmaster@neoregon.net"/>
    </rdf:Alt>
</s:EmailAddys>
</rdf:Description>
</RDF>
```

Here, any one of the items listed in the container value for `EmailAddys` is an acceptable value without regard to the other items. This container has to have at least one member, or list item. The first item in the list will be identified by the value _1 and serve as the default value.

Statements

In order to identify specifically which resource you are describing with your RDF statements, you have to us an `id` attribute. The use of the `id` attribute enables you to create stacked `Description` statements that can then be parsed to collect all of the information about the resource through a series of referents.

The following example uses a bag to compile a list of pages located within the Wallowa Valley Community Web site. The container lists the pages, while the `Description` statement identifies Heather Williamson as the creator of the site. This example lists nothing about the pages as individuals in the original container, but it uses a descriptor statement pointing to the page to identify that page's creator:

```
<rdf:Bag ID="pages">
  <rdf:li resource="http://wallowavalley.com/index.html" />
  <rdf:li resource="http://wallowavalley.com/about.html" />
  <rdf:li resource="http://wallowavalley.com/art.html" />
  <rdf:li resource="http://wallowavalley.com/kids.html" />
  <rdf:li resource="http://wallowavalley.com/lodging.html" />
  <rdf:li resource="http://wallowavalley.com/shops.html" />
</rdf:Bag>

<rdf:Description about="#pages">
  <s:Creator>Heather Williamson</s:Creator>
</rdf:Description>
<rdf:Description about="http://wallowavalley.com/index.html">
  <s:Creator>Heather Williamson</s:Creator>
</rdf:Description>
<rdf:Description about="http://wallowavalley.com/about.html">
  <s:Creator>Luis de Texas</s:Creator>
</rdf:Description>
<rdf:Description about="http://wallowavalley.com/doc/art.html">
  <s:Creator>Luis de Texas</s:Creator>
</rdf:Description>
<rdf:Description about="http://wallowavalley.com/doc/kid.html">
  <s:Creator>Belle</s:Creator>
</rdf:Description>
<rdf:Description about="http://wallowavalley.com/lodging.html">
  <s:Creator>Heather Williamson</s:Creator>
</rdf:Description>
<rdf:Description about="http://wallowavalley.com/shop.html">
  <s:Creator>Belle</s:Creator>
</rdf:Description>
```

URI Patterns

Another use of metadata is to make global statements about all of the documents used in a Web site or about all of the authors of those documents. In most cases it will be impractical to list each resource separately. Not only is that a huge duplication of work, but it is unnecessary. Using a series of predefined URI patterns, you can refer to all of the resources in a bag whose resource identifiers meet specific requirements.

This process uses the `aboutEach` or the `aboutEachPrefix` property to select the specific bag members that are affected by the descriptors. The `aboutEach` property provides a URI link to another descriptor block describing the bag. The `aboutEachPrefix` is a string that is used to select all the contents of a bag whose URIs begin with the contents of the string.

For example, if the two resources http://wallowavalley.com/doc/art and http://wallowavalley.com/doc/kid exist, we can specify that each has a copyright property with the following code:

```
<rdf:Description aboutEachPrefix="http://wallowavalley.com/doc">
  <s:Copyright>© 2001, Cat's Back Consulting
  </s:Copyright>
</rdf:Description>
```

If the two resources http://wallowavalley.com/doc/art and http://wallowavalley.com/doc/kid are the only two resources whose URIs start with the "http://wallowavalley.com/doc/" string, then the preceding code is equivalent to both of the following alternative RDF statements which follow:

- The following example uses multiple `Description` statements to set matching information for multiple resources.

```
<rdf:Description about="http://wallowavalley.com/doc/art.htm">
  <s:Copyright>© 2001, Cat's Back Consulting </s:Copyright>
</rdf:Description>
<rdf:Description about="http://wallowavalley.com/doc/kid.htm">
  <s:Copyright>© 2001, Cat's Back Consulting </s:Copyright>
</rdf:Description>
```

- The following example uses `aboutEach` to identify a statement referencing a bag.

```
<rdf:Description aboutEach="#docpages">
  <s:Copyright>© 2001, Cat's Back Consulting </s:Copyright>
</rdf:Description>
<rdf:Bag ID="docpages">
  <rdf:li resource="http://wallowavalley.com/doc/art.htm"/>
  <rdf:li resource="http://wallowavalley.com/doc/kid.htm"/>
</rdf:Bag>
```

Summary

RDF statements are used to format metadata to describe a document and a document's parts, making it easy to understand by both people and machines. RDF is the primary framework that has been defined as a means of standardizing metadata. The rigid structure that RDF imposes supports a standardized metadata system, providing for the exchange of metadata that has been defined by different resource communities. The RDF Schema describes how RDF should be used to describe RDF vocabularies.

The RDF model uses namespace declarations to identify the resources used in the markup of a document. The following is the namespace for RDF:

```
<RDF xmlns="http://www.w3.org/TR/REC-rdf-syntax#">
```

The use of namespaces within the RDF model enables you to point your document to multiple resources including the Dublin Core:

```
<xmlns:DC="http://www.purl.org/DC#">
```

An RDF description is composed of resources, properties, and statements. RDF descriptors describe resources. A resource might be an entire Web page (http://www.w3.org/index.htm) or any other document or portion of a document that has a URI. A property is a specific characteristic, attribute, or relationship that can be used to describe a resource. Statements are made up of an RDF property and its value.

Part VI

XML in Action

Chapter 26

XHTML

Extensible Hypertext Markup Language (XHTML) is the reformulation of HTML 4.01 into XML. This language is the next step in the development of Hypertext Markup Language (HTML), and XHTML will be slowly adopted as the default language of most Web browsers. Because the language is formulated into XML, which has more rigid rules for how information must appear and how it can be formatted, XHTML serves as the first step in enabling Web developers to process XHTML documents using XML tools, as well as opening up the possibility for the extension of the HTML vocabulary by making the incorporation of other XML document types and syntax into your XHTML documents easier.

What Is XHTML

XHTML is the future of HTML. The content and formatting of documents on the Internet will not be controlled by a single language or necessarily found in a single document. As of the first quarter of 2001, the current version of the XHTML recommendation is 1.0. This recommendation is simply a combination of HTML 4.01 vocabulary and the XML document syntax.

All XHTML documents are also XML-compliant documents. XHTML has reformulated the three HTML 4 documents types into applications of XML. The reformulation was done in such a way that with some careful adjustments, your new XHTML document will also be HTML 4 compatible and, therefore, viewable in all of the current HTML 4–compliant Web browsers. The migration of HTML to XHTML provides a variety of benefits to the developer. These benefits include

- Conformance with both HTML and XML documenting-viewing applications and editors. XHTML documents can be created, viewed, modified, and validated using both XML and HTML tools.
- Script reliance on either the HTML or the XML Document Object Model (DOM) for the creation of applications within your Web document.
- As XML, and therefore XHTML, evolves, more Web browsers and other XML applications will be able to access the information in your documents.
- Documents written to conform to XHTML 1.0 can potentially perform better in the current Web tools than they when written to conform to HTML.
- HTML is not designed for use with palm or cellular applications, which are supported by a more rigid XML format.

Because XHTML is simply the next step in the continual development of HTML, you can stay compatible with the past technology, as well as be sure to go forward with new technology, something that HTML could not do.

HTML to XHTML Conversions

Currently one of the biggest implementations of XHTML is the conversion of existing HTML documents into this new, more highly structure format. When converting from HTML to XHTML, there are a few rules that you must keep in mind:

- All element and attribute names must be lowercase.
- All attribute values must be enclosed in quotation marks.
- The root element of the document must be `<html>`.
- The `<!DOCTYPE>` declaration must precede the root element in the document:

```
<!DOCTYPE html PUBLIC "-//W3C//DTD XHTML 1.0 Transitional//EN"
"http://www.w3.org/TR/xhtml1/xhtml-tranistional.dtd">
<!DOCTYPE html PUBLIC "-//W3C//DTD XHTML 1.0 Strict//EN"
"http://www.w3.org/TR/xhtml1/DTD/xhtml1-strict.dtd">
```

- The default namespace associated with the root element must be `http://www.w3.org/1999/xhtml`
- All elements must be closed. Empty elements must be closed with a forward slash before the closing >, for instance, `<br /> and <img.../>`. Nonempty elements must be closed using a standard end tag.
- In instances in which an element is not normally empty, but sometimes is empty, use the complete set of tags. For instance, use `<p></p>` not `<p />`.
- The use of external style sheets is suggested if your style sheet uses any of the following characters: `<, &, ]]>,` or `--`.
- The use of external scripts is suggested if your script uses any of the following characters: `<, &, ]]>, or --`.

Note *Because XHTML documents, like XML documents, are permitted to remove comments from their content, enclosing scripts and style sheets within comment brackets will not necessarily work in older browsers as a means of hiding a style sheet or script from nonsupporting Web browsers.*

- Line breaks and extra white space found in attribute values are handled inconsistently and, therefore, should be avoided.
- When creating transitional documents, use both the `lang` and `xml:lang` attributes when specifying the language of an element. This enables older browsers to view the document properly. When used together, the value of the `xml:lang` attribute will take precedence.
- Use the `id` attribute, not the `name` attribute, to identify elements. The `id` attribute isn't supported in all Web browsers, specifically version of Netscape prior to 4.5, so you will need to provide matching `id` and `name` attributes to

support older Web browsers. The name attribute isn't supported in XHTML documents, because it is not defined as an attribute of type ID.

- To specify the character encoding used in your XHTML document, use both the XML declaration <?xml version="1.0" encoding="EUC-JP"?> and a matching meta http-equiv element such as <meta http-equiv="Content-type" content="text/html; charset="EUC-JP"' />. When these attributes are used together, supporting applications will use the XML declaration.
- Boolean attributes, such as checked, nowrap, compact, and resize are not correctly supported in XML browsers, although they will continue to be used for HTML browsers. For support in XML browsers, use the complete statement such as checked=checked.
- When an ampersand (&) appears in an attribute value, it must be displayed as the character entity: & . This creates problems when working with addresses containing ampersands within *href* attributes, as they will need to be expressed as http://website.com/cgi-bin/sendmail.pl?id=guest&name=user rather than http://website.dom/cgi-bin/sendmail.pl?id=guest&name=user.

Element Conversions

All of the empty elements, as well as those that we typically don't close, such as <p>, must be made to conform to the new XHTML standard if you wish to use XHTML as the primary base of your documents. All of the empty elements, as well as those that were not required to be closed in HTML 4, are shown in Table 26-1 with their previously acceptable HTML markup and their new XHTML version.

HTML Element	XHTML Element
<AREA>	<area />
<BASE>	<base />
<COLGROUP>	<colgroup> ... </colgroup>
<DD>	<dd> ... </dd>
<DT>	<dt> ... </dt>

Table 26-1. *HTML to XHTML Converted Elements*

HTML Element	XHTML Element
<FRAME>	<frame />
<HR>	<hr />
<IMG>	<img />
<INPUT>	<input />
<LI>	<li> ... </li>
<LINK>	<link />
<META>	</meta>
<OPTION>	<option> ... </option>
<P>	<p> ... </p>
<PARAM>	<param />
<TD>	<td> ... </td>
<TFOOT>	<tfoot> ... </tfoot>
<TH>	<th> ... </th>
<THEAD>	<thead> ... </thead>
<TR>	<tr> ... </tr>

Table 26-1. *HTML to XHTML Converted Elements* (continued)

A Quick Conversion from HTML to XHTML

Take, for instance, the following HTML document. It shows the basic structure of an HTML document with a variety of common usages of HTML elements, including some that are empty and others that have an opening but no closing element:

```
<html>
<head>
<title>This is a sample document. >/title>
</head>
<body>
   <img src="mylogo.gif" alt="company logo" height="100" width="300">
   <p>
```

```
      This is just some test text.<br>
      This is more test text.
    <form>
       <input type="text" value="12">
    </form>
</body>
</html>
```

To convert the previous sample code into XHTML, you need to use the proper <html> and namespace statement, as well as close the open and empty elements appropriately, as shown in bold in the following code:

```
<?xml version="1.0" encoding="Latin1"?>
<!DOCTYPE html PUBLIC "-//W3C//DTD XHTML 1.0 Transitional//EN"
"http://www.w3.org/TR/xhtml1/xhtml-tranistional.dtd">
<html xmlns="http://www.w3.org/1999/xhtml">
<head>
<title>This is a sample document. >/title>
<meta http-equiv="Content-type" content="text/html; charset="EUC-JP"' />
</head>
<body>
   <img src="mylogo.gif" alt="company logo" height="100" width="300" />
<p>
     This is just some test text.<br />
     This is more test text. </p>
  <form>
     <input type="text" value="12" />
</form>
</body>
</html>
```

Future XHTML Modules

The modularization of XHTML work that is being explored at the World Wide Web Consortium (W3C) is going ahead full steam at the start of the new millennium. During this process, XHTML is being broken down into a series of modules that enable Web browsers and other applications to support only those portions of the XHTML specification that are needed for their particular work. These modules include

- **Structure Module** The Structure Module includes directives for elements that control the physical structure of the document, such as `body`, `head`, `html`, and `title`.

- **Text Module** The Text Module defines the basic text elements such as `abbr, acronym, address, blockquote, br, cite, code, dfn, div, em, h1, h2, h3, h4, h5, h6, kbd, p, pre, q, samp, span, strong,` and `var`.
- **Hypertext Module** The Hypertext Module only supports the `<a> element to create links.`
- **List Module** The List Module provides for list-oriented elements including `dl, dt, dd, ol, ul,` and `li`.
- **Presentation Module** The Presentation Module provides the minimum markup for creating simple presentations. These elements include `b, big, hr, i, small, sub, sup,` and `tt`.
- **Edit Module** The Edit Module is used to provide elements and attributes for use in creating editorial marks in your text. These elements include `del and ins`.
- **Bidirectional Text Module** The Bidirectional Text Module defines the `bdo` element, which can be used to control the direction that text is displayed on your screen.
- **Forms Module** The elements provided as part of the Forms Module enable you to create form-related content on your documents. Forms elements include `form, input, label, select, option, button, fieldset, legend, optgroup,` and `textarea`.
- **Table Module** The Table Module provides all the elements that can be used to create table structures in your documents. These elements include `caption, table, td, th, tr, col, colgroup, tbody, thead,` and `tfoot`.
- **Image Module** The Image Module provides for the support of a single-image element `img` that enables the embedding of basic images within your documents.
- **Client-Side Image Map Module** The Client-Side Image Map Module provides for the use of client-side image maps within your document. This module supports the `area` element and its attributes.

These modules can be used alone or in conjunction with each other to create the functionality in your application and document that you are looking for. If your application provides support for a module, it must provide support for all of the elements contained within that module.

Structure Module

The XHTML proposed Structure Module defines the primary elements that define an XHTML document. These elements provide the foundation for the creation of elements containing content, as well as provide the associations used for adding style sheets to XHTML documents. Table 26-2 lists all of the elements and attributes that are included in the Structure Module.

The syntax displayed in the Content column of this table shows the Document Type Definition (DTD) structure for this element as it is used in XML.

The `<html>` element serves as the root element of the document and must contain the `xmlns` attribute to meet with the XHTML specification.

Text Module

The Text Module contains all of the elements that are used in traditional HTML documents to control the appearance of text. Table 26-3 lists all of the elements and attributes available as part of this module.

The syntax displayed in the Content column of this table shows the DTD structure for this element as it is used in XML.

Element	Attributes	Content
body	Core Attributes: name, id, title Language Attributes: xml:lang Event Attributes: onclick, ondblclick, onmousedown, onmouseup, onmouseover, onmousemove, onmouseout, onkeypress, onkeydown, onkeyup Other Attributes: style	(Heading Text elements | Block Text elements | List elements)*
head	Language Attributes: xml:lang Other Attributes: profile	<title>
html	Language Attributes: xml:lang Other Attributes: version, xmlns (URI="http://www.w3.org/1999/xhtml")	<head>, <body>
title	Language Attributes: xml:lang	PCDATA

Table 26-2. *XHTML Structure Model Elements and Attributes*

Element	Attribute	Content
abbr	Core Attributes: name, id, title Language Attributes: xml:lang Event Attributes: onclick, ondblclick, onmousedown, onmouseup, onmouseover, onmousemove, onmouseout, onkeypress, onkeydown, onkeyup Other Attributes: style	(PCDATA | Inline Text elements)*
acronym	Core Attributes: name, id, title Language Attributes: xml:lang Event Attributes: onclick, ondblclick, onmousedown, onmouseup, onmouseover, onmousemove, onmouseout, onkeypress, onkeydown, onkeyup Other Attributes: style	(PCDATA | Inline Text elements)*
address	Core Attributes: name, id, title Language Attributes: xml:lang Event Attributes: onclick, ondblclick, onmousedown, onmouseup, onmouseover, onmousemove, onmouseout, onkeypress, onkeydown, onkeyup Other Attributes: style	(PCDATA | Inline Text elements)*
blockquote	Core Attributes: name, id, title Language Attributes: xml:lang Event Attributes: onclick, ondblclick, onmousedown, onmouseup, onmouseover, onmousemove, onmouseout, onkeypress, onkeydown, onkeyup Other Attributes: style, cite(url)	(PCDATA | Block Text elements | List elements)*
br	Core Attributes: name, id, title Language Attributes: xml:lang	EMPTY

Table 26-3. *Text Module Elements and Attributes*

Element	Attribute	Content
cite	Core Attributes: name, id, title Language Attributes: xml:lang Event Attributes: onclick, ondblclick, onmousedown, onmouseup, onmouseover, onmousemove, onmouseout, onkeypress, onkeydown, onkeyup Other Attributes: style	(PCDATA | Inline Text elements)*
code	Core Attributes: name, id, title Language Attributes: xml:lang Event Attributes: onclick, ondblclick, onmousedown, onmouseup, onmouseover, onmousemove, onmouseout, onkeypress, onkeydown, onkeyup Other Attributes: style	(PCDATA | Inline Text elements)*
dfn	Core Attributes: name, id, title Language Attributes: xml:lang Event Attributes: onclick, ondblclick, onmousedown, onmouseup, onmouseover, onmousemove, onmouseout, onkeypress, onkeydown, onkeyup Other Attributes: style	(PCDATA | Inline Text elements)*
div	Core Attributes: name, id, title Language Attributes: xml:lang Event Attributes: onclick, ondblclick, onmousedown, onmouseup, onmouseover, onmousemove, onmouseout, onkeypress, onkeydown, onkeyup Other Attributes: style	(Heading Text elements | Block Text elements | List elements)*

Table 26-3. *Text Module Elements and Attributes* (continued)

Element	Attribute	Content
em	Core Attributes: name, id, title Language Attributes: xml:lang Event Attributes: onclick, ondblclick, onmousedown, onmouseup, onmouseover, onmousemove, onmouseout, onkeypress, onkeydown, onkeyup Other Attributes: style	(PCDATA | Inline Text elements)*
h1	Core Attributes: name, id, title Language Attributes: xml:lang Event Attributes: onclick, ondblclick, onmousedown, onmouseup, onmouseover, onmousemove, onmouseout, onkeypress, onkeydown, onkeyup Other Attributes: style	(PCDATA | Inline Text elements)*
h2	Core Attributes: name, id, title Language Attributes: xml:lang Event Attributes: onclick, ondblclick, onmousedown, onmouseup, onmouseover, onmousemove, onmouseout, onkeypress, onkeydown, onkeyup Other Attributes: style	(PCDATA | Inline Text elements)*
h3	Core Attributes: name, id, title Language Attributes: xml:lang Event Attributes: onclick, ondblclick, onmousedown, onmouseup, onmouseover, onmousemove, onmouseout, onkeypress, onkeydown, onkeyup Other Attributes: style	(PCDATA | Inline Text elements)*

Table 26-3. *Text Module Elements and Attributes* (continued)

Element	Attribute	Content
h4	Core Attributes: name, id, title Language Attributes: xml:lang Event Attributes: onclick, ondblclick, onmousedown, onmouseup, onmouseover, onmousemove, onmouseout, onkeypress, onkeydown, onkeyup Other Attributes: style	(PCDATA | Inline Text elements)*
h5	Core Attributes: name, id, title Language Attributes: xml:lang Event Attributes: onclick, ondblclick, onmousedown, onmouseup, onmouseover, onmousemove, onmouseout, onkeypress, onkeydown, onkeyup Other Attributes: style	(PCDATA | Inline Text elements)*
h6	Core Attributes: name, id, title Language Attributes: xml:lang Event Attributes: onclick, ondblclick, onmousedown, onmouseup, onmouseover, onmousemove, onmouseout, onkeypress, onkeydown, onkeyup Other Attributes: style	(PCDATA | Inline Text elements)*
kbd	Core Attributes: name, id, title Language Attributes: xml:lang Event Attributes: onclick, ondblclick, onmousedown, onmouseup, onmouseover, onmousemove, onmouseout, onkeypress, onkeydown, onkeyup Other Attributes: style	(PCDATA | Inline Text elements)*

Table 26-3. *Text Module Elements and Attributes* (continued)

Element	Attribute	Content
`p`	Core Attributes: `name, id, title` Language Attributes: `xml:lang` Event Attributes: `onclick, ondblclick, onmousedown, onmouseup, onmouseover, onmousemove, onmouseout, onkeypress, onkeydown, onkeyup` Other Attributes: `style`	(PCDATA | Inline Text elements)*
`pre`	Core Attributes: `name, id, title` Language Attributes: `xml:lang` Event Attributes: `onclick, ondblclick, onmousedown, onmouseup, onmouseover, onmousemove, onmouseout, onkeypress, onkeydown, onkeyup` Other Attributes: `style`	(PCDATA | Inline Text elements)*
`q`	Core Attributes: `name, id, title` Language Attributes: `xml:lang` Event Attributes: `onclick, ondblclick, onmousedown, onmouseup, onmouseover, onmousemove, onmouseout, onkeypress, onkeydown, onkeyup` Other Attributes: `style`	(PCDATA | Inline Text elements)*
`samp`	Core Attributes: `name, id, title` Language Attributes: `xml:lang` Event Attributes: `onclick, ondblclick, onmousedown, onmouseup, onmouseover, onmousemove, onmouseout, onkeypress, onkeydown, onkeyup` Other Attributes: `style`	(PCDATA | Inline Text elements)*

Table 26-3. *Text Module Elements and Attributes* (continued)

Element	Attribute	Content
span	Core Attributes: name, id, title Language Attributes: xml:lang Event Attributes: onclick, ondblclick, onmousedown, onmouseup, onmouseover, onmousemove, onmouseout, onkeypress, onkeydown, onkeyup Other Attributes: style	(PCDATA | Inline Text elements)*
strong	Core Attributes: name, id, title Language Attributes: xml:lang Event Attributes: onclick, ondblclick, onmousedown, onmouseup, onmouseover, onmousemove, onmouseout, onkeypress, onkeydown, onkeyup Other Attributes: style	(PCDATA | Inline Text elements)*
var	Core Attributes: name, id, title Language Attributes: xml:lang Event Attributes: onclick, ondblclick, onmousedown, onmouseup, onmouseover, onmousemove, onmouseout, onkeypress, onkeydown, onkeyup Other Attributes: style	(PCDATA | Inline Text elements)*

Table 26-3. *Text Module Elements and Attributes* (continued)

The Text Module provides the predefined content sets shown in Table 26-4.

Element Set	Element Names
Heading	h1 | h2 | h3 | h4 | h5 | h6
Block	address | blockquote | div | p | pre

Table 26-4. *Text Module Element Sets*

Element Set	Element Names
Inline	abbr | acronym | br | cite | code | dfn | em | kbd | q | samp | span | strong | var
Flow	Heading set | Block set | Inline set

Table 26-4. *Text Module Element Sets* (continued)

Hypertext Module

The Hypertext Module is used to provide the element used to define hypertext links: `<a>`. This is the only linking element provided in the XHTML 1.0 specification. The `<a>` element is defined in Table 26-5.

Note *When using the Hypertext Module with the Text Module, the* `<a>` *element becomes a part of the Inline set of the Text Module.*

Element	Attributes	Content
a	Core Attributes: name, id, title Language Attributes: xml:lang Event Attributes: onclick, ondblclick, onmousedown, onmouseup, onmouseover, onmousemove, onmouseout, onkeypress, onkeydown, onkeyup Other Attributes: style accesskey, charset, href, hreflang, rel, rev, tabindex, type	(PCDATA | Inline Text elements: <a>)*

Table 26-5. *Hypertext Module Elements and Attributes*

List Module

The List Module contains definitions for all of the list-oriented elements. All of the elements in the List Module are specified in Table 26-6.

Elements	Attributes	Content
dl	Core Attributes: name, id, title Language Attributes: xml:lang Event Attributes: onclick, ondblclick, onmousedown, onmouseup, onmouseover, onmousemove, onmouseout, onkeypress, onkeydown, onkeyup Other Attributes: style	(<dt> | <dd>)*
dt	Core Attributes: name, id, title Language Attributes: xml:lang Event Attributes: onclick, ondblclick, onmousedown, onmouseup, onmouseover, onmousemove, onmouseout, onkeypress, onkeydown, onkeyup Other Attributes: style	(PCDATA | Inline Text elements)*
dd	Core Attributes: name, id, title Language Attributes: xml:lang Event Attributes: onclick, ondblclick, onmousedown, onmouseup, onmouseover, onmousemove, onmouseout, onkeypress, onkeydown, onkeyup Other Attributes: style	(PCDATA | Inline Text elements)*
ol	Core Attributes: name, id, title Language Attributes: xml:lang Event Attributes: onclick, ondblclick, onmousedown, onmouseup, onmouseover, onmousemove, onmouseout, onkeypress, onkeydown, onkeyup Other Attributes: style	<li>+

Table 26-6. *List Module Elements and Attributes*

Elements	Attributes	Content
ul	Core Attributes: name, id, title Language Attributes: xml:lang Event Attributes: onclick, ondblclick, onmousedown, onmouseup, onmouseover, onmousemove, onmouseout, onkeypress, onkeydown, onkeyup Other Attributes: style	<ul>+
li	Core Attributes: name, id, title Language Attributes: xml:lang Event Attributes: onclick, ondblclick, onmousedown, onmouseup, onmouseover, onmousemove, onmouseout, onkeypress, onkeydown, onkeyup Other Attributes: style	(PCDATA | Inline Text elements)*

Table 26-6. *List Module Elements and Attributes* (continued)

Note *The syntax displayed in the Content column of this table shows the DTD structure for this element as it is used in XML.*

The minimal content of the List Module's content is `(dl | ol | ul)+`. When this module is used in conjunction with the Text Module, the `<dl>`, `<ol>`, and `<ul>` elements are added to the Flow set of the Text Module.

Presentation Module

The Presentation Module is actually an extension of the Text Module. This module is used to define the elements, attributes, and content for controlling simple presentation markup. Table 26-7 provides a list of the elements, attributes, and content of the Presentation Module.

Note *The syntax displayed in the Content column of this table shows the DTD structure for this element as it is used in XML.*

Elements	Attributes	Content
b	Core Attributes: name, id, title Language Attributes: xml:lang Event Attributes: onclick, ondblclick, onmousedown, onmouseup, onmouseover, onmousemove, onmouseout, onkeypress, onkeydown, onkeyup Other Attributes: style	(PCDATA | Inline Text elements)*
big	Core Attributes: name, id, title Language Attributes: xml:lang Event Attributes: onclick, ondblclick, onmousedown, onmouseup, onmouseover, onmousemove, onmouseout, onkeypress, onkeydown, onkeyup Other Attributes: style	(PCDATA | Inline Text elements)*
hr	Core Attributes: name, id, title Language Attributes: xml:lang Event Attributes: onclick, ondblclick, onmousedown, onmouseup, onmouseover, onmousemove, onmouseout, onkeypress, onkeydown, onkeyup Other Attributes: style	EMPTY
i	Core Attributes: name, id, title Language Attributes: xml:lang Event Attributes: onclick, ondblclick, onmousedown, onmouseup, onmouseover, onmousemove, onmouseout, onkeypress, onkeydown, onkeyup Other Attributes: style	(PCDATA | Inline Text elements)*

Table 26-7. *Presentation Module Elements and Attributes*

Elements	Attributes	Content
small	Core Attributes: name, id, title Language Attributes: xml:lang Event Attributes: onclick, ondblclick, onmousedown, onmouseup, onmouseover, onmousemove, onmouseout, onkeypress, onkeydown, onkeyup Other Attributes: style	(PCDATA | Inline Text elements)*
sub	Core Attributes: name, id, title Language Attributes: xml:lang Event Attributes: onclick, ondblclick, onmousedown, onmouseup, onmouseover, onmousemove, onmouseout, onkeypress, onkeydown, onkeyup Other Attributes: style	(PCDATA | Inline Text elements)*
sup	Core Attributes: name, id, title Language Attributes: xml:lang Event Attributes: onclick, ondblclick, onmousedown, onmouseup, onmouseover, onmousemove, onmouseout, onkeypress, onkeydown, onkeyup Other Attributes: style	(PCDATA | Inline Text elements)*
tt	Core Attributes: name, id, title Language Attributes: xml:lang Event Attributes: onclick, ondblclick, onmousedown, onmouseup, onmouseover, onmousemove, onmouseout, onkeypress, onkeydown, onkeyup Other Attributes: style	(PCDATA | Inline Text elements)*

Table 26-7. *Presentation Module Elements and Attributes* (continued)

When you use the Presentation Module in conjunction with the Text Module, the elements are added to different portions of the Text Module, as shown in Table 26-8.

Element	Text Module Set
<b>	Inline Set
<big>	Inline Set
<hr>	Block Set
<i>	Inline Set
<small>	Inline Set
<sub>	Inline Set
<sup>	Inline Set
<tt>	Inline Set

Table 26-8. *Presentation Module Element Allocations*

Edit Module

The Edit Module is used to define the elements that can be used to provide revision marks or other editing related markup to your XHTML documents. Table 26-9 lists the elements that are used in this module.

Note *The syntax displayed in the Content column of this table shows the DTD structure for this element as it is used in XML.*

Element	Attribute	Content
del	Core Attributes: name, id, title Language Attributes: xml:lang Event Attributes: onclick, ondblclick, onmousedown, onmouseup, onmouseover, onmousemove, onmouseout, onkeypress, onkeydown, onkeyup Other Attributes: style, cite, datetime	(PCDATA | Inline Text elements)*

Table 26-9. *Edit Module Elements and Attributes*

Element	Attribute	Content
ins	Core Attributes: name, id, title Language Attributes: xml:lang Event Attributes: onclick, ondblclick, onmousedown, onmouseup, onmouseover, onmousemove, onmouseout, onkeypress, onkeydown, onkeyup Other Attributes: style, cite, datetime	(PCDATA | Inline Text elements)*

Table 26-9. *Edit Module Elements and Attributes* (continued)

When this module is used in conjunction with the Text Module, both the <del> and the <ins> elements are added to the Text Module's Inline element set and are therefore used as if they were normal text elements.

Bidirectional Text Module

The Bidirectional Text Module defines the element, <bdo>, which declares the direction that text flows within your document. The <bdo> element is described in Table 26-10.

Note *The syntax displayed in the Content column of this table shows the DTD structure for this element as it is used in XML.*

When used with the Text Module, the <bdo> element becomes a part of the Inline element set. The use of this module will also add the use of the attribute dir to all other elements that use the xml:lang attribute.

Element	Attribute	Content
bdo	Core Attributes: name, id, title Other Attributes: dire* ("ltr" | "rtl")	(PCDATA | Inline Text elements)*

Table 26-10. *Bidirectional Text Module Elements and Attributes*

Forms Module

There are two possible implementations of Forms Module: Basic and Form. The Basic Module provides access to the primary form elements that were originally created with the HTML 2 and HTML 3 specifications. The Form Module includes other forms elements that were created with the HTML 4 specification. All of the elements that are part of either or both of the Forms Modules are listed in Table 26-11.

Element	Attribute	Content	Forms Module
form	Core Attributes: name, id, title Language Attributes: xml:lang Event Attributes: onclick, ondblclick, onmousedown, onmouseup, onmouseover, onmousemove, onmouseout, onkeypress, onkeydown, onkeyup Other Attributes: style, accept (Form), accept-charset (Form), action, method, enctype	Basic Content: (Heading Text elements | Block Text elements - <form>) Form Content: (Heading Text elements | Block Text elements | fieldset)*	Basic, Form
input	Core Attributes: name, id, title Language Attributes: xml:lang Event Attributes: onclick, ondblclick, onmousedown, onmouseup, onmouseover, onmousemove, onmouseout, onkeypress, onkeydown, onkeyup Other Attributes: style, accept (Form), accesskey, alt (Form), checked, disabled (Form), maxlength, name, readonly (Form), size, src, tabindex (Form), type, value	EMPTY	Basic, Form

Table 26-11. *Forms Module Elements and Attributes*

Element	Attribute	Content	Forms Module
label	Core Attributes: name, id, title Language Attributes: xml:lang Event Attributes: onclick, ondblclick, onmousedown, onmouseup, onmouseover, onmousemove, onmouseout, onkeypress, onkeydown, onkeyup Other Attributes: style, accesskey, for	(PCDATA | Inline text elements - label)*	Basic, Form
select	Core Attributes: name, id, title Language Attributes: xml:lang Event Attributes: onclick, ondblclick, onmousedown, onmouseup, onmouseover, onmousemove, onmouseout, onkeypress, onkeydown, onkeyup Other Attributes: style, disabled (Form), multiple, name, size, tabindex (Form)	Basic Content: option+ Form Content: (optgroup | option)+	Basic, Form
option	Core Attributes: name, id, title Language Attributes: xml:lang Event Attributes: onclick, ondblclick, onmousedown, onmouseup, onmouseover, onmousemove, onmouseout, onkeypress, onkeydown, onkeyup Other Attributes: style, disabled (Form), label (Form), selected, value	Basic Content: Inline text elements Form Content: PCDATA	Basic, Form

Table 26-11. *Forms Module Elements and Attributes* (continued)

Element	Attribute	Content	Forms Module
textarea	Core Attributes: name, id, title Language Attributes: xml:lang Event Attributes: onclick, ondblclick, onmousedown, onmouseup, onmouseover, onmousemove, onmouseout, onkeypress, onkeydown, onkeyup Other Attributes: style, accesskey, cols, disabled (Form), name, readonly (Form), rows, tabindex (Form)	PCDATA	Basic, Form
button	Core Attributes: name, id, title Language Attributes: xml:lang Event Attributes: onclick, ondblclick, onmousedown, onmouseup, onmouseover, onmousemove, onmouseout, onkeypress, onkeydown, onkeyup Other Attributes: style, accesskey, disabled, name, tabindex, type, value	(PCDATA | Heading text elements | List elements | Block text elements - form | Inline text elements - formctrl)*	Form
fieldset	Core Attributes: name, id, title Language Attributes: xml:lang Event Attributes: onclick, ondblclick, onmousedown, onmouseup, onmouseover, onmousemove, onmouseout, onkeypress, onkeydown, onkeyup Other Attributes: style	(PCDATA | Inline text elements | Flow)*	Form

Table 26-11. *Forms Module Elements and Attributes* (continued)

Element	Attribute	Content	Forms Module
legend	Core Attributes: name, id, title Language Attributes: xml:lang Event Attributes: onclick, ondblclick, onmousedown, onmouseup, onmouseover, onmousemove, onmouseout, onkeypress, onkeydown, onkeyup Other Attributes: style, accesskey	(PCDATA | Inline text elements)*	Form
optgroup	Core Attributes: name, id, title Language Attributes: xml:lang Event Attributes: onclick, ondblclick, onmousedown, onmouseup, onmouseover, onmousemove, onmouseout, onkeypress, onkeydown, onkeyup Other Attributes: style, disabled, label	option+	Form

Table 26-11. *Forms Module Elements and Attributes* (continued)

Note *The syntax displayed in the Content column of this table shows the DTD structure for this element as it is used in XML. The (Form) designate near some of the Attributes in Table 26-11 note the use of that attribute only in the Form implementation of the Forms Modules.*

The Form Modules define two content sets: the Form content set with the elements <form> and <fieldset>, and the Formctrl content set with the elements <input>, <select>, <textarea>, <label>, and <button>. When the Form Module is used, all of the Form content set elements are added to the Block set of the Text Module, while all of the elements in the Formctrl content set are added to the Inline set of the Text Module. As you can see from Table 26-11, the Basic Form Module is simply a subset of the Form Module. You can't use these Form Modules together within a single document.

Table Module

There are two Tables-related Modules that have been developed for use with XHTML: Basic Tables Module and Tables Module. The Basic Tables Module provides just the primarily used table-related elements, whereas the Tables Module provides support for all of the elements available with HTML 4 that were used to create tables. All of these elements are shown in Table 26-12.

Note *The syntax displayed in the Content column of this table shows the DTD structure for this element as it is used in XML. The (Table) designate near some of the Attributes in Table 26-12 note the use of that attribute only in the Form implementation of the Forms Modules.*

Element	Attribute	Content	Module
caption	Core Attributes: name, id, title Language Attributes: xml:lang Event Attributes: onclick, ondblclick, onmousedown, onmouseup, onmouseover, onmousemove, onmouseout, onkeypress, onkeydown, onkeyup Other Attributes: style	(PCDATA | Inline text elements)*	Basic, Tables
table	Core Attributes: name, id, title Language Attributes: xml:lang Event Attributes: onclick, ondblclick, onmousedown, onmouseup, onmouseover, onmousemove, onmouseout, onkeypress, onkeydown, onkeyup Other Attributes: style, border (Tables), cellpadding (Tables), cellspacing (Tables), datapagessize (Tables), frame (Tables), rules (Tables), summary, width	Basic Content: caption?, tr+ Tables Content: caption?, (col* | colgroup*), ((thead?, tfoot?, tbody+) | (tr+))	Basic, Tables

Table 26-12. *Table Module Elements and Attributes*

Element	Attribute	Content	Module
td	Core Attributes: name, id, title Language Attributes: xml:lang Event Attributes: onclick, ondblclick, onmousedown, onmouseup, onmouseover, onmousemove, onmouseout, onkeypress, onkeydown, onkeyup Other Attributes: style, abbr, align, axis, char (Tables), charoff (Tables), colspan, headers, rowspan, scope, valign	Basic Content: (PCDATA | Flow text elements—table)* Tables Content: (PCDATA | Flow text elements)*	Basic, Tables
th	Core Attributes: name, id, title Language Attributes: xml:lang Event Attributes: onclick, ondblclick, onmousedown, onmouseup, onmouseover, onmousemove, onmouseout, onkeypress, onkeydown, onkeyup Other Attributes: style, abbr, align, axis, char (Tables), charoff (Tables), colspan, headers, rowspan, scope, valign	Basic Content: (PCDATA | Flow text elements - table)* Tables Content: (PCDATA | Flow text elements)*	Basic, Tables
tr	Core Attributes: name, id, title Language Attributes: xml:lang Event Attributes: onclick, ondblclick, onmousedown, onmouseup, onmouseover, onmousemove, onmouseout, onkeypress, onkeydown, onkeyup Other Attributes: style, align, char (Tables), charoff (Tables), valign	Basic Content: (td)+ Tables Content: (td | th)+	Basic, Tables

Table 26-12. *Table Module Elements and Attributes* (continued)

Element	Attribute	Content	Module
col	Core Attributes: name, id, title Language Attributes: xml:lang Event Attributes: onclick, ondblclick, onmousedown, onmouseup, onmouseover, onmousemove, onmouseout, onkeypress, onkeydown, onkeyup Other Attributes: style, align, char, charoff, span, valign, width	EMPTY	Tables
colgroup	Core Attributes: name, id, title Language Attributes: xml:lang Event Attributes: onclick, ondblclick, onmousedown, onmouseup, onmouseover, onmousemove, onmouseout, onkeypress, onkeydown, onkeyup Other Attributes: style, align, char, charoff, span, valign, width	col*	Tables
tbody	Core Attributes: name, id, title Language Attributes: xml:lang Event Attributes: onclick, ondblclick, onmousedown, onmouseup, onmouseover, onmousemove, onmouseout, onkeypress, onkeydown, onkeyup Other Attributes: style, align, char, charoff, valign	tr+	Tables

Table 26-12. *Table Module Elements and Attributes* (continued)

Element	Attribute	Content	Module
thead	Core Attributes: name, id, title Language Attributes: xml:lang Event Attributes: onclick, ondblclick, onmousedown, onmouseup, onmouseover, onmousemove, onmouseout, onkeypress, onkeydown, onkeyup Other Attributes: style, align, char, charoff, valign	tr+	Tables
tfoot	Core Attributes: name, id, title Language Attributes: xml:lang Event Attributes: onclick, ondblclick, onmousedown, onmouseup, onmouseover, onmousemove, onmouseout, onkeypress, onkeydown, onkeyup Other Attributes: style, align, char, charoff, valign	tr+	Tables

Table 26-12. *Table Module Elements and Attributes* (continued)

Image Module

The Image Module adds the controls enabling you to insert images into your XHTML documents. The XHTML 1.0 specification only included the `<img />` element, which enables you to insert any JPG, GIF, or PNG image into your XHTML document. The `<img />` element is described in Table 26-13.

The syntax displayed in the Content column of this table shows the DTD structure for this element as it is used in XML.

The `<img />` element creates an inline element that is added to the Inline element set of the Text Module when the Image Module is used in an application.

Element	Attribute	Content
img	Core Attributes: name, id, title Language Attributes: xml:lang Event Attributes: onclick, ondblclick, onmousedown, onmouseup, onmouseover, onmousemove, onmouseout, onkeypress, onkeydown, onkeyup Other Attributes: style, alt, height. longdesc, src, width	EMPTY

Table 26-13. *Image Module Elements and Attributes*

Client-Side Image Map Module

The Client-Side Image Map Module provides information on the <area> and the <a> elements that can be used to create a mapping of hot links over an image created with the <img /> element discussed in the previous section on the Image Module. Table 26-14 explains how the <area> and <a> elements are used.

Note *The syntax displayed in the Content column of this table shows the DTD structure for this element as it is used in XML.*

Element	Attribute	Content
a	coords, shape	EMPTY
area	Core Attributes: name, id, title Language Attributes: xml:lang Event Attributes: onclick, ondblclick, onmousedown, onmouseup, onmouseover, onmousemove, onmouseout, onkeypress, onkeydown, onkeyup Other Attributes: style, accesskey, coords, shape	EMPTY

Table 26-14. *Client-Side Image Map Module Elements and Attributes*

The `<area>` and `<a>` elements are typically contained in a `<map>` element on an HTML or XHTML document and are invisible inline elements that have no effect on the layout of your XHTML document.

Summary

The change from HTML to XHTML enables document developers to start working toward the separation of content from formatting, which is the ultimate goal of XML. The XHTML specification has provided Web developers with a huge boost toward the change and progression into the world of XML.

Because XHTML is based on XML, all XHTML documents are also XML-compliant documents. The reformulation of HTML into XHTML was done so that, with some careful planning, your new XHTML documents will be HTML 4 compatible and therefore viewable in all of the current HTML 4 compliant Web browsers.

The next step in the development of XHTML is the modularization of XHTML into a variety of modules that can be used with a wider selection of hardware and software applications such as Palm devices, Windows CE machines, and cellular phones. These modules include

- **Structure Module** The Structure Module includes directives for elements that control the physical structure of the document, such as `body, head, html,` and `title.`
- **Text Module** The Text Module defines the basic text elements such as `abbr, acronym, address, blockquote, br, cite, code, dfn, div, em, h1, h2, h3, h4, h5, h6, kbd, p, pre, q, samp, span, strong,` and `var.`
- **Hypertext Module** The Hypertext Module only supports the `<a>` element to create links.
- **List Module** The List Module provides for list-oriented elements including `dl, dt, dd, ol, ul,` and `li.`
- **Presentation Module** The Presentation Module provides the minimum markup for creating simple presentations. These elements include `b, big, hr, i, small, sub, sup,` and `tt.`
- **Edit Module** The Edit Module is used to provide elements and attributes for use in creating editorial marks in your text. These elements include `del` and `ins.`
- **Bidirectional Text Module** The Bidirectional Text Module defines the `bdo` element, which can be used to control the direction that text is displayed on your screen.
- **Forms Module** The elements provided as part of the Forms Module enable you to create form-related content in your documents. Forms elements include

form, input, label, select, option, button, fieldset, legend, optgroup, and textarea.

- **Table Module** The Table Module provides all the elements that can be used to create table structures within your documents. These elements include caption, table, td, th, tr, col, colgroup, tbody, thead, and tfoot.
- **Image Module** The Image Module provides for the support of a single-image element img that enables the embedding of basic images within your documents.
- **Client-Side Image Map Module** The Client-Side Image Map Module provides for the use of client-side image maps in your document. This module supports the area element and its attributes.

These modules can be used alone or in conjunction with each other to create the functionality in your application and document that you are looking for.

Chapter 27

Manipulating XML with JavaScript

XML is a language used to control the organization and content of a document, not to provide scripts. Therefore you may imagine that there are few direct methods to incorporate JavaScript in an XML document. XHTML allows you to do so using the traditional HTML `<script>` element with `CDATA` content. The Mozilla project incorporates scripts in XML documents using XUL, and Internet Explorer allows you to incorporate scripts through the use of the still buggy `html:script` element. However, if you want your scripts to work for everyone, I've found the best route to take is to incorporate your scripts within an XSLT transformation and let the script be dealt with as if you were viewing a standard HTML document.

The Process

In order to incorporate scripts with your XML information, you must create a variety of documents. Each document has a specific role within the process of adding scripts to your document. The following are the steps for this process:

1. Create your XML document.
2. Ensure that it is valid using a Document Type Definition (DTD) or a Schema.
3. Use XSLT to transform your XML information into HTML.
4. Write a script that will perform your specified task with the HTML results of the XSL transformation.
5. Adjust the XSL Transformations (XSLT) code to incorporate the script and any other changes required by the script so that it works properly with your transformed XML information.

This seems like a very short process, but there are plenty of problems that can come up. Most of the problems happen when trying to get the XSL transformations to occur correctly.

The XML Document

The XML document provides the storage location for all of the information used in the example given in this chapter. The following document describes an inventory list; as we move through the chapter, this document will be modified by both XSLT and JavaScript:

```
<?xml version="1.0" encoding="UTF-8"?>
<!-- edited with XML Spy v3.5 (http://www.xmlspy.com) by Heather
(Wagonboss.net) -->
<?xml-stylesheet type="text/xsl" href="sample27.xsl"?>
<InvList xmlns:xsi="http://www.w3.org/2000/10/XMLSchema-instance"
```

```
xsi:noNamespaceSchemaLocation="D:\Osborne-McGraw\XML-
ComRef\Chapter27\sample27.xsd">
  <ItemInfo LastUpdated="2005-02-01">
    <ItemName>Widget Works Pro</ItemName>
    <ItemNum>W22-34</ItemNum>
    <ItemDesc>
      This is the perfect Widget for all major projects.
    </ItemDesc>
    <ItemCost>14.55</ItemCost>
    <ItemLocation>Chicago</ItemLocation>
    <NumInStock>2345</NumInStock>
  </ItemInfo>
  <ItemInfo LastUpdated="2004-12-09">
    <ItemName>Widget Basics</ItemName>
    <ItemNum>W22-03</ItemNum>
    <ItemDesc>Widget for smaller jobs.</ItemDesc>
    <ItemCost>9.06</ItemCost>
    <ItemLocation>SanDiego</ItemLocation>
    <NumInStock>123333</NumInStock>
  </ItemInfo>
  <ItemInfo LastUpdated="2003-13-19">
    <ItemName>Widget Regular</ItemName>
    <ItemNum>W22-19</ItemNum>
    <ItemDesc>
       Widget for the majority of jobs you will encounter
    </ItemDesc>
    <ItemCost>12.34</ItemCost>
    <ItemLocation>Overseas</ItemLocation>
    <NumInStock>40325</NumInStock>
  </ItemInfo>
</InvList>
```

Our Schema

With the XML document created, be sure to validate it against a Schema or a DTD. Although this isn't strictly necessary, it does ensure that the information you are working with is well-formed and valid and that the document will hold no surprises for your XSL transformation. The following Schema validates the inventory list created in the previous XML document:

```
<?xml version="1.0" encoding="UTF-8"?>
<xsd:schema xmlns:xsd="http://www.w3.org/2000/10/XMLSchema"
```

```
            elementFormDefault="qualified"
            ttributeFormDefault="unqualified">
<xsd:complexType name="Item">
  <xsd:annotation>
    <xsd:documentation>
     Individual Item Entry
    </xsd:documentation>
  </xsd:annotation>
  <xsd:sequence>
    <xsd:element name="ItemName" type="xsd:string"/>
    <xsd:element name="ItemNum">
      <xsd:simpleType>
        <xsd:restriction base="xsd:string">
          <xsd:pattern value=".\d\d-\d\d"/>
        </xsd:restriction>
      </xsd:simpleType>
    </xsd:element>
    <xsd:element name="ItemDesc" type="xsd:string"/>
    <xsd:element name="ItemCost" type="xsd:decimal"/>
    <xsd:element name="ItemLocation">
      <xsd:simpleType>
        <xsd:restriction base="xsd:string">
          <xsd:enumeration value="Chicago"/>
          <xsd:enumeration value="SanDiego"/>
          <xsd:enumeration value="Overseas"/>
        </xsd:restriction>
      </xsd:simpleType>
    </xsd:element>
    <xsd:element name="NumInStock" type="xsd:int"/>
  </xsd:sequence>
  <xsd:attribute name="LastUpdated"
                 type="xsd:date" use="required"/>
</xsd:complexType>
<xsd:complexType name="Inventory">
  <xsd:annotation>
    <xsd:documentation>
    Inventory list - root element
    </xsd:documentation>
  </xsd:annotation>
  <xsd:sequence>
    <xsd:element name="ItemInfo"  type="Item"
                 minOccurs="0" maxOccurs="unbounded"/>
```

```
    </xsd:sequence>
  </xsd:complexType>
  <xsd:element name="InvList" type="Inventory"/>
  <xsd:element name="ItemInfo" type="Item"/>
</xsd:schema>
```

Our Style Sheet

You can't add scripts directly to your XML document, so you must use XSLT to transform the XML data into Hypertext Markup Language (HTML) or another format that can incorporate the script itself. The following XSLT document converts the basic XML document, described in the previous document, into HTML:

```
<?xml version="1.0" encoding="UTF-8"?>
<xsl:stylesheet version="1.0"
     xmlns:xsl="http://www.w3.org/1999/XSL/Transform"
     xmlns="http://www.w3.org/TR/REC-html40">

  <xsl:output method="xml" version="1.0"
              encoding="UTF-8" omit-xml-declaration="no"
              indent="no" media-type="text/html" />

  <xsl:template match="InvList">
   <html>
    <head>
     <title>
       Inventory List
     </title>
     <style type="text/css">
       @page {
            margin-left: 15px;
            margin-bottom: 30px;
            margin-right: 15px;
        }
        h1 {
            font-family: Verdana, Arial, sans-serif ;
            font-size: larger;
            background-color: yellow;
            border-bottom-style: double;
            color: Black;
```

```
          }
       </style>
     </head>
     <body>
       <xsl:for-each select="ItemInfo">
         <h1>
           <xsl:value-of select="ItemName" />
         </h1>
         <blockquote>
            Item Number: <xsl:value-of select="ItemNum" />
            <br />
            Item Description: <xsl:value-of select="ItemDesc" />
            <br />
            Item Cost: $<xsl:value-of select="ItemCost" />
            <br />
            Item Location: <xsl:value-of select="ItemLocation" />
            <br />
            Num. In Stock: <xsl:value-of select="NumInStock" />
         </blockquote>
       </xsl:for-each>
     </body>
    </html>
  </xsl:template>
</xsl:stylesheet>
```

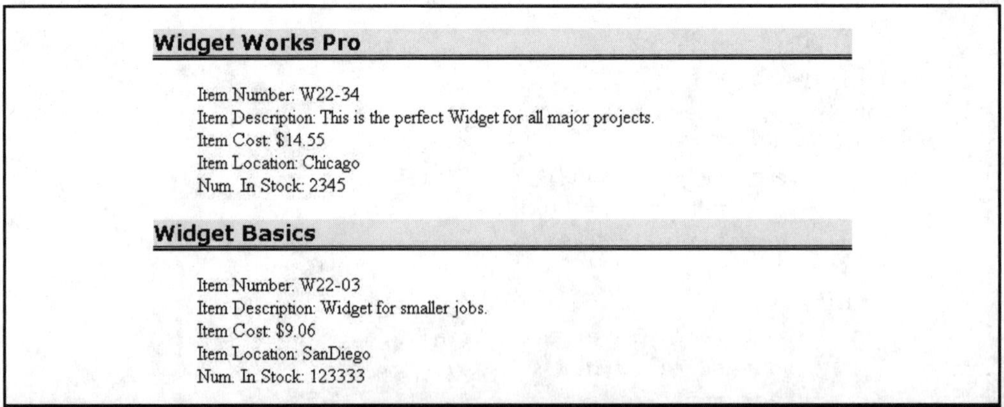

Widget Works Pro

Item Number: W22-34
Item Description: This is the perfect Widget for all major projects.
Item Cost: $14.55
Item Location: Chicago
Num. In Stock: 2345

Widget Basics

Item Number: W22-03
Item Description: Widget for smaller jobs.
Item Cost: $9.06
Item Location: SanDiego
Num. In Stock: 123333

Figure 27-1. *The document is formatted with XSLT before adding script information.*

Writing the Script

If you're familiar with a scripting language, writing the script might be the easiest part of the process. The script that is used in this example simply changes the visibility property of a layer created with a HTML <div> element. Now create a short script to manipulate your XML document. You can use the following script that simply adjusts a property for each item, such as the visibility of a layer:

```
var bwr = navigator.appName;
var ver = parseInt(navigator.appVersion, 10);
NS4 = ( bwr == "Netscape" && ver == 4 ) ? 1 : 0;
NS6 = ( bwr == "Netscape" && ver == 6 ) ? 1 : 0;
IE4 = ( bwr == "Microsoft Internet Explorer" && ver == 4 ) ? 1 : 0;
IE5 = ( bwr == "Microsoft Internet Explorer" && ver == 5 ) ? 1 : 0;
 if (NS4 || NS6) {
   doc = "document";
   styl = "";
  }
  else if (IE4 || IE5) {
   doc = "document.all";
   styl = ".style";
  }
function ChangeProp (layerName, theProp, theValue) {
  var usedLyr = eval(doc + '["' + layerName + '"]' + styl);
  eval('usedLyr.' + theProp + '="' + theValue + '"');
}
```

This script includes a function that has to be called using the onclick event associated with a button provided for showing each inventory item. In order for this to happen, you have to associate each layer with a button created within the XSL style sheet. This is shown in the next section.

In the following section, each of these documents are put together to create a script-enabled document that works with the content of your XML document.

Putting It All Together

When putting together the script with the XSL document, you need to add the script itself between <script> tags in the <head> section of the code of your XSL document, as shown in the following code. The script is in bold to make it easier to find:

```
<?xml version="1.0" encoding="UTF-8"?>
<xsl:stylesheet version="1.0"
```

```
   xmlns:xsl="http://www.w3.org/1999/XSL/Transform"
   xmlns="http://www.w3.org/TR/REC-html40">

<xsl:output method="xml" version="1.0"
            encoding="UTF-8" omit-xml-declaration="no"
            indent="no" media-type="text/html" />

<xsl:template match="InvList">
 <html>
  <head>
   <title>
     Inventory List
   </title>
   <style type="text/css">
     @page {
          margin-left: 15px;
          margin-bottom: 30px;
          margin-right: 15px;
      }
      h1 {
          font-family: Verdana, Arial, sans-serif ;
          font-size: larger;
          background-color: yellow;
          border-bottom-style: double;
          color: Black;
       }
   </style>
   <script type="text/javascript">
    <!--
    var bwr = navigator.appName;
    var ver = parseInt(navigator.appVersion, 10);
    NS4 =(bwr=="Netscape" && ver==4) ? 1 : 0;
    NS6 =(bwr=="Netscape" && ver==6) ? 1 : 0;
    IE4 =(bwr=="Microsoft Internet Explorer" && ver==4) ? 1 : 0;
    IE5 =(bwr=="Microsoft Internet Explorer" && ver==5) ? 1 : 0;
   if (NS4 || NS6) {
     doc = "document";
     styl = "";
   }
   else if (IE4 || IE5) {
     doc = "document.all";
     styl = ".style";
```

```
    }
    function ChangeProp (layerName, theProp, theValue) {
      var usedLyr = eval(doc + '["' + layerName + '"]' + styl);
      eval('usedLyr.' + theProp + '="' + theValue + '"');
    }
    -->
    </script>
  </head>
```

Now the remainder of the XSL template needs to be adjusted so that it places the item information in individual layers so the information is not just running down the HTML document. This is done with the incorporation of positioned <div> elements included within the code. You also need to adjust the <body> element so that it makes all of the layers invisible when the document loads. This is done using the `onload` event as shown in the following code. The <div> element statements are shown in bold to make them easier to find:

```
<body>
  <xsl:for-each select="ItemInfo">
  <div id="{@Name}"
       style="position:absolute;
              left:6px; top:78px;
              width:412px; height:111px;
              z-index:2">
    <h1>
      <xsl:value-of select="ItemName" />
    </h1>
    <blockquote>
       Item Number: <xsl:value-of select="ItemNum" />
       <br />
       Item Description: <xsl:value-of select="ItemDesc" />
       <br />
       Item Cost: $<xsl:value-of select="ItemCost" />
       <br />
       Item Location: <xsl:value-of select="ItemLocation" />
       <br />
       Num. In Stock: <xsl:value-of select="NumInStock" />
    </blockquote>
  </div>
  </xsl:for-each>
</body>
```

```
    </html>
  </xsl:template>
</xsl:stylesheet>
```

The <div> element is placed in the <xsl:for-each> statements because you want each <div> to be placed in the same location with the same formatted information that we previously created in our XSL document.

In addition to your standard HTML <div> element, you need to specify a separate identifier to be used with each layer. This is done using the {@Name} statement shown in bold in the following example:

```
<div id="{@Name}"
     style="position:absolute;
            left:6px; top:78px;
            width:412px; height:111px;
            z-index:2">
```

You also need to adjust the <body> element so that it makes all of the layers invisible when the document loads. This is done using the onload event shown in the following code:

```
<body onload="ChangeProp('1','visiblity','hidden');
              ChangeProp('2','visiblity','hidden');
              ChangeProp('3','visiblity','hidden')">
```

There is one last thing that you need to do for your script to work in your XML document: you have to add one additional layer to contain the buttons that call the ChangeProp() function and alter the visibility property of the individual layers containing the formatted XML data. This code must appear prior to the <xsl:for-each> statement, since you only want it to appear on your document once:

```
<div id="Layer1"
     style="position:absolute;
            left:8px; top:5px;
            width:408px; height:49px;
            z-index:1">
  <form method="post" action="">
    <input type="button" name="WidgetPro" value="Widget Pro"
onClick="ChangeProp('1','visiblity','hidden')" />
    <input type="button" name="WidgetBasic" value="Widget Basic"
           onClick="ChangeProp('2','visiblity','hidden')" />
    <input type="button" name="WidgetReg" value="Widget Regular"
           onClick="ChangeProp('3','visiblity','hidden')" />
  </form>
</div>
```

Note *You must put the closing slash at the end of each of your <input> elements in order for the XSLT document to be well-formed and to transform your information properly.*

The following is your completed XSLT document:

```
<?xml version="1.0" encoding="UTF-8"?>
<xsl:stylesheet version="1.0"
     xmlns:xsl="http://www.w3.org/1999/XSL/Transform"
xmlns="http://www.w3.org/TR/REC-html40">

  <xsl:output method="xml" version="1.0"
            encoding="UTF-8" omit-xml-declaration="no"
            indent="no" media-type="text/html" />

  <xsl:template match="InvList">
   <html>
    <head>
     <title>
       Inventory List
     </title>
     <style type="text/css">
       @page {
            margin-left: 15px;
            margin-bottom: 30px;
            margin-right: 15px;
        }
        h1 {
            font-family: Verdana, Arial, sans-serif ;
            font-size: larger;
            background-color: yellow;
            border-bottom-style: double;
            color: Black;
         }
     </style>
     <script type="text/javascript">
     <!--
     var bwr = navigator.appName;
    var ver = parseInt(navigator.appVersion, 10);
    NS4= ( bwr=="Netscape" && ver==4) ? 1 : 0;
    NS6= ( bwr=="Netscape" && ver==6) ? 1 : 0;
    IE4= ( bwr=="Microsoft Internet Explorer" && ver==4) ? 1 : 0;
    IE5= ( bwr=="Microsoft Internet Explorer" && ver==5) ? 1 : 0;
```

```
  if (NS4 || NS6) {
    doc = "document";
    styl = "";
  }
  else if (IE4 || IE5) {
    doc = "document.all";
    styl = ".style";
  }
  function ChangeProp (layerName, theProp, theValue) {
    var usedLyr = eval(doc + '["' + layerName + '"]' + styl);
    eval('usedLyr.' + theProp + '="' + theValue + '"');
  }
  -->
  </script>
 </head>
 <body onload="ChangeProp('1','visiblity','hidden');
              ChangeProp('2','visiblity','hidden');
              ChangeProp('3','visiblity','hidden')">
  <div id="Layer1"
       style="position:absolute; left:8px; top:5px;
             width:408px; height:49px; z-index:1">
   <form method="post" action="">
       <input type="button" name="WidgetPro"
        value="Widget Pro"
        onClick="ChangeProp('1','visiblity','hidden')">
       <input type="button" name="WidgetBasic"
        value="Widget Basic"
        onClick="ChangeProp('2','visiblity','hidden')">
       <input type="button" name="WidgetReg"
        value="Widget Regular"
        onClick="ChangeProp('3','visiblity','hidden')">
   </form>
  </div>
   <xsl:for-each select="ItemInfo">
   <div id="{@Name}"
        style="position:absolute;
              left:6px; top:78px;
              width:412px; height:111px;
              z-index:2">
     <h1>
       <xsl:value-of select="ItemName" />
     </h1>
```

```
          <blockquote>
             Item Number: <xsl:value-of select="ItemNum" />
             <br />
             Item Description: <xsl:value-of select="ItemDesc" />
             <br />
             Item Cost: $<xsl:value-of select="ItemCost" />
             <br />
             Item Location: <xsl:value-of select="ItemLocation" />
             <br />
             Num. In Stock: <xsl:value-of select="NumInStock" />
          </blockquote>
        </div>
        </xsl:for-each>
      </body>
    </html>
  </xsl:template>
</xsl:stylesheet>
```

Summary

To incorporate scripts in your XML information, you must create a variety of documents. Each document has a specific role in the process of adding scripts to your document. The following are the steps for this process:

1. Create your XML document.
2. Ensure that it is valid using a DTD or a Schema.
3. Use XSLT to transform your XML information into HTML.
4. Write a script that will perform your specified task with the HTML results of the XSL transformation.
5. Adjust the XSLT code to incorporate the script and any other changes required by the script so that it works properly with your transformed XML information.

In Chapter 28, you will see how to convert information in a flat-file database into XML using a Common Gateway Interface (CGI) script.

The Complete Reference

Chapter 28

Collecting and Writing Data with CGI

One of the most popular uses of Common Gateway Interface (CGI) on the Internet is to read a flat-file database. In all of the XML articles and books that you read, there is a lot of discussion of using XML as a universal means of viewing information within a database. There are many ways to do this, including using a proprietary program's conversion process to read and convert the information in the database. Of course, using a proprietary program isn't an option in all cases. That is why in this chapter, we will discuss how you can create your own converter using CGI.

This chapter doesn't teach you CGI code. If you do not know CGI/Practical Extraction and Report Language (perl), you will need to read the Perl Developers Guide *written by Edward Peschko and Michelle De Wolfe and published by Osborne/McGraw-Hill.*

The example in this chapter uses a flat-file database, rather than using the data from an Oracle or MySQL database.

Setting Up the Variables and Opening the Script

The first step to converting your flat-file database to an XML document is to start formatting the CGI script appropriately.

The first line of your CGI script must direct the script to the location of perl on your server. In the following example, it is at `!/usr/bin/perl`:

```
#!/usr/bin/perl -T
```

Following the opening statement designating the location of perl on the server are the introductory comments, all preceded by a pound (#) symbol. These comments simply give you an introduction to the script and what it is supposed to do. In this case, it also names the author and copyright information for the script:

```
#                 Application Information                      #
# Application Name: CGI - Text to XML
# Application Authors:
# Version: 1.0
# Last Modified: 01MAR01
#
# Copyright:
#    You may use this code according to the terms specified in
#    the "Artistic License" included with this distribution. The
#    license can be found in the "Documentation" subdirectory as
#    a file named README.LICENSE.
```

```
#
# Description:
#     This program converts information in a flat-file database into
#     an XML document.
#
```

Once you have described your program with comments, you need to specify the variables that will be used when working with your information. The first of these will be the two files that are being manipulated in this CGI program: the database file represented by the `$database_file` variable, and the XML document represented by the `$xml_file` variable. The following code creates these two variables.

```
$database_file = "./sample.txt";
$xml_file = "./sample.xml";
```

After defining these two variables, you will need to specify the other perl libraries that will be used to actually do the processing of the information within the database, as well as save the data to the XML file after it has been formatted.

```
#                       Require Libraries.                        #
# Require the necessary files within the perl library.
# ($lib is the location of the Library directory where the files
# associated with the default PERL installation are installed.
# Set $lib = "." if you do not have a Library directory.
#
# The cig-lib.pl, cgi-lib.sol, auth-lib.pl, and date.pl Perl
# files are libraries allowing the reading of the database
# without spending too much time re-creating the wheel.
#

$lib = "./Library";
&CgiRequire("$lib/cgi-lib.pl", "$lib/cgi-lib.sol",
         "$lib/auth-lib.pl", "$lib/date.pl");
```

Format of the Flat-File Database

When you are attempting to read from your database, you first have to define the order of information contained within the database. The CGI program must have this information in order to properly encode the data in your resulting XML document. The following code identifies the format of the information in the flat database file. When the CGI program reads the data from the database, it will be ordered to fit in this particular structure:

```
%FIELD_ARRAY = ( 'DBID', 'dbid',
                 'Contact', 'contact',
                 'Company', 'company',
                 'Email', 'email',
                 'City', 'city',
                 'State', 'state');
@field_names = ("DBID", "Contact", "Company", "Email", "City",
                "State");
@field_values = ("dbid", "contact", "company", "email", "city",
                 "state");
```

This code can be used to identify the following database records:

ID	Contact	Company	Email	City	State
1	Heather	Cat's Claw	heather@catsclaw.com	Enterprise	TX
2	Luis	Cat's Claw	luis@catsclaw.com	Enterprise	TX
3	Ann	Watch Pocket Creations	ann@watchpkt.com	Orlando	OH

Creating the XML File

After you have set up the variables for reading and working with the other perl library files, you need to create and open a new XML document file. This is done using the `new()` `File:IO` method included in the perl `cgi-lib.pl` file:

```
new(XMLDOC, "sample.xml")
```

You must create and open the XML document prior to starting any of the writing processes, shown in the next section, since all data must be written directly to that XML document in order to be saved.

Opening the Database and Starting the Loop

With your XML file opened, you are ready to start writing information to the file. The information that must first be written to any XML document is the XML processing instruction and the opening root element, in this case `<AddressBook>`:

```
#  Write the XML document header information
#  and the root element <AddressBook> for the
#  entire XML document.
```

```
# ##
print XMLDOC qq! "<?xml version="1.0" standalone="yes"?>\n" !;
print XMLDOC "<AddressBook>\n";
```

If your XML document will be using a DTD, Schema, or style sheet, you will need to add the appropriate declarations for those elements in this section.

If you wish to print your information to the screen rather than a file, do not use the XMLDOC variable in the `print` *statements.*

Once you have written the appropriate heading information to your XML document, you must open the database and prepare to read information from it. In this case, the `open()` function opens the file specified in the variable `$database_file` with the identifier `DATABASE` for easy reference throughout the remainder of the CGI program. If there is an error opening the database, an error message is displayed to let the user know what and where a problem occurred.

```
# Grab the listings for all the entries in the file. Make sure
# that if you are unable to open the database file,
# a useful message is sent back to the user for debugging.
# Do this using the open_error subroutine in cgi-lib.sol passing
# the routine the location of the database file.
      open (DATABASE, "$database_file") || &CgiDie ("I am sorry, but I
      was unable to open the data file. The value I have is $database_file.
Check the path and the permissions.");
```

Reading the Data

Once you have opened both your XML document and your database, you are ready to read the information from the database. This is done using a `while` loop that will read each record from the database until the end of the database is reached. In the process of performing this `while` loop, all of the information in the database is separated into its respective variables:

```
# Loop through each record in the database.
#
while (<DATABASE>)
 {
  ($dbid, $contact, $company, $email, $city, $state) = split (/\|/,$_);
```

Writing Your Data

With the separated data, you are now ready to write each formatted line to your XMLDOC document. Each document is written in turn, providing the appropriate XML element structure around each variable so they are formatted properly within the final XML document. The `\n` rule at the end of each `print` statement inserts a line break in your XML document designated by the XMLDOC file.

```
#  Write each record for the database
#
print XMLDOC "<ContactRecord>\n";
print XMLDOC "<ID>$ID</ID>\n";
print XMLDOC "<Contact>$Contact</Contact>\n";
print XMLDOC "<Company>$Company</Company>\n";
print XMLDOC "<Email>$Email</Email>\n";
print XMLDOC "<City>$ID</City>\n";
print XMLDOC "<State>$ID</State>\n";
print XMLDOC "</ContactRecord>\n";
```

Now you need to close the `while` loop, using a simple closing curly bracket shown in the following example code:

```
#  Close of WHILE Loop Writing Each Record
}
```

With the `while` loop closed, the closing element of the XML document is ready to be applied. The following `print` statement adds the closing `<AddressBook>` element to the XMLDOC document:

```
#  Write closing root-element.
#
print XMLDOC "</AddressBook>\n";
```

Saving Your XML File and Ending the Program

The last thing to do at this point is close and save your XML document so that the changes you have made are permanently stored. This is done with a single `close()` statement:

```
close(XMLDOC);
```

The Complete Script

You have seen all of the pieces of this script separated out, but sometimes it is easiest to understand the overall flow of the script by seeing the script in one document. The following CGI script is the combination of each piece that was discussed in the previous sections:

```
#!/usr/bin/perl -T
#                  Application Information                       #
# Application Name: CGI - Text to XML
# Application Authors:
# Version: 1.0
# Last Modified: 01MAR01
#
# Copyright:
#     You may use this code according to the terms specified in
#     the "Artistic License" included with this distribution.  The
#     license can be found in the "Documentation" subdirectory as
#     a file named README.LICENSE.
#
# Description:
#    This program converts information in a flat-file database into
#    and XML document.
#
##
$database_file = "./sample.txt";
$xml_file = "./sample.xml";

#                      Required Libraries.                       #
# Require the necessary files within the Perl library.
# ($lib is the location of the Library directory where the files
# associated with the default PERL installation are installed.
# Set $lib = "." if you do not have a Library directory.
#
# The cig-lib.pl, cgi-lib.sol, auth-lib.pl, and date.pl Perl
# files are libraries allowing the reading of the database
# without spending to much time re-creating the wheel.
#
  $lib = "./Library";
  &CgiRequire("$lib/cgi-lib.pl", "$lib/cgi-lib.sol",
          "$lib/auth-lib.pl", "$lib/date.pl");
%FIELD_ARRAY = ( 'DBID', 'dbid',
                 'Contact', 'contact',
```

```
                 'Company', 'company',
                 'Email', 'email',
                 'City', 'city',
                 'State', 'state');
@field_names = ("DBID", "Contact", "Company", "Email", "City",
                "State");
@field_values = ("dbid", "contact", "company", "email", "city",
                 "state");
##
#   Create/Open XML document
##
new(XMLDOC, "sample.xml")
##
#  Write the XML document header information
#  and the root element <AddressBook> for the
#  entire XML document
# ##
print XMLDOC qq! "<?xml version="1.0" standalone="yes"?>\n" !;
print XMLDOC "<AddressBook>\n";
##
# Grab the listings for all the entries in the file.  Make sure
# that if you are unable to open the database file,
# a useful message is sent back to the user for debugging.
# Do this using the open_error subroutine in cgi-lib.sol passing
# the routine the location of the database file.
##
      open (DATABASE, "$database_file") || &CgiDie ("I am sorry, but I
     was unable to open the data file. The value I have is $database_file.
Would you please check the path and the permissions.");
##
# Loop through each record in the database.
##

while (<DATABASE>)
 {
  ($dbid, $contact, $company, $email, $city, $state) = split (/\|/,$_);
```

```
##
#  Write each record for the database.
##
print XMLDOC "<ContactRecord>\n";
print XMLDOC "<ID>$ID</ID>\n";
print XMLDOC "<Contact>$Contact</Contact>\n";
print XMLDOC "<Company>$Company</Company>\n";
print XMLDOC "<Email>$Email</Email>\n";
print XMLDOC "<City>$ID</City>\n";
print XMLDOC "<State>$ID</State>\n";
print XMLDOC "</ContactRecord>\n";

}  #  Close WHILE Loop Writing Each Record
##
#  Write closing root element and close the document
##
print XMLDOC "</AddressBook>\n";
close(XMLDOC);
```

Summary

When using CGI to convert information from a database to an XML document, the function is the same as if you were converting the information into an HTML file. There are a variety of locations on the Internet to get sample programs that will assist you in the process of performing this conversion, although you will need to modify the script from these sample programs in order to change the conversion to XML rather than HTML.

In the next part, Part VII you will learn about some of the more popular XML child languages that are currently in use on the Internet and in educational institutions around the world.

Part VII

XML Child Languages

Chapter 29

SYMM and SMIL

Synchronized Multimedia Integration Language (SMIL, pronounced "smile") is a markup language that is similar to Hypertext Markup Language (HTML) that enables you to add tags to a text document so that you can easily combine and synchronize text, still images, animation, audio, and video. You can then turn that document into a lively new Web site or multimedia CD-ROM with enough bells and whistles to impress even the most jaded friends or customers.

SYMM Basics

The work that the World Wide Web Consortium (W3C) has been doing on Synchronized Multimedia Modules (SYMM) is based on SMIL 1.0. The SYMM modularization project allows for the breakup of SMIL into a variety of modules, or component parts, that can be separated and used in a variety of other applications. For instance, you can use a layout module in a variety of applications to control the basic design of your application or document. You can use a timing module to control the synchronization of events contained within the document or application.

By modularizing SMIL without changing its content, you give it a much wider realm of possible uses than just the control of Internet multimedia content. The constant development of the SYMM module structure allows a collective look at all the activity taking place in the development of HTML, Extensible Markup Language (XML), Extensible Stylesheet Language (XSL), and Cascading Style Sheets (CSS). By combining this overall look at SMIL and its brethren, the group of developers working on SYMM can modify or suggest modifications to SMIL that use the preexisting standards and commands to provide the same type of functionality that it's already providing, but in a more familiar manner for the developer. We all know that the more comfortable developers are with the tools they're using, the more they'll use them.

Understanding SMIL

SMIL documents are compact enough to store on the Internet, providing all viewers with a high-end multimedia experience without the slow download times inherent in most other multimedia formats. You can use SMIL to enhance multimedia presentations on CD-ROMs, spruce up a computer-based training session, or increase the entertainment value in a RealPlayer multimedia presentation. You can apply SMIL to any type of project as long as you have the SMIL software (such as RealPlayer 8) available to read the document.

SMIL opens up a world of possibilities for you. When you add multimedia to your data offerings, such as your Web site, you can offer visitors a video demonstration of your latest product, provide a tour of the house that you're trying to sell, or put together multimedia help files and product tutorials as technical support for your customers. SMIL also gives you the capability control the timing of when events take place, so you can vary what the viewer sees at a particular time during a presentation.

Because SMIL simply directs the playing of each of the parts of your presentation, it doesn't interfere with the existing quality of your media files, nor does it add any degradation to the files due to playing and positioning instructions. So if you start with top-quality parts, you can end up with a top-quality product.

SMIL Editors and Players

SMIL is constantly growing and attracting more support every month. A perfect example of this is RealNetworks constant development of new tools that both play and create SMIL documents. Apple QuickTime has joined the bandwagon by increasing its support for SMIL in the QuickTime 4.1 version of the software. Other small, relatively unknown companies are also adding support or developing products for SMIL. The SMIL players currently available are shown in Table 29-1.

Software Name	Web Address	Description
Apple QuickTime 4.1	http://www.apple.com/quicktime/	Apple QuickTime runs proprietary QuickTime video files, as well as SMIL documents containing QuickTime-supported files.
Internet Explorer 5.5	http://msdn.Microsoft.com/downloads	Internet Explorer (IE) 5.5 provides support for some SMIL 2.0 modules, although IE is referring to these modules as "HTML+TIME support". IE only supports SMIL if it is embedded within an HTML document.
Oratrix GriNS Player	http://www.oratrix.com/GriNS/index.html	This player allows you to play both RealPlayer G2 and SMIL files.

Table 29-1. *Available SMIL Players*

Software Name	Web Address	Description
RealNetworks RealPlayer	http://www.real.com	The RealPlayer shows both RealPlayer proprietary video and audio documents, as well as SMIL files containing RealVideo and audio multimedia content.

Table 29-1. *Available SMIL Players* (continued)

The ability to watch SMIL action has often been offset by the difficulty to create it. The SMIL editors currently available are listed in Table 29-2.

Note *SMIL is easily created in a text editor such as Windows Notepad or, on a Macintosh, BBEdit. You do not require a special editor to create SMIL documents, but these editors can come in handy when trying to manage all of your multimedia elements and set up timing correctly for the playing of the presentation.*

Software Name	Web Address
Allaire Homesite	http://www.allaire.com
Oratrix GriNS	http://www.oratrix.com/GriNS/index.html
RealNetworks RealSlideshow 2	http://www.real.com
Sausage Software's SMIL Composer	http://www.sausage.com/supertoolz/toolz/stsmil.html
Veon's Studio	http://www.veon.com

Table 29-2. *SMIL Editors*

SMIL and HTML

If you look at an HTML and SMIL document side by side (see Table 29-3), you can see a number of similarities. Although the basic structure of HTML and SMIL documents is practically the same, they both use different namespaces. The namespace identifying SMIL is located at http://www.w3.org/TR/REC-smil/2000/SMIL20/LC/.

Like HTML, SMIL uses a series of elements (or tags), such as the <head> and <body>, to identify each section of the presentation and each item, such as a particular piece of video or a text blurb, that is added to the document. Elements are simply placeholders on the document that tell the SMIL player or the Web browser what type of information it's reading and how to display that information.

The only major difference in the primary document structure between SMIL and HTML is that with SMIL you start with a `<smil>` tag instead of with an `<html>` tag. Regarding all other aspects, the format of these languages is the same:

- All element names are enclosed in angle brackets (<>).
- Each element has an opening and closing element marker.
- The closing element marker has an additional forward slash that identifies it as the close of a preceding tag.

Each of these requirements is based upon SMIL being just one aspect of XML.

HTML Document	SMIL Presentation
`<html>`	`<smil>`
`<head>`	`<head>`
`<meta>`	`<meta/>`
`</head>`	`</head>`
`<body>`	`<body>`
Content of document	*Content of presentation*
`</body>`	`</body>`
`</html>`	`</smil>`

Table 29-3. *Standard SMIL and HTML Document Structure*

Note *SMIL requires that you close the* `<meta>` *tag with a forward slash, as shown in Table 29-3, before the closing angle bracket. In HTML documents, that slash isn't necessary and actually causes some Web browsers to display documents incorrectly. SMIL's XML foundation dictates the requirement for closing your meta tags.*

SMIL Media Elements

If you have ever built a standard Web page, you are already familiar with many of the media types that you use with SMIL. All of the text, video, images, and sound files that you use on your HTML pages are media. Media is simply a global term applied to the various types of images, animation, text, sound bytes, and video that can be played and displayed. Table 29-4 provides a list of all the media elements that can load your different media types, available with SMIL 2.0.

Media Element	Example	Description
`<animation>`	`<animation src="url" type = "application/gif">`	Adds animations, which are typically GIFs with multiple images stored within them. Each frame, or image, is created individually and then, using some type of GIF animation compilation program, are placed into the proper sequential order with timing controls added.
`<audio>`	`<audio src = "http://www.mydomain.com/smilsong.mid" type = "audio/midi">`	Inserts an audio file, which can be a WAV, MIDI, Real Audio, or other audio format, as long as the SMIL player supports that particular audio format.

Table 29-4. *SMIL Media Elements*

Media Element	Example	Description
<img>	`<img src = "url" type = "MIME type">`	Adds images to your document. SMIL players typically support GIF, JPEG, and PNG image formats
<text>	`text src = "http://www.mydomain.com/smiltext.txt" type = "text/plain">`	Adds stationary text, which can be formatted with CSS, to your presentation document.
<textstream>	`<textstream src = "http://www.mydomain.com/smil.html" type = "text/html">`	Adds a scrolling marquee to your presentation document. The appearance of this text may be formatted using CSS.
<video>	`<video src = "http://www.mydomain.com/smillogo.mpg" type = "video/mpeg">`	Adds a video file—MPEG, Real Movie, QuickTime Movie, or any other type of movie file that is supported by the SMIL player being used—to your document.

Table 29-4. *SMIL Media Elements* (continued)

The sample SMIL presentation shown in Figure 29-1 uses animations, audio, text, and images to create a quick introduction to the RealPlayer SMIL player. This SMIL presentation ships with RealPlayer 8 as firstrun.smi.

Figure 29-1. *An SMIL presentation is used as a quick introduction to SMIL and RealPlayer.*

Unknown Media Types

There will be times when you will want to add information to your SMIL presentation, but you won't be sure which type of media will be used there, which will happen frequently if your SMIL presentations are being created by scripts. To deal with this, SMIL provides you with the `<ref>` element, which refers you to a general media object. When you are using the `<ref>` element, you should provide more than the minimum required attributes. This is to ensure that the SMIL player knows exactly what to do with the media type you are adding to your presentation. All of the attributes available with SMIL media elements are listed in Table 29-5 in the following section.

SMIL Media Attributes

As you may have noted from the previous sections, SMIL media elements also have a variety of attributes associated with them. Typically there are only two attributes that are required in a media element declaration: `src` and `type`. In addition to these attributes, there are many others that provide more detailed information about how to manipulate the media element you are defining. Table 29-5 provides a list of all the SMIL Media object attributes that are available.

Name	Example(s)	Description
abstract	abstract="Photo of Department Manager J. Hall"	Provides a description of the content contained within the element.
alt	alt=""Mug shot of Jim Hall"	Provides alternative text information for SMIL players that don't support the particular media type that was used and is strongly recommended for all media objects, but the enforcement of this usage has been left in the hands of the SMIL authoring tools.
author	author="Heather"	Identifies the name of the person who created this particular media object.
begin	begin="ImgObject.click" begin=5s" begin="song.begin+2s"	Provides the starting time for the playing of this object or another object by the clock, in reference to another object, or in response to a user interaction; see "Setting Up SMIL Timing" later in this chapter.
clipBegin	clipBegin="smtpe= 01:31:00"	Provides the specific time for beginning the playing of a portion, or clip, of a media object. For more information on the `clipBegin` attribute, see "Setting Up SMIL Timing" later in this chapter.
clipEnd	clipEnd="song=5s"	Provides the specific time for stopping the playing of a portion, or clip, of a media object. For more information on the `clipEnd` attribute, see "Setting Up SMIL Timing" later in this chapter.

Table 29-5. *SMIL Media Attributes*

Name	Example(s)	Description
copyright	copyright="Copyright 2005, H. Williamson"	Provides the copyright of the content that is identified by this media element.
end	end="song.begin+2s"	Provides the ending time for the playing of this object or another object by the clock, in reference to another object, or in response to a user interaction; see "Setting Up SMIL Timing" later in this chapter.
longdesc	longdesc="http://mydomain.com/longdesc.html"	Provides a link to a file that contains a long description of the current media object. If the media object is being used as a link to another destination, this attribute will often contain the information about that destination.
port	port="1234-1235"	Provides the Real Time Transport Protocol/Real Time Streaming Protocol (RTP/RTSP) port identifier for the media object if it is being transferred using RTP but without using RTSP.
readIndex	readIndex="1"	Provides the indexing value that controls the order in which screen readers will read out the text provided in `longdesc` and `alt` attributes. The default is 0, with those objects having a positive `readIndex` value read first from the lowest to the highest value.
region	region="region name"	Specifies the region that the media object should be placed within.

Table 29-5. *SMIL Media Attributes* (continued)

Name	Example(s)	Description
rtpformat	rtpformat="96,98"	Provides a list of media formats that are available to use with the RTP file transfer.
src	src"SMILaudio.au"	Provides the address/URI of the media object being added.
strip Repeat	stripRepeat=""true"	Removes the built-in repeat value from the media object so that animated GIFs can't repeat indefinitely and songs will only play once.
title	title="Song: Row Row Row Your Boat"	Provides the title of the object that is being added to the presentation. This text is often used as a tool tip on visual SMIL players.
transport	transport="RTP"	Provides a name for the transport protocol being used to deliver the media object.
type	type="audio/basic"	Provides the MIME type of the object that is being added to the SMIL presentation.
xml:lang	xml:lang="en-US"	Provides the natural language of the element.

Table 29-5. *SMIL Media Attributes* (continued)

All of these attributes are valid with the various media types identified within SMIL presentations, although some will not be necessary at all times and/or may never be used in your presentation.

SMIL Layout and Formatting Elements

SMIL documents use a variety of formatting elements and layout elements to control the structural appearance of your document. SMIL has very few controls, actually, to affect the appearance of your information, as far as boldface fonts and changing font faces go. It has to rely upon CSS to make this type of formatting adjustments. The following sections cover the primary layout and formatting elements associated with SMIL.

Setting Up the Presentation: <smil>, <head>, *and* <body>

Just like an HTML document, a SMIL presentation consists of a root tag (<smil>) and a head (<head>) and body (<body>) section.

The <smil> Element

Every SMIL presentation has to start and end with the <smil> and </smil> tags. Without this element, the software reading the presentation doesn't know whether to treat the elements included in this section of a document as HTML, SMIL, or Klingon.

The <smil> elements provide the primary structure that identifies everything between its opening and closing element as SMIL code so that the document browser can interpret the information properly. There are several attributes available to use with the <smil> element. Each of these attributes provides additional information about the entire SMIL presentation. This allows the SMIL code to be referenced as part of another document while simultaneously clueing in the Web browser or other viewing software that the document it is viewing is based on XML. The attributes used with the <smil> element, shown in Table 29-6, each have their own purpose in defining the SMIL presentation.

The <head> Element

The <head> element probably looks very familiar if you've ever done any HTML development. In SMIL presentations, the <head> serves a similar function as the <head> element in an HTML document: the <head> element provides a place for both storing information about the information in the document using <meta> and <metadata> elements (see the section "Using Meta Information" later in this Chapter) and controls the physical location of the presentation's content using the <switch> and <layout> elements. All of the attributes associated with the <head> element are listed in Table 29-6.

The <body> Element

The final part of your SMIL presentation's basic document structure is the <body>. In the <body>, you place all the images, text, multimedia, and audio instructions for creating your presentation, as well as the timing controls that affect when the information is displayed or heard. As with the <head> and <smil> elements, the <body> element supports a few attributes that are displayed in detail in Table 29-6. The attributes that are supported by the <body> element will have "body" listed in the Supporting Elements column.

The <smil>, <head>, and <body> Attributes

You also have a series of attributes associated with each of these elements. An attribute provides additional information about the element. For example, an attribute of your head would be hair. Each attribute has a *value*. This value defines the existing state of the attribute. For example, the value of the hair attribute of your head could be brunette or blond.

Attribute	Example	Supporting Element	Description
class	class="smil-media"	<smil> <head> <body>	Provides a way of identifying SMIL content as part of a group. For example, you could have three <smil> sections in a single HTML document, each having the class "smil-media". The id attribute identifies individual "smil-media" class elements.
id	id="video1"	<smil> <head> <body>	Provides a uniquely identifiable name for the SMIL content. It is imperative to use the id attribute when you are including SMIL content within another document and plan on using scripting languages to manipulate it dynamically from within the SMIL players, as discussed in Chapter 1.
profile	profile="http://www.w3.org/TR/SMIL-Boston"	<head>	Identifies the current set of definitions that identify the DTD to which this is matched. DTDs provide a detailed list of the elements and attributes that can be used in a specific type of document. The SMIL DTD provides definitions of all of the elements and attributes that can be used within SMIL documents. The document address specified here may or may not be the same as one of your "xmlns:" statements located in the <smil> element.

Table 29-6. *<smil>, <head>, and <body> Elements*

Attribute	Example	Supporting Element	Description
title	title="Fred's Video Debut"	<smil> <head> <body>	Provides additional information about the <smil> object. It may or may not be used by the SMIL player or the Web browser, to provide a page title for the software's title bar. You can place long strings of text within the content of this attribute or a simple identifier such as "Fred's movie." The use of this attribute is almost entirely dependent upon the SMIL player viewing the document.
xml:lang	xml:lang="en"	<smil> <head> <body>	An XML-based element that identifies the language used in an element. A variety of language codes are available, such as "en" for English, with variations such as "en-GB" for Great Britain's English (or the queen's English) and "en-US" for America's version. For more information on XML elements and attributes, go to the W3C site located at http://www.w3.org/TR/REC-xml.
xmlns	xmlns:smil=" http://www.w3.org/SMIL-Boston.dtd"	<smil>	Identifies the XML namespace used by SMIL. An XML namespace is a means of identifying the origin of all the elements in a document. In other words, an XML namespace provides the address of the document that specifies the individual elements used within the SMIL document. You can use this attribute as many times in the document as you have element origins.

Table 29-6. *<smil>*, <head>, *and* <body> *Elements* (continued)

Using Meta Information

This SMIL `<meta>` element works similarly to the `<meta>` element in an HTML document: it provides metadata, or information about the information, in the SMIL presentation. The `<meta>` element in SMIL follows the same structure as the `<meta>` element in XML and HTML documents

Generally, the most important information to record for each presentation includes the author, copyright, description, and keywords, although their importance may not necessarily fall in that order. If you are placing your SMIL presentation on the Internet, then the description and keywords information will likely be your primary concern, since search engines and other services providing a way for people to find your presentation use this information. The copyright information helps secure your presentation's content against those who might want to steal it. With the changes in copyright law for Internet content, the publication of a copyright statement is required for the protection of your content. On intranets, or internal networks, the author may be the most important piece of information to store with the document, as this allows everyone in the organization to find the person responsible for your great, or not so great, work.

Let's think about this book for a moment. If you were to write down the meta information on this book your list might look like this:

```
Book Title="XML: The Complete Reference"
```

Author="Heather Williamson"

Publisher="Osborne/McGraw-Hill"

Copyright="Copyright © 2000, Osborne/McGraw-Hill.
All rights reserved."

Description="Everything you want to know about XML."

Keywords="XML, xml, extensible markup language, xslt, xsl, css"

When written as `<meta>` elements, this information would be placed within each element's `name`, `http-equiv`, and `content` attributes:

- **`name`** Marks the identifier for the information provided in the `content attribute`
- **`http-equiv`** Provides a marker for information that will need to be processed by the XML browser and SMIL player
- **`content`** Provides the value that should be associated with the `name` or `http-equiv` statement that is identified

Note *For the majority of SMIL players, the* `name` *and* `http-equiv` *attributes are completely interchangeable.*

XML CHILD LANGUAGES

Some samples of <meta> elements that would be applied to our SMIL presentation are shown in the following code sample. The <meta> tag information is placed within the <head> element between its opening and closing tags:

```
<meta name="Author"
      content="Heather"/>
<meta name="Keywords"
      content=" XML, xml, extensible markup language, xslt, xsl,
css"/>
<meta name="Description"
      content=" Everything you want to know about XML."/>
<!-- This Refresh tag loads the second version of this
     video 60 seconds after this page loads.-->
<meta http-equiv="Refresh"
      content="60,URL:chapter2.smi"/>
<!-- This Robots meta tag allows search engines to index
     this page, and follow any links it contains.-->
<meta http-equiv="Robots"
      content="index,follow"/>
```

In addition to the <meta> element, you can include <metadata> elements in your presentation that provide meta information about the particular pieces of content in the presentation. Just as the <meta> element is used to identify information about the overall presentation, the <metadata> element is used to identify information about the individual parts of the presentation. To continue with our book example used previously, the meta information on this book includes the book title, author, copyright, description, and keywords for the entire book. It does not take into account individual parts of the book. If you wanted to define additional information about this chapter, then you would use <metadata> elements to do so.

The <metadata> elements require the use of XML namespaces, discussed in Chapter 7, to identify each reference properly, and the <metadata> elements work in a fashion very similar to <meta> tags. Because of the use of XML namespaces, <metadata> elements can have more than the standard `name`, `http-equiv`, and `content` attributes. These elements can use any of the attribute identifiers that have been made available through the XML namespace references. <metadata> elements also differ from <meta> elements in the fact that <metadata> elements can have child elements. A sample of the complexity of a <metadata> element is shown in the following code:

```
<metadata id="meta-rdf">
<!-- This code identifies the sources of the XML namespace
references used throughout the
```

```
     metadata -->
  <rdf:RDF
    xmlns:rdf = "http://www.w3.org/22-rdf-syntax-ns#"
    xmlns:dc = "http://purl.org/metadata/dublin_core#"
    xmlns:smilmetadata = "http://www.w3.org/AudioVideo/smil-ns#"/>
<!-- Metadata about the SMIL presentation -
     These elements and attributes have been defined
     in the rdf, dc, and smilmetadata documents referenced
     in the above rdf:RDF declaration -->
  <rdf:Description
      about="http://www.mysite.com/Chapter29.smi"
      dc:Title="XML:CR Chapter29"
      dc:Description="XML:CR Chapter 29 - Discussion of SMIL"
      dc:Publisher="Osborne/McGraw-Hill"
      dc:Date="2005-10-12"
      dc:Rights="Copyright 2005 Heather Williamson"
      dc:Format="text/smil" >
  </rdf:Description>
</metadata>
```

To understand this code better, read Chapter 7 and Chapter 25.

Metadata is not required for SMIL documents to display properly or to be accessible by individuals all over the Internet, but it does make the sharing of information between the various organizations easier. Metadata will become increasingly important as software improves and uses this information to provide more personalized services for each interaction you have with your computer and the software that runs on it.

Using <layout>

The <layout> element is primarily a container to define how the individual regions of your SMIL presentation will be positioned within your document. In other words, the layout element is like the stage of a play that is used to contain all of the scenes, actors, and props. This element contains all of the individual region identifiers, which, if we think back to our stage analogy, would be areas such as stage right, stage left, backstage, and so on.

The <layout> element must be contained within the <head> of the SMIL presentation, as shown in bold text in the following example. The <root-layout> and <region> elements are covered later in this chapter:

```
<smil>
<head>
   <layout>
```

```
      <root-layout... />
      <region... />
      <region... />
   </layout>
</head>
<body>
   <!-- Body Information and content go here -->
</body>
</smil>
```

There is just one attribute that is used with the <layout> element: type. This attribute is used to specify which language should be used to lay out the elements. The default value is "text/smil-basic-layout". This value informs the SMIL presentation player that a version of SMIL compatible with the SMIL 1.0 and SMIL Layout Level 0 (from SMIL 2.0) syntax is being used:

```
<layout type="text/smil-basic-layout">
```

Note *If the SMIL presentation software that you are using does not recognize the SMIL language specified within the type attribute, all of the elements contained within the <layout> element should be ignored until the closing </layout> element is encountered.*

The <layout> element can contain three other elements: <root-layout>, <viewport>, and <region>. All of which are discussed in the next three sections of this chapter.

Using <root-layout>

The <root-layout> element has one job: to control the visual appearance of your presentation screen. This element sets the width, height, backgroundColor, and title of your SMIL presentation playing window. Because you can only have one background for your presentation, you can only have one <root-layout> element within your layout. If you were to add more than one <root-layout> element for any presentation, you would create an error and your presentation would, in most SMIL players, not be displayed.

The <root-layout> element is an empty element. It doesn't have any children or contain other elements within itself. For example, as you saw with the <layout> element, you can have both <root-layout> and <region> elements within its opening and closing tags. The <root-layout> element is like the HTML <img> element. It doesn't have a closing tag, and all of the information pertinent to use with the element is contained within itself through the use of attributes, which are listed in Table 29-7.

Attribute	Description
backgroundColor or background-color	Identifies the color used as the background behind the various text, image and the video objects placed on your SMIL presentation
height	Sets the vertical size of the box that the entire presentation must be included within
title	Provides additional information about the presentation background area
width	Sets the horizontal size of the box that the entire presentation must be included within

Table 29-7. <root-layout> *Attributes*

Using <region>

All of the information on a SMIL presentation is placed inside the presentation using a *region*. A <region> is basically a box that has been set aside to store information, whether text, images, video, or audio. You can have as many different regions on your document as you want, and each of these regions can contain multiple objects.

Take a look at the following sample code. In this code, the <layout> and <root-layout> elements define the working area of the presentation. Then the <region> element defines an area that will have text displayed within it. The <text> element found within the body of the SMIL document identifies the name of the region that it will be placed in:

```
<smil>
   <head>
      <layout>
         <root-layout width="300" height="300" />
         <region id="text_region" top="5"  left ="5"
                 height="290" width="290"/>
      </layout>
   </head>
   <body>
      <text region="text_region"
            src="new_text.html" dur="10s" />
   </body>
</smil>
```

This code specifically creates a 300 by 300 pixel presentation screen using the `<root-layout>` element with a single region in it that starts 5 pixels down (`top`) and 5 pixels in (`left`) from the upper-left corner of the presentation area. It defines the size of the region to be 290 pixels tall (`height`) and 290 pixels wide (`width`) so that it is framed by the presentation area with 5 pixels of space on either side (300[total]– 290 [`region`] – 5 [`left and top`] = 5 [`right` and `bottom`]). All of the attributes used by the `<region>` element are listed in Table 29-8.

Attributes	Description
`backgroundColor` or `background-color`	Defines the color that should be used as the background behind the various text, image, and video objects placed on your SMIL presentation. The value is one of the CSS accepted color values.
`bottom`	Identifies the location of the bottom edge of the region. This is a measurement in pixels.
`fit`	Controls the behavior that will result if the contents of a region are bigger than the region's dimensions. Available values are `fill` Forces the contents of the region to be stretched or shrunk so that the object exactly fits the size of the region. `hidden` If the object is smaller than the region, it will fill up as much of the region as it would naturally take, starting in the upper-left corner. If the object is larger than the region, it will fill up the entire region, and any portions of the image outside of the region will be cropped. `meet` Scales the object until one of its dimensions, either height or width, matches that of the region. `scroll` Adds scroll bars to the edges of the region if the contents of the region extend past the regions boundaries. `slice` Scales the object so that its maintains its proportions, taking up the entire region either horizontally or vertically, but will extend itself so that only one edge of the object is cropped, therefore retaining is proper proportion.

Table 29-8. `<region>` *Attributes*

Attributes	Description
`height`	Sets the vertical size of the box that the entire presentation must be included within. This is a measurement in pixels.
`left`	Identifies the location of the left edge of the region. This is a measurement in pixels.
`regionName`	This text string identifies the name of the region.
`right`	This attribute identifies the location of the right edge of the region. This is a measurement in pixels.
`showBackground`	This attribute controls whether the background color of a region is visible. It has the following values: `always` Shows the background color whether the `region` has any content or not. `whenActive` Shows the background color of the region when there is some type of media object currently active within the region.
`top`	Identifies the location of the top edge of the region measured in pixels.
`width`	Sets the horizontal size of the box, measured in pixels, that the entire presentation must be included within.
`z-index`	Controls the vertical stacking order of the regions on your SMIL presentation. Can be set to integer values, of which the highest values appear above lower values.

Table 29-8. *`<region>` Attributes* (continued)

Note *All `<region>` elements are placed relative to their position and size of their parent element, which in SMIL documents is the `<layout>` element. Since the size and position of the `layout` element is defined using the `<root-layout>` element, the `<region>` elements are then positioned relative to the dimensions specified in the `<root-layout>` element, rather than the `<layout>` element.*

Using <viewport>

Most presentations use a single window to display the presentation. With the advent of the SMIL 2 specification and its additional layout elements, you can now have multiple presentation windows. When using multiple presentation windows, the original window, which is the source of the primary SMIL document, is called the root window. This is the window that was first created, and it serves as the creator of the other windows. When you use the <viewport> element in your original presentation window, to create multiple windows, each of the new windows shows a different portion of the presentation.

The multiple layout windows defined by the <viewport> element aren't like HTML frames. The <viewport> element actually opens multiple copies of your SMIL player, each showing a different part of your presentation. Being able to define information for multiple windows with a single presentation enables you to create a table of contents in one window that can interact with the actual content of a book presentation in a second window, as shown in the following example code. Some of the code is boldface to help the <viewport> element and its attributes stand out.

```
<layout>
   <!-- Open  the first window (100 x 250), call it TOC,
        give it the title Table of Contents, which
        should appear in the SMIL Player's title
        bar if the title attribute is supported. -->
   <viewport id="TOC"
             title="Table of Contents"
             width="100"
             height="250">
<!-- Draw in the region that will contain the actual
           Table of Contents entries. This region takes
           Up 100% of the Viewport window. -->
      <region id="TOC_Entries"
              title="Contents Entries"
              height="100%"
              fit="meet"/>
   </viewport>
<!-- Open the second window (600 x 250), call it
        contents, give it the title Book Contents, which
        should appear in the SMIL Player's title
        bar if the title attribute is supported. -->
   <viewport id="contents"
             title="Book Contents"
             width="600"
             height="250">
```

```
<!-- Draw in the region that will contain the actual
          book pages. This region takes
          Up 90% of the Viewport window. -->
  <region id="pages"
               title="page text"
               top="90%"
               fit="meet"/>
  </viewport>
</layout>
```

When you're using the <viewport> element to organize your regions, you need to be aware that each region can only be assigned to one window at a time. This means that you can't have "region1" assigned to both a "TOC" and a "contents" window. You need to create separate regions for each top-level window. Yes, this means that you have to have unique names for all your regions.

Providing Display Options

There may be a time when you need to provide an alternate document layout depending upon who is looking at your SMIL presentation. This alternative layout can be created using a <switch> element within your presentation's <head>. In the following code, you can see a <switch> statement that loads one of a series of layouts dependent upon the baud rate that is available for downloading the document. Within each of the <layout> elements is the systemBitrate test attribute that is used to accompany the <switch> element that is used to perform the text. The systemBitrate attribute is only valid when the <layout> element is included within a <switch>:

```
<smil>
<head>
   <switch>
      <layout systemBitrate="50000">
        ...
      </layout>
      <layout systemBitrate="24000">
        ...
      </layout>
      <layout systemBitrate="2400">
        ...
      </layout>
   </switch>
</head>
<body>
```

```
    <!-- Body Information and content go here -->
</body>
</smil>
```

The available testing attributes that can be used with the <switch> element are covered in Table 29-9.

Test Attribute	Syntax	Description
systemAudioDesc	systemAudioDesc= "[on | off]"	Tests for the SMIL player's preference settings for displaying closed audio descriptions or audio captions for visually challenged individuals, for your presentations.
systemBitrate	systemBitrate=" *integer*"	Specifies the approximate bandwidth, in bits per second, that is available for the presentation on the current connection.
systemCaptions	systemCaptions= "on" | "off"	Specifies a text caption to appear in conjunction with an audio file.
systemComponent	systemComponent= "string"	This is an open-ended test that enables you to test the various components of a SMIL player. You can use this test to see if the SMIL player tests for JavaScript or Java, for instance. The exact string that you need to use varies depending on the SMIL player that your visitor is using.

Table 29-9. <switch> *Element Testing Attributes*

Test Attribute	Syntax	Description
systemCPU	systemCPU="*cpu-code*"	Determines the type of CPU in use by the visitor's computer
systemLanguage	systemLangauge="*languagecode*"	Specifies one of the supported primary language codes
systemOperatingSystem	systemOperatingSystem="*os-code*"	Determines the operating system currently used by the presentation visitor
systemOverdubOrSubtitle	systemOverdubOrSubtitle="[overdub | subtitle]"	Tests the SMIL player's preference settings for receiving overdubbing or subtitles with the audio and video tracks
systemRequired	systemRequired="*namespaceprefix*"	Compares the name of the XML namespace to those namespaces supported by the SMIL player.
systemScreenDepth	systemScreenDepth=" [1 | 4 | 8 | 24 | 32 | *integer*]"	Tests the number of colors that are supported by the screen's color palette, based on the number of bits that are required for displaying the presentation on screen.
systemScreenSize	systemScreenSize="*height* X *width*"	Tests the resolution of the visitor's monitor and compares it to the available screen dimensions.

Table 29-9. <switch> *Element Testing Attributes* (continued)

Note

These attributes can be applied to any media element, or the <par>, <seq>, *or* <excl> *elements, which control the display order of your media elements, discussed in the next section.*

Setting Up SMIL Timing

SMIL timing is broken down into categories, much like the real world. SMIL's categories of time are *global time* and *local time*. Global time is also called *document time* because you use it to control all the overall timing issues within your SMIL presentation. You use local time to control the individual objects that are playing within your presentation. Global time is like the everyday happenings of the world: The crash of an airplane may not directly affect your life at the exact second that it happens, but it may affect your neighbor in a very personal way, which, ultimately, may come back to affect you.

Global time affects everything in your presentation. For instance, the start of the presentation is a global time setting. This time affects all of the individual objects within the presentation because they can't start until the presentation starts. Local time works something like your own personal schedule. You get up, drink your coffee, drive to work, park your car, get to your desk, and begin the day's tasks. Local time provides a way of measuring an object's time. For instance, you can start a video playing in your presentation without affecting any other objects in that presentation, unless those other objects, a text file for instance, are directly looking for the start of that video so they can start their own local time processes. There are three ways that local time can be measured:

- **Active time** The measurement of the element's or object's active duration. Active time begins to be measured whenever an object, such as a video, starts to play and ends when that video stops playing.
- **Simple time** A measurement that's relative to the start of the playing of an object. This time measurement serves as an offset to the playing of a video, for example.
- **Media time** A measurement of the intrinsic duration of a particular type of media.

Synchronizing Your Site

There are two types of synchronization that can be accomplished using SMIL: *hard sync* and *soft sync*. Hard sync is the most restrictive of the synchronization methods, requiring that the entire presentation be constrained to single timing graph that must be strictly followed by all software. In a hard sync system, interference factors such as network congestion and slow connections affect the playback of the entire document. Hard sync will stop the playing of the entire document while the software waits for more information to load. Soft sync is easier on the software. It allows for a looser implementation of the timing system by the software itself. This means that in a soft sync document, elements are slowed down by the interruptions caused by slow connections and congested networks on an individual basis. With the release of SMIL 2.0, you can now define which of your SMIL elements must remain within a hard sync relationship and which of them can use a soft sync, or slip, relationship.

SMIL defines some elements and attributes that are used to control and coordinate the timing and synchronization of your presentation's media elements, including still images, text, and vector-based graphics, as well as intrinsically time-based media such as videos, audio tracks, and animation files. The three elements that are used to control the synchronization of your elements are

- **<seq>** Plays its child elements one after another in a sequence
- **<par>** Plays the child elements as a group, in parallel
- **<excl>** Plays one child element at a time, but without imposing any specific order

Each of these elements works as a time container, allowing you to group your media elements together in a coordinated timeline.

Using <seq>

The primary element to force an order of appearance for your media elements is <seq>. This element identifies the sequence of elements that will play, one after another, within its area of the presentation. This element uses the order of the media elements, as found within the SMIL document, to control the playback order of the elements contained within the presentation. Imagine a presentation with a video, text block, and an audio file. If, for example, it were created with the following SMIL code, it would be

```
<seq>
   <video.../>
   <img.../>
   <textarea.../>
</seq>
```

Using <par>

The primary element that allows parallel playing of your media types is <par>. This element identifies the series of elements that will play together, based upon the values of their `begin`, `end`, and `dur` attributes, within it's area of the presentation. The order of the media elements, as found within the SMIL document, has no control over the playback order of the elements. The playback order can be simultaneous or widely varied over time, depending upon the value of each element's `begin` attribute. Imagine a presentation with a video, text block, and an audio file. If, for example, it were created with the following SMIL code, the `video`, image (`img`), and `textarea` content would appear simultaneously:

```
<par>
   <video id="vid1".../>
   <img id="img1".../>
   <textarea id="txt1".../>
</par>
```

Using the <par> element, each of your media types starts as soon as the <par> block is started. In other words, there is no waiting for the `video` to stop playing before the image element can be displayed. The video, img, and textarea elements all use the par element as their begin marker. So as soon as the <par> element is loaded, all of the media located between the opening and closing <par> tags will load and begin playing. The <par> element will have a duration as long as the length of its longest media child. This means that if one of its media child elements has an indefinite duration, then the <par> itself will be indefinite.

Using <excl>

If you don't care about your media elements occurring in a specific order, but only want them to occur one at a time, you can use the <excl> element. This element will play all of its media children in any order ordained by the individual media element's begin attributes, but only one at a time (exclusively). In the following sample code, the textarea element starts playing as soon as the <excl> element is reached. Three seconds after the <excl> element is started, the video will start. Two seconds after the video ends (video.end+2s), the image will display for 15 seconds:

```
<excl>
   <video id="vid1" begin="+3s".../>
   <img id="img1" begin="video.end+2s" dur="15s".../>
   <textarea id="txt1" dur="10s".../>
</excl>
```

The Timing and Synchronization Attributes

There are a variety of attributes using for timing and synchronization of your presentation, all listed in Table 29-10.

Linking Between Objects and Presentations

Using links, you can control not only your destination as you could with HTML, but you can also control what happens to your existing document, how the new document is loaded, where within the new document you will arrive, and how you can view multiple documents altogether. This is all related to the same technology being developed with XML Linking Language (XLink), discussed in Chapter 24. There are two elements that allow you to create links within SMIL presentations: <a> and <area>.

Using <a>

The <a> element in SMIL functions very similarly to the <a> element in HTML. Using this element, you can create a link from your current presentation to any point within

Attribute Name	Example	Description
begin	begin="5s"	The beginning of an object's playing time.
clipBegin	clipBegin="3s"	Specifies the beginning of a section, or clip, of a continuous media object as offset from the start of the media object.
clipEnd	clipEnd="150s"	Specifies the end of a subclip of a continuous media object as offset from the start of the media object.
dur	dur="indefinite"	Sets the duration of the media element's playing time. Three values are available: **Time in second** (For example 10s, where *s* stands for seconds.) The clock value must be a positive number greater than zero. Negative or zero values are ignored or found as an error. **`Media`** The intrinsic duration of the media element itself. **`Indefinite`** Forces the duration of an element to last forever
end	end="15s"	Stops the playing of an object even if the object's duration, specified by the `dur` element, has not completed.
endsync	endsync = "all"	Synchronizes the ending of two elements.

Table 29-10. *Timing and Synchronization Attributes*

Attribute Name	Example	Description
fillDefault	fillDefault = (remove | freeze | hold | transition | auto | inherit)	Defines the default value for the fill behavior for an element and all descendents.
max	max="15s"	Sets the maximum duration for the display of the media object.
min	min="media"	Sets the minimum duration for the display of the media object.
repeatCount	repeatCount= "3"	Specifies the number of iterations of the simple duration.
repeatDur	repeatDur= "indefinite"	Specifies the total duration for repeat.
restart	restart = "never"	Specifies when and how the media element should restart its playing cycle.
sync Behavior	syncBehavior="canSlip "	Enables an author to control a hard sync relationship to the parent time container or allow it to slip with respect to the time container.
syncMaster	syncMaster = (true | false)	A Boolean attribute used on media elements and time containers to force other elements in the time container to synchronize their playback to this element.
sync Tolerance	syncTolerance = "1s"	Identifies the amount of tolerance allowed for the associated synchronization element.

Table 29-10. *Timing and Synchronization Attributes* (continued)

another presentation. Just as with HTML, there are a variety of rules that must be met when using the <a> link within your SMIL presentation, although these rules may differ some from HTML:

- The <a> element has no effect on positioning.
- The <a> element must have an `href` attribute to designate the destination of the link.
- The <a> element cannot be nested within other <a> elements.
- The <a> element does not have any affect upon the synchronization of other elements within your SMIL document.

SMIL allows you to specify several ways that your link can be triggered, allowing anything from a user's mouse click to the press of key to an event occurring elsewhere in the presentation. Because SMIL has a whole variety of timing systems, your links also have to be activated within a specific time, for instance, if your link is a part of a text element that is only visible for a specific amount of time. If you think about a text file, you know that it doesn't have any intrinsic time duration. You have to use a `fill="freeze"` attribute with your text objects, in addition to a `dur="indefinite"` attribute to force the contents of your text file to stay visible during the entire duration of your presentation as shown in the following code.

```
<a href="new.smi"
      target="toggle_region">
   <text src="title_text.txt"
         region="text_region"/>
</a>
```

Note *The <a> element has been deprecated in favor of the <area> element, although it is still supported through the SMIL 2.0 specification. If you are developing documents that will have a long shelf life, I'd suggest not using this element and creating all of your links using the <area> element discussed in the next section.*

Using <area>

The <area> element allows you to associate a link with only a part of a single media object, such as a corner of a video or a specific spot on an image. The <a> link only allows you to create a link out of a complete media object. It allows you to identify the specific spatial coordinates of a media object and create a map that matches those locations with a destination document. The <area> element also allows you to link to a specific time within the playing duration of its destination object.

<area> elements are placed within the boundaries of your media element so that, unlike HTML, they are linked by element enclosure, rather than a unique name:

```
<img src="mystreetsigns.gif">
  <area shape="poly"
        coords="0,0,0,100,100,100,100,0,0,0" />
</img>
```

The <area> element is an empty element and cannot have any children. It must be enclosed by the media element tags, which can normally be expressed as empty elements. The use of the <area> element forces the media elements to have both an opening and closing tag.

Link Attributes

There are quite a few attributes that are associated with the <a> and <area> elements. These attributes are shown in Table 29-11.

Attribute Name	Example	Description
accesskey	accesskey="A"	Assigns a keyboard character or character combination that will activate the link when pressed
actuate	actuate="onRequest"	Controls whether the link is triggered by the media element, to which it is assigned, becoming active, or whether a presentation viewer has to click the link
alt	alt="This is my link"	Provides alternative text to describe the link
coords	coords="0,0,0,100,100, 100,100,0,0,0"	Provides the coordinates of each corner of the area drawn on your image

Table 29-11. *Link Attributes Associated with the <a> and <area> Elements*

Attribute Name	Example	Description
destination Level	destinationLevel="25%"	Controls the volume of the destination documents audio elements
destination Playstate	destinationPlaystate= "pause"	Controls how the destination document is opened: currently playing or paused
external	external="true"	Controls whether or not the computer itself will control which software application loads the destination of the link or whether the current SMIL player will open the destination file
href	href="mysample.smi"	Provides the address of the destination of the link
nohref	nohref	Allows the area element to not have an address or href attribute
shape	shape="poly"	Controls the shape of the area being drawn on the image
show	show="new"	Controls how the presentation will be will be opened
sourceLevel	sourceLevel="25%"	Controls the volume of the current document's audio elements when the link is pressed
sourcePlay state	sourcePlaystate="stop"	Controls what happens to the source document: whether it will close or simply pause

Table 29-11. *Link Attributes Associated with the <a> and <area> Elements* (continued)

Attribute Name	Example	Description
tabindex	tabindex="2"	Provides the numerical value representing the order of appearance of this link when the tab key is being used to navigate the presentation
target	target="region_name"	Provides the name of the window or region that should contain the contents of the destination of the link once that link is activated

Table 29-11. *Link Attributes Associated with the* <a> *and* <area> *Elements* (continued)

Creating SMIL Animations and Transformations

SMIL provides a mechanism to incorporate animations and transformations within your presentations by enabling you to control the settings of the various attributes associated with the media element you're modifying.

Animation Effects

Four elements work together or individually to create your fully animated presentation. They include

- **<animate>** The generic animation element, allowing you to animate or change the values of any media element's attribute
- **<animateMotion>** Animation focused on moving an object from one location to another location
- **<animateColor>** Allows the alteration of colors that are set by attributes on objects within your presentation
- **<set>** Allows you to set the values of attributes for specified durations

The preceding elements use some combination of the attributes identified in Table 29-12.

Attribute Name	Example	Description
attributeName	attributeName="width"	Specifies the name of the attribute that will have its values altered
attributeType	attributeType="CSS"	Specifies the type of attribute that will have its values altered
targetElement	targetElement="img"	Identifies the element with which the attribute is associated
accumulate	accumulate="sum"	Selects whether the animation effect will be cumulative or will constantly repeat
additive	additive="replace"	Controls whether the values in the animation will increase or decrease as the animation runs
from	from="10"	Selects the beginning value of the attribute
to	to="100"	Selects the ending value of the attribute
by	by="5"	Selects the incremental value that the attribute will be changed by

Table 29-12. *Animation Element Attributes*

You can use these elements and attributes to create simple effects, as shown in the following example, which would take quite a bit of programming in a scripting language for a standard HTML document:

```
<text class="PlainText">
   This will highlight if you mouse over it...
```

```
    <animateColor attributeName="color"
         to="black"
         begin="mouseover"
         end="mouseout" />
</text>
```

Transformation Effects

Transformation effects allow you to add the fade and wipe effects to your SMIL presentation. These effects are similar to those that are available with the filter effects provided with Microsoft's Internet Explorer extensions. Fade effects essentially fade your screen from the current image to either another image or a flat color. Wipe effects essentially use a wiping motion to clear the screen of one image and replace it with another.

The only element used to create transformations is the `<transition>` element. This element has a variety of attributes that define the duration of the transition, the type of the transition, and how that transition is used. A large variety of other transition types are included in SMIL. These transition effects are broken down into five categories, which are described below:

- **Edge wipes** Wipe effects that occur along the edge of your object. An example of an edge wipe is a left-to-right moving bar that reveals a new image to the left of the bar and the old image to the right of the bar, as the bar moves across the image, until only the new image is visible.
- **Iris wipes** Wipe effects that expand from the center of the media like an eye opening up.
- **Clock wipes** Wipe effects that have a rotating arm, reaching from the center of the object to its edge, that replace the old image with the new as they sweep around the center of the object.
- **Matrix wipes** Wipe effects that occur by replacing squares in the old image with portions of the new image in a specified pattern.
- **Non-SMPTE wipes** These are the wipe effects that don't really fall into another category and have not been identified by the Society of Motion Picture and Television Engineers (SMPTE). They include such things as snake wipes that update your screen in a random pattern and other wipe effects that have not been standardized for use in television and movies.

The transition element has a variety of attributes that are associated with it and are used to define the transition taking place:

- **`type`** Identifies the type of transition to take place
- **`subtype`** Identifies the specific transition within the selected type category
- **`dur`** The length of the transition

- **startProgress** The point at which the transition should start
- **endProgress** The point at which the transition should end
- **direction** The direction the transition will move
- **faceColor** Controls the change of a fade transition to a specific color
- **borderWidth** Sets the width of the border of the transition area
- **borderColor** Sets the color of the border of the transition area

In the following example, a single transition has been created that fades the old image to black before allowing the new image to appear. This transition is used with each image, as you can see by the addition of the `transOut` attribute associated with each `<img>` element. I have boldfaced the lines of transition code to help you spot them easier:

```
<smil>
  <head>
    ...
    <transition id="fadeblack"
                type="fade"
                subtype="fadeToColor"
                fadeColor="#000000"
                dur="1s"/>
  </head>
  <body>
    ...
    <par>
      <img src="rat.jpg"
           dur="5s"
           transOut="fadeblack"... />
      <img src="mouse.jpg"
           dur="5s"
           transOut="fadeblack" ... />
<img src="hamster.jpg"
           dur="5s"
           transOut="fadeblack" ... />
<img src="gerbil.jpg"
           dur="5s"
           transOut="fadeblack"... />
</par>
    ...
  </body>
</smil>
```

Summary

SMIL documents provide a fast, cheap, and easy way to create multimedia presentations that can be viewed by anyone over the Internet, as long as they have a SMIL compatible player such as RealPlayer or Apple QuickTime. There are a host of SMIL players and editors available, and more are becoming available every month. As the popularity of SMIL grows, so will the number of editors and players that are available to use with it.

SMIL is based on XML, and, therefore, it uses the same rules for element and attribute name structure, as well as syntax structure, that exist within XML itself. SMIL provides you with the majority of tools that you need to format and place text, image, video, audio, and animated media on the Internet, and format it so it appears with the appropriate timing, links, animations, and transformations that you require to create professional documents.

Chapter 30

Using Scalable Vector Graphics (SVG)

Scalable Vector Graphics (SVG) is used to describe two-dimensional vector-based graphics in HTML and other document formats. SVG is based on XML and incorporates controls for working with animations, groups, filters, and templates. This chapter introduces SVG and provides a basic reference of the primary elements included in SVG that create vector graphics.

A Quick Look at SVG

The Scalable Vector Graphics format has been inspired by the development of the Vector Markup Language (VML) and Precision Graphic Markup Language (PGML) and is on its way to becoming one of the most highly developed technologies on the Internet. The original working draft was released by the World Wide Web Consortium in February of 1999 and became a Candidate Recommendation, November 2000. You can find the most recent SVG specification proposal at http://www.w3.org/TR/SVG.

SVG is an application of XML 1.0 that allows for the encoding of vector information, which is used to describe 2D graphics, and style sheet markup to identify how a vector based graphic should be displayed in Internet Explorer 5 or Netscape Navigator 6. This combination allows us to incorporate full vector graphics and images in the current document, without using imbedded animations or images.

Note *Vector graphics use math formulas to draw your images, whereas the standard Internet image formats such as GIF and JPEG images use bitmap to draw the image. In other words, GIF and JPEG images use a series of colored dots to make your images appear correctly.*

SVG identifies the markup of vector graphic information in the same way, using many of the same attributes, that HTML marks up textual information. SVG uses a series of markup commands that describe the paths of series of connected lines and curves. By using markup, you can dramatically decrease the amount of time it takes to display images on your HTML/XML pages. It also makes it possible for the graphics on the page to be altered quickly with the changing of a style sheet setting, not the exchange of an image.

SVG markup can be used with Cascading Style Sheets in the same manner as HTML markup in order to determine the layout of the graphics that it creates. The simple five-pointed star shown in Figure 30-1 is drawn using the following SVG code.

Figure 30-1. *An organically shaped five-pointed star*

```
<?xml version="1.0" standalone="no"?>
<!DOCTYPE svg PUBLIC "-//W3C//DTD SVG 20001102//EN"
  "http://www.w3.org/TR/2000/CR-SVG-20001102/DTD/svg-20001101.dtd">
<svg width="500" height="500">
   <path
      d="M199.622 8 C232.811 8.20081 214.367 125.34 244.106 146
.834 C273.845 168.328 378.115 128.556 392.764 146.834 C407.411
165.111 288.235 200.134 272.414 233.353 C256.593 266.572 354.851
 370.833 318.92 372.187 C282.989 373.541 236.235 290.282 199.622
 285.667 C163.01 281.052 87.0879 415.467 80.3243 371.141 C73.5607
 326.816 133.607 269.383 126.83 233.353 C120.054 197.324 -3.37061
 163.915 7.53222 146.834 C18.4351 129.753 119.407 137.661 155.138
 146.834 C190.87 156.007 166.434 7.79919 199.622 8 z"
     style="stroke-miterlimit:4;stroke-linejoin:miter;
            stroke-width:5;stroke-opacity:1;stroke:rgb(255,0,0);
            fill-opacity:1;fill:rgb(0,0,255);opacity:1"/>
</svg>
```

SVG has been designed to work in the existing HTML and CSS constructs. This allows browsers and their developers to avoid reinventing the wheel to implement different representations and implementations for existing HTML or CSS functions. In the case of HTML, the document workflow is used to generate information and control locations of characters. In SVG, these same systems are used to generate and place vector paths and their related objects.

SVG Syntax

SVG documents have a similar base layout to other types of XML documents. This layout provides a basic structure from which SVG documents or embedded SVG elements can be created. For instance, the following example provides the basic structure of an SVG document. This document uses the `<?xml?>` declaration statement to identify this document as being part of the XML document family, and then the `!DOCTYPE` processing instruction is used to point to the DTD used to verify the contents of the SVG document. You can see that the `<svg>` element also has a namespace declaration added. This is to assist in the integration of the SVG document with others. If you are only using SVG content in your document, the namespace declaration is not necessary.

```
<?xml version="1.0" standalone="no"?>
<!DOCTYPE svg PUBLIC "-//W3C//DTD SVG 20001102//EN"
```

```
"http://www.w3.org/TR/2000/CR-SVG-20001102/DTD/svg-20001101.dtd">
<svg width="100%" height="100%"
    xmlns = "http://www.w3.org/2000/SVG">
  <desc> <!--Add description of graphic here --> </desc>
  <g>
    <!--Add graphic creating elements  here -->
  </g>
</svg>
```

If you were including the SVG content in another document, HTML for example, you would need to declare the svg namespace, but not include the <?xml?> declaration. If you were including your SVG image in an XHTML document, the <?xml?> declaration would be used for the XHTML document, as well as the SVG content. You can see a simple merging of SVG content and an XHTML document in the following template example.

```
<?xml version="1.0" standalone="no"?>
<!DOCTYPE svg PUBLIC "-//W3C//DTD SVG 20001102//EN"
  "http://www.w3.org/TR/2000/CR-SVG-20001102/DTD/svg-20001101.dtd">
<html xml:lang="en" lang="en"
      svg:xmlns = http://www.w3.org/2000/SVG >
<head>
  <title> <!-- Add a title here --> </title>
</head>
<body>
 <h1> <!-- Add Heading Text here --></h1>
 <svg:svg width="100%" height="100%">
  <svg:desc> <!--Add description of graphic here --> </svg:desc>
  <svg:g>
    <!--Add graphic creating elements  here -->
  </svg:g>
 </svg:svg>
 <!-- Add closing HTML code here -->
</body>
</html>
```

A third way of incorporating SVG documents into your XHTML documents is through the use of the XHTML <embed> element. This element allows you to embed your SVG file directly into your HTML document as an object. The following code shows you how the <embed> element works:

```
<?xml version="1.0" standalone="no"?>
<!DOCTYPE svg PUBLIC "-//W3C//DTD SVG 20001102//EN"
  "http://www.w3.org/TR/2000/CR-SVG-20001102/DTD/svg-20001101.dtd">
<html xml:lang="en" lang="en"
      svg:xmlns = http://www.w3.org/2000/SVG >
<head>
  <title> <!-- Add a title here --> </title>
</head>
<body>
 <h1> <!-- Add Heading Text here --></h1>
 <embed src="somefile.svg" ... />
 <!-- Add closing HTML code here -->
</body>
</html>
```

There are two aspects of SVG code that you must familiarize yourself with to become proficient with SVG: datatypes and syntax.

SVG DataTypes

SVG uses the basic datatypes that are available with many other XML applications. These datatypes include

- ***<integer>*** A numerical value ranging from –2147483648 to 2147483648. This is the same as a `long value` in an XML Schema.
- ***<number>*** A real number value that can be specified differently for each attribute or style sheet property to which it is applied. Most values specified as a <number> datatype will allow any real number in decimal notation.
- ***<length>*** A measurement of distance that is a combination of a `number` and a unit identifier such as `mm` (millimeter), `in` (inch), `cm` (centimeter), `px` (pixels), `pt` (points), or `em` (the length of the `m` character in the currently used base font for the document or viewing application).
- ***<coordinate>*** A length based upon the (x,y) Cartesian positioning system used in the document. On most documents viewed through your computer monitor, this will be a measurement in pixels.

- ***enumerated list*** A list of comma-separated property values that are valid for the element.
- ***<angle>*** A `number` optionally followed by an angle unit identifier such as `deg` (degrees), `grad` (gradients), or `rad` (radians).
- ***<color>*** A name (`red`) or RGB value (`#FF0000`) representing a color to be displayed. Valid values for this datatype include those values that are supported by the CSS2 specification.
- ***<paint>*** A value representing the type settings available for filling an object with color. This can be either `none`, `currentColor`, `<color>`, or `<uri>`.
- ***<percentage>*** A `<number>` followed by the percentage (`%`) sign that represents a relative portion of a dimension of another object.
- ***<transform-list>*** A space separated list of the transformation values: `matrix`, `translate`, `scale`, `rotate`, `skewX`, and `skewY`.
- ***<uri>*** A Uniform Resource Identifier representing a file to be referenced or loaded in a document.
- ***<frequency>*** A non-negative `number` followed by one of the frequency unit identifiers `Hz` (Hertz) or `kHz` (kilohertz) that applies only to aural properties.
- ***<time>*** A measurement of time, such as `13ms` (milliseconds) or `13s` (seconds), that controls the duration of an animation or other timed transformation.

SVG Elements

SVG uses a variety of elements to draw your vector images exactly as you wish them to be. All of the elements supported by the SVG candidate recommendation are listed in Table 30-1.

Element	Syntax	Description
a	<a *attributeValues*> (desc | title | metadata | defs | path | text | rect | circle | ellipse | line | polyline | polygon | use | image | svg | g | view | switch | a | altGlyphDef | script | style | symbol | marker | clipPath | mask | linearGradient | readialGradient | pattern | filter | cursor | font | animate | set | animateMotion | animateColor | animateTransform | color-profile | font-face)* </a>	Creates a link between a specified destination and a specific portion of your drawing

Table 30-1. *SVG Elements*

Element	Syntax	Description
altGlyph	<altGlyph *attributeList*> (*#PCDATA* | altGlyph)* </altGlyph>	Provides controls over the character glyphs used to render specific character data
altGlyphDef	<altGlyph *attributeList*> (glyphRef+ | altGlyphItem+)* </altGlyph>	Defines a set of possible glyph substitutions
altGlyphItem	<altGlyphItem *attributeList*> (glyphRef+ | altGlyphItem)* </altGlyphItem>	Defines a set of possible glyph substitutions
animate	<animate *attributeList*> (desc | title | metadata)* </animate>	Used to animate a single attribute or property over the course of time
animateColor	<animateColor *attributeList*> (desc | title | metadata)* </animateColor>	Specifies a color transformation on an object
animateMotion	<animateMotion *attributeList*> (desc | title | metadata | mpath)* </animateMotion>	Defines a path that a referenced element will move along

Table 30-1. *SVG Elements* (continued)

Element	Syntax	Description
animateTransform	<animateTransform *attributeList*> (desc | title | metadata)* </animateTransform>	Animates an attribute on an element allowing the animation to control the translation, rotation, scaling, and/or skewing of the element
circle	<circle *attributeList*> (desc | title | metadata | animate | set | animateMotion | animateColor | animateTransform)* </circle>	Defines a circle based on a center point and a radius
clipPath	<clipPath *attributeList*> (desc | title | metadata | path | text | rect | circle | ellipse | line | polyline | polygon | use | animate | set | animateMotion | animateColor | animateTransform) </clipPath>	Defines how an object will be clipped
color-profile	<color-profile *attributeList*> (desc | title | metadata) </color-profile>	Selects a color profile to use with the current object

Table 30-1. *SVG Elements* (continued)

Element	Syntax	Description
cursor	<cursor *attributeList*> (desc | title | metadata) </cursor>	Defines a platform independent customized cursor
defs	<defs *attributeValues*> (desc | title | metadata | defs | path | text | rect | circle | ellipse | line | polyline | polygon | use | image | svg | g | view | switch | a | altGlyphDef | script | style | symbol | marker | clipPath | mask | linearGradient | readialGradient | pattern | filter | cursor | font | animate | set | animateMotion | animateColor | animateTransform | color-profile | font-face)* </defs>	A container element for other referenced elements
desc	<desc *attributeList*> *#PCDATA* </desc>	Provides descriptive text of SVG block, group, or individual object

Table 30-1. *SVG Elements* (continued)

Element	Syntax	Description
ellipse	`<ellipse attributeList> (desc | title | metadata | animate | set | animateMotion | animateColor | animateTransform)* </ellipse>`	Specifies an ellipse of specific height and width
filter	`<filter attributeList> (desc | title | metadata | feBlend | feFlood | feColorMatrix | feCompnentTransfer | feComposite | feConvolveMatrix | feDiffuseLighting | feDisplacementMap | feGaussianBlur | feImage | feMerge | feMorphology | feOffset | feSpecularLighting | feTile | feTurbulence | animate | set)* </filter>`	Defines the different filter effects that can be applied to your images
font	`<font attributeList> (desc | title | metadata | font-face | missing-glyph (glyph | hkern | vkern)*)* </font>`	Defines a font for use with SVG

Table 30-1. *SVG Elements* (continued)

Element	Syntax	Description
font-face	<font-face *attributeList*> (desc | title | metadata | font-face-src | definition-src) </font-face>	Corresponds to the @font-face CSS2 rule, and is used to describe the characteristics of any font, SVG or otherwise
g	<g *attributelist*> (desc | title | metadata | defs | path | text | rect | circle | ellipse | line | polyline | polygon | use | image | svg | g | view | switch | a | altGlyphDef | script | style | symbol | marker | clipPath | mask | linearGradient | readialGradient | pattern | filter | cursor | font | animate | set | animateMotion | animateColor | animateTransform | color-profile | font-face)* </g>	Groups and names collections of drawing elements

Table 30-1. *SVG Elements* (continued)

Element	Syntax	Description
glyph	<glyph *attributelist*> (desc | title | metadata | defs | path | text | rect | circle | ellipse | line | polyline | polygon | use | image | svg | g | view | switch | a | altGlyphDef | script | style | symbol | marker | clipPath | mask | linearGradient | readialGradient | pattern | filter | cursor | font | animate | set | animateMotion | animateColor | animateTransform | color-profile | font-face)* </glyph>	Defines the individual graphics that create character glyphs
glyphRef	<glyphRef *attributeList* />	Defines a possible set of glyphs to use
image	<image *attributeList*> (desc | title | metadata | animate | set | animateMotion | animateColor | animateTransform | image)* </image>	Displays a bitmapped image that has been loaded from an external source

Table 30-1. *SVG Elements* (continued)

Element	Syntax	Description
line	<line *attributeList*> (desc | title | metadata | animate | set | animateMotion | animateColor | animateTransform | image)* </line>	Specifies a straight line
linearGradient	<linearGradient attributeList> (desc | title | metadata (stop | animate | set | animateTransform | linearGradient)*) </linearGradient>	Fills a shape using a linear, either horizontal or vertical, color gradient
marker	<marker *attributelist*> (desc | title | metadata | defs | path | text | rect | circle | ellipse | line | polyline | polygon | use | image | svg | g | view | switch | a | altGlyphDef | script | style | symbol | marker | clipPath | mask | linearGradient | readialGradient | pattern | filter | cursor | font | animate | set | animateMotion | animateColor | animateTransform | color-profile | font-face)* </marker>	Defines the graphics that are to be used for drawing arrowheads and polymarkers on <path>, <line>, <polyline>, and <polygon> elements

Table 30-1. *SVG Elements* (continued)

Element	Syntax	Description
mask	<mask *attributelist*> (desc | title | metadata | defs | path | text | rect | circle | ellipse | line | polyline | polygon | use | image | svg | g | view | switch | a | altGlyphDef | script | style | symbol | marker | clipPath | mask | linearGradient | readialGradient | pattern | filter | cursor | font | animate | set | animateMotion | animateColor | animateTransform | color-profile | font-face)* </mask>	Defines an image or shape that is used to mask out a section of another shape
metadata	<metadata *attributeList*> (*#PCDATA* | metadata)* </metadata>	Provides additional information on the objects being used in the document
path	<path *attributelist*> (desc | title | metadata | animate | set | animateMotion | animateColor | animateTransform)* </path>	Defines the shape that makes up the shape being defined

Table 30-1. *SVG Elements* (continued)

Element	Syntax	Description
pattern	<svg *attributelist*> (desc | title | metadata | defs | path | text | rect | circle | ellipse | line | polyline | polygon | use | image | svg | g | view | switch | a | altGlyphDef | script | style| symbol | marker | clipPath | mask | linearGradient | readialGradient | pattern | filter | cursor | font | animate | set | animateMotion | animateColor | animateTransform | color-profile | font-face)* </svg>	Fills or strokes an object using a predefined tiled graphic object
polygon	<polygon *attributeList*> (desc | title | metadata | animate | set | animateMotion | animateColor | animateTransform | image)* </polygon>	Defines shape drawn from a set of connected straight line segments

Table 30-1. *SVG Elements* (continued)

Element	Syntax	Description
polyline	<polyline *attributeList*> (desc | title | metadata | animate | set | animateMotion | animateColor | animateTransform)* </polyline>	Specifies a line flowing between a variety of set points
radialGradient	<radialGradient attributeList> (desc | title | metadata (stop | animate | set | animateTransform | radialGradient)*) </radialGradient>	Fills a shape using a radial (circular) color gradient
rect	<rect *attributeList*> (desc | title | metadata | animate | set | animateMotion | animateColor | animateTransform)* </rect>	Specifies a rectangle of a specific height and width
script	<script *attributeList*> *#PCDATA* </script>	Provides for the inclusion of internal scripts within your SVG document
set	<set *attributeList*> (desc | title | metadata)* </set>	Provides a means of setting the value of an attribute for a specified length of time
stop	<stop *attributeList*> (animate | set | animateMotion | animateColor | stop)* </stop>	Defines the change of colors in a gradient

Table 30-1. *SVG Elements* (continued)

Element	Syntax	Description
style	`<style attributelist> #PCDATA </style>`	Allows style sheets to be embedded directly in SVG content
svg	`<svg attributelist> (desc | title | metadata | defs | path | text | rect | circle | ellipse | line | polyline | polygon | use | image | svg | g | view | switch | a | altGlyphDef | script | style | symbol | marker | clipPath | mask | linearGradient | readialGradient | pattern | filter | cursor | font | animate | set | animateMotion | animateColor | animateTransform | color-profile | font-face)* </svg>`	Root element for all SVG documents or SVG content within documents

Table 30-1. *SVG Elements* (continued)

Element	Syntax	Description
switch	<switch *attributelist*> (desc | title | metadata | path | text | rect | circle | ellipse | line | polyline | polygon | use | image | svg | g | view | switch | a | foreignObject | animate | set | animateMotion | animateColor | animateTransform)* </switch>	Provides the ability to alternate between views
symbol	<symbol *attributelist*> (desc | title | metadata | defs | path | text | rect | circle | ellipse | line | polyline | polygon | use | image | svg | g | view | switch | a | altGlyphDef | script | style | symbol | marker | clipPath | mask | linearGradient | readialGradient | pattern | filter | cursor | font | animate | set | animateMotion | animateColor | animateTransform | color-profile | font-face)* </symbol>	Defines graphical template objects, which can then be instantiated by the <use> element

Table 30-1. *SVG Elements* (continued)

Element	Syntax	Description
text	<text *attributeList*> (*#PCDATA* | desc | title | metadata | tspan | tref | textPath | a | altGlyph | animate | set | animateMotion | animateColor | animateTransform | image)* </text>	Defines text that should appear as a graphical element on your document
textPath	<textPath *attributeList*> (*#PCDATA* | desc | title | metadata | tspan | tref | a | altGlyph | animate | set | animateColor)* </textPath>	Draws text along the shape of a specified path element
title	<title *attributeList*> *#PCDATA* </title>	Used as a tooltip when the mouse moves over objects
tref	<tref *attributeList*> (desc | title | metadata | animate | set | animateColor)* </tref>	References the textual content of <text> elements
tspan	<tspan *attributeList*> (*#PCDATA* | desc | title | metadata | tspan | tref | a | altGlyph | animate | set | animateColor)* </tspan>	Adjusts the location of text using absolute or relative coordinate values

Table 30-1. *SVG Elements* (continued)

Element	Syntax	Description
use	<use *attributeList*> (desc | title | metadata | animate | set | animateMotion | animateColor | animateTransform | use)* </use>	Instantiates a template object created by the <symbol> element or any other external object file, such as an image or video
view	<view *attributeList*> (desc | title | metadata)* </view>	Defines specific views of the object that can be changed using scripts

Table 30-1. *SVG Elements* (continued)

SVG Attributes

SVG elements use a large variety of attributes to define further the elements that are included in SVG documents. Table 30-2 provides a list of the attributes used with SVG and the elements that they can be applied to.

Attribute	Values	Elements	Default Value
alignment-baseline	auto | baseline | top | before-edge | text-top | text-before-edge | middle | bottom | after-edge | text-bottom | text-after-edge | ideographic | lower | hanging | mathematical | inherit	<text>, <tspan>, <tref>, <altGlyph>, <textPath>	auto

Table 30-2. *SVG Attribute Values and Applicable Elements*

Attribute	Values	Elements	Default Value
baseline-shift	baseline | sub | super | <*percentage*> | <*length*> | inherit	<text>, <tspan>, <tref>, <altGlyph>, and <textPath>	baseline
clip	<*shape*> | auto | inherit	<svg>	auto
clip-path	<*uri*> | none | inherit	All elements	none
clip-rule	nonzero | evenodd | inherit	Graphics elements within a <clipPath> element	nonzero
color	<*color*> | inherit	<fill>, <stroke>, <stop-color>, <flood-color>, <lighting-color>	Depends on user agent
color-interpolation	auto | sRGB | linearRGB | inherit	Color interpolation and compositing operations	sRGB
color-profile	auto | sRGB | (<uri> | <local-profile>)+ | inherit	<image>elements that refer to raster images	auto
color-rendering	auto | optimizeSpeed | optimizeQuality | inherit	Color interpolation and compositing operations	auto

Table 30-2. *SVG Attribute Values and Applicable Elements* (continued)

Attribute	Values	Elements	Default Value
cursor	[[<uri> ,]* [auto | crosshair | default | pointer | move | e-resize | ne-resize | nw-resize | n-resize | se-resize | sw-resize | s-resize | w-resize| text | wait | help]] | inherit	Container elements and graphics elements	auto
direction	ltr | rtl | inherit	<text>, <tspan>, <tref>, and <textPath>	ltr
display	inline | block | list-item | run-in | compact | marker | table | inline-table | table-row-group | table-header-group | table-footer-group | table-row | table-column-group | table-column | table-cell | table-caption | none | inherit	All elements	inline

Table 30-2. *SVG Attribute Values and Applicable Elements* (continued)

Attribute	Values	Elements	Default Value
dominant-baseline	auto | autosense-script | no-change | reset| ideographic | lower | hanging | mathematical | inherit	<text>, <tspan>, <tref>, <altGlyph>, <textPath>	auto
enable-background	accumulate | new [*<x>* *<y>* *<width>* *<height>*] | inherit	Container elements	accumulate
fill	*<paint>* (See Specifying paint)	All elements	black
fill-opacity	*<opacity-value>* | inherit	All elements	1
fill-rule	nonzero | evenodd | inherit	All elements	nonzero
filter	*<uri>* | none | inherit	Graphics and container elements	none
flood-color	currentColor |<color> [icc-color(<name> [,<icccolorvalue>]*)] | inherit	<feFlood>	black
flood-opacity	*<alphavalue>* | inherit	<feFlood>	1

Table 30-2. *SVG Attribute Values and Applicable Elements* (continued)

<table>
<tr><th>Attribute</th><th>Values</th><th>Elements</th><th>Default Value</th></tr>
<tr><td>font</td><td>[['font-style' || 'font-variant' || 'font-weight']? 'font-size' [/ 'line-height']? 'font-family'] | caption | icon | menu | message-box | small-caption | status-bar | inherit</td><td><text>, <tspan>, <tref>, <altGlyph>, <textPath></td><td>See individual properties</td></tr>
<tr><td>font-family</td><td>[[*<family-name>* | *<generic-family>*],]* [*<family-name>* | *<generic-family>*] | inherit</td><td><text>, <tspan>, <tref>, <altGlyph>, <textPath></td><td>Depends on user agent</td></tr>
<tr><td>font-size</td><td>*<absolute-size>* | *<relative-size>* | *<length>* | *<percentage>* | inherit</td><td><text>, <tspan>, <tref>, <altGlyph>, <textPath></td><td>medium</td></tr>
<tr><td>font-size-adjust</td><td>*<number>* | none | inherit</td><td><text>, <tspan>, <tref>, <altGlyph>, <textPath></td><td>none</td></tr>
</table>

Table 30-2. *SVG Attribute Values and Applicable Elements* (continued)

Attribute	Values	Elements	Default Value
font-stretch	normal | wider | narrower | ultra-condensed | extra-condensed | condensed | semi-condensed | semi-expanded | expanded | extra-expanded | ultra-expanded | inherit	<text>, <tspan>, <tref>, <altGlyph>, <textPath>	normal
font-style	normal | italic | oblique | inherit	<text>, <tspan>, <tref>, <altGlyph>, <textPath>	normal
font-variant	normal | small-caps | inherit	<text>, <tspan>, <tref>, <altGlyph>, <textPath>	normal
font-weight	normal | bold | bolder | lighter | 100 | 200 | 300 | 400 | 500 | 600 | 700 | 800 | 900 | inherit	<text>, <tspan>, <tref>, <altGlyph>, <textPath>	normal
glyph-orientation-horizontal	<*angle*> | inherit	<text>, <tspan>, <tref>, <altGlyph>, <textPath>	0
glyph-orientation-vertical	<*angle*> | auto | inherit	<text>, <tspan>, <tref>, <altGlyph>, <textPath>	auto

Table 30-2. *SVG Attribute Values and Applicable Elements* (continued)

Attribute	Values	Elements	Default Value
image-rendering	auto | optimizeSpeed | optimizeQuality | inherit	Images	auto
kerning	auto | *<length>* | inherit	<text>, <tspan>, <tref>, <altGlyph>, <textPath>	auto
letter-spacing	normal | *<length>* | inherit	<text>, <tspan>, <tref>, <altGlyph>, <textPath>	normal
lighting-color	currentColor |<color> [icc-color(<name> [,<icccolorvalue>]*)] | inherit	<feDiffuse Lighting> and <feSpecular Lighting>	white
marker	See individual properties	<path>, <line>, <polyline>, <polygon>	See individual properties
marker-end		All elements	
marker-mid		All elements	
marker-start	none | inherit |*<uri>*	<path>, <line>, <polyline>, <polygon>	none
mask	*<uri>* | none | inherit	All elements	none
opacity	*<alphavalue>* | inherit	All elements	1
overflow	visible | hidden | scroll | auto | inherit	Elements that establish a new viewport	See prose

Table 30-2. *SVG Attribute Values and Applicable Elements* (continued)

Attribute	Values	Elements	Default Value
pointer-events	visiblePainted | visibleFill | visibleStroke | visible | painted | fill | stroke | all | none | inherit	Container elements and graphics elements	visiblePainted
shape-rendering	auto | optimizeSpeed | crispEdges | geometricPrecision | inherit	All shape elements	auto
stop-color	currentColor |*<color>* [icc-color(*<name>* [,*<icccolorvalue>*]*)] | inherit	<stop>	black
stop-opacity	*<alphavalue>* | inherit	<stop>	1
stroke	*<paint>* (See Specifying paint)	All Shape elements	none
stroke-dasharray	none | *<dasharray>* | inherit	All Shape elements	none
stroke-dashoffset	*<dashoffset>* | inherit	All Shape elements	0
stroke-linecap	butt | round | square | inherit	All Shape elements	butt
stroke-linejoin	miter | round | bevel | inherit	All Shape elements	miter
stroke-miterlimit	*<miterlimit>* | inherit	All Shape elements	4

Table 30-2. *SVG Attribute Values and Applicable Elements* (continued)

Attribute	Values	Elements	Default Value
stroke-opacity	<*opacity-value*> | inherit	All Shape elements	1
stroke-width	<*width*> | inherit	All Shape elements	1
text-anchor	start | middle | end | inherit	<text>, <tspan>, <tref>, <altGlyph>, <textPath>	start
text-decoration	none | [underline || overline || line-through || blink] | inherit	<text>, <tspan>, <tref>, <altGlyph>, <textPath>	none
text-rendering	auto | optimizeSpeed | optimize Legibility | geometric Precision | inherit	<text>	auto
unicode-bidi	normal | embed | bidi-override | inherit	<text>, <tspan>, <tref>, <textPath>	normal
visibility	visible | hidden | collapse | inherit		inherit
word-spacing	normal | <*length*> | inherit	<text>, <tspan>, <tref>, <altGlyph>, <textPath>	normal
writing-mode	lr-tb | rl-tb | tb-rl | lr | rl | tb | inherit	<text>	lr-tb

Table 30-2. *SVG Attribute Values and Applicable Elements* (continued)

An SVG Example

All of the elements and attributes discussed in this chapter can be used together to create your own SVG images that are viewable in Internet Explorer 5.5 with a plug-in or Mozilla, the precursor to Netscape Navigator 6. You can be sure of seeing your SVG code by using the Adobe SVG Plug-in available at the Adobe Web site (http://www.adobe.com/svg/). The following code, which creates the image shown in Figure 30-2, draws a triangle and circle with filter effects applied, as well as adding text that will be drawn and formatted across the bottom of the image.

Note *The following code was created using Jasc WebDraw, a native SVG drawing program. You can download this tool at http://www.jasc.com*

```
<?xml version="1.0" standalone="no"?>
<!DOCTYPE svg PUBLIC "-//W3C//DTD SVG 20001102//EN"
"http://www.w3.org/TR/2000/CR-SVG-20001102/DTD/svg-20001102.dtd">
<svg width="500" height="500">

   <linearGradient id="cyan-magenta-yellow_1"
         x1="0%" y1="0%" x2="100%" y2="60%"
         spreadMethod="pad" gradientUnits="objectBoundingBox">
      <stop offset="0%"
            style="stop-color:rgb(0,255,255);stop-opacity:1"/>
      <stop offset="49%"
            style="stop-color:rgb(255,0,255);stop-opacity:1"/>
      <stop offset="100%"
            style="stop-color:rgb(255,255,0);stop-opacity:1"/>
   </linearGradient>
   <radialGradient id="red-yellow-red"
        cx="49%" cy="50%" r="50%" fx="50%" fy="50%"
        spreadMethod="pad" gradientUnits="objectBoundingBox">
      <stop offset="10%"
            style="stop-color:rgb(255,0,0);stop-opacity:1"/>
      <stop offset="50%"
            style="stop-color:rgb(255,255,0);stop-opacity:1"/>
      <stop offset="90%"
           style="stop-color:rgb(255,0,0);stop-opacity:1"/>
   </radialGradient>
   <linearGradient id="black-white"
         x1="0%" y1="0%" x2="100%" y2="0%"
         spreadMethod="pad" gradientUnits="objectBoundingBox">
      <stop offset="0%"
```

```
            style="stop-color:rgb(0,0,0);stop-opacity:1"/>
      <stop offset="100%"
            style="stop-color:rgb(255,255,255);stop-opacity:1"/>
   </linearGradient>
   <linearGradient id="cyan-magenta-yellow"
         x1="0%" y1="0%" x2="100%" y2="0%"
         spreadMethod="pad" gradientUnits="objectBoundingBox">
      <stop offset="0%"
            style="stop-color:rgb(0,255,255);stop-opacity:1"/>
      <stop offset="49%"
            style="stop-color:rgb(255,0,255);stop-opacity:1"/>
      <stop offset="100%"
            style="stop-color:rgb(255,255,0);stop-opacity:1"/>
   </linearGradient>
   <path d="M235.837 4.90106 L477.667 483.333 L-5.99328 483.333 z"
         style="stroke-miterlimit:4;stroke-linejoin:miter;
         stroke-width:8;stroke-opacity:1;
         stroke:url(#cyan-magenta-yellow);
         fill-opacity:1;fill:rgb(128,0,128);opacity:1"/>
   <ellipse cx="229.667" cy="205.167"
            rx="155" ry="156.5"
            style="stroke-width:9;stroke-opacity:1;
            stroke:rgb(0,0,0);fill-opacity:1;
            fill:url(#red-yellow-red);
            opacity:0.79"/>
   <text x="148" y="430"
         transform="matrix(2.35816 0 0 1.94842 -288.481 -441.848)"
         style="font-family:Harrington;font-size:28;
            stroke-width:1;stroke-opacity:1;
            stroke:url(#cyan-magenta-yellow_1);
            fill-opacity:1;fill:rgb(255,255,255);opacity:1">
     Raven&apos;s Eye</text>
   <text x="191.667" y="447"
         transform="matrix(3.86848 0 0 1.75546 -667.525 -326.839)"
         style="font-family:Arial;font-size:31;stroke-width:1;
         stroke-opacity:0.89;stroke:rgb(255,255,255);
         fill-opacity:1;fill:rgb(255,255,255);opacity:1">
      Travel</text>
</svg>

<!-- Generated by Jasc WebDraw PR4(tm) on 02/26/01 00:19:14 -->
```

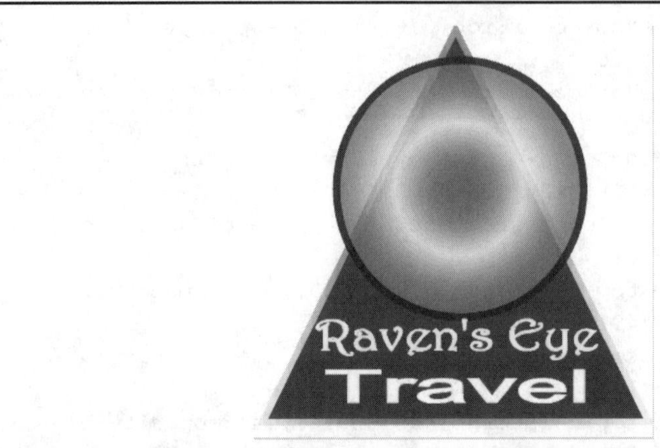

Figure 30-2. *This drawing uses effects and filters to create a simple SVG graphic*

Summary

In this chapter we looked at developing Scalable Vector Graphics for use with Internet Explorer 5.5 and Netscape Navigator 6. SVG graphics are used to describe two-dimensional vector based graphics in HTML and other document formats. SVG uses a series of markup commands that describe the paths of series of connected lines and curves. By using markup, you can dramatically decrease the amount of time it takes to display images on your HTML/XML pages. SVG is based on XML and incorporates controls for working with animations, groups, filters, and templates. SVG has been designed to work within the existing HTML and CSS constructs, allowing browsers and their developers to avoid reinventing the wheel to implement different representations and implementations for existing HTML or CSS functions.

The Complete Reference

Chapter 31

Scientific Languages: MathML and CML

You have heard a dozen times by now that XML is a language that can be used to create languages that organizations and industries can standardize in order to further the sharing of information. The creation of the Mathematical Markup Language (MathML) and the Chemical Markup Language (CML) are working examples of how you can use XML to share information with people who are scattered all over the world and are on a wide variety of computer platforms.

Both MathML and CML are constantly undergoing improvements and expansion. The World Wide Web Consortium (W3C) is developing MathML, and you can follow the developments in the MathML specification by visiting http://www.w3.org/Math. CML has its own development committee, and you can follow the development of the CML language by visiting the CML home page located at http://www.xml-cml.org.

The Language of Mathematicians: MathML

Mathematics has been a hot topic for the world since history was first recorded. It has only taken us ten years to be able to efficiently display math on the most popular information dispersal tool of the twenty-first century. With the completion of the MathML 1.0 specification and the upcoming completion of MathML 2.0, mathematicians and scientists around the world can display mathematical equations meaningfully.

The MathML committee's goal was the creation of a language allowing mathematics to be viewed and processed on the Web as text rather than unusable images. MathML controls both the vertical and horizontal alignment of characters in equations displayed on XML or Hypertext Markup Language (HTML) pages. It enables document authors to describe all mathematical notations and values while correctly representing both their structure and content.

MathML Elements

MathML currently defines more than 150 elements to show mathematical notation correctly. The 28 elements that are listed in the following sections are those that are used to control the presentation, not necessarily the meaning, of the content. You can study the remaining MathML commands at the W3C Web site at http://www.w3.org/Math.

Using <math>

In order to include MathML expressions in an HTML document, you must specify a single top-level math element. This element must serve as the bounds on all other MathML content. Both <math> tags must always be expressed, and it is illegal for one <math> element to contain another. You can have any number of child elements contained within your <math> tags. The following MathML code will display x + y correctly:

```
<math style="display"
     xmlns="http://www.w3.org/1998/Math/MathML">
  <mfenced>
   <mrow>
```

```
        <mi> x </mi>
        <mo> + </mo>
        <mi> y </mi>
      </mrow>
    </mfenced>
  </math>
```

Using <maction>

The <maction> element is used to bind a particular action to an expression. For example, you may want your readers to be able to toggle between a shorthand and longhand expression. You might also want to be able to provide specific information on the status line or as a tool tip that would help your reader understand what is happening with your equation. The <maction> element provides you with all of these capabilities. You, as the document author, simply need to decide how the information will be displayed best and set the element's attributes respectively.

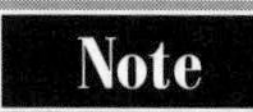

You can read about all of the attributes used with MathML elements by looking at the MathML specification located at http://www.w3.org/MathML.

The following example code shows you how to create nested pop-up menu items for your expressions:

```
<math style="display"
      xmlns="http://www.w3.org/1998/Math/MathML">
   <maction actiontype="menu" selection="1">
      <mtext> Menu option 1 </mtext>
      <mtext> Menu option 2 </mtext>
      <maction actiontype="menu" selection="1">
         <mtext> Option A </mtext>
         <mtext> Option B </mtext>
      </maction>
      <mtext> Menu option 3 </mtext>
   </maction>
</math>
```

Using <maligngroup/>

When working with mathematical equations, one of the most important items to be aware of is alignment. By changing the alignment of an equation set, you can change the numbers that the equation works with. When you specify an alignment using MathML, you need to be sure to specify the specific points that are to be aligned in each equation and the beginning of the alignment group. You must also specify which parts of the equation do not have any alignment needs. The <maligngroup> element provides you with part of this function. This tag is displayed as a zero-width element on your documents, so you need not worry about the tag changing the appearance of the remaining text of your document.

The alignment groups start at the first <maligngroup> element. You need to place the <maligngroup> element before each group of characters that you wish to have aligned in your document. You can only use this element in an existing alignment structure such as the <mtable> or <mrow> elements. Any other use of the <maligngroup> element will be ignored.

The following example code uses these two equations and aligns them so they can properly be worked in our HTML documents:

```
8.5x + 2y = 0
6x - 1y = 2
```

The code for properly aligning these two equations follows:

```
<mtable groupalign="decimalpoint left left decimalpoint
 left left decimalpoint">
<mtd>
   <mrow>
      <mrow>
         <maligngroup/>
         <mn> 8.5 </mn>
         <mo> &InvisibleTimes; </mo>
         <maligngroup/>
         <mi> x </mi>
      </mrow>
      <maligngroup/>
      <mo> + </mo>
      <mrow>
         <maligngroup/>
         <mn> 2 </mn>
         <mo> &InvisibleTimes; </mo>
         <maligngroup/>
         <mi> y </mi>
      </mrow>
   </mrow>
   <maligngroup/>
   <mo> = </mo>
   <maligngroup/>
   <mn> 0 </mn>
</mtd>
<mtd>
   <mrow>
      <mrow>
         <maligngroup/>
         <mn> 6 </mn>
         <mo> &InvisibleTimes; </mo>
```

```
            <maligngroup/>
            <mi> x </mi>
        </mrow>
        <maligngroup/>
        <mo> - </mo>
        <mrow>
            <maligngroup/>
            <mn> 1</mn>
            <mo> &InvisibleTimes; </mo>
            <maligngroup/>
            <mi> y </mi>
        </mrow>
    </mrow>
    <maligngroup/>
    <mo> = </mo>
    <maligngroup/>
    <mrow>
        <mn> 2 </mn>
    </mrow>
</mtd>
</mtable>
```


Using <malignmark/>

The <malignmark> element is used with the <maligngroup/> element when there has been no groupalign attribute specified or when a special character needs to be used as an alignment marker. The following example code uses the <malignmark> element to align the decimal points of the two statements:

```
 1.8x
+ 18y
-----
1099
```

The MathML code is shown here:

```
<mtd>
    <mrow>
        <mrow>
            <maligngroup/>
            <mn> <malignmark edge="right">.8 </mn>
            <mo> &InvisibleTimes; </mo>
            <maligngroup/>
            <mi><malignmark edge="left"> x </mi>
```

```
        </mrow>
        <maligngroup/>
        <mo> <malignmark edge="right">+ </mo>
        <mrow>
            <maligngroup/>
            <mn> 18 <malignmark edge="left"></mn>
            <mo> &InvisibleTimes; </mo>
            <maligngroup/>
            <mi> <malignmark edge="right">y </mi>
        </mrow>
    </mrow>
    <maligngroup/>
    <mo><malignmark edge="right"> = </mo>
    <maligngroup/>
    <mrow>
        <mn> <malignmark edge="right">1099 </mn>
    </mrow>
</mtd>
```

Using <merror>

The <merror> element displays its contents as an error message. This can be done in a variety of ways, including displaying the contents in a vivid color, blinking the contents, or altering the element's content's background color. This element was designed to provide MathML generating programs with a standard way of reporting syntax error in data. Although the function of the <merror> element was outlined, there are no rules as to the format of the error messages it could contain. Let's assume that the applications developers will make the error messages as easy for viewers to read as possible.

The <merror> element can contain any expression or expression sequence. If there is more than one argument or expression, its entire contents are treated as a single <mrow> element.

Using <mfenced>

The <mfenced> element is used to provide a way in which to express the common equation breakdowns involving fences such as braces, brackets, and parentheses. It has also been expanded to include separators, such as commas, that often occur between arguments. The <mfenced> element is used to represent a pair of fences. If you need to show a single fence character, use the <mo> element instead.

An <mfenced> element is capable of containing none or multiple arguments enclosed in an <mrow> statement. For nested parenthetical statements, the use of nested <mrow> elements is required around the <mfenced> expressions.

The following MathML code will display x + y correctly:

```
<mfenced>
   <mrow>
      <mi> x </mi>
      <mo> + </mo>
      <mi> y </mi>
   </mrow>
</mfenced>
```

Using <mfrac>

The <mfrac> element is used to display fractions, although you can use it to mark up any fraction-like object such as a binomial coefficient.

The following code is used to create a properly displayed fraction 1/2:

```
<mrow>
   <mfrac linethickness="1">
      <mn> 1 </mn>
      <mn> 2 </mn>
   </mfrac>
</mrow>
```

Using <mi>

The <mi> element is used to represent a symbolic name or text that represents an identifier. Identifiers can be designated in part or whole as variables, function names, or symbolic constants. Because <mi> is a presentation element, its contents should be rendered as an identifier, although individual user agents may function differently. You need to be aware that not all math identifiers will be represented by the <mi> element. If a variable is either subscripted or primed, it will be represented using the <msub> or <msup> elements.

In addition to this rule, the names of symbolic constants should be displayed using the <mi> element. For example:

- <mi> π </mi>
- <mi> sin </mi>
- <mi> ⅇ </mi>

With MathML, identifiers are designed to include function names such as sin, cos, and tan. Using MathML, you can write expressions such as tan x using the &ApplyFunction operator, as shown in the following code:

```
<mrow>
  <mi> tan </mi>
  <mo> &ApplyFunction; </mo>
  <mi> x </mi>
</mrow>
```

Using <mmultiscripts>

The <mmultiscripts> element is used to display presubscripts and tensor notations. If you wish to render any number of vertically aligned pairs of subscripts and superscripts attached to a single base expression, you have to use <mmultiscripts>. You can use postscripts and prescripts—the former appearing to the right of your base expression and the latter to the left. Any missing sub- or superscript must be represented by an empty <none/> element.

Generally, in a <mmultiscripts> element arrangement, the argument sequence is composed of a base expression and then zero or more pairs of vertically aligned subscripts and superscripts.

The following example code shows both a prescript and a postscript using subscripts without matching superscripts to represent the equation:

$_0F_5(:a;d)$

```
<mrow>
  <mrow>
    <mmultiscripts>
      <mi> F </mi>
      <mn> 5 </mn>
      <none/>
      <mprescripts/>
      <mn> 0 </mn>
      <none/>
    </mmultiscripts>
    <mo> &ApplyFunction; </mo>
  </mrow>
  <mo> ( </mo>
  <mrow>
    <mo> ; </mo>
    <mi> a </mi>
    <mo> ; </mo>
    <mi> d </mi>
  </mrow>
<mo> ) </mo>
</mrow>
```

Using <mn>

The <mn> element is used to display a *numeric literal* or other data that should be displayed as a number. A numeric literal is simply a sequence of digits, possibly including a decimal point, that represents an unsigned integer or real number. Because the true definition of a number depends upon the context that it is being used, negative numbers, complex numbers, ratios, and numeric constants should be displayed using other MathML tags such as the <mfrac> or the <mi> elements.

The following lines of code show a variety of ways to display numerical values using the <mn> element, which forces these values to be treated as a number:

```
<mn> 16 </mn>
<mn> 16,000,000 </mn>
<mn> 4.1e9 </mn>
<mn> MCMLXIX </mn>
<mn> 0.987 </mn>
<mn> 0xDEAF </mn>
<mn> twenty five </mn>
```

Using <mo>

If you need to identify an operator in MathML, use the <mo> element. MathML includes a sophisticated mechanism that enables you to deal with the complicated nature of mathematical notation of operators. Because of this built-in flexibility, you can use the <mo> operator to include tildes, braces, brackets, parentheses, or other notations not normally thought of as operators. Table 31-1 shows some of these common operators.

Symbol or Code	Description
+	addition
–	subtraction
/	division
*	multiplication
<	less than
>	greater than
≤	less than or equal to
≥	greater than or equal to
¬	not sign
±	vertical plus/minus sign
×	multiplication symbol
÷	division symbol

Table 31-1. *Operators Used with the MathML <mi> Element*

Although the <mo> element has been designed to render mathematical operators, it can't display all operators without help. In some cases, they need the assistance of elements such as <msub>, <msup>, or <mfrac>.

There are some operators that are invisible yet require specific spacing or other layout effects within the representation of an equation. These operators have specific entity references that are displayed in the <mo> element. Some of these invisible operators are

- **⁢** (⁢) Used for equations such as *2x* where the multiplication of 2 and x is implied rather than outwardly stated using the multiplication sign (*)
- **⁡** (⁡) Used for equations like *f(x)* and *sin x* where you need to apply the listed function to the numerical identifier
- **⁣** (⁣) Used in statements such as *m* 12 where a comma is implied, but not necessarily stated, in normal mathematical notation

```
<mo> + </mo>   <!— Addition sign «—>
<mo> &InvisibleTimes; </mo>   <!— Multiply «—>
<mo> &lt; </mo>  <!— Less Than «—>
<mo> &le; </mo>  <!— Less than or Equal To «—>
<mo> ++ </mo>
<mo> &sum; </mo>
<mo> .NOT. </mo>
<mo> and </mo>
```

Using <mover>

The <mover> element enables you to create an *overscript* within your expression. Overscripts can be used as either accent marks or limits. One of the most common uses of an overscript is with the repetitive character mark commonly seen in the results of long division expressions.

The following example code, and Figure 31-1, displays two versions of two equations. The first of each set is drawn as an accent mark, the second is drawn as a limit:

```
<mrow>
   <mover accent="true">
      <mi> z </mi>
      <mo> &hat; </mo>
   </mover>
   <mtext>   vs   </mtext>
   <mover accent="false">
      <mi> z </mi>
      <mo> &hat; </mo>
   </mover>
</mrow>
```

Figure 31-1. *Using the accent attribute can create the impression of a true accent mark or a limit mark.*

Using <mpadded>

The <mpadded> element enables you to control the overall size and dimensions taken up by its contents. Although this element does not stretch or shrink the content of the tags, it does create the appearance of bounds around the expression it contains. This allows you to control more accurately how the user agent will display your content. You can use the <mpadded> element to contain as many expressions as you need. If there are multiple expressions in the element's contents, they will all be treated as if they were bound by an inferred <mrow> command.

The following code examples show how the <mpadded> attributes can be used to control the bounding box dimensions:

```
<mpadded width="+9em"> ... </mpadded>
<mpadded lspace="+70%"> ... </mpadded>
<mpadded width="- 1 height"> ... </mpadded>
<mpadded depth="90%"> ... </mpadded>
<mpadded width="10% width"> ... </mpadded>
<mpadded height="8 width"> ... </mpadded>
<mpadded length="3.0 width"> ... </mpadded>
```

Using <mphantom>

The <mphantom> element can't be seen by the viewer, but it maintains the size and dimensions that its content would normally require. One use for <mphantom> is to align segments of expressions by invisibly copying its subexpressions. The expressions contained within <mphantom> tags should use the same spacing rules as those contained in an <mrow> element. This element can accept an unlimited number of expressions.

The following code example uses the <mphantom> element as a means of ensuring the alignment of corresponding variables in the numerator and denominator of a fraction. The goal is to create an equation. This method forces the following equation to render as it is displayed here

```
a + b + c
---------
a     + c
```

rather than here

```
a + b + c
---------
  a + c
```

The following code is the MathML representation of this equation:

```
<mfrac>
   <mrow>
      <mi> a </mi>
      <mo> + </mo>
      <mi> b </mi>
      <mo> + </mo>
      <mi> c </mi>
   </mrow>
   <mrow>
      <mi> a </mi>
      <mphantom>
         <mo form="infix"> + </mo>
         <mi> b </mi>
      </mphantom>
      <mo> + </mo>
      <mi> c </mi>
   </mrow>
</mfrac>
```

Using <mroot>

The <mroot> element is used to construct radicals with indices such as a cube root. This element requires two arguments: the first is the base value being evaluated, and the second is the index value with which the base is being evaluated. The syntax for this element is

```
<mroot> ... </mroot>
```

This code displays the equation $(a+b)^2$ being evaluated for its cube root:

```
<math style="display"
      xmlns="http://www.w3.org/1998/Math/MathML">
<mtable>
   <mtd>
      <mroot>
         <msup>
         <mfenced>
         <mrow>
            <mi>a</mi>
            <mo>+</mo>
            <mi>b</mi>
```

```
            </mrow>
            </mfenced>
            <mn>2</mn>
            </msup>
            <mn> 3</mn>
         </mroot>
      </mtd>
   </mtable>
   </math>
```

Using <mrow>

At its most basic, the <mrow> element is used to group together any number of subexpressions. These expressions generally consist of a series of <mo> elements (operators) acting upon a series of expressions that function as operands. The <mrow> element creates horizontally grouped rows of arguments. This element provides a means of allowing user agents to insert line breaks into an expression automatically without forcing document authors to specify explicitly how and where the breaks should occur on various sizes of displays.

Other elements, such as <mfenced> or <msqrt>, automatically treat their arguments as if they were contained in an <mrow> element. Similarly, if an <mrow> element contains a single argument, that element will be treated as if it were alone. If an <mrow> element contains multiple arguments, then they need to be grouped in the same logical way they would be on paper by a mathematician. This grouping is necessary to ensure that the expression is read properly in audio renderings by user agents. If the <mrow> elements are not grouped properly, you could easily change the expression "A plus B squared" into something more closely resembling "A plus B multiplied by 2." Proper grouping also enables user agents to insert line breaks when needed, and at appropriate locations in order to avoid distortion of the meaning of the equation.

You can display a standard algebraic equation such as 2x + y + 3z = 0 in MathML using the following nested <mrow> elements:

```
<mrow>
  <mrow>
     <mn> 2 </mn>
     <mo> &InvisibleTimes; </mo>
     <mi> x </mi>
  </mrow>
  <mo> + </mo>
  <mi> y </mi>
  <mo> + </mo>
  <mrow>
     <mn> 3 </mn>
     <mo> &InvisibleTimes; </mo>
```

```
        <mi> z </mi>
      </mrow>
      <mo> = </mo>
      <mn> 0 </mn>
    </mrow>
```

Using <ms>

The <ms> element is used to represent string literals commonly found in algebraic systems or those that are interpreted through a programming system. Generally, string literals are displayed between quotation marks for easy identification.

Using <mspace/>

A document author can use the <mspace/> element to display blank spaces of any desired dimensions within an expression. Because the space is controlled by setting attributes, and the default value for each of its attributes is either 0em or 0ex, this element is not useful without its attributes specified. <mspace/> is not the only element that can be used to create space within an equation.

Using <msqrt>

The <msqrt> element evaluates the given equation for its square root. If there is more than one argument within the <msqrt> element tags, the entire contents will be treated as is they were contained within a single <mrow> element. The syntax for this element is

```
<msqrt>arguments... </msqrt>
```

This code displays the equation $(a+b)^3$ being evaluated for its square root:

```
<math style="display"
      xmlns="http://www.w3.org/1998/Math/MathML">
<mtable>
   <mtd>
      <msqrt>
         <msup>
         <mfenced>
         <mrow>
            <mi>a</mi>
            <mo>+</mo>
            <mi>b</mi>
         </mrow>
         </mfenced>
         <mn>3</mn>
         </msup>
      </msqrt>
   </mtd>
</mtable>
</math>
```

Using <mstyle>

The <mstyle> element enables the document creator to force style changes that control how the contents of an element are rendered. This element can use any attribute accepted by any MathML presentation element. Because this element enables you to use any of the attributes valid for other presentation elements, you can use it to change the default value of any of its child elements.

The following example code enables you to control the background and text colors of your equations:

```
<mstyle fontcolor="#FF0000" background="#0000FF">
   <mrow>
      <mi>y</mi>
      <mo>&InvisibleTimes;</mo>
      <mfenced>  <mi>t</mi>  </mfenced>
   </mrow>
   <mo> = </mo>
   <mrow>
      <mrow>
         <mfrac> <mn>5</mn><mn>2</mn></mfrac>
         <mo>&InvisibleTimes;</mo>
         <msup>
            <mi>e</mi>
            <mi>t</mi>
         </msup>
      </mrow>
      <mo> - </mo>
      <mrow>
         <mn>2</mn>
         <mo>&InvisibleTimes;</mo>
         <msup>
            <mi>e</mi>
            <mrow>
               <mn>2</mn>
               <mo>&InvisibleTimes;</mo>
               <mi>t</mi>
            </mrow>
         </msup>
      </mrow>
      <mo>+</mo>
      <mrow>
         <mfrac> <mn>1</mn><mn>2</mn></mfrac>
         <mo>&InvisibleTimes;</mo>
         <msup>
```

```
                <mi>e</mi>
                <mrow>
                    <mn>3</mn>
                    <mo>&InvisibleTimes;</mo>
                    <mi>t</mi>
                </mrow>
            </msup>
        </mrow>
    </mrow>
</mstyle>
```

Using <msub>

The <msub>element is used to create a subscript attached to either an identifier or a number. Whenever you use the <msub> element, you increase the script level by one. This causes the attributes controlling the font size of the subscript to be set automatically. The syntax for <msub> is

```
<msub> base subscript</msub>
```

Using <msubsup>

This element enables you to control the distance between the base and the subscript and superscript. As with the <msub> element, the <msubsup> element increases the script level by one, causing an automatic shift in the size of the rendered font. The syntax for the <msubsup> element is

```
<msubsup>base subscript superscript</msubsup>
```

Using <msup>

The <msup>element enables the document author to control the placement and content of a superscript. Whenever you use the <msup> element, you increase the script level by one. This causes the attributes controlling the font size of the superscript to be set automatically. The syntax for <msup> is

```
<msup> base superscript </msup>
```

Using <mtable>

The <mtable> element is used to lay out a matrix or a table. The <mtr> and <mtd> elements are used within <mtable> tags to provided a designation of both each row and table cell. <mtable> elements that don't use <mtr> tags are treated as a one-column row essentially inferring the <mtr> designation. Similarly, if an expression is not included in an <mtd> element, that expression is treated as a single table entry by inferring the <mtd> tags. When specifying a series of rows for a table that has a nonstandard number of columns, the short rows will be padded on the right side with empty implied <mtd> elements. This forces the number of columns in all rows to match across the table.

Note *You must display the parentheses bordering the matrix in <mo> elements because they are not automatically displayed as part of* <mtable>.

The following code shows a 3 by 3 matrix laid out using MathML:

```
<mrow>
   <mo> ( </mo>
   <mtable>
      <mtr> <mn>1</mn> <mn>2</mn> <mn>6</mn> </mtr>
      <mtr> <mn>-1</mn> <mn>1</mn> <mn>4</mn> </mtr>
      <mtr> <mn>1</mn> <mn>0</mn> <mn>1</mn> </mtr>
   </mtable>
   <mo> ) </mo>
</mrow>
```

Using <mtd>

The <mtd> element is used to identify a single entry in a matrix or a table that is a direct subexpression of an <mtr> element. You can place any number of arguments in a single <mtd> element block. All of the arguments will be treated as a single <mtd> expression.

The code in this example uses the <mtd> element is used as a frame to create the following expression:

```
8.5x + 2y + z = 199
```

```
<mtable>
   <mtd>
      <mrow>
         <mn> 8.5</mn>
         <mo> &InvisibleTimes; </mo>
         <mi> x </mi>
      </mrow>
      <mo> + </mo>
      <mrow>
         <mn> 2</mn>
         <mo> &InvisibleTimes; </mo>
         <mi> y </mi>
      </mrow>
      <mo> + </mo>
      <mrow>
         <mi> z </mi>
      </mrow>
      <mo> = </mo>
      <mrow>
         <mn> 199</mn>
```

```
        </mrow>
    </mtd>
</mtable>
```

Using <mtext>

The <mtext> element's main job is to display text that needs to be displayed as itself and not as part of an equation. Most often, this element will be used to show commentary text used to explain the mathematical process being displayed. You can use <mtext> to assist with controlling the spacing of characters by using invisible characters to create what is referred to as *renderable white space*. These types of characters are used to provide delays or affect the rhythm of speech in audio renderers. Some of the invisible characters that can affect spacing are listed here:

- **
** Starts a new line without an indent
- **&IndentingNewLine;** Starts a new line with an indent
- **** Does not allow a line break to occur at this location
- **&GoodBreak;** Specifies an acceptable location for a line break if needed
- **&BadBreak;** Specifies that this is a bad location for a line break to occur if one is needed on this line

The following example code shows a variety of ways that you can use <mtext> to display text that adds meaning or descriptions of the equations shown or alters the spacing used in the equations:

```
<mtext> Algorithm 3: </mtext>
<mtext>   </mtext>
<mtext>    </mtext>
<mtext> /* a comment */ </mtext>
```

Using <mtr>

As with the <tr> element used in standard HTML, the <mtr> element represents a single row in a table or matrix. You can only use the <mtr> element as a subexpression of <mtable>. As with <tr>, each argument of <mtr> is placed in its individual column, starting with the leftmost column. This element can be inferred, and in such instances, it can only have a single argument. This creates a single column table.

When specifying a series of rows for a table that has a nonstandard number of columns, the short rows will be padded on the right side with empty, implied <mtd> elements. This forces the number of columns in all rows to match across the table. You can use the rowspan and columnspan attributes to force your <mtr> elements to take up more columns than normal. This limits the number of inferred <mtd> elements that need to be created.

The code in this example uses the <mtr> element as a frame to create the following matrix (see also Figure 31-2):

$$\begin{pmatrix} X & 0 & X \\ 0 & X & 2 \\ 1 & 0 & 0 \end{pmatrix}$$

Figure 31-2. *A standard 3 by 3 matrix used for evaluating **X** looks like this.*

```
<mrow>
   <mo> ( </mo>
   <mtable>
      <mtr> <mi>x</mi > <mn>0</mn> <mi>x</mi > </mtr>
      <mtr> <mn>0</mn> < mi >x</mi > < mi >2x</mi > </mtr>
      <mtr> <mn>1</mn> <mn>0</mn> <mn>0</mn> </mtr>
   </mtable>
   <mo> ) </mo>
</mrow>
```

Using <munder>

The <munder> attribute is used to attach an underscript to a base character, equation, or value. The syntax for <munder> is

```
<munder> base underscript </munder>
```

The following example code displays two versions of an equation shown in Figure 31-3. The first set is drawn as an accent mark, the second is drawn as a limit:

```
<mrow>
   <munder accentunder="true">
      <mrow>
         <mi> a </mi>
         <mo> + </mo>
         <mi> b </mi>
         <mo> - </mo>
         <mi> c </mi>
      </mrow>
      <mo> &UnderBrace; </mo>
   </munder>
   <mtext>   vs   </mtext>
   <munder accentunder="false">
```

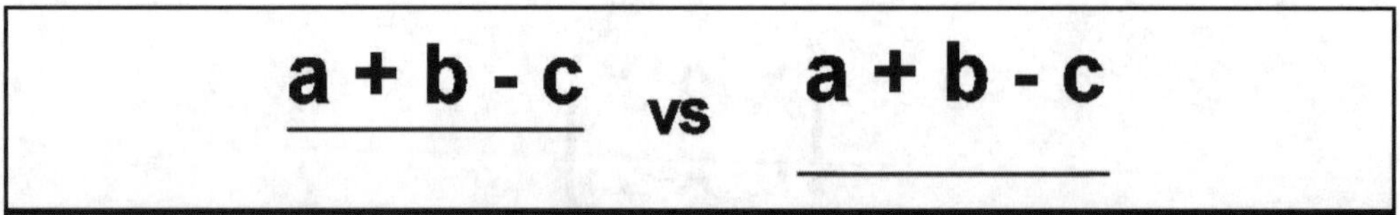

a + b - c vs a + b - c

Figure 31-3. *Mathematics uses both limits and accent marks to control how an equation is evaluated.*

```
      <mrow>
         <mi> a </mi>
         <mo> + </mo>
         <mi> b </mi>
         <mo> - </mo>
         <mi> c </mi>
      </mrow>
      <mo> &UnderBrace; </mo>
   </munder>
</mrow>
```

Using <munderover>

The <munderover> element provides document authors with a means of applying both an overscript and an underscript to a base simultaneously. This element places the underscript and overscript equally vertically spaced in relation to the base to which they are applied. The difference in the vertical spacing, between setting the underscript and overscript using the <mover> and <munder> elements or the <munderover> element, is too small to be noticed on a low resolution display. It is noticeable on high-resolution devices such as printers or when using large fonts. In addition to these differences, it is more accurate to attach both the underscript and overscript to the same base.

```
<munderover> base underscript overscript </munderover>
```

MathML Examples

The following example shows how to use some of the MathML elements in an HTML document to display math functions and processes correctly:

```
<html>
<head>
   <title> Embedding MathML in an HTML document </title>
</head>
```

```
<body>
   <!-- This equation is  (a+b)^2. -->
   <h3> (a+b)<sup>2</sup> expressed using MathML </h3>
   <math style="display"
   xmlns="http://www.w3.org/1998/Math/MathML">
      <mtable>
        <mtd>
         <msup>
         <mfenced>
         <mrow>
            <mi>a</mi>
            <mo>+</mo>
            <mi>b</mi>
         </mrow>
         </mfenced>
         <mn>2</mn>
         </msup>
    </mtd>
 </mtable>
</math>

</-- This equation is A= [ x y] over [ z u ] -->
<img src="mathml.gif"> <font size=+3>expressed using mathml </font><p>
<math style="display" xmlns="http://www.w3.org/1998/Math/MathML">
   <mtable>
      <mrow>
         <mi>A</mi>
         <mo>=</mo>
         <mfenced open="[" close="]">
            <mtable>
               <mtr>
                  <mtd><mi>x</mi></mtd>
                  <mtd><mi>y</mi></mtd>
               </mtr>
               <mtr>
                  <mtd><mi>z</mi></mtd>
                  <mtd><mi>w</mi></mtd>
                </mtr>
            </mtable>
         </mfenced>
      </mrow>
```

```
    </mtable>
</math>
</html>
```

The Language of Chemists: CML

CML merges the power of XML with the complexity of chemical information. CML and its associated tools provide chemists with the ability to convert their current proprietary formatted documents and publications into well formatted and well structured documents that can be read by chemists, and the chemically inclined, from all over the world and without requiring special expensive software.

CML was initially created as a means of mapping molecules, their reactions, and their components. Like all XML-based languages, you can extend CML so that it displays reports, synthetic recipes, or instrumental or computer output.

CML Elements

CML has been designed with ease of understanding in mind so that it is possible for the average chemist to understand and use it. In order to accomplish this, it has been broken down into only 24 elements, each of which is described in the following sections:

- **<angle>** Specialized data type used to define the coordinate and line systems used when drawing 2-D molecular structures based upon Cartesian, fractional, or other types of coordinate systems
- **<atom>** Used to contain the individual elements that define the atom
- **<atomArray>** Used to contain a series of atom descriptions
- **<bond>, <bondArray>** Defines a bond or a set of bonds linking two atoms in a molecular structure
- **<coordinate2>, <coordinate3>** Specialized data type used to define the coordinates used when drawing 2-D molecular structures based on Cartesian, fractional, or other coordinate systems
- **<crystal>** Container used to define the crystallographic information that defines the spaces, cell dimensions, and symmetry that is required of the crystalline structure
- **<electron>** Container holding the information that defines the electrons and their actions that are taken within the bonds of the molecule
- **<feature>** Provides annotations for protein sequences
- **<float>, <floatArray>, <floatMatrix>** Standard data-type identifying numerical floating point values or those values as they are held within an array or a matrix
- **<formula>** Container for the chemical formula that creates the molecule

- **<integer>, <integerArray>** Standard data-type identifying numerical integer values or those numerical values held within an array structure
- **<link>** Defines a hyperlink between molecular components
- **<list>** Standard data-type that provides descriptive information about its container element
- **<molecule>** Generic container used to hold all of the atoms, bonds, and other molecules that are combined to create a chemical structure
- **<reaction>** Container that defines the chemical reactions that occur between various atoms and bonds within a molecule
- **<sequence>** Container for describing the protein sequence used in the bonding of a molecule
- **<string>, <stringArray>** Standard data-type identifying text values or those text values held within an array structure that are used to define the atom, molecule, or bond to which they are applied
- **<torsion>** Specialized data-type used to define the coordinate and line systems used when drawing 2-D molecular structures based upon Cartesian, fractional, or other types of coordinate systems

All of these elements work together to define individual atoms, the bonds between those atoms, and the molecules that those atoms and bonds create.

CML Examples

The following CML example was copied from the ChiMeraL Web site at http://www.ch.ic.ac.uk/chimeral/. This example combines two molecules: C6 H10 and C3 H4 O. These are combined, with heat, and result in C9 H14 O. The following example code draws these two molecules, provides the instructions for their reaction, and then provides their bonded outcome. You can see the results of the code on screen in Figure 31-4, which follows the code.

```
<?xml version="1.0"?>
<?xml-stylesheet type="text/xsl" href="reaction.xsl" ?>
<document>

<!-- CML document - simple reaction example -->
<!-- karne@innocent.com - 7/4/00 -->
<!-- file converted from: MDL .mol and JCAMP-DX -->
<!-- contains example of how to markup
     a simple A + B = C reaction -->
<cml title="Simple Reaction" id="cml_simple"
```

```
xmlns="x-schema:cml_schema_ie_02.xml">
   <reaction title="Diels-Alder cycloaddition"
             id="simple_rxn_1" convention="stepwise">

      <string title="description">
        Simple example of a A + B -> C reaction.
        See source for further information.</string>
       <float title="yield" units="%">88</float>
       <string title="notes">
         taken from Vollhardt and Schore</string>
       <list title="reactionStep" id="simple_s_1">
          <string title="description">cycloaddition</string>
          <float title="yield" convention="%">88</float>
          <string title="notes">one step</string>
          <link title="reactant"
                href="simple_mol_reactant1" id="simple_lk_1"/>
          <link title="reactant"
                href="simple_mol_reactant2" id="simple_lk_2"/>
          <link title="reagent" id="simple_lk_3">
             <integer title="index">1</integer>
            <string title="solvent">Acetonitrile</string>
             <string title="temperature"
                    convention="degC">100</string>
             <string title="duration"
                    convention="hours">3</string>
             <string title="notes">reflux</string>
          </link>
          <link title="reagent" id="simple_lk_4">
            <integer title="index">2</integer>
            <string title="notes">workup</string>
          </link>
          <link title="product"
               href="simple_mol_product" id="simple_lk_5"/>
          <!-- also catalyst, intermediate, transition state as needed -->
      </list>
   </reaction>
   <!-- reactants -->
   <molecule title="2,3-Dimethyl-1,3-butadiene" id="simple_mol_reactant1">
      <formula>C6 H10</formula>
      <!-- atom list -->
      <list title="atoms">
         <atom id="r1_a_1">
```

```
      <integer builtin="atomId">1</integer>
      <float builtin="x3" units="A">5.4000</float>
      <float builtin="y3" units="A">-3.4000</float>
      <float builtin="z3" units="A">0.0000</float>
      <string builtin="elementType">C</string>
   </atom>
   <atom id="r1_a_2">
      <integer builtin="atomId">2</integer>
      <float builtin="x3" units="A">5.3958</float>
      <float builtin="y3" units="A">-4.2250</float>
      <float builtin="z3" units="A">0.0000</float>
      <string builtin="elementType">C</string>
   </atom>
   <atom id="r1_a_3">
      <integer builtin="atomId">3</integer>
      <float builtin="x3" units="A">5.9833</float>
      <float builtin="y3" units="A">-2.8125</float>
      <float builtin="z3" units="A">0.0000</float>
      <string builtin="elementType">C</string>
   </atom>
   <atom id="r1_a_4">
      <integer builtin="atomId">4</integer>
      <float builtin="x3" units="A">4.8083</float>
      <float builtin="y3" units="A">-4.8083</float>
      <float builtin="z3" units="A">0.0000</float>
      <string builtin="elementType">C</string>
   </atom>
   <atom id="r1_a_5">
      <integer builtin="atomId">5</integer>
      <float builtin="x3" units="A">5.9792</float>
      <float builtin="y3" units="A">-4.8083</float>
      <float builtin="z3" units="A">0.0000</float>
      <string builtin="elementType">C</string>
   </atom>
   <atom id="r1_a_6">
      <integer builtin="atomId">6</integer>
      <float builtin="x3" units="A">4.8125</float>
      <float builtin="y3" units="A">-2.8125</float>
      <float builtin="z3" units="A">0.0000</float>
      <string builtin="elementType">C</string>
   </atom>
</list>
```

```
    <list title="bonds">
      <bond id="r1_b_1">
        <integer title="bondId">1</integer>
        <integer builtin="atomRef">1</integer>
        <integer builtin="atomRef">2</integer>
        <integer builtin="order" convention="MDL">1</integer>
      </bond>
      <bond id="r1_b_2">
        <integer title="bondId">2</integer>
        <integer builtin="atomRef">2</integer>
        <integer builtin="atomRef">4</integer>
        <integer builtin="order" convention="MDL">1</integer>
      </bond>
      <bond id="r1_b_3">
        <integer title="bondId">3</integer>
        <integer builtin="atomRef">2</integer>
        <integer builtin="atomRef">5</integer>
        <integer builtin="order" convention="MDL">2</integer>
      </bond>
      <bond id="r1_b_4">
       <integer title="bondId">4</integer>
       <integer builtin="atomRef">1</integer>
       <integer builtin="atomRef">3</integer>
       <integer builtin="order" convention="MDL">2</integer>
      </bond>
      <bond id="r1_b_5">
       <integer title="bondId">5</integer>
       <integer builtin="atomRef">1</integer>
       <integer builtin="atomRef">6</integer>
       <integer builtin="order" convention="MDL">1</integer>
      </bond>
    </list>
  </molecule>
  <molecule title="Propenal" id="simple_mol_reactant2">
    <formula>C3 H4 O</formula>
    <!-- atom list -->
    <list title="atoms">
     <atom id="r2_a_1">
       <integer builtin="atomId">1</integer>
       <float builtin="x3" units="A">0.9083</float>
       <float builtin="y3" units="A">-1.3750</float>
       <float builtin="z3" units="A">0.0000</float>
```

```
    <string builtin="elementType">C</string>
  </atom>
  <atom id="r2_a_2">
    <integer builtin="atomId">2</integer>
    <float builtin="x3" units="A">0.9042</float>
    <float builtin="y3" units="A">-2.2000</float>
    <float builtin="z3" units="A">0.0000</float>
    <string builtin="elementType">C</string>
  </atom>
  <atom id="r2_a_3">
    <integer builtin="atomId">3</integer>
    <float builtin="x3" units="A">0.3208</float>
    <float builtin="y3" units="A">-0.7875</float>
    <float builtin="z3" units="A">0.0000</float>
    <string builtin="elementType">H</string>
  </atom>
  <atom id="r2_a_4">
          <integer builtin="atomId">4</integer>
          <float builtin="x3" units="A">1.4917</float>
          <float builtin="y3" units="A">-0.7875</float>
          <float builtin="z3" units="A">0.0000</float>
          <string builtin="elementType">C</string>
        </atom>
        <atom id="r2_a_5">
          <integer builtin="atomId">5</integer>
          <float builtin="x3" units="A">1.4875</float>
          <float builtin="y3" units="A">0.0375</float>
          <float builtin="z3" units="A">0.0000</float>
          <string builtin="elementType">O</string>
        </atom>
      </list>
      <list title="bonds">
         <bond id="r2_b_1">
           <integer title="bondId">1</integer>
           <integer builtin="atomRef">1</integer>
           <integer builtin="atomRef">3</integer>
           <integer builtin="order" convention="MDL">1</integer>
        </bond>
        <bond id="r2_b_2">
           <integer title="bondId">2</integer>
           <integer builtin="atomRef">1</integer>
           <integer builtin="atomRef">2</integer>
```

```
          <integer builtin="order" convention="MDL">2</integer>
        </bond>
        <bond id="r2_b_3">
          <integer title="bondId">3</integer>
          <integer builtin="atomRef">1</integer>
          <integer builtin="atomRef">4</integer>
          <integer builtin="order" convention="MDL">1</integer>
        </bond>
        <bond id="r2_b_4">
          <integer title="bondId">4</integer>
          <integer builtin="atomRef">4</integer>
          <integer builtin="atomRef">5</integer>
          <integer builtin="order" convention="MDL">2</integer>
        </bond>
      </list>
    </molecule>
    <!-- reagents -->
    <!-- products -->
    <molecule title="Diels-Alder adduct" id="simple_mol_product">
       <formula>C9 H14 O</formula>
       <!-- atom list -->
       <list title="atoms">
          <atom id="p_a_1">
            <integer builtin="atomId">1</integer>
            <float builtin="x3" units="A">4.0375</float>
            <float builtin="y3" units="A">0.9292</float>
            <float builtin="z3" units="A">0.0000</float>
            <string builtin="elementType">C</string>
          </atom>
          <atom id="p_a_2">
            <integer builtin="atomId">2</integer>
            <float builtin="x3" units="A">4.0333</float>
            <float builtin="y3" units="A">0.1042</float>
            <float builtin="z3" units="A">0.0000</float>
            <string builtin="elementType">C</string>
          </atom>
          <atom id="p_a_3">
            <integer builtin="atomId">3</integer>
            <float builtin="x3" units="A">4.7418</float>
            <float builtin="y3" units="A">-0.3096</float>
            <float builtin="z3" units="A">0.0000</float>
            <string builtin="elementType">C</string>
```

```
</atom>
<atom id="p_a_4">
  <integer builtin="atomId">4</integer>
  <float builtin="x3" units="A">5.4589</float>
  <float builtin="y3" units="A">0.0970</float>
  <float builtin="z3" units="A">0.0000</float>
  <string builtin="elementType">C</string>
</atom>
<atom id="p_a_5">
  <integer builtin="atomId">5</integer>
  <float builtin="x3" units="A">5.4631</float>
  <float builtin="y3" units="A">0.9220</float>
  <float builtin="z3" units="A">0.0000</float>
  <string builtin="elementType">C</string>
</atom>
<atom id="p_a_6">
  <integer builtin="atomId">6</integer>
  <float builtin="x3" units="A">4.7501</float>
  <float builtin="y3" units="A">1.3404</float>
  <float builtin="z3" units="A">0.0000</float>
  <string builtin="elementType">C</string>
</atom>
<atom id="p_a_7">
  <integer builtin="atomId">7</integer>
  <float builtin="x3" units="A">3.3208</float>
  <float builtin="y3" units="A">1.3417</float>
  <float builtin="z3" units="A">0.0000</float>
  <string builtin="elementType">C</string>
</atom>
<atom id="p_a_8">
  <integer builtin="atomId">8</integer>
  <float builtin="x3" units="A">3.3167</float>
  <float builtin="y3" units="A">-0.3042</float>
  <float builtin="z3" units="A">0.0000</float>
  <string builtin="elementType">C</string>
</atom>
<atom id="p_a_9">
  <integer builtin="atomId">9</integer>
  <float builtin="x3" units="A">6.1750</float>
  <float builtin="y3" units="A">1.3417</float>
  <float builtin="z3" units="A">0.0000</float>
  <string builtin="elementType">C</string>
```

```
      </atom>
      <atom id="p_a_10">
        <integer builtin="atomId">10</integer>
        <float builtin="x3" units="A">6.1708</float>
        <float builtin="y3" units="A">2.1667</float>
        <float builtin="z3" units="A">0.0000</float>
        <string builtin="elementType">O</string>
      </atom>
    </list>
    <list title="bonds">
      <bond id="p_b_1">
        <integer title="bondId">1</integer>
        <integer builtin="atomRef">4</integer>
        <integer builtin="atomRef">5</integer>
        <integer builtin="order" convention="MDL">1</integer>
      </bond>
      <bond id="p_b_2">
        <integer title="bondId">2</integer>
        <integer builtin="atomRef">5</integer>
        <integer builtin="atomRef">6</integer>
        <integer builtin="order" convention="MDL">1</integer>
      </bond>
      <bond id="p_b_3">
        <integer title="bondId">3</integer>
        <integer builtin="atomRef">1</integer>
        <integer builtin="atomRef">2</integer>
        <integer builtin="order" convention="MDL">2</integer>
      </bond>
      <bond id="p_b_4">
        <integer title="bondId">4</integer>
        <integer builtin="atomRef">1</integer>
        <integer builtin="atomRef">7</integer>
        <integer builtin="order" convention="MDL">1</integer>
      </bond>
      <bond id="p_b_5">
        <integer title="bondId">5</integer>
        <integer builtin="atomRef">1</integer>
        <integer builtin="atomRef">6</integer>
        <integer builtin="order" convention="MDL">1</integer>
      </bond>
      <bond id="p_b_6">
        <integer title="bondId">6</integer>
```

```
      <integer builtin="atomRef">2</integer>
      <integer builtin="atomRef">8</integer>
      <integer builtin="order" convention="MDL">1</integer>
    </bond>
    <bond id="p_b_7">
      <integer title="bondId">7</integer>
      <integer builtin="atomRef">2</integer>
      <integer builtin="atomRef">3</integer>
      <integer builtin="order" convention="MDL">1</integer>
    </bond>
    <bond id="p_b_8">
      <integer title="bondId">8</integer>
      <integer builtin="atomRef">5</integer>
      <integer builtin="atomRef">9</integer>
      <integer builtin="order" convention="MDL">1</integer>
    </bond>
    <bond id="p_b_9">
       <integer title="bondId">9</integer>
       <integer builtin="atomRef">3</integer>
       <integer builtin="atomRef">4</integer>
       <integer builtin="order" convention="MDL">1</integer>
    </bond>
    <bond id="p_b_10">
      <integer title="bondId">10</integer>
      <integer builtin="atomRef">9</integer>
      <integer builtin="atomRef">10</integer>
      <integer builtin="order" convention="MDL">2</integer>
    </bond>
   </list>
 </molecule>
</cml>
</document>
```

Summary

Both MathML and CML are standardized languages that are used by the scientific community to assist in the display of complex equations representing mathematical or chemical constructs. MathML allows mathematics to be viewed and processed on the Web as text, rather than as unusable images, by controlling both the display and vertical and horizontal alignment of characters in equations displayed on XML or HTML pages. The release of the MathML 2.0 specification is expected in 2001.

CML was initially created as a means of mapping molecules, their reactions, and their components. Like all XML-based languages, you can extend CML so that it reports synthetic recipes in either instrumental or computer output. CML has been designed with ease of understanding in mind, so that it is possible for the average chemist to understand and use it. It is kept simple by using only 24 elements to describe the molecules, atoms, bonds, and reactions that occur with the joining of various molecules and atoms.

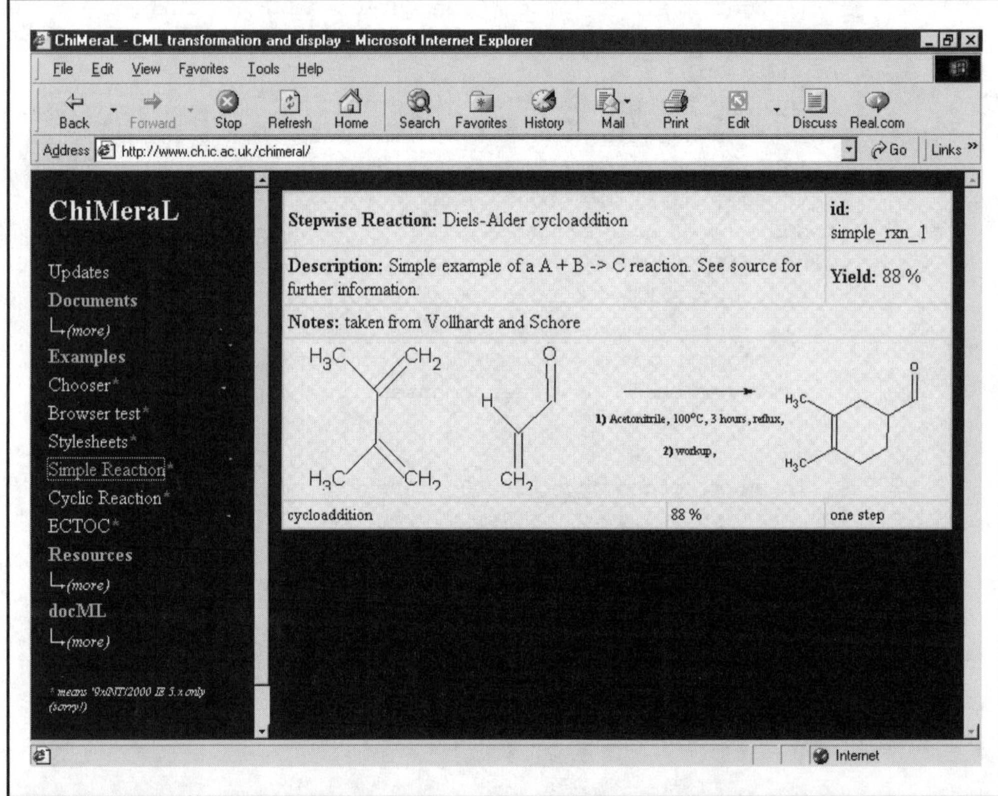

Figure 31-4. *CML can be used to map both molecules, their reactions, and the results of those reactions in both text and 2-D drawings.*

The Complete Reference

Part VIII

The Appendixes

Appendix A

DTD Key Codes and a Sample DTD

Document Type Definitions (DTDs) were discussed in detail in this book in Part II, "Working with DTDs." The essence of those chapters has been incorporated here. This chapter adds a highly commented version of the Extensible Hypertext Markup Language (XHTML) 1.0 Strict DTD.

DTD Elements

Each element declaration is identified with the following basic syntax:

```
<!ELEMENT elementname content>
```

This syntax can be further explored by taking a look at its individual parts:

- ***elementname*** This is the name of the element (for example, POET, DOCUMENT, or AUTHOR).
- ***content*** Each element has a set of allowable content. The DTD identifies the type of content that can be used with any particular element. The valid content-type options for your elements are shown in Table A-1.

The content model specified within the DTD's <!ELEMENT> statement identifies the valid contents of the element. An element's content model is specified using the syntax shown in Table A-2.

Content Type	Description	Example
EMPTY	Allows no content. The element may contain attributes.	`<!ELEMENT IMAGE EMPTY>`
ANY	May contain any content.	`<!ELEMENT ADDRESSBOOK ANY>`
Mixed content	Allows either element names or character data (#PCDATA).	`<!ELEMENT ADDRESSBOOK (NAME | NICKNAME | #PCDATA)>`
Children	Only child elements, no text, can be used within the element. The child elements can contain text.	`<!ELEMENT CONTACT ( NAME, STREET, CITY, PHONE)>`

Table A-1. *Valid Types of Content for XML Elements*

Markup	Definition	Example
(...)	Delimits a group.	
A | B	Either A or B occurs, but not both. In the example, the record either has a PAGER record or a CELL record but not both.	<!ELEMENT CONTACT (PAGER | CELL)
A , B	Both A and B occur, in that order. In the example, the CONTACT record could only have six child elements, and one character data element, all of which have to occur and must occur in the order they are listed.	<!ELEMENT CONTACT (NAME, STREET, SUITE, CITY, STATE, ZIP, #PCDATA)>
A & B	Both A and B occur in any order. In the example, the contact's NAME may occur before or after a selection of text.	<!ELEMENT CONTACT (NAME & #PCDATA)>
A?	A occurs zero or one time. In the example, the element NAME has to occur either one time or not at all within the CONTACT element.	<!ELEMENT CONTACT (NAME?)>
A*	A occurs zero or more times. In the example, the element STREET can occur any number of times or not at all within the CONTACT element.	<!ELEMENT CONTACT (STREET*)>
A+	A occurs one or more times. In the example, the ADDRESSBOOK must have at least one CONTACT record within it.	<!ELEMENT ADDRESSBOOK (CONTACT+)>

Table A-2. *DTD Element Content Model Rules*

Attribute Declarations

Attributes, like elements, have a specific format that must be used for their DTD specification. The basic structure is quite simple:

```
<!ATTLIST element_name attribute_name attribute_type
default_value>
```

This syntax can be further explored by taking a look at its individual parts:

- `<!ATTLIST>` Notifies your parser that you are identifying an attribute
- *`element_name`* Specifies an element that has already been declared, or is going to be declared, within the DTD
- *`attribute_name`* Identifier used to distinctly identify this attribute
- *`attribute_type`* One of the valid attribute types including
  - `CDATA`
  - `ENTITY, ENTITIES`
  - `Enumerated`
  - `ID`
  - `IDREF, IDREFS`
  - `NMTOKEN, NMTOKENS`
  - `NOTATION`
- *`default_value`* Specifies the default value of the attribute or one of the three default values, `#REQUIRED`, `#IMPLIED`, and `#FIXED`, included in the XML specification

In XML there are two predefined attributes. These attributes, like all others, must be declared in the DTD in order to have a valid document when the parser is processing the document. The following are these attributes:

- `xml:space` Descriptor for the treatment of white space in your element
- `xml:lang` Descriptor for the language used to write the element

DTD General Entities

The following are the rules for working with general entity references:

- You cannot use general entity references to refer to parts of text that will only be used within the DTD. If you wish to merge information in the DTD, you will need to use a parameter entity.
- You cannot use the ampersand (`&`), percent symbol (`%`), or the double-quotation mark (`"`) in your entity value directly. They can be included using their character reference, shown in Table A-3, as another entity within your current entity. Declare the default XML entities in your DTD if you are unsure of the support level of the XML browsers and parsers that will be viewing your document.

General Entity Representation (Character Reference)	Character Being Represented	Entity Declaration
`&`	& (ampersand)	`<!ENTITY amp "&:#38;">`
`'`	' (apostrophe)	`<!ENTITY amp "'">`
`>`	> (greater-than)	`<!ENTITY amp ">">`
`<`	< (less-than)	`<!ENTITY amp "&:#60;">`
`"`	" (quotation mark)	`<!ENTITY amp """>`

Table A-3. *XML Built-in General Entities*

Internal General Entities

The standard syntax for an internal general entity is quite simple. It provides an abbreviation for text that will be placed in the XML document:

```
<!ENTITY entity-name "entity-value">
```

This syntax can be further explored by taking a look at its individual parts:

- *entity-name* Can only contain alphanumeric characters, periods, dashes, underscores, or colons. `Entity-names` must begin with a letter or an underscore. Colons are typically used to demark namespace prefixes, so they should be avoided for clarity's sake unless necessary.
- *entity-value* Can contain any valid XML-formatted text and must be enclosed in quotation marks.

The following is the syntax to use an internal general entity in your XML document:

```
&entity-name;
```

You can embed entities within other entities, but be sure to not create recursive references.

APPENDIXES

External General Entities

The following is the syntax for specifying an external general entity:

```
<!ENTITY entity-name SYSTEM "entity-URI">
```

This syntax can be further explored by taking a look at its individual parts:

- *entity-name* Name of the entity that you will refer to in your XML document
- *entity-URI* Address, whether absolute or relative, of the resource providing the additional content

The syntax to use an external general entity within your XML document is the same as that for an internal general entity:

```
&entity-name;
```

Parameter Entities

Parameter entities use a separate notation system than general entities. Whereas general entities are referenced within the document using a leading ampersand (&), a parameter entity is referenced in the DTD with a percent sign (%). Unlike general entities, parameter entities cannot appear in the XML document at all.

Parameter entities are declared in the DTD using syntax very similar to that used by general entities with the only change being the addition of a percent sign (%) before the *entity-name*:

```
<!ENTITY % entity-name entity-definition>
```

Notations

The declaration statement used to identify a notation is similar to that used to express an external entity. You provide a name for the file type, rather than the entity, use either the SYSTEM or PUBLIC identifier, and then provide an external identifier, such as a Multipurpose Internet Mail Extensions (MIME) type, for the file type, as seen in the following syntax statement:

```
<!NOTATION file_type (SYSTEM|PUBLIC "public id")
"external_identifier">
```

External Unparsed Entities

Files that contain information that XML processors cannot parse are called *external unparsed entities*. The XML parser makes no attempt whatsoever to comprehend the data these files contain, it simply passes the information about the file to the XML processor to, in turn, pass it on to some type of application that can read the information contained within the file.

In the DTD, XML uses ENTITY references and attributes referencing those entities to access a specific location, provided with the ENTITY reference, that stores the specific content that is intended to be a part of the XML document. The following is an example of a standard unparsed external entity declaration statement:

```
<!ENTITY entity-name SYSTEM NDATA notation_name>
```

DTD Comments

DTD comments are used to provide instructions in an XML DTD for the programmer and anyone performing follow-up maintenance. They are not interpreted by the user agent viewing the document. Comments are often used in the following situations:

- To add comments to specific sections of code found in a DTD
- To hide code that is still being developed
- To note changes that were made to previous versions of the document
- To note the author and editing date of the document

Comments can be on a single line or on multiple lines, as shown in the following example:

```
<!--This is a comment -->
<!--Comments can have multiple lines.
    If they do, they will appear like this. -->
```

Any text found between the comment markers is not visible to a site visitor when run through an XML parser and browser. Do not place more than two dashes in line together within a comment. This causes some older parsers to truncate your comment, and any portion of your comment past the multiple dashes will be visible to your visitors.

Conditional Statements

Conditional statements provide you with a way to ignore or include information in your DTD specifically. The structure of the `IGNORE` statement is shown in the following code:

```
<![ IGNORE
   Declaration statements to be ignored
]]>
```

You can wrap as many elements, entities, notations, and attributes within the `IGNORE` statement as you wish. You can imbed `IGNORE` statements in other `IGNORE` statements.

There is only one restriction on the use of IGNORE statements: they must include an entire declaration, which also means that they cannot be used to ignore half of a declaration statement.

In addition to the IGNORE statement you can also use the INCLUDE statement to ensure that the declarations in the DTD are read. The syntax of the INCLUDE statement is exactly like the IGNORE statement:

```
<![ INCLUDE
   Declarations to be included
]]>
```

When you are nesting INCLUDE and IGNORE statements there are two restrictions on action:

- An IGNORE statement in an INCLUDE statement will be ignored.
- An INCLUDE statement in an IGNORE statement will be ignored.

Processing Instructions

Processing instructions (PIs) provide a method allowing you to incorporate information into your XML documents that are meant for a specific proprietary application. PIs can provide a lot of information to the XML processor if the processor has been programmed to understand and work with the information being displayed. PIs can provide additional information about the programs required to view the contents of unparsed external entities, run external programs, and set up style sheets and other accessory documents to your XML code.

All PIs are found between <? and ?> brackets. The instruction itself, occurring between these brackets, must contain a valid XML-formatted name, called the *target*, followed by the data providing the meat of the PI. There are two restrictions on naming your PIs. First, your name cannot start with xml; this string is reserved for uses that are either currently or may be specified within the XML standard itself. Second, you cannot include the ?> closing delimiter anywhere in the PI other than as a closing to the instruction; this closing delimiter would close your PI without giving the intended application a chance to work with the instructions.

Sample DTD: The Strict XHTML DTD

In Chapter 26 of this book, XHTML is the topic of conversation. The following DTD provides you with all of the information required to parse and validate your XHTML documents correctly. If you read through this DTD, you can discover the various elements and attributes that are supported in strict XHTML, and you can create your documents accordingly.

```
<!--
   Extensible HTML version 1.0 Strict DTD
   This is the same as HTML 4.0 Strict except for
   changes due to the differences between XML and SGML.
   Namespace = http://www.w3.org/1999/xhtml
   For further information, see: http://www.w3.org/TR/xhtml1
   Copyright (c) 1998-2000 W3C (MIT, INRIA, Keio),
   All Rights Reserved.
   This DTD module is identified by the PUBLIC and SYSTEM
   identifiers: PUBLIC "-//W3C//DTD XHTML 1.0 Strict//EN"
   SYSTEM "http://www.w3.org/TR/xhtml1/DTD/xhtml1-strict.dtd"
   $Revision: 1.1 $
   $Date: 2000/01/26 14:08:56 $
-->

<!--================= Character Mnemonic Entities ====================-->
<!ENTITY % HTMLlat1 PUBLIC
   "-//W3C//ENTITIES Latin 1 for XHTML//EN"
   "xhtml-lat1.ent">
%HTMLlat1;
<!ENTITY % HTMLsymbol PUBLIC
   "-//W3C//ENTITIES Symbols for XHTML//EN"
   "xhtml-symbol.ent">
%HTMLsymbol;
<!ENTITY % HTMLspecial PUBLIC
   "-//W3C//ENTITIES Special for XHTML//EN"
   "xhtml-special.ent">
%HTMLspecial;

<!--=================== Imported Names ==============================-->
<!ENTITY % ContentType "CDATA">
    <!-- media type, as per [RFC2045] -->
<!ENTITY % ContentTypes "CDATA">
    <!-- comma-separated list of media types, as per [RFC2045] -->
<!ENTITY % Charset "CDATA">
    <!-- a character encoding, as per [RFC2045] -->
<!ENTITY % Charsets "CDATA">
    <!-- a space separated list of character encodings, as per [RFC2045] -->
<!ENTITY % LanguageCode "NMTOKEN">
    <!-- a language code, as per [RFC1766] -->
<!ENTITY % Character "CDATA">
    <!-- a single character from [ISO10646] -->
<!ENTITY % Number "CDATA">
```

```
    <!-- one or more digits -->
<!ENTITY % LinkTypes "CDATA">
    <!-- space-separated list of link types -->
<!ENTITY % MediaDesc "CDATA">
    <!-- single or comma-separated list of media descriptors -->
<!ENTITY % URI "CDATA">
    <!-- a Uniform Resource Identifier, see [RFC2396] -->
<!ENTITY % UriList "CDATA">
    <!-- a space separated list of Uniform Resource Identifiers -->
<!ENTITY % Datetime "CDATA">
    <!-- date and time information. ISO date format -->
<!ENTITY % Script "CDATA">
    <!-- script expression -->
<!ENTITY % StyleSheet "CDATA">
    <!-- style sheet data -->
<!ENTITY % Text "CDATA">
    <!-- used for titles etc. -->
<!ENTITY % FrameTarget "NMTOKEN">
    <!-- render in this frame -->
<!ENTITY % Length "CDATA">
    <!-- nn for pixels or nn% for percentage length -->
<!ENTITY % MultiLength "CDATA">
    <!-- pixel, percentage, or relative -->
<!ENTITY % MultiLengths "CDATA">
    <!-- comma-separated list of MultiLength -->
<!ENTITY % Pixels "CDATA">
    <!-- integer representing length in pixels -->
<!-- these are used for image maps -->
<!ENTITY % Shape "(rect|circle|poly|default)">
<!ENTITY % Coords "CDATA">
    <!-- comma-separated list of lengths -->

<!--=================== Generic Attributes ========================-->
<!-- core attributes common to most elements
  id       document-wide unique id
  class    space separated list of classes
  style    associated style info
  title    advisory title/amplification
-->
<!ENTITY % coreattrs
 "id          ID             #IMPLIED
  class       CDATA          #IMPLIED
```

```
  style       %StyleSheet;   #IMPLIED
  title       %Text;         #IMPLIED"
  >
<!-- internationalization attributes
  lang        language code (backwards compatible)
  xml:lang    language code (as per XML 1.0 spec)
  dir         direction for weak/neutral text
-->
<!ENTITY % i18n
 "lang        %LanguageCode; #IMPLIED
  xml:lang    %LanguageCode; #IMPLIED
  dir         (ltr|rtl)      #IMPLIED"
  >
<!-- attributes for common UI events
  onclick     a pointer button was clicked
  ondblclick  a pointer button was double-clicked
  onmousedown a pointer button was pressed down
  onmouseup   a pointer button was released
  onouseover  a pointer was moved over the element
  onmousemove a pointer was moved onto the element
  onmouseout  a pointer was moved away from the element
  onkeypress  a key was pressed and released
  onkeydown   a key was pressed down
  onkeyup     a key was released
-->
<!ENTITY % events
 "onclick     %Script;       #IMPLIED
  ondblclick  %Script;       #IMPLIED
  onmousedown %Script;       #IMPLIED
  onmouseup   %Script;       #IMPLIED
  onmouseover %Script;       #IMPLIED
  onmousemove %Script;       #IMPLIED
  onmouseout  %Script;       #IMPLIED
  onkeypress  %Script;       #IMPLIED
  onkeydown   %Script;       #IMPLIED
  onkeyup     %Script;       #IMPLIED"
  >
<!-- attributes for elements that can get the focus
  accesskey   accessibility key character
  tabindex    position in tabbing order
  onfocus     the element got the focus
  onblur      the element lost the focus
```

```
-->
<!ENTITY % focus
 "accesskey   %Character;    #IMPLIED
  tabindex    %Number;       #IMPLIED
  onfocus     %Script;       #IMPLIED
  onblur      %Script;       #IMPLIED"
  >
<!ENTITY % attrs "%coreattrs; %i18n; %events;">

<!--=================== Text Elements ==================================>
<!ENTITY % special
   "br | span | bdo | object | img | map">
<!ENTITY % fontstyle "tt | i | b | big | small">
<!ENTITY % phrase "em | strong | dfn | code | q | sub | sup |
                  samp | kbd | var | cite | abbr | acronym">
<!ENTITY % inline.forms "input | select | textarea | label | button">
<!-- these can occur at block or inline level -->
<!ENTITY % misc "ins | del | script | noscript">
<!ENTITY % inline "a | %special; | %fontstyle; | %phrase; | %inline.forms;">
<!-- %Inline; covers inline or "text-level" elements -->
<!ENTITY % Inline "(#PCDATA | %inline; | %misc;)*">

<!--================== Block Level Elements ============================>
<!ENTITY % heading "h1|h2|h3|h4|h5|h6">
<!ENTITY % lists "ul | ol | dl">
<!ENTITY % blocktext "pre | hr | blockquote | address">
<!ENTITY % block
     "p | %heading; | div | %lists; | %blocktext; | fieldset | table">
       <!ENTITY % Block "(%block; | form | %misc;)*">
       <!-- %Flow; mixes Block and Inline and is used for list items etc. -->
       <!ENTITY % Flow "(#PCDATA | %block; | form | %inline; | %misc;)*">

       <!--================== Content Models for Exclusions ================>
       <!-- a elements use %Inline; excluding a -->
       <!ENTITY % a.content
          "(#PCDATA | %special; | %fontstyle; | %phrase; | %inline.forms; |
       %misc;)*">
       <!-- pre uses %Inline excluding img, object, big, small, sub, or sup
       -->
       <!ENTITY % pre.content
          "(#PCDATA | a | br | span | bdo | map | tt | i | b |
             %phrase; | %inline.forms;)*">
```

```
<!-- form uses %Block; excluding form -->
<!ENTITY % form.content "(%block; | %misc;)*">
<!-- button uses %Flow; but excludes a, formc and form controls -->
<!ENTITY % button.content
   "(#PCDATA | p | %heading; | div | %lists; | %blocktext; |
    table | %special; | %fontstyle; | %phrase; | %misc;)*">

<!--================== Document Structure ==============================-->
<!-- the namespace URI designates the document profile -->
<!ELEMENT html (head, body)>
<!ATTLIST html
  %i18n;
  xmlns       %URI;          #FIXED 'http://www.w3.org/1999/xhtml'
  >

<!--================== Document Head ===================================-->
<!ENTITY % head.misc "(script|style|meta|link|object)*">
<!-- content model is %head.misc; combined with a single
     title and an optional base element in any order -->
<!ELEMENT head (%head.misc;,
     ((title, %head.misc;, (base, %head.misc;)?) |
      (base, %head.misc;, (title, %head.misc;))))>
<!ATTLIST head
  %i18n;
  profile     %URI;          #IMPLIED
  >
<!-- The title element is not considered part of the flow of text.
       It should be displayed, for example, as the page header or
       window title. Exactly one title is required per document.
    -->
<!ELEMENT title (#PCDATA)>
<!ATTLIST title %i18n;>
<!-- document base URI -->
<!ELEMENT base EMPTY>
<!ATTLIST base
  href        %URI;          #IMPLIED
  >
<!-- generic metainformation -->
<!ELEMENT meta EMPTY>
<!ATTLIST meta
  %i18n;
  http-equiv  CDATA          #IMPLIED
```

```
  name        CDATA          #IMPLIED
  content     CDATA          #REQUIRED
  scheme      CDATA          #IMPLIED
  >
<!--
  Relationship values can be used in principle:
   a) for document specific toolbars/menus when used
      with the link element in document head, e.g.
      start, contents, previous, next, index, end, help
   b) to link to a separate style sheet (rel="stylesheet")
   c) to make a link to a script (rel="script")
   d) by style sheets to control how collections of
      html nodes are rendered into printed documents
   e) to make a link to a printable version of this document,
      e.g. a PostScript or PDF version
     (rel="alternate" media="print")
-->
<!ELEMENT link EMPTY>
<!ATTLIST link
  %attrs;
  charset     %Charset;      #IMPLIED
  href        %URI;          #IMPLIED
  hreflang    %LanguageCode; #IMPLIED
  type        %ContentType;  #IMPLIED
  rel         %LinkTypes;    #IMPLIED
  rev         %LinkTypes;    #IMPLIED
  media       %MediaDesc;    #IMPLIED
  >
<!-- style info, which may include CDATA sections -->
<!ELEMENT style (#PCDATA)>
<!ATTLIST style
  %i18n;
  type        %ContentType;  #REQUIRED
  media       %MediaDesc;    #IMPLIED
  title       %Text;         #IMPLIED
  xml:space   (preserve)     #FIXED 'preserve'
  >
<!-- script statements, which may include CDATA sections -->
<!ELEMENT script (#PCDATA)>
<!ATTLIST script
  charset     %Charset;      #IMPLIED
  type        %ContentType;  #REQUIRED
```

```
  src         %URI;           #IMPLIED
  defer       (defer)         #IMPLIED
  xml:space   (preserve)      #FIXED 'preserve'
  >
<!-- alternate content container for non script-based rendering -->
<!ELEMENT noscript %Block;>
<!ATTLIST noscript
  %attrs;
  >

<!--=================== Document Body ==============================-->
<!ELEMENT body %Block;>
<!ATTLIST body
  %attrs;
  onload          %Script;   #IMPLIED
  onunload        %Script;   #IMPLIED
  >
<!ELEMENT div %Flow;>  <!-- generic language/style container -->
<!ATTLIST div
  %attrs;
  >

<!--=================== Paragraphs =================================-->
<!ELEMENT p %Inline;>
<!ATTLIST p
  %attrs;
  >

<!--=================== Headings ===================================-->
<!-- There are six levels of headings from h1 (the most important)
  to h6 (the least important).
-->
<!ELEMENT h1  %Inline;>
<!ATTLIST h1
   %attrs;
   >
<!ELEMENT h2 %Inline;>
<!ATTLIST h2
   %attrs;
   >
<!ELEMENT h3 %Inline;>
<!ATTLIST h3
```

```
    %attrs;
    >
<!ELEMENT h4 %Inline;>
<!ATTLIST h4
    %attrs;
    >
<!ELEMENT h5 %Inline;>
<!ATTLIST h5
    %attrs;
    >
<!ELEMENT h6 %Inline;>
<!ATTLIST h6
    %attrs;
    >

<!--==================== Lists =========================================-->
<!-- Unordered list -->
<!ELEMENT ul (li)+>
<!ATTLIST ul
  %attrs;
  >
<!-- Ordered (numbered) list -->
<!ELEMENT ol (li)+>
<!ATTLIST ol
  %attrs;
  >
<!-- List item -->
<!ELEMENT li %Flow;>
<!ATTLIST li
  %attrs;
  >
<!-- Definition lists - dt for term, dd for its definition -->
<!ELEMENT dl (dt|dd)+>
<!ATTLIST dl
  %attrs;
  >
<!ELEMENT dt %Inline;>
<!ATTLIST dt
  %attrs;
  >
<!ELEMENT dd %Flow;>
<!ATTLIST dd
```

```
  %attrs;
  >

<!--==================== Address =====================================-->
<!-- Information on author -->
<!ELEMENT address %Inline;>
<!ATTLIST address
  %attrs;
  >

<!--==================== Horizontal Rule =============================-->
<!ELEMENT hr EMPTY>
<!ATTLIST hr
  %attrs;
  >

<!--==================== Preformatted Text ===========================-->
<!-- Content is %Inline; excluding "img|object|big|small|sub|sup" -->
<!ELEMENT pre %pre.content;>
<!ATTLIST pre
  %attrs;
  xml:space (preserve) #FIXED 'preserve'
  >

<!--==================== Blocklike Quotes ============================-->
<!ELEMENT blockquote %Block;>
<!ATTLIST blockquote
  %attrs;
  cite        %URI;           #IMPLIED
  >

<!--==================== Inserted/Deleted Text========================-->
<!-- ins/del are allowed in block and inline content, but its
  inappropriate to include block content within an ins element
  occurring in inline content.
-->
<!ELEMENT ins %Flow;>
<!ATTLIST ins
  %attrs;
  cite        %URI;           #IMPLIED
  datetime    %Datetime;      #IMPLIED
```

```
  >
<!ELEMENT del %Flow;>
<!ATTLIST del
  %attrs;
  cite          %URI;           #IMPLIED
  datetime      %Datetime;      #IMPLIED
  >

<!--=================== Anchor Element ================================-->
<!-- content is %Inline; except that anchors shouldn't be nested -->
<!ELEMENT a %a.content;>
<!ATTLIST a
  %attrs;
  charset       %Charset;       #IMPLIED
  type          %ContentType;   #IMPLIED
  name          NMTOKEN         #IMPLIED
  href          %URI;           #IMPLIED
  hreflang      %LanguageCode;  #IMPLIED
  rel           %LinkTypes;     #IMPLIED
  rev           %LinkTypes;     #IMPLIED
  accesskey     %Character;     #IMPLIED
  shape         %Shape;         "rect"
  coords        %Coords;        #IMPLIED
  tabindex      %Number;        #IMPLIED
  onfocus       %Script;        #IMPLIED
  onblur        %Script;        #IMPLIED
  >

<!--===================== Inline Elements ===========================-->
<!ELEMENT span %Inline;> <!-- generic language/style container -->
<!ATTLIST span
  %attrs;
  >
<!ELEMENT bdo %Inline;>  <!-- I18N BiDi override -->
<!ATTLIST bdo
  %coreattrs;
  %events;
  lang          %LanguageCode;  #IMPLIED
  xml:lang      %LanguageCode;  #IMPLIED
  dir           (ltr|rtl)       #REQUIRED
  >
<!ELEMENT br EMPTY>   <!-- forced line break -->
```

```
<!ATTLIST br
  %coreattrs;
  >
<!ELEMENT em %Inline;>   <!-- emphasis -->
<!ATTLIST em %attrs;>
<!ELEMENT strong %Inline;>   <!-- strong emphasis -->
<!ATTLIST strong %attrs;>
<!ELEMENT dfn %Inline;>   <!-- definitional -->
<!ATTLIST dfn %attrs;>
<!ELEMENT code %Inline;>   <!-- program code -->
<!ATTLIST code %attrs;>
<!ELEMENT samp %Inline;>   <!-- sample -->
<!ATTLIST samp %attrs;>
<!ELEMENT kbd %Inline;>  <!-- something user would type -->
<!ATTLIST kbd %attrs;>
<!ELEMENT var %Inline;>   <!-- variable -->
<!ATTLIST var %attrs;>
<!ELEMENT cite %Inline;>   <!-- citation -->
<!ATTLIST cite %attrs;>
<!ELEMENT abbr %Inline;>   <!-- abbreviation -->
<!ATTLIST abbr %attrs;>
<!ELEMENT acronym %Inline;>   <!-- acronym -->
<!ATTLIST acronym %attrs;>
<!ELEMENT q %Inline;>   <!-- inlined quote -->
<!ATTLIST q
  %attrs;
  cite        %URI;          #IMPLIED
  >
<!ELEMENT sub %Inline;> <!-- subscript -->
<!ATTLIST sub %attrs;>
<!ELEMENT sup %Inline;> <!-- superscript -->
<!ATTLIST sup %attrs;>
<!ELEMENT tt %Inline;>   <!-- fixed pitch font -->
<!ATTLIST tt %attrs;>
<!ELEMENT i %Inline;>   <!-- italic font -->
<!ATTLIST i %attrs;>
<!ELEMENT b %Inline;>   <!-- bold font -->
<!ATTLIST b %attrs;>
<!ELEMENT big %Inline;>   <!-- bigger font -->
<!ATTLIST big %attrs;>
<!ELEMENT small %Inline;>   <!-- smaller font -->
<!ATTLIST small %attrs;>
```

```
<!--===================== Object ================================-->
<!-- Object is used to embed objects as part of HTML pages.
  param elements should precede other content. Parameters
  can also be expressed as attribute/value pairs on the
  object element itself when brevity is desired.
-->
<!ELEMENT object
    (#PCDATA | param | %block; | form | %inline; | %misc;)*>
<!ATTLIST object
  %attrs;
  declare     (declare)       #IMPLIED
  classid     %URI;           #IMPLIED
  codebase    %URI;           #IMPLIED
  data        %URI;           #IMPLIED
  type        %ContentType;   #IMPLIED
  codetype    %ContentType;   #IMPLIED
  archive     %UriList;       #IMPLIED
  standby     %Text;          #IMPLIED
  height      %Length;        #IMPLIED
  width       %Length;        #IMPLIED
  usemap      %URI;           #IMPLIED
  name        NMTOKEN         #IMPLIED
  tabindex    %Number;        #IMPLIED
  >
<!-- param is used to supply a named property value.
  In XML it would seem natural to follow RDF and support an
  abbreviated syntax where the param elements are replaced
  by attribute value pairs on the object start tag.
-->
<!ELEMENT param EMPTY>
<!ATTLIST param
  id          ID              #IMPLIED
  name        CDATA           #IMPLIED
  value       CDATA           #IMPLIED
  valuetype   (data|ref|object) "data"
  type        %ContentType;   #IMPLIED
  >

<!--=================== Images ========================================-->
<!-- To avoid accessibility problems for people who aren't
   able to see the image, you should provide a text
```

```
    description using the alt and longdesc attributes.
    In addition, avoid the use of server-side image maps.
    Note that in this DTD there is no name attribute. That
    is only available in the transitional and frameset DTD.
-->
<!ELEMENT img EMPTY>
<!ATTLIST img
  %attrs;
  src         %URI;          #REQUIRED
  alt         %Text;         #REQUIRED
  longdesc    %URI;          #IMPLIED
  height      %Length;       #IMPLIED
  width       %Length;       #IMPLIED
  usemap      %URI;          #IMPLIED
  ismap       (ismap)        #IMPLIED
  >
<!-- usemap points to a map element which may be in this document
  or an external document, although the latter is not widely supported
-->

<!--================== Client-side Image Maps ===============-->
<!-- These can be placed in the same document or grouped in a
  separate document although this isn't yet widely supported -->
<!ELEMENT map ((%block; | form | %misc;)+ | area+)>
<!ATTLIST map
  %i18n;
  %events;
  id          ID             #REQUIRED
  class       CDATA          #IMPLIED
  style       %StyleSheet;   #IMPLIED
  title       %Text;         #IMPLIED
  name        NMTOKEN        #IMPLIED
  >
<!ELEMENT area EMPTY>
<!ATTLIST area
  %attrs;
  shape       %Shape;        "rect"
  coords      %Coords;       #IMPLIED
  href        %URI;          #IMPLIED
  nohref      (nohref)       #IMPLIED
  alt         %Text;         #REQUIRED
  tabindex    %Number;       #IMPLIED
```

```
  accesskey   %Character;    #IMPLIED
  onfocus     %Script;       #IMPLIED
  onblur      %Script;       #IMPLIED
  >

<!--================ Forms ===============================-->
<!ELEMENT form %form.content;>
   <!-- forms shouldn't be nested -->
<!ATTLIST form
  %attrs;
  action      %URI;          #REQUIRED
  method      (get|post)     "get"
  enctype     %ContentType;  "application/x-www-form-urlencoded"
  onsubmit    %Script;       #IMPLIED
  onreset     %Script;       #IMPLIED
  accept      %ContentTypes; #IMPLIED
  accept-charset %Charsets;  #IMPLIED
  >
<!--   Each label must not contain more than ONE field
  Label elements shouldn't be nested.
-->
<!ELEMENT label %Inline;>
<!ATTLIST label
  %attrs;
  for         IDREF          #IMPLIED
  accesskey   %Character;    #IMPLIED
  onfocus     %Script;       #IMPLIED
  onblur      %Script;       #IMPLIED
  >
<!ENTITY % InputType
  "(text | password | checkbox |
    radio | submit | reset |
    file | hidden | image | button)"
   >
<!-- the name attribute is required for all
     but submit & reset -->
<!ELEMENT input EMPTY>     <!-- form control -->
<!ATTLIST input
  %attrs;
  type        %InputType;    "text"
  name        CDATA          #IMPLIED
  value       CDATA          #IMPLIED
```

```
  checked     (checked)       #IMPLIED
  disabled    (disabled)      #IMPLIED
  readonly    (readonly)      #IMPLIED
  size        CDATA           #IMPLIED
  maxlength   %Number;        #IMPLIED
  src         %URI;           #IMPLIED
  alt         CDATA           #IMPLIED
  usemap      %URI;           #IMPLIED
  tabindex    %Number;        #IMPLIED
  accesskey   %Character;     #IMPLIED
  onfocus     %Script;        #IMPLIED
  onblur      %Script;        #IMPLIED
  onselect    %Script;        #IMPLIED
  onchange    %Script;        #IMPLIED
  accept      %ContentTypes;  #IMPLIED
  >
<!ELEMENT select (optgroup|option)+>
    <!-- option selector -->
<!ATTLIST select
  %attrs;
  name        CDATA           #IMPLIED
  size        %Number;        #IMPLIED
  multiple    (multiple)      #IMPLIED
  disabled    (disabled)      #IMPLIED
  tabindex    %Number;        #IMPLIED
  onfocus     %Script;        #IMPLIED
  onblur      %Script;        #IMPLIED
  onchange    %Script;        #IMPLIED
  >
<!ELEMENT optgroup (option)+>
    <!-- option group -->
<!ATTLIST optgroup
  %attrs;
  disabled    (disabled)      #IMPLIED
  label       %Text;          #REQUIRED
  >
<!ELEMENT option (#PCDATA)>
    <!-- selectable choice -->
<!ATTLIST option
  %attrs;
  selected    (selected)      #IMPLIED
  disabled    (disabled)      #IMPLIED
```

APPENDIXES

```
  label       %Text;          #IMPLIED
  value       CDATA           #IMPLIED
  >
<!ELEMENT textarea (#PCDATA)>
   <!-- multi-line text field -->
<!ATTLIST textarea
  %attrs;
  name        CDATA           #IMPLIED
  rows        %Number;        #REQUIRED
  cols        %Number;        #REQUIRED
  disabled    (disabled)      #IMPLIED
  readonly    (readonly)      #IMPLIED
  tabindex    %Number;        #IMPLIED
  accesskey   %Character;     #IMPLIED
  onfocus     %Script;        #IMPLIED
  onblur      %Script;        #IMPLIED
  onselect    %Script;        #IMPLIED
  onchange    %Script;        #IMPLIED
  >
<!-- The fieldset element is used to group form fields.
  Only one legend element should occur in the content
  and if present should only be preceded by white space.
-->
<!ELEMENT fieldset
    (#PCDATA | legend | %block; | form | %inline; | %misc;)*>
<!ATTLIST fieldset
  %attrs;
  >
<!ELEMENT legend %Inline;>
   <!-- fieldset label -->
<!ATTLIST legend
  %attrs;
  accesskey   %Character;     #IMPLIED
  >
<!--  Content is %Flow; excluding a, form and form controls
-->
<!ELEMENT button %button.content;>
    <!-- push button -->
<!ATTLIST button
  %attrs;
  name        CDATA           #IMPLIED
  value       CDATA           #IMPLIED
```

```
  type        (button|submit|reset) "submit"
  disabled    (disabled)       #IMPLIED
  tabindex    %Number;         #IMPLIED
  accesskey   %Character;      #IMPLIED
  onfocus     %Script;         #IMPLIED
  onblur      %Script;         #IMPLIED
  >

<!--====================== Tables ======================-->
<!-- Derived from IETF HTML table standard, see [RFC1942] -->
<!--  The border attribute sets the thickness of the frame
 around the table. The default units are screen pixels.
 The frame attribute specifies which parts of the frame around
 the table should be rendered. The values are not the same as
 CALS to avoid a name clash with the valign attribute.
-->
<!ENTITY % TFrame
   "(void|above|below|hsides|lhs|rhs|vsides|box|border)">
<!--  The rules attribute defines which rules to draw between
 cells:  If rules is absent then assume:
     "none" if border is absent or border="0" otherwise "all"
-->
<!ENTITY % TRules "(none | groups | rows | cols | all)">
  <!-- horizontal placement of table relative to document -->
<!ENTITY % TAlign "(left|center|right)">
<!-- horizontal alignment attributes for cell contents
  char        alignment char, e.g. char=':'
  charoff     offset for alignment char
-->
<!ENTITY % cellhalign
  "align      (left|center|right|justify|char) #IMPLIED
   char       %Character;      #IMPLIED
   charoff    %Length;         #IMPLIED"
  >
<!-- vertical alignment attributes for cell contents -->
<!ENTITY % cellvalign
  "valign     (top|middle|bottom|baseline) #IMPLIED"
  >
<!ELEMENT table
    (caption?, (col*|colgroup*), thead?, tfoot?, (tbody+|tr+))>
<!ELEMENT caption  %Inline;>
<!ELEMENT thead    (tr)+>
```

```
<!ELEMENT tfoot    (tr)+>
<!ELEMENT tbody    (tr)+>
<!ELEMENT colgroup (col)*>
<!ELEMENT col      EMPTY>
<!ELEMENT tr       (th|td)+>
<!ELEMENT th       %Flow;>
<!ELEMENT td       %Flow;>
<!ATTLIST table
  %attrs;
  summary     %Text;         #IMPLIED
  width       %Length;       #IMPLIED
  border      %Pixels;       #IMPLIED
  frame       %TFrame;       #IMPLIED
  rules       %TRules;       #IMPLIED
  cellspacing %Length;       #IMPLIED
  cellpadding %Length;       #IMPLIED
  >
<!ENTITY % CAlign "(top|bottom|left|right)">
<!ATTLIST caption
  %attrs;
  >
<!-- colgroup groups a set of col elements. It allows you to
group several semantically related columns together.
-->
<!ATTLIST colgroup
  %attrs;
  span        %Number;       "1"
  width       %MultiLength;  #IMPLIED
  %cellhalign;
  %cellvalign;
  >
<!--  col elements define the alignment properties for cells in
 one or more columns.
 The width attribute specifies the width of the columns, e.g.
    width=64        width in screen pixels
    width=0.5*      relative width of 0.5
 The span attribute causes the attributes of one
 col element to apply to more than one column.
-->
<!ATTLIST col
  %attrs;
  span        %Number;       "1"
```

```
  width       %MultiLength;  #IMPLIED
  %cellhalign;
  %cellvalign;
  >
<!-- Use thead to duplicate headers when breaking table
    across page boundaries, or for static headers when
    tbody sections are rendered in scrolling panel.
    Use tfoot to duplicate footers when breaking table
    across page boundaries, or for static footers when
    tbody sections are rendered in scrolling panel.
    Use multiple tbody sections when rules are needed
    between groups of table rows.
-->
<!ATTLIST thead
  %attrs;
  %cellhalign;
  %cellvalign;
  >
<!ATTLIST tfoot
  %attrs;
  %cellhalign;
  %cellvalign;
  >
<!ATTLIST tbody
  %attrs;
  %cellhalign;
  %cellvalign;
  >
<!ATTLIST tr
  %attrs;
  %cellhalign;
  %cellvalign;
  >
<!-- Scope is simpler than headers attribute for common
  tables -->
<!ENTITY % Scope "(row|col|rowgroup|colgroup)">
<!-- th is for headers, td for data and for cells acting as
  both -->
<!ATTLIST th
  %attrs;
  abbr        %Text;         #IMPLIED
  axis        CDATA          #IMPLIED
```

```
  headers     IDREFS        #IMPLIED
  scope       %Scope;       #IMPLIED
  rowspan     %Number;      "1"
  colspan     %Number;      "1"
  %cellhalign;
  %cellvalign;
  >
<!ATTLIST td
  %attrs;
  abbr        %Text;        #IMPLIED
  axis        CDATA         #IMPLIED
  headers     IDREFS        #IMPLIED
  scope       %Scope;       #IMPLIED
  rowspan     %Number;      "1"
  colspan     %Number;      "1"
  %cellhalign;
  %cellvalign;
  >
```

Appendix B

CSS Language Reference

This is a quick overview of all the Cascading Style Sheet (CSS) properties that can be used with XML documents. The information provided here is terse, but it should assist you when you need the style sheet property for proper formatting of your document.

Basic Concepts and @-Rules

This section defines some of the basic terms and functions used with CSSs found in XML documents.

Comments

Insert a text comment into your CSS code.

Syntax

```
/* comment text */
```

Example Stylesheet

```
/* Control the appearance of TITLE elements */
TITLE  { font: Arial;
         font-size: 4; }
```

<?xml-stylesheet...?>

Links to an external style sheet from in your XML document. This statement appears following the XML declaration.

Syntax

```
<?xml-stylesheet type="mime type value" href="URL"?>
```

Example Stylesheet

```
<?xml version="1.0" standalone="no"?>
<?xml-stylesheet type="text/css" href="sonnet.css"?>
<SONNET> … </SONNET>
```

Selectors

Selectors designate the specific XML element(s) to which style sheet properties are applied. You can select any number of properties that you wish.

Syntax

```
ELEMENT { descriptors; }
ELEMENT, ELEMENT, ELEMENT { descriptors; }
```

Example Stylesheet

```
SONNET         { line-height: 18pt;
                 color: purple; }
SONNET, VERSE { font: Arial; }
```

for the following XML document:

```
<?xml version="1.0" standalone="no"?>
<?xml-stylesheet type="text/css" href="sonnet.css"?>
<SONNET>
   <VERSE> … </VERSE>
</SONNET>
```

Contextual Selector

Contextual selectors are used to control the appearance of elements that are found in other specified elements. You can specify that the `<LINE>` elements in a `<STANZA>` element appear in blue, while a `<LINE>` element in a `<REFRAIN>` element appears in red.

Syntax

```
ELEMENT ELEMENT ELEMENT { descriptors; }
```

Example Stylesheet

```
STANZA LINE  { color: blue; }
REFRAIN LINE { color: red; }
```

for the following XML document:

```
<?xml version="1.0" standalone="no"?>
<?xml-stylesheet type="text/css" href="sonnet.css"?>
<SONNET>
   <STANZA>
      <LINE> … </LINE>
      <LINE> … </LINE>
   </STANZA>
```

```
    <REFRAIN>
        <LINE> … </LINE>
        <LINE> … </LINE>
    </REFRAIN>
</SONNET>
```

class Selector

Class selectors allow you to select specific elements from in the entire list of elements of their type. For example, you could have a series of <POEM> elements, some with a class of haiku, and others with a class of sonnet. You can format each of these classes of poems differently.

Note *Class selectors are only guaranteed to work for HTML and XHTML—no guarantees for XML*

Syntax

```
ELEMENT.class { descriptors; }
```

Example Stylesheet

```
POEM.haiku    { font: Arial; }
POEM.sonnet   { font: Times New Roman;}
.haiku        { color: red;
                line-height: 14pt;
                font-size: 4; }
.sonnet       { color: purple;
                line-height: 12pt;
                font-size: inherit }
```

for the following XML document:

```
<?xml version="1.0" standalone="no"?>
<?xml-stylesheet type="text/css" href="poetry.css"?>
<POETRY>
    <POEM class="haiku">
        <LINE class="haiku"> … </LINE>
        <LINE class="haiku"> … </LINE>
    </POEM>
    <POEM class="sonnet">
        <LINE class="sonnet"> … </LINE>
        <LINE class="sonnet"> … </LINE>
```

```
    </POEM>
</POETRY>
```

ID selector

This selector is used to select elements with a specified ID attribute value that has been specified by a Document Type Definition (DTD) and validated by a parser, no matter what the element type.

Syntax

```
#id { descriptors; }
```

Example Stylesheet

```
#Shakespeare   { border-bottom: 2 inset black; }
#Chaucer       { border-left: 5 ridge green; }
```

for the following XML document:

```
<?xml version="1.0" standalone="no"?>
<?xml-stylesheet type="text/css" href="poetry.css"?>
<POETRY>
   <POEM id="Shakespeare"> ... </POEM>
   <POEM id="Chaucer"> ... </POEM>
</POETRY>
```

@charset

This rule is used to identify the character encoding or set of UNICODE characters used by the current style sheet property to which it is applied.

Syntax

```
@charset "character set identifier";
```

Example Stylesheet

```
@charset "ANSI_X3.4-1968"
```

@fontface

This CSS statement allows you to designate a specific font or font family to appear in your document. If your font can't be found on the computer viewing your document, this statement allows the visitor to download that font from any source you specify.

Syntax

```
@font-face { descriptors; }
```

Example Stylesheet

```
@font-face { font-family: "Comic Sans";
              src: url(http://site.com/fonts/comicsans.ttf);
}
```

Available Descriptors

font-family	font-size	font-weight
font-variant	font-style	font-face
font-set	src	

@import

This statement allows you to specify a style sheet to import for your document. In this fashion you can embed style sheets with .css extensions in your existing style sheets. You can only have one `@import` statement in a document.

Syntax

```
@import url (web address) mediatype
```

Example Stylesheet

```
@import url (print.css) print;
@import url (video.css) tv, screen;
@import url (voices.css) aural;
```

@media

This rule identifies and defines the media that is to be affected by the style sheet declarations you are making. You have as many `@media` statements in your document as you wish.

Syntax

```
@media mediatype { descriptors;}
```

Example Stylesheet

```
@media screen {
    POEM { font-size: 3;
           line-height: 14;
           color: Black; }
    AUTHOR  { font-size: 2;
              line-height: 18;
              color: green; }}
@media print {
    POEM { font-size: 12;
           line-height: 14;
           color: black; }
    AUTHOR { font-size: 10;
             line-height: 18;
             color: green; }}
@media screen, print {
    POEM { border-size: 1 } }
```

Available Media Types

all	aural	braille
embossed	handheld	print
projection	screen	tty
tv		

@page

This statement is only available with Web browsers or XML browsers that are compatible with the CSS2 specification. It is used to control how your printed page appears.

Syntax

```
@page { descriptors;}
```

Example Stylesheet

```
@page       { size: landscape;
              marks: crop; }
@page:left  { margin-top: 10cm;
              margin-bottom: 10cm;
              margin-left:  5cm;
              margin-right: 10cm; }
```

Available Descriptors

`:first`	`:left`	`:right`
all `margin` attributes	`mark`	`size`

!important

By declaring a property `!important`, you will add more force to the specification, making it harder to be overwritten by a viewer's software. This declaration will override any normal ruling specified in a reader's user agent software. An important declaration in the viewer's software will override a normal declaration in the documents. If a user's style has been declared `!important`, it will override an `!important` declaration in the author's document. By declaring a property `!important`, you are declaring all of that property's subproperties important also.

Syntax

```
ELEMENT { descriptors !important }
```

Example Stylesheet

```
POEM { color: maroon !important;
     font-family: Verdana, Helvetica !important;
     font-style: bold; }
```

Pseudo-Elements and Pseudo-Classes

Pseudo-elements and pseudo-classes provide access to the elements, element states, and positions in a document that aren't otherwise accessible.

:active

This anchor pseudo-class is applied only when the link is being selected by the user. This pseudo-element allows you to control the color of your anchors while they are active.

Syntax

```
ELEMENT:active { descriptor }
```

Example Stylesheet

```
POEM:active { color: green }
```

Available Descriptor

```
color
```

:after

This pseudo-element is used to insert the information specified in the `content` parameter after every instance of the tag or tags that it has been applied to. This pseudo-element must be used with the `content` descriptor.

Syntax

```
ELEMENT:after { content:description }
```

Example Stylesheet

```
POEM:after { content: url("greenball.gif") }
```

Available Descriptor

```
content
```

:before

The `:before` pseudo-element is used to insert the information specified in the `content` parameter before every instance of the tag or tags that it has been applied to. This pseudo-element must be used with the `content` descriptor.

Syntax

```
ELEMENT:before { content:description }
```

Example Stylesheet

```
POEM:before { content: url("blueball.gif") }
```

Available Descriptor

```
content
```

:first

This pseudo-class is only applied to the `@page` rule. Using this pseudo-class, you can apply information directly to the page layout of the first printed page of your document.

Syntax

```
@page:first { descriptors; }
```

Example Stylesheet

```
@page:first  { margin-top: 10cm;
               margin-bottom: 10cm;
               margin-left:  5cm;
               margin-right: 10cm; }
```

Available Descriptors

All `margin` properties

:first-child

This pseudo-element is used to select the first child-element of the designated element and to apply the style sheet descriptors to that element. This match is only made if the specified child element is actually the first element following the specified parent. For example, the example here selects the `<LINE>` element if it is in a format similar to

```
<POEM>
   <LINE> This is a line of a poem.</LINE>
</POEM>
```

but not

```
<POEM>
   <AUTHOR> The Fabulous Me </AUTHOR>
   <LINE> This is a line of a poem.</LINE>
</POEM>
```

Syntax

```
parent-Element > child-Element:first-child { descriptors; }
```

Example Stylesheet

```
POEM > LINE:first-child { color:blue; }
```

:first-letter

This pseudo-element is used to create graphical effects, such as drop caps, in your XML documents.

Syntax

```
ELEMENT:first-letter { descriptors; }
```

Example Stylesheet

```
POEM:first-letter { font-size: 7;
                    font-style: italic;
                    font-weight: bold;
                    float: left; }
LINE:first-letter { color: red; }
```

Available Descriptors

All `background` properties	`clear`
All `border` properties	`color`
All `margin` properties	`line-height`
All `padding` properties	`text-decoration`
All `font` properties	`float`
`text-transform`	

:first-line

This statement is used to apply its descriptors to the first line of the specified block element.

Syntax

```
Element:first-line { descriptors; }
```

Example Stylesheet

```
POEM:first-line  { color: red;
                   font-size: 3;>
```

Available Descriptors

All background properties	All font properties	
clear	color	float
letter-spacing	text-decoration	text-transform
vertical-align	word-spacing	

:focus

This pseudo-class is applied to fields or other elements that are currently active and allow keyboard input.

Syntax

```
ELEMENT:focus { descriptors }
```

Example Stylesheet

```
LINE:focus { background: aqua }
```

Available Descriptors

All font properties	All background properties	color

:hover

This pseudo-class is applied to links when the mouse is moved over them.

Syntax

```
ELEMENT:hover { descriptors; }
```

Example Stylesheet

```
A:link { color: red; }
```

Available Descriptors

All `font` properties

All `background` properties

`color`

:lang

This pseudo-class is used to identify a specific set of style sheet properties that are dependant upon the language the document is written in.

Syntax

```
ELEMENT:lang(langid) { descriptors }
```

The `langid` is any of the valid language types, such as `fr` for French and `en` for English.

Example Stylesheet

```
POEM:lang (fr) { font: "Verdana" }
```

Available Descriptors

All CSS properties

:left

This pseudo-class is applied to `@page` rule and is used to set the margins of the left side of your page.

Syntax

```
@page:left { descriptors; }
```

Example Stylesheet

```
@page:left  { margin-top: 10cm;
              margin-bottom: 10cm;
              margin-left:  5cm;
              margin-right: 10cm;}
```

Available Descriptors

All `margin` properties

:link

This anchor pseudo-class is applied to all selected links on your document. This pseudo-element allows you to control the color of your anchors while they are active.

Syntax

```
ELEMENT:link { descriptors }
```

Example Stylesheet

```
POEM:link { color: green }
```

Available Descriptors

```
color
```

:right

This pseudo-class is applied to `@page` rule and is used to set the margins of the right side of your page.

Syntax

```
@page:right {descriptors;}
```

Example Stylesheet

```
@page:right  { margin-top: 10mm;
               margin-bottom: 10px;
```

```
margin-left:  5cm;
margin-right: 10cm; }
```

Available Descriptors

All `margin` properties

:visited

This anchor pseudo-class is applied to all visited links on your document. This pseudo-element allows you to control the color of your anchors after they have been used.

Syntax

```
ELEMENT:visited { descriptors }
```

Example Stylesheet

```
POEM:visited { color: green }
```

Available Descriptors

```
color
```

Units of Measurement

When reading the syntax and value lists for each of these properties, you will see a variety of options listed such as `<length>` and `<percentage>`. The descriptions for these values are listed here.

<length>

Sets the numerical value and unit of distance to measure the length of an element.

`em`	Measurement based upon the height of the letter *m* in the current font.
`ex`	Measurement based upon the height of the letter *x* in the current font.
`px`	Pixel
`in`	Inch
`cm`	Centimeter
`mm`	Millimeter
`pt`	Point
`pc`	Pica

<percentage>

This setting is a length or height measurement based upon the total height or width of the current element's parent containment block.

<color>

Properties that ask for a color can use one of the following color name values or Red-Green-Blue (RGB) numerical values.

Color Names

Color name values break down into two groups. The first are those colors that are standardized with the World Wide Web Consortium (W3C). The second group of color names is a development by Microsoft and is therefore only available to Microsoft clients.

HTML 4.0 List

Aqua	Black	Blue	Fuchsia
Gray	Green	Lime	Maroon
Navy	Olive	Purple	Red
Silver	Teal	White	Yellow

Microsoft Extended List

AliceBlue	Antique	White	Aquamarine
Azure	Beige	Bisque	BlanceDalmond
BlueViolet	Brown	Burlywood	CadetBlue
Chartreuse	Chocolate	Coral	Cornflower
Cornsilk	Crimson	Cyan	DarkBlue
DarkCyan	DarkGoldenrod	Darkgray	DarkGreen
DarkKhaki	DarkMagenta	DarkOliveGreen	DarkOrange
DarkOrchid	DarkRed	DarkSalmon	DarkSeaGreen
DarkSlateBlue	DarkSlateGray	DarkTurquoise	DarkViolet
DeepPink	DeepSkyBlue	DimGray	DodgerBlue
FireBrick	FloralWhite	ForestGreen	Gainsboro
GhostWhite	Gold	GoldenRod	GreenYellow
HoneyDew	HotPink	IndianRed	Indigo

Ivory	Khaki	Lavender	LavenderBlush
LawnGreen	LemonChiffon	LightBlue	LightCoral
LightCyan	LightGoldenrodYellow	LightGreen	LightSkyBlue
LightSlateGray	LightSteelBlue	LightYellow	LimeGreen
Linen	Magenta	MediumAquamarine	MediumBlue
MediumOrchid	MediumPurple	MediumSeaGreen	MediumSlateBlue
MediumSpringGreen	MediumTurquoise	MediumVioletRed	MidnightBlue
MintCream	MistyRose	Moccasin	NavajoWhite
OldLace	OliveDrab	Orange	OrangeRed
Orchid	PaleGoldenrod	PaleGreen	PaleTurquoise
PaleVioletRed	PapayaWhip	PeachPuff	Peru
Pink	Plum	PowderBlue	RosyBrown
RoyalBlue	SaddleBrown	Salmon	SandyBrown
SeaGreen	SeaShell	Sienna	SkyBlue
SlateBlue	SlateGray	Snow	SpringGreen
SteelBlue	Tan	Thistle	Tomato
Turquoise	Violet	Wheat	WhiteSmoke
YellowGreen			

RGB Value

Red-Green-Blue (RGB) values identify the numerical amounts of each of those colors to add to the "pot" when creating a color for your style. There are four formats that can be used:

`(RRR, GGG, BBB)`	Sets the color value based upon an integer between 1 and 256 for each color red, green, and blue.
`(R%, G%, B%)`	Sets the color value based upon the percentage of red, green, and blue in the resulting color.
`#xxx`	Uses single digit hex notation to identify the color you wish to use. This format is the most limiting of the four when considering potential color values.
`#xxxxxx`	Uses double-digit hex notation to identify the color you wish to use. This is the most common method of identifying colors on the Internet.

URI

Uniform Resource Identifiers (URIs) identify the address of a resource that should be used with the element to which a style with this value is applied. URIs can be specified using one of two notations:

`url("`*`fileaddress`*`")`	This identifies the address of the resource as a specific URL and can be used to reference remote files.
`fileaddress`	This identifies the address of the resource, but due to confusion when used with some properties, it only identifies local resources.

Font and Text Properties

All of these properties are available to control the formatting of text objects in your XML documents.

font

This property is used to set all of the font attributes for your selected element.

Syntax

```
font:[ [font-style || font-variant || font-weight ]
      font-size [/line-height] font-family] | caption
      | icon | menu | messagebox | smallcaption | statusbar | inherit
```

Values

font-style	*font-variant*	*font-weight*
font-size	*line-height*	*font-family*
caption	icon	menu
messagebox	smallcaption	statusbar
inherit (default)		

Example Stylesheet

```
{ font:  italic small-caps lighter 12pt "Comic Sans"}
```

font-family

This property sets the family name or generic-family name for the font you wish to use for this element.

Syntax

```
font-family: <family-name> || <generic-family>
```

Values

The default value is set by the XML Browser

<family-name>	A comma delimited list of font family names such as Lucida or Times New Roman.
<generic-family>	A comma-delimited list of serif, sans serif, cursive, fantasy, and monospace.

Example Stylesheet

```
{ font-family: "Times New Roman"; }
{ font-family: "Arial"; }
{ font-family: "serif"; }
{ font-family: "fantasy"; }
```

font-size

This property sets the size of the font used to display the element specified. The interpretation of this setting is based on the configuration of the current XML browsing software.

Syntax

```
font-size: <absolute-size> | <relative-size> | <length> |
<percentage> | inherit
```

Values

<absolute-size>: xx-small, x-small, small, medium (default), large, x-large, xx-large	*<relative-size>*: larger, smaller	*<length>*
<percentage>	inherit	

font-size-adjust

Controls the width of a font, selected using the font-family property, in relation to its height. This setting allows you to control the aspect of width to height of your fonts, with the wider the font, the more legible it is at smaller sizes in comparison to narrower fonts.

Syntax

```
font-size-adjust: <number> | none | inherit
```

Values

<number>	none (default)	inherit

Example Stylesheet

```
{font-size-adjust: '".56"'
 font-family: "Verdana, Times New Roman, Helvetica";}
```

font-stretch

Controls the kerning of a font.

Syntax

```
font-stretch: normal | wider | narrower | ultracondensed |
extracondensed | condensed | semicondensed | semiexpanded |
expanded | extraexpanded | ultraexpanded
```

Values

normal (default)	wider	narrower
ultracondensed	extracondensed	condensed
semicondensed	semiexpanded	expanded
extraexpanded	ultraexpanded	

Example Stylesheet

```
{ font-stretch: wider;
  font-family: Verdana;
  font-size: 4; }
```

font-style

Controls the style, either italic or oblique, used to display the font.

Syntax

```
font-style: normal | italic | oblique | inherit
```

Values

`normal` (default) `italic` `oblique`

`inherit`

Example Stylesheet

```
{ font-style: italic;
  font-weight: bold; }
```

Controls the use of small caps with your fonts.

Syntax

```
font-variant: normal | small-caps | inherit
```

Values

`normal` (default) `small-caps` `inherit`

Example Stylesheet

```
{ font-variant: "small-caps"; }
```


font-weight

Controls the weight, or thickness, of the font used.

Syntax

```
font-weight: normal | bold | bolder | lighter | 100 | 200 | 300 |
00 | 500 | 600 | 700 | 800 | 900 | inherit
```

Values

The numerical values specify an incremental increase in the thickness of the font.

normal (default—same as a value of 400)	bold (same as a value of 700)	bolder
lighter	100	200
300	400	500
600	700	800
900	inherit	

Example Stylesheet

```
{ font-weight: bold; }
{ font-weight: 900; }
```

letter-spacing

Controls the amount of white space between characters.

Syntax

```
letter-spacing: normal | <length> | <percentage> | inherit
```

Values

normal (default)	*<length>*
<percentage>	inherit

Example Stylesheet

```
{ letter-spacing: "2"; }
{ letter-spacing: "normal"; }
{ letter-spacing: "10%"; }
```

line-height

Controls the height of each line of text.

Syntax

```
line-height: normal | <number> | <length> | <percentage> | inherit
```

Values

`normal` (default)

<length>

<percentage>

<number>

`inherit`

Example Stylesheet

```
{ line-height: "2"; }
{ line-height: "normal"; }
{ line-height: "10%"; }
```

text-align

Controls the alignment of text in a specified element.

Syntax

```
text-align: left | right | center | justify | <string> | inherit
```

Values

The default value for this property is controlled by the XML browser.

`left`

`right`

`center`

`justify`

<string>

`inherit`

Example Stylesheet

```
{ text-align: left; }
{ text-align: justify; }
{ text-align: "."; }
```

text-decoration

Controls the addition of decorative properties to an element.

Syntax

```
text-decoration: none | [underline || overline || line-through ||
blink] | inherit
```

Values

none (default)	underline	overline
line-through	blink	inherit

Example Stylesheet

```
{ text-decoration: underline }
{ text-decoration: blink }
```

text-indent

Controls the indentation amount of the first line of a paragraph.

Syntax

```
text-indent: <length> | <percentage> | inherit
```

Values

The default value for this property is zero.

<length>	*<percentage>*	inherit

Example Stylesheet

```
{ text-indent: ".5in" }
{ text-indent: "2%" }
{ text-indent: "15px" }
```

text-shadow

Controls the application of a shadow, including color and length, to the text content of an element.

Syntax

```
text-shadow: none | [<color> || <horiz-length> <vert-length>
blur-length>] | inherit
```

Values

none (default)	<color>
<length> measurement for horizontal, vertical, and blur dimensions.	inherit

Example Stylesheet

```
{ text-shadow: "red 5px 5px 3px" }
{ text-shadow: "blue 10px 5px 10px" }
{ text-shadow: "none" }
```

text-transform

Controls the capitalization style used to display the text, no matter how it is typed into the original XML document.

Syntax

```
text-transform: capitalize | uppercase | lowercase | none | inherit
```

Values

capitalize	uppercase	lowercase
none (default)	inherit	

Example Stylesheet

```
{ text-transform: "lowercase" }
{ text-transform: "capitalize" }
```

vertical-align

Controls the vertical alignment of the text in an inline element.

Syntax

```
vertical-align:Baseline | sub | super | top | text-top | middle |
bottom | text-bottom | <percentage> | <length> | inherit
```

Values

baseline (default)	sub	super
top	text-top	middle
bottom	text-bottom	*<percentage>*
<length>	inherit	

Example Stylesheet

```
{ vertical-align: baseline }
{ vertical-align: 10% }
{ vertical-align: 5px }
```

word-spacing

Controls the amount of space found between words.

Syntax

```
word-spacing: normal | <length> | inherit
```

Values

normal (default)	*<length>*	inherit

Example Stylesheet

```
{ word-spacing: 10px }
{ word-spacing: .5in }
```

Color and Background Properties

These properties control the background settings and the color of the element.

background

A catch-all setting to set all of the background properties simultaneously.

Syntax

```
background: [background-color || background-image ||
background-repeat || background-attachment ||
background-position ] | inherit
```

Values

background-color property	*background-image* property	*background-repeat* property
background-attachment property	*background-position* property	inherit

Example Stylesheet

```
{ background: "red repeat-x fixed" }
{ background: "image.gif no-repeat fixed top" }
```

background-attachment

Controls the whether the background image scrolls with the page or remains fixed in the XML browser screen.

Syntax

```
background-attachment: scroll | fixed | inherit
```

Values

`scroll` (default)	`fixed`	`inherit`

Example Stylesheet

```
{ background-attachment: fixed }
```

background-color

Sets the background color of the element.

Syntax

```
background-color: <color> | transparent | inherit
```

Value

<color> transparent (default) inherit

Example Stylesheet

```
{ background-color: red }
{ background-color: transparent }
```

background-image

Sets the background image of the element

Syntax

```
background-image: uri("uri") | none | inherit
```

Values

uri*("uri")* none (default) inherit

Example Stylesheet

```
{ background-image: uri("gift.gif")}
{ background-image: none }
```

background-position

Controls the initial horizontal and vertical placement of the background image.

Syntax

```
background-position: [<percentage> | <length>] || [top | center |
bottom] || [left | center | right] || inherit
```

Values

The default value for this property is zero percent. This pair uses a horizontal and then vertical percentage or length.

<percentage>	*<length>*	top
center (vertical)	bottom	left
center (horizontal)	right	inherit

Example Stylesheet

```
{ background-position: "100% 10%" }
{ background-position: "1in 2in" }
{ background-position: "10px 30px" }
{ background-position: "top left" }
{ background-position: "center center" }
```

background-repeat

This controls the method to propagate the background on the XML browser window.

Syntax

```
background-repeat: repeat | repeat-x | repeat-y | no-repeat | inherit
```

Values

`repeat` (default—repeat the background in standard tile fashion)	`repeat-x` (repeat horizontally only)
`repeat-y` (repeat vertically only)	`no-repeat` (do not repeat the background at all)
`inherit`	

Example Stylesheet

```
{ background-repeat: repeat-x }
{ background-repeat: no-repeat }
```

color

This property controls the color of your elements.

Syntax

```
color: <color> | <RGB Value> | transparent | inherit
```

Values

The default value of this property is a setting of the XML browser.

<color>	*<RGB Value>*
transparent	inherit

Example Stylesheet

```
{ color: red }
{ color: #FF0000 }
{ color: transparent }
```

Generated Content and Cursors

CSS allows you to create your own content and customize your document cursors using the `content` and `cursor` properties.

content

Controls the addition of automatically generated information in the XML document. This property is used in conjunction with `:before` and `:after`.

Syntax

```
content: [<string> | <uri> | <counter> | attr(x) | open-quote |
close-quote | no-open-quote | no-close-quote]+ | inherit
```

Values

<string>	*<uri>*	*<counter>*
attr(*x*)	open-quote	close-quote
no-open-quote	no-close-quote	inherit

Example Stylesheet

```
POEM: before { content: "blueball.gif" }
POEM: before { content: no-close-quote }
POEM: after { content: close-quote }
```

counter-increment

Allows the creation of a number for each iteration of an element in your document.

Syntax

```
counter-increment: [<identifier> <integer>] | none | inherit
```

Values

<identifier>

<integer>

none (default)

inherit

Example Stylesheet

```
LINE {counter-increment: par-num }
POEM { counter-reset: par-num }
LINE: before { content: counter(par-num, lower-roman) "." }
```

counter-reset

Resets the value of the counter whenever the element is encountered.

Syntax

```
counter-reset:  [<identifier> <integer>] | none | inherit
```

Values

<identifier>

<integer>

none (default)

inherit

Example Stylesheet

```
LINE { counter-increment: par-num }
POEM { counter-reset: par-num }
LINE:before { content: counter(par-num, lower-roman) "." }
```

cursor

Controls the type of cursor displayed when the mouse is placed over an element.

Syntax

```
cursor:  [ [auto | crosshair | default | pointer | move |
e-resize | ne-resize | nw-resize | n-resize | se-resize |
sw-resize | s-resize | e-resize | w-resize | text | wait |
help] || <uri>] | inherit
```

Values

`auto` (default)	`crosshair`	`default`
`pointer`	`move`	`e-resize`
`ne-resize`	`nw-resize`	`n-resize`
`se-resize`	`sw-resize`	`s-resize`
`e-resize`	`w-resize`	`text`
`wait`	`help`	*<uri>*
`inherit`		

Example Stylesheet

```
{ cursor: "text" }
{ cursor: "wait" }
```

Containment Box Properties

These properties are used to control the appearance of the element's containment box.

border

A shortcut property to set all of the border properties including *border-color, border-style,* and *border-width.*

Syntax

```
border: [border-color || border-style || border-width] | inherit
```

Values

border-color	*border-style*
border-width	`inherit`

Example Stylesheet

```
{ border: red inset 2px }
{ border: green thin }
{ border: inset inverted }
```

border-bottom

A shortcut property to set all of the bottom border properties including `border-bottom-color`, `border-bottom-style`, and `border-bottom-width`.

Syntax

```
border-bottom: [border-bottom-color || border-bottom-style ||
               border-bottom-width] | inherit
```

Values

border-bottom-color property	*border-bottom-style* property
border-bottom-width property	`inherit`

Example Stylesheet

```
{ border-bottom: red inset 2px }
{ border-bottom: green thin }
{ border-bottom: inset inverted }
```

border-bottom-color

Controls the color of an element's bottom border.

Syntax

```
border-bottom-color: <colorname> | <#RGB> | invert | inherit
```

Values

<colorname>	*<#RGB>*
`invert` (default)	`inherit`

Example Stylesheet

```
{ border-bottom-color: red }
{ border-bottom-color: #FF0000 }
{ border-bottom-color: invert }
```

border-bottom-style

Controls the style used to draw the bottom border.

Syntax

```
border-bottom-style: none | hidden | dotted | dashed | solid |
double | grooved | ridge | inset | outset | inherit
```

Values

none (default)	hidden	dotted
dashed	solid	double
grooved	ridge	inset
outset	inherit	

Example Stylesheet

```
{ border-bottom-style: hidden }
{ border-top-style: inset }
```

border-bottom-width

Controls the width of a box's bottom border.

Syntax

```
border-bottom-width: medium | thin | thick | inherit
```

Values

medium (default)	thin
thick	inherit

Example Stylesheet

```
{ border-bottom-width: thin }
{ border-bottom-width: thick }
```

border-collapse

Forces the borders of a table to collapse in on themselves.

Syntax

```
border-collapse: collapse | separate | inherit
```

Values

`collapse` `separate` (default) `inherit`

Example Stylesheet

```
{ border-collapse: collapse }
```

border-color

Controls the color of an element's border.

Syntax

```
border-color: <colorname> | <#rgb> | invert | inherit
```

Values

<*colorname*> <#*RGB*>

`invert` (default) `inherit`

Example Stylesheet

```
{ border-color: red }
{ border-color: #FF0000 }
{ border-color: invert }
```

border-left

A shortcut property to set all of the left border properties, including `border-left-color`, `border-left-style`, and `border-left-width`.

Syntax

```
border-left: [border-bottom-color || border-bottom-style ||
border-bottom-width] | inherit
```

Values

border-left-color property	*border-left-style* property
border-left-width property	inherit

Example Stylesheet

```
{ border-left: red inset 2px }
{ border-left: green thin }
{ border-left: inset inverted }
```

border-left-color

Controls the color of an element's left border.

Syntax

```
border-left-color: <colorname> | <#RGB> | invert | inherit
```

Values

<colorname>	*<#RGB>*
invert (default)	inherit

Example Stylesheet

```
{ border-left-color: red }
{ border-left-color: #FF0000 }
{ border-left-color: invert }
```

border-left-style

Controls the style used to draw the left border.

Syntax

```
border-left-style: none | hidden | dotted | dashed | solid |
double | grooved | ridge | inset | outset | inherit
```

Values

none (default)	hidden	dotted
dashed	solid	double
grooved	ridge	inset
outset	inherit	

Example Stylesheet

```
{ border-left-style: hidden }
{ border-left-style: inset }
```

border-left-width

Controls the width of a box's left border.

Syntax

```
border-left-width: medium | thin | thick | inherit
```

Values

medium (default)	thin
thick	inherit

Example Stylesheet

```
{ border-left-width: thin }
{ border-left-width: thick }
```

border-right

A shortcut property to set all of the right border properties including `border-right-color`, `border-right-style`, and `border-right-width`.

Syntax

```
border-right: [border-right-color || border-right-style ||
border-right-width] | inherit
```

Values

border-right-color property	*border-right-style* property
border-right-width property	`inherit`

Example Stylesheet

```
{ border-right: red inset 2px }
{ border-right: green thin }
{ border-right: inset inverted }
```

border-right-color

Controls the color of an element's right border.

Syntax

```
border-right-color: <colorname> | <#RGB> | invert | inherit
```

Values

<colorname>	*<#RGB>*
`invert` (default)	`inherit`

Example Stylesheet

```
{ border-right-color: red }
{ border-right-color: #FF0000 }
{ border-right-color: invert }
```

border-right-style

Controls the style used to draw the right border.

Syntax

```
border-right-style: none | hidden | dotted | dashed | solid |
double | grooved | ridge | inset | outset | inherit
```

Values

none (default)	hidden	dotted
dashed	solid	double
grooved	ridge	inset
outset	inherit	

Example Stylesheet

```
{ border-right-style: hidden }
{ border-top-style: inset }
```

border-right-width

Controls the width of a box's right border.

Syntax

```
border-right-width: medium | thin | thick | inherit
```

Values

medium (default)	thin
thick	inherit

Example Stylesheet

```
{ border-right-width: thin }
{ border-right-width: thick }
```

border-style

Controls the style used to draw the border.

Syntax

```
border-style: none | hidden | dotted | dashed | solid | double |
grooved | ridge | inset | outset | inherit
```

Values

none (default)	hidden	dotted
dashed	solid	double
grooved	ridge	inset
outset	inherit	

Example Stylesheet

```
{ border-style: hidden }
{ border-style: inset }
```

border-top

A shortcut property to set all of the top border properties including `border-top-color`, `border-top-style`, and `border-top-width`.

Syntax

```
border-top: [border-top-color || border-top-style ||
border-top-width] | inherit
```

Values

border-top-color property	*border-top-style* property
border-top-width property	inherit

Example Stylesheet

```
{ border-top: red inset 2px }
{ border-top: green thin }
{ border-top: inset inverted }
```

border-top-color

Controls the color of an element's top border.

Syntax

```
border-top-color: <colorname> | <#RGB> | invert | inherit
```

Values

<colorname>	*<#RGB>*
invert (default)	inherit

Example Stylesheet

```
{ border-top-color: red }
{ border-top-color: #FF0000 }
{ border-top-color: invert }
```

border-top-style

Controls the style used to draw the top border.

Syntax

```
border-top-style: none | hidden | dotted | dashed | solid |
double | grooved | ridge | inset | outset | inherit
```

Values

none (default)	hidden	dotted
dashed	solid	double
grooved	ridge	inset
outset	inherit	

Example Stylesheet

```
{ border-top-style: hidden }
{ border-top-style: inset }
```

border-top-width

Controls the width of a box's top border.

Syntax

```
border-top-width: medium | thin | thick | inherit
```

Values

`medium` (default)

`thin`

`thick`

`inherit`

Example Stylesheet

```
{ border-top-width: thin }
{ border-top-width: thick }
```

border-width

Controls the width of a box's border.

Syntax

```
border-width: medium | thin | thick | inherit
```

Values

`medium` (default)

`thick`

`thin`

`inherit`

Example Stylesheet

```
{ border-width: thin }
{ border-width: thick }
```

bottom

Controls the distance between the bottom edge of an element's object box and the bottom edge of the containment box or page.

Syntax

```
bottom: <length> | <percentage> | auto | inherit
```

Values

<length>

<percentage>

auto (default)

inherit

Example Stylesheet

```
{ bottom: 1cm }
{ bottom: auto }
{ bottom: 1mm }
{ bottom: 1px }
{ bottom: 15%}
```

clear

Controls whether an element allows a floating object on either its left or right side so that text can be properly placed around the floating object.

Syntax

```
clear: none | left | right | both | inherit
```

Values

none (default)

left

right

both

inherit

Example Stylesheet

```
{ clear: left }
{ clear: right }
```

clip

Identifies the portion of an element's content that is visible when rendered by an XML browser.

Syntax

```
clip: <shape> | auto | inherit
```

Values

`<shape>` (`rect` [rectangle]) is currently the only valid shape that can be used with this value.

`inherit`	`auto (default)`

Example Stylesheet

```
{ clip: rect }
{ clip: auto }
```

float

Specifies whether a containment box should float to the left, right, or not at all in relation to the element's parent containment box.

Syntax

```
float: left | right | none | inherit
```

Values

`left`	`right`
`none` (default)	`inherit`

Example Stylesheet

```
{ float: left }
{ float: right }
```

height

Controls the height of boxes created by block-level elements.

Syntax

```
height: <length> | <percentage> | auto | inherit
```

Values

<length>	*<percentage>*
auto (default)	inherit

Example Stylesheet

```
{ height: 10px }
{ height: 15% }
{ height: 1cm }
```

left

Controls the distance between the left edge of an element's object box and the right edge of the containment box or page.

Syntax

left: *<length>* | *<percentage>* | auto | inherit

Values

<length>	*<percentage>*
auto (default)	inherit

Example Stylesheet

```
{ left: 1cm }
{ left: auto }
{ left: 1mm }
{ left: 1px }
{ left: 15% }
```

margin

Controls the margins on the page. This is a shorthand property to set all four margins simultaneously.

Syntax

margin: *<margin-width>* {1,4} | inherit

Values

```
<margin-width>                    inherit
```

Example Stylesheet

```
{ margin-width: 10px 20px 15px } /* Sets top to 10 px, left and
                                 right to 20px, bottom to 15px */
{ margin-width: 10mm 20mm } /* Sets top & bottom to 10mm, left &
                            right to 20mm */
{ margin-width: 1cm 2cm 3cm 4cm } /* Sets top
                                 to 1cm, right to 2cm, left to
                                 3cm, and  bottom to 4cm*/
```

margin-bottom

Sets the dimensions of the bottom page or element box margin.

Syntax

```
margin-bottom: <margin-width> | inherit
```

Values

The default value for this property is 0.

```
<margin-width>                    inherit
```

Example Stylesheet

```
{ margin-bottom: 1cm }
{ margin-bottom: 1in }
```

margin-left

Sets the dimensions of the left page or element box margin.

Syntax

```
margin-left: <margin-width> | inherit
```

Values

The default value for this property is 0.

<margin-width>	inherit

Example Stylesheet

```
{ margin-left: 1cm }
{ margin-left: 1in }
```

margin-right

Sets the dimensions of the right page or element box margin.

Syntax

```
margin-right: <margin-width> | inherit
```

Values

The default value for this property is 0.

<margin-width>	inherit

Example Stylesheet

```
{ margin-right: 1cm }
{ margin-right: 1in }
```

margin-top

Sets the dimensions of the top page or element box margin.

Syntax

```
margin-top: <margin-width> | inherit
```

Values

The default value for this property is 0.

<margin-width>	inherit

Example Stylesheet

```
{ margin-top: 1cm }
{ margin-top: 1in }
```

marker-offset

Specifies the distance between the edge of the marker box, or the vertical space taken up by list markers, and the edge of your principal box.

Syntax

```
marker-offset: <length> | auto | inherit
```

Values

<*length*> auto (default) inherit

Example Stylesheet

```
{ marker-offset: 6cm }
```

marks

Controls the appearance of printer and alignment marks on the pages.

Syntax

```
marks: [crop || cross] | none | inherit
```

Values

crop cross
none (default) inherit

Example Stylesheet

```
{ marks: crop }
{ marks: cross }
```

max-height

Sets the maximum available height for the element's containment box.

Syntax

```
max-height: <length> | <percentage> | none | inherit
```

Values

The default value of this property is `100` percent.

<length>	*<percentage>*
none	inherit

Example Stylesheet

```
{ max-height: 300px }
{ max-height: 150% }
{ max-height: 150pc }
```

max-width

Sets the maximum available width for the element's containment box.

Syntax

```
max-width: <length> | <percentage> | none | inherit
```

Values

The default value of this property is `100` percent.

<length>	*<percentage>*
none	inherit

Example Stylesheet

```
{ max-width: 400px }
{ max-width: 99% }
{ max-width: 100pc }
```

min-height

Sets the minimum available height for the element's containment box.

Syntax

```
min-height: <length> | <percentage> | none | inherit
```

Values

The default value of this property is 0.

<length>	*<percentage>*
none	inherit

Example Stylesheet

```
{ min-height: 3px }
{ min-height: 10% }
{ min-height: 1pc }
```

min-width

Sets the minimum available width for the element's containment box.

Syntax

```
max-height: <length> | <percentage> | none | inherit
```

Values

The default value of this property is set by the XML browser.

<length>	*<percentage>*
none	inherit

Example Stylesheet

```
{ min-width: 100px }
{ min-width: 1% }
{ min-width: 3pc }
```

orphans

Specifies the minimum number of lines in a paragraph that must be reserved at the bottom of a page when a paragraph is broken between two pages.

Syntax

```
orphans: <integer> | inherit
```

Value

The default value of this property is 2 .

<integer> inherit

Example Stylesheet

```
{ orphans: 4 }
{ orphans: 1 }
```

outline

A shortcut property to set all of the outline properties including `outline-color`, `outline-style`, and `outline-width`.

Syntax

```
outline: [outline-color || outline-style || outline-width] | inherit
```

Values

outline-color property

outline-style property

outline-width property

inherit

Example Stylesheet

```
{ outline: red inset 2px }
{ outline: green thin }
{ outline: inset inverted }
```

outline-color

Controls the color of an element's outline.

Syntax

```
outline-color: <colorname> | <#RGB> | invert | inherit
```

Values

<colorname>

<#RGB>

invert (default)

inherit

Example Stylesheet

```
{ outline-color: red }
{ outline-color: #FF0000 }
{ outline-color: invert }
```

outline-style

Controls the style used to draw the outline.

Syntax

```
outline-style: none | hidden | dotted | dashed | solid |
double | grooved | ridge | inset | outset | inherit
```

Values

none (default)	hidden	dotted
dashed	solid	double
grooved	ridge	inset
outset	inherit	

Example Stylesheet

```
{ outline-style: hidden }
{ outline-style: inset }
```

outline-width

Controls the width of an outline of a box.

Syntax

```
outline-width: medium | thin | thick | inherit
```

Values

medium (default)	thin
thick	inherit

Example Stylesheet

```
{ outline-width: thin }
{ outline-width: thick }
```

overflow

Controls how information that more than fills a designated layer or containment box size should be treated.

Syntax

```
overflow: visible | hidden | scroll | auto | inherit
```

Values

`visible` (default)	`hidden`	`scroll`
`auto`	`inherit`	

Example Stylesheet

```
{ overflow: hidden }
{ overflow: scroll }
```

padding

Controls the amount of padding between the page edge and the elements it contains. This is a shorthand property to set all four padding settings simultaneously.

Syntax

```
padding: <padding-width> {1,4} | inherit
```

Values

<padding-width>	`inherit`

Example Stylesheet

```
{ padding: 10px 20px 15px } /* Sets top to 10 px, left and right
                               to 20px, bottom to 15px */
{ padding: 10mm 20mm }      /* Sets top and bottom to 10mm, left
                               and right to 20mm */
```

```
{ padding: 1cm 2cm 3cm 4cm } /* Sets top to 1cm, right to 2cm,
                                left to 3cm, and  bottom to 4cm*/
```

padding-bottom

Sets the dimensions of the padding appearing at the bottom page or element box.

Syntax

```
padding-bottom: <padding-width> | inherit
```

Values

The default value for this property is `0`.

<padding-width>	inherit

Example Stylesheet

```
{ padding-bottom: 1cm }
{ padding-bottom: 1in }
```

padding-left

Sets the dimensions of the padding appearing at the left edge of the page or element box.

Syntax

```
padding-left: <padding-width> | inherit
```

Values

The default value for this property is `0`.

<padding-width>	inherit

Example Stylesheet

```
{ padding-left: 1cm }
{ padding-left: 1in }
```

padding-right

Sets the dimensions of the padding appearing at the right edge of the page or element box.

Syntax

```
padding-right: <padding-width> | inherit
```

Values

The default value for this property is zero.

```
<padding-width>                 inherit
```

Example Stylesheet

```
{ padding-right: 1cm }
{ padding-right: 1in }
```

padding-top

Sets the dimensions of the padding appearing at the top edge of the page or element box.

Syntax

```
padding-top: <padding-width> | inherit
```

Values

The default value for this property is zero.

```
<padding-width>                 inherit
```

Example Stylesheet

```
{ padding-top: 1cm }
{ padding-top: 1in }
```

page

This property works in conjunction with the @page rule to define a variety of page sizes.

Syntax

```
page: identifier | inherit
```

Values

```
identifier                      inherit
```

Example Stylesheet

```
@page rotated { size: landscape }
@page skinny  { size: 4″ 14″ }
POEM  { page: rotated }
HAIKU { page: skinny }
```

page-break-after

Controls whether a page break will appear after this element.

Syntax

```
page-break-after: auto | always | avoid | left | right | inherit
```

Values

auto (default)	always	avoid
left	right	inherit

Example Stylesheet

```
{ page-break-after: always } /* A new page always starts

after this element*/
{ page-break-after: avoid } /* A page break never
                               occurs after this element */
```

page-break-before

Controls whether a page break will appear before this element.

Syntax

```
page-break-before: auto | always | avoid | left | right | inherit
```

Values

auto (default)	always	avoid
left	right	inherit

Example Stylesheet

```
{ page-break-before: always } /* A new page always starts

before this element*/
{ page-break-before: avoid } /*
A page break never
                                    occurs before this element */
```

page-break-inside

Allows or prohibits the insertion of a page break inside the current object.

Syntax

```
page-break-inside: avoid | auto | inherit
```

Values

`avoid` `auto` (default) `inherit`

Example Stylesheet

```
{ page-break-inside: avoid } /* No page break allowed*/
{ page-break-inside: auto } /* The printer decides where

the pages break. */
```

position

Controls how the object is positioned in relation to the other elements on the page.

Syntax

```
position: static | relative | absolute | fixed | inherit
```

Values

`static` `relative` (default) `absolute`
`fixed` `inherit`

Example Stylesheet

```
{ position: absolute;
   top: 60px;
   left: 100px; }  /*Sets an absolutely positioned box 60px down
                     and 100px left of the top corner of the page,
                     or this element's containment box. */
{ position: fixed;
  top: 100px;
  left: 50px } /*Sets fixed positioned box 100px down and
                 50px left from the top corner of the document
                 window. This box does not move when the page is
                 scrolled. */
```

quotes

Specifies the quotation marks to use with any number of embedded quotes.

Syntax

quotes: [*<string>* *<string>*]+ | none | inherit

Values

The default value of this property is dependant upon the XML browser.

<string> none inherit

Example Stylesheet

```
{ quotes: "" "" "<" ">" }
{ quotes: '"' '"' "' " "' " }
```

right

Controls the distance between the right edge of an element's object box and the right edge of the containment box or page.

Syntax

right: *<length>* | *<percentage>* | auto | inherit

Values

<length>
<percentage>
auto (default)
inherit

Example Stylesheet

```
{ right: 1cm }
{ right: auto }
{ right: 1mm }
{ right: 1px }
{ right: 15% }
```

size

Sets the size and layout of the printed page.

Syntax

```
size: <length>{1,2} | auto | portrait | landscape | inherit
```

Values

<length>
auto (default)
portrait
landscape
inherit

Example Stylesheet

```
{ size: portrait } /* Creates standard portrait 8.5x11" page */
{ size: 6in 8in }  /* Creates a 6x8in page */
```

top

Controls the distance between the top edge of an element's object box and the left edge of the containment box or page.

Syntax

```
top: <length> | <percentage> | auto | inherit
```

Values

<length>	*<percentage>*
auto (default)	inherit

Example Stylesheet

```
{ top: 1cm }
{ top: auto }
{ top: 1mm }
{ top: 1px }
{ top: 15% }
```

visibility

Controls how the content of an element is rendered.

Syntax

```
visibility: inherit | visible | collapse | hidden
```

Values

inherit (default)	visible
collapse	hidden

Example Stylesheet

```
{ visibility: visible }  /* Element is visible */
{ visibility: hidden }   /* Element is not visible but
                            affects document layout */
{ visibility: collapse } /* Element is not visible and
                            does not affect layout */
```

widows

Specifies the minimum number of lines in a paragraph that must be placed at the top of a page when a paragraph is broken between two pages.

Syntax

```
widows: <integer> | inherit
```

Values

The default value of this property is 2.

<integer>	inherit

Example Stylesheet

```
{ widows: 4 }
{ widows: 1 }
```

width

Controls the width of boxes created by block-level elements.

Syntax

```
width: <length> | <percentage> | auto | inherit
```

Values

<length>	*<percentage>*
auto (default)	inherit

Example Stylesheet

```
{ width: 10px }
{ width: 15% }
{ width: 1cm }
```

z-index

Controls the indexing and stacking value of layers of information.

Syntax

```
z-index: auto | <integer> | inherit
```

Values

`auto` (default) <*integer*> `inherit`

Example Stylesheet

```
{ z-index: 0 } /* Bottom-most level layer—unless
                  negative numbers are used */
{ z-index: 2 } /* Layer shown at level 2 */
```

Classification Properties

These properties are used to identify the classifications of specific elements, mostly in relation to how they are displayed for external formatting of the element.

direction

This property controls the direction that letters are written. You can specify that a paragraph is being written from right to left or left to right, depending upon the language being used and requirements of the document itself.

Syntax

```
direction: ltr | rtl | inherit
```

Values

`ltr` (default: left to right) `rtl` (right to left) `inherit`

Example Stylesheet

```
{ language: "English-GB";
  direction: ltr; }
{ language: "Hebrew";
  direction: rtl; }
```

display

Controls the treatment of the element so that it is treated as a block of information or as an inline element.

Syntax

```
display: inline | block | list-item | none | run-in | compact |
marker | table | inline-table | table-row-group |
table-column-group | table-header-group | table-footer-group |
table-row | table-cell | table-caption | inherit
```

Values

`inline` (default)	`block`	`list-item`
`none`	`run-in`	`compact`
`marker`	`table`	`inline-table`
`table-row-group`	`table-column-group`	`table-header-group`
`table-footer-group`	`table-row`	`table-cell`
`table-caption`	`inherit`	

Example Stylesheet

```
{ display: block }
{ display: table }
```

list-style

This shorthand property controls the other `list-style` property settings such as `list-style-type`, `list-style-image`, and `list-style-position`.

Syntax

```
list-style: [list-style-type || list-style-position ||
list-style-image] | inherit
```

Values

`list-style-type` property	*`list-style-position`* property
`list-style-image` property	`inherit`

Example Stylesheet

```
{ list-style: lower-roman inside }
{ list-style: circle outside }
{ list-style: url(ball.gif) inside }
```

list-style-image

Identifies the image that should appear in place of the bullet or numeric character to set off items of the list.

Syntax

```
list-style-image: <uri> | none | inherit
```

Values

<uri>	none (default)	inherit

Example Stylesheet

```
{ list-style-image: none }
{ list-style-image: url("ball.gif") }
```

list-style-position

Controls the position of the list item identifier, commonly a bullet or number, in relation to the boundaries of the list.

Syntax

```
list-style-position: inside | outside | inherit
```

Values

inside	outside (default)	inherit

Example Stylesheet

```
{ list-style-position: outside }
{ list-style-position: inside }
```

list-style-type

Controls the style of character that is placed at the beginning of a list to identify each item in that list.

Syntax

```
list-style-type: disc | circle | square | decimal |
decimal-leading-zero | lower-roman | upper-roman |
lower-alpha | upper-alpha | lower-greek | lower-latin |
upper-latin | hebrew | armenian | georgian | cjk-ideographic |
hiragana | katakana | hiragana-iroha | katakana-iroha | none |
inherit
```

Values

disc (default)	circle	square
decimal	decimal-leading-zero	lower-roman
upper-roman	lower-alpha	upper-alpha
lower-greek	lower-latin	upper-latin
hebrew	armenian	georgian
cjk-ideographic	hiragana	katakana
hiragana-iroha	katakana-iroha	none
inherit		

Example Stylesheet

```
{ list-style-type: lower-roman }
{ list-style-type: circle }
{ list-style-type: georgian }
```

unicode-bidi

Controls how the direction property is enforced with UNICODE text.

Syntax

```
unicode-bidi: normal | embed | bidi-override | inherit
```

Values

normal (default)	embed
bidi-override	inherit

Example Stylesheet

```
{ unicode-bidi: embed }
{ unicode-bidi: bidi-override }
```

white-space

Controls the treatment of white space found in elements.

Note *You can use this property in conjunction with* `xml:space`.

Syntax

```
white-space: normal | pre | nowrap | inherit
```

Values

normal (default)	pre
nowrap	inherit

Example Stylesheet

```
{ white-space: pre }    /* prevents the user agent from
                         collapsing white space */
{ white-space: nowrap } /* collapses white space
                        and prevents line breaks in it*/
```

Table Properties

These properties are used to control the appearance and formatting of tables.

caption-side

Controls the position of the caption box of a table-structured element.

Syntax

```
caption-side: top | bottom | left | right | inherit
```

Values

`top` (default)	`bottom`	`left`
`right`	`inherit`	

Example Stylesheet

```
{ caption-side: top }
```

cell-spacing

Controls the specific amount of space between cells in a table.

Syntax

cell-spacing: none | *<length>* | inherit

Values

`none` (default)	*<length>*	`inherit`

Example Stylesheet

```
{ cell-spacing: 2 }
```

column-span

Identifies the number of columns in a table that the current element spans.

Syntax

column-span: *<integer>* | inherit

Values

The default value of this property is `1`.

<integer>	`inherit`

Example Stylesheet

```
{ column-span: 4 } /* this cell spans 4 columns */
```

empty-cells

This property controls how borders around empty cells are treated.

Syntax

```
empty-cells: show | hide | inherit
```

Values

show hide inherit

Example Stylesheet

```
{ empty-cells: show }
{ empty-cells: hide }
```

table-layout

Sets the constraints on the layout of the table, providing the XML browser with a set of instructions for laying out the table.

Syntax

```
table-layout: auto | fixed | inherit
```

Values

auto (default) fixed inherit

Example Stylesheet

```
{ table-layout: auto } /* XML browser can display the
                          table as it wishes */
{ table-layout: fixed } /* XML browser must follow
                           the CSS guidelines */
```

Aural Properties

These properties control the reading of the XML document through a voice synthesizing program.

azimuth

Controls the horizontal special relationship of the voices, allowing you to add depth to your range of speakers. This allows you to have your voices appear from multiple angles.

Syntax

```
azimuth: <angle> | [left-side | far-left | left | center-left
| center | center-right | right | far-right | right-side]
  | behind | leftwards | rightwards | inherit
```

Values

`<angle>` (a range of 0–360 degrees)	`left-side` (270 degrees)
`far-left` (300 degrees)	`left` (320 degrees)
`center-left` (340 degrees)	`center` (default–0 degrees)
`center-right` (20 degrees)	`right` (40 degrees)
`far-right` (60 degrees)	`right-side` (90 degrees)
`behind` (reverses the degree so that is sounds as if it is coming from behind you)	`leftwards` (20 degree increments left)
`rightwards` (20 degree increments right)	`inherit`

Example Stylesheet

```
{ azimuth: 30deg }
{ azimuth: far-right }
{ azimuth: behind far-left }
{ azimuth: behind }
```

cue

Controls the `cue-before` and `cue-after` properties, setting up sound elements timed with the loading of an element.

Syntax

```
cue: cue-before | cue-after | inherit
```

APPENDIXES

Values

`cue-before` `cue-after` `inherit`

Example Stylesheet

```
{ cue: url("growl.wav") url("cat.wav") }
{ cue: url("growl.wav") }
```

cue-after

Identifies the sound to play after the selected element has loaded.

Syntax

cue-after: *<uri>* | none | inherit

Values

<uri> none (default) inherit

Example Stylesheet

```
{ cue-after: url("growl.wav") }
{ cue-after: none }
{ cue-after: inherit }
```

cue-before

Identifies the sound to play before the selected element has loaded.

Syntax

cue-before: *<uri>* | none | inherit

Values

<uri> none (default) inherit

Example Stylesheet

```
{ cue-before: url("growl.wav") }
{ cue-after: none }
{ cue-after: inherit }
```

elevation

Controls the apparent height of the speaker in reference to your position.

Syntax

```
elevation: <angle> | below | level | above | below | higher |
lower | inherit
```

Values

<angle>	below	level (default)
above	below	higher
lower	inherit	

Example Stylesheet

```
{ elevation: lower }
{ elevation: above }
{ elevation: 15deg }
```

pause

This is a shorthand control to set the amount of time to pause the reading of a document before and after the creation of the specified element.

Syntax

```
pause: [ [<time> | <percentage>]{1,2}] | inherit
```

Values

The default value for this property is controlled by the XML browser.

<time>	*<percentage>*	inherit

Example Stylesheet

```
{ pause: 30ms 6ms }
{ pause: 15% }
```

pause-after

Controls the amount of time to pause the reading of a document after the creation of the specified element.

Syntax

```
pause-after: <time> | <percentage> | inherit
```

Values

The default value for this property is controlled by the XML browser.

<time>	*<percentage>*	inherit

Example Stylesheet

```
{ pause-after: 6ms }
{ pause-after: 15% }
```

pause-before

Controls the amount of time to pause the reading of a document before the creation of the specified element.

Syntax

```
pause-before: <time> | <percentage> | inherit
```

Values

The default value for this property is controlled by the XML browser.

<time>	*<percentage>*	inherit

Example Stylesheet

```
{ pause-before: 30ms }
{ pause-before: 15% }
```

pitch

Controls the frequency of the speech synthesizer for a particular element.

Syntax

```
pitch: <frequency> | x-low | low | medium | high | x-high | inherit
```

Values

`<frequency>` (the hertz value of the pitch)

`x-low`

`low`

`medium` (default)

`high`

`x-high`

`inherit`

Example Stylesheet

```
{ pitch: x-low }
{ pitch: 165 }
```

pitch-range

Controls the acceptable variations of the average pitch of the speech synthesizer for a particular element.

Syntax

```
pitch-range: <number> | inherit
```

Values

The default value for this property is `50`.

<number> (range is between 0 and 100.)

`inherit`

Example Stylesheet

```
{ pitch-range: 25 }
```

play-during

Controls the sound to play while the contents of an element are spoken. This can be used to provide background music to monologs and plays.

Syntax

```
play-during: <uri> | mix? repeat? | auto | none | inherit
```

Values

<*uri*>	mix?	repeat?
auto	none (default)	inherit

Example Stylesheet

```
{ play-during: url(purrrr.wav) repeat; }
```

richness

Controls the richness or brightness, also referred to as the depth, of the voice used by the speech synthesizer.

Syntax

```
richness: <number> | inherit
```

Values

The default value of this property is 50.

<*number*>	inherit

Example Stylesheet

```
{ richness: 25 }
```

speak

Controls how the speech synthesizer reads the text of an element.

Syntax

```
speak: normal | none | spell-out | inhert
```

Values

`normal` (default)

`none`

`spell-out`

`inherit`

Example Stylesheet

```
{ speak: spell-out } /*Reads each character */
{ speak: normal }    /* Reads the words*/
```

speak-header

Controls how the text content of header cells on a table will be spoken.

Syntax

```
speak-header: once | always | inherit
```

Values

`once` (default)

`always`

`inherit`

Example Stylesheet

```
{ speak-header: once } /* Header is stated only once.*/
{ speak-header: always } /* Header  repeats for each cell. */
```

speak-numeral

Controls how individual digits in a number are read.

Syntax

```
speak-numeral: digits | continuous | inherit
```

Values

digits	continuous (default)	inherit

Example Stylesheet

```
{ speak-numeral: digits } /* number is read as digits
                     one-two-three*/
{ speak-numeral: continuous } /* number is read as
                     one hundred twenty-three */
```

speak-punctuation

Controls how a speech synthesizer will read punctuation.

Syntax

```
speak-punctuation: code | none | inherit
```

Values

code	none (default)	inherit

Example Stylesheet

```
{ speak-punctuation: code } /*all punctuation is spoken*/
{ speak-punctuation: none } /*no punctuation is spoken,
                     but pauses are inserted*/
```

speech-rate

Controls the speed at which your speech synthesizer will read text.

Syntax

```
speech-rate:  <number> | x-slow | slow | medium | fast |
   x-fast | faster | slower | inherit
```

Values

<number> (number of words per minute spoken)	`x-slow` (80 wpm)	`slow` (120 wpm)
`medium` (default 180–200 wpm)	`fast` (300 wpm)	`x-fast` (500 wpm)
`faster` (increments 40 wpm)	`slower` (decrements 40 wpm)	`inherit`

Example Stylesheet

```
{ speech-rate: 150 }
{ speech-rate: slow }
```

stress

Controls the amount of stress to apply specific characters in the language being spoken.

Syntax

```
stress: <number> | inherit
```

Values

The default value for this property is `50`.

<number> (A number between 1 and 100)	`inherit`

Example Stylesheet

```
{ stress: 60 }
```

voice-family

Provides a prioritized list of voice family names and generic voice names used by speech synthesizers.

Syntax

```
voice-family: [<specific-voice> || <generic-voice> list] | inherit
```

Values

The default value for this property is set by the XML browser.

<*specific-voice*>	<generic-voice> (male, female, child)	inherit

Example Stylesheet

```
{ voice-family: male }
{ voice-family: announcer }
{ voice-family: child }
{ voice-family: clown }
```

volume

Controls the volume of the reading of an individual element.

Syntax

```
volume: <number> | <percentage> | silent | x-soft | soft |
medium | loud | x-loud | inherit
```

Values

<*number*>	<*percentage*>	silent
x-soft	soft	medium (default)
loud	x-loud	inherit

Example Stylesheet

```
{ volume: x-soft }
{ volume: 50% }
```

The Complete Reference

Appendix C

XSL Formatting Objects Reference

This is a quick overview of all the XSL formatting Objects and properties that can be used with XML documents. The information provided here is terse, but should assist you when looking for the syntax of the style sheet property you need for proper formatting of your document.

XSL Formatting Objects

This section contains summaries of each of the defined formatting objects used with XSL. Included with each formatting object name is a definition of its common usage, a list of properties that it supports, a list of areas that it generates, and the object's constraints.

Declarations, Pagination, and Layout

These objects are used to control the overall layout of the document.

fo:root

This is the top node of the formatting object tree, holding a `fo:layout-master-set` formatting object (containing all masters used in the document), an optional `fo:declarations`, and one or more `fo:page-sequence` objects.

Areas: None

Contents: `(layout-master-set,declarations?,page-sequence+)`

fo:declarations

Groups global declarations for a style sheet.

Areas: None

Contents: `(color-profile)+`

fo:color-profile

Declares an ICC Color Profile for a style sheet.

Areas: None

Contents: `EMPTY`

Properties:

src	color-profile-name	rendering-intent

fo:page-sequence

Specifies how to create a (sub-)sequence of pages within a document. The pages created by the `fo:page-sequence` command have a variety of constraints that must be followed in order for the sub pages to be properly created.

- **The Pages Must Be Complete.** Each page must be treated as a complete page descendant of the parent.
- **The Flow-Map Must Maintain its Correct Associations**. All of the pages that are created by the `fo:page-sequence` action must be able to be properly referenced by their appropriate flow-name, and their region reference areas.
- **Area-Class Associations Must Be Maintained**. Any areas of the pages created by the `fo:page-sequence` must be properly associated with their appropriate area-classes, and descendants of appropriate areas.

The stackable areas of any given class must be properly stacked in regard to their reference areas.

Areas: Generates a sequence of viewport/reference pairs.
Returns the `page-viewport-areas`.

Contents:

```
(title?,static-content*,flow)
```

Properties:

country	format	language
letter-value	grouping-separator	grouping-size
id	initial-page-number	force-page-count
master-name		

fo:layout-master-set

A wrapper around all masters used in the document, including `page-sequence-masters`, `page-masters`, and `region-masters`.

Areas: Generates no area directly, but the masters that are children of `fo:layout-master-set` generate pages specified by `fo:page-sequence`.

Contents:

```
(simple-page-master|page-sequence-master)+
```

fo:page-sequence-master

Specifies the constraints on and the order in which a given set of page-masters will be used in generating a sequence of pages.

Areas: Generates no area directly, but is used by the fo:page-sequence formatting object to generate pages.

Contents:

```
(single-page-master-reference|repeatable-page-master-reference|
repeatable-page-master-alternatives)+
```

Properties:

master-name

fo:single-page-master-reference

The simplest sub-sequence-specifier, specifying a single instance of a single page-master.

Areas: Generates no area directly, but is used by the fo:page-sequence formatting object to generate pages.

Contents:

EMPTY

Properties:

master-name

fo:repeatable-page-master-reference

A simple sub-sequence-specifier identifying sub-sequence consisting of repeated instances of a single page-master.

Areas: Generates no area directly, but is used by the fo:page-sequence formatting object to generate pages.

Contents:

EMPTY

Properties:

master-name maximum-repeats

fo:repeatable-page-master-alternatives

A complex sub-sequence-specifier, identifying a sub-sequence consisting of repeated instances of a set of alternative page-masters.

Areas: Generates no area directly, but is used by the fo:page-sequence formatting object to generate pages.

Contents:

```
(conditional-page-master-reference+)
```

Properties:

```
maximum-repeats
```

fo:conditional-page-master-reference

Identifies a page-master used when the conditions on its use are satisfied. This object contains a reference to the same master-name specified in the fo:simple-page-master object. There are three traits, page-position, odd-or-even, and blank-or-not-blank that specify conditions on the use of the referenced page-master. All of these subconditions must be true for the condition of the fo:conditional-page-master-reference to be true.

Areas: Generates no area directly, but is used by the fo:page-sequence formatting object to generate pages.

Contents:

```
EMPTY
```

Properties:

master-name	page-position
odd-or-even	blank-or-not-blank

fo:simple-page-master

Assists in the generation of pages and specifies the geometry of the page that can be subdivided into up to five regions: region-body, region-before, region-after, region-start, and region-end. When a page-master is used in the generation of a page, the height and width of the content rectangle of the pages viewing are determined using the computed values of the page-height and page-width properties. If these properties have explicit values, they are then used to set the height and width settings on the page-viewport-area. If either of these options is set to "auto", the page-viewport-area size is determined from the size of the media, or in the case of continuous media, the size of the XML document browser window.

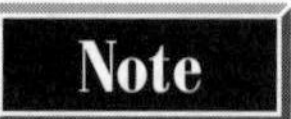

There are a lot of restrictions and constraints on the use of this object. If you have questions on its use please check out the XSLT Recommendation at http://www.w3.org/.

Areas: Generates no area directly, but is used in the generation of pages by a fo:page-sequence.

Contents:

```
(region-body,region-before?,region-after?,region-start?,region-end?)
```

Properties:

master-name	page-height	page-width
reference-orientation	writing-mode	Common Margin Properties-Block

fo:region-body

Used to specify a viewport/reference pair located in the center of a simple-page-master.

Areas: Generates one region-viewport-area and one region-reference-area whenever a fo:simple-page-master with a fo:region-body as a child is used to generate a page.

Contents:

```
EMPTY
```

Properties:

Common Border, Padding, and Background Properties	Common Margin Properties-Block	
clip	column-count	column-gap
display-align	overflow	region-name
reference-orientation	writing-mode	

fo:region-before

Used to specify a viewport/reference pair located on the before side of a simple-page-master.

Areas: Generates one `region-viewport-area` and one `region-reference-area` whenever a `fo:simple-page-master` with a `fo:region-body` as a child is used to generate a page.

Contents:

```
EMPTY
```

Properties:

`clip`	`display-align`	`extent`
`overflow`	`precedence`	`region-name`
`reference-orientation`	`writing-mode`	Common `Border`, `Padding`, and `Background` Properties

fo:region-after

Used to specify a viewport/reference pair located on the after side of a `simple-page-master`.

Areas: Generates one `region-viewport-area` and one `region-reference-area` whenever a `fo:simple-page-master` with a `fo:region-body` as a child is used to generate a page.

Contents:

```
EMPTY
```

Properties:

`clip`	`display-alin`	`extent`
`overflow`	`precedence`	`region-name`
`reference-orientation`	`writing-mode`	Common `Border`, `Padding`, and `Background` Properties

fo:region-start

Used to specify a viewport/reference pair located on the start side of a `simple-page-master`.

Areas: Generates one region-viewport-area and one region-reference-area whenever a `fo:simple-page-master` with a `fo:region-body` as a child is used to generate a page.

Contents:

EMPTY

Properties:

clip	display-alin	extent
overflow	precedence	region-name
reference-orientation	writing-mode	Common Border, Padding, and Background Properties

fo:region-end

Used to specify a viewport/reference pair located on the end side of a `simple-page-master`.

Areas: Generates one region-viewport-area and one region-reference-area whenever a `fo:simple-page-master` with a `fo:region-body` as a child is used to generate a page.

Contents:

EMPTY

Properties:

clip	display-align	extent
overflow	precedence	region-name
reference-orientation	writing-mode	Common Border, Padding, and Background Properties

fo:flow

Creates a sequence of flow objects that supplies the flowing text content that is distributed into pages.

Areas: Does not generate any areas, but does return a sequence of areas created by concatenating the sequences of areas returned by each of its children.

Contents:

```
(%block;)+
```

Additionally this object may contain a sequence of zero or more `fo:markers` as its initial children.

Properties:

```
flow-name
```

fo:static-content

Holds a sequence, or a tree, of formatting objects to be presented within a single region, or that are to be repeated in a series of regions with the same name.

Areas: Does not generate any areas, but returns the sequence of areas created by concatenating the areas returned by each of its children.

Contents:

```
(%block;)+
```

Properties:

```
flow-name
```

fo:title

Associates a title with a given document.

Areas: Returns the sequence of areas returned by the flow its children.

Contents:

```
(#PCDATA|%inline;)*
```

Properties:

Common `Accessibility` Properties	Common `Aural` Properties	Common `Border`, `Padding`, and `Background` Properties
Common `Font` Properties	Common `Margin` Properties-Inline	
`baseline-shift`	`color`	`line-height`
`line-height-shift-adjustment`	`visibility`	`z-index`

Block-Level Objects

These objects are used to control the formatting of block formatted document content.

fo:block

Used for formatting paragraphs, titles, headlines, captions for figures and tables, and many other block type objects.

Areas: Generates one or more normal `block-areas`.

Contents:

```
(#PCDATA|%inline;|%block;)*
```

May also include a sequence of zero or more `fo:markers` as its initial children, optionally followed by an `fo:initial-property-set`.

Table C-1 shows the `fo:block` properties.

Common Accessibility Properties	Common Aural Properties	Common Border, Padding, and Background Properties
Common Font Properties	Common Hyphenation Properties	Common Margin Properties-Block
break-after	break-before	color
font-height-override-after	font-height-override-before	hyphenation-keep
hyphenation-ladder-count	id	keep-together
keep-with-next	keep-with-previous	last-line-end-indent
linefeed-treatment	line-height	line-height-shift-adjustment
line-stacking-strategy	orphans	relative-position
space-treatment	span	text-align
text-align-last	text-indent	visibility
white-space-collapse	widows	wrap-option
z-index		

Table C-1. `fo:block` *Formatting Properties*

fo:block-container

Used to create a block-level reference area containing text blocks with different writing-modes.

Areas: Generates one or more viewport/reference pairs.

Returns these areas and any `page-level-out-of-line` areas returned by its children.

Contents:

```
(%block;)+
```

May have a sequence of zero or more `fo:markers` as its initial children if this object does not generate an absolutely positioned area.

Properties:

Common Absolute `Position` Properties	Common `Border`, `Padding`, and `Background` Properties	Common `Margin` Properties-Block
`block-progression-dimension`	`break-after`	`break-before`
`clip`	`display-align`	`height`
`id`	`inline-progression-dimension`	`keep-together`
`keep-with-next`	`keep-with-previous`	`overflow`
`reference-orientation`	`span`	`width`
`writing-mode`		

Inline-Level Objects

These objects are used to control the formatting of inline formatted document content.

fo:bidi-override

When the UNICODE-bidi algorithm fails, this inline object forces a string of text to be written a specific direction. Bidi references a bidirectional algorithm that determines when text flows right to left, or left to right. The Unicode-bidi algorithm attempts to guess the text direction, and set it if necessary.

Areas: Generates one or more normal inline areas.

Contents:

```
(#PCDATA|%inline;)*
```

This object may have a sequence of zero or more `fo:markers` as its initial children.

Properties:

Common `Aural` Properties	Common `Font` Properties	
`color`	`direction`	`id`
`letter-spacing`	`line-height`	`line-height-shift-adjustment`
`relative-position`	`score-spaces`	`text-shadow`
`text-transform`	`unicode-bidi`	`word-spacing`

fo:character

Represents a character that is mapped to a specified glyph for presentation purposes.

Areas: Generates and returns a single normal inline-area.

Contents:

EMPTY

Table C-2 shows the `fo:character` properties.

Common `Aural` Properties	Common `Border, Padding,` and `Background` Properties	Common `Font` Properties
Common `Hyphenation` Properties	Common `Margin` Properties-Inline	
`alignment-adjust`	`treat-as-word-space`	`baseline-identifier`
`baseline-shift`	`character`	`color`
`dominant-baseline`	`font-height-override-after`	`font-height-override-before`
`glyph-orientation-horizontal`	`glyph-orientation-vertical`	`id`
`keep-with-next`	`keep-with-previous`	`letter-spacing`

Table C-2. `fo:character` *Properties*

line-height	line-height-shift-adjustment	relative-position
score-spaces	suppress-at-line-break	text-decoration
text-shadow	text-transform	word-spacing

Table C-2. fo:character *Properties* (continued)

fo:initial-property-set

Specifies the formatting properties for the first line of an fo:block object.

It is analogous to the CSS first-line *pseudo-element.*

Areas: Does not generate or return any areas, but simply reserves a set of traits applicable to the first line-area of a block.

Contents:

EMPTY

Properties:

Common Accessibility Properties	Common Aural Properties	Common Border, Padding, and Background Properties
Common Font Properties		
color	id	letter-spacing
line-height	line-height-shift-adjustment	relative-position
score-spaces	text-decoration	text-shadow
text-transform	word-spacing	

fo:external-graphic

Used to specify an inline graphic whose data resides outside of the area specified by the fo:element tree.

APPENDIXES

Areas: Generates and returns one inline-level viewport-area and one reference-area containing the external graphic.

Contents:

```
EMPTY
```

Table C-3 shows the `fo:external-graphic` properties.

fo:instream-foreign-object

Formats inline graphics, or other generic objects, with the data residing as one of its descendants.

Areas: Generates and returns one inline `viewport-area` and one `reference-area` containing the `instream-foreign-object`.

Contents: This object has children from a non-XSL namespace, and is therefore permitted the structure identified within that namespace.

Common `Accessibility` Properties	Common `Aural` Properties	Common `Border, Padding, and Background` Properties
Common `Margin` Properties-Inline		
`alignment-adjust`	`baseline-identifier`	`baseline-shift`
`block-progression-dimension`	`content-height`	`content-type`
`content-width`	`dominant-baseline`	`height`
`id`	`inline-progression-dimension`	`keep-with-next`
`keep-with-previous`	`line-height`	`line-height-shift-adjustment`
`relative-position`	`overflow`	`scaling`
`scaling-method`	`src`	`width`

Table C-3. `fo:external-graphic` *Properties*

Common Accessibility Properties	Common Aural Properties	Common Border, Padding, and Background Properties
Common Margin Properties-Inline		
alignment-adjust	baseline-identifier	baseline-shift
block-progression-dimension	content-height	content-type
content-width	dominant-baseline	height
id	inline-progression-dimension	keep-with-next
keep-with-previous	line-height	line-height-shift-adjustment
overflow	relative-position	scaling
scaling-method	width	

Table C-4. fo:instream-foreign-object *Properties*

Table C-4 shows the fo:instream-foreign-object properties.

fo:inline

Formats a portion of text within a background or enclosing it in a border.

Areas: Generates one or more inline areas.

Returns these areas, any page-level-out-of-line areas, as well as any reference-level-out-of-line areas returned by its children.

Contents:

```
(#PCDATA|%inline;)*
```

May have a sequence of zero or more fo:markers as its initial children.

Properties:

Common Accessibility Properties	Common Aural Properties	Common Border, Padding, and Background Properties
Common Font Properties	Common Margin Properties-Inline	
alignment-adjust	baseline-identifier	baseline-shift
color	dominant-baseline	id
keep-together	keep-with-next	keep-with-previous
line-height	line-height-shift-adjustment	relative-position
text-decoration	visibility	z-index

fo:inline-container

Used to create an inline reference area often used for containing text with varying writing styles.

Areas: Generates one or more viewport/reference pairs. The viewport-areas generated by this object are inline-level areas. This object returns these areas and any page-level-out-of-line areas returned by its children.

Contents:

```
(%block;)+
```

May have a sequence of zero or more fo:markers as its initial children.

Properties:

Common Border, Padding, and Background Properties	Common Margin Properties-Inline	
alignment-adjust	baseline-identifier	baseline-shift
block-progression-dimension	clip	display-align
dominant-baseline	height	id
inline-progression-dimension	keep-together	keep-with-next

keep-with-previous	line-height	line-height-shift-adjustment
overflow	reference-orientation	relative-position
width	writing-mode	

fo:leader

Used to create leader characters in table of contents, entry fields, and horizontal rules. Leaders are the little dots or lines that you see between the text of a table of content entry and the page number the entry starts on.

Areas: Generates and returns a single normal `inline-area`.

Contents:

```
(#PCDATA|%inline;)*
```

The content can contain an `fo:leader`, or `fo:inline-container` as a descendant. Table C-5 shows the `fo:leader` properties.

Common Accessibility Properties	Common Aural Properties	Common Border, Padding, and Background Properties
Common Font Properties	Common Margin Properties-Inline	
alignment-adjust	baseline-identifier	baseline-shift
color	dominant-baseline	font-height-override-after
Font-height-override-before	id	leader-alignment
leader-length	leader-pattern	leader-pattern-width
relative-position	rule-style	rule-thickness
letter-spacing	line-height	line-height-shift-adjustment
text-shadow	visibility	word-spacing
z-index		

Table C-5. `fo:leader` *Properties*

fo:page-number

Used to create an inline-area containing a page number for the current page.

Areas: Generates and returns a single normal inline-area.

Contents:

EMPTY

Properties:

Common Accessibility Properties	Common Aural Properties	Common Border, Padding, and Background Properties
Common Font Properties	Common Margin Properties-Inline	
alignment-adjust	baseline-identifier	baseline-shift
dominant-baseline	id	keep-with-next
keep-with-previous	letter-spacing	line-height
line-height-shift-adjustment	relative-position	score-spaces
text-decoration	text-shadow	text-transform
word-spacing		

fo:page-number-citation

References the page number for the page containing the normal area being cited.

This works well for adding page-numbers to table of contents, cross-reference, or index entries.

Areas: Generates and returns a single normal inline-area.

Contents:

EMPTY

Properties:

Common Accessibility Properties	Common Aural Properties	Common Border, Padding, and Background Properties
Common Font Properties	Common Margin Properties-Inline	
alignment-adjust	baseline-identifier	baseline-shift
dominant-baseline	id	keep-with-next
keep-with-previous	letter-spacing	line-height
line-height-shift-adjustment	ref-id	relative-position
score-spaces	text-decoration	text-shadow
text-transform	word-spacing	

Table Formatting Objects

These objects are used to format tables, and all of their associated cells, rows, and captions.

fo:table-and-caption

Used for formatting a table and its caption.

Areas: Generates one or more inline areas.

Returns these areas, any page-level-out-of-line areas, as well as any reference-level-out-of-line areas returned by its children.

Contents:

```
(table-caption?,table)
```

May have a sequence of zero or more fo:markers as its initial children.

Properties:

Common Accessibility Properties	Common Aural Properties	Common Border, Padding, and Background Properties
Common Margin Properties-Block	caption-side	id
keep-together	relative-position	

fo:table

Used for formatting the flow and visual layout of a table into its rows, columns, and cells.

Areas: Generates one or more block areas.

Returns these areas, any page-level-out-of-line areas, as well as any reference-level-out-of-line areas returned by its children.

Contents:

```
(table-column*,table-header?,table-footer?,table-body+)
```

May have a sequence of zero or more fo:markers as its initial children.

Properties:

Common Accessibility Properties	Common Aural Properties	Common Border, Padding, and Background Properties
Common Margin Properties-Block		
block-progression-dimension	border-collapse	border-separation
break-after	break-before	id
inline-progression-dimension	height	keep-together
keep-with-next	keep-with-previous	relative-position
table-layout	table-omit-footer-at-break	table-omit-header-at-break
width	writing-mode	

fo:table-column

Contains formatting controls for specifying the characteristics applicable only to cells that are in a single specified column.

Areas: Does not generate or return any areas, although it holds a series of traits providing constraints on the column widths and a specification of some presentation characteristics.

Contents:

```
EMPTY
```

Properties:

Common Border, Padding, and Background Properties	column-number	column-width
number-columns-repeated	number-columns-spanned	visibility

fo:table-caption

Used to manipulate the block level object containing the text caption for a table.

Areas: Generates one or more normal reference-areas, and returns these reference-areas as well as any page-level-out-of-line areas returned by its children.

Contents:

```
(%block;)+
```

May have a sequence of zero or more fo:markers as its initial children.

Properties:

Common Accessibility Properties	Common Aural Properties	Common Border, Padding, and Background Properties
block-progression-dimension	height	id
inline-progression-dimension	keep-together	relative-position
width		

fo:table-header

Used to specify the formatting for the block object containing the table header information.

Areas: Does not generate any areas, although it does return the sequence of areas generated by joining the areas returned by its children.

Contents:

```
(table-row+|table-cell+)
```

This object must have at least one fo:table-row as its child, or alternatively fo:table-cell.

Properties:

Common Accessibility Properties	Common Aural Properties	Common Border, Padding, and Background Properties
id	relative-position	

fo:table-footer

Contains the content of the table footer.

Areas: Does not generate any areas, although it does return the sequence of areas generated by joining the areas returned by its children.

Contents:

```
(table-row+|table-cell+)
```

Properties:

Common Accessibility Properties	Common Aural Properties	Common Border, Padding, and Background Properties
id	relative-position	

fo:table-body

Contains the contents of the table body.

Areas: Does not generate any areas, although it does return the sequence of areas generated by joining the areas returned by its children.

Contents:

```
(table-row+|table-cell+)
```

Properties:

Common Accessibility Properties	Common Aural Properties	Common Border, Padding, and Background Properties
id	relative-position	

fo:table-row

Groups table-cells into rows.

Areas: Does not generate any areas, although it does return the sequence of areas generated by joining the areas returned by its children.

Contents:

```
(table-cell+)
```

Properties:

Common Accessibility Properties	Common Aural Properties	Common Border, Padding, and Background Properties
block-progression-dimension	break-after	break-before
id	height	keep-together
keep-with-next	keep-with-previous	relative-position

fo:table-cell

Groups content to be placed in a table-cell.

Areas: Generates one or more normal reference-areas; returning these reference-areas and any page-level-out-of-line areas returned by its children.

Contents:

```
(%block;)+
```

May have a sequence of zero or more fo:markers as its initial children.

Properties:

Common Accessibility Properties	Common Aural Properties	Common Border, Padding, and Background Properties
block-progression-dimension	column-number	display-align
relative-align	empty-cells	ends-row
height	id	number-columns-spanned
number-rows-spanned	relative-position	starts-row
width		

List Formatting Objects

These objects are used to control the appearance and formatting of list type objects used within your documents.

fo:list-block

Formats a list.

Areas: Generates one or more normal `block-areas`; returning these areas, any `page-level-out-of-line` areas, and any `reference-level-out-of-line` areas returned by its children.

Contents:

```
(list-item+)
```

May have a sequence of zero or more `fo:markers` as its initial children.

Properties:

Common `Accessibility` Properties	Common `Aural` Properties	Common `Border, Padding, and Background` Properties
Common `Margin` Properties-Block	`break-after`	`break-before`
`id`	`keep-together`	`keep-with-next`
`keep-with-previous`	`provisional-distance-between-starts`	`provisional-label-separation`
`relative-position`		

fo:list-item

Contains the label and the body of an item in a list.

Areas: Generates one or more normal block-areas; returning these areas, any page-level-out-of-line areas, and any reference-level-out-of-line areas returned by its children.

Contents:

```
(list-item-label,list-item-body)
```

May have a sequence of zero or more `fo:markers` as its initial children.

Properties:

Common Accessibility Properties	Common Aural Properties	Common Border, Padding, and Background Properties
Common Margin Properties-Block		
break-after	break-before	id
keep-together	keep-with-next	keep-with-previous
relative-align	relative-position	

fo:list-item-body

Contains the content of the body of a list-item.

Areas: Does not generate any areas, although it does return the sequence of areas generated by joining the areas returned by its children.

Contents:

```
(%block;)+
```

May have a sequence of zero or more fo:markers as its initial children.

Properties:

Common Accessibility Properties	id	keep-together

fo:list-item-label

Contains the contents of the label of a list-item, which is often used to either enumerate, identify, or adorn the list-item's body.

Areas: Does not generate any areas, although it does return the sequence of areas generated by joining the areas returned by its children.

Contents:

```
(%block;)+
```

May have a sequence of zero or more fo:markers as its initial children.

Properties:

Common Accessibility Properties	id	keep-together

Link and Multi-Formatting Objects

These objects are use to control the appearance and actions taken with links.

fo:simple-link

Represents the start resource of a simple one-directional single-target link.

Areas: Generates one or more normal `inline-areas`; returning these areas, any `page-level-out-of-line` areas, and any `reference-level-out-of-line` areas returned by its children.

Contents:

```
(#PCDATA|%inline;|%block;)*
```

May have a sequence of zero or more `fo:markers` as its initial children.

Properties:

Common `Accessibility` Properties	Common `Aural` Properties	Common `Border`, Padding, and `Background` Properties
Common `Margin` Properties-Inline		
`alignment-adjust`	`baseline-identifier`	`baseline-shift`
`destination-placement-offset`	`dominant-baseline`	`external-destination`
`id`	`indicate-destination`	`internal-destination`
`keep-with-next`	`keep-with-previous`	`line-height`
`line-height-shift-adjustment`	`relative-position`	`show-destination`

fo:multi-switch

This object is used to control the switching mechanism that allows you to have multiple sets of formatting properties for your document objects.

This functionality is useful for setting up interactive tasks like drop-down menus, changing between next/previous views, and having multiple targets available for a single button.

Areas: Does not generate any areas; although it returns the sequence of areas that are created from its currently selected set of options.

Contents:

```
(multi-case+)
```

Properties:

Common `Accessibility` Properties	`auto-restore`	`id`

fo:multi-case

Groups formatting objects so that this objects parent can either show or hide the property set as a group.

Areas: Does not generate any areas, although it does return the sequence of areas generated by joining the areas returned by its children.

Contents:

```
(#PCDATA|%inline;|%block;)*
```

Properties:

Common `Accessibility` Properties	`id`	`case-name`
`case-title`	`starting-state`	

fo:multi-toggle

Establishes the area that can activate the switching from one `fo:multi-case` object's set of properties to another.

Areas: Does not generate any areas; it only returns the sequence of areas created by combining the areas returned by each of its children.

Contents:

```
(#PCDATA|%inline;|%block;)*
```

Properties:

Common `Accessibility` Properties	`id`	`switch-to`

fo:multi-properties

Allows you to switch between two or more sets of properties associated with a specific section of your document content.

This formatting object can be used to give varying appearances to a specific portion of your document content, such as using the change in a link color, to reformat the content of the document.

Areas: Does not generate any areas; it only returns the sequence of areas created by concatenating the areas returned by each of its children.

Contents:

```
(multi-property-set+,wrapper)
```

Properties:

Common `Accessibility` Properties	`id`

fo:multi-property-set

Sets an alternative set of formatting properties for the child objects of the `fo:wrapper` child of this object.

Areas: Does not generate or return any areas.

Constraints: None

Contents:

```
EMPTY
```

Properties:

`id`	`active-state`

Out-of-Line Formatting Objects

Controls the formatting of floating objects within your documents.

fo:float

Used to cause an image or other content to be positioned within an object so that the other content will flow around and alongside the image.

Areas: Generates a single inline-area with no children, and one or more `block-areas` that share the same `area-class` ("xsl-before-float", "`xsl-side-float`" or "`xsl-normal`").

Contents:

```
(%block;)+
```

Not permitted to have an `fo:float`, `fo:footnote`, `fo:marker`, or an `fo:block-container` object, which generates an absolutely positioned area, as descendants.

Properties:

float	clear

fo:footnote

Produces footnote-citations within both the region-body of a page and a corresponding footnote in a separate area nearer the after-edge, or bottom edge, of the page.

Areas: Does not generate any areas, although it returns the areas generated and returned by its child fo:inline formatting objects.

Contents:

```
(inline,footnote-body)
```

Not permitted to have an fo:float, fo:footnote, fo:marker, or an fo:block-container object, which generates an absolutely positioned area, as descendants.

fo:footnote-body

Generates the footnote content.

Areas: Generates and returns one or more block-level areas with area-class "xsl-footnote".

Contents:

```
(%block;)+
```

Other Formatting Objects

Control the properties of formatting objects not otherwise identified in the XSL specification.

fo:wrapper

Used to specify inherited properties for a group of formatting objects.

Areas: Does not generate any areas, but returns the sequence of areas created by concatenating the areas returned by each its children.

Contents:

```
(#PCDATA|%inline;|%block;)*
```

In addition this formatting object may have a sequence of zero or more fo:markers as its initial children.

Properties:

```
id
```

fo:marker

When used in conjunction with `fo:retrieve-marker` this produces running headers or footers.

Areas: Does not directly generate any area, although its children may be retrieved and formatted from within an `fo:static-content` object.

Contents:

```
(#PCDATA|%inline;|%block;)*
```

May contain any of the formatting objects permitted as a replacement for `fo:retrieve-marker` objects that retrieve an `fo:marker`'s children.

Properties:

```
marker-class-name
```

fo:retrieve-marker

Is used in conjunction with `fo:marker` to create a running header of footer.

Areas: Does not directly generate any area.

Contents:

```
EMPTY
```

Properties:

```
retrieve-class-name    retrieve-boundary    retrieve-position
```

Formatting Properties

These properties are listed in tables here showing just their values, default value, inherited status, and the portion of the implementation of XSL to which they belong. If you need more information on these properties visit the World Wide Web Consortium Web site located at: http://www.w3.org/TR/xsl.

There are three levels of conformance to this specification: Basic, Extended and Complete. The Basic level only includes the formatting objects and properties required to create a basic page or aural rendering of the document. The Extended level includes everything other than the shorthand properties. The Complete level includes everything in the complete specification.

Accessibility Properties

Accessibility properties control the relationship of the current element, to the other elements in the document, or the document itself.

Property	Values	Default Value	Inherited	Conformance Level
role	<string> | none | inherit	none	no	Basic
source-document	<uri>+ | none | inherit	none	no	Basic

Absolute Position Properties

These properties control the position of an element or layer within the visible layout of a document.

Property	Values	Default Value	Inherited	Conformance Level
absolute-position	auto | absolute | fixed | inherit	auto	no	Complete
bottom	<length> | <percentage> | auto | inherit	auto	no	Extended
left	<length> | <percentage> | auto | inherit	auto	no	Extended
position	static | relative | absolute | fixed | inherit	static	no	Complete
right	<length> | <percentage> | auto | inherit	auto	no	Extended
top	<length> | <percentage> | auto | inherit	auto	no	Extended

Border, Padding, and Background Properties

These properties, shown in Table C-6, control the appearance of the borders and backgrounds of the document content.

Property	Values	Default Value	Inherited	Conformance Level
background	[<Background-color> || <background-image> || <background-repeat> || <background-attachment> || <background-position> |]]inherit	Not defined for shorthand properties	no	Complete
background-attachment	scroll | fixed | inherit	scroll	no	Extended
background-color	<color> | transparent | inherit	transparent	no	Basic
background-image	<uri> | none | inherit	none	no	Extended
background-position	[[<percentage> | <length>]{1,2} | [[top | center | bottom] || [left | center | right]]] | inherit	0% 0%	no	Complete
background-position-horizontal	<percentage> | <length> | left | center | right | inherit	0%	no	Extended
background-position-vertical	<percentage> | <length> | top | center | bottom | inherit	0%	no	Extended
background-repeat	repeat | repeat-x | repeat-y | no-repeat | inherit	repeat	no	Extended
border	[<border-width> || <border-style> || <color>] | inherit	See individual properties	no	Complete

Table C-6. *Border, Padding, and Background Properties*

Property	Values	Default Value	Inherited	Conformance Level
border-after-color	<color> | inherit	The value of the 'color' property	no	Basic
border-after-style	<border-style> | inherit	none	no	Basic
border-after-width	<border-width> | <length-conditional> | inherit	medium	no	Basic
border-before-color	<color> | inherit	The value of the 'color' property	no	Basic
border-before-style	<border-style> | inherit	none	no	Basic
border-before-width	<border-width> | <length-conditional> | inherit	medium	no	Basic
border-bottom	[<border-top-width> || <border-style> || <color>] | inherit	See individual properties	no	Complete
border-bottom-color	<color> | inherit	The value of the 'color' property	no	Basic
border-bottom-style	<border-style> | inherit	none	no	Basic
border-bottom-width	<border-width> | inherit	medium	no	Basic
border-color	<color>{1,4} | transparent | inherit	See individual properties	no	Complete
border-end-color	<color> | inherit	The value of the 'color' property	no	Basic

Table C-6. *Border, Padding, and Background Properties* (continued)

Property	Values	Default Value	Inherited	Conformance Level
border-end-style	<border-style> | inherit	none	no	Basic
border-end-width	<border-width> | inherit	medium	no	Basic
border-left	[<border-top-width> || <border-style> || <color>] | inherit	See individual properties	no	Complete
border-left-color	<color> | inherit	The value of the 'color' property	no	Basic
border-left-style	<border-style> | inherit	none	no	Basic
border-left-width	<border-width> | inherit	medium	no	Basic
border-right	[<border-top-width> || <border-style> || <color>] | inherit	See individual properties	no	Complete
border-right-color	<color> | inherit	The value of the 'color' property	no	Basic
border-right-style	<border-style> | inherit	none	no	Basic
border-right-width	<border-width> | inherit	medium	no	Basic
border-spacing	<length> <length>? | inherit	0pt	yes	Complete
border-start-color	<color> | inherit	The value of the 'color' property	no	Basic
border-start-style	<border-style> | inherit	none	no	Basic
border-start-width	<border-width> | inherit	medium	no	Basic
border-style	<border-style>{1,4} | inherit	See individual properties	no	Complete

Table C-6. *Border, Padding, and Background Properties* (continued)

Property	Values	Default Value	Inherited	Conformance Level
border-top	[<border-top-width> || <border-style> || <color>] | inherit	See individual properties	no	Complete
border-top-color	<color> | inherit	The value of the 'color' property	no	Basic
border-top-style	<border-style> | inherit	none	no	Basic
border-top-width	<border-width> | inherit	medium	no	Basic
border-width	<border-width>{1,4} | inherit	See individual properties	no	Complete
padding	<padding-width>{1,4} | inherit	Not defined for shorthand properties	no	Complete
padding-after	<padding-width> | <length-conditional> | inherit	0pt	no	Basic
padding-before	<padding-width> | <length-conditional> | inherit	0pt	no	Basic
padding-bottom	<padding-width> | inherit	0pt	no	Basic
padding-end	<padding-width> | inherit	0pt	no	Basic
padding-left	<padding-width> | inherit	0pt	no	Basic
padding-right	<padding-width> | inherit	0pt	no	Basic
padding-start	<padding-width> | inherit	0pt	no	Basic
padding-top	<padding-width> | inherit	0pt	no	Basic

Table C-6. *Border, Padding, and Background Properties* (continued)

Font Properties

These properties, shown in Table C-7, control the appearance of the text that is used to display the content of the document.

<table>
<tr><th>Property</th><th>Values</th><th>Default Value</th><th>Inherited</th><th>Conformance Level</th></tr>
<tr><td>font</td><td>[[<font-style> || <font-variant> || <font-weight>]? <font-size> [/ <line-height>]? <font-family>] | caption | icon | menu | message-box | small-caption | status-bar | inherit</td><td>See individual properties</td><td>yes</td><td>Complete</td></tr>
<tr><td>font-family</td><td>[[<family-name> | <generic-family>],]* [<family-name> | <generic-family>] | inherit</td><td>Depends on user agent</td><td>yes</td><td>Basic</td></tr>
<tr><td>font-size</td><td><absolute-size> | <relative-size> | <length> | <percentage> | inherit</td><td>medium</td><td>Yes, the computed value is inherited</td><td>Basic</td></tr>
<tr><td>font-size-adjust</td><td><number> | none | inherit</td><td>none</td><td>yes</td><td>Extended</td></tr>
<tr><td>font-stretch</td><td>normal | wider | narrower | ultra-condensed | extra-condensed | condensed | semi-condensed | semi-expanded | expanded | extra-expanded | ultra-expanded |inherit</td><td>normal</td><td>yes</td><td>Extended</td></tr>
</table>

Table C-7. *Font Properties*

Property	Values	Default Value	Inherited	Conformance Level
font-style	normal | italic | oblique | backslant | inherit	normal	yes	Basic
font-variant	normal | small-caps | inherit	normal	yes	Basic
font-weight	normal | bold | bolder | lighter | 100 | 200 | 300 | 400 | 500 | 600 | 700 | 800 | 900 | inherit	normal	yes	Basic

Table C-7. *Font Properties* (continued)

Table Properties

The Table properties shown in Table C-8 are used to control all aspects of the table from borders to captions.

Property	Values	Default Value	Inherited	Conformance Level
border-collapse	collapse | separate | inherit	collapse	yes	Extended
border-separation	<length-bp-ip-direction> | inherit	.block-progression -direction= "0pt".inline-progressio-direction="0pt"	yes	Extended
caption-side	before | after | start | end | top | bottom | left | right | inherit	before	yes	Complete

Table C-8. *Table Properties*

APPENDIXES

Property	Values	Default Value	Inherited	Conformance Level
column-number	<number>	See prose	no	Basic
column-width	<length>	See prose	no	Basic
empty-cells	show | hide | inherit	show	yes	Extended
ends-row	yes | no	no	no	Extended
number-columns-repeated	<number>	1	no	Basic
number-columns-spanned	<number>	1	no	Basic
number-rows-spanned	<number>	1	no	Basic
starts-row	yes | no	no	no	Extended
table-layout	auto | fixed | inherit	auto	no	Extended
table-omit-footer-at-break	yes | no	no	no	Extended
table-omit-header-at-break	yes | no	no	no	Extended

Table C-8. *Table Properties* (continued)

Hyphenation Properties

The hyphenation properties, shown in Table C-9, allow you to control how character hyphenations occur within the document for each country or language the document is displayed in.

Property	Values	Default Value	Inherited	Conformance Level
country	none | <country> | inherit	none	yes	Extended
hyphenate	false | true | inherit	FALSE	yes	Extended
hyphenation-character	<character> | inherit	The unicode hyphen character u+2010	yes	Extended
hyphenation-push-character-count	<number> | inherit	2	yes	Extended
hyphenation-remain-character-count	<number> | inherit	2	yes	Extended
language	none | <language> | inherit	none	yes	Extended
script	none | auto | <script> | inherit	auto	yes	Extended

Table C-9. *Hyphenation Properties*

Margin Properties-Block

Block Margin properties, shown in Table C-10, are used to control the appearance of the margins and indentations of each block element.

Property	Values	Default Value	Inherited	Conformance Level
end-indent	<length> | inherit	0pt	yes	Basic
margin	<margin-width> {1,4} | inherit	Not defined for shorthand properties	no	Complete
margin-bottom	<margin-width> | inherit	0	no	Basic
margin-left	<margin-width> | inherit	0pt	no	Basic
margin-right	<margin-width> | inherit	0pt	no	Basic
margin-top	<margin-width> | inherit	0	no	Basic
space-after	<space> | inherit	space.minimum=0pt, .optimum=0pt, .maximum=0pt, .conditionality= discard, .precedence=0	no	Basic
space-before	<space> | inherit	space.minimum=0pt, .optimum=0pt, .maximum=0pt, .conditionality= discard, .precedence=0	no	Basic
start-indent	<length> | inherit	0pt	yes	Basic

Table C-10. *Area Alignment Properties*

Margin Properties-Inline

These properties are used to control the appearance of the margins and indentations of each inline element.

Property	Values	Default Value	Inherited	Conformance Level
space-end	<space> | inherit	space.minimum=0pt, .optimum=0pt, .maximum=0pt, .conditionality=discard, .precedence=0	no	Basic
space-start	<space> | inherit	space.minimum=0pt, .optimum=0pt, .maximum=0pt, .conditionality=discard, .precedence=0	no	Basic

Area Alignment Properties

The alignment properties, shown in Table C-11, are used to control the alignment of the individual block elements in your document's visual display.

Property	Values	Default Value	Inherited	Conformance Level
alignment-adjust	auto | <percentage> | <length> | inherit	auto	no	Basic
baseline-identifier	baseline | before-edge | text-before-edge | middle | after-edge | text-after-edge | ideographic | alphabetic | hanging | mathematical | inherit	Object dependent	no	Basic
baseline-shift	baseline | sub | super | <percentage> | <length> | inherit	baseline	no	Basic
display-align	auto | before | center | after | inherit	auto	yes	Basic
dominant-baseline	auto | autosense-script | no-change | reset-size | ideographic | alphabetic | hanging | mathematical | inherit	auto	no	Basic
relative-align	before | baseline | inherit	before	yes	Basic

Table C-11. *Area Alignment Properties* (continued)

APPENDIXES

Area Dimension Properties

These properties, shown in Table C-12, control the dimensions (height, width, etc.) of the elements displayed in your XML document.

Property	Values	Default Value	Inherited	Conformance Level
block-progression-dimension	auto | <length> | <percentage> | <length-range> | inherit	auto	no	Extended
content-height	auto | <length> | <percentage> | inherit	auto	no	Extended
content-width	auto | <length> | <percentage> | inherit	auto	no	Extended
height	<length> | <percentage> | auto | inherit	auto	no	Basic
inline-progression-dimension	auto | <length> | <percentage> | <length-range> | inherit	auto	no	Basic
max-height	<length> | <percentage> | none | inherit	0pt	no	Basic
max-width	<length> | <percentage> | none | inherit	none	no	Basic
min-height	<length> | <percentage> | inherit	0pt	no	Basic
min-width	<length> | <percentage> | inherit	Depends on UA	no	Basic
scaling	uniform | non-uniform | inherit	uniform	no	Extended
scaling-method	auto | integer-pixels | resample-any-method | inherit	auto	no	Extended

Table C-12. *Area Dimension Properties*

Property	Values	Default Value	Inherited	Conformance Level
size	<length>{1,2} | auto | landscape | portrait | inherit	auto	N/A [is optional]	Complete
width	<length> | <percentage> | auto | inherit	auto	no	Basic

Table C-12. *Area Dimension Properties* (continued)

Block and Line-Related Properties

These properties, shown in Table C-13, are used to control the line height of block objects.

Property	Values	Default Value	Inherited	Conformance Level
hyphenation-keep	auto | column | page | inherit	none	yes	Extended
hyphenation-ladder-count	no-limit | <number> | inherit	no-limit	yes	Extended
last-line-end-indent	<length> | <percentage> | inherit	0pt	yes	Extended
linefeed-treatment	ignore | preserve | treat-as-space | inherit	treat-as-space	yes	Extended
line-height	normal | <length> | <number> | <percentage> | <space> | inherit	normal	yes	Basic
line-height-shift-adjustment	consider-shifts | disregard-shifts | inherit	consider-shifts	yes	Extended

Table C-13. *Block and Line-Related properties*

Property	Values	Default Value	Inherited	Conformance Level
line-stacking-strategy	line-height | font-height | max-height | inherit	line-height	yes	Basic
space-treatment	ignore | preserve | inherit	preserve	yes	Extended
text-align	start | center | end | justify | inside | outside | left | right | <string> | inherit	start	yes	Basic
text-align-last	relative | start | center | end | justify | inside | outside | left | right | <string> | inherit	relative	yes	Extended
text-indent	<length> | <percentage> | inherit	0pt	yes	Basic
vertical-align	baseline | middle | sub | super | text-top | text-bottom | <percentage> | <length> | top | bottom | inherit	baseline	no	Complete
white-space	normal | pre | nowrap | inherit	normal	yes	Complete
white-space-collapse	false | true | inherit	TRUE	yes	Extended
wrap-option	no-wrap | wrap | inherit	wrap	yes	Basic

Table C-13. *Block and Line-Related properties* (continued)

Character Properties

These properties, shown in Table C-14, control the appearance, or display characters.

Property	Values	Default Value	Inherited	Conformance Level
character	<character>	N/A, value is required	No, a value is required	Basic
letter-spacing	normal | <length> | <space> | inherit	normal	Yes	Extended
suppress-at-line-break	auto | suppress | retain | inherit	auto	no	Extended
text-decoration	none | [[underline | no-underline] || [overline | no-overline] || [line-through | no-line-through] || [blink | no-blink]] | inherit	none	No, but see prose	Extended
text-shadow	none | [<color> || <length> <length> <length>? ,]* [<color> || <length> <length> <length>?] | inherit	none	No, see prose	Extended
text-transform	capitalize | uppercase | lowercase | none |	none	yes	Extended
treat-as-word-space	auto | yes | no | inherit	auto	no	Extended
word-spacing	normal | <length> | <space> | inherit	normal	yes	Extended

Table C-14. *Character Properties*

Color-Related Properties

These properties control the color associated with each element.

Property	Values	Default Value	Inherited	Conformance Level
color	<color> | inherit	Depends on user agent	yes	Basic
color-profile-name	<name> | inherit		no	Extended
rendering-intent	auto | perceptual | relative-colorimetric | saturation | absolute-colorimetric | inherit	auto	no	Extended

Float-Related Properties

These properties control the appearance of floating elements on your documents.

Property	Values	Default Value	Inherited	Conformance Level
clear	start | end | left | right | both | none | inherit	none	no	Extended
float	before | start | end | left | right | none | inherit	none	no	Extended

Keeps and Breaks Properties

These properties, shown in Table C-15, control how text appears on your document in the same manner as widows and orphans controls, and page breaks are implemented within other document formats.

Property	Values	Default Value	Inherited	Conformance Level
break-after	auto | column | page | even-page | odd-page | inherit	auto	no	Basic
break-before	auto | column | page | even-page | odd-page | inherit	auto	no	Basic
keep-together	<keep> | inherit	.within-line=auto, .within-column=auto, .within-page=auto	yes	Extended.
keep-with-next	<keep> | inherit	.within-line=auto, .within-column=auto, .within-page=auto	no	Basic
keep-with-previous	<keep> | inherit	.within-line=auto, .within-column=auto, .within-page=auto	no	Basic
orphans	<integer> | inherit	2	yes	Basic
widows	<integer> | inherit	2	yes	Basic

Table C-15. *Keeps and Breaks Properties*

Layout-Related Properties

These properties control the appearance of elements that extend past their allotted boundaries.

Property	Values	Default Value	Inherited	Conformance Level
clip	<shape> | auto | inherit	auto	no	Basic
overflow	visible | hidden | scroll | auto | inherit	auto	no	Basic
reference-orientation	0 | 90 | 180 | 270 | -90 | -180 | -270 | inherit	0	Yes (see prose)	Basic
relative-position	auto | static | relative | inherit	static	no	Extended
span	none | all | inherit	none	no	Extended

Leader and Rule Properties

These properties, shown in Table C-16, set the appearance of text leaders within your elements.

Properties for Links

This property controls the appearance of a link based upon its current selection state.

Property	Values	Default Value	Inherited	Conformance Level
active-state	link | visited | active | hover | focus	No, a value is required	no	Extended

Property	Values	Default Value	Inherited	Conformance Level
leader-alignment	none | reference-area | page | inherit	none	yes	Extended
leader-length	<length-range> | inherit	leader-length. minimum=0pt, .optimum=12.0pt, .maximum=100%	yes	Basic
leader-pattern	space | rule | dots | use-content | inherit	space	yes	Basic

Table C-16. *Leader and Ruler Properties*

Property	Values	Default Value	Inherited	Conformance Level
leader-pattern-width	use-font-metrics | <length> | inherit	use-font-metrics	yes	Extended
Rule-style	none | dotted | dashed | solid | double | groove | ridge | inherit	solid	yes	Basic
rule-thickness	<length>	1.0pt	yes	Basic

Table C-16. *Leader and Ruler Properties* (continued)

Document Properties

These properties, shown in Table C-17, control the settings of the document independent of the document's content.

Properties for Markers

These properties control the appearance and function of document markers within the visual appearance of your XML document.

Property	Values	Default Value	Inherited	Conformance Level
marker-class-name	<name>	An empty name	No, a value is required	Extended
retrieve-boundary	page | page-sequence | document	page-sequence	no	Extended
retrieve-class-name	<name>	An empty name	No, a value is required	Extended
retrieve-position	first-starting-within-page | first-including-carryover | last-starting-within-page | last-ending-within-page	first-starting-within-page	no	Extended
span	none | all | inherit	none	no	Extended

Property	Values	Default Value	Inherited	Conformance Level
auto-restore	yes | no	no	yes	Extended
case-name	<name>	None, a value is required	No, a value is required	Extended
case-title	<string>	None, a value is required	No, a value is required	Extended
destination-placement-offset	<length>	0pt	no	Extended
external-destination	<uri-reference>	Null string	no	Extended
indicate-destination	yes | no	no	no	Extended
internal-destination	null string | <idref>	Null string	no	Extended
show-destination	replace | new	replace	no	Extended
starting-state	show | hide	show	no	Extended
switch-to	xsl-preceding | xsl-following | xsl-any | <name>[<name>]*	xsl-any	no	Extended
xml:lang	<country-language> | inherit	Not defined for shorthand properties	yes	Complete

Table C-17. *Document Properties* (continued)

Properties for Number to String Conversion

These properties control the conversion between numbers and strings.

Property	Values	Default Value	Inherited	Conformance Level
format	<string>	1	no	Basic
grouping-separator	<character>	No separator	no	Basic
grouping-size	<number>	No grouping	no	Basic
letter-value	auto | alphabetic | traditional	auto	no	Basic

Pagination and Layout Properties

These properties, shown in Table C-18, control the layout and pagination of your XML document.

Property	Values	Default Value	Inherited	Conformance Level
Blank-or-not-blank	blank | not-blank | any | inherit	any	no	Extended
column-count	<number> | inherit	1	no	Extended
column-gap	<length> | <percentage> | inherit	12.0pt	no	Extended
extent	<length> | <percentage> | inherit	0.0pt	no	Extended
flow-name	<name>	An empty name	No, a value is required	Basic
force-page-count	auto | even | odd | end-on-even | end-on-odd | no-force | inherit	auto	no	Extended

Table C-18. *Pagination and Layout Properties*

Property	Values	Default Value	Inherited	Conformance Level
initial-page-number	auto | auto-odd | auto-even | <number> | inherit	auto	no	Basic
master-name	<name>	An empty name	No, a value is required	Basic
maximum-repeats	<number> | no-limit | inherit	no-limit	no	Extended
odd-or-even	odd | even | any | inherit	any	no	Extended
page-break-after	auto | always | avoid | left | right | inherit	auto	no	Basic
page-break-before	auto | always | avoid | left | right | inherit	auto	no	Basic
page-break-inside	avoid | auto | inherit	auto	yes	Complete
page-height	auto | indefinite | <length> | inherit	auto	no	Basic
page-position	first | last | rest | any | inherit	any	no	Extended
page-width	auto | indefinite | <length> | inherit	auto	no	Basic
precedence	true | false | inherit	FALSE	no	Basic
region-name	xsl-region-body | xsl-region-start | xsl-region-end | xsl-region-before | xsl-region-after | xsl-before-float-separator | xsl-footnote-separator | <name>	See prose	No, a value is required	Basic

Table C-18. *Pagination and Layout Properties* (continued)

Writing-Mode-Related Properties

These properties control how the writing of your document is done. It includes settings for controlling finite font appearance and the directional flow of your text.

Property	Values	Default Value	Inherited	Conformance Level
direction	ltr | rtl | inherit	ltr	yes	Basic
font-height-override-after	use-font-metrics | <length> | inherit	Use-font-metrics	no	Extended
font-height-override-before	use-font-metrics | <length> | inherit	Use-font-metrics	no	Extended
glyph-orientation-horizontal	<angle> | inherit	0	yes	Extended
glyph-orientation-vertical	auto | <angle> | inherit	auto	yes	Extended
unicode-bidi	normal | embed | bidi-override | inherit	normal	no	Extended
writing-mode	lr-tb | rl-tb | tb-rl | lr | rl | tb | inherit	lr-tb	Yes, see prose	Basic

Miscellaneous Properties

These properties, shown in Table C-19, provide everything from identifiers to control over the content types of your document.

Aural Properties

These properties, shown in Table C-20, control the aural, or sound, associated with displaying your XML document through a text synthesizer.

Property	Values	Default Value	Inherited	Conformance Level
content-type	<string> | auto	auto	no	Basic
id	<id>	See prose	No, see prose	Basic
provisional-distance-between-starts	<length> | inherit	24.0pt	yes	Basic
provisional-label-separation	<length> | inherit	6.0pt	yes	Basic
ref-id	<idref> | inherit	None, value required	no	Basic
score-spaces	true | false | inherit	TRUE	yes	Extended
src	<uri> | inherit	None, value required	no	Basic
visibility	visible | hidden | collapse | inherit	visible	no	Basic
z-index	auto | <integer> | inherit	auto	no	Basic

Table C-19. *Miscellaneous Properties*

Property	Values	Default Value	Inherited	Conformance Level
azimuth	<angle> | [[left-side | far-left | left | center-left | center | center-right | right | far-right | right-side] || behind] | leftwards | rightwards | inherit	center	yes	Basic
cue	<cue-before> || <cue-after> | inherit	Not defined for shorthand properties	no	Complete
cue-after	<uri> | none | inherit	none	no	Basic
cue-before	<uri> | none | inherit	none	no	Basic
elevation	<angle> | below | level | above | higher | lower | inherit	level	yes	Basic
pause	[<time> | <percentage>] {1,2} | inherit	Depends on user agent	no	Complete
pause-after	<time> | <percentage> | inherit	Depends on user agent	no	Basic
pause-before	<time> | <percentage> | inherit	Depends on user agent	no	Basic
pitch	<frequency> | x-low | low | medium | high | x-high | inherit	medium	yes	Basic
pitch-range	<number> | inherit	50	yes	Basic

Table C-20. *Aural Properties*

APPENDIXES

<table>
<tr><th>Property</th><th>Values</th><th>Default Value</th><th>Inherited</th><th>Conformance Level</th></tr>
<tr><td>play-during</td><td><uri> mix? repeat? | auto | none | inherit</td><td>auto</td><td>no</td><td>Basic</td></tr>
<tr><td>richness</td><td><number> | inherit</td><td>50</td><td>yes</td><td>Basic</td></tr>
<tr><td>speak</td><td>normal | none | spell-out | inherit</td><td>normal</td><td>yes</td><td>Basic</td></tr>
<tr><td>speak-header</td><td>once | always | inherit</td><td>once</td><td>yes</td><td>Basic</td></tr>
<tr><td>speak-numeral</td><td>digits | continuous | inherit</td><td>continuous</td><td>yes</td><td>Basic</td></tr>
<tr><td>speak-punctuation</td><td>code | none | inherit</td><td>none</td><td>yes</td><td>Basic</td></tr>
<tr><td>speech-rate</td><td><number> | x-slow | slow | medium | fast | x-fast | faster | slower | inherit</td><td>medium</td><td>yes</td><td>Basic</td></tr>
<tr><td>stress</td><td><number> | inherit</td><td>50</td><td>yes</td><td>Basic</td></tr>
<tr><td>voice-family</td><td>[[<specific-voice> | <generic-voice>],]* [<specific-voice> | <generic-voice>] | inherit</td><td>Depends on user agent</td><td>yes</td><td>Basic</td></tr>
<tr><td>volume</td><td><number> | <percentage> | silent | x-soft | soft | medium | loud | x-loud | inherit</td><td>medium</td><td>yes</td><td>Basic</td></tr>
</table>

Table C-20. *Aural Properties* (continued)

Appendix D

UNICODE Character Sets

XML documents use the UNICODE character sets as their native language, and although many XML browsers will display these characters within the limitations of their currently available fonts, there aren't many text editors that allow you to type them in the first place. This means that you will end up dealing with your UNICODE characters in one of several ways.

- Use the encoding declaration to indicate which character encoding you're using:

```
<?xml version="1.0" encoding="ISO-8859-1"?>
```

- Convert your document from your localized character set, such as ISO-Latin-1UTF-8, to strict UNICODE, such as UTF-8 or UTF-16.
- Type the characters using either hex or decimal notation as an integer between 0 and 65,535, prefaced by `"&#"` and followed by a semicolon (;). If you are going to write your UNICODE in hex notation, your number will need prefaced by `"&#x"`.

If you are going to need a large amount of UNICODE text, definitely use a converter, but otherwise you can use the direct entry of your UNICODE Character References.

The various languages supported by UNICODE are placed in the file in a variety of language blocks identified in Table D-1.

ISO Language Blocks	Character Range	Spoken Language Support
Basic Latin	0–127	ASCII and American English
Latin-1 Supplement	126–255	Used with the Basic Latin block for Danish, Dutch, English, Faroese, Flemish, German, Hawaiian, Icelandic, Indonesian, Irish, Italian, Norwegian, Portuguese, Spanish, Swahili, and Swedish

Table D-1. *UNICODE Character Mappings*

ISO Language Blocks	Character Range	Spoken Language Support
Latin Extended-A	256–383	In conjunction with Basic Latin and Latin-1, supplement covers Afrikaans, Breton, Basque, Catalan, Czech, Esperanto, Estonian, French, Frisian, Greenlandic, Hungarian, Latvian, Lithuanian, Maltese, Polish, Provençal, Rhaeto-Romanic, Romanian, Romany, Slovak, Slovenian, Sorbian, Turkish, and Welsh.
Latin Extended-B	383–591	Extends Latin languages to cover African languages, Croatian digraphs for Serbian Cyrillic letters, the Pinyin transcription of Chinese, and Sami characters.
IPA Extensions	592–686	International Phonetic Alphabet
Spacing Modifier Letters	687–766	Symbols that change the previous letter
Combining Diacritical Marks	767–879	Diacritical marks such as ~, ', and ? that are combined with the previous character to create a new, joined character.
Greek	880–1023	Modern Greek

Table D-1. *UNICODE Character Mappings* (continued)

ISO Language Blocks	Character Range	Spoken Language Support
Cyrillic	1024–1279	Russian, many Slavic languages (Ukrainian, Byelorussian, and others), and many non-Slavic languages of Russian states (Azerbaijani, Chechen, Tajik, and others)
Armenian	1326–1423	Armenian
Hebrew	1424–1535	Hebrew, Judezmo, early Aramaic, and Yiddish
Arabic	1536–1791	Arabic, Kurdish, Pashto, Persian, Sindhi, and classical Turkish
Devanagari	2304–2431	Hindi, Nepali, Sanskrit, and other languages of India including Awadhi, Bagheli, Bhatneri, Bhili, Bihari, Braj Bhasha, Chhattisgarhi, Garhwali, Gondi, Harauti, Ho, Jaipuri, Kachchhi, Kanauji, Konkani, Kului, Kumaoni, Kurku, Kurukh, Marwari, Mundari, Newari, Palpa, and Santali
Bengali	2432–2559	Bengali, Assamese, Daphla, Garo, Hallam, Khasi, Manipuri, Mizo, Naga, Munda, Rian, and Santali
Gurmukhi	2560–2686	Punjabi
Gujarati	2687–2815	Gujarati
Oriya	2816–2943	Khondi, Oriya, and Santali
Tamil	2944–3071	Badaga and Tamil

Table D-1. *UNICODE Character Mappings* (continued)

ISO Language Blocks	Character Range	Spoken Language Support
Telugu	3072–3199	Gondi, Lambadi, and Telugu
Kannada	3200–3327	Kannada and Tulu
Malalayam	3326–3455	Malalayam
Thai	3584–3711	Kuy, Lavna, Pali, and Thai
Lao	3712–3839	Lao
Tibetan	3840–4031	Himalayan languages
Georgian	4256–4351	Georgian (from the former Russian state)
Hangul Jamo	4352–4607	Alphabetic components of Korean Hangul
Latin Extended Additional	7680–7935	Latin letters such as *a* and *e* combined with diacritical marks
Greek Extended	7936–8191	Greek letters combined with diacritical marks
General Punctuation	8192–8303	Punctuation marks
Superscripts and Subscripts	8304–8351	Superscripts and subscripts
Currency Symbols	8352–8399	Currency symbols not already provided for
Combining Marks for Symbols	8400–8446	Makes diacritical marks span two or more characters
Letterlike Symbols	8447–8526	Letterlike symbols such as ™ and ?
Number Forms	8527–8591	Fractions and Roman numerals
Arrows	8592–8703	Arrows
Mathematical Operators	8704–8959	Mathematical operators not already specified

Table D-1. *UNICODE Character Mappings* (continued)

ISO Language Blocks	Character Range	Spoken Language Support
Miscellaneous Technical	8960–9039	Crop marks, bracket notation from quantum mechanics, symbols needed for the APL programming language, plus others
Control Pictures	9216–9279	Images of ASCII control characters
Optical Character Recognition	9280–9311	OCR-A and the magnetic ink character recognition (MICR)
Enclosed Alphanumerics	9312–9471	Letters and numbers in circles and parentheses such as © and ®
Box Drawing	9472–9599	Characters used for drawing boxes
Block Elements	9600–9631	Monospaced terminal graphics used in DOS and other text-based terminals
Geometric Shapes	9632–9726	Rectangles, squares, triangles, and others
Miscellaneous Symbols	9727–9983	Various miscellaneous symbols such as chess pieces and card symbols
Dingbats	9984–10175	Zapf Dingbat characters
CJK Symbols and Punctuation	12286–12351	Chinese, Japanese, and Korean (CJK) symbols and punctuation
Hiragana	12352–12446	Set of Japanese cursive syllables
Katakana	12447–12543	Set of noncursive syllables used to write Western words such as *computer* in Japanese

Table D-1. *UNICODE Character Mappings* (continued)

ISO Language Blocks	Character Range	Spoken Language Support
Bopomofo	12544–12591	Chinese phonetic alphabet
Hangul Compatibility Jamo	12592–12686	Korean characters
Kanbun	12687–12703	Japanese marks used to identify the reading order of classical Chinese
Enclosed CJK Letters and Months	12800–13055	Hangul and Katakana characters enclosed in circles and parentheses
CJK Compatibility	13056–13311	Characters needed to encode KSC 5601 and CNS 11643
CJK Unified Ideographs	19966–40959	Han ideographs used for Chinese, Japanese, and Korean
Hangul Syllables	44032–55203	A Korean table of syllables
Surrogates	55296–57343	Unused, but will allow for the extension of UNICODE to over one million different characters
Private Use	57344–63743	For software developers private use
CJK Compatibility Ideographs	63744–64255	Extra Han ideographs needed to maintain compatibility with existing standards
Alphabetic Presentation Forms	64256–64335	Ligatures and variants sometimes used in Latin, Armenian, and Hebrew
Arabic Presentation Forms	64336–65023	Variants of assorted Arabic characters

Table D-1. *UNICODE Character Mappings* (continued)

ISO Language Blocks	Character Range	Spoken Language Support
Combining Half Marks	65056–65071	Combines multiple diacritical marks into a single diacritical mark spanning multiple characters
CJK Compatibility Forms	65072–65103	Mostly vertical variants of Han ideographs used in Taiwan
Small Form Variants	65104–65135	Small version of ASCII punctuation
Additional Arabic Presentation Forms	65136–65279	Variations of assorted Arabic characters
Half-width and Full-width Forms	65280–65519	Characters allowing conversion between Chinese and Japanese encodings of the same character
Specials	65520–65535	Special characters used to control UNICODE files including the nonbreaking space and the byte order mark

Table D-1. *UNICODE Character Mappings* (continued)

Math-Related Character Codes

Table D-2 offers samples of mathematical character codes used by the Mathematical Markup Language (MathML) and the Chemical Markup Language (CML) discussed in Chapter 31.

Hex Code	Name	Description	Group
219E	Larr	two-head left arrow	ISOAMSA
E200	xlArr	long left double-arrow	ISOAMSA
E201	xlarr	long left arrow	ISOAMSA
E202	xhArr	long left and right double-arrow	ISOAMSA
E203	xharr	long left and right arrow	ISOAMSA
E204	xrArr	long right double-arrow	ISOAMSA
E205	xrarr	long right arrow	ISOAMSA
E206	lBarr	left doubly broken arrow	ISOAMSA
E207	rBarr	right doubly broken arrow	ISOAMSA
E208	xmap	long map stop	ISOAMSA
E209	RBarr	two-headed right-broken arrow	ISOAMSA
E20A	swarhk	SW arrow-hooked	ISOAMSA
E20B	searhk	SE arrow-hooked	ISOAMSA
E20C	nwarhk	NW arrow-hooked	ISOAMSA
E20D	nearhk	NE arrow-hooked	ISOAMSA
E20E	nesear	NE and SE arrows	ISOAMSA
E20F	midcir	mid, circle below	ISOAMSA
E20F	seswar	SE and SW arrows	ISOAMSA
E210	swnwar	SW and NW arrows	ISOAMSA
E211	nwnear	NW and NE arrows	ISOAMSA
E212	Map	two-headed map stop	ISOAMSA
E214	lfisht	left fishtail	ISOAMSA
E215	rfisht	right fishtail	ISOAMSA
E216	duarr	down arrow, up arrow	ISOAMSA
E217	duhar	down harp, up harp	ISOAMSA

Table D-2. *Mathematical Character Codes Used by MathML and CML*

Hex Code	Name	Description	Group
E218	udhar	up harp, down harp	ISOAMSA
E219	cudarrr	right, curved, down arrow	ISOAMSA
E219	rdca	right, down curved, arrow	ISOAMSA
E21A	ldca	left, down curved, arrow	ISOAMSA
E21B	nrarrw	not right arrow-wavy	ISOAMSA
E21C	rarrc	right arrow-curved	ISOAMSA
E21D	nrarrc	not right arrow-curved	ISOAMSA
E21E	rarrpl	right arrow, plus	ISOAMSA
E220	larrbfs	left arrow-bar, filled square	ISOAMSA
E221	rarrbfs	right arrow-bar, filled square	ISOAMSA
E222	larrfs	left arrow, filled square	ISOAMSA
E223	rarrfs	right arrow, filled square	ISOAMSA
E224	rHar	right harpoon-up over right harpoon-down	ISOAMSA
E225	lHar	left harpoon-up over left harpoon-down	ISOAMSA
E226	uHar	up harpoon-left, up harpoon-right	ISOAMSA
E227	dHar	down harpoon-left, down harpoon-right	ISOAMSA
E228	ldrushar	left-down-right-up harpoon	ISOAMSA
E229	lurdshar	left-up-right-down harpoon	ISOAMSA
E22A	ruluhar	right harpoon-up over left harpoon-up	ISOAMSA
E22B	luruhar	left harpoon-up over right harpoon-up	ISOAMSA
E22C	ldrdhar	left harpoon-down over right harpoon-down	ISOAMSA

Table D-2. *Mathematical Character Codes Used by MathML and CML* (continued)

Hex Code	Name	Description	Group
E22D	rdldhar	right harpoon-down over left harpoon-down	ISOAMSA
E22E	lharul	left harpoon-up over long dash	ISOAMSA
E22F	lrhard	right harpoon-down below long dash	ISOAMSA
E230	rharul	right harpoon-up over long dash	ISOAMSA
E231	llhard	left harpoon-down below long dash	ISOAMSA
E232	srarr	short right arrow	ISOAMSA
E233	slarr	short left arrow	ISOAMSA
E234	simrarr	similar, right arrow below	ISOAMSA
E235	rarrap	approximate, right arrow above	ISOAMSA
E236	erarr	equal, right arrow below	ISOAMSA
E237	Uarrocir	up two-headed arrow above circle	ISOAMSA
E238	DDotrahd	right arrow with dotted stem	ISOAMSA
E239	Rarrtl	right two-headed arrow with tail	ISOAMSA
E23B	rAtail	right double arrow-tail	ISOAMSA
E23C	latail	left arrow-tail	ISOAMSA
E23D	lAtail	left double arrow-tail	ISOAMSA
E23E	cudarrl	left, curved, down arrow	ISOAMSA
E23F	larrpl	left arrow, plus	ISOAMSA
E240	harrcir	left and right arrow with a circle	ISOAMSA
E241	roarr	right open arrow	ISOAMSA

Table D-2. *Mathematical Character Codes Used by MathML and CML* (continued)

Hex Code	Name	Description	Group
E242	loarr	left open arrow	ISOAMSA
E243	hoarr	horizontal open arrow	ISOAMSA
E244	zigrarr	right zigzag arrow	ISOAMSA
E248	angzarr	angle with down zigzag arrow	ISOAMSA
E249	curarrm	curved right arrow with minus	ISOAMSA
E24A	cularrp	curved left arrow with plus	ISOAMSA
E24B	ufisht	up fish tail	ISOAMSA
E24C	dfisht	down fish tail	ISOAMSA
E24D	rarrsim	right arrow, similar	ISOAMSA
E24E	larrsim	left arrow, similar	ISOAMSA
E250	cirmid	circle, mid below	ISOAMSA
E402	lbarr	left broken arrow	ISOAMSA
E405	rbarr	right broken arrow	ISOAMSA
228E	xuplus	big u plus	ISOAMSB
228E	uplus	plus-sign in union	ISOAMSB
229E	plusb	plus-sign in box	ISOAMSB
25EC	tridot	dot in triangle	ISOAMSB
E207	ac	most positive	ISOAMSB
E251	amalg	amalgamation or coproduct	ISOAMSB
E259	iprod	interior product	ISOAMSB
E25A	plusdu	plus sign, dot below	ISOAMSB
E25B	minusdu	minus sign, dot below	ISOAMSB
E25C	loplus	plus sign in left half-circle	ISOAMSB
E25D	roplus	plus sign in right half-circle	ISOAMSB
E25E	lotimes	multiply sign in left half-circle	ISOAMSB

Table D-2. *Mathematical Character Codes Used by MathML and CML* (continued)

Hex Code	Name	Description	Group
E260	ohbar	circle with horizontal bar	ISOAMSB
E261	capdot	intersection with dot	ISOAMSB
E262	subdot	subset with dot	ISOAMSB
E263	supdot	superset with dot	ISOAMSB
E264	smashp	smash product	ISOAMSB
E265	wedbar	wedge, bar below	ISOAMSB
E266	pluscir	plus, small circle above	ISOAMSB
E267	pluse	plus, equals	ISOAMSB
E268	eplus	equal, plus	ISOAMSB
E269	plustwo	plus, two; Nim-addition	ISOAMSB
E26A	plusacir	plus, circumflex accent above	ISOAMSB
E26B	simplus	plus, similar above	ISOAMSB
E26C	plussim	plus, similar below	ISOAMSB
E26D	timesd	times, dot	ISOAMSB
E26E	cupcap	union above intersection	ISOAMSB
E26F	capcup	intersection above union	ISOAMSB
E270	cupbrcap	union, bar, intersection	ISOAMSB
E271	capbrcup	intersection, bar, union	ISOAMSB
E272	cupcup	union, union, joined	ISOAMSB
E273	capcap	intersection, intersection, joined	ISOAMSB
E274	cups	union, serifs	ISOAMSB
E275	caps	intersection, serifs	ISOAMSB
E276	sqcups	square union, serifs	ISOAMSB
E277	sqcaps	square intersection, serifs	ISOAMSB
E278	ccups	closed union, serifs	ISOAMSB
E279	ccaps	closed intersection, serifs	ISOAMSB

Table D-2. *Mathematical Character Codes Used by MathML and CML* (continued)

Hex Code	Name	Description	Group
E27A	ccupssm	closed union, serifs, smash product	ISOAMSB
E27B	triplus	plus in triangle	ISOAMSB
E27C	triminus	minus in triangle	ISOAMSB
E27D	tritime	multiply in triangle	ISOAMSB
E27E	trisb	triangle, serifs at bottom	ISOAMSB
E27F	solb	solidus in square	ISOAMSB
E280	bsolb	reverse solidus in square	ISOAMSB
E281	capand	intersection, and	ISOAMSB
E282	cupor	union, or	ISOAMSB
E283	ncup	bar, union	ISOAMSB
E284	ncap	bar, intersection	ISOAMSB
E285	odiv	divide in circle	ISOAMSB
E286	odsold	dot, solidus, dot in circle	ISOAMSB
E287	ofcir	filled circle in circle	ISOAMSB
E288	olt	less-than in circle	ISOAMSB
E289	ogt	greater-than in circle	ISOAMSB
E28A	opar	parallel in circle	ISOAMSB
E28B	operp	perpendicular in circle	ISOAMSB
E28C	otimes	multiply sign in double circle	ISOAMSB
E28D	otimesas	multiply sign in circle, circumflex accent	ISOAMSB
E28E	timesbar	multiply sign, bar below	ISOAMSB
E28F	race	reverse most positive, line below	ISOAMSB
E290	acE	most positive, two lines below	ISOAMSB
E409	olcir	large circle in circle	ISOAMSB

Table D-2. *Mathematical Character Codes Used by MathML and CML* (continued)

Hex Code	Name	Description	Group
E40A	omid	vertical bar in circle	ISOAMSB
E40B	ovbar	circle with vertical bar	ISOAMSB
E40D	rotimes	multiply sign in right half circle	ISOAMSB
E844	ssetmn	small reverse solidus	ISOAMSB
231E	dlcorn	lower-left corner	ISOAMSC
E291	rpargt	right parenthesis, greater-than	ISOAMSC
E292	lparlt	left parenthesis, less-than	ISOAMSC
E293	rmoust	right moustache	ISOAMSC
E294	lmoust	left moustache	ISOAMSC
E295	ltrPar	double right parenthesis, less	ISOAMSC
E296	gtlPar	double left parenthesis, greater	ISOAMSC
E297	langd	left angle, dot	ISOAMSC
E298	rangd	right angle, dot	ISOAMSC
E299	lbrke	left bracket, equal	ISOAMSC
E29A	rbrke	right bracket, equal	ISOAMSC
E29B	lbrkslu	left bracket, solidus top corner	ISOAMSC
E29C	rbrksld	right bracket, solidus bottom corner	ISOAMSC
E29D	lbrksld	left bracket, solidus bottom corner	ISOAMSC
E29E	rbrkslu	right bracket, solidus top corner	ISOAMSC
22EA	nltri	not left triangle	ISOAMSN
22EB	nrtri	not right triangle	ISOAMSN
22EC	nltrie	not left triangle, equals	ISOAMSN
22ED	nrtrie	not right triangle, equals	ISOAMSN

Table D-2. *Mathematical Character Codes Used by MathML and CML* (continued)

Hex Code	Name	Description	Group
E2A1	gvnE	greater-than, vertical, not double equals	ISOAMSN
E2A2	lnap	less, not approximate	ISOAMSN
E2A4	lvnE	less, vertical, not double equals	ISOAMSN
E2A6	nge	not greater-than-or-equal	ISOAMSN
E2A7	nle	not less-than-or-equal	ISOAMSN
E2AA	nsmid	negated short mid	ISOAMSN
E2AB	nspar	not short par	ISOAMSN
E2B3	prnE	precedes, not double equals	ISOAMSN
E2B5	scnE	succeeds, not double equals	ISOAMSN
E2B8	vsubnE	subset not double equals, variant	ISOAMSN
E2B9	vsubne	subset, not equals, variant	ISOAMSN
E2BA	vsupne	superset, not equals, variant	ISOAMSN
E2BB	vsupnE	super not double equals, variant	ISOAMSN
E2BC	napid	not approximately identical to	ISOAMSN
E2C5	ncongdot	not congruent, dot	ISOAMSN
E2C6	nvap	not, vertical, approximate	ISOAMSN
E2C7	napE	not approximately equal or equal to	ISOAMSN
E2C8	parsim	parallel, similar	ISOAMSN
E2C9	nLt	not, vertical, much less than	ISOAMSN
E2CA	nGt	not, vertical, much greater than	ISOAMSN
E2CB	nLtv	not much less than, variant	ISOAMSN
E2CC	nGtv	not much greater than, variant	ISOAMSN

Table D-2. *Mathematical Character Codes Used by MathML and CML* (continued)

Hex Code	Name	Description	Group
E2CD	nLl	not triple less than	ISOAMSN
E2CE	nGg	not triple greater than	ISOAMSN
E2CF	nvrtrie	not, vertical, right triangle, equals	ISOAMSN
E2D0	nvltrie	not, vertical, left triangle, equals	ISOAMSN
E2D1	rnmid	reverse nmid	ISOAMSN
E411	gnap	greater, not approximate	ISOAMSN
E412	npre	not precedes, equals	ISOAMSN
E413	nsce	not succeeds, equals	ISOAMSN
E415	nvsim	not, vertical, similar	ISOAMSN
E416	solbar	solidus, bar through	ISOAMSN
E2D3	empty	letter O slashed	ISOAMSO
E2D4	jmath	small j, no dot	ISOAMSO
E2D5	plank	Planck's over 2pi	ISOAMSO
E2D6	ange	angle, equal	ISOAMSO
E2D7	range	reverse angle, equal	ISOAMSO
E2D8	nang	not, vertical, angle	ISOAMSO
E2D9	angmsdaa	angle-measured, arrow, up, right	ISOAMSO
E2DA	angmsdab	angle-measured, arrow, up, left	ISOAMSO
E2DC	angmsdac	angle-measured, arrow, down, left	ISOAMSO
E2DD	angmsdae	angle-measured, arrow, right, up	ISOAMSO
E2DE	angmsdaf	angle-measured, arrow, left, up	ISOAMSO

Table D-2. *Mathematical Character Codes Used by MathML and CML* (continued)

Hex Code	Name	Description	Group
E2DF	angmsdag	angle-measured, arrow, right, down	ISOAMSO
E2E0	angmsdah	angle-measured, arrow, left, down	ISOAMSO
E2E1	angrtvbd	right angle-measured, dot	ISOAMSO
E2E2	urtri	upper-right triangle	ISOAMSO
E2E3	lrtri	lower-right triangle	ISOAMSO
E2E4	ultri	upper-left triangle	ISOAMSO
E2E5	lltri	lower-left triangle	ISOAMSO
E2E6	boxbox	two joined squares	ISOAMSO
E2E7	demptyv	circle, slash, bar above	ISOAMSO
E2E8	cemptyv	circle, slash, small circle above	ISOAMSO
E2E9	raemptyv	circle, slash, right arrow above	ISOAMSO
E2EA	laemptyv	circle, slash, left arrow above	ISOAMSO
E2EB	vzigzag	vertical zigzag line	ISOAMSO
E2EC	trpezium	trapezium	ISOAMSO
E2ED	bsemi	reverse semicolon	ISOAMSO
E2EE	bbrk	bottom square bracket	ISOAMSO
E2EF	tbrk	top square bracket	ISOAMSO
E418	angrtvb	right angle-measured	ISOAMSO
E419	bbrktbrk	bottom above top square bracket	ISOAMSO
E41A	bemptyv	reversed circle, slash	ISOAMSO
E41B	cirE	circle, two horizontal stroked to the right	ISOAMSO
E41C	cirscir	circle, small circle to the right	ISOAMSO
E41D	oS	capital S in circle	ISOAMSO

Table D-2. *Mathematical Character Codes Used by MathML and CML* (continued)

Hex Code	Name	Description	Group
E301	smid	short mid	ISOAMSR
E302	spar	short parallel	ISOAMSR
E303	ssmile	small up curve	ISOAMSR
E306	thkap	thick approximate	ISOAMSR
E309	eDDot	equal with four dots	ISOAMSR
E30A	mlcp	transversal intersection	ISOAMSR
E30B	siml	similar, less	ISOAMSR
E30C	simg	similar, greater	ISOAMSR
E30D	Vbar	double vertical, bar (under)	ISOAMSR
E30E	Colone	double colon, equals	ISOAMSR
E30F	Dashv	double dash, vertical	ISOAMSR
E310	vBar	vertical, double bar (under)	ISOAMSR
E311	Barv	vertical, double bar (over)	ISOAMSR
E312	vBarv	double bar, vertical over and under	ISOAMSR
E313	Vdashl	vertical, dash (long)	ISOAMSR
E314	congdot	congruent, dot	ISOAMSR
E315	apE	approximately equal or equal to	ISOAMSR
E317	Esim	equal, similar	ISOAMSR
E318	equivDD	equivalent, four dots above	ISOAMSR
E319	sdote	equal, dot below	ISOAMSR
E31A	mcomma	minus, comma above	ISOAMSR
E31B	forkv	fork, variant	ISOAMSR
E31C	topfork	fork with top	ISOAMSR
E31D	lesdot	less-than-or-equal, slanted, dot inside	ISOAMSR

Table D-2. *Mathematical Character Codes Used by MathML and CML* (continued)

Hex Code	Name	Description	Group
E31E	gesdot	greater-than-or-equal, slanted, dot inside	ISOAMSR
E31F	lesdoto	less-than-or-equal, slanted, dot above	ISOAMSR
E320	gesdoto	greater-than-or-equal, slanted, dot above	ISOAMSR
E321	lesdotor	less-than-or-equal, slanted, dot above right	ISOAMSR
E322	gesdotol	greater-than-or-equal, slanted, dot above left	ISOAMSR
E323	elsdot	equal-or-less, slanted, dot inside	ISOAMSR
E324	egsdot	equal-or-greater, slanted, dot inside	ISOAMSR
E325	ltcir	less than, circle inside	ISOAMSR
E326	gtcir	greater than, circle inside	ISOAMSR
E327	el	equal-or-less	ISOAMSR
E328	eg	equal-or-greater	ISOAMSR
E329	ltquest	less than, question mark above	ISOAMSR
E32A	gtquest	greater than, question mark above	ISOAMSR
E32B	lesg	less, equal, slanted, greater	ISOAMSR
E32C	gesl	greater, equal, slanted, less	ISOAMSR
E32D	lgE	less, greater, equal	ISOAMSR
E32E	glE	greater, less, equal	ISOAMSR
E32F	glj	greater, less, overlapping	ISOAMSR
E330	gla	greater, less, apart	ISOAMSR
E331	lesges	less, equal, slanted, greater, equal, slanted	ISOAMSR

Table D-2. *Mathematical Character Codes Used by MathML and CML* (continued)

Hex Code	Name	Description	Group
E332	gesles	greater, equal, slanted, less, equal, slanted	ISOAMSR
E333	lsime	less, similar, equal	ISOAMSR
E334	gsime	greater, similar, equal	ISOAMSR
E335	lsimg	less, similar, greater	ISOAMSR
E336	gsiml	greater, similar, less	ISOAMSR
E337	simlE	similar, less, equal	ISOAMSR
E338	simgE	similar, greater, equal	ISOAMSR
E339	smt	smaller than	ISOAMSR
E33A	lat	larger than	ISOAMSR
E33B	smte	smaller than or equal	ISOAMSR
E33C	late	larger than or equal	ISOAMSR
E33D	smtes	smaller than or equal, slanted	ISOAMSR
E33E	lates	larger than or equal, slanted	ISOAMSR
E33F	subrarr	subset, right arrow	ISOAMSR
E340	suplarr	superset, left arrow	ISOAMSR
E341	subplus	subset, plus	ISOAMSR
E342	supplus	superset, plus	ISOAMSR
E343	submult	subset, multiply	ISOAMSR
E344	supmult	superset, multiply	ISOAMSR
E345	subsim	subset, similar	ISOAMSR
E346	supsim	superset, similar	ISOAMSR
E347	subsup	subset above superset	ISOAMSR
E348	supsub	superset above subset	ISOAMSR
E349	subsub	subset above subset	ISOAMSR
E34A	supsup	superset above superset	ISOAMSR
E34B	suphsub	superset, subset	ISOAMSR

Table D-2. *Mathematical Character Codes Used by MathML and CML* (continued)

Hex Code	Name	Description	Group
E34C	supdsub	superset, subset, dash joining them	ISOAMSR
E34D	bsolhsub	reverse solidus, subset	ISOAMSR
E34E	suphsol	superset, solidus	ISOAMSR
E34F	subedot	subset, equals, dot	ISOAMSR
E350	supedot	superset, equals, dot	ISOAMSR
E351	csub	subset, closed	ISOAMSR
E352	csup	superset, closed	ISOAMSR
E353	csube	subset, closed, equals	ISOAMSR
E354	csupe	superset, closed, equals	ISOAMSR
E355	ltcc	less than, closed by curve	ISOAMSR
E356	gtcc	greater than, closed by curve	ISOAMSR
E357	lescc	less than, closed by curve, equal, slanted	ISOAMSR
E358	gescc	greater than, closed by curve, equal, slanted	ISOAMSR
E359	rtriltri	right triangle above left triangle	ISOAMSR
E35C	Pr	double precedes	ISOAMSR
E35D	Sc	double succeeds	ISOAMSR
E35E	ltlarr	less than, left arrow	ISOAMSR
E35F	gtrarr	greater than, right arrow	ISOAMSR
E420	bepsi	such that	ISOAMSR
E421	ges	greater-than-or-equal, slanted	ISOAMSR
E425	les	less-than-or-equals, slant	ISOAMSR
E426	sfrown	small down curve	ISOAMSR
E429	thksim	thick similar	ISOAMSR

Table D-2. *Mathematical Character Codes Used by MathML and CML* (continued)

Hex Code	Name	Description	Group
E43E	hbenzenb	horizontal benzene ring, one double binding	ISOCHEM
E440	hbenzend	horizontal benzene ring, one double binding	ISOCHEM
E441	hbenzene	horizontal benzene ring, one double binding	ISOCHEM
E445	hbenzeni	horizontal benzene ring, two double bindings	ISOCHEM
E42A	benzena	benzene ring, one double binding	ISOCHEM
E42B	benzenb	benzene ring, one double binding	ISOCHEM
E42C	benzenc	benzene ring, one double binding	ISOCHEM
E42D	benzend	benzene ring, one double binding	ISOCHEM
E42E	benzene	benzene ring, one double binding	ISOCHEM
E42F	benzenf	benzene ring, one double binding	ISOCHEM
E430	benzeng	benzene ring, two double bindings	ISOCHEM
E431	benzenh	benzene ring, two double bindings	ISOCHEM
E432	benzeni	benzene ring, two double bindings	ISOCHEM
E433	benzenj	benzene ring, two double bindings	ISOCHEM
E434	benzenk	benzene ring, two double bindings	ISOCHEM
E435	benzenl	benzene ring, two double bindings	ISOCHEM

Table D-2. *Mathematical Character Codes Used by MathML and CML* (continued)

Hex Code	Name	Description	Group
E436	benzenm	benzene ring, two double bindings	ISOCHEM
E437	benzenn	benzene ring, two double bindings	ISOCHEM
E438	benzeno	benzene ring, two double bindings	ISOCHEM
E439	benzenp	benzene ring, three double bindings	ISOCHEM
E43A	benzenq	benzene ring, three double bindings	ISOCHEM
E43B	benzenr	benzene ring, circle	ISOCHEM
E43C	benzen	benzene ring	ISOCHEM
E43D	hbenzena	horizontal benzene ring, one double binding	ISOCHEM
E43F	hbenzenc	horizontal benzene ring, one double binding	ISOCHEM
E442	hbenzenf	horizontal benzene ring, one double binding	ISOCHEM
E443	hbenzeng	horizontal benzene ring, two double bindings	ISOCHEM
E444	hbenzenh	horizontal benzene ring, two double bindings	ISOCHEM
E446	hbenzenj	horizontal benzene ring, two double bindings	ISOCHEM
E447	hbenzenk	horizontal benzene ring, two double bindings	ISOCHEM
E448	hbenzenl	horizontal benzene ring, two double bindings	ISOCHEM
E449	hbenzenm	horizontal benzene ring, two double bindings	ISOCHEM

Table D-2. *Mathematical Character Codes Used by MathML and CML* (continued)

Hex Code	Name	Description	Group
E44A	hbenzenn	horizontal benzene ring, two double bindings	ISOCHEM
E44B	hbenzeno	horizontal benzene ring, two double bindings	ISOCHEM
E44C	hbenzenp	horizontal benzene ring, three double bindings	ISOCHEM
E44D	hbenzenq	horizontal benzene ring, three double bindings	ISOCHEM
E44E	hbenzenr	horizontal benzene ring, circle	ISOCHEM
E44F	hbenzen	horizontal benzene ring	ISOCHEM
E450	uml	umlaut mark	ISODIA
E47C	Afr	fraktur letter A	ISOMFRK
E47D	Bfr	fraktur letter B	ISOMFRK
E47E	Cfr	fraktur letter C	ISOMFRK
E47F	Dfr	fraktur letter D	ISOMFRK
E480	Efr	fraktur letter E	ISOMFRK
E481	Ffr	fraktur letter F	ISOMFRK
E482	Gfr	fraktur letter G	ISOMFRK
E483	Hfr	fraktur letter H	ISOMFRK
E484	Ifr	fraktur letter I	ISOMFRK
E485	Jfr	fraktur letter J	ISOMFRK
E486	Kfr	fraktur letter K	ISOMFRK
E487	Lfr	fraktur letter L	ISOMFRK
E488	Mfr	fraktur letter M	ISOMFRK
E489	Nfr	fraktur letter N	ISOMFRK
E48A	Ofr	fraktur letter O	ISOMFRK
E48B	Pfr	fraktur letter P	ISOMFRK

Table D-2. *Mathematical Character Codes Used by MathML and CML* (continued)

Hex Code	Name	Description	Group
E48C	Qfr	fraktur letter Q	ISOMFRK
E48D	Rfr	fraktur letter R	ISOMFRK
E48E	Sfr	fraktur letter S	ISOMFRK
E48F	Tfr	fraktur letter T	ISOMFRK
E490	Ufr	fraktur letter U	ISOMFRK
E492	Wfr	fraktur letter W	ISOMFRK
E493	Xfr	fraktur letter X	ISOMFRK
E494	Yfr	fraktur letter Y	ISOMFRK
E495	afr	fraktur letter a	ISOMFRK
E496	bfr	fraktur letter b	ISOMFRK
E497	cfr	fraktur letter c	ISOMFRK
E498	dfr	fraktur letter d	ISOMFRK
E499	efr	fraktur letter e	ISOMFRK
E49A	ffr	fraktur letter f	ISOMFRK
E49B	gfr	fraktur letter g	ISOMFRK
E49C	hfr	fraktur letter h	ISOMFRK
E49D	ifr	fraktur letter i	ISOMFRK
E49E	jfr	fraktur letter j	ISOMFRK
E49F	kfr	fraktur letter k	ISOMFRK
E4A0	lfr	fraktur letter l	ISOMFRK
E4A1	mfr	fraktur letter m	ISOMFRK
E4A2	nfr	fraktur letter n	ISOMFRK
E4A3	ofr	fraktur letter o	ISOMFRK
E4A4	pfr	fraktur letter p	ISOMFRK
E4A5	qfr	fraktur letter q	ISOMFRK
E4A6	rfr	fraktur letter r	ISOMFRK

Table D-2. *Mathematical Character Codes Used by MathML and CML* (continued)

Hex Code	Name	Description	Group
E4A7	sfr	fraktur letter s	ISOMFRK
E4A8	tfr	fraktur letter t	ISOMFRK
E4A9	ufr	fraktur letter u	ISOMFRK
E4AA	vfr	fraktur letter v	ISOMFRK
E4AB	wfr	fraktur letter w	ISOMFRK
E4AC	xfr	fraktur letter x	ISOMFRK
E4AD	yfr	fraktur letter y	ISOMFRK
E4AE	zfr	fraktur letter z	ISOMFRK
E4B0	Bopf	open face letter B	ISOMOPF
E4B1	Dopf	open face letter D	ISOMOPF
E4B2	Eopf	open face letter E	ISOMOPF
E4B3	Fopf	open face letter F	ISOMOPF
E4B4	Gopf	open face letter G	ISOMOPF
E4B5	Hopf	open face letter H	ISOMOPF
E4B6	Iopf	open face letter I	ISOMOPF
E4B7	Jopf	open face letter J	ISOMOPF
E4B8	Kopf	open face letter K	ISOMOPF
E4B9	Lopf	open face letter L	ISOMOPF
E4BA	Mopf	open face letter M	ISOMOPF
E4BB	Nopf	open face letter N	ISOMOPF
E4BC	Oopf	open face letter O	ISOMOPF
E4BD	Sopf	open face letter S	ISOMOPF
E4BE	Topf	open face letter T	ISOMOPF
E4AF	Aopf	open face letter A	ISOMOPF
E4C0	Vopf	open face letter V	ISOMOPF
E4C1	Wopf	Weierstrass p	ISOMOPF

Table D-2. *Mathematical Character Codes Used by MathML and CML* (continued)

Hex Code	Name	Description	Group
E4C2	Xopf	open face letter X	ISOMOPF
E4C3	Yopf	open face letter Y	ISOMOPF
E4C4	Zopf	open face letter Z	ISOMOPF
E4C5	Ascr	script letter A	ISOMSCR
E4C6	Bscr	script letter B	ISOMSCR
E4C7	Cscr	script letter C	ISOMSCR
E4C8	Dscr	script letter D	ISOMSCR
E4C9	Escr	script letter E	ISOMSCR
E4CA	Fscr	script letter F	ISOMSCR
E4CB	Gscr	script letter G	ISOMSCR
E4CC	Hscr	script letter H	ISOMSCR
E4CD	Iscr	script letter I	ISOMSCR
E4CE	Jscr	script letter J	ISOMSCR
E4CF	Kscr	script letter K	ISOMSCR
E4D0	Lscr	script letter L	ISOMSCR
E4D1	Mscr	script letter M	ISOMSCR
E4D2	Nscr	script letter N	ISOMSCR
E4D3	Oscr	script letter O	ISOMSCR
E4D4	Pscr	script letter P	ISOMSCR
E4D5	Qscr	script letter Q	ISOMSCR
E4D6	Rscr	script letter R	ISOMSCR
E4D7	Sscr	script letter S	ISOMSCR
E4D8	Tscr	script letter T	ISOMSCR
E4D9	Uscr	script letter U	ISOMSCR
E4DA	Vscr	script letter V	ISOMSCR
E4DB	Wscr	script letter W	ISOMSCR

Table D-2. *Mathematical Character Codes Used by MathML and CML* (continued)

Hex Code	Name	Description	Group
E4DC	Xscr	script letter X	ISOMSCR
E4DD	Yscr	script letter Y	ISOMSCR
E4DE	Zscr	script letter Z	ISOMSCR
E4DF	ascr	script letter a	ISOMSCR
E4E0	bscr	script letter b	ISOMSCR
E4E1	cscr	script letter c	ISOMSCR
E4E2	dscr	script letter d	ISOMSCR
E4E3	escr	script letter e	ISOMSCR
E4E4	fscr	script letter f	ISOMSCR
E4E5	gscr	script letter g	ISOMSCR
E4E6	hscr	script letter h	ISOMSCR
E4E7	iscr	script letter i	ISOMSCR
E4E8	jscr	script letter j	ISOMSCR
E4E9	kscr	script letter k	ISOMSCR
E4EA	lscr	script letter l	ISOMSCR
E4EB	mscr	script letter m	ISOMSCR
E4EC	nscr	script letter n	ISOMSCR
E4ED	oscr	script letter o	ISOMSCR
E4EE	pscr	script letter p	ISOMSCR
E4EF	qscr	script letter q	ISOMSCR
E4F0	sscr	script letter s	ISOMSCR
E4F1	tscr	script letter t	ISOMSCR
E4F2	uscr	script letter u	ISOMSCR
E4F3	vscr	script letter v	ISOMSCR
E4F4	wscr	script letter w	ISOMSCR
E4F5	xscr	script letter x	ISOMSCR

Table D-2. *Mathematical Character Codes Used by MathML and CML* (continued)

Hex Code	Name	Description	Group
E4F6	yscr	script letter y	ISOMSCR
E4F7	zscr	script letter z	ISOMSCR
E4F8	hyphen	hyphen	ISONUM
25EA	squarfbr	square, filled bottom-right corner	ISOPUB
E4F9	blank	significant blank symbol	ISOPUB
E4FB	diamondf	diamond, filled	ISOPUB
E4FC	diamonfb	diamond, filled bottom half	ISOPUB
E4FD	diamonfl	diamond, filled left half	ISOPUB
E4FE	diamonfr	diamond, filled right half	ISOPUB
E4FF	diamonft	diamond, filled top half	ISOPUB
E500	fjlig	small fj ligature	ISOPUB
E501	lozf	lozenge, filled	ISOPUB
E502	marker	histogram marker	ISOPUB
E503	mldr	em leader	ISOPUB
E504	rect	rectangle, open	ISOPUB
E505	sext	sextile (6-pointed star)	ISOPUB
E506	squarfbl	square, filled bottom-left corner	ISOPUB
E507	squarfb	square, filled bottom half	ISOPUB
E508	squarftr	square, filled top-right corner	ISOPUB
E509	squarft	square, filled top half	ISOPUB
FB00	fflig	small ff ligature	ISOPUB
FB01	filig	small fi ligature	ISOPUB
FB02	fllig	small fl ligature	ISOPUB
FB03	ffilig	small ffi ligature	ISOPUB

Table D-2. *Mathematical Character Codes Used by MathML and CML* (continued)

Hex Code	Name	Description	Group
FB04	ffllig	small ffl ligature	ISOPUB
25A1	squ	square, open	ISOPUB
25AA	squf	/blacksquare -sq bullet, filled	ISOPUB
22EE	vellip	vertical ellipsis	ISOPUB
230E	urcrop	upward right crop mark	ISOPUB
E4FA	circle	circle, open	ISOPUB
221E	infin	/infty infinity	ISOTECH
222E	conint	contour integral operator	ISOTECH
22EF	ctdot	/cdots, three dots, centered	ISOTECH
232E	profalar	all-around profile	ISOTECH
E364	fnof	function of (italic, small f)	ISOTECH
E365	iff	/iff if and only if	ISOTECH
E36A	lowast	low asterisk	ISOTECH
E370	notinva	negated set membership, variant	ISOTECH
E371	qprime	quadruple prime	ISOTECH
E372	iinfin	infinity sign, incomplete	ISOTECH
E376	pointint	integral around a point operator	ISOTECH
E377	quatint	quaternion integral operator	ISOTECH
E378	qint	quadruple integral operator	ISOTECH
E379	lopar	left open parenthesis	ISOTECH
E37A	ropar	right open parenthesis	ISOTECH
E37B	notinvb	negated set membership, variant	ISOTECH
E37C	notinvc	negated set membership, variant	ISOTECH

Table D-2. *Mathematical Character Codes Used by MathML and CML* (continued)

Hex Code	Name	Description	Group
E37D	notnivb	contains, variant	ISOTECH
E37E	notnivc	contains, variant	ISOTECH
E380	strns	straightness	ISOTECH
E381	fltns	flatness	ISOTECH
E382	parsl	parallel, slanted	ISOTECH
E383	topcir	top, circle below	ISOTECH
E384	eparsl	parallel, slanted, equal; homothetically congruent to	ISOTECH
E385	smeparsl	similar, parallel, slanted, equal	ISOTECH
E386	eqvparsl	equivalent, equal; congruent and parallel	ISOTECH
E387	bnequiv	reverse not equivalent	ISOTECH
E388	bne	reverse not equal	ISOTECH
E389	nparsl	not parallel, slanted	ISOTECH
E38A	nedot	not equal, dot	ISOTECH
E38B	simdot	similar, dot	ISOTECH
E38D	nhpar	not, horizontal, parallel	ISOTECH
E38E	nvinfin	not, vertical, infinity	ISOTECH
E390	npart	not partial differential	ISOTECH
E392	orv	or with middle stem	ISOTECH
E393	ord	or, horizontal dash	ISOTECH
E396	fpartint	finite part integral	ISOTECH
E397	rppolint	line integration, rectangular path around pole	ISOTECH
E398	scpolint	line integration, semicircular path around pole	ISOTECH

Table D-2. *Mathematical Character Codes Used by MathML and CML* (continued)

Hex Code	Name	Description	Group
E399	npolint	line integration, not including the pole	ISOTECH
E39A	intlarhk	integral, left arrow with hook	ISOTECH
E39C	isindot	set membership, dot above	ISOTECH
E39D	notindot	negated set membership, dot above	ISOTECH
E39E	isinE	set membership, two horizontal strokes	ISOTECH
E3A0	disin	set membership, long horizontal stroke	ISOTECH
E3A1	nisd	contains, long horizontal stroke	ISOTECH
E3A2	isinsv	large set membership, vertical bar on horizontal stroke	ISOTECH
E3A4	isins	set membership, vertical bar on horizontal stroke	ISOTECH
E3A5	nis	contains, vertical bar on horizontal stroke	ISOTECH
E3A7	elinters	electrical intersection	ISOTECH
E3A8	olcross	circle, cross	ISOTECH
E3A9	dsol	solidus, bar above	ISOTECH
E3AA	dwangle	large downward pointing angle	ISOTECH
E3AE	orslope	sloping large or	ISOTECH
E50B	imped	impedance	ISOTECH
E50C	infintie	tie, infinity	ISOTECH
E50D	notinE	negated set membership, two horizontal strokes	ISOTECH
E50E	oror	two logical or	ISOTECH

Table D-2. *Mathematical Character Codes Used by MathML and CML* (continued)

Hex Code	Name	Description	Group
E36E	andand	two logical and	ISOTECH
E38C	apacir	approximate, circumflex accent	ISOTECH
E391	andv	and with middle stem	ISOTECH
E394	andd	and, horizontal dash	ISOTECH
E395	cirfnint	circulation function	ISOTECH
E39B	awint	anti clockwise integration	ISOTECH
E3A3	xnis	large contains, vertical bar on horizontal stroke	ISOTECH
E3A6	acd	ac current	ISOTECH
E3AB	uwangle	large upward pointing angle	ISOTECH
E3AD	bNot	reverse not with two horizontal strokes	ISOTECH
E50A	andslope	sloping large and	ISOTECH
226E	nlt	not less-than	ISOAMSN
226E	nvlt	not, vertical, less-than	ISOAMSN
223E	mstpos	most positive	ISOAMSR
224E	bump	bumpy equals	ISOAMSR
227E	prap	precedes, approximate	ISOAMSR
227E	prsim	precedes, similar	ISOAMSR
227E	scE	succeeds, double equals	ISOAMSR
039E	Xi	capital Xi, Greek	ISOGRK3
002E	period	full stop, period	ISONUM
003E	gt	greater-than sign	ISONUM
00A0	nbsp	no break (required) space	ISONUM
00A1	iexcl	inverted exclamation mark	ISONUM
00A2	cent	cent sign	ISONUM

Table D-2. *Mathematical Character Codes Used by MathML and CML* (continued)

Hex Code	Name	Description	Group
00A3	pound	pound sign	ISONUM
00A4	curren	general currency sign	ISONUM
00A5	yen	yen sign	ISONUM
00A6	brvbar	broken (vertical) bar	ISONUM
00A7	sect	section sign	ISONUM
00A9	copy	copyright sign	ISONUM
00AA	ordf	ordinal indicator, feminine	ISONUM
00AB	laquo	angle quotation mark, left	ISONUM
00AC	not	/neg /lnot not sign	ISONUM
00AD	shy	soft hyphen	ISONUM
00AF	reg	registered sign	ISONUM
00B0	deg	degree sign	ISONUM
00B1	plusmn	plus-or-minus sign	ISONUM
00B2	sup2	superscript two	ISONUM
00B3	sup3	superscript three	ISONUM
00B5	micro	micro sign	ISONUM
00B6	para	pilcrow (paragraph sign)	ISONUM
00B7	middot	middle dot	ISONUM
00B9	sup1	superscript one	ISONUM
00BA	ordm	ordinal indicator, masculine	ISONUM
00BB	raquo	angle quotation mark, right	ISONUM
00BC	frac14	fraction one-quarter	ISONUM
00BD	frac12	fraction one-half	ISONUM
00BD	half	fraction one-half	ISONUM
00BE	frac34	fraction three-quarters	ISONUM
00BF	iquest	inverted question mark	ISONUM

Table D-2. *Mathematical Character Codes Used by MathML and CML* (continued)

Hex Code	Name	Description	Group
00D7	times	multiply sign	ISONUM
00F7	divide	divide sign	ISONUM
215E	frac78	fraction seven-eighths	ISONUM
201E	ldquor	rising double quote, left (low)	ISOPUB
211E	rx	pharmaceutical prescription (Rx)	ISOPUB
260E	phone	telephone symbol	ISOPUB
266E	natur	music natural	ISOPUB
002B	plus	plus sign	ISONUM
002C	comma	comma	ISONUM
002F	sol	solidus	ISONUM
03A0	Pi	capital Pi, Greek	ISOGRK3
03A3	Sigma	capital Sigma, Greek	ISOGRK3
03A6	Phi	capital Phi, Greek	ISOGRK3
03A8	Psi	capital Psi, Greek	ISOGRK3
03A9	Omega	capital Omega, Greek	ISOGRK3
03B1	alpha	small alpha, Greek	ISOGRK3
03B2	beta	small beta, Greek	ISOGRK3
03B3	gamma	small gamma, Greek	ISOGRK3
03B4	delta	small delta, Greek	ISOGRK3
03B5	epsiv	rounded small epsilon, Greek	ISOGRK3
03B6	zeta	small zeta, Greek	ISOGRK3
03B7	eta	small eta, Greek	ISOGRK3
03B8	theta	straight theta, small theta, Greek	ISOGRK3
03B9	iota	small iota, Greek	ISOGRK3

Table D-2. *Mathematical Character Codes Used by MathML and CML* (continued)

Hex Code	Name	Description	Group
03BA	kappa	small kappa, Greek	ISOGRK3
03BB	lambda	small lambda, Greek	ISOGRK3
03BC	mu	small mu, Greek	ISOGRK3
03BD	nu	small nu, Greek	ISOGRK3
03BE	omicron	small omicron, Greek	ISOGRK3
03BE	xi	small xi, Greek	ISOGRK3
03C0	pi	small pi, Greek	ISOGRK3
03C1	rho	small rho, Greek	ISOGRK3
03C2	sigmav	terminal sigma, Greek	ISOGRK3
03C3	sigma	small sigma, Greek	ISOGRK3
03C4	tau	small tau, Greek	ISOGRK3
03C5	upsi	small upsilon, Greek	ISOGRK3
03C6	phi	small phi, Greek	ISOGRK3
03C7	chi	small chi, Greek	ISOGRK3
03C8	psi	small psi, Greek	ISOGRK3
03C9	omega	small omega, Greek	ISOGRK3
03D1	thetav	curly or open theta	ISOGRK3
03D2	Upsi	capital Upsilon, Greek	ISOGRK3
03D5	phiv	curly or open small phi, Greek	ISOGRK3
03D6	piv	rounded small pi (pomega), Greek	ISOGRK3
03DC	Gammad	capital digamma	ISOGRK3
03DC	gammad	digamma, old Greek	ISOGRK3
03F0	kappav	rounded small kappa, Greek	ISOGRK3
03F1	rhov	rounded small rho, Greek	ISOGRK3
003A	colon	colon	ISONUM

Table D-2. *Mathematical Character Codes Used by MathML and CML* (continued)

Hex Code	Name	Description	Group
003B	semi	semicolon	ISONUM
003C	lt	less-than sign	ISONUM
003D	equals	equals sign	ISONUM
003F	quest	question mark	ISONUM
005B	lsqb	left square bracket	ISONUM
005C	bsol	/backslash reverse solidus	ISONUM
005D	rsqb	right square bracket	ISONUM
005F	lowbar	low line	ISONUM
007B	lcub	left curly bracket	ISONUM
007D	rcub	right curly bracket	ISONUM
007C	verbar	vertical bar	ISONUM
20DB	tdot	three dots above	ISOTECH
20DC	DotDot	four dots above	ISOTECH
21A0	Rarr	two-headed right-arrow	ISOAMSA
21A1	Darr	down two-headed arrow	ISOAMSA
21A2	larrtl	left arrow-tailed	ISOAMSA
21A3	rarrtl	right arrow-tailed	ISOAMSA
21A3	ratail	right arrow-tail	ISOAMSA
21A6	map	map-stop	ISOAMSA
21A9	larrhk	left arrow-hooked	ISOAMSA
21AA	rarrhk	right arrow-hooked	ISOAMSA
21AB	larrlp	left arrow-looped	ISOAMSA
21AC	rarrlp	right arrow-looped	ISOAMSA
21AD	harrw	left and right arrow-wavy	ISOAMSA
21AE	nharr	not left and right arrow	ISOAMSA
21B0	lsh	lsh	ISOAMSA

Table D-2. *Mathematical Character Codes Used by MathML and CML* (continued)

Hex Code	Name	Description	Group
21B1	rsh	rsh	ISOAMSA
21B2	ldsh	left down angled arrow	ISOAMSA
21B3	rdsh	right down angled arrow	ISOAMSA
21B6	cularr	left curved arrow	ISOAMSA
21B7	curarr	right curved arrow	ISOAMSA
21BA	olarr	left arrow in circle	ISOAMSA
21BB	orarr	right arrow in circle	ISOAMSA
21BC	lharu	left harpoon-up	ISOAMSA
21BD	lhard	left harpoon-down	ISOAMSA
21BE	uharr	up harp-r	ISOAMSA
21BF	uharl	up harpoon-left	ISOAMSA
21C0	rharu	right harpoon-up	ISOAMSA
21C1	rhard	right harpoon-down	ISOAMSA
21C2	dharr	down harpoon-right	ISOAMSA
21C3	dharl	down harpoon-left	ISOAMSA
21C4	rlarr	right arrow over left arrow	ISOAMSA
21C5	udarr	up arrow, down arrow	ISOAMSA
21C6	lrarr	left arrow over right arrow	ISOAMSA
21C7	llarr	two left arrows	ISOAMSA
21C8	uuarr	two up arrows	ISOAMSA
21C9	rrarr	two right arrows	ISOAMSA
21CA	ddarr	two down arrows	ISOAMSA
21CB	lrhar	left harp over r	ISOAMSA
21CC	rlhar	right harp over l	ISOAMSA
21CD	nlArr	not implied by	ISOAMSA
21CD	nvlArr	not, vertical, left double arrow	ISOAMSA

Table D-2. *Mathematical Character Codes Used by MathML and CML* (continued)

Hex Code	Name	Description	Group
21CE	nhArr	not left and right double arrow	ISOAMSA
21CE	nvhArr	not, vertical, left and right double arrow	ISOAMSA
21CF	nrArr	not implies	ISOAMSA
21CF	nvrArr	not, vertical, right double arrow	ISOAMSA
21D1	uArr	up double arrow	ISOAMSA
21D3	dArr	down double arrow	ISOAMSA
21D4	hArr	left and right double arrow	ISOAMSA
21D5	vArr	up and down double arrow	ISOAMSA
21D6	nwArr	NW pointing double arrow	ISOAMSA
21D7	neArr	NE pointing double arrow	ISOAMSA
21D8	seArr	SE pointing double arrow	ISOAMSA
21D9	swArr	SW pointing double arrow	ISOAMSA
21DA	lAarr	left triple arrow	ISOAMSA
21DB	rAarr	right triple arrow	ISOAMSA
21DD	dzigrarr	right long zigzag arrow	ISOAMSA
0021	excl	exclamation mark	ISONUM
21D0	lArr	is implied by	ISOTECH
21D2	rArr	implies	ISOTECH
22B6	origof	original of	ISOAMSA
22B7	imof	image of	ISOAMSA
22B8	mumap	multimap	ISOAMSA
22A0	timesb	multiply sign in box	ISOAMSB
22A1	sdotb	small dot in box	ISOAMSB
22B9	hercon	hermitian conjugate matrix	ISOAMSB

Table D-2. *Mathematical Character Codes Used by MathML and CML* (continued)

Hex Code	Name	Description	Group
22BA	intcal	intercal	ISOAMSB
22BC	barwed	logical and, bar above	ISOAMSB
22BD	barvee	bar, vee	ISOAMSB
22C0	xwedge	logical or operator	ISOAMSB
22C1	xvee	logical and operator	ISOAMSB
22C2	xcap	intersection operator	ISOAMSB
22C3	xcup	union operator	ISOAMSB
22C4	diam	open diamond	ISOAMSB
22C5	sdot	small middle dot	ISOAMSB
22C6	sstarf	small star, filled, low	ISOAMSB
22C7	divonx	division on times	ISOAMSB
22C9	ltimes	times sign, left closed	ISOAMSB
22CA	rtimes	times sign, right closed	ISOAMSB
22CB	lthree	left three times	ISOAMSB
22CC	rthree	right three times	ISOAMSB
22CE	cuvee	curly logical or	ISOAMSB
22CF	cuwed	curly logical and	ISOAMSB
0022	nprcue	not curly precedes, equals	ISOAMSN
22AC	nvdash	not vertical, dash	ISOAMSN
22AD	nvDash	not vertical, double dash	ISOAMSN
22AE	nVdash	not double vertical, dash	ISOAMSN
22AF	nVDash	not double vertical, double dash	ISOAMSN
22A2	vdash	vertical, dash	ISOAMSR
22A3	dashv	dash, vertical	ISOAMSR
22A7	models	models	ISOAMSR

Table D-2. *Mathematical Character Codes Used by MathML and CML* (continued)

Hex Code	Name	Description	Group
22A8	vDash	vertical, double dash	ISOAMSR
22A9	Vdash	double vertical, dash	ISOAMSR
22AA	Vvdash	triple vertical, dash	ISOAMSR
22AB	VDash	double vertical, double dash	ISOAMSR
22B0	prurel	element precedes under relation	ISOAMSR
22B2	vltri	left triangle, open, variant	ISOAMSR
22B3	vrtri	right triangle, open, variant	ISOAMSR
22B4	ltrie	left triangle, equals	ISOAMSR
22B5	rtrie	right triangle, equals	ISOAMSR
22C8	bowtie	bow tie	ISOAMSR
22CD	bsime	reverse similar, equals	ISOAMSR
22D0	Sub	double subset	ISOAMSR
22D1	Sup	double superset	ISOAMSR
22D4	fork	pitch fork	ISOAMSR
22D6	ltdot	less than, with dot	ISOAMSR
22D7	gtdot	greater than, with dot	ISOAMSR
22D8	Ll	triple less-than	ISOAMSR
22D9	Gg	triple greater-than	ISOAMSR
22DA	lEg	less, double equals, greater	ISOAMSR
22DA	leg	less, equals, greater	ISOAMSR
22DB	gEl	greater-than, double equals, less	ISOAMSR
22DB	gel	greater, equals, less	ISOAMSR
22DC	els	equal-or-less, slanted	ISOAMSR
22DD	egs	equal-or-greater, slanted	ISOAMSR

Table D-2. *Mathematical Character Codes Used by MathML and CML* (continued)

Hex Code	Name	Description	Group
22DE	cuepr	curly equals, precedes	ISOAMSR
22DF	cuesc	curly equals, succeeds	ISOAMSR
0022	quot	quotation mark	ISONUM
22A4	top	top	ISOTECH
22A5	bottom	bottom	ISOTECH
22A5	perp	perpendicular	ISOTECH
22D5	epar	parallel, equal; equal or parallel	ISOTECH
22F1	dtdot	/ddots, three dots, descending	ISOTECH
22BE	vangrt	right angle, variant (with arc)	ISOTECH
22F0	utdot	three dots, ascending	ISOTECH
0023	num	number sign	ISONUM
0024	dollar	dollar sign	ISONUM
25B3	xutri	big up triangle, open	ISOAMSB
25BD	xdtri	big down triangle, open	ISOAMSB
25CB	xcirc	large circle	ISOAMSB
0025	percnt	percent sign	ISONUM
25B8	rtrif	right triangle, filled	ISOPUB
25B9	rtri	right triangle, open	ISOPUB
25BE	dtrif	down triangle, filled	ISOPUB
25BF	dtri	down triangle, open	ISOPUB
25C2	ltrif	left triangle, filled	ISOPUB
25C3	ltri	left triangle, open	ISOPUB
25CA	loz	lozenge or total mark	ISOPUB
25B4	utrif	up triangle, filled	ISOPUB
25B5	utri	up triangle, open	ISOPUB

Table D-2. *Mathematical Character Codes Used by MathML and CML* (continued)

Hex Code	Name	Description	Group
25CF	circlef	circle, filled	ISOPUB
25D0	circlefl	circle, filled left half [Harvey ball]	ISOPUB
25D1	circlefr	circle, filled right half	ISOPUB
25D2	circlefb	circle, filled bottom half	ISOPUB
25D3	circleft	circle, filled top half	ISOPUB
25A0	squarf	square, filled	ISOTECH
25A1	square	square	ISOTECH
0026	amp	ampersand	ISONUM
0027	apos	apostrophe	ISONUM
0028	lpar	left parenthesis	ISONUM
0029	rpar	right parenthesis	ISONUM
030A	ring	ring	ISODIA
030B	dblac	double acute accent	ISODIA
030C	caron	caron	ISODIA
039B	Lambda	capital Lambda, Greek	ISOGRK3
0040	commat	commercial at	ISONUM
0131	imath	small i, no dot	ISOAMSO
200A	hairsp	hair space	ISOPUB
201C	ldquo	double quotation mark, left	ISONUM
201D	rdquo	double quotation mark, right	ISONUM
201A	lsquor	rising single quote, left (low)	ISOPUB
201B	rdquor	rising double quote, right (high)	ISOPUB
201F	rsquor	rising single quote, right (high)	ISOPUB
210F	plankv	variant Planck's over 2pi	ISOAMSO

Table D-2. *Mathematical Character Codes Used by MathML and CML* (continued)

Hex Code	Name	Description	Group
210B	hamilt	Hamiltonian (script capital H)	ISOTECH
211C	real	real	ISOAMSO
211A	Qopf	open face letter Q	ISOMOPF
211D	Ropf	open face letter R	ISOMOPF
211B	rscr	script letter r	ISOMSCR
212B	angst	Angstrom capital A, ring	ISOTECH
212C	bernou	Bernoulli function (script capital B)	ISOTECH
215B	frac18	fraction one-eighth	ISONUM
215C	frac38	fraction three-eighths	ISONUM
215D	frac58	fraction five-eighths	ISONUM
215A	frac56	fraction five-sixths	ISOPUB
219A	nlarr	not left arrow	ISOAMSA
219B	nrarr	not right arrow	ISOAMSA
219D	rarrw	right arrow-wavy	ISOAMSA
219F	Uarr	up two-headed arrow	ISOAMSA
0220	nsccue	not succeeds, curly equals	ISOAMSN
220A	epsi	small epsilon, Greek	ISOGRK3
220A	isin	set membership	ISOTECH
220B	niv	contains, variant	ISOTECH
220C	notni	negated contains	ISOTECH
220C	notniva	negated contains, variant	ISOTECH
220D	ni	contains	ISOTECH
221D	vprop	proportional, variant	ISOAMSR
221A	radic	/surd radical	ISOTECH
221D	prop	is proportional to	ISOTECH

Table D-2. *Mathematical Character Codes Used by MathML and CML* (continued)

Hex Code	Name	Description	Group
221F	angrt	right (90-degree) angle	ISOTECH
222A	cup	union or logical sum	ISOTECH
222B	int	integral operator	ISOTECH
222C	Int	double integral operator	ISOTECH
222D	tint	triple integral operator	ISOTECH
222F	Conint	double contour integral operator	ISOTECH
223D	bsim	reverse similar	ISOAMSR
223A	mDDot	minus with four dots, geometric properties	ISOAMSR
223B	homtht	homothetic	ISOAMSR
223C	sim	similar	ISOTECH
224A	ape	approximate, equals	ISOAMSR
224B	apid	approximately identical to	ISOAMSR
224D	asymp	asymptotically equal to	ISOAMSR
224F	bumpe	bumpy equals, equals	ISOAMSR
225A	veebar	logical or, equals	ISOAMSB
225B	easter	equal, asterisk above	ISOAMSR
225C	trie	triangle, equals	ISOAMSR
225F	equest	equal with question mark	ISOAMSR
226F	ngt	not greater than	ISOAMSN
226F	nvgt	not, vertical, greater than	ISOAMSN
226A	Lt	double less-than sign	ISOAMSR
226B	Gt	double greater than sign	ISOAMSR
226C	twixt	between	ISOAMSR
227A	pr	precedes	ISOAMSR
227B	sc	succeeds	ISOAMSR

Table D-2. *Mathematical Character Codes Used by MathML and CML* (continued)

Hex Code	Name	Description	Group
227C	prcue	precedes, curly equals	ISOAMSR
227C	prE	precedes, double equals	ISOAMSR
227C	pre	precedes, equals	ISOAMSR
227D	sccue	succeeds, curly equals	ISOAMSR
227D	sce	succeeds, equals	ISOAMSR
227F	scap	succeeds, approximate	ISOAMSR
227F	scsim	succeeds, similar	ISOAMSR
228D	cupdot	union, with dot	ISOAMSB
228A	subnE	subset, not double equals	ISOAMSN
228A	subne	subset, not equals	ISOAMSN
228B	supnE	superset, not double equals	ISOAMSN
228B	supne	superset, not equals	ISOAMSN
228F	sqsub	square subset	ISOAMSR
229A	ocir	small circle in circle	ISOAMSB
229B	oast	asterisk in circle	ISOAMSB
229D	odash	hyphen in circle	ISOAMSB
229F	minusb	minus sign in box	ISOAMSB
230A	lfloor	left floor	ISOAMSC
230B	rfloor	right floor	ISOAMSC
230C	drcrop	downward right crop mark	ISOPUB
230D	dlcrop	downward left crop mark	ISOPUB
230F	ulcrop	upward left crop mark	ISOPUB
231C	ulcorn	upper-left corner	ISOAMSC
231D	urcorn	upper-right corner	ISOAMSC
231F	drcorn	lower-right corner	ISOAMSC
232D	cylcty	cylindricity	ISOTECH

Table D-2. *Mathematical Character Codes Used by MathML and CML* (continued)

Hex Code	Name	Description	Group
266D	flat	musical flat	ISOPUB
266F	sharp	musical sharp	ISOPUB
0300	grave	grave accent	ISODIA
300A	Lang	left angle bracket, double	ISOTECH
300B	Rang	right angle bracket, double	ISOTECH
0301	acute	acute accent	ISODIA
301A	lobrk	left open bracket	ISOTECH
301B	robrk	right open bracket	ISOTECH
0303	tilde	tilde	ISODIA
0304	macr	macron	ISODIA
0305	breve	breve	ISODIA
0306	dot	dot above	ISODIA
0308	die	dieresis	ISODIA
0308	Dot	dieresis or umlaut mark	ISOTECH
0327	cedil	cedilla	ISODIA
0328	ogon	ogonek	ISODIA
0393	Gamma	capital Gamma, Greek	ISOGRK3
0394	Delta	capital Delta, Greek	ISOGRK3
0398	Theta	capital Theta, Greek	ISOGRK3
2002	ensp	en space (half an em)	ISOPUB
2003	emsp	em space	ISOPUB
2004	emsp13	third of an em space	ISOPUB
2005	emsp14	quarter of an em space	ISOPUB
2007	numsp	digit space (width of a number)	ISOPUB
2008	puncsp	punctuation space (width of comma)	ISOPUB

Table D-2. *Mathematical Character Codes Used by MathML and CML* (continued)

Hex Code	Name	Description	Group
2009	thinsp	thin space (sixth of an em)	ISOPUB
2010	dash	hyphen (true graphic)	ISOPUB
2013	ndash	en dash	ISOPUB
2014	mdash	em dash	ISOPUB
2015	horbar	horizontal bar	ISONUM
2016	Verbar	double vertical bar	ISOTECH
2018	lsquo	single quotation mark, left	ISONUM
2019	rsquo	single quotation mark, right	ISONUM
2020	dagger	dagger	ISOPUB
2021	Dagger	double dagger	ISOPUB
2022	bull	round bullet, filled	ISOPUB
2025	nldr	double baseline dot (en leader)	ISOPUB
2026	hellip	ellipsis (horizontal)	ISOPUB
2030	permil	per thousand	ISOTECH
2031	pertenk	per 10 thousand	ISOTECH
2032	prime	/prime prime or minute	ISOTECH
2033	Prime	double prime or second	ISOTECH
2034	tprime	triple prime	ISOTECH
2035	bprime	reverse prime	ISOAMSO
2038	caret	caret (insertion mark)	ISOPUB
2043	hybull	rectangle, filled (hyphen bullet)	ISOPUB
2102	Copf	open face letter C	ISOMOPF
2105	incare	in-care-of symbol	ISOPUB
2111	image	imaginary	ISOAMSO

Table D-2. *Mathematical Character Codes Used by MathML and CML* (continued)

APPENDIXES

Hex Code	Name	Description	Group
2112	lagran	Lagrangian (script capital L)	ISOTECH
2113	ell	cursive small l	ISOAMSO
2117	copysr	sound recording copyright sign	ISOPUB
2118	weierp	Weierstrass p	ISOAMSO
2119	Popf	open face letter P	ISOMOPF
2122	trade	trade mark sign	ISONUM
2124	Zfr	fraktur letter Z	ISOMFRK
2126	ohm	ohm sign	ISONUM
2127	mho	conductance	ISOAMSO
2129	iiota	inverted iota	ISOAMSO
2133	phmmat	physics M-matrix (script capital M)	ISOTECH
2134	order	order of (script small o)	ISOTECH
2135	aleph	/aleph aleph, Hebrew	ISOTECH
2136	beth	beth, Hebrew	ISOAMSO
2137	gimel	gimel, Hebrew	ISOAMSO
2138	daleth	daleth, Hebrew	ISOAMSO
2153	frac13	fraction one-third	ISOPUB
2155	frac15	fraction one-fifth	ISOPUB
2156	frac25	fraction two-fifths	ISOPUB
2157	frac35	fraction three-fifths	ISOPUB
2158	frac45	fraction four-fifths	ISOPUB
2159	frac16	fraction one-sixth	ISOPUB
2190	larr	leftward arrow	ISONUM
2191	uarr	upward arrow	ISONUM

Table D-2. *Mathematical Character Codes Used by MathML and CML* (continued)

Hex Code	Name	Description	Group
2192	rarr	rightward arrow	ISONUM
2193	darr	downward arrow	ISONUM
2194	harr	left and right arrow	ISOAMSA
2195	varr	up and down arrow	ISOAMSA
2196	nwarr	NW pointing arrow	ISOAMSA
2198	searr	SE pointing arrow	ISOAMSA
2199	swarr	SW pointing arrow	ISOAMSA
2200	nsqsube	not, square subset, equals	ISOAMSN
2200	forall	/forall, for all	ISOTECH
2201	comp	complement sign	ISOAMSO
2202	part	/partial partial differential	ISOTECH
2203	exist	/exists at least one exists	ISOTECH
2204	nexist	negated exists	ISOAMSO
2205	emptyv	circle, slash	ISOAMSO
2207	nabla	del, Hamilton operator	ISOTECH
2208	isinv	set membership, variant	ISOTECH
2209	notin	negated set membership	ISOTECH
2210	coprod	coproduct operator	ISOAMSB
2211	sum	summation operator	ISOAMSB
2212	minus	minus sign	ISOTECH
2213	mnplus	minus-or-plus sign	ISOTECH
2214	plusdo	plus sign, dot above	ISOAMSB
2216	setmn	reverse solidus	ISOAMSB
2217	midast	centered asterisk	ISOAMSB
2218	cir	circle, open	ISOPUB
2218	compfn	composite function (small circle)	ISOTECH

Table D-2. *Mathematical Character Codes Used by MathML and CML* (continued)

Hex Code	Name	Description	Group
2220	ang	angle	ISOAMSO
2221	angmsd	angle-measured	ISOAMSO
2222	angsph	/sphericalangle, angle-spherical	ISOTECH
2223	mid	mid	ISOAMSR
2224	nmid	negated mid	ISOAMSN
2225	par	parallel	ISOTECH
2226	npar	not parallel	ISOAMSN
2227	and	logical and	ISOTECH
2228	or	logical or	ISOTECH
2229	cap	intersection	ISOTECH
2230	Cconint	triple contour integral operator	ISOTECH
2231	cwint	clockwise integral	ISOTECH
2232	cwconint	contour integral, clockwise	ISOTECH
2233	awconint	contour integral, anti-clockwise	ISOTECH
2234	there4	therefore	ISOTECH
2235	bcong	because	ISOAMSR
2236	ratio	ratio	ISOAMSR
2238	minusd	minus sign, dot above	ISOAMSB
2240	wreath	wreath product	ISOAMSB
2241	nsim	not similar	ISOAMSN
2242	esim	equals, similar	ISOAMSR
2243	sime	similar, equals	ISOTECH
2244	nsime	not similar, equals	ISOAMSN
2245	cong	congruent with	ISOTECH

Table D-2. *Mathematical Character Codes Used by MathML and CML* (continued)

Hex Code	Name	Description	Group
2246	simne	similar, not equals	ISOAMSN
2247	ncong	not congruent with	ISOAMSN
2248	ap	approximate	ISOTECH
2249	nap	not approximate	ISOAMSN
2250	esdot	equals, single dot above	ISOAMSR
2251	eDot	equals, even dots	ISOAMSR
2252	efDot	equals, falling dots	ISOAMSR
2253	erDot	equals, rising dots	ISOAMSR
2254	colone	colon, equals	ISOAMSR
2254	frac23	fraction two-thirds	ISOPUB
2255	ecolon	equals, colon	ISOAMSR
2256	ecir	circle on equals sign	ISOAMSR
2257	cire	circle, equals	ISOAMSR
2259	wedgeq	corresponds to (wedge, equals)	ISOTECH
2260	ne	not equal	ISOTECH
2261	equiv	identical with	ISOTECH
2262	nequiv	not identical with	ISOAMSN
2264	le	less-than-or-equal	ISOTECH
2265	ge	greater-than-or-equal	ISOTECH
2266	lE	less, double equals	ISOAMSR
2267	gE	greater, double equals	ISOAMSR
2268	lnE	less, not double equals	ISOAMSN
2268	lne	less, not equals	ISOAMSN
2269	gnE	greater, not double equals	ISOAMSN
2269	gne	greater, not equals	ISOAMSN

Table D-2. *Mathematical Character Codes Used by MathML and CML* (continued)

Hex Code	Name	Description	Group
2270	nlE	not less, double equals	ISOAMSN
2270	nles	not less-or-equals, slant	ISOAMSN
2270	nvle	not, vertical, less-than-or-equal	ISOAMSN
2271	ngE	not greater, double equals	ISOAMSN
2271	nges	not greater-than-or-equals, slanted	ISOAMSN
2271	nvge	not, vertical, greater-than-or-equal	ISOAMSN
2272	lap	less, approximate	ISOAMSR
2272	lsim	less, similar	ISOAMSR
2273	gap	greater, approximate	ISOAMSR
2273	gsim	greater, similar	ISOAMSR
2274	nlsim	not less, similar	ISOAMSN
2275	ngsim	not greater, similar	ISOAMSN
2276	lg	less, greater	ISOAMSR
2277	gl	greater, less	ISOAMSR
2278	ntlg	not less, greater	ISOAMSN
2278	ntvlg	not, vertical, less, greater	ISOAMSN
2279	ntgl	not greater, less	ISOAMSN
2279	ntvgl	not, vertical, greater, less	ISOAMSN
2280	npr	not precedes	ISOAMSN
2281	nsc	not succeeds	ISOAMSN
2282	sub	subset or is implied by	ISOTECH
2283	sup	superset or implies	ISOTECH
2284	nsub	not subset	ISOAMSN
2285	nsup	not superset	ISOAMSN

Table D-2. *Mathematical Character Codes Used by MathML and CML* (continued)

Hex Code	Name	Description	Group
2285	vnsub	not superset, variant	ISOAMSN
2286	subE	subset, double equals	ISOAMSR
2286	sube	subset, equals	ISOTECH
2287	supE	superset, double equals	ISOAMSR
2287	supe	superset, equals	ISOTECH
2288	nsubE	not subset, double equals	ISOAMSN
2288	nsube	not subset, equals	ISOAMSN
2289	nsupE	not superset, double equals	ISOAMSN
2289	nsupe	not superset, equals	ISOAMSN
2290	sqsup	square superset	ISOAMSR
2291	sqsube	square subset, equals	ISOAMSR
2292	sqsupe	square superset, equals	ISOAMSR
2293	sqcap	square intersection	ISOAMSB
2294	sqcup	square union	ISOAMSB
2294	xsqcup	square union operator	ISOAMSB
2295	oplus	plus sign in circle	ISOAMSB
2295	xoplus	circle plus operator	ISOAMSB
2296	ominus	minus sign in circle	ISOAMSB
2297	otimes	multiply sign in circle	ISOAMSB
2297	xotime	circle times operator	ISOAMSB
2298	osol	solidus in circle	ISOAMSB
2299	odot	middle dot in circle	ISOAMSB
2299	xodot	circle dot operator	ISOAMSB
2306	Barwed	logical and, double bar above	ISOAMSB
2308	lceil	left ceiling	ISOAMSC
2309	rceil	right ceiling	ISOAMSC

Table D-2. *Mathematical Character Codes Used by MathML and CML* (continued)

Hex Code	Name	Description	Group
2310	bnot	reverse not	ISOTECH
2312	profline	profile of a line	ISOTECH
2313	profsurf	profile of a surface	ISOTECH
2315	telrec	telephone recorder symbol	ISOPUB
2316	target	register mark or target	ISOPUB
2322	frown	down curve	ISOAMSR
2323	smile	up curve	ISOAMSR
2336	topbot	top and bottom	ISOTECH
2580	uhblk	upper half block	ISOPUB
2584	lhblk	lower half block	ISOPUB
2588	block	full block	ISOPUB
2591	blk14	25 percent shaded block	ISOPUB
2592	blk12	50 percent shaded block	ISOPUB
2593	blk34	75 percent shaded block	ISOPUB
2605	starf	star, filled	ISOPUB
2612	cross	ballot cross	ISOPUB
2640	female	Venus, female	ISOPUB
2642	male	Mars, male	ISOPUB
2660	spades	spades suit symbol	ISOPUB
2661	hearts	heart suit symbol	ISOPUB
2662	diams	diamond suit symbol	ISOPUB
2663	clubs	club suit symbol	ISOPUB
2669	sung	music note (sung text sign)	ISONUM
2713	check	tick, check mark	ISOPUB
2720	malt	maltese cross	ISOPUB
3008	lang	left angle bracket	ISOTECH

Table D-2. *Mathematical Character Codes Used by MathML and CML* (continued)

Hex Code	Name	Description	Group
3009	rang	right angle bracket	ISOTECH
3014	lbbrk	left broken bracket	ISOTECH
3015	rbbrk	right broken bracket	ISOTECH
3018	loang	left open angular bracket	ISOTECH
3019	roang	right open angular bracket	ISOTECH
2200	nsqsupe	not, square superset, equals	ISOAMSN
2200	lnsim	less, not similar	ISOAMSN
2200	gnsim	greater, not similar	ISOAMSN
2500	squarfl	square, filled left half	ISOPUB
2200	prnap	precedes, not approximate	ISOAMSN
2200	prnsim	precedes, not similar	ISOAMSN
2500	squarfr	square, filled right half	ISOPUB
2200	scnap	succeeds, not approximate	ISOAMSN
2200	scnsim	succeeds, not similar	ISOAMSN
2500	squarftl	square, filled top-left corner	ISOPUB

Table D-2. *Mathematical Character Codes Used by MathML and CML* (continued)

Index

SYMBOLS

" (double-quotation mark), 127
% (percent symbol)
    entity restrictions, 127
    referencing parameter entities, 134
' (apostrophe), entity references, 67
/ (forward slash)
    location paths and, 287–288
    using with closing element tags, 66
{} (curly brackets), attribute value templates, 342
<, (less-than sign), entity references, 67
<> (angle brackets), using with element names, 66
> (greater-than sign), entity references, 67
@media, CSS media types, 255–256
@import, CSS media types, 257
& (ampersand)
    entity references, 67, 134
    entity restrictions, 127

A

<a> element
    SMIL, 652, 655
    XLink, 516
abbreviated syntax, RDF, 556–557
absolute positioning, CSS, 246
abstract elements, using with Schemas, 494
accessibility, CSS, 176–178
Acrobat Reader. *See* Adobe Acrobat PDF reader
:active, CSS pseudo-classes, 195
actuate attribute, XLink, 523–524
Adobe Acrobat PDF reader
    Formatting Objects to PDF (FOP), 279–281
    native XSL-FO renderer, 278
Adobe SVG Plug-in, 692
:after, CSS pseudo-elements, 194, 231–233
algebra expressions. *See* XML Queries, algebra
<aligngroup/> element, MathML, 697–699
alignment options, CSS text, 204–205
<all>, Schema constraints, 478–479
alternative objects, RDF containers, 560
Amaya browser, 22–23
ampersand (&)
    entity references, 67, 134
    entity restrictions, 127
angle brackets (<>), using with element names, 66
animation effects, SMIL, 658–660
annotation element, Schemas, 475–476
Antenna House, XSL Formatter, 412
API (Application Programming Interface), 19
apostrophe ('), entity references, 67
appInfo element, Schema annotations, 475
Application Programming Interface (API), 19
applications, sorting order, 177
applications/xml, 549
arc, XLink, 517, 529–530
arcrole attribute, XLink, 523–524
Are You Well-Formed (RUWF), 29
<area> element, HTML, 516–517
<area> element, SMIL, 655–656
area model, XSL style sheets, 179
ASCII, 541
atomic data, XML Query Algebra, 506–507
<!ATTLIST> statement, 144
<attribute> element, Schemas, 454
attribute nodes, 286, 320–322
attribute value templates (AVTs), 342–344
    restrictions on, 344
    use of, 342–344
attributes, 74–90, 142–158
    ambiguity of, 76–77
    default namespaces and, 96
    defining, 143–144
    enhancing elements, 79–81
    enhancing empty elements, 83
    identifying, 56
    lack of extensibility of, 76–78
    metadata and, 75–76
    multiple attributes, 82, 152–156
    naming, 81–82
    overview of, 74–75, 142–143
    predefined, xml:lang, 157
    predefined, xml:space, 156–157
    rules for, 81–82
    sharing, 83
    using with XML tags, 7
    values of, 82
    vs. elements, 74–75, 143
    when to use, 75
attributes, default values
    #FIXED, 152
    #IMPLIED, 151–152
    #REQUIRED, 150–151
    using quotes for defining, 150
attributes, predefined
    xml:lang, 157
    xml:space, 156–157
attributes, Schemas, 470–483
    annotations, 475–476
    checking for specification changes, 473
    constraints, 476–479
    constraints, <all>, 478–479
    constraints, <choice>, 476–477
    constraints, <sequence>, 477–478
    creating unique elements and attributes, 479–480
    entities values and, 482
    groups, 473–475
    groups, improving readability, 475

groups, location, 474–475
list of descriptions, 470–473
namespaces and, 480–481
attributes, SMIL, 632–635, 653–654
attributes, style sheets, 84–89
adding, 84–85
CCS, 86
XSL, 86–89
attributes, SVG, 683–691
attributes, types
CDATA, 145–146
ENTITY or ENTITIES, 146–147
enumerated, 147
ID, 147–148
IDREF or IDREFS, 148–149
NMTOKEN or NMTOKENS, 149
NOTATION, 149–150
attributes, XHTML
Bidirectional Text Module, 587
Client-Side Image Map Module, 596
Edit Module, 586–587
Forms Module, 588–591
Hypertext Module, 581
Image Module, 596
List Module, 582–583
Presentation Module, 584–585
Table Module, 592–595
Text Module, 574–580
attributes, XLink, 519–524
to, 524
from, 524
actuate, 523–524
arcrole, 523–524
href, 522
label, 524
role, 523
show, 523
title, 523
type, 520–521
attributes, XSLT, 340–342, 359–360
aural style sheets, 257–261
attributes of, 258–261
overview of, 257
authoring tools. *See* editors
AVTs. *See* attribute value templates (AVTs)
axes, XPath location steps, 292–294
list of, 292–293
short cuts, 294
axes, XPointer, 540

B

backgrounds, CSS object boxes, 217–221
background-attachment property, 217–218
background-color property, 218
background-image property, 218–219
background-position property, 219–220
background property, 221
background-repeat property, 220–221
Backus-Naur-Form (BNF) grammar, 11
bag objects, RDF containers, 558–559
bare names, XPointer, 539
:before, CSS pseudo-elements, 194, 230–231
behavior, XLink, 517
Bidirectional Text Module, XHTML, 587
binary data, 66
block formatting, 408
block objects, CSS, 242–243
BNF (Backus-Naur-Form) grammar, 11
<body> element
HTML, 607–608
SMIL, attributes, 637–638
SMIL, overview, 636
Boolean
values, 506
XPath functions, 305–307
borders, CSS object boxes, 207–210
border-collapse property, 210–211
border-color property, 210
border property, 207–208
border-style property, 209
border-width property, 208
bottom positioning, CSS, 250
browsers. *See also* Internet Explorer; Netscape Navigator
Amaya browser, 22–23
XHTML and, 568
XLink and, 517
built-in nodes, XSLT, 320–322

C

candidate nodes, 295
Canonical XML, 15
Cascading Style Sheets (CSS), 186–227
adding to documents, 187
attributes and, 56, 86
basic statement, 186–187
compared with XSL, 174, 181–182, 264–265
conflict resolution, 329
creating style sheets, 221–226
deciding which type of stylesheet to use, 181–182
features, 174–178
selecting classes, 192
selecting elements, 191–192
selecting IDs, 193
selecting in context, 193
selector patterns, 188–191
separating content from formatting, 6
standards, 12
SVG and, 664–665
using pseudo-classes, 194–196
using pseudo-elements, 193–194
versions, 230
XPointer and, 537
Cascading Style Sheets (CSS), fonts
setting color, 201–202
setting family, 197
setting shorthand, 200–201
setting size, 197–198
setting style, 199
setting variant, 199
setting weight, 200
settings stretch, 198–199

Cascading Style Sheets (CSS), modification and formatting effects, 230–262
adding content, 230–233
adding content, :after, 231–233
adding content, :before, 230–231
aural style sheets, 257–261
creating counters and automatic numbering, 233–234
cursors, 253–254
display property values, block, 242–243
display property values, compact and run-in, 243
display property values, inline, 241–242
display property values, marker, 243–244
display property values, none, 243
display property values, tables, 243–244
media types, 255–257
media types, @import, 257
media types, @media, 255–256
object importance, 254
overflow and clip properties, 252–253
positioning, absolute, 246
positioning, bottom, 250
positioning, fixed, 246–247
positioning, left, 249
positioning, relative, 245–246
positioning, right, 249
positioning, stacking elements with z-index property, 247–248
positioning, top, 249
pseudo-classes and pseudo-elements, 234–240
pseudo-classes and pseudo-elements, :first-child, 235
pseudo-classes and pseudo-elements, :first-letter, 237–240
pseudo-classes and pseudo-elements, :first-line, 235–237
size, 250–251
size, height, 251
size, width, 251
visibility, 252
Cascading Style Sheets (CSS), object boxes
adding padding, 215–217
setting backgrounds, 217–221
setting border-collapse, 210–211
setting borders, 207–210
setting margins, 213–215
setting outlines, 211–213
Cascading Style Sheets (CSS), text
setting alignment, 204–205
setting letter-spacing, 202
setting line-height, 203
setting text-align, 203–204
setting word-spacing, 204
text-decoration property, 205–206
text-indent property, 205
text-shadow property, 206
text-transform property, 206–207
CDATA. *See* character data (CDATA)
cdata-section-elements attribute, 359–360
cellular devices, XHTML, 568
CGI. *See* Common Gateway Interface (CGI), database conversion
character data (CDATA)
attribute type for, 145–146
in DTD elements, 112–113
element content and, 66–67
using in elements, 42
character encoding values, XML declarations, 62–65
characters, XPointer
escaping characters for use in XML text, 541–542
escaping characters in URLs, 541
escaping specific characters, 541
Chemical Markup Language (CML), 716–726
elements, 716–717
examples, 717–725
overview of, 696
child elements
namespace declaration and, 96–97
well-formed documents and, 71–72
child languages. *See* Synchronized Multimedia Integration Language (SMIL)
child objects, XML, 39
child sequence, XPointer, 540
<choice>, Schema constraints, its classes, CSS, 192
Client-Side Image Map Module, XHTML, 596–597
clip property, CSS, 252–253
closing tags, elements, 66
CML. *See* Chemical Markup Language (CML)
code
adding comments to, 43–45
including and importing, 354–357
colons (:), element names and
color, CSS fonts, 201–202
comma-separated values (CSV), 267
comment nodes
as built-in template rule, 322
defined, 287
comments
compared with annotations, 475
DTDs and, 118–119, 165–167
rules governing, 44
XML code and, 43–45
XSLT and, 315–317
Common Gateway Interface (CGI), database conversion, 614–621
creating XML file, 615–616
format of flat-file database, 615–616
opening database and starting the loop, 616–617
reading data, 617
saving and closing, 618
setting up variables and opening the script, 614–615
summary of script for, 618–621
writing data, 618
compact, CSS display property values, 243
compatibility, CSS stylesheets, 175
complex elements, Schemas, 454–456
<complexType> element, 437, 454–456
compositor elements, Schemas, 435
conditional processing, XSLT
xsl:choose, 332–334
xsl:if, 332
conditional statements, 165–167
function of, 165
IGNORE, 166–167
INCLUDE, 166–167

conflict resolution, template rules, 329–331
constraints, Schemas, 476–479
<all> attribute, 478–479
<choice> attribute, 476–477
compared with ID attributes, 489
<sequence> attribute, 477–478
containers, RDF
alternative objects, 560
bag objects, 558–559
defined, 557
sequence objects, 559
syntax for, 558
content
controlling, 114–117
defined, 114
DTD rules, 115
elements and, 66–67
content property, CSS, 230–233
:after, 231–233
:before, 230–231
content, XHTML
Bidirectional Text Module, 587
Client-Side Image Map Module, 596
Edit Module, 586–587
Forms Module, 588–591
Hypertext Module, 581
Image Module, 596
List Module, 582–583
Presentation Module, 584–585
Table Module, 592–595
Text Module, 574–580
content, XSL-FO documents, 405–410
block vs. inline formatting, 408
content that varies page to page, 410
fixed content, 408–409
overview, 405–407
context node, XPath, 291
conversions
converting XSL to PDF, 410–411
HTML to XHTML, 568–572
XML to HTML, 603–604
conversions, databases. *See* Common Gateway Interface (CGI), database conversion
Core Object Model, DOM, 19
counter-increment property, CSS, 233–234
counter property, CSS, 233–234
counter-reset property, CSS, 233–234
counters, CSS, 233–234
CSV (comma-separated values), 267
curly brackets ({}), 342
current(), XSLT functions, 383–385
cursors, CSS, 253–254

D

data
difficulty of expressing non-textual data in XLM, 162–163
representation in XML Query, 504
structure, 45
SVG types, 667–668
data () function, XML Query Algebra, 506
data, non-XML
conditional statements, 165–167
notations, 160–162
processing instructions, 167–169
unparsed external entities, 162–165
data organization, 48–57
adding detail to personal information databases, 49–51
creating levels of information, 48–49
ensuring data meets DOM requirements, 56–57
identifying attributes, 56
identifying elements, 51–56
databases, converting. *See* Common Gateway Interface (CGI), database conversion
databases, information management in, 48–51
declarations
Schemas, 494
XML, 430–434
XSL-FO, 398
description statement, RDF, 560
descriptor, CSS stylesheets, 177
display options, SMIL, 647–649
display properties, XSL-FO, 413–414
display property values, CSS
block, 242–243
compact and run-in, 243
inline, 241–242
marker, 243–244
none, 243
overview of, 240–241
tables, 243–244
<div> element, HTML, 605, 607–608
doctype-public attribute, XSLT, 359
<!DOCTYPE> statements, 107–109, 137
doctype-system attribute, XSLT, 359
Document Object Model (DOM)
data organization and, 56–57
scripting and, 19
XHTML and, 568
Document Style Semantics and Specification Language (DSSSL), 266–267
Document Type Definitions (DTDs), 104–119
adding to documents, 105–108
adding to documents, embedding, 107–108
adding to documents, linking, 106–107
adding to documents, overview, 105–106
comments and, 118–119
compared with Schemas, 430–434, 489
conditional statements and, 165–167
content model rules and, 115
elements, controlling content, 114–117
elements, declaring type, 109–114
entities, DTD entity, 138–140
entities, external, 165
function of, 104
namespaces and, 97–100
parsers and, 29–31
processing instructions and, 168
public vs. system, 108–109
RDF Schema and, 553
standards for, 11

validation, 6, 29–31, 104–105, 601
XML 1.0 and, 428
XML Query and, 502
document (), XSLT functions, 369–371
documentation element, Schemas, 475
documents. *See also* Extensible Markup Language (XML), simple documents; XSL Formatting Objects (XSL-FO), documents
adding CSSs to, 187
adding DTDs to, 105–108
adding DTDs to, embedding, 107–108
adding DTDs to, linking, 106–107
adding DTDs to, overview, 105–106
basics, 60–65
basics, root elements, 65
basics, <?xml> declarations, 60–65
default namespaces for, 96
editors, 22–27
editors, XMetaL (SoftQuad), 23
editors, XML Authority (Extensibility), 23–25
editors, XML Instance (Extensibility), 25–26
editors, XML Spy (Icon Information Systems), 26–27
identifying namespaces in, 94–95
syntax of qualified names, 96
validating with DTDs, 104–105
DOM. *See* Document Object Model (DOM)
double-quotation mark ("), 127
DSSSL (Document Style Semantics and Specification Language), 266–267
DTD entities. *See* entities, DTD
DTDs. *See* Document Type Definitions (DTDs)
Dublin Core, RDF specification, 552

E

Edit Module, XHTML, 586–587
editors, 22–27, 439–440
SMIL, 627–628
Turbo XML, 439–441
XMetaL (SoftQuad), 23
XML Authority (Extensibility), 23–25
XML Instance (Extensibility), 25–26
XML Spy, 439
XML Spy (Icon Information Systems), 26–27
XSL/XSLT software, 272–274
element attributes. *See* attributes
<element> element, 454
element nodes
built-in template rules and, 319–320
defined, 286
element sets, XHTML Text Module, 580–581
<!ELEMENT> statement, 109–113
elements, 39, 66–71
attributes, comparing with, 74–75, 143
attributes, using with, 79–81, 83
content, 66–67, 114–117
converting HTML to XHTML, 570–571
empty elements, 117–118
empty tags, 68
global vs. local declarations, 489–492
identifying, 51–56
including unparsed entities in, 164
layering, 42–43
naming, 68–71
opening and closing tags, 66
overview of, 39
stacking with z-index property, 247–248
substitution groups and, 493–494
verbose form of commands, 70–71
elements, CML, 716–717
elements, CSS, 191–192
elements, DTD
content types, 110
declaring, 109–113
syntax of, 109–110
elements, MathML
<aligngroup/>, 697–699
<maction>, 696–697
<malignmark/>, 699–700
<math>, 696–697
<merror>, 700
<mfenced>, 700–701
<mfrac>, 701
<mi>, 701
<mmultiscripts>, 702
<mn>, 702–703
<mo>, 703–704
<mover>, 704–705
<mphantom>, 705–706
<mroot>, 706–707
<mrow>, 707–708
<ms>, 708
<mspace>, 708
<msqrt>, 708
<mstyle>, 709–710
<msub>, 710
<msubsup>, 710
<msup>, 710
<mtable>, 710–711
<mtd>, 711–712
<mtext>, 712
<mtr>, 712–713
<munder>, 713–714
<munderover>, 714
elements, Schemas
catalog of, 437–438
content, 464–466
content, attributes and simple values, 464–465
content, empty, 466
content, mixed, 465
groups, 463–464
syntax and descriptions, 446–453
target namespaces and, 486–488
types, 454–463
types, complex, 454–456
types, defining custom, 461–463
types, simple, 456–460
elements, SMIL, 635–649
display options, 647–649
<layout>, 641–642
media elements, 630–632
presentation setup, 636–638

<region>, 643–645
<root-layout>, 642–643
using meta information, 639–641
<viewport>, 646–647
elements, SVG, 668–683
elements, XHTML
Bidirectional Text Module, 587
Client-Side Image Map Module, 596
Edit Module, 586–587
Forms Module, 588–591
Hypertext Module, 581
Image Module, 596
List Module, 582–583
Presentation Module, 584–585
Table Module, 592–595
Text Module, 574–580
<embed> element, XHTML, 666–667
empty elements, DTDs, 117–118
empty tags, 68, 143
encoding attribute, XSLT, 359
end-point
range function and, 544
XPointer function and, 548
engines. *See* processors
entities, DTD, 122–140
defined, 122
embedding entities within entities, 127
external entities, overview, 123
general entities, external, 130–134
general entities, internal, 125–127
general entities, overview, 124
general entities, predefined, 128
general entities, restrictions, 127–128
internal entities, overview, 123
parameter entities, external, 138–140
parameter entities, internal, 135–137
parameter entities, overview, 124–125
understanding, 122–123
entities, Schemas, 482
ENTITY or ENTITIES attribute, CDATA, 146–147
" (quotation mark), entity references, 67
entity references
defined, 66–67
using with CDATA attributes, 146
<!ENTITY> statement
internal general entities and, 125–127
parameter entities and, 135–136
enumerated attributes, 147
<enumeration> element, Schema, 461
escaping, XPointers, 540–542
characters in URLs, 541
characters in XML text, 541–542
specific characters, 541
<excl> element, SMIL, 652
extended links, XLink, 519, 526–528
extensibility, of attributes, 76–78
Extensible Hypertext Markup Language (XHTML), 568–598
Bidirectional Text Module, 587
Client-Side Image Map Module, 596–597
Edit Module, 586–587
<embed> element, 666–667
Forms module, 588–591
HTML to XHTML conversions, 568–572
HTML to XHTML conversions, element conversions, 570–571
HTML to XHTML conversions, example, 571–572
HTML to XHTML conversions, rules for, 569–570
Hypertext Module, 581
Image module, 595–596
List Module, 582–583
overview of, 568
Presentation Module, 584–586
scripts and, 600
standards, 16
Structure Module, 573–574
Table module, 592–595
Text Module, 574–581
Extensible Markup Language (XML), 4–20
DOM, 19
formatting with CSSs, 186
general requirements, 6
SGML as foundation of, 4–5
software, nonvalidating parsers, 16–17
software, validating parsers, 18
text, escaping characters, 541–542
using as meta language, 9–10
using tags to describe structure, 7–9
XML 1.0, basic XML standards in, 10–11
XML 1.0, DTDs and, 428
XML 1.0, nonvalidating parsers and, 28
Extensible Markup Language (XML), simple documents, 36–46
commenting code, 43–44
data structures and organization, 45
elements, 39
linking XSLT to, 268
parsing, 41
structure, 36–39
using layers of elements, 42–43
writing, 40
Extensible Markup Language (XML), standards
Canonical XML, 15
Cascading Style Sheets (CSS), 12
Document Type Definitions (DTDs), 11
Extensible Stylesheet Language (XSL), 12
RDF Schema, 15
XHTML, 16
XLinks, 14
XML 1.0, 10–11
XML Digital Signatures, 15
XML namespaces, 11
XML Query Language, 13
XML Schemas, 13
XPath, 14
XPointers, 14
Extensible Stylesheet Language (XSL), 264–281. *See also* XSL Formatting Objects (XSL-FO); XSL Transformations (XSLT)
attributes and, 56, 86–89
comparing with CSS, 174, 179–181
deciding which type of stylesheet to use, 181–182
features, 179–181
history of, 265–267
need for, 264–265

software, 272–277
software, processors, 274–277
software, editing/authoring tools, 272–274
standards, 12
external entities
general, 130–134
overview, 123
parameter, 138–140

F

facets, creating datatypes with, 456
filename extensions, XSL-FO, 398
:first-child, pseudo-classes, 195, 235
:first-letter, pseudo-elements, 194, 237–240
:first-line, pseudo-elements, 194, 235–237
:first, pseudo-classes, 195
#FIXED, attribute default values, 152
fixed positioning, CSS, 246–247
flat-file databases, converting. *See* Common Gateway Interface (CGI), database conversion
flow objects, XSL, 265
fo:block, 408, 422
fo:color-profile, 398
:focus, pseudo-classes, 195
fo:declarations, 398
fo:external-graphic, 414
fo:flow, 410, 413, 420
fo:inline, 408
fo:layout-master-set, 399
fonts, CSS, 197–202
font color property, 201–202
font-family property, 197
font shorthand, 200–201
font-size property, 197–198
font-stretch property, 198–199
font-style property, 199
font-variant property, 199
font-weight property, 200
FOP (Formatting Objects to PDF), 279–281, 410–411, 422–423
fo:page-sequence, 398–399
fo:page-sequence-master, 404
format-number(), 380–382
formatting
XML, 8
XSL, 267
XSL-FO, 408
Formatting Objects to PDF (FOP), 279–281, 410–411, 422–423
formatting, SMIL. *See* layout and formatting elements, SMIL
formatting, XSLT numbers, 375–383
format-number(), 380–382
xsl:decimal-format, 382–383
xsl:number, 375–380
Forms module, XHTML, 588–591
fo:root element, 398
forward slash (/)
location paths and, 287–288
using with closing element tags, 66
fo:simple-page-master, 400–401
fo:static-content, 408–409, 413, 418–420
fo:table-cell, 422
fo:table-row, 422
fragment identifiers, 542
from attribute, XLink, 524
Frontier XML Syntax Checker, 29
full form, XPointer, 538–539
functions, XPath, 300–309
Boolean, 305–307
node-set, 300–302
numeric, 307–309
string, 302–305
functions, XPointers, 540, 543–548
end-point, 548
here, 546–547
location-set, 543
origin, 547
point, 544
range, 544
range-to, 546
start-point, 547–548
string-range, 544–546
functions, XSLT, 369–395
current(), 383–385
document (), 369–371
generate-id(), 387–394
keys, 371–375
keys, key(), 372–375
keys, xsl:key, 372
numbering and number formatting, 375–383
numbering and number formatting, format-number(), 380–382
numbering and number formatting, xsl:decimal-format, 382–383
numbering and number formatting, xsl:number, 375–380
system-property(), 394–395
unparsed-entity-uri(), 385–387

G

general entities
built-in, 124
external, 130–134
internal, 125–127
overview, 124
restrictions, 127–128
General Markup Language (GML), 5
generate-id(), XSLT functions, 387–394
GIF files
notations for, 160
vector graphics and, 664
global attributes, XLinks, 518–519
global elements
compared with DTDs, 489
vs. local, 489–492
global parameters, XSLT, 352–353
global time, SMIL, 650
global variables, XSLT, 348
GMIL (General Markup Language), 5
graphics, vector-based. *See* Scalable Vector Graphics (SVG)
greater-than sign (>), entity references, 67
<group> element, Schemas, 464

groups, Schema attributes, 473–475
    improving readability, 474–475
    location of, 474–475

H

halign, CSS text alignment options, 205
hard sync, SMIL, 650
<head> element, SMIL
    attributes of, 637–638
    overview of, 636
height property, CSS size, 251
Hello World. *See* Extensible Markup Language (XML), simple documents
here (), XPointer, 546–547
hierarchical structure, Schemas, 435–437
:hover, pseudo-classes, 196
href attribute, XLink, 522
HTML. *See* Hypertext Markup Language (HTML)
HTML Object Model, DOM, 19
html:script, 600
hypertext links, 516. *See also* XML Linking Language (XLink)
Hypertext Markup Language (HTML)
    <a> element, 516
    attributes, 74–75
    compared with SMIL, 629–630
    compared with XML, 4, 60
    compared with XSL-FO, 270, 408
    conversions, HTML to XHTML, 568–572
    conversions, XML to HTML, 603–604
    <div> element, 605, 607–608
    formatting with CSSs, 186
    limitations of, 6, 130
    mixing HTML code with XML code, 481
    scripts and, 600
    SVG and, 664–665
    XSL standards and, 264
Hypertext Module, XHTML, 581

I

id attribute
    drawbacks, 371
    RDF statements, 560
ID attribute
    attribute types and, 147–148
    Schemas and, 489
    XPointer and, 539
id function, XPointer, 539
identifiers, notations and, 160–161
IDREF/IDREFS attribute
    attribute types and, 148–149
    node identity and, 502
    using with Schemas, 489
IDs, CSS, 193
IE (Internet Explorer). *See* Internet Explorer (IE)
IETF (Internet Engineering Task Force), 161
IGNORE conditional statement, 166–167
Image module, XHTML, 595–596
images, adding to XSL-FO documents, 414–415
#IMPLIED, attribute default values, 151–152
@import, CSS media types, 257
INCLUDE conditional statement, 166–167
<include> element, Schemas, 492–493
indent attribute, XSLT, 360
information
    adding detail to personal information databases, 49–51
    creating levels of, 48–49
    designing outline of, 52
    formatting data as needed, 55
inline formatting, 408
inline object boxes, CSS display property values, 241–242
<input> element, HTML, 608
instance documents, 429
integer values, 506
internal entities
    general, 125–127
    overview, 123
    parameter, 135–137
Internationalized URI (IURI), 541
Internet Engineering Task Force (IETF), 161
Internet Explorer (IE)
    MathML and, 93
    MSXML and, 60–72, 276
    nonvalidating parsers, 27
    viewing SVG images, 692
iteration, XML Query Algebra, 507
IURI (Internationalized URI), 541

J

Jasc WebDraw, 692
JavaScript
    CSS and, 176
    scripting languages and, 56
JavaScript, manipulating XML document, 600–611
    combining the script with XSL document, 605–611
    sample XML document, 600–601
    Schema validation, 601–603
    using XSLT to transform document into scriptable format, 603–604
    writing the script, 605
join, XML Query Algebra, 509
JPEG files
    notations for, 160–161
    vector graphics and, 664

K

keys, XSLT, 371–375
    key(), 372–375
    sorting, 335
    xsl:key, 372

L

label attribute, XLink, 524
:lang, CSS pseudo-elements, 194
languages, writing modes, 180–181
layout and formatting elements, SMIL, 635–649
    display options, 647–649

<layout>, 641–642
presentation setup, 636–638
<region>, 643–645
<root-layout>, 642–643
using meta information, 639–641
<viewport>, 646–647
<layout> element, SMIL, 641–642
layout master sets, XSL-FO, 399–404
defined, 398
page layouts, 400–403
page sequences, 404
layout, SVG, 665–667
:left, CSS pseudo-classes, 196
left positioning, CSS, 249
less-than sign (<), entity references, 67
letter-spacing attribute, CSS text, 202
line-height property, CSS text, 203
:link, CSS pseudo-classes, 196
linking controls, XSL, 180–181
links. *See also* XML Pointer Language (XPointers)
links, SMIL
<a>, 652, 655
<area>, 655–656
attributes, 656–658
links, XLink, 524–531
arc, 529–530
extended, 526–528
locator, 528–529
resource, 530–531
simple, 524–526
title, 531
List Module, XHTML, 582–583
local elements, vs. global, 494
local time, SMIL, 650
location functions, XPointer
location-set, 543
point, 544
range, 544–546
location paths, XPath
defined, 287
examples, 297–299
location-set function, XPointer, 543
location steps, XPath, 291–297
defined, 287
syntax, axis, 292–294
syntax, node test, 295–296
syntax, predicate, 296–297
locator link, XLink, 528–529
looping, template rules and, 327–329
LT XML, 30
LTG XML Well-Formedness Checker and Validator, 32

M

<maction> element, MathML, 696–697
maintenance, CSS stylesheets, 175
<malignmark/> element, MathML, 699–700
margins, CSS object boxes, 213–215
margin-bottom property, 215
margin-left property, 215
margin property, 214–215
margin-right property, 215
margin-top property, 215
marker, CSS display property values, 243–244
<math> element, MathML, 696–697
Mathematical Markup Language (MathML), 696–716
as derivative of XML, 92–94
examples, 714–716
limitations of DTDs and, 428
Mathematical Markup Language (MathML), elements
<aligngroup/>, 697–699
<maction>, 696–697
<malignmark/>, 699–700
<math>, 696–697
<merror>, 700
<mfenced>, 700–701
<mfrac>, 701
<mi>, 701
<mmultiscripts>, 702
<mn>, 702–703
<mo>, 703–704
<mover>, 704–705
<mphantom>, 705–706
<mroot>, 706–707
<mrow>, 707–708
<ms>, 708
<mspace>, 708
<msqrt>, 708
<mstyle>, 709–710
<msub>, 710
<msubsup>, 710
<msup>, 710
<mtable>, 710–711
<mtd>, 711–712
<mtext>, 712
<mtr>, 712–713
<munder>, 713–714
<munderover>, 714
max-height property, CSS size, 250
max-width property, CSS size, 250
<maxInclusive> element, Schemas, 461
@media, CSS media types, 255–256
media elements, SMIL, 630–635
attributes, 632–635
list of, 630–631
unknown types, 632
media-type attribute, XSLT, 360
media types
CSS, 255–257
CSS, @import, 257
CSS, list of, 256
CSS, @media, 255–256
XPointer, 549
<merror> element, MathML, 700
messages, issuing from style sheets, 367–369
<meta> element, SMIL, 639–641
meta information, SMIL, 639–641
meta languages, 9–10
metadata
RDF data model and, 552
using attributes with, 75–76
method attribute, XSLT, 359

<mfenced> element, MathML, 700–701
<mfrac> element, MathML, 701
<mi> element, MathML, 701
min-height property, CSS size, 250
min-width property, CSS size, 250
<minInclusive> element, Schemas, 461
<mmultiscripts> element, MathML, 702
<mn> element, MathML, 702–703
<mo> element, MathML, 703–704
modular style sheets, 353
modules, XHTML
  Bidirectional Text Module, 587
  Client-Side Image Map Module, 596–597
  Edit Module, 586–587
  Forms Module, 588–591
  Hypertext Module, 581
  Image Module, 595–596
  List Module, 582–583
  overview of, 572–573
  Presentation Module, 584–586
  Structure Module, 573–574
  Table Module, 592–595
  Text Module, 574–581
molecules, mapping with CML, 726
<mover> element, MathML, 704–705
Mozilla, 692
<mphantom> element, MathML, 705–706
<mroot> element, MathML, 706–707
<mrow> element, MathML, 707–708
<ms> element, MathML, 708
<mspace> element, MathML, 708
<msqrt> element, MathML, 708
<mstyle> element, MathML, 709–710
<msub> element, MathML, 710
<msubsup> element, MathML, 710
<msup> element, MathML, 710
MSXML
  handling of white space by, 157
  Internet Explorer and, 22
  using DTDs to validate documents, 113–114
  XSLT processors and, 276–277
<mtable> element, MathML, 710–711
<mtd> element, MathML, 711–712
<mtext> element, MathML, 712
<mtr> element, MathML, 712–713
multimedia, Synchronized Multimedia Modules (SYMM), 626. *See also* Synchronized Multimedia Integration Language (SMIL)
multiple attributes, 152–156
multiple documents, 492–493
<munder> element, MathML, 713–714
<munderover> element, MathML, 714

N

<name> element, Schemas, 464
name space nodes, 287
names attribute sets, XSLT, 340–342
namespaces, 92–100
  adding to DTDs, 97–100
  document, default, 96
  document, identifying, 94–95
  document, syntax of qualified names, 96
  notation for declaring, 94
  overview of, 92–94
  RDF, 553
  Schema attribute values, 480–481
  target namespace, undeclared, 486–488
  target namespace, with Schemas, 486–488
  XLink, 518–519
  XML standards, 11
naming
  attributes, 81–82
  elements, 68–71
  elements, case sensitivity, 69
  elements, rules for, 68
Netscape Navigator
  nonvalidating parser in, 27
  viewing SVG images, 692
NMTOKEN/NMTOKENS attribute, CDATA, 149
node-set function, XPath, 300–302
node test, XPath, 295–296
nodes
  copying to result tree, current node only, 361–362
  copying to result tree, entire branch, 362–364
  current() function and, 383–385
  effect of sorting on node position, 337
  getting processor to identify, 387–394
  reference values and, 502
  testing for existence of, 297
  types, 286–287
  values, 299–300
none, CSS display property values, 243
nontextual data, 162–163
nonvalidating parsers, 16–17
  available online, 28–29
  basic varieties, 28
  Frontier XML Syntax Checker, 29
  overview, 27–28
  RUWF (Are You Well-Formed), 29
NOTATION attribute, CDATA, 149–150
notations, 160–162
  declaration statement for, 160–161
  functions of, 160
  identifiers for, 160–161
Notepad, writing XML documents with, 40
numbering and number formatting, XSLT, 375–383
  format-number(), 380–382
  xsl:decimal-format, 382–383
  xsl:number, 375–380
numeric functions, XPath, 307–309
numeric operators, 308–309

O

object boxes, CSS, 207–217
  backgrounds, 217–221
  border-collapse, 210–211
  borders, 207–210
  margins, 213–215
  outlines, 211–213
  padding, 215–217

object importance, CSS, 254
offset, relative positioning and, 245
omit-xml-declaration attribute, XSLT, 359
onload event, 607–608
opening tags
  attributes in, 143
  elements in, 66
origin, XPointer function, 547
outlines, CSS object boxes, 211–213
  outline-color property, 212
  outline property, 211
  outline-style property, 212–213
  outline-width property, 213
overflow property, CSS, 252–253

P

padding, CSS object boxes, 215–217
  batting-top property, 217
  padding-bottom property, 216
  padding-left property, 216
  padding property, 215–216
  padding-right property, 217
page layouts, XSL-FO, 400–403
page sequences, XSL-FO, 398–399, 404
paging, XSL style sheets, 179
palm devices, XHTML and, 568
<par> element, SMIL, 651–652
parameter entities
  declaration statements for, 138
  external, 138–140
  internal, 135–137
  overview, 124–125
  syntax for, 135
parent objects, XML structure, 39
parsers, 27–33, 441–442
  MSXML3 parser, 105
  nonvalidating, 16–17
  nonvalidating, available online, 28–29
  nonvalidating, basic varieties, 28
  nonvalidating, Frontier XML Syntax Checker, 29
  nonvalidating, overview, 27–28
  nonvalidating, RUWF (Are You Well-Formed), 29
  validating, 18
  validating, available online, 31–32
  validating, LTG XML Well-Formedness Checker and Validator, 32
  validating, overview, 29–30
  validating, Richard Tobins Well-Formedness Checker, 32
  validating, Schema checkers, 33
  validating, STG Validating Parser, 32
  validating, validation requirements and, 30–31
parsing
  simple XML document, 41
  using DTDs for document validation, 104
  well-formed documents and, 72
  white space handling and, 157
<pattern> element, Schemas, 461
PDF (Portable Document Format), 410–411
PDF reader, Adobe Acrobat
  Formatting Objects to PDF (FOP), 279–281
  native XSL-FO renderer, 278
percent symbol (%)
  entity restrictions, 127
  referencing parameter entities, 134
personal information. *See* information
PGML (Precision Graphic Markup Language), 664
PI nodes, 287, 322
PIs. *See* processing instructions (PIs)
players, SMIL, 627–628
point function, XPointer, 544
Portable Document Format (PDF), 410–411
position properties, CSS
  absolute, 246
  bottom, 250
  fixed, 246–247
  left, 249
  relative, 245–246
  right, 249
  stacking elements with z-index property, 247–248
  top, 249
Precision Graphic Markup Language (PGML), 664
predicates, XPath, 296–297
  compound predicates, 297
  logical test, 296
  testing for node existence, 297
predicates, XPointer, 540
Presentation Module, XHTML, 584–586
processing instructions (PIs), 167–169
  function of, 167
  naming, 168
  PI nodes, 287, 322
  placement and format of, 167–168
  relationship to container, 285
  XSLT, 315–317
processing sequence, XSLT template rules, 326–327
processors
  identifying nodes with, 387–394
  system-property() and, 394–395
  XSLT, 274–277
  XSLT, MSXML, 276–277
  XSLT, overview of, 274
  XSLT, Saxon, 275
projection, XML Query Algebra, 506
properties
  RDF, 554
  selector and, 178
properties, CSS
  first-letter, 238–240
  position, absolute, 246
  position, bottom, 250
  position, fixed, 246–247
  position, left, 249
  position, relative, 245–246
  position, right, 249
  position, top, 249
  stacking elements with z-index property, 247–248
pseudo-classes, CSS, 194–196
  basis of, 234–235
  :first-child, 235
pseudo-elements, CSS, 193–194
  :first-letter, 237–240
  :first-line, 235–237

PUBLIC document type
  referencing, 109
  vs. SYSTEM document type, 108
public identifier strings, 109
PUBLIC identifiers, 161

Q

qualified attributes, 96
qualified names, 96
quantification, XML Query Algebra, 508–509
queries. *See* XML Queries
quotation mark ("), entity references, 67

R

range function, XPointer, 544
range-to function, XPointer, 546
RDF. *See* Resource Description Framework (RDF)
RealPlayer, 632
ref attribute, 438
<ref> element, SMIL, 632
<region> element, SMIL, 643–645
regions, XSL-FO, 401
relative positioning, CSS, 245–246
remote resources, using locator links with, 528–529
#REQUIRED, attribute default values, 150–151
Resource Description Framework (RDF), 552–563
  basic syntax, abbreviated, 556–557
  basic syntax, serialized, 555–556
  containers, alternative objects, 560
  containers, bag objects, 558–559
  containers, sequence objects, 559
  containers, syntax, 558
  implementing, 553–557
  overview of, 552–553
  properties, 554
  RDF Schema and, 553
  resources, 554
  standards, 15
  statements, 554–555, 560–561
  URI patterns, 561–562
resource link, XLink, 530–531
resources
  RDF, 554
  remote, 528–529
  URI, 517
<restriction> element, Schemas, 461
result trees, 284–286
result trees, XSLT
  attribute value templates, 342–344
  creating attributes with xsl:attribute, 339–342
  creating elements with xsl:element, 338–339
  special output, cdata-section-elements attribute, 359–360
  special output, indent attribute, 360
  special output, media-type attribute, 360
  special output, method attribute, 359
  special output, overview, 358–359
  special output, version and other attributes, 359
Richard Tobins Well-Formedness Checker, 32
:right, CSS pseudo-classes, 196
right positioning, CSS, 249
role attribute, XLink, 523
root elements
  documents and, 65
  DTDs, 111
  fo:root element, 398
  namespace and, 97
  style sheets and, 309
  xsl:stylesheet element, 310–312
<root-layout> element, SMIL, 642–643
root nodes
  as built-in template rule, 319–320
  defined, 286
root objects, XML, 39
rules. *See also* template rules, XSLT
  attributes, 81–82
  comments, 44
  converting HTML to XHTML, 569–570
  DTDs, 115
  elements, 75
  naming elements, 68
run-in, CSS display property values, 243
RUWF (Are You Well-Formed), 29

S

Saxon, XSLT processors, 275
Scalable Vector Graphics (SVG), 664–694
  example of, 692–694
  overview of, 664–665
  specifications, 664
  syntax, 665–683
  syntax, attributes, 683–691
  syntax, data types, 667–668
  syntax, elements, 668–683
  syntax, layout, 665–667
  XSL and, 267
Schema checkers, 33
Schema definition language (XSD), 428
Schemas, 428–443
  compared with DTDs, 430–434, 489
  defined, 428–429
  RDF Schema, 553
  restricting element contents with, 162
  software, editors, 439–440
  software, validators and parsers, 441–442
  standards, 13
  using with XML Query, 502
  validating documents with, 104
  validation, 486, 601–603
  writing, 434–438
  writing, catalog of elements, 437–438
  writing, hierarchical structure, 435–437
Schemas, advanced, 486–495
  abstract elements, 494
  constraints vs. ID attributes, 489
  global vs. local declarations, 489–492
  substitution groups, 493–494
  target namespaces and, 486–488
  undeclared target name spaces, 486–488
  using as multiple documents, 492–493
Schemas, attributes, 470–483
  annotations, 475–476

checking for specification changes, 473
constraints, 476–479
constraints, <all>, 478–479
constraints, <choice>, 476–477
constraints, <sequence>, 477–478
creating unique elements and attributes, 479–480
entities values and, 482
groups, 473–475
groups, improving readability, 475
groups, location, 474–475
list of descriptions, 470–473
namespaces and, 480–481
Schemas, elements
content, 464–466
content, attributes and simple values, 464–465
content, empty, 466
content, mixed, 465
groups, 463–464
overview of, 429
syntax and descriptions, 446–453
types, 454–463
types, complex, 454–456
types, defining custom, 461–463
types, simple, 456–460
schemes, XPointer, 536–538
scripts. *See also* Common Gateway Interface (CGI), database conversion; JavaScript
CSS stylesheets and, 176
XHTML and, 568
scrolling, XSL style sheets, 179
selecting in context, CSS, 193
selection, XML Query Algebra, 507–508
selectors, CSS, 177
overview of, 186–187
pseudo-classes, 234–240
selector patterns, 188–191
selectors, XSL style sheets, 179
<seq> element, SMIL, 651
sequence objects, RDF containers, 559
<sequence>, Schema constraints, 477–478
serialized syntax, RDF, 555–556
SGML (Standard Generalized Markup Language), 4–5, 266
sharing, attributes, 83
shorthand properties, CSS fonts, 200–201
shorthand properties, CSS object boxes
background, 221
border, 207–208
margin, 214–215
outline, 211
padding, 215–216
show attribute, XLink, 523
simple links, XLink
defined, 519–520
overview of, 524–526
<simpleType>, Schemas, 457–460
size, CSS, 250–251
height, 251
width, 251
SMIL, 626–662
animation effects, 658–660
compared with HTML, 629–630
editors and players, 627–628
limitations of DTDs and, 428
media elements, 630–635
overview of, 626–627
synchronization, 650–652
transformation effects, 660–661
<smil> element, SMIL, 636
SMIL, formatting elements, 635–649
display options, 647–649
<layout>, 641–642
presentation setup, 636–638
<region>, 643–645
<root-layout>, 642–643
using meta information, 639–641
<viewport>, 646–647
SMIL, linking
<a>, 652, 655
<area>, 655–656
attributes, 656–658
SMIL, media elements
list out of, 630–631
SMIL attributes, 632–635
unknown types, 632
SMIL, synchronization
attributes, 653–654
<excl>, 652
<par>, 651–652
<seq>, 651
SMIL, timing
attributes, 653–654
categories, 650
soft sync, SMIL, 650
software, Schemas
editors, 439–440
validators and parsers, 441–442
software, XML
nonvalidating parsers, 16–17
validating parsers, 18
software, XSL-FO
Formatting Objects to PDF (FOP), 279–281
native renderers, 278–279
software, XSL/XSLT, 272–277
editing/authoring tools, 272–274
processors, 274–277
sorting
applications, 177
XML Query Algebra, 510
sorting, XSLT
attributes for, 334–335
effect on node position, 337
on multiple keys, 335
xsl:apply-templates, 335–336
xsl:for-each, 336–337
source trees, 284–286
specifications
DSSSL (Document Style Semantics and Specification Language), 552
RDF (Dublin Core), 552
SVG, 664
XBase, 531–532
XLink, 516

XML Query, 500
XPointer, 537
XSL, 264
standalone attribute, XSLT, 359
standalone documents, 61
Standard Generalized Markup Language (SGML), 4–5, 266
standards
Canonical XML, 15
CSS, 12
DTDs, 11
RDF Schema, 15
XHTML, 16
XLinks, 14
XML 1.0, 10–11
XML Digital Signatures, 15
XML namespaces, 11
XML Query Language, 13
XML Schemas, 13
XPath, 14
XPointer, 14
XSL, 12
start-point, 544, 547–548
STG Validating Parser, 32
string functions, XPath, 302–305
string-range, XPointer, 544–546
strings
string-range function and, 544–546
values, 506
XPointer, 538
structure
CSS style sheets, 175
XSL-FO documents, 398–399
Structure Module, XHTML, 573–574
structure, XML documents, 7–9, 36–39
style attribute, CSS, 187
style sheets, 84–89, 174–182. *See also* Cascading Style Sheets (CSS); Extensible Stylesheet Language (XSL); XSL Transformations (XSLT), style sheet structure
adding to documents, 84–85
comparing XSL with CSS, 174, 179–181, 264–265
controlling formatting with, 8
creating, 221–226
deciding which type to use, 181–182
defined, 174
issuing messages from, 367–369
substitution groups, 493–494
SVG. *See* Scalable Vector Graphics (SVG)
<svg> element, 665
<switch> element, SMIL, 647–649
SYMM (Synchronized Multimedia Modules), 626
synchronization, SMIL, 650–652
attributes, 653–654
<excl>, 652
<par>, 651–652
<seq>, 651
Synchronized Multimedia Integration Language (SMIL). *See* SMIL
Synchronized Multimedia Modules (SYMM), 626
syntax
bare names, 539
child sequence, 540
full form, 538–539
RDF, abbreviated, 556–557
RDF, containers, 558
RDF, serialized, 555–556
Schema elements, 446–453
SVG, 665–683
SVG, attributes, 683–691
SVG, data types, 667–668
SVG, elements, 668–683
SVG, layout, 665–667
XLink, 517–518
XPointers, 538–540
SYSTEM document type
referencing, 108–109
vs. PUBLIC document type, 108
system-property(), XSLT functions, 394–395

T

Table module, XHTML, 592–595
tables
CSS, 243–244
XSL-FO, 415–423
tags
closing, 66
empty, 68
metadata and, 9–10
opening, 66
using to describe XML structure, 7–9
target namespaces
undeclared, 489
use of, 486
template rules, 267
template rules, XSLT
built-in, 319–322
built-in, processing instruction and comment nodes, 322
built-in, root and all element nodes, 319–320
built-in, text and attribute nodes, 320–322
conflict resolution, 329–331
explicit, 322–326
looping within, 327–329
overview of, 317–319
processing sequence of, 326–327
templates
XSL standard and, 266
XSL style sheets and, 87–88
text
CDATA attributes, 145
content, 114
XSLT, 314–315
text, CSS, 202–207
alignment options, 204–205
letter-spacing attribute, 202
line-height property, 203
text-align attribute, 203–204
text-decoration property, 205–206
text-indent property, 205
text-shadow property, 206
text-transform property, 206–207
word-spacing attribute, 204
text editors, writing XML documents with, 40

Text Module, XHTML, 574–581
text nodes
 as built-in template rule, 320–322
 defined, 286–287
text/xml, 549
timing, SMIL
 attributes, 653–654
 categories, 650
title attribute, XLink, 523
title link, XLink, 531
to attribute, XLink, 524
top-level elements
 XSL, 268
 XSLT, 313
top positioning, CSS, 249
transformation effects, SMIL, 660–661
transformation principle, XSL, 265
<transition> element, SMIL, 660
traversal, XLink
 arc of, 530
 defined, 517
tree structure
 XML documents, 37
 XSL style sheets, 179
 XSLT, 284
Turbo XML, 439–441
type attribute, XLink, 520–521
types, XML Query, 504

U

UNICODE characters, 541–542
Uniform Resource Identifier (URI)
 href attribute and, 522
 node identity and, 502
 RDF and, 553–554
 resource links and, 530–531
 URI patterns, 561–562
 XLink and, 517
 XML Namespaces and, 11
 XPointer and, 536
Uniform Resource Locators (URLs)
 escaping characters and, 541
 referencing DTDs, 106
<unique> element, Schemas, 479
unparsed-entity-uri(), XSLT functions, 385–387
unparsed external entities, 162–165
URI. *See* Uniform Resource Identifier (URI)
URLs. *See* Uniform Resource Locators (URLs)

V

validating parsers
 available online, 31–32
 LTG XML Well-Formedness Checker and Validator, 32
 overview, 29–30
 Richard Tobins Well-Formedness Checker, 32
 Schema checkers, 33
 software for, 18, 441–442
 STG Validating Parser, 32
 validation requirements, 30–31
valign, CSS text alignment, 204–205
values
 of attributes, 82
 of properties, 178
variables, XSLT
 attributes, 345–347
 global, 348
 result tree fragments and, 349–350
 scope, 347
vector graphics. *See* Scalable Vector Graphics (SVG)
Vector Markup Language (VML), 664
version attribute, XSLT, 359
<viewport> element, SMIL, 646–647
visibility property, CSS, 252
:visited, CSS pseudo-classes, 196
VML (Vector Markup Language), 664

W

W3C Validator for XML Schema, 441–442
well-formed documents, 60–72
 checking with nonvalidating parsers, 27
 child elements, 71–72
 defined, 7
 document basics, 60–65
 document basics, root elements, 65
 document basics, <?xml> declarations, 60–65
 elements, 66–71
 elements, content, 66–67, 66–67
 elements, empty tags, 68
 elements, naming, 68–71
 elements, opening and closing tags, 66
 XSLT as, 309
width property, CSS size, 251
Windows Notepad, writing XML documents with, 40
word-spacing attribute, CSS text, 204
World Wide Web Consortium (W3C)
 Amaya browser, 22–23
 CSSs, 186
 RDF specification, 552
 SVG, 664
 SYMM, 626
 XHTML modularization, 572
 XLink, 516
 XML, 10
 XML namespaces, 92
 XSL, 179, 264
writing modes, CSS and XSL, 180

X

XBase, 531–532
Xerces Java, 442
XHTML. *See* Extensible Hypertext Markup Language (XHTML)
XLink. *See* XML Linking Language (XLink)
xlink prefix, 518
XMetaL (SoftQuad), 23
XML Authority (Extensibility), 23–25
<?xml> declarations, 60–65
 character encoding values, 62–65
 standalone documents and, 61

XML Digital Signatures, 15
XML (Extensible Markup Language). *See* Extensible Markup Language (XML)
XML Information Set, 501
XML Infoset, 500
XML Instance (Extensibility), 25–26
XML Linking Language (XLink), 516–533
function of, 516–517
namespace, 518–519
standards, 14
syntax, 517–518
XBase and, 531–532
XML Linking Language (XLink), attributes, 519–524
from, 524
to, 524
actuate, 523–524
arcrole, 523–524
href, 522
label, 524
role, 523
show, 523
title, 523
type, 520–521
XML Linking Language (XLink), links, 524–531
arc, 529–530
extended, 526–528
locator, 528–529
resource, 530–531
simple, 524–526
title, 531
XML Path (XPath), 287–309
context, 291
functions, 300–309
functions, Boolean, 305–307
functions, node-set, 300–302
functions, numeric, 307–309
functions, string, 302–305
location path examples, 297–299
location step syntax, 291–297
location step syntax, axis, 292–294
location step syntax, node test, 295–296
location step syntax, predicate, 296–297
node values, 299–300
overview of, 287–291
path navigation with, 506
standards, 14
XPointer and, 536
XML Pointer Language (XPointers), 536–549
escaping, 540–542
escaping, characters for use in XML text, 541–542
escaping, characters in URLs, 541
escaping, specific characters, 541
function of, 536
functions, 543–548
functions, end-point, 548
functions, here, 546–547
functions, location-set, 543
functions, origin, 547
functions, point, 544
functions, range, 544
functions, range-to, 546
functions, start-point, 547–548
functions, string-range, 544–546
node identity and, 502
node isolation in, 287
overview of, 536
schemes, 536–538
standards, 14
syntax, 538–540
syntax, bare names, 539
syntax, child sequence, 540
syntax, full form, 538–539
XML Queries
algebra, 502–510
algebra, atomic data, 506–507
algebra, data and types, 504–506
algebra, global and local variables, 506
algebra, iteration, 507
algebra, join, 509
algebra, overview, 502–504
algebra, projection, 506
algebra, quantification, 508–509
algebra, selection, 507–508
algebra, sorting, 510
model for, 501–502
requirements, 500–501
standards, 13
use cases, 500
using, 510–512
XML Schemas. *See* Schemas
XML Spy (Icon Information Systems), 26–27, 273–274, 439
<?xml-stylesheet?>, 187
xml:base attribute, 531–532
xml:lang, predefined attributes, 157
xmlns scheme, 537
xml:space, predefined attributes, 156–157
XPath. *See* XML Path (XPath)
XPointer. *See* XML Pointer Language (XPointers)
XPointer scheme, 537, 539
xsd, as Schema prefix, 435
xsd:schema, 435
XSL (Extensible Stylesheet Language). *See* Extensible Stylesheet Language (XSL)
XSL-FO. *See* XSL Formatting Objects (XSL-FO)
XSL Formatter (Antenna House), 278–279, 412
XSL Formatting Objects (XSL-FO)
comparing with XSLT, 277
complexity of style sheets in, 270–272
emphasis on presentation vs. content, 269–270
software, formatting objects-to-PDF converters, 279–281
software, native renderers, 278–279
XSL standards and, 264
XSL Formatting Objects (XSL-FO), documents, 398–424
adding content, 405–410
adding content, block vs. inline formatting, 408
adding content, content that varies page to page, 410
adding content, fixed content, 408–409
adding content, overview, 405–407
inserting images, 414–415
layout master sets, 399–404
layout master sets, page layouts, 400–403

layout master sets, page sequences, 404
modifying display properties, 413–414
structure of, 398–399
tabular output, 415–423
viewing, 410–412
XSL Transformations (XSLT), 267–272
comparing with XSL-FO, 277
conditional processing, 331–334
conditional processing, xsl:choose, 332–334
conditional processing, xsl:if, 332
copying nodes to result tree, 360–364
copying nodes to result tree, current node only, 361–362
copying nodes to result tree, entire branch, 362–364
generating XSL-FO documents with, 399
importing code with xsl:import, 354–357
including code with xsl:include, 353–354
incorporating scripts using, 600
issuing messages from style sheets, 367–369
linking to XML documents, 268
software, 272–277
software, processors, 274–277
software, editing/authoring tools, 272–274
style sheet structure, 268–269
template rule modes, 364–367
transforming XML document into scriptable format, 603–604
viewing attribute values with, 143
XPath and, 536
XSL standards and, 264
XSL Transformations (XSLT), basic concepts, 284–287
nodes and node types, 286–287
source and result trees, 284–286
XSL Transformations (XSLT), functions, 369–395
current(), 383–385
document (), 369–371
generate-id(), 387–394
keys, 371–375
keys, key(), 372–375
keys, xsl:key, 372
numbering and number formatting, 375–383
numbering and number formatting, format-number(), 380–382
numbering and number formatting, xsl:decimal-format, 382–383
numbering and number formatting, xsl:number, 375–380
system-property(), 394–395
unparsed-entity-uri(), 385–387
XSL Transformations (XSLT), parameters, 350–353
global, 352–353
using with named templates, 350–352
XSL Transformations (XSLT), result tree content, 338–344
attribute value templates, 342–344
creating attributes with xsl:attribute, 339–342
creating elements with xsl:element, 338–339
XSL Transformations (XSLT), sorting, 334–337
attributes, 334–335
effect on node position, 337
on multiple keys, 335
xsl:apply-templates, 335–336
xsl:for-each, 336–337
XSL Transformations (XSLT), special output, 358–360
cdata-section-elements attribute, 359–360
indent attribute, 360
media-type attribute, 360
method attribute, 359
overview, 358–359
version and other attributes, 359
XSL Transformations (XSLT), style sheet structure, 309–317
comment and PI elements, 315–317
other elements, 313–314
text elements, 314–315
top-level elements, 313
xsl:stylesheet element, 310–312
XSL Transformations (XSLT), template rules, 317–331
built-in, 319–322
conflict resolution, 329–331
explicit, 322–326
looping within, 327–329
overview of, 317–319
processing sequence of, 326–327
XSL Transformations (XSLT), variables
attributes, 345–347
global, 348
parameters, 350–353
result tree fragments and, 349–350
scope, 347
xsl:apply-templates, 335–336, 364–367, 418
xsl:attribute, 339–342
xsl:choose structure, 332–334, 422
xsl:comment, 316
xsl:copy, 361–362
xsl:copy-of, 362–364
xsl:decimal-format, 382–383
xsl:element, 338–339
xsl:for-each, 336–337
xsl:if element, 332
xsl:import, 354–357
xsl:include, 353–354
xsl:key, 372
xsl:message, 367–369
xsl:number, 375–380
xsl:processing-instruction, 317
xsl:sort element, 334
xsl:stylesheet element
exclude-result-prefixes attribute, 312
extension-element-prefixes attribute, 311–312
function of, 310
id attribute, 311
[other namespace declarations] attribute, 310–311
top-level elements, 268
version attribute, 310
XSLT, 310–312
xsl:template element, 268. *See also* template rules, XSLT
importance of, 313
template rules and, 317
xsl:text element, 314
xsl:variable. *See* variables, XSLT

Z

z-index property, CSS positioning, 233–234, 247–248

INTERNATIONAL CONTACT INFORMATION

AUSTRALIA
McGraw-Hill Book Company Australia Pty. Ltd.
TEL +61-2-9417-9899
FAX +61-2-9417-5687
http://www.mcgraw-hill.com.au
books-it_sydney@mcgraw-hill.com

CANADA
McGraw-Hill Ryerson Ltd.
TEL +905-430-5000
FAX +905-430-5020
http://www.mcgrawhill.ca

GREECE, MIDDLE EAST, NORTHERN AFRICA
McGraw-Hill Hellas
TEL +30-1-656-0990-3-4
FAX +30-1-654-5525

MEXICO (Also serving Latin America)
McGraw-Hill Interamericana Editores S.A. de C.V.
TEL +525-117-1583
FAX +525-117-1589
http://www.mcgraw-hill.com.mx
fernando_castellanos@mcgraw-hill.com

SINGAPORE (Serving Asia)
McGraw-Hill Book Company
TEL +65-863-1580
FAX +65-862-3354
http://www.mcgraw-hill.com.sg
mghasia@mcgraw-hill.com

SOUTH AFRICA
McGraw-Hill South Africa
TEL +27-11-622-7512
FAX +27-11-622-9045
robyn_swanepoel@mcgraw-hill.com

UNITED KINGDOM & EUROPE (Excluding Southern Europe)
McGraw-Hill Education Europe
TEL +44-1-628-502500
FAX +44-1-628-770224
http://www.mcgraw-hill.co.uk
computing_neurope@mcgraw-hill.com

ALL OTHER INQUIRIES Contact:
Osborne/McGraw-Hill
TEL +1-510-549-6600
FAX +1-510-883-7600
http://www.osborne.com
omg_international@mcgraw-hill.com